EXAMKRACKERS MCAT®

101 PASSAGES:
CARS

CRITICAL ANALYSIS AND REASONING SKILLS

OSOTE
PUBLISHING

Major Contributors:

Leena Asfour

Jennifer Birk-Goldschmidt, M.S.

Erik Davies

Teresa Jiang

Laura Neubauer

Lauren Nadler

Eileen Robinson

Henry Rosen

Sara Streett, Ph.D.

J. Van Etten

Eric Ward

Contributors:

Kaitlyn Barkley

David Collins

Caroline Dunne

Ian Magruder

Art Director:

Erin Daniel

Designer:

Dana Kelley

Copyright © 2016 by Examkrackers, Inc.,

All rights reserved under International and Pan-American Copyright Conventions.

Published in the United States of America by Osote Publishing, New Jersey.

ISBN 10: 1-893858-90-1

ISBN 13: 978-1-893858-90-9

To purchase additional copies of this book or other books of the 101 Passage series, call 1-888-572-2536.

Examkrackers.com

Osote.com

PHOTOCOPYING & DISTRIBUTION POLICY

The illustrations and all other content in this book are copyrighted material owned by Osote Publishing. Please do not reproduce any of the content, illustrations, charts, graphs, photos, etc., on email lists or websites.

Photocopying the pages so that the book can then be resold is a violation of copyright.

Schools and co-ops MAY NOT PHOTOCOPY any portion of this book. For more information, please contact Osote Publishing: email: support@osote.com or contact Examkrackers: email: support@examkrackers.com or phone 1.888.KRACKEM.

Read this First

Practice is essential to your success on the MCAT®, and Examkrackers practice materials provide the best MCAT® simulation available. Using this book to prepare for the Critical Analysis and Reasoning Skills (CARS) section is the best way to develop the skills you will need to get a high score.

Your score will increase as you hone your abilities for the CARS section. Learning to organize the passage and to align yourself with the author's opinion not only results in a high score but also prepares you for your future work as a doctor. Organizing information you receive from a patient and listening for what they care about is the beginning of every healing encounter. MCAT® practice is medical practice.

Below you will find information on:

- How to begin: Assess your CARS MCAT® skills
- MCAT® simulation and timing
- How to use this book to increase your MCAT® score
    Test review
    Change: Making commitments
    Smart practice
- Scoring
- Complete MCAT® preparation with Examkrackers

How to Begin: Assess Your CARS MCAT® Skills

This book begins with two "warm-up" passages. Use them to familiarize yourself with the look, feel, and format of CARS passages and questions. Give yourself about fifteen minutes to take the warm-up test. While working through the two passages and the associated questions, observe yourself and notice your own approach. Immediately after taking the warm-up test, look at the following checklist of strategies and skills taught in the Examkrackers *Reasoning Skills Manual*. Based on the passages and questions in the warm-up, evaluate which skills come naturally to you and which skills you will work to build as you continue through this book.

- Energy
- Focus
- Confidence
- Timing
- Animated reading
- Narrating the passage
- Finding the author's voice
- Constructing the main idea
- Simplifying the questions and answers
- Identifying question types
- Eliminating answers
- Tolerating uncertainty
- Not going back to the passage
- Building a spectrum.

Choose two or three skills to focus on throughout Test 1 and continue to build new skills as you proceed through the book. Return to this page and check off strategies and skills as you master them.

MCAT® Simulation and Timing

MCAT® SIMULATION

The 101 CARS passages and associated questions in this book were carefully designed to exactly simulate the content, length, style, tone, difficulty and format of real AAMC CARS MCAT® test sections, passages, questions, and answer choices. Just like the real CARS section, each test has nine passages and 53 questions, and the array of question types is the same as the real CARS MCAT®.

When you are ready to take your first simulated CARS test, choose an environment that is not familiar or comfortable, e.g. a public library, not your couch at home. Ensure that you will maximize focus and minimize distraction for one sitting of at least 90 minutes. If needed, you may use disposable earplugs, just as you are allowed on MCAT® day. Treat each practice test like MCAT® day. Learn not to look at or answer your telephone, not to stare out the window, or get up at all during the test to get a drink or to go to the bathroom. This will build your focus and stamina to increase your score.

It is always a good idea to mark up the multiple choice questions *on the test itself* as you go through them. If 'A' can't be correct, then mark it off and go to 'B'. If 'B' is *possible*, circle it, and go to 'C', and so on. That way you are eliminating and narrowing choices that are *not possible* or are *less likely*. Using the process of elimination is a very helpful technique on the MCAT®. The computer-based test allows the use of strikethrough and highlight functions to help narrow down choices. It is best not to write your answers or considerations on a separate piece of notebook paper, as this does not simulate MCAT® day.

TIMING

Examkrackers 101 books are great tools with which to master MCAT® timing before MCAT® day. In order to get a high score on the MCAT®, it is important to finish each section completely, within the time allotted. The tests in this book can be taken timed or untimed. As you initially practice brand-new skills, you may want to go slowly in order to master them. But, remember that only timed tests accurately simulate MCAT® day and allow you to work on your timing.

Take a 5-second break before reading each passage. Look at the clock only once, at the halfway point (the 27th question). If the timer is before the 45-minute mark, slow down. If it is after the 45-minute mark, speed up. Developing an intuitive sense for good MCAT® timing and pace is an essential skill. With practice, you will come to know whether you are on-pace without looking at a clock. You will notice when you are slowing down or rushing, so you can adjust your speed accordingly.

If you run out of time on a test, consider where you spent the time that you could save. For instance, remember not to go back to the passage while answering questions, as the main idea you constructed is what you need to choose the best answer and this cannot be found by looking back at the passage. Once you are comfortable with timing and finishing on time, only go back to the passage when you know exactly where you are going in the passage and what you are looking for. As you take timed tests and gain comfort with CARS MCAT® skills, your timing will improve.

Make a schedule and distribute these 11 tests throughout your study period. If you are studying over a ten-week period, take one test from this book every week on the same day. Do not save all the tests for the few weeks immediately prior to the MCAT®, as MCAT® skills require time and practice to develop . Between tests, give yourself adequate time to review the test you take each week. Consciously plan what you will do differently on the next test in order to increase your CARS MCAT® score.

How to Use This Book to Increase Your MCAT® Score:

TEST REVIEW

Test review is the single most important thing you can do to change your MCAT® score. Reviewing the questions you get wrong, the questions you mark and even those you got right will help you learn what is working and what is not. Every question you get wrong is a gift, an opportunity to increase your score. Always think about how questions you get wrong are valuable – they are the pearls that will lead you directly to a higher MCAT® score.

Leave plenty of time for your review of each test. Review each test the same day, very soon after you take it, so you remember well how you solved the questions.

Leave ninety minutes to take each test and at least ninety minutes to review it with a short break between test and review.

Immediately after completing a test, take notes on what happened during the test. Then, take a short break for an hour or less. Next, sit down and check your answers. At the end of each test, you will be directed to the page in the back of the book where you can find the answers and answer explanations for that test. Every page of the tests has a tab and footer telling you the test number you are taking. Every page of the answers and explanations has a tab and footer telling you which test is being covered. Always be sure these match when checking your answers. There is no need to flip through pages and pages of explanations looking for the right test.

Make a list of question numbers you marked and/or got wrong. Do not yet read the answer explanations.

Compare your score to the last practice test you took. Your raw score is the number you answered correctly out of 53. Did your raw score increase since the last test? If it did, what did you do differently? Make a note to keep doing what worked. If it did not, what was different today? Make a commitment to change strategies that did not work.

It also helps to review those questions you got right in order to reinforce the approach, skills, and confidence that allowed you to solve those problems well.

Retake the questions you answered incorrectly before looking at the answer explanations. This allows you to build the most important MCAT® muscles of all: problem solving and independent thinking. Once you see the answer explanation, you lose the opportunity to learn how to solve the MCAT® question yourself. This may sometimes require multiple attempts, but the purpose of practice is for you to learn how to solve the questions. "Critical analysis" and "reasoning skills" are processes that require practice. Reading the explanation of how to get to the right answer should come only after you have tried your hardest to find your own way there.

Once you have made a second attempt, read the answer explanation for each question you got wrong in order to learn to think in ways that will get you a high score. Examkrackers answer explanations are process-oriented. They show you the reasoning process that leads to the elimination of each weak answer and the selection of the best answer. Our answer explanations will help you identify new strategies that work and will help you learn to think like the MCAT® to bring a high score.

CHANGE: MAKING COMMITMENTS

Immediately after each test, assess how it went. Write down specific commitments for future practice: what is needed next to build your CARS MCAT® skills? What are you doing right that you want to do more of? What is not working that you want to change?

Commitments work best when they are specific. Commitments work best when old, bad habits are directly linked to new, good habits. I can make a general commitment not to speed on the highway tomorrow, but inevitably I will find myself speeding again unless I have a specific, new plan. "When… Then…" commitments are most powerful.

When I do speed, then I will immediately slow down to 54 mph.

Similarly:

When I have negative thinking while taking the test,
Then I will take a five-second break and focus only on the question in front of me.

Or

When I have trouble understanding what I am reading,
Then I will take a five-second break and resume reading as if the passage were a children's story.

When you commit to avoiding the mistakes that led you to incorrect answers in one test, you will see improvement in your raw score on the next test.

Look toward the next date you will take a practice test. After each test review, document your commitments and keep them ready at hand to look over before you begin on the day of your next practice test.

There are two kinds of practice: practice that is repetitive and practice that is smart. Practice that is repetitive, in which you do the same thing over and over again, will reinforce skills that you already have but unfortunately, reinforces the very habits that are not working.

Smart practice not only builds new skills but is efficient and effective. It is not how much you practice, but how you practice. Smart practice means paying attention before, during and after each test.

1. Before each test, review your commitments to focus on the skills you want to build with this practice.

2. Be self-aware during each test. Notice what you are doing when you are reading passages and solving MCAT® questions. What are you thinking or feeling, what is going well, what is getting in your way, what MCAT® skills you are still struggling with?

3. Immediately after each test, evaluate how the commitments helped. If your score increased, what did you do differently that accounts for the increase? Write down a commitment to continue with this new skill. If your score decreased, what in your approach or environment was different? Write down a commitment to replace what is not working.

Scoring Your Practice Tests

Your raw score on each test in this book is a ratio of the number of questions you answered correctly over the total number of questions, 53. The best way to utilize your raw score is to be sure it increases with each practice test you take.

Please note: Even if Examkrackers derived a scaled score by analyzing the data from thousands of students, it would not accurately predict your AAMC MCAT® score. Examkrackers practice materials include a higher proportion of medium and difficult questions than the AAMC MCAT® and fewer easy questions in order to maximize your score increase. Since our students are at different stages of preparation for the MCAT® they do not represent the MCAT® day student population. For these reasons, a scaled score we could derive would not accurately predict your AAMC MCAT® score. Only a scaled score from the AAMC can accurately predict your AAMC MCAT® score.

Your goal is to get more questions right and fewer wrong with each Examkrackers practice test you take. Document your progress. A higher score with each practice test reflects that you are using the questions you get wrong and those you get right to learn and practice new skills that will increase your score. Increasing raw scores show that you are building the MCAT® skills that bring a high score on MCAT® day.

Complete Your MCAT® Preparation

To complete your preparation for the CARS MCAT® section, use this book along with Examkrackers Reasoning Skills manual and the Examkrackers Comprehensive MCAT® Course. Together these tools provide in-depth instruction in the skills needed to get a high score on the CARS MCAT® section.

To prepare fully for the four sections of the MCAT®, Examkrackers Complete Study Package includes six manuals packed with content review, MCAT® strategy, and guided practice. The corresponding MCAT® 101 Passages series allows you to practice the methods and build the skills taught in Examkrackers study manuals.

Examkrackers Live MCAT® Hotline is a service available ten hours per week so your questions can be addressed directly and interactively by expert, high scoring MCAT® instructors.

EK-Tests are the best full length simulated MCAT® product available on the market. Each electronic test matches the MCAT® in sources, style, format, length, question types, and skills and content tested. Tools to maximize review and score improvement are built-in.

Regularly visit the Examkrackers Forums where students' questions are answered and any errata are posted. Go to www.examkrackers.com or call 1.888.KRACKEM to learn more about Examkrackers materials, support and live MCAT® preparation, both online and in-person.

Toward your success!

TABLE OF CONTENTS

WARM-UP

0

Passages: 2

Time: 15 minutes

INSTRUCTIONS: Use these warm-up passages and questions to become familiar with the MCAT® CARS section and to assess your skills before beginning Practice Test 1.

Each passage is followed by associated questions. Read the passage, then select the best answer to each question. If you are unsure of the answer, rule out incorrect choices and select from the remaining options. Indicate your answer beside the option you choose.

Passage 1 (Questions 1-4)

This passage was adapted from "Food Sovereignty: Power, Gender, and the Right to Food." Patel R. *PLoS Medicine.* 2012. doi: 10.1371/journal.pmed.1001223 for use under the terms of the Creative Commons CC BY 3.0 license (http://creativecommons.org/licenses/by/3.0/legalcode).

One of the most enduring misconceptions about hunger is that it is primarily the result of a deficit in global food production. If this were so, we might expect food to be absent at times and in places where people die of hunger. Yet economist Amartya Sen has shown that in the majority of cases of widespread famine-related death since WWII, food has been available within the famine-affected area. People have died not for want of food, but for want of the entitlement to eat it. Questions about hunger and its attendant pathologies, therefore, ought to begin with questions about social and political configurations around power over food, rather than about the mere presence or absence of food in the vicinity of a hungry individual.

Although no single commonly agreed-upon definition of hunger exists, two common standards prevail: "undernourishment" and "food security." The former refers to the number of people "whose dietary energy consumption is continuously below a minimum dietary energy requirement for maintaining a healthy life and carrying out a light physical activity." Undernourishment is a condition suffered by individuals. It is, however, usually established not through individual surveys but through an analysis of a country's food availability, household purchasing power, and entitlements. Current estimates put the worldwide number of undernourished people at nearly one billion.

The concept of "food security" attempts to capture the notion of hunger as a deficit not of calories, but as a violation of a broader set of social, economic, and physical conditions. In 1996, the Food and Agriculture Organization of the United Nations (FAO) established at its World Food Summit the most widely agreed-upon definition that "Food security, at the individual, household, national, regional and global levels [is achieved] when all people, at all times, have physical and economic access to sufficient, safe and nutritious food to meet their dietary needs and food preferences for an active and healthy life."

By definition, more people are food insecure than are undernourished, and food insecurity precedes undernourishment. Although there are few people in the United States whose calorie intake is continuously below the threshold of maintaining a healthy life, there are many who, at some point during any given year, are unable to meet their food needs. Many US citizens live in food-insecure households, and the distribution of food insecurity is uneven. For instance, more than one-third of all female-headed households were food insecure in 2010, compared to only one-fourth of male-headed households.

Since food insecurity is a broader measure than that of undernourishment, it has been linked to both hunger and obesity, particularly among women. If hunger is a symptom of a lack of control over the socioeconomic context in which one attempts to eat, it is not unreasonable to understand that lack of control as correlated with factors associated with obesity too. It is possible to have sufficient calories, but insufficiently nutritious food for a healthy life. Armed with this understanding, and with persistent evidence across countries of women and girls' disempowerment compared to men and boys, it becomes easier to appreciate the systematically higher rates of food insecurity among women.

Question 1

Based on the passage, which of the following assumptions is most likely to be true?

○ A. Food secure individuals are well-nourished.
○ B. Food insecure individuals will become undernourished.
○ C. Undernourished individuals can be food secure.
○ D. Well-nourished individuals are food secure.

Question 2

Which of the following assertions in the passage does the author support with examples or evidence?

○ A. The greatest misconception about hunger is that it is primarily due to a deficit in global food production.
○ B. Undernourishment is a condition suffered by individuals.
○ C. More people are food insecure than undernourished.
○ D. It is possible to have sufficient calories but insufficient nutrition for a healthy life.

Question 3

When using the term "for want of the entitlement to eat it" (paragraph 1), the author seems to mean the ability to:

○ A. receive food.
○ B. find food to consume.
○ C. produce food.
○ D. consume food in excess.

Question 4

It may be inferred from the passage that female-headed households can become more food secure by:

○ A. transferring power to a man.
○ B. relocating to another area.
○ C. applying for help from the government.
○ D. becoming more powerful in the community.

Passage 2 (Questions 5-8)

Since the feminist movement in the 1960s, sexism has been an important research subject for both sociologists and linguists. According to the Sapir-Whorf Hypothesis, language not only comes into being under the influence of society and culture but also affects people's perceptions of reality and the world in turn. News, as one of the pragmatic uses of language, shares the same attribute: shaped by and reshapes society. As news media has become the major channel for people to obtain authoritative information, feminist media research has entered a prosperous stage and has drawn attention both at home and abroad.

Addressed terms are used to ascertain people's roles and positions in the society, reflecting and affecting people's perceptions about others. However, compared with male politicians who have the same power and influence, female politicians tend to have more addressed terms, which make their positions and roles weaker and vaguer. It is often found that the addressed terms of male politicians are either in their full names, in the form of "Mr. + surname," or in the form of "title + full name/surname," with no mention of their roles as fathers or husbands. In the 2008 United States presidential election, Barack Hussein Obama was commonly addressed as Barack Obama, Mr. Obama, and Senator Barack Obama. However, his rival in the Democratic Party, Hillary Diane Rodham Clinton, was addressed in terms like Mrs. Clinton, and was frequently referred to as the wife of a former US president. Other famous female leaders, such as Margaret Thatcher and Angela Merkel, are often addressed as Mrs. Thatcher and Mrs. Merkel, and their roles as mothers, daughters, and wives are frequently mentioned in reports.

Mr. and Mrs. are respectively the honorific title of males and females, but the former is used for the sake of respect, with no indication of marital status, while the latter shows not only respect but also marital status, which puts women in a position subordinate to their husbands. Women are classified into the married "Mrs." and unmarried "Miss," while all men are "Mr." As Dale Spender commented, "the practice of labeling women as married or single also serves supremely sexist ends…there is no tension between the representation of women as sex objects and male ownership rights over women and this has been resolved by an explicit and most visible device of designating the married status of women."

Margaret Gibbon found in one study that when reading a riddle (a boy whose father has already died in an accident was sent to hospital, but the surgeon refused to operate on him because "he's my son"), people are confused because they have a stereotyped image of surgeons as men and have difficulty envisioning surgeons as women. Females are always semantically absent from professional and prestigious occupations, which are usually considered exclusive to males (i.e., lawyer, pilot, doctor, judge, mayor, governor, administrator, etc.). When these occupations are taken by women, people add "woman," "lady," or "female" in front of these words. This practice establishes men as the norm and women as derivative.

Furthermore, many female terms which start out as harmless or positive undergo semantic degradation while their masculine counterparts do not. Governess, which referred to female rulers at the beginning, can be used now only to refer to a family tutor. "Governor," however, retains its original meaning of lord. Other words such as duchess or mayoress not only indicate the position itself but also suggest marital status, denoting "the wife of." While many words change meaning over time, a clear pattern has emerged among the corpus of gendered terms.

This passage was adapted from "Sexism in News: A Comparative Study on the Portray of Female and Male Politicians in *The New York Times*." Dai H, Xu X. *Open Journal of Modern Linguistics*. 2014. 4 doi: 10.4236/ojml.2014.45061 for use under the terms of the Creative Commons CC BY 4.0 license (https://creativecommons.org/licenses/by/4.0/legalcode).

Question 5

A woman wants to apply for jobs and does not know how to sign her email. What advice would the author be most likely to give?

- **A.** She should sign as "Miss + Full Name."
- **B.** She should sign as "Ms. + Full Name."
- **C.** She should sign as "Mrs. + Full Name."
- ○ **D.** She should sign with "Lady + Profession" before her full name.

Question 6

The author suggests that sexism in the media is most difficult for females because:

- ○ **A.** most journalists are male.
- ○ **B.** female politicians are still the minority.
- **C.** language norms are more derogatory towards females.
- ○ **D.** women tend to hold less respected jobs.

Question 7

The author's argument about sexism in language would be most challenged by the finding that:

- ● **A.** readers of a newspaper that used sexist language to cover an election still voted for the female candidate.
- ○ **B.** most women reported that they did not notice sexism in the media.
- ⊘ **C.** most women reported that they did notice sexism in the media, but were not bothered by it.
- ○ **D.** most men reported that they felt sexist language had affected them.

Question 8

According to the passage, female politicians are particularly likely to experience sexist language if:

- ○ **A.** they are inexperienced.
- ○ **B.** they run for a national election.
- ○ **C.** they are attractive.
- ⊘ **D.** they have a family.

STOP. If you finish before time is called, check your work. You may go back to any question in this test.

ANSWERS & EXPLANATIONS for the Warm-Up Passages can be found on p. 179.

TEST ①

Number of Questions: 53
Time: 90 minutes

INSTRUCTIONS: Each passage is followed by associated questions. Read the passage, then select the best answer to each question. If you are unsure of the answer, rule out incorrect choices and select from the remaining options. Indicate your answer beside the option you choose.

Passage 1 (Questions 1-6)

The traditional rationale for history's inclusion in public education is based predominantly on the idea that the transmission of a positive story about the national past will inculcate in young people a sense of loyalty to the state and a reassuring and positive sense of identity and belonging. Until the 1970s, the story or narrative that was told in history lessons in England was essentially positive, uncritical, and unproblematic. The idea that more than one story might be told was not a feature of school history.

England moved away from this 'traditional' model of school history with the first National Curriculum for history, which mandated a balance between British, European, and World history, and between political, economic, social, and cultural history. It also placed significant emphasis on the importance of developing pupils' critical literacy, including the idea that young people should learn that the past could be interpreted in different ways.

A number of newspaper articles and high profile academic historians have lamented the fact that because of this move away from traditional school history, young people appear to know nothing of their nation's past. Politicians and policymakers also expressed concern about the move away from the use of school history to inculcate national pride.

The new curriculum's opposition assumes that a return to traditional school history will serve to increase the motivation and engagement of pupils and the proportion of pupils who continue their studies beyond the age at which the subject becomes optional. Currently, only 30% of pupils in England choose to continue to study history once it becomes an optional subject. Research suggests that this is due to school policies on examination entries rather than pupil disengagement with the subject, with schools opting to enter less-able pupils for 'easier' examination subjects. A majority of pupils in the 1970s thought that the subject was 'useless and boring,' while recently a far higher proportion of pupils considered history to be interesting and useful.

Recent government statements about history in schools might be seen as a renewed attempt at 'cultural restorationism': the attempt to use the education system as a means of promoting values and dispositions associated with ideological positions and preferences. Events such as the 7/7 bombings in the UK led to calls to strengthen education for social cohesion in the increasingly multicultural and multi-ethnic Britain. The assumption that teaching a positive story of the national past will promote social cohesion is an illusory and untested one. Research has found that a majority of young people in England did not agree that 'a common history promotes common bonds.'

The weaknesses and flaws in the current arrangements for the teaching of history include over-reliance on short 'snippets' from sources, a reduction in the time allocated to history in English schools, and unsatisfactory and ineffective forms of assessing pupil progress in history. However, the attempt to bring back the traditional model of history education runs the risk of reverting to a form of school history that is outmoded and of limited relevance to young people growing up in the twenty-first century. In an era when students have access to alternative ways of learning about the past to a much greater degree than in the 1970s, putting forward an unproblematically positive portrayal of the national story is a dubious and probably doomed enterprise.

The desired form of school history depends on what sort of citizens the state wants to cultivate. Is it better to have citizens who are loyal or who are discerning in their ability to handle information? Only time will tell.

Question 1

Based on the passage, the author would most likely support changes to the science curriculum that include:

- A. the transition from alchemy to modern chemistry.
- B. acknowledgement of great scientists from England.
- C. an abbreviated summary of the scientific method.
- D. interactive experiments and models.

Question 2

Which of the following opinions discussed in the passage has the LEAST supporting or opposing evidence?

- A. The youth of England are losing their patriotism.
- B. Nationalism is important now more than ever.
- C. Students are losing interest in their history lessons.
- D. Knowing the past is the best way to create a better future.

Question 3

Based on the information in the passage, it is most reasonable to conclude that the author wrote this passage in order to:

- A. identify flaws in the current history curriculum.
- B. defend the National Curriculum.
- C. criticize the traditional idea of nationalism.
- D. propose changes for history education.

Question 4

Suppose a country successfully employed cultural restorationism as defined in the passage. Which of the following statements is most likely to be true about that country?

- A. All of the students would receive the same education.
- B. The majority of people would be in the same political party.
- C. Much of the population would support anti-terrorism laws.
- D. Many of the churches would preach similar sermons.

Question 5

Which of the following views is most in line with the author's opinion of the traditional history curriculum?

- ○ A. It was rooted in government propaganda.
- ○ B. It taught important historical information to its contemporaries.
- ○ C. It neglected newly recognized historical facts.
- ● D. It failed to adapt to changing cultural norms.

Question 6

A new study found that England awarded more master's degrees in history after the integration of the National Curriculum than before its implementation. How does this finding affect the author's argument about the National Curriculum? → *this claim is made in the article*

- ● A. It would support the claim that current students find history interesting.
- ○ B. It would substantiate the claim that recent students opt out of history when it is no longer required.
- ○ C. It would reiterate the claim that past students disliked the traditional curriculum.
- ○ D. It would negate the claim that the current curriculum is flawed.

Passage 2 (Questions 7-12)

While it is generally known that the founders of Alcoholics Anonymous (AA) got their start in recovery through the evangelistic, Christian-oriented Oxford Group, many rank-and-file members are mostly unaware of the large debt owed there. Early AA members worked hard to distance the organization from these roots. However, many things were borrowed, many undercurrents remain, and many debts are still owed to AA's Christian roots.

Among its innovations, AA introduced a very different approach to the will. Rather than a will that is functional but misdirected, the group presented a will that was partly disabled by its vulnerability to alcohol. This represents a crucial theological insight, for it moves AA away from the temptation of a moralistic, judgmental and perfectionistic understanding of the problem (that is, sin) and actually puts it more in line with evangelical Christian traditions.

This concept of a partially paralyzed will calls up some ancient theological battles. For instance, are we able to choose recovery from sin, or is our will in a bondage that can only be loosened with divine help? And if instead our will is neutral, thus free to pursue good or evil, then why do we hesitate to say that persons struggling with addiction are fully responsible for their plight? In calling into question the certainty of biological determinism, AA implicitly critiques the notion that human beings are at liberty to choose good or evil.

Yet this move has also led in an unexpected direction, bringing back a concept of evil. While mainstream Christianity derides a belief in a literal devil, it has concomitantly lost a way to conceptualize "evil forces." The addiction recovery model may unknowingly fight against this loss. Indeed, the popularity of calling many types of human dysfunction "addiction" may gain some of its popularity by explaining how dangerous substances or disordered processes can tempt and control the individual. In this way, it offers an explanation and a warning to a contemporary culture in which science seems to have promised much but has also delivered many dangerous and unintended consequences.

In effect, early AA actually took more seriously the nuances embedded in the concept of evil. One sub-classification, "moral evil," also known as sin, involves human cooperation, one's own, or that of another, implying that one can be a victim of another's sin. However, AA also implicitly considers the idea of "radical evil," *i.e.*, non-moral evil, which cannot be clearly attributed to human wrongdoing. It does this by identifying a substance and disease process that is cunning, baffling, powerful, and essentially without clear cause. In this way, it comes close to contemporary theological understandings of "radical evil" as unlinked to personal wrongdoing, yet still exerting a powerful influence. AA does this by objectifying the foe and containing it in a physical substance just waiting to ruin one's life if one succumbs to it.

While alcohol is not identified as a universal diabolic power dangerous to everyone, persons with significant recovery may also find its power greatly reduced. It is nevertheless important to note that this highlighting of alcohol's power over those people who are susceptible effectively externalizes radical evil, because although one may be vulnerable to it, there is a sure way to block it out:

total abstinence. Yet the ever-expanding addiction metaphor skates close to re-introducing a more universal human vulnerability to radical evil by showing how addiction can come along even with necessary substances and processes, like food and sex.

Question 7

The author relies most heavily on which argument to support the claim that AA's understanding of human willpower differs from that of its Christian ideological predecessors?

- **A.** AA asserts that alcohol is an evil force that is beyond the ability of human willpower to overcome.
- **B.** AA has been more effective in giving form to an otherwise symbolic enemy.
- **C.** AA believes that human will can choose good as easily as it can choose evil.
- **D.** AA views alcohol as impairing the willpower of some more than others.

Question 8

The author of the passage would most likely agree with which of the following conclusions concerning the nature of addiction?

- **A.** Addiction is more of a moral evil than a radical evil.
- **B.** All humans may be prone to some form of addiction.
- **C.** People are most likely to resolve their addictions in a judgment-free setting.
- **D.** Biological factors play no role in human addiction.

Question 9

The passage describes Christian theology and the beliefs of AA as similar in that both:

- **A.** call into question the teachings and consequences of science.
- **B.** believe sin is largely the result of external forces.
- **C.** argue that humans are endowed with unfettered free will.
- **D.** view food as a source of addiction for a subset of humans.

Question 10

The author stops short of calling the AA conception of alcohol a traditional, evangelical example of radical evil because:

- **A.** resisting it is at least somewhat within a human's control.
- **B.** alcohol has the power to shatter an individual's livelihood.
- **C.** the addictive nature of alcohol is external to individual willpower.
- **D.** too many other types of human dysfunction exist to single out alcoholism.

Question 11

Which finding, if true, would most strongly *undermine* AA's view of alcohol as an externalized threat?

- **A.** Alcoholism is predominantly acquired as a function of habit rather than heredity.
- **B.** Binge drinking is the strongest predictor of addiction to alcohol.
- **C.** The physiological effects of withdrawal make abstinence from alcohol excruciating.
- **D.** The overwhelming majority of those who complete rehabilitation for addiction relapse.

Question 12

Which scenario would the author see as the *weakest* example of radical evil?

- **A.** After a devastating flood, residents of a village resort to theft from neighboring peoples.
- **B.** When his wife is in labor, a man drives nearly twice the speed limit on the way to the hospital.
- **C.** To prevent her son from going to prison, a mother provides false testimony, implicating a neighbor.
- **D.** A father, beset with mental illness, verbally abuses his partner and children.

Next ▶

Passage 3 (Questions 13-18)

Playing violent video games or watching violent TV/movies has commonly been believed to allow people to "vent" their aggressive inclinations and therefore behave less aggressively after playing/watching. This is known as the aggression catharsis hypothesis—the idea that "venting" aggression through exposure to media violence reduces the risk of later aggressive behavior.

Therapeutic catharsis, on the other hand, is the concept that allowing oneself to feel and express one's feelings helps to maintain mental health. This clinical focus on the beneficial effects of expressing one's emotions in a therapeutic context, thereby allowing oneself to avoid or resolve potential conflicts, has received empirical support. The aggression catharsis hypothesis states that viewing others' aggression (either in person or via the media) reduces viewers' aggressive feelings and behaviors. A. A. Brill, who introduced Freudian psychoanalysis to the United States, recommended attending prize fights once a month to reduce the aggressive drive.

There is empirical evidence that when people learn about and believe in catharsis, they change their choices and behaviors based on their beliefs. In one study, participants were randomly assigned to read a fake newspaper article that either refuted the catharsis hypothesis, supported it, or was unrelated to it, and then all were insulted and angered. After being angered, they read descriptions of eight video games and rated how much they wanted to play them. Angered participants who read the pro-catharsis argument wanted to play the violent video games the most.

When angered, behaving aggressively feels pleasurable. This may be interpreted by people to suggest that they would behave less aggressively after engaging in violent media. Viewing media violence or playing a violent video game can indeed provide short-term enjoyment or distraction from a difficult situation. In this sense, then, media violence can reduce the immediate risk of aggression, because if we leave a frustrating situation and go home to play a violent video game, we are using the media to help cope with our difficult feelings at that moment. Using media as a distraction or coping technique is not, however, the same thing as reducing our tendency to respond aggressively. It is removing us from the situation, which could equally be done by going for lunch. → faulty interpretation

People often say they get an "adrenaline rush" when they play violent video games. There is evidence that violent video games result in increased physiological arousal, including increased heart rate, blood pressure, and release of stress hormones into the blood stream. This is part of why media violence is so exciting and fun to watch. The problem is that this stress response is an acute response system, not a chronic system. The stress response was not designed to stay active for hours, but when playing a violent video game, it can. Feeling tired or "spent" after playing a violent video game can make us feel like we are now relaxed, and we likely interpret that to mean that catharsis has occurred. In fact, all it means is that our bodies are tired of the stress of playing a violent game, and we have now spent hours priming our aggressive thoughts, feelings, and attitudes, often having them reinforced by the game. → misinterpretation

This passage was adapted from "Catharsis and Media Violence: A Conceptual Analysis." Gentile DA. *Societies*. 2013. 3 doi: 10.3390/soc3040491 for use under the terms of the Creative Commons CC BY 3.0 license (https://creativecommons.org/licenses/by/3.0/legalcode).

Question 13

The main thesis of the passage is that:

- A. using media violence as a coping strategy reduces the short-term probability of behaving aggressively.
- B. based on empirical evidence, engaging in media violence affects people's aggressive behaviors.
- C. people's interpretations of their reactions to media violence are faulty.
- D. playing violent video games causes chronic stress, which inevitably leads to aggression.

Question 14

Given the information in the passage, which of the following situations best reflects the author's description of "therapeutic catharsis" (paragraph 2)?

- A. Punching a pillow to let off steam
- B. Taking deep breaths and burying one's feelings
- C. Going to a comedic film as a distraction
- D. Watching a wrestling match to reduce aggressive drive

Question 15

According to the passage, it is reasonable to conclude that all of the following are true about media EXCEPT:

- A. media evokes a range of emotions.
- B. media diverts our attention from what we truly care about.
- C. media takes on a variety of forms.
- D. media can be employed in a therapeutic context.

Question 16

Research has shown that people who speak to a therapist when they are angry are less likely to behave aggressively. Based on passage information, would this finding change the author's opinion about the aggression catharsis hypothesis?

- A. Yes, because speaking to a therapist is a coping strategy that has now been shown to decrease aggressive tendencies.
- B. Yes, because the author does not believe people can effectively vent their anger.
- C. No, because aggression catharsis is not achieved by vocalizing one's feelings.
- D. No, because the author already claims that there is a clinical benefit to aggression catharsis.

Question 17

Based on passage information, one could reasonably conclude that the human stress response:

A. has adapted to be active for various time periods depending on human need.

B. can cause dangerous physiological symptoms, including cardiac events.

C. only reinforces aggressive feelings.

D. is provoked in response to simulated threats.

Question 18

The information in this passage would be of most use to:

A. a psychiatrist seeking to understand the source of a patient's anger.

B. an educational consultant determining why students who say they are happy are often referred to guidance counselors for behavioral health concerns.

C. a film director coaching her actors to leverage their own emotions when expressing what their characters are feeling.

D. an army general conducting research into how to harness the stress response and apply it productively to wartime efforts.

Passage 4 (Questions 19-24)

Musical actors compete not only in terms of offering their labor. Rather, comparable to models in the fashion industries or actors in public theatres, they offer their entire embodied self. Hence, further developing their own identity as part of their employability is a permanent task for them. One important aspect of this ongoing identity management is to create a personalized profile that distinguishes one actor from another, allowing him or her to stand out in the crowd.

Actors at the beginning of their careers have a much clearer understanding of their labor market in terms of roles, forms of engagements, and institutional settings. Young actors know of the necessity to build up a role profile and to collect numerous experiences in musical productions. Professional resilience is acquired by collecting as many valuable experiences as possible as a musical performer. Therefore, they invest time and effort in creating an ideal musical performer's CV by associating themselves with reputable employers, big theatres, prominent locations and, of course, many star roles. Once this has been achieved, future auditions will be passed more easily, or might even be skipped completely. This sort of adaptive orientation in building up a positional identity is fundamentally *telescopic*, as it is clearly focused on a particular image.

The networking strategies within the logic of adaptability, which are utilized by more experienced actors, differ significantly from those of the neophytes. These networks encompass many more actors, are differentiated in several layers, and are more extensive in spatial terms. Experienced musical actors usually keep in touch with many actors from the business. This layer within their network has grown organically as their array of former colleagues and collaborators expands with each successive engagement.

These more complex, multilayered professional networks of more experienced musical actors have their advantages in a labor market that is largely over-supplied and in which demand for veteran actors is stagnant or even shrinking. Broad networks are helpful in the sense that they provide advance access to information about auditions. Sometimes they might even generate invitations to auditions, so that the first round of competition can be skipped. However, invitations do not allow for these competitive situations to be circumvented completely. Also, as their careers progress, musical actors increasingly realize that the possibilities to build up their reputations are rather restricted. In the long run, it is possible to build a reputation within a network, but constructing a public reputation is almost impossible.

Moreover, experienced actors are very aware of the limited efficiency of their networking activities. The initiation and maintenance of strategic ties through socializing, for instance, requires their presence at business events, such as first night celebrations or festivals. They have to stay for hours in order to find an appropriate occasion to approach the person they wish to contact. Ephemeral ties to former colleagues require some effort to be maintained, despite the ubiquity of social media. With increasing experience, musical actors realize that they initially overestimated the enabling effects of networks while at the same time they underestimated the effort required to build up and maintain their networks.

Next ▶

Recently graduated musical actors employ a strategy geared towards adaptation. At the beginning of a career, the main emphasis is on getting into the market. Musical actors with 10–15 years of professional experience exemplify labor market strategies towards *adaptability*. This becomes necessary in a volatile and over-saturated labor market in which public reputation turns out to be unattainable and the demand for older stage ages drops dramatically.

This passage was adapted from "Once You are in You Might Need to Get Out: Adaptation and Adaptability in Volatile Labor Markets – The Case of Musical Actors." Ibert O, Schmidt S. 2014. *Soc. Sci.* 3 doi: 10.3390/socsci3010001 for use under the terms of the Creative Commons CC BY 4.0 license (http://creativecommons.org/licenses/by/4.0/legalcode).

Question 19

According to the author, the networks of more established performers differ from those of neophytes in which of the following ways?

I. They are built around a narrower sampling of the performers' abilities.

II. These networks are more helpful for learning about auditions in distant cities.

III. They provide more advantages in the audition process.

- **A.** II only
- **B.** I and II
- **C.** I and III
- **D.** II and III

Question 20

Which of the following is most like the labor market for more experienced performers?

- **A.** A desktop computer whose interface must be continuously redesigned despite a consumer base that prefers laptops
- **B.** An aging politician who has lost touch with the needs of her electorate
- **C.** A former runway model who has returned to college to acquire the credentials necessary to enter another industry
- **D.** A former professional athlete who practices his sport by coaching youth leagues, since his injuries preclude his ability to play at a high level

Question 21

The author implies that strategies of adaptation and those of adaptability differ in that:

- **A.** the former is naïve, while the latter is more mature.
- **B.** the former is newer, while the latter is more dated.
- **C.** the former is more optimistic about market conditions, while the latter is more pessimistic.
- **D.** the former is narrower, while the latter is broader.

Question 22

The passage implies that younger actors are most likely to be successful by:

- **A.** etching out a niche audience.
- **B.** emphasizing their unique qualities in auditions.
- **C.** crafting a narrow public image.
- **D.** broadening professional networks at opening night galas.

Question 23

Directors prefer to cast performers with whom they are familiar from previous work. If true, how does this statement affect the views presented in the passage?

- **A.** It neither contradicts information presented in the passage nor seriously undermines the central thesis.
- **B.** It does not contradict information presented in the passage, but it seriously compromises the central thesis.
- **C.** It contradicts information presented in the passage without seriously undermining the central thesis.
- **D.** It contradicts information presented in the passage while seriously compromising the central thesis.

Question 24

The author's use of the word "telescopic" in the second paragraph most likely refers to a performer who:

- **A.** wishes to project a narrow range of professional personas.
- **B.** cherry-picks audition opportunities to land the perfect role.
- **C.** remains mindful of a future where his or her market opportunities will be diminished.
- **D.** attempts only the most challenging roles to demonstrate versatility.

Passage 5 (Questions 25-29)

Observational studies collect data on people in their natural environments and usually do not impose risks on subjects that are greater than the risks ordinarily encountered in daily life, or "minimal risks" as defined under federal research regulations. A field study of pesticide applicators that measures pesticide residue on subjects before and after the workday would impose few risks beyond the risk of loss of confidentiality. Although the subjects would be exposed to pesticides at work, this exposure would have occurred even if they did not participate in the study - it is not a risk imposed by the study.

A field study was designed by the Environmental Protection Agency (EPA) concerning pesticides in the environment surrounding children. Families with high pesticide use were invited to participate in the study, and the investigators planned to take both surface wipe samples from around the home and urine samples from the children. Parents were asked to record their children's activity on camera, were given monetary compensation for the cameras, and were not required to start using pesticides to be included in the study. Critics complained that the study was an intentional exposure study that treated children like guinea pigs. They alleged that the study targeted low-income groups and that monetary support constituted an unacceptable conflict of interest. EPA officials were unable to convince politicians and the public that the study should go forward.

Experimental studies may impose risks on research subjects that are more than minimal. The EPA conducts studies on the effects of air pollution on the human respiratory system. Scientists measure subjects' responses to various exposures, and monitor the subjects' medical conditions. Some experiments that expose subjects to pollutants involve a bronchoscopy, an insertion of a tube, to examine the airway and collect a small piece of lung tissue for analysis. The risks of a bronchoscopy include bronchial spasms, difficulty breathing, bleeding, cardiac arrhythmias, infections, hoarseness, and a 0.1% chance of death.

Imposing more than minimal risks on subjects who are not expected to receive any benefits from the research can be appropriately justified if the study is expected to yield important benefits for society. Trials of new drugs on healthy subjects usually involve risks that can be ethically justified, according to most commentators, because they are a necessary step in treating diseases.

Environmental health research experiments do not produce new medical treatments, but these studies can be justified if they are expected to protect public health. It is essential for investigators to take precautions to minimize risks to subjects, such as using criteria to disqualify potential subjects who have an increased risk for developing health problems, follow-up with subjects after the testing period, and implementing effective procedures for reporting adverse events.

Some environmental health studies impose risks on third parties. A study of agricultural workers may impose risks on farmers who employ the workers. The federal research regulations only mention the obligation to minimize risks to research subjects, so some writers have questioned whether researchers should address these risks at all. Others have argued that there is an ethical obligation to address third party risks based on the notion of avoiding harm.

Some private companies have conducted pesticide experiments on human subjects, exposing people to minute amounts of chemicals that can be toxic in larger doses. Commentators have argued that these experiments are unethical because companies designed these experiments to generate data to convince regulatory agencies to weaken pesticide registration rules. Others argue that some pesticide experiments can be justified if they are expected to yield important public health benefits and if these important endeavors satisfy stringent scientific and ethical standards.

This passage was adapted from "Environmental Health Research Involving Human Subjects: Ethical Issues." Resnik DB. *Environmental Health Insights.* 2008. 2, for use under the terms of the Creative Commons CC BY 3.0 license (http://creativecommons.org/licenses/by/3.0/legalcode).

Question 25

The passage suggests that "minimal risk" can be ambiguous because:

- **A.** every risk affects a subject in a distinct way.
- **B.** risks can be interpreted dissimilarly depending on the interpreter.
- **C.** the risk can change based on the manner of data collection.
- **D.** a risk that is minimal to one person may be more than minimal to a third party.

Question 26

Based on the information in the passage, which of these situations would the author consider to be most similar to minimal risk?

- **A.** Getting a parking ticket at a research conference
- **B.** Waking up with a sore neck after sleeping on a friend's couch
- **C.** Stepping on gum on the usual walk to work
- **D.** Getting a flat tire while picking up a friend from jail

Question 27

A new observational study was approved to monitor the effects of a failing waste water treatment system on the human body. Based on the information in the passage, the study was likely approved because:

- **A.** the study was unpublicized, so potential critics were unaware of impending harm.
- **B.** researchers hypothesized that consuming the waste water would not endanger the study subjects.
- **C.** information from the study could be used in a review of the waste water treatment system.
- **D.** the subjects in the study would be provided with resources to move away from the treatment system.

Question 28

It can reasonably be concluded that the author discussed the effects on third parties in order to:

- A. reiterate the ambiguous nature of the term "minimal risk."
- B. provide context for why risks need to be continuously examined.
- C. emphasize how environmental health studies differ from other types of studies.
- D. suggest that industry standards regarding risk do not always translate to actual studies.

Question 29

Based on the information in the passage, it is reasonable to conclude that the author believes experimental studies most differ from observational studies in that:

- A. observational studies impose only minimal risks.
- B. experimental studies require greater justification.
- C. observational studies do not lead to new medical treatments.
- D. experimental studies often have greater consequences.

Passage 6 (Questions 30-35)

The audience of the TV show *Mad Men* finds pleasure in the tiny details that make the contemporary television series look so convincingly like the set of an old movie. The show instigated a full-blown consumer fever for all things mid-century: fashions, lifestyles, and the art of consumer America. Magazines like GQ, Vogue, and Vanity Fair not only put the stars of the show on their covers but also present readers with style instructions for their own lives. The US clothing retailer Banana Republic used the distinctive 1960s look as inspiration for a nationwide fashion campaign. Second-hand shopping also boomed to create personal vintage *Mad Men*-esque looks. These trends attest to the show's status as a social meme.

Not everyone is crazy for *Mad Men*. The show's ability to generate consumer heat has been interpreted by some television and cultural critics as direct evidence of its weakness as genuine television art. *Mad Men* has been accused of being primarily interested in selling audiences on life in the 1960s in the midst of the baby boom, trading consumer nostalgia for genuine historicity. Mark Greif remarks, "The less you think about the plot, the more you are free to luxuriate in the low sofas and Eames chairs and shiny IBM typewriters." He takes exception to the way the show invites the audience to take pleasure in looking at the past, even while it draws attention to the many undesirable aspects of that history, such as sexism, racism, and homophobia.

Other critics note that there exists a substantial body of film scholarship that draws attention to the way in which props and costumes are foregrounded in costume films, period pieces and melodramas. In analyzing such genres, scholars point to the alternative narratives that are established via the metaphoric language of period objects and actions. Often the spectator is aware that objects possess a significance beyond themselves and their immediate function, but ultimately is excluded from their exact codified meaning. For example, the purchase of a fainting couch may be no mere acquired antique but an object expression of sublimated and conflicting desires of a character for a more traditional past and a liberated future.

The essayist Daniel Mendelsohn proposed that the audience's enjoyment of the show's mid-century aesthetics demonstrates a failure to fully conceive the significance of the past. *Mad Men*'s appeal to a young demographic, Mendelsohn suggests, is an example of inauthentic nostalgia, saying, "only those who cannot remember the period would long to return there, and only then because they are lured by a world made of appealing surfaces." Other reviewers agree, saying *Mad Men* is "a delicious but ultimately meaningless immersion in style over substance."

Mad Men mobilizes objects and visual design from mid-century America to establish the role of material things in characterizing the complexity of individuals, their relationships to one another, and society more broadly. Audiences delight in undertaking the work of understanding these relationships within the frame of the narrative and also delight in mobilizing similar objects to similar ends in their own lives, as through second-hand shopping. This practice demonstrates how the past exists through textual traces in a cultural and ideological conversation with the present. Old items are desirable not only because they represent an alternative to the present but, more specifically, because they represent an alternative to contemporary modes of consumption and production.

This passage was adapted from "Seeing the World Second Hand: *Mad Men* and the Vintage Consumer." Hamilton C. *Cultural Studies Review*. 2012. 18(2) doi:10.5130/csr.v18i2.2766 for use under the terms of the Creative Commons CC BY 4.0 license (https://creativecommons.org/licenses/by/4.0/legalcode).

Question 30

Based on the passage, with which of the following statements about *Mad Men* is the author most likely to agree?

- A. *Mad Men* should be taught in film courses as a model for characterization.
- B. The show is a complex period piece that is unduly attacked by critics.
- C. The beautifully captured images are not matched by an elegantly executed plot line.
- D. Each well-dressed character is undermined by a sense of emptiness.

Question 31

Which of the following most closely represents a social meme as presented in the passage?

- A. A celebrity that induces young girls to wear only red lipstick and stiletto heels
- B. A movie that causes one fan to start looking for UFOs and another to become an astronaut
- C. A picture that is used on several Internet sites to signify an unpopular opinion
- D. A dystopian novel that popularizes a new hairstyle and also instigates a rise in archery classes

Question 32

Consumer nostalgia, as described in the passage, refers to:

- A. a marketing campaign by the producers of *Mad Men*.
- B. a fond remembrance of items from the past.
- C. the use of longing for old objects to sell the TV show.
- D. the viewers' desire to remember their past purchases.

Question 33

Which of the following, if true, would provide the greatest support for Greif's argument (paragraph 2)?

- A. An advertisement for an episode with a successful and well-dressed gay couple attracted media attention.
- B. The top comments on an episode featuring Vietnam soldiers remarked upon the crispness of the soldiers' uniforms.
- C. The main characters of *Mad Men* are Caucasian, while people of color play supportive and comical roles.
- D. An underlying theme of the show is the way women in well-furnished homes support their families and themselves .

Question 34

In the film *2001: A Space Odyssey*, a pen floats through the spaceship to signify man losing control of his tools. Which reference in the passage most closely relates to this scene?

- A. The shiny IBM typewriters used in *Mad Men*
- B. The old items that present an alternate form of consumption
- C. The description of a fainting couch
- D. Material things that connect individuals

Question 35

If a study found that the audience of *Mad Men* is evenly split between millennials and baby boomers, which of the following would be true?

- A. Mendelsohn's argument would be weakened because a generation that lived in the 1960s appreciates the television program.
- B. Mendelsohn's argument would be upheld because the older viewers are unlikely to remember the negative aspects of the period.
- C. Mendelsohn's argument would be further supported because older generations are often selectively nostalgic.
- D. Mendelsohn's argument would not be affected because these age groups are irrelevant to the argument.

Next ▶

Passage 7 (Questions 36-41)

Many patients admitted to the medical or surgical ward in hospitals are malnourished, yet a significant number of these at-risk patients remain undetected. Malnutrition has been shown to independently increase mortality, length of stay, and risk of readmission, affecting patient flow and health care costs. Costs of a malnourished patient's care amount, on average, to $2,000 more than the costs for a well-nourished patient's care. Undetected malnutrition is of particular concern both during admission and upon discharge, as patients who do not receive adequate nutritional care are at increased risk for complications related to their conditions.

Malnutrition has long been recognized as a serious clinical issue, especially for older adults, the subgroup of the hospital population that presents as most likely to be malnourished and to have significant barriers to food intake. Advocates have pushed for increased prevention efforts and a greater focus on nutrition in medical education. Despite this emphasis on hospital malnutrition over the past few decades, recent studies indicate that the prevalence of malnutrition at admission remains high, and patients and hospitals continue to suffer the consequences.

A number of organizational, environmental, and patient-specific factors contribute to malnutrition in hospitals. For example, lack of communication between patients, staff, and food services leads to patients receiving food they will not or cannot eat. Furthermore, hospitals are not necessarily designed or managed outright to support the diverse needs of their patients, which can make it difficult to provide the best care (including nutritional care).

Hospital management needs to sponsor the actions taken to improve the nutrition culture. Awareness is a first step, as hospital management may or may not be aware of the prevalence and implications of malnutrition. Management should translate evidence into policy and protocols that support and sustain context-specific changes revolving around patient-centered care. Service providers must protect patients from the risks of inadequate food and fluid intake by: (1) providing appropriate and nutrient-dense food; (2) meeting religious and cultural needs; and (3) supporting intake of food and fluid, i.e., ensuring eating assistance. Studies have shown that hospital budgets affect flexibility in the variety of the menu, food availability outside of meal times, and ability to meet the diverse needs of patients. Without investment in food, staff is unable to improve the institutional nutrition culture. With a consistent rate of patient malnutrition, dieticians and diet technicians especially may descend into a spiral of low morale.

On the other hand, patients need to recognize that eating is their way of contributing to their own recovery and that adequate food intake has a positive effect on their treatment goals and successful discharge. Patients can be empowered through the knowledge and understanding that their care is improved when they treat food like medicine. While in the hospital, patients may become frustrated by the inability to eat independently and may be reluctant to ask for help from busy staff. Staff needs to be aware of the barriers to food intake and understand the mechanisms to avoid exacerbating the issue. For example, staff can suggest to family members that they visit during mealtimes, which can ensure patients have social interaction and assistance eating, thereby improving food intake without taking staff time. However, these changes ultimately can only be enacted when hospitals provide adequate staff training and support.

The importance of adequate nutrition does not end when a person is discharged from the hospital, which must be made clear to the patient and family. Having hospital management provide nutrition-related materials at discharge specific to the patient's needs may assist with this transition. These materials can include information regarding support services available in the community (e.g. home delivery meal programs), information for their general practitioners, or materials that assist patients and their families with eating strategies at home.

This passage was adapted from "Becoming Food Aware in Hospital: A Narrative Review to Advance the Culture of Nutrition Care in Hospitals." Laur C, McCullough J, Davidson B, and Keller H. *Healthcare*. 2015. 5(1) doi: 10.3390/healthcare3020393 for use under the terms of the Creative Commons CC BY 4.0 license (https://creativecommons.org/licenses/by/4.0/legalcode).

Question 36

According to the passage, all of the following contribute to malnutrition in hospitals EXCEPT:

A. a lack of sufficient funds to purchase a variety of food.

B. a failure to provide patients with food they want to eat.

C. an absence of nutritional care pamphlets with information on how to improve eating.

D. a lack of personnel available to help patients eat.

Question 37

Which of the following situations best reflects the author's argument about the current role of hospital staff?

A. Sergeants are sensitive to the complaints of their lower-ranked soldiers, but cannot resolve those complaints without directives from their superiors.

B. The staff members at a small boutique not only manage but also own shares of the store.

C. Chefs at a restaurant design meals they believe their diners will enjoy.

D. An employee in the financial division of a company provides input into which goods and services will be purchased over the next year.

Question 38

A new study finds that when hospitalized patients are counseled about the positive effects of appropriate nutrition on health, the prevalence of malnutrition remains steady. The author would be LEAST likely to recommend:

○ **A.** developing a promotional campaign directed at hospital management around the need for adequate nutrition.

○ **B.** inducing hospitals to provide better staff training on strategies to improve eating.

○ **C.** increasing patient-centered educational efforts that use different media to stress to patients the importance of nutrition.

○ **D.** providing supplementary grants to hospitals who have identified a gap in their food budgets.

Question 39

Based on the passage, a high prevalence of malnutrition among patients causes which of the following?

  I. Rising health care costs that exceed hospital budgets

  II. Increased risk of exacerbating patient illnesses

  III. Negative attitudes among hospital staff

○ **A.** II only

○ **B.** I and II

○ **C.** I and III

● **D.** II and III

Question 40

The ideas discussed in this passage would likely be of most use to:

● **A.** an advocate.

○ **B.** a family caregiver.

○ **C.** a hospital dietician.

○ **D.** a patient.

Question 41

Based on the passage, which of the following strategies has most likely already been undertaken in an attempt to improve patient nourishment?

○ **A.** Inviting community-based support services into the hospital to provide educational programming around nutrition

○ **B.** Increasing communication between hospital food services and patients to ensure that patients are given food they can eat

● **C.** Incorporating nutrition-focused curriculum into medical school lectures

○ **D.** Decreasing admissions of older adult patients, which is the patient subgroup most likely to experience malnutrition

Passage 8 (Questions 42-46)

Metaphor analysis today is valued for its implied ideological meaning. Metaphorical expressions are analyzed with the purpose of reconstructing their underlying conceptual frames and restoring their moral matrix or hidden ideological value. Metaphors are thus seen as both tools of thought and mechanisms reflecting our worldviews. Recent research has shown that different understandings of metaphors depend on the narratives in which these metaphors are embedded. Discourse, at this point, should be perceived as an interactive narrative constructing social identities and ideologies.

Cognitive linguists perceive metaphor as a reflection of general conceptual organization, categorization principles, and processing mechanisms. In this view, metaphor is seen as a specific mental mapping and a neural co-activation influencing the way people think, reason, and imagine in their everyday life. More importantly, metaphorical thought is used constantly, and people act on their metaphors. Metaphors may vary from person to a person, so not all forms of reasoning are universal. The analysis of metaphors, in its turn, leads to various and dissimilar observations about views or ideologies.

In this context, ideology refers to a form of socially shared and distributed cognition or a system of socially shared beliefs that may control many manifestations of social practice. It is assumed that ideologies and their structures influence attitudes, mental models, and the choice of discourse structures. Metaphor as both a mental model and a discourse structure can be explored for its ideological implications and evaluation patterns. According to English professor Andrew Goatly, most metaphorical models "have ideological implications, in the sense that they are recruited and used by those exerting economic, scientific, political, or personal power."

Consider a few examples of metaphors, imagining what sort of ideology they create, reinforce, or enact. Take, for instance, the conventional IMPORTANCE IS SIZE metaphor, by which the source domain of size or height is used for or mapped onto various overlapping positive qualities such as importance, power, authority, status, success, and so on. In everyday language, this metaphor can be illustrated by the following metaphorical expressions: a big decision, make a big thing of, a big day, great men, a big name, a top man/woman, high places, at the peak of one's career, and so on. The use of this metaphor has made size or height an ideological symbol of power, success, achievement, and importance. As noted by Goatly, the symbolism of height as power is especially noticeable in constructing high buildings. A non-linguistic act that occurred on September 11th, 2001 provided a somber reminder of the ideological power of this metaphor when terrorists attacked the World Trade Center with the purpose of reducing the power, success, and importance of the United States on the global stage.

Another example of the prevalence of metaphors can be found in higher education mission statements. Many perceive the university as a business person driven by self-interest, competing in the market for supremacy, building an ever stronger resume as it increases its number of students, staff, and achievements. The metaphors evoked therein are conservative in nature and are based on the positive evaluation of such underlying concepts as strong leadership, competitiveness for superiority, hierarchical relationships, and quantifiable quality.

It should be further noted that metaphors allow consumers of ideas to understand the complexity of perceptions and expectations. The narrative of universities' mission statements reflects both the values of a speaker and the expected values of an addressee. The representation of a higher institution in competitive and commercial terms mirrors what the speakers expect from their addressees' reaction to the provided narrative.

This passage was adapted from "EU Universities' Mission Statements: What is Popularized by Metaphors." Arcimaviciene L. SAGE Open. 2015. doi: 10.1177/2158244015584378 for use under the terms of the Creative Commons CC BY 3.0 license (http://creativecommons.org/licenses/by/3.0/legalcode).

Question 42

The central thesis of this passage is that:

○ **A.** metaphors are an integral part of university mission statements.

○ **B.** metaphors are underrated and often unnoticed in society.

○ **C.** poetic language can be used as a tool of understanding.

○ **D.** the interpretation and influence of metaphors can vary by situation and person.

Question 43

According to the passage, it is reasonable to conclude that the interpretation of metaphors:

○ **A.** reflects societal beliefs.

○ **B.** instructs individuals to act in certain ways.

○ **C.** prompts intellectual discussion.

○ **D.** influences spiritual beliefs.

Question 44

The ideas discussed in this passage would likely be of most use to:

○ **A.** a writer.

● **B.** an advertiser. → public rxns to metaphors

○ **C.** an editor.

○ **D.** a dean of a university.

Question 45

The author's explanation of ideology in relation to metaphors would be most challenged by the finding that:

○ **A.** metaphors are often employed by struggling businesses.

○ **B.** Americans report that they almost never notice metaphors in everyday life. → notice vs. influence

● **C.** businesses report that they do not use metaphors as a method of influence.

○ **D.** businesses have dissimilar reasons for deploying metaphors.

Question 46

Based on information in the passage, which of the following vehicles would a newly-promoted CEO be most likely to purchase?

○ **A.** An expensive sports car

○ **B.** A bulky SUV → importance is vs size

○ **C.** A compact convertible

○ **D.** A one-seat motorcycle

Passage 9 (Questions 47-53)

The popular Bengali novelist and short story writer Sharatchandra Chattopadhyay's reputation is of a daradī [sympathetic] and maramī [compassionate] novelist and short story writer. Sharat lived and wrote in the 19th century, a time that witnessed the completion of the British domination of India. This domination was accompanied by Western efforts to educate the "natives," with a view to awaken them to their own cultural heritage as well as transform them into useful, faithful, and pliable subjects.

This dawn of colonial enlightenment touched the women of the middle and upper classes who had hitherto been deprived of education by their society, which had until this point firmly believed that an educated female eventually becomes either a widow or a whore. As early as 1819, the future leader of the Brāhmo movement objected to the prevailing belief that women were nitwits by pointing out the unfairness of making such a judgment without allowing them to prove themselves in education. In the same year, Christian missionaries started the first public school for girls.

During this time, patriotic Bengali literature highlighted the figure of the woman, married as well as widowed. One journal coined the term strīsvādhīnatā [freedom of women] and began publishing articles on the predicament of women, suggesting ways and means to eradicate their handicaps in society.

Sharatchandra's ideal woman is first and foremost a maternal figure—nurturing, benevolent, indulgent, and long-suffering. Her primordial motherhood is couched in a related concept, that of a loyal wife—a true follower of her husband. Sharat's significant and popular female characters are generally young and pretty widows or frustrated and unloved married women mostly from high-caste families—whether from the genteel household or a menial maid or a fallen woman, an indigent housewife forced to sell her body due to the exigencies of circumstance. They display either maternal and filial piety or an erotic sentiment toward socially tabooed male characters. However, they harbor a phobic disdain for active sexuality—a reflection of Sharat's personal predilection, somewhat reminiscent of the Puritans of early modern England. The most progressive and aggressive among them adhere scrupulously to the traditional social ethos in respect of love and marriage.

Sharatchandra wrote a scholarly article on women in which he appeared as a self-appointed advocate of Indian (especially Bengali) womanhood. In his moral economy, women's worth in society is diminished due to the plenitude of their supply, and he took the self-centered, cowardly, misogynistic patriarchy to task for failing to give the women their due. Beneath the veneer of his liberal and egalitarian attitude toward women, Sharat nevertheless found them lacking in the wherewithal to claim their place under the sun.

Sharat once described his views as the following: "The guiding principle of society… cannot be transgressed or challenged… Nor can it be claimed that it is a mark of cowardice to sacrifice one's legitimate rights at the altar of society." As a current literary critic has put it, this mentality "rendered Sharat's work popular but at the expense of its artistic excellence." No doubt Sharatchandra has raised some serious concerns about widows' and married

women's rights, and yet he denied his fictional female characters any recognition in this regard, thereby catering to the social biases of many of his readers, and thus ensuring his popularity. The qualities that made his stories popular were those of his prose style: transparency, pathos, and simple elegance. His works never aimed to propose a new utopia.

This passage was adapted from "Sharatchandra's Caste and Gender Consciousness: A Reassessment." Sil N. *SAGE Open*. 2015. 5(1) doi: 10.1177/2158244014564360 for use under the terms of the Creative Commons CC BY 4.0 license (https://creativecommons.org/licenses/by/4.0/legalcode).

Question 47

The author's apparent attitude towards the British domination of India is:

- O **A.** grateful.
- O **B.** outraged.
- O **C.** scornful.
- O **D.** ambivalent.

Question 48

Which of the following, if true, would most *weaken* the author's argument about Sharatchandra's writing?

- O **A.** Sharatchandra's work derives its popularity from its expressive descriptions of relationships between men and women.
- O **B.** Sharatchandra published a number of novels that rejected the burgeoning belief that women should be allowed to find employment outside the home.
- O **C.** Sharatchandra was praised for attacking the social prejudices that affected women of his time.
- ● **D.** Sharatchandra wrote with the idea that his books would incite a social revolution.

Question 49

According to passage information about Sharatchandra's literary female characters, which of the following plot synopses is most likely?

- **A.** A beautiful young widow courts three men from her village, all of whom vie for her attention.
- **B.** A married woman pines for her neighbor but does not act out of respect for her in-laws.
- **C.** A teenage girl who dreams of leaving her small town works diligently to earn her high school degree.
- O **D.** A well-to-do woman, frustrated with her loveless marriage, seeks divorce.

Question 50

Which of the following conclusions about women in nineteenth century India can be inferred from the passage?

- A. All women were given the opportunity to receive an education.
- B. Women were expected to either get married or become prostitutes.
- C. Women were considered intellectually inferior to men.
- D. Women were not encouraged to express their sexuality.

Question 51

According to passage information, the best way to ensure the popularity of a literary work is to:

- A. write female characters who adhere to traditional social ideals of love and marriage.
- B. employ complex, winding prose.
- C. represent the dominant cultural views of the time.
- D. make a strong statement about contemporary injustices.

Question 52

It is reasonable to conclude that all of the following describe Sharatchandra's ideal woman EXCEPT:

- A. she is a motherly figure to her many children.
- B. she is well-educated.
- C. she is willing to endure hardship for her family.
- D. she is chaste.

Question 53

The ideas discussed in this passage would likely be of most use to:

- A. a political analyst dissecting a presidential candidate's decision to present one view on the gender income gap in his written platform and another view in a debate.
- B. a literary critic correlating events and relationships in Sharatchandra's own life with his views on women.
- C. a historian studying the timeline between Indian women gaining the right to education and being granted the right to vote.
- D. a journalist reporting on women's rights to accessible and affordable contraception across multiple nations.

STOP. If you finish before time is called, check your work. You may go back to any question in this test.

ANSWERS & EXPLANATIONS for Test 1 can be found on p. 183.

TEST ②

Number of Questions: 53
Time: 90 minutes

INSTRUCTIONS: Each passage is followed by associated questions. Read the passage, then select the best answer to each question. If you are unsure of the answer, rule out incorrect choices and select from the remaining options. Indicate your answer beside the option you choose.

Passage 1 (Questions 1-7)

It is clear that culture does matter in the clinic. Cultural factors shape health-related beliefs, behaviors, and values. But large claims about the value of cultural competence for the art of professional care-giving around the world are simply not supported by robust evaluation research showing that systematic attention to culture really improves clinical services. This lack of evidence is a failure of outcome research to take culture seriously enough to routinely assess the cost-effectiveness of culturally-informed therapeutic practices, not a lack of effort to introduce culturally-informed strategies into clinical settings.

One major problem with the idea of cultural competency is that it suggests culture can be reduced to a technical skill for which clinicians can be trained to develop expertise. This problem stems from how culture is defined in medicine, which contrasts strikingly with its current use in anthropology—the field in which the concept of culture originated. Culture in medicine is often made synonymous with ethnicity, nationality, and language. Patients of a given ethnicity are assumed to have a core set of beliefs about illness owing to fixed ethnic traits.

Cultural competency becomes a series of "do's and don'ts" that define how to treat a patient of a given ethnic background. The idea of isolated societies with shared cultural meanings would be rejected by anthropologists today, since it leads to dangerous stereotyping as if entire societies or ethnic groups could be described by these simple slogans. In anthropology today, culture is not seen as homogenous or static.

Anthropologists emphasize that culture is not a single variable but rather comprises multiple variables, affecting all aspects of experience. Culture is inseparable from economic, political, religious, psychological, and biological conditions. Culture is a process through which ordinary activities and conditions take on an emotional tone and moral meaning for participants. Cultural processes include the embodiment of meaning in psychophysiological reactions, the development of interpersonal attachments, the serious performance of religious practices, common-sense interpretations, and the cultivation of collective and individual identity. Cultural processes frequently differ within the same ethnic or social group because of differences in age cohort, gender, political association, class, religion, ethnicity, and even personality.

It is of course legitimate and highly desirable for clinicians to be sensitive to cultural difference, and to attempt to provide care that deals with cultural issues from an anthropological perspective. The optimal way to do this is to train clinicians in ethnography. "Ethnography" is the technical term used in anthropology for its core methodology. It refers to an anthropologist's description of what life is like in a "local world," a specific setting in a society—usually one different from that of the anthropologist's world. Traditionally, the ethnographer visits a foreign country, learns the language, and, systematically, describes social patterns in a particular village, neighborhood, or network. What sets this apart from other methods of social research is the importance placed on understanding the native's point of view. The ethnographer practices an intensive and imaginative empathy for the experience of the natives—appreciating and humanely engaging with their foreignness, and understanding their religion, moral values, and everyday practices.

Ethnography eschews the "trait list approach" that understands culture as a set of already-known factors. Ethnography emphasizes engagement with others and with the practices that people undertake in their local worlds. It also emphasizes the ambivalence that many people feel as a result of being between worlds in a way that cultural competency does not. And ethnography eschews the technical mastery that the term "competency" suggests. Anthropologists and clinicians share a common belief—i.e., the primacy of experience. The clinician, as an anthropologist of sorts, can empathize with the lived experience of the patient's illness and can try to understand the illness as the patient understands, feels, perceives, and responds to it.

This passage was adapted from "Anthropology in the clinic: The problem of cultural competency and how to fix it." Kleinman A, Benson P. *PLoS Med.* 2006. 3(10): e294. DOI: 10.1371/journal.pmed.0030294 for use under the terms of the Creative Commons CC BY 2.0 license (https://creativecommons.org/licenses/by/2.0/legalcode).

Question 1

Which of the following statements is most strongly supported by evidence in the passage?

- O **A.** Healthcare-related behaviors and values are determined by cultural factors.
- O **B.** Anthropologists eschew the idea of culture as a homogenous or fixed entity within a group.
- O **C.** Large claims about the value of culturally-sensitive research are poorly supported because outcome research fails to routinely assess the cost-effectiveness of culturally-informed therapeutic practices.
- **D.** Anthropology emphasizes an understanding of a cultural native's point of view more than ethnography does.

Question 2

Which example best illustrates "ethnography" as it is discussed in the passage?

- O **A.** A police officer requests to work in the neighborhood she grew up in.
- O **B.** A professor requests student feedback on his course and does not make any changes for the next year.
- O **C.** A tourist attempts to use the local language to ask for directions to the train station.
- **D.** An author interviews residents of Beijing about their everyday lives in the city as research for her next book.

Question 3

Based on the passage, the author's opinion of "cultural competency" is most likely that:

A. it is a skill for which people can be trained to develop expertise.

B. it unfairly attributes the same set of cultural traits to people of a certain ethnicity.

C. it is preferable to ethnography because it accounts for the variations in cultural beliefs among people of the same ethnicity.

D. it correctly equates culture with economic, political, religious, psychological, and biological conditions.

Question 4

An anthropologist is employed by a prominent teaching hospital to educate physicians on how to improve cultural awareness. According to the passage, this is most likely because:

A. anthropologists are trained to acknowledge variations in cultural beliefs among people of the same ethnic group.

B. physicians cannot understand cultural variability within an ethnic group.

C. anthropologists acknowledge that culture is constantly evolving and competency in a particular culture is not a reasonable goal.

D. anthropologists emphasize that culture is composed of multiple variables including a person's economic, geographic, and political experiences.

Question 5

It can be reasonably concluded that the purpose of educating physicians on cultural awareness is:

A. to equip physicians to address medical issues that especially affect a particular ethnic group.

B. to prepare physicians to address various cultural barriers among patients of distinct ethnic groups.

C. to help the physicians empathize with their patients and provide more culturally sensitive treatments.

D. to make physicians more understanding of differing beliefs amongst their patients.

Question 6

According to the passage, how does ethnography differ from "cultural competency?"

A. Cultural competency characterizes culture as a set of economic, political, religious, and health parameters.

B. Cultural competency assumes that ethnicity is homogenous among members of the same ethnic group.

C. Ethnography characterizes culture as a set of economic, political, religious, and health parameters.

D. Ethnography assumes that ethnicity is homogenous among members of the same ethnic group.

Question 7

The author would be least likely to disagree with which of the following statements regarding the cultural practices of Chinese people?

A. Chinese people strongly believe that acupuncture is an effective cure for chronic lower back pain.

B. Chinese people always have poor medication adherence because Chinese culture discourages medication for preventative measures.

C. Most Chinese people believe that Eastern medicine is preferable to Western medicine.

D. Some Chinese people take herbal supplements in addition to the Western medications they are prescribed.

Passage 2 (Questions 8-13)

The law notoriously lags behind advancements in technology. The initial explosion of cybercrimes in the 21st century left the American criminal justice system woefully unprepared. The courts struggled to confront the emerging crimes of computer hacking, Internet viruses, and sexting with traditional criminal statutes. Forced to work within the confines of criminal laws already on the books, trespassing, theft, and child pornography statutes were stretched to new limits. While the federal and state governments eventually updated their laws, the technology gap remains. The slow response time of state and federal legislatures perpetuates a legal system constantly trying to "catch up" with innovation. In addition, a two hundred year old constitution is asked to confront modern technological issues that the founding fathers never imagined.

The search and seizure clause of the Fourth Amendment was recently evaluated in relation to cell phone privacy when the Supreme Court consolidated the cases of David Leon Riley and Brima Wurie in a groundbreaking case regarding the evolution of privacy in the digital age. In separate incidents, both men had their cell phones searched during arrest, even though the officers lacked a warrant authorizing the search of private property. The information contained on their cell phones ultimately led to convictions for additional offenses. Riley was initially stopped in California for a traffic violation but was eventually arrested after an inventory search revealed two loaded handguns under the hood of his car. During the search incident to arrest, Riley's cell phone was removed from the pocket of his pants and searched preliminarily by the police officer on scene. A review of text messages and contacts indicated membership in the Bloods street gang. Two hours after the arrest, a detective further analyzed Riley's cell phone without a warrant at the police station. The detective discovered photographs of Riley standing near a car allegedly used in a drive-by shooting. Riley was ultimately convicted for attempted murder, assault with a semiautomatic firearm, and firing at an occupied vehicle, and was sentenced to 15 years to life in prison for his involvement in the drive-by shooting.

Nearly 41 years after the development of the first mobile phone, the Supreme Court in *Riley v. California* issued its first major privacy ruling regarding such devices. In a unanimous decision, the justices emphatically ruled that the search of a suspect's cell phone incident to arrest requires a warrant. Conceding that *Riley v. California* will now make the job of law enforcement more difficult, the Court emphasized the unique attributes of cell phones and the cost of maintaining personal privacy. Local, state, and federal law enforcement agencies must now confront the real-world impact of *Riley* in criminal investigations.

The unanimous decision spent a significant amount of time examining the characteristics of a cell phone. When compared to other physical objects, the Court emphasized the vast quantitative and qualitative differences of the modern phone. They highlighted the immense storage capacity and variety of data contained on cell phones, which Chief Justice Roberts noted could just "as easily be called cameras, video players, rolodexes, calendars, tape recorders, libraries, diaries, albums, televisions, maps, or newspapers."

Accordingly, a warrantless search of a cell phone implicates a substantially greater violation of privacy than the standard review of the contents of a wallet or cigarette packet. The Court noted that 90 percent of adults in America essentially have "on their person a digital record of nearly every aspect of their lives–from the mundane to the intimate." A detailed examination of a cell phone is analogous to an exhaustive search of an entire home.

This passage was adapted from "The Cost of Privacy: *Riley v. California's* Impact on Cell Phone Searches." Moore JL, Langton J, and Pochron J. *Journal of Digital Forensics, Security, and Law.* 2014. 9(3) for use under the terms of the Creative Commons CC BY 4.0 license (https://creativecommons.org/licenses/by/4.0/legalcode).

Question 8

A film adaptation of the events in the passage is being created. Which of the following characters would the author most likely depict as the hero or heroes?

- ○ **A.** Legislators
- ○ **B.** David Riley
- ○ **C.** Police officers
- ⊘ **D.** Chief Justice Roberts

Question 9

According to the passage, the best way to gain information from a possible suspect in a crime is:

- ○ **A.** to question the suspect until satisfied with the answers.
- ⊘ **B.** to search whatever objects the law permits.
- ○ **C.** to trust the suspect's testimony until he or she is proven guilty.
- ○ **D.** to gather information by any means necessary.

Question 10

Based on the passage, it is reasonable to conclude that under current law a warrant is required to search:

- I. a cell phone.
- II. a wallet.
- III. a house.

- ○ **A.** I only
- ○ **B.** II and III only
- ⊘ **C.** I and III only
- ○ **D.** I, II, and III

Question 11

Which of the following conclusions would be most in agreement with a theme of the passage?

- A. The technology gap in law enforcement is currently a significant issue.
- B. The founding fathers did not prepare the country well for the future.
- C. Courts have not been able to reach an agreement about cybercrimes.
- D. Cybercrimes have only presented a problem in the last five years.

Question 12

Which of the following findings, if true, would most *weaken* the author's argument about cell phones and law enforcement?

- A. Individuals keep just as much personal information on iPads as on cell phones.
- B. Police officers report that the new law will make law enforcement more difficult.
- C. Cell phones usually reveal only information that is also posted on social media.
- D. Cell phone sales have decreased over the last ten years.

Question 13

The author's argument about the law and technology suggests that they would likely *support* which of the following?

- A. Legislation requiring a warrant to search an iPad or tablet
- B. Funding to hire more police officers in response to the *Riley v. California* outcome
- C. A public service announcement warning the American public that their cell phones cannot be searched without a warrant
- D. Altering the justice system so that technological issues are addressed more quickly

Passage 3 (Questions 14-19)

We are now entering an era of uncertainty as to the very possibility of maintaining *architecture as an art* in a society that has leveled it to the point of invisibility. How we communicate architectural strategy, and how we both represent ideas and process them is pertinent to the standing of the profession in an increasingly specialized construction industry. The question of architectural representation is not simply one of aesthetic refinement. Today hand drawings in architecture are all but eclipsed by their digital counterparts. These geometrical drawings are created out of facts abstracted from the human situation in which they are primarily organized and from which they have meaning. However, while digitized modeling brings an unprecedented freedom to explore form and complexity, digital space remains simulated space. In the age of digital building, it is unclear what fills the void left by the decline of other forms of representation. It is therefore problematic to argue for other forms of drawing to be incorporated into architectural design, in terms of their legitimacy, meaning, and contribution to the design process. At the same time it is equally problematic to consider the computer as the *only* design tool.

Consider that collage is a "paper technology" in terms of its role in describing relations that are inscribed in space and time. The phrase "paper technologies" was coined in an article by science historian Dr. Te Hessen that looked at the ongoing value of the paper notebook in a digital age. "The phenomenon of paper persists," writes Hessen. "In spite of all the computers sitting on desks and organigrams of virtual filing systems, paper has proven stubborn and enduring, although its capacities and speed are no match for electronic data processing." Despite the Internet and the arrival of the paperless office, our paper consumption has gone up. The reasons for this may be various, but the quality of paper itself, which the computer cannot simulate, must account for the persistent use of the material. The materiality of paper has a spatiality that the screen cannot simulate and, as such, it promotes a kind of thinking, one might say spontaneity, which is not otherwise available. Yet, the easily transmissible nature of digital design makes it a more practical tool for design revision.

Our understanding of space has been petrified in the modes of representation from which it grew, but which are still practiced, the dominating representation being perspective. On the one hand, perspectival representation allows us to connect with "global space." On the other hand, it fuels a distancing from the world for what it actually is. An exploration of the material conditions of space, the relationship to the body, rhythms of use and so forth, is substituted for a more abstract grasp of dimension, geometry and seductively visualized space.

The notion of "space" is a relatively new concept in our civilization. It is taken for granted today that space is that which is described by a dimensional, geometrically defined presence. But this is forgetting the derivative nature of space: it is already assuming that space exists independently of its context, its history, and the cultures and movements that frequent it. If we look back to primordial architecture, we see that it was made up of places that only looked like space: we can describe such structures as being spatially ordered. This kind of space has to do with time: there is no sense of space, but a spatiality that is structured temporally. During the Renaissance, with the invention of perspective drawing, there was a radical and lasting shift, in terms of representation, changing "processional space" into perspectival space. The spatial order that previously belonged to the life of the city, its beliefs, processions, and spaces that structured dialogues between religious, political, and economic life now could be transformed into a singular vision. As a scene became understood geometrically and drawn as mathematical perspective, perhaps it also became further removed from the experience it depicts.

This passage was adapted from "Elevating Mallarmé's Shipwreck." Dernie D. *Buildings*. 2013. 3 doi: 10.3390/buildings3020324 for use under the terms of the Creative Commons CC BY 3.0 license (https://creativecommons.org/licenses/by/3.0/legalcode).

Question 14

If architectural design solely utilized perspectival drawing techniques, the author would react by:

- **A.** praising the new, widely applicable understanding of space.
- **B.** advocating for further innovations that improve the realism of architectural drawing.
- **C.** lamenting the loss of the human connection to architecture that characterized processional drawing.
- **D.** asserting that the precision possible in digital modeling should be integrated into paper drawing.

Question 15

The author's opinion of architectural drawing would be most directly opposed by which perspective?

- **A.** Digital architectural renderings allow for a complexity of design that far exceeds that of paper drawing.
- **B.** Paper drawing conveys an authenticity that is lost in digital design.
- **C.** Traditional hand drawing of architecture has spatiality superior to that of digital design.
- **D.** Digital architectural design is as connected to the human experience of architecture as hand drawing is.

Question 16

Which of the following statements from the passage was least supported by evidence?

- **A.** It is unclear what fills the void left by the decline of other forms of representation.
- **B.** Our current notion of space assumes that space exists independently of its context.
- **C.** Our understanding of space has been petrified in modes of representation.
- **D.** Perspectival representation fuels a distancing from the world for what it actually is.

Question 17

Based on the information about "space" presented in paragraph 4, it can most reasonably be inferred that:

- **A.** a drawing style originating in the Renaissance introduced temporality into the current understanding of space.
- **B.** temporally structured spatiality is characteristic of modern architecture.
- **C.** the current concept of space originated after the Renaissance.
- **D.** geometrical forms shaped the pre-Renaissance conception of space.

Question 18

The author's description of "simulated space" in architecture most closely parallels which of the following examples?

- **A.** Auto-tuned vocal music
- **B.** A cheap brass miniature of a famous landmark
- **C.** A smudged print of a painting from the Renaissance
- **D.** Newspaper printed on a traditional printing press

Question 19

According to the author, paper technologies are persistently utilized because:

- **A.** paper is more easily portable than digital design technologies.
- **B.** paper technology is more widely available than digital design tools.
- **C.** the qualities of various papers lend themselves to a variety of drawing techniques.
- **D.** paper allows for a more intuitive design process.

Passage 4 (Questions 20-24)

Simón Bolivar once commented that revolutions should be observed close at hand but that they needed to be analyzed and assessed guarding a certain distance. The distance he appeared to have in mind was literal, physical distance, but the suggestion is also valid if we take it as a metaphor. Indeed, we could understand the academic disciplines used to interpret revolutions, or social change in general, as attempts to systematize mechanisms designed to produce a healthy distance between what is being observed and the conclusions which are drawn from it.

In the case of revolutions, the need for observing them close at hand is particularly marked because secondhand sources are notoriously unreliable, in the sense that they are almost inevitably colored by the political proclivities of the observer in a situation which is always sharply polarized. Venezuela under Chávez is just one of the most recent cases. Distance is also particularly necessary because revolutions tend to question longstanding assumptions, reveal powerful but neglected undercurrents which need to be interpreted in new ways and, not least important, can be better understood with the benefit of a comparative perspective.

Several novels examining contemporary Venezuela have been published in recent years—all written in English by foreigners, educated abroad, and almost all Anglo-Saxons to boot. This provides an additional dimension to the problem because there is a certain Nativist tradition which argues that foreigners (and particularly Anglo-Saxons), are incapable of fully understanding Latin American culture and/or history or politics, precisely because there is a cultural gap which is extremely difficult to bridge.

In fact these foreign authors, in very different ways, make what I consider substantial contributions to our understanding of the impact of the Bolivarian revolution. It appears to me of particular interest to examine how each of them has broached the problem of combining close-up observation with those academic tools which offer, even more so than any physical distance, that perspective which Bolívar regarded as so necessary. Significantly, most authors took advantage of a year spent abroad in order to write their respective books. Foreigners are clearly capable of providing revealing analyses, on the condition that they succeed in observing the revolution close at hand.

However, Bolívar did not have foreigners in mind when he made this commentary. He was thinking of himself and his colleagues, who had been totally immersed in the War of Independence and therefore faced the problem of standing back and taking distance from the events. It could be argued that the same problem faces those Venezuelans currently engaged in the Bolivarian revolution, whatever their political inclinations. Despite an abundant academic production dedicated to the Chávez period, Venezuelans tend to write articles which broach aspects of the experience but eschew attempts to offer overall interpretations such as those we have been analyzing here.

This passage was adapted from "Venezuela's Bolivarian Revolution as Seen through Foreign Eyes." Parker D. *European Review of Latin American and Caribbean Studies*. 2009. 87 doi: 10.18352/erlacs.9606 for use under the terms of the Creative Commons CC BY 3.0 license (http://creativecommons.org/licenses/by/3.0/legalcode).

Question 20

Based on the passage, how would the author advise an American news network to cover a Peruvian revolution?

- A. Contact local Peruvians to broadcast their views.
- B. Send an American to Peru to cover the story.
- C. Send a native Peruvian to his hometown to cover the story.
- D. Report all of their information from the studio.

Question 21

Which finding would provide the most support for Nativist claims?

- A. Anglo-Saxon reporters who travel all over the world are published in the most prestigious journals.
- B. Anglo-Saxon reporters who extensively research events from home are published in the most prestigious journals.
- C. Latin American reporters who specialize in Latin American politics are published in the most prestigious journals.
- D. Latin American reporters who study global politics are published in the most prestigious journals.

Question 22

Who would qualify as a "notoriously unreliable" secondhand source if another country was reporting on an American election?

- A. Liberal Democrat
- B. Moderate Republican
- C. Foreign correspondent
- D. Debate moderator

new perspetive

Question 23

Which of the following is NOT a reason given by the passage for why reporters must maintain some distance when analyzing revolutions?

○ **A.** They can provide a fresh interpretation of the new order.

○ **B.** They can more easily forgo old beliefs.

○ **C.** They can compare the situation to that of another country.

○ **D.** They can report honestly without fear of repercussion.

Question 24

Why does the author mention Simón Bolivar?

○ **A.** To engage a wider audience with a familiar name

○ **B.** To support their own beliefs with those of a respected Venezuelan

○ **C.** To criticize the precedent set by Bolivar

○ **D.** To gain the respect of a Venezuelan audience

Passage 5 (Questions 25-29)

The health of people in different socioeconomic strata is disparate whether measured by education, type of employment, or income level, but those living in poverty exhibit the worst health status. In the United States there are over 45 million uninsured or underinsured people who by definition have restricted access to healthcare. Although not all of them are unemployed or underemployed, there is no doubt that occupational status affects insurance status, which affects health status. There is also convincing evidence that low socioeconomic status causes poor health, as does race. Having established that there are people who have a lack of healthcare access due to multi-factorial etiologies, the question arises as to whether the intervention necessary to assist them is something that should be considered a privilege, or a right.

Many have argued on behalf of the existence of "the soul," a concept perpetuated in many religions and philosophies. Aristotle hypothesized the existence, content, and necessary conditions of the soul. Putting aside the concepts of good and evil, souls need nourishment. They have sensation (pain, pleasure, desire) and they can think, calculate, and imagine. Would it not be right and prudent to assist this entity called "soul" (that moves through a society by using a body which needs nurture or nutrition to slow or prevent its decay) to endure and persist as long as possible in the midst of others like itself? To press the argument further, would humankind not be better off if the vehicle of social interaction was cared for and nourished, not only by itself, but assisted and nurtured by other such vehicles in a society? Would there not be an alteration in its growth, perception, calculation, and imagination resulting in a higher probability of positive consequences or actions?

The existence of humans is not for their use only as a means to accomplish a task. We are not a means to someone else's pleasure or well-being. If people should not be treated as things, then it must be recognized that all people have an absolute worth simply because they exist. You must "act in such a way that you always treat humanity, whether in your own person or in the person of any other, never simply as a means, but at the same time as an end." This statement has been called the Formula of Humanity. Kant explains that society depends upon interactions between people—we all serve each other's interests at one time or another, but we are never to be treated only as a means.

Kant also claims that "The motive of morality is quite different from that of interest or desire. It rules us absolutely and necessarily; we feel its power even when we are most defying it. It is not one consideration to be balanced against others, but rather a compelling dictate that can be ignored, but never refuted." We can politically ignore the force of morality, but it will always be there. The question of healthcare access for all people will be a persistent moral and politico-economic imperative.

If healthcare access becomes a right, difficulties will invariably ensue. Do the elderly receive liver transplants? Can a person who is morbidly obese receive a reoperation for coronary artery bypass grafting? Can a patient with diabetes receive a second kidney transplant? How much is enough healthcare access? Will healthcare delivery become a tiered process? Are we wise enough to make the necessary and correct decisions? Who will be society's proxy to make such decisions? There are no clear answers.

This passage was adapted from "Healthcare access as a right, not a privilege: a construct of Western thought." Papadimos TJ. *Philosophy, Ethics, and Humanities in Medicine*. 2007. 2(2) doi: 10.1186/1747-5341-2-2 for use under the terms of the Creative Commons CC BY 2.0 license (http://creativecommons.org/licenses/by/2.0/legalcode).

Question 25

Which of the following assertions is most supported by evidence or explanation in the passage?

- A. Unemployed Americans make up a large proportion of uninsured citizens.
- B. Healthcare access has recently been a controversial topic.
- C. Access to healthcare should not necessarily be a right extended to all humans.
- D. Healthcare access should be considered an issue of human morality.

Question 26

The author's attitude towards universal healthcare access is best described as:

- A. cautious.
- B. unsure.
- C. supportive.
- D. analytical.

Question 27

Given the information in the passage, one can reasonably assume that universal healthcare access:

- A. would succeed by providing nourishment for the soul.
- B. would attempt to treat every incident of disease.
- C. would cost Americans and the government a significant amount of money.
- D. would complicate the healthcare system.

Question 28

Which of the following findings, if true, would most *support* the author's argument about universal healthcare access?

- A. Countries with universal healthcare experience fewer deaths by preventable diseases.
- B. Doctors often report wanting to help patients even if they are uninsured.
- C. Many Americans would vote in favor of universal healthcare.
- D. Most hospitals report that they could treat more patients than they generally see each day.

Question 29

Based on the passage, the author would be most likely to *oppose* which of the following proposals?

- A. Legislation requiring all citizens to sign up for health insurance
- B. A system where health insurance is primarily provided by employers
- C. Research investigating universal healthcare in other countries
- D. A tax increase to fund a universal healthcare system

Passage 6 (Questions 30-35)

Rap music has been one of the main pillars of the American music industry and urban youth culture since the 1980s, when this previously local culture found a mainstream market. This period, known as the "Golden Era," from roughly the mid-1980s to the mid-1990s, demarcated the era in which hip-hop diversified itself, with many sub-genres such as conscious rap, jazz rap, gangsta rap, and hardcore hip-hop emerging. Despite this range, gangsta rap attracted the most media attention, largely due to its lyrics and music videos marked by drugs, firearms, cars, and voluptuous women. These aspects linked rap music to the action movie industry, played on deep-seated racial stereotypes in American culture, and gave a sensationalist aspect to gangsta rap. Not by chance, the genesis of this subgenre occurred on the American West Coast, home to artists like Dr. Dre, Snoop Dogg, and Tupac Shakur. At the time Los Angeles was considered by rappers and hip-hoppers to be an extremely violent and uncultured place—a "Wild West" as compared to New York, the birthplace of hip-hop culture, in which highly sophisticated artists such as Grandmaster Flash, Nas, and Wu-Tang Clan had emerged.

Twenty years later, another Angelino rapper came on the scene with a gangsta thematic, but this time through the internet, primarily on YouTube. Tyler, the Creator, born Tyler Okonma, attracted attention through his prodigious talent and internet savviness, reaching success in an independent way. Tyler started to rise as one of the main revelations in contemporary rap due to his notable productions: leading and founding the Odd Future hip-hop collective at 16 years old, releasing his first solo and self-financed album *Bastard* at 18, scoring a YouTube sensation with the "Yonkers" video clip, winning two 2011 Video Music Awards at age 20, and being nominated for two 2013 Grammy Awards at 22 years old. His stripped, nihilist, and sometimes extreme spirit pushes against the grain of a mainstream hip-hop that talks mostly about getting rich, famous, and powerful. His lyrics range from personal dramas like being fatherless and having relationship problems to more outrageous themes involving fantasies and ultraviolent chants.

Owing to his propensity to talk openly and freely about his insecurities, thoughts, and bizarre sexual fantasies, Tyler gained much media attention and success. Because he views his tracks as fictional like movies, he feels free to engage topics based on aesthetic considerations. Recently he has suggested that he will leave the music industry to become a filmmaker, and in 2013, he began shooting his first film. In an interview for *The Drone*, he explained that he understands his lyrics as nothing more than "telling a story," an argument that has been used by other rappers, such as the legendary Tupac Shakur, who emphasized his role as a businessman. Notably, Dr. Dre took the same stance when he talked about leaving a seminal gangsta rap group: "I'm here to make money, I don't consider myself no gangsta—making records is my job."

Rather than use violence to show virility and power in gangland, Tyler uses violent themes to compensate for his feelings of personal failure and as a challenge to entertainment industry, which frequently uses such themes with no greater consequences. The way he speaks freely about his feelings and frustrations serves as a counterpoint to the monstrous imagery he creates in his music.

Some of Tyler, the Creator's music is indeed unsettling, and I often found certain material difficult to reconcile with the aims of even the most dispassionate inquiry. However, reading his text as an (at times surprisingly transparent) admission of masculine lack, rather than as a declaration of masculine power, reduces the sexual hostility represented in Tyler, the Creator's music to a frantic, somewhat pathetic compensation. The dramatic, hysterical, and conflicted tone of his polyvocal texts exposes the inherent vulnerabilities of dominant constructions of Black masculinity, and with them, the actual source of his resentment.

This passage was adapted from "Beyond Gangsta: Hip Hop, Skate Culture and Web Culture in the music of Tyler, the Creator." Marques GS. *Art and Design Review*. 2015. 3 doi: 10.4236/adr.2015.31002 for use under the terms of the Creative Commons CC BY 4.0 license (https://creativecommons.org/licenses/by/4.0/legalcode).

Question 30

According to the passage, the primary factor contributing to the spread of rap music into the mainstream market involved:

- **A.** the incorporation of rap music into action movies.
- **B.** the support of popular rappers.
- **C.** the creation of multiple rapping styles.
- **D.** the expansion of rap music to the West Coast.

Question 31

The passage suggests that audiences offended by Tyler, the Creator's music may benefit from:

  I. understanding his individuality in the genre.
  II. ignoring the lyrics due to their fictional nature.
  III. recognizing his frustration with stereotypes.

- **A.** I only
- **B.** II only
- **C.** I and III only
- **D.** II and III only

Question 32

Given the passage discussion, which of the following is most likely to be the topic of a song written by Tyler, the Creator?

- A. Acquiring money to fund his cinematic adventures
- B. The amount of fame the internet can provide
- C. Violent tendencies and desires
- D. Drinking alcohol and partying

Question 33

Which of the following assertions is supported by strong evidence in the passage?

- A. Tyler, the Creator does not regret his past because it inspired his music.
- B. Gangsta rappers are more successful than rappers from other genres.
- C. Tyler, the Creator is commended for his honesty in the industry.
- D. Rap music is constantly evolving in modern society.

Question 34

The passage author would be likely to oppose which of the following?

- A. Censoring rap music for children
- B. Separating gangsta rap from the movie industry
- C. Grouping all rap music together
- D. Listening to rap music

Question 35

Which of the following actions most resembles those of Tyler, the Creator expressing his feelings in his lyrics?

- A. A boy training extensively for a race and winning first place
- B. A girl bragging about her grades even though she performs poorly
- C. A student faking knowledge about an upcoming political election
- D. A journalist dreading writing for a new section of the newspaper

Passage 7 (Questions 36-40)

Developmental and life-course perspectives on crime suggest that contextual factors in life and events and choices throughout the life course influence patterns of delinquency. Sampson and Laub's age-graded life-course theory of crime and other social control perspectives suggest that family and religion may be especially important influences on patterns of delinquency because they are primary sources of social control, support and integration. In a recent study, Petts examined whether family and religious characteristics influence individual-level delinquency trajectories from early adolescence through young adulthood. The results suggest that residing with two parents deters youths from becoming delinquent and that supportive parenting practices reduce their likelihood of becoming involved in delinquent behavior early in adolescence. Although numerous studies have examined the relationship between family and religion on delinquency, there have not been studies of the relationship between parents, friends, and religion on substance use among adults.

Studies on substance use have implicated gender as an important determinant of behavior and outcomes. The convergence hypothesis predicts that men and women would adopt similar patterns of drinking as their social roles converge. Based on the logic of the convergence hypothesis, role-related changes connected to women's labor force participation would not only challenge traditional family roles, but would also transform the attitudes of both men and women in other domains, including the appropriateness of certain types of social behavior, such as alcohol consumption. Contrary to the convergence hypothesis, adolescent and adult males still drink more frequently and consume larger quantities of alcohol than their female counterparts.

According to Smith, religious institutions provide resources, such as support networks and teaching, to help individuals cope with and find meaning in stressful events. These resources may be especially beneficial to adults who are at high risk for substance use. Rohrbaugh and Jessor identify several processes of internalized social control through which personal religiosity may influence behavior. They maintain that religion sensitizes individuals to moral issues and acceptable standards of behavior, and it offers a deity as a source of punishment and wrath. Thus, active religious involvement should foster an interest in abiding by religious precepts. High religious participation should be related to reduced substance use because the fear of divine punishment would make a person less likely to disobey the rules of the faith. Most studies on the association of religion with substance use have found an inverse, contemporaneous relationship.

The positive effect of formal social integration on substance use supports Hirschi's contention that attachment to organizations works as a social control. The significant effects for frequency of attending religious services on smoking and drinking are consistent with Neil and Kahn's observation that engagement with religious communities might also benefit older adults in particular by providing opportunities for socialization and social support in later life. Similarly, Levin and Taylor suggest that older adults may have been socialized to value religiosity and spirituality more than younger people.

Peer relationships are considered the primary factor involved in whether youth decide to engage in and maintain substance use, and peers reinforce substance use behaviors. Several studies have found that substance-using youth are more likely to have substance-using friends. A body of literature stresses that the social capital that is available in open networks produces advantages for teenagers and young adults. Bott explored the effects of open and diffused networks and pointed out that with the freedom afforded by open networks, other important relations (e.g. strong ties and significant others) can have their influence enhanced.

One recent study found that an adult's relationships with their mother and father have distinct impacts on smoking and drinking behavior. Other studies have documented that substance abuse occurs in certain patterns throughout familial generations. Further investigation may elucidate these recurring findings. The lack of a significant effect for relationship with friends suggests that peer relationships may not have an influence on adult substance use. The findings support general social control perspective that family and religion are primary sources of social control, support, and integration.

This passage was adapted from "Gender Differences in Social Relationships, Social Integration and Substance Use." Jones-Johnson G, DeLisi M, Hochstetler A, Johnson WR, and Frishman N. *Sociology Mind*. 2013. 3(1) doi: 10.4236/sm.2013.31016 for use under the terms of the Creative Commons CC BY 3.0 license (http://creativecommons.org/licenses/by/3.0/legalcode).

Question 36

A 30-year-old male who has struggled with alcoholism is afraid he will relapse. What advice would the author be most likely to give him?

- ○ **A.** Share these thoughts with friends for support.
- ○ **B.** Contact his mother or father to develop a relationship.
- ○ **C.** Attend a religious service.
- ○ **D.** Consult with female friends and relatives, since they are less likely to consume alcohol.

Question 37

Which passage assertion is *least* supported by evidence?

- ○ **A.** Contextual factors, events, and choices throughout the life course influence patterns of delinquency.
- ○ **B.** Studies on substance use have implicated gender as an important determinant of behavior and outcomes.
- ○ **C.** Religious resources may be especially beneficial to adults who are at high risk for substance use.
- ○ **D.** Older adults may have been socialized to value religiosity and spirituality more than younger people.

Question 38

A new movie is marketed as a realistic tale of a teen addicted to drugs. Based on the passage, which of the following statements is most likely to be true?

- ○ **A.** The protagonist's father left the family when he was a baby.
- ○ **B.** The teen's friends first provided him with drugs.
- ○ **C.** The protagonist is a loner and does not have social support.
- ○ **D.** The film concludes with a religious awakening.

Question 39

According to the passage, religious institutions:

- ○ **A.** are only helpful in the context of stressful life events.
- ○ **B.** inspire individuals mainly through fear.
- ○ **C.** are primarily comprised of older individuals.
- ○ **D.** can be social organizations.

Question 40

The passage points out that relationships with mothers or fathers affect substance use behaviors in distinct ways. Which of the following is most likely NOT a reason that the author mentions this?

- ○ **A.** To stress that parenting is a team effort
- ○ **B.** To promote further research investigating this finding
- ○ **C.** To acknowledge the role of heredity in substance use
- ○ **D.** To suggest how many factors can affect substance use

Next ▶

Passage 8 (Questions 41-47)

Over many generations, human beings have developed socio-technical practices to protect them from vulnerabilities and to respond to shocks, thereby increasing socialization of risk and vulnerability. Increasing socialization means that people took into consideration those around them, starting with small groups, families, and tribes. To those they loved they extended cooperation, perhaps the earliest form of human resilience. The development of various kinds of communitarian structures and practices to deal with these vulnerabilities represents a resilient whole that protects humans from risk and suffering.

Research carried out after the Second World War about the effects of Allied bombing on the German economy was among the first systematic studies of resilience in a social system . While economists' findings indicated that Allied bombing was ineffective, policymakers sided with Pentagon officials who maintained that strategic bombing had been decisive in bringing about the war's conclusion. Just a few years later, the methodologies developed in the course of retrospective studies on the global conflict would find a new object of investigation in research on the anticipated effects of nuclear war on the United States, leading to more precise data about the aggregate economy. Aggregate data offered insights about the present state of the economy, but recognizing their inability to predict future conditions, economists engineered more sophisticated models. These new models of the economy moved from thinking about aggregates to thinking about interconnected flows of capital, examining the post-attack capabilities of industrial facilities through the lens of "critical networks." Vulnerability and hence resilience were thus reconceptualized.

These models, in turn, figured in the strategic management of the US president's Wage and Price Control policy announced in 1971, triggered by rising unemployment rates. This policy once again brought economists to work alongside engineers from operations research. Their continued efforts resulted in increasing reliance on probability in their models of risk; in the shift from modeling the national economy to models of financial markets; to notions of stress tests applied not to physical objects but to financial instruments; to the use of models by banks to make decisions about trades; and eventually to the use of models as a regulatory device. Thus, from the first systematic studies of resilience we find an unbroken link of conceptual and methodological developments, moving from the field of security to the field of securities and leading to contemporary models of risk—models, moreover, which take into account that other actors are also using models in attempts to design resilience in response to risky futures.

Models of risk, however, can themselves be risky. The real purpose and function of the market is to provide an arena for the mutual observation of observers—in this context, competing financial institutions. The most interesting aspect of the circularity of observations (observers observing observers) pertains to uncertainty about the future. And the most troubling aspect is that models that predict the future can and will, by being used by rival traders, bring about a different world than the one predicted. This is a diabolical circularity: the more a prediction is followed, the more it will modify the conditions on which it was based, and thereby change the world. Or, as the Yankee philosopher Yogi Berra so aptly stated: "The future ain't what it used to be."

Any model needs to make assumptions about the actions of others. Things get really interesting when models become more sophisticated and begin to take into account that others are not simply acting but are acting on the basis of models (which themselves take into account that others are using models, each of which is probability-based). As models become more sophisticated, more powerful, and better able to take into account model risk, prices become more volatile and the system as a whole less predictable.

Passage was adapted from "On Resilience." Stark D. *Soc. Sci.* 2014. 3 doi: 10.3390/socsci3010060 for use under the terms of the Creative Commons CC BY 4.0 license (http://creativecommons.org/licenses/by/4.0/legalcode).

Question 41

In the author's view, models of risk in the financial industry:

○ **A.** predict the actions of others within a narrow range of probability.

○ **B.** destabilize the market by making unfounded predictions about the actions of traders.

○ **C.** deliberately attempt to skew the accuracy of rivals' models.

○ **D.** alter the very prices they attempt to predict.

Question 42

The passage states that models of risk originally were created in order to:

○ **A.** predict the consequences of nuclear war.

○ **B.** better understand fluctuations in the national economy.

○ **C.** mitigate price volatility in the market for securities.

○ **D.** obfuscate the predictive ability of alternative trading models.

Question 43

On the basis of the information presented in the passage, which of the following scenarios would best allow a company's financial models to fulfill their intended purpose?

○ **A.** The government offers more accurate data concerning the aggregate economy.

○ **B.** Traders are unable to determine the models being used by competitors.

○ **C.** Economists revert from the use of probabilistic models back to models used before the Second World War.

○ **D.** No rival companies in the industry employ the use of models.

Question 44

The author would be most likely to support which of the following remedies to the problem described in the passage?

○ **A.** An alternative means to assess risk beyond the use of models

○ **B.** Government regulation to prohibit the use of models

○ **C.** Cooperation on the part of financial institutions to develop less risky models

○ **D.** An industry-wide prohibition of model variables that account for the models of others

Question 45

The "critical networks" discussed in the second paragraph most likely refer to:

○ **A.** the supply chain, an area of vulnerability in national security in the event of a nuclear attack.

○ **B.** the tendency of risk models to affect the models of other market observers.

○ **C.** the web of likely American allies and adversaries in the event of a global nuclear conflict.

○ **D.** the tendency of models to produce additional information that impacts later models.

Question 46

In the author's view, which of the following situations is most similar to the problem with the use of information posed by models of risk in today's financial markets?

○ **A.** A presidential candidate learns that one of her senior advisors has been relaying campaign secrets to a major rival.

○ **B.** A quarterback of a professional football team selects a poor play on the basis of faulty statistics about the opposing team.

○ **C.** Two young people are in love but never confess their feelings for one another because both are waiting for the other to speak up first.

○ **D.** People in a remote village fish freely from a pond, depleting the pond of its fish and depriving the village of a valuable food source.

Question 47

Which saying could best replace the Yogi Berra quotation without changing the author's argument?

○ **A.** "Only by acceptance of the past can you alter it."

○ **B.** "Who controls the past controls the future. Who controls the present controls the past."

○ **C.** "The past, the present and the future are really one: they are today."

○ **D.** "Study the past, if you would divine the future."

Passage 9 (Questions 48-53)

Human rights theory holds that human beings possess basic interests that ought never to be violated. These interests are so strong that they merit rights, a kind of protective shield that safeguards them from violation. No matter how great a benefit is at stake, one's right to life trumps any reason someone else may have to violate it.

Accordingly, the inviolable rights view holds that a person cannot be killed in order to harvest that person's body parts, even if dozens of other humans might benefit from that person's organs, bone marrow, or stem cells.

Most people think that humans alone deserve inviolable rights, because they uniquely possess certain capacities. Yet the problem with this argument is that not all humans thought to deserve rights share whatever capacity is deemed necessary for rights. For instance, people with severe cognitive disabilities deserve inviolable rights, yet may not share the capacity to be rational or use language.

What, then, does ground a claim to inviolable rights? According to animal rights theorists, it is the capacity for sentience, the ability to be aware of one's surroundings and to experience pain that grounds this claim. Sentient beings are selves—that is, they have a distinctive subjective experience of their own lives and of the world. They are vulnerable to pleasure and pain, to frustration and satisfaction, to joy and suffering, or to fear and death. On this view, if a being is sentient, then that being has certain basic interests in need of protection.

Several have objected to the argument that animal sentience supports a claim to inviolable animal rights. According to philosopher Carl Cohen, even if animal sentience may generate certain obligations on the part of humans to animals, it cannot generate anything close to animal rights. The reason is that animals are of a fundamentally different kind from humans, such that "rights pertain to [humans] as humans", and never to animals. However, given that he recognizes the strength of the argument that not all humans share any one capacity that uniquely grants them rights, Cohen is at pains to explain why humans and animals are of a morally different kind. If they do not all share one capacity that grants them moral status, then why is being biologically human morally relevant? Absent the ability to rely on some supposedly shared human capacity, Cohen's principle amounts to pure speciesism, or the arbitrary privileging of one's species over another.

An animal rights approach to whether rights ought to hinge on higher cognition might be to imagine Telepaths. Telepaths are an alien species with cognitive capacities far beyond our own, including their impressive capacity to communicate telepathically. Imagine that Telepaths come to Earth, enslave the human race and defend their actions on the grounds that humans have inferior mental capacities. Naturally, we, the enslaved, would think the Telepaths morally abhorrent. Regardless of our relatively feeble capacities, humans would protest, "we have our own lives to lead, our own experience of the world, our own sense of how our lives go better or worse."

Insofar as the same is true for animals, one cannot condemn the Telepaths' violation of human rights without also condemning humans' violation of animal rights. As a matter of consistency, if one thinks that all sentient humans deserve the right not to be subject to experimentation against their will, one must likewise hold that all sentient animals deserve this right.

This passage was adapted from "Against the Use of Knowledge Gained from Animal Experimentation." Tuvel R. *Societies*. 2015. 5(1) doi:10.3390/soc5010220 for use under the terms of the Creative Commons CC BY 4.0 license (http://creativecommons.org/licenses/by/4.0/legalcode).

Question 48

The author claims that most people think inviolable rights derive from:

○ **A.** sentience.

○ **B.** the ability to reason.

○ **C.** susceptibility to emotion.

○ **D.** arbitrary designation.

Question 49

Based on information in the passage, Carl Cohen distinguishes humans and animals morally for the reason that:

○ **A.** humans exhibit characteristics of sentience.

○ **B.** animals can experience neither pain nor pleasure.

○ **C.** humans constitute a distinctive species.

○ **D.** animals do not share a capacity for higher cognition.

Question 50

The author brings up Telepaths in order to show that:

○ **A.** humans are vulnerable as a species.

○ **B.** inviolable rights are applied arbitrarily.

○ **C.** some species have higher cognitive abilities than others.

○ **D.** human rights are inviolable.

Question 51

The passage suggests that animal rights theorists would likely NOT consider which of the following characteristics as a qualifier for inviolable rights?

    I. High cognitive capacity

    II. Vulnerability to death

    III. Ability to use language

○ **A.** I only

○ **B.** I and III only

○ **C.** II and III only

○ **D.** I, II, and III

Question 52

New legislation concerning animal testing is being considered. The author would most fully support the legislation if:

○ **A.** it protected animals that can reason from being killed for research.

○ **B.** it distinguished humans and animals as different kinds of beings.

○ **C.** it stipulated that animal testing must be conducted humanely.

○ **D.** it prohibited non-consensual testing on sentient beings.

Question 53

Which of the following conclusions can most reasonably be drawn from the author's definition of sentience?

○ **A.** Only some animals are sentient.

○ **B.** Sentience is more universal than higher cognition.

○ **C.** Higher cognition is a precondition for sentience.

○ **D.** Sentient beings only feel basic emotions.

STOP. If you finish before time is called, check your work. You may go back to any question in this test.

ANSWERS & EXPLANATIONS for Test 2 can be found on p. 197.

TEST ③

Number of Questions: 53
Time: 90 minutes

Passage 1 (Questions 1-6)

The diffusion and appropriation of mobile technologies have made it possible for information, knowledge, and service industry work to be performed from almost anywhere and at any time. The ubiquity of these technologies has altered traditional boundaries between work and private life. According to the International Telecommunication Union, worldwide subscriptions to mobile phones reached six billion in 2012. A leading digital measurement company reporting key trends in the U.S. smartphone industry reports a 7% increase in the number of people in the United States who owned smartphones during the first quarter of 2014 compared to November 2013. Similar remarkable increases in mobile phone use have been reported in other parts of the globe. As of February 2014, roughly three-fourths of the South Korean population was using smartphones. It is now commonplace for individuals to exchange work-related messages at home or personal communications at work. For many users, mobile technologies have extended work engagement beyond the period and locus of paid employment. In doing so, mobile technologies have not only changed the pattern of work and private life but also perceptions about the role of technology in the home and work-life balance.

While mobile technologies provide opportunities for individuals to organize work tasks in resourceful ways to create more private time, the relationship between work and mobile technology is complicated and paradoxical. One possible benefit is that workers may use technology in a way that maximizes the amount and quality of time allocated for private activities.

At the other extreme, technology-enabled mobility can facilitate an imbalance in which work dominates private life. The influence of mobile technology on social relationships goes beyond business sector boundaries, in such a way that how mobile communication technology influences social networks has become crucial in policymaking. Information and knowledge are being digitized, reducing the need for workers to be where work and information are located. Concepts such as telework and the virtual office can complicate this balance as employees attempt to deal with flexibility and sculpt the permeability of their own work and personal/family life boundaries.

One study of mobile and non-mobile employees at a major information technology company showed that while some employees reported that mobility had helped them balance work and family life, a majority of mobile employees indicated that balancing their work and home life is "difficult" or "very difficult." The newly found fluidity of space, time, and context creates an entirely new milieu in which individuals must scope new boundaries and new relationships to create entirely new forms of work and private life. The concern is how people engaged in such transformations make sense of their experiences managing the perceived boundaries between their work and private lives.

The advent of mobile technologies has provoked discussion about whether technology that facilitates working at home enhances work-life balance or just creates new forms of imbalance. There is evidence that home-based employees have mixed feelings about its effects on work-life balance. While they are positive about their greater flexibility, they also note the blurred boundary between work and family, increased workload, longer working hours, and the potential for burnout. Perhaps at the heart of this idea of balance is what sociologist Leslie Perlow describes as "the inherent time famine." It is a sense that people ". . . have insufficient time to meet all of the demands on them from work and their lives outside of work." Thus, "their feeling [is] of having too much to do and not enough time in which to do it."

This passage was adapted from "Making Sense of Mobile Technology: The Integration of Work and Private Life." Pauleen D, Campbell J, Harmer B, and Intezari A. *SAGE Open*. 2015. doi: 10.1177/2158244015583859 for use under the terms of the Creative Commons CC BY 4.0 license (http://creativecommons.org/licenses/by/4.0/legalcode).

Question 1

According to the passage, mobile technology use by professionals:

- **A.** is always harmful to the individual's personal life.
- **B.** can vary in its efficacy depending on the individual user.
- **C.** is always beneficial to the company.
- **D.** is only beneficial to the company if the individual has developed work/life boundaries.

Question 2

How would the author most likely react if hired by a company that encouraged mobile technology use?

- **A.** They would refuse to participate in that practice.
- **B.** They would limit their technology use at work to one device.
- **C.** They would set up strict "work" hours and "personal" hours.
- **D.** They would ask coworkers for advice about finding work/life balance.

Question 3

Technology is a beast that eats at personal time. What evidence from the passage would most support this claim?

- **A.** It is now customary for individuals to exchange personal communications at work.
- **B.** Information and knowledge are being digitalized, so workers do not need to be where work and information are located.
- **C.** The blurred boundary from mobile technology leads to increased workload, longer working hours, and greater potential for burnout.
- **D.** Time famine makes individuals feel like there is insufficient time to meet all of the demands on them from work and their lives outside of work.

Question 4

Which of the following conclusions can be inferred from the passage?

○ **A.** Most Americans now have a cell phone.

○ **B.** Work-life imbalance is specific to American technology users.

○ **C.** The feeling of "time famine" is a recent development.

○ **D.** Many technology users are not paid for the full amount of time that they work.

Question 5

Which of the following technological devices would the author most recommend using in order to maintain work-life balance?

○ **A.** Cell phone

○ **B.** Laptop

○ **C.** Desktop computer

○ **D.** Online server

Question 6

A CEO proposes that employees have a separate cell phone strictly for work purposes. Would the author be likely to support this proposal?

○ **A.** Yes, as long as employees turned off their personal phone while at work and vice versa.

○ **B.** Yes, as long as employees left their work cell phones at the office.

○ **C.** No, because employees could still be tempted to work from home using another device.

○ **D.** No, because it could lead to more stress for the employees.

Passage 2 (Questions 7-11)

Bhutan is the only country in the world that is formally committed to the pursuit of happiness as a central policy goal. Gross National Happiness (GNH) is the guiding development strategy, a unique operational vision that rejects pure economic growth for its own sake in favor of integrated multidimensionality. A singular focus on economic or environmental policy is replaced by an understanding of policy domains that continually interact deeply with one another.

This approach to happiness rooted in interdependent conditions is distinctly grounded in Mahayana Buddhism. Key is the disarticulation of "happiness" from individual pleasure, in favor of a subtle understanding of multiple evolving synergies, where radical acceptance of the world is paired with radical intervention in the world. The happiness that GNH strives to foster is a state of consciousness known as *"sukha."* Unlike notions of happiness as immediate pleasure fulfillment, *sukha* is a deeper, more stable understanding of happiness as "a state of flourishing that arises from mental balance and insight into the nature of reality."

Already this notion of happiness presents as a paradox for the West, where GNH is sometimes dismissed as utopian and vague. However, annual economic growth in Bhutan has been second only to China in the region alongside an internationally recognized record on environmental conservation. Paralleling socioeconomic advances such as free health care and free education has been a purposeful process of decentralization and democratization.

In *Money, Sex, War, Karma,* Buddhist scholar David Loy presents a familiar argument: our Judeo-Christian heritage has given those of us in the West a false dichotomy between humans and nature, while our Greek heritage has given us a similar distinction between the social and the natural. The result is a variety of worldviews that construct the "environment" as resource and technology as resource extractor. Loy goes further to speculate collective analogs to individual suffering, expressed in the structures of our societies, all of which posit and value the atomized, reified individual. By "reified individual," Loy means the Cartesian Self, imagined as a stand-alone entity: coherent over time, self-directed, and conceptually distinct from the networks that create and sustain it.

However, as Buddhist scholar Andrew Olendzki notes, "interdependence" in the West, tends to rest upon spatial metaphors. As such it reprises the whole lineage of "substantialist" thinking that compromises an accurate understanding of interdependence and calcifies the nominal forms of language that stress nouns and their qualities. In everything from our literature to our legal system, the individual Self is assumed to be a noun instead of a series of verbs or trajectory of events or continual process of development and becoming. In Western versions of interdependence, relation is retained, in the idea of a "web of life" or the "coupling" of distinct elements. However, process is lost: Self—or anything that can be said to have an identity—is not understood as a perpetually evolving set of probabilities, constantly interacting with all other probabilities within the networks or environments that provide its context.

Thinking through and activating new policies that engage "interdependence" and "coupling" can be naïve, perhaps self-defeating. Our entrenched substantialist assumptions make us ill-equipped to understand interdependence as the combination of interrelation and evolution. This is because to isolate an entity or principle—essentially, to define it—is to conceptually "take it out of time," so that it retains its stand-alone status that can persist *through* time *as* an identity. We often fail to recognize that the definition and conceptualization of interdependence itself has a complex and disputed history that is still unresolved, even in those cultures and histories that have thought about it for centuries. An understanding of interdependence, as in Bhutan, can simultaneously encourage progress in economic and in personal arenas.

This passage was adapted from "Happy Environments: Bhutan, Interdependence and the West." Schroeder R, Schroeder K. *Sustainability*. 2014. 6(6):3521-3533. doi: 10.3390/su6063521 for use under the terms of the Creative Commons CC BY 4.0 license (https://creativecommons.org/licenses/by/4.0/legalcode).

Question 7

Why is Bhutan integrating the pursuit of happiness into policy?

- ○ **A.** The majority of its people practice Mahayana Buddhism and aspire to achieve *"sukha."*
- ○ **B.** For the Bhutanese, happiness is a prerequisite to economic success.
- ○ **C.** Bhutan's culture is strongly influenced by Mahayana Buddhism, which focuses on the desires of the reified Self.
- ○ **D.** The beliefs of Bhutanese people are influenced by Mahayana Buddhism, which emphasizes interdependence.

Question 8

The author implies that Western conceptions of "interdependence" are:

- ○ **A.** intrinsically flawed because of their disregard for the traits that characterize an identity.
- ○ **B.** nuanced in their understanding of the continual process of identity formation.
- ○ **C.** problematic due to their focus on a noun's qualities rather than on its evolution.
- ○ **D.** idealistic because the assumption that a noun's traits are immobile is prerequisite to this belief system.

Question 9

Suppose GNH focused on maximizing individual citizens' happiness rather than on *sukha*. How would this affect the author's argument?

- ○ **A.** The argument would be weakened, because this focus on the reified Self results in the same fallacies present in Western conceptions of interdependence.
- ○ **B.** The argument would be weakened, because this makes the GNH more understandable to people with a Western perspective.
- ○ **C.** The argument would be strengthened, because emphasizing immediate pleasure promotes individuals' mental stability.
- ○ **D.** The argument would be strengthened, because this would reinforce the notion that Bhutanese individuals share a unified goal in supporting both the economic success and pristine environment of their country.

Question 10

According to the passage, people who ascribe to western cultural values are "ill-equipped to understand interdependence as the combination of interrelation and evolution." Which statement provides evidence for this assertion?

- ○ **A.** Westerners have a false dichotomy between humans and nature.
- ○ **B.** Identity is not understood by Westerners as a perpetually evolving set of probabilities.
- ○ **C.** Western worldviews construct the "environment" as resource.
- ○ **D.** Bhutan has an understanding of policy domains that continually interact deeply with one another.

Question 11

If Western cultures were to solely utilize fossil fuels as their source of energy, Loy's explanation would be that:

- ○ **A.** their Judean-Christian heritage makes Westerners incapable of understanding that the environment does not solely function as a resource.
- ○ **B.** Westerners' focus on the Cartesian self inhibits their ability to empathize with issues that do not immediately affect them.
- ○ **C.** support for the reified individual by Western society's structure promotes a disregard for the environment's value aside from being a resource.
- ○ **D.** their Greek heritage limits Westerners' awareness of the interconnectedness between humans and nature.

Passage 3 (Questions 12-15)

The exponentially-growing body of work on the human brain of the past few decades has not only taught us a lot about how the brain does cognition, but also has had a profound influence on other disciplines that study cognition and behavior. A notable example, interestingly enough, is philosophy. A small movement dedicated to applying neuroscience to traditional philosophical problems and using philosophical methods to illuminate issues in neuroscience began about twenty-five years ago and has been gaining momentum ever since. The central thought behind it is that certain basic questions about human cognition, questions that have been studied in many cases for millennia, will be answered only by a philosophically sophisticated grasp of what contemporary neuroscience teaches us about how the human brain processes information.

The evidence for this proposition is now overwhelming. The philosophical problem of perception has been transformed by new knowledge about the vision systems in the brain. Our understanding of memory has been deepened by knowing that two quite different systems in the brain are involved in short- and long-term memory. Knowing something about how language is implemented in the brain has transformed our understanding of the structure of language, especially the structure of many breakdowns in language, and so on. On the other hand, a great deal is still unclear about the implications of this new knowledge of the brain. Are cognitive functions localized in the brain in the way assumed by most recent work on brain imaging? Does it even make sense to think of cognitive activity being localized in such a way? Does knowing about the areas active in the brain when we are conscious of something hold any promise for helping with long-standing puzzles about the nature and role of consciousness?

In much early philosophy of science, the notion of law is central, as in the Deductive-Nomological theory of scientific explanation. While the nomological view of science seems entirely applicable to sciences such as physics, there is a real question as to whether it is appropriate for life sciences such as biology and neuroscience. One challenge is based on the seeming teleological character, or purpose that is imposed by humans, of biological systems. A teleological approach can integrate neuroscience, psychology and biology.

Another challenge to the hegemony of nomological explanation comes from philosophers of neuroscience who argue that explanations in terms of laws at the very least need to be supplemented by explanations in terms of mechanisms. Nomological explanations, as conceived by the Deductive-Nomological model, involve showing that a description of the target phenomenon is logically deducible from a statement of general law. Advocates of the mechanistic model of explanation claim that adequate explanations of certain target phenomena can be given by describing how the phenomena results from various processes and sub-processes. Cellular respiration is explained by appeal to various chemical reactions and the areas in the cell where these reactions take place. Laws are not completely abandoned, but they are supplemented.

One main reason why neuroscience raises issues such as these in stark form is that, while there is clearly an enormous amount of structure in the brain (the human brain is made up of roughly 100,000,000,000 neurons), neuroscience has had very little success in finding general laws that all or nearly all brains instantiate. Maybe for at least the complex kinds of activity that underpin cognition, it will turn out that there are no such laws, just masses and masses of individually-distinct (though still highly structured) events.

A related challenge to logical positivist philosophy of science questions whether scientific theories are best considered to be sets of sentences. Perhaps the vector space model of neural representation should replace the view of representations as sentences. This would completely recast our view of the enterprise of scientific theorizing, hypothesis testing, and explanation.

This passage was adapted from "The Philosophy and Neuroscience Movement." Kenari MA. *Art and Design Review*. 2014. 2 doi: 10.4236/adr.2014.22004 for use under the terms of the Creative Commons CC BY 4.0 license (https://creativecommons.org/licenses/by/4.0/legalcode).

Question 12

Which aspect of neuroscience has NOT been clarified by philosophy?

- ○ **A.** Vision
- ○ **B.** Syntax
- ○ **C.** Recall
- ○ **D.** Reflection

Question 13

Based on the description in the fifth paragraph, which of the following environments is most analogous to the brain?

- ○ **A.** A colorful forest
- ○ **B.** A vast desert
- ○ **C.** A large swimming pool
- ○ **D.** A standard dam

Question 14

The author appears to differ from earlier philosophers because he:

- ○ **A.** has devoted his studies to the philosophy of neuroscience.
- ○ **B.** argues for the philosophical study of all scientific concepts.
- ○ **C.** questions the nomological view of science.
- ○ **D.** believes that scientific theories need to be remodeled.

Question 15

The author would most likely favor a college course that:

- ○ **A.** studies the intricacies of neurological processes.
- ○ **B.** combines the study of ethics with science.
- ○ **C.** approaches scientific concepts with skepticism.
- ○ **D.** reevaluates basic questions of science.

Passage 4 (Questions 16-20)

Prostate cancer (PCa) is the most frequently diagnosed cancer and was the sixth leading cause of cancer death among men worldwide in 2012. Over the past two decades, PCa incidence has been increasing rapidly, influenced by prostate specific antigen (PSA) screening among both symptomatic and asymptomatic men—a practice that was adopted in the 1990s—as well as by the detection of latent cancer in prostate surgery. There are few population-based organized programs for PCa in Europe (in contrast to cervical and breast cancer), while opportunistic testing (case-finding) among men with or without urological symptoms is rather common. Some researchers have claimed that the shift to earlier-stage diagnosis is evidence of the effectiveness of screening. Others argue that diagnosing PCa early may not necessarily lead to fewer deaths, or that PSA screening may simply be detecting more dormant cancers, which has led to some controversy over the unproven benefits of screening for prostate cancer. Recently, the U.S. Preventive Services Task Force (USPSTF) concluded that PSA screening has no net benefit and that the potential harms may outweigh the benefits.

However, the "no-screening" policy may be a bad investment at the societal level because only persons with certain personality dispositions may have the motivation to seek help from a physician at the time of symptom presentation, while others may not. The "no-screening" policy may cost more in terms of treating advanced diseases and missing a significant number of cancer cases. As PSA screening is no longer recommended, there may be an increased need for interventions that increase men's participation in office-based initial screenings. Men are not a homogeneous group, and it is important to consider the influence that these several factors, especially dispositional factors (including personality), have on health service use. Knowing the personality characteristics of a man may facilitate active participation of both clinician and patient in the decision-making process.

Personality is a significant predictor in describing behavior, and thus, it is important to test the relationship between personality and PSA screening behavior. As every behavior is influenced by making certain decisions, which a person makes according to his values and preferences, personality might have an influence on screening decisions. As the USPSTF recommends against systematic PSA-based screening for prostate cancer, it is important to offer office-based initial screening to those age-eligible men whose personal characteristics indicate the capacity for compliance.

Education is predictive of the intention to attend PSA testing. Educated people may be more informed about health services and take more precautions with their health. In addition, it seems that worrying about health and prudence and self-discipline are the key motivational factors for utilizing PSA testing. It is worth noting that real behavior requires not only motivation but also the capacity to put decisions into practice. Neurotic people obviously do not have the emotional capacity to behave in the desired manner because these subjects may be more affected by stress and experience less social support. Their general negative affectivity may induce dissatisfaction with PSA testing, therefore leading to less actual testing. Conscientious men manage to put testing and treatment plans into practice because they have enough self-

control to set goals and realize them. It is also noteworthy that while extroverted men do not tend to worry about visiting a doctor, they do have enough energy and enthusiasm to attend testing when needed. Considering these dispositions, it is possible to improve predictions of men's health behaviors, as well as to help make decisions on management and service provision.

This passage was adapted from "Personality and Utilization of Prostate Cancer Testing: Evidence for the Influence of Neuroticism and Conscientiousness." Neeme M, Aavik A, Aavik T, and Punab M. *SAGE Open*. 2015. doi: 10.1177/2158244015593324 for use under the terms of the Creative Commons CC BY 4.0 license (http://creativecommons.org/licenses/by/4.0/legalcode).

Question 16

The passage implies that the recent increase in diagnosis of PCa is a result of:

○ **A.** unhealthy habits in neurotic patients.

○ **B.** an increase in the frequency of men visiting physicians.

○ **C.** the expansion of diagnostic criteria.

○ **D.** the implementation of screening recommendations.

Question 17

According to the author, concluding PSA screening is not a beneficial technique is:

○ **A.** discouraging but necessary.

○ **B.** only partly true.

○ **C.** a theory without evidence.

○ **D.** a setback to cancer treatment.

Question 18

The author's primary criticism of the USPSTF's recommendation, as presented in the passage, points to its failure to consider patients':

    I. disposition.

    II. expenses.

    III. heterogeneity.

○ **A.** I only

○ **B.** I and II only

○ **C.** I and III only

○ **D.** II and III only

Question 19

Which of the following, if true, would most support the author's conclusion regarding screening recommendations?

○ **A.** The implementation of screening recommendations for breast cancer significantly reduced the incidence of death.

○ **B.** Conscientious individuals have been shown to reliably follow treatment plans regarding cancer screening.

○ **C.** Physicians report noticing common personality traits within the first five minutes of a patient visit.

○ **D.** Most cancer research is devoted to screening rather than to treatment and outcomes.

Question 20

The author's argument about screening recommendations suggests that they would most likely oppose which of the following?

○ **A.** Recommending strict screening of all women for cervical cancer

○ **B.** Implementing standard cancer treatments for all patients

○ **C.** Funding to research the USPSTF's claim

○ **D.** Recommending PSA screening for all men

Passage 5 (Questions 21-27)

Prior to the late 20th century, the body of scholarly literature concerning the black church fell into a dichotomy of characterizing the role of black churches as being *either* an opiate or accommodative to the oppressive status quo, *or* liberatory and resistant to the status quo of oppression. The accommodative half of the dichotomy refers to black churches that ignored or downplayed inequality and accepted the normative claims and practices of white society. For example, black churches during the Reconstruction era (c.1865–1877) have been characterized as accommodative due to their acceptance of the prevailing Victorian standards of morality and calls for assimilation into white society. Numerous churches, particularly the National Baptist Convention, created temperance organizations to counter vices that presented stereotypical images of blacks to whites.

The resistant half of the dichotomy refers to black churches that viewed Christianity as a mechanism for liberation, affirmed their black heritage, and challenged the status quo of inequality. Historically, resistance has referred to protest, community action, and political involvement. The Progressive National Baptist Convention, formed by Dr. Martin Luther King, Jr. in protest of the National Baptist Convention's inaction on demanding civil liberties, embodied the resistant strain of the black church. Beyond its active involvement in the Civil Rights Movement, it supported the Black Power Movement and was one of the earliest groups to oppose the Vietnam War.

Leading up to the Civil Rights Movement, scholars tended to agree that black churches did little to address racial inequality among blacks and that they were more accommodating than resistant. While scholar W.E.B. Du Bois acknowledged that one function of organized religion in black communities was to provide a sense of community and shelter from the racism of the outside world, he also observed how black churches could simultaneously uphold the status quo of race, class, and gender oppression by reinforcing divisions based on economics, abiding Jim Crow segregation, and denying women access to leadership positions. Sociologist Gunnar Myrdal, in his 1944 report on race relations in the United States, *An American Dilemma*, argued that although some black ministers took part in protesting racism, on the whole black churches were conservative institutions, their ministers lacking in education and unequipped to lead a national movement demanding civil rights.

The notion of accommodation carries a submissive tone of uncritical acceptance, but scholars have neglected the viewpoint that black churches may have assumed an accommodative posture as a survival strategy. Black churches during the Reconstruction era have been characterized as accommodationist because of their emphasis on Victorian morality and assimilation into white society, couched in the language of "racial uplift" and self-help. Racial uplift involved moral, economic, social, and educational improvement, which drew upon Victorian morals stressing self-discipline, low tolerance of crime, sexual restraint, and generally "respectable" (*i.e.*, middle-class) behavior. In many post-Civil War black churches, blacks were encouraged to abstain from alcohol and tobacco and to become educated. On the one hand, this behavior upheld white, middle-class values. On the other hand, by encouraging blacks to present themselves as citizens worthy of equal treatment, the seemingly accommodative behavior of some black churches actually challenged the dominant narrative that blacks were uncivilized and would never participate as equal members of the United States democracy. It is also important to note that in a context in which black churches faced violent consequences for challenging the status quo, such as church burnings and bombings, they represented not an escapist institution focused on achieving salvation in the afterlife but, rather, solace for a community under assault.

This passage was adapted from "Whither Shall We Go? The Past and Present of Black Churches and the Public Sphere." Barber KH. *Religions*. 2015. 6(1) doi:10.3390/rel6010245 for use under the terms of the Creative Commons CC BY 4.0 license (https://creativecommons.org/licenses/by/4.0/legalcode).

Question 21

From the author's perspective, black churches in the post-Civil War era should be viewed as:

- ○ **A.** occupying a spectrum rather than a binary.
- ○ **B.** ascribing to prevailing white values.
- ○ **C.** intent on negating the social order.
- ○ **D.** ill-equipped to effect social change.

Question 22

The passage most forcefully criticizes the scholarship regarding the black church for assuming that:

- ○ **A.** Victorian morality is superior to that of the black community.
- ○ **B.** black values and middle-class values are mutually exclusive.
- ○ **C.** black churches were not unified in the struggle for civil rights.
- ○ **D.** accommodation can never carry subversive undertones.

Question 23

The author most probably cites W.E.B. Du Bois and Gunnar Myrdal in order to:

- ○ **A.** present scholars with viewpoints more closely aligned to her own.
- ○ **B.** provide examples of the ways in which the black church was resistant to oppression.
- ○ **C.** paint black churches as multidimensional against portrayals to the contrary.
- ○ **D.** criticize their views of the black church as unfit to disrupt the oppressive status quo.

Question 24

The author appears to believe that the prevailing expectation that blacks conform to Victorian values was:

- ○ **A.** the best way for the black community to improve its social status.
- ○ **B.** ironic in light of the eventual failure of the temperance movement.
- ○ **C.** unjust but presented an opportunity to advance the cause of racial equality.
- ○ **D.** a secondary concern to gender oppression and classism within the black church's own ranks.

Question 25

Which of the following strategies would be most effective to develop the argument that accommodative behavior served multiple ends?

- ○ **A.** Provide examples of how offering protection enabled churches to resist oppression
- ○ **B.** Rebut churches who believed that Victorian values were the key to liberation
- ○ **C.** Counter the racist undertones underlying the call for "racial uplift"
- ○ **D.** Describe the protections that accommodation offered the black community

Question 26

Same-sex marriage was legalized across the United States beginning in 2015. Were proponents of legalization to follow the example of the National Baptist Convention in advocating their cause, they would likely:

- ○ **A.** encourage same-sex couples to fashion their marriages around traditional norms.
- ○ **B.** align themselves with social movements of other oppressed groups.
- ○ **C.** assert that their marriages are identical to those of heterosexual couples.
- ○ **D.** unite within an established church committed to equal rights for same-sex couples.

Question 27

It is reasonable to assume that the passage author believes the best histories of social movements:

- ○ **A.** validate rival movements with differing means to a shared end.
- ○ **B.** give equal weight to dissenting arguments.
- ○ **C.** provide context to the movements' imperfections.
- ○ **D.** judge scholarship of the era from the viewpoints of the past rather than the present.

Next ▶

Passage 6 (Questions 28-33)

The "right to health" has been recognized as a basic human right for at least the past half-century, since international adoption of the Universal Declaration of Human Rights (UDHR) in 1948. Currently, the right to health has been formally recognized by 56 national governments, in the form of constitutional or statutory provisions. The features of a healthcare system that is able to guarantee a comprehensive "right to the highest level of attainable health" for the citizenry of a given nation-state may be complicated by a variety of social and political obstacles.

Despite a general awareness within the scholarly community that the right to health may not be available universally, investigations of this right have in large part been limited in scope. Debates frequently center on the structure, elements, and functions of health systems located within nations, thereby defining the state-centric platform from which citizens can access a right to health. An implicit assumption of this discourse is that the nation-state is the guarantor of first resort for the social rights of its recognized citizenry, either through state action or through the promotion of such efforts in the private sector.

Many politicians believe migratory health is adequately addressed, especially for those who migrate between nations by choice or as refugees. Both the citizens of a state who reside within its borders, as well as legal immigrants and refugees, face a host of well-documented barriers to healthcare, but still are able to achieve their right to health. Both recognized citizens and legal immigrants often do have access to these admittedly imperfect healthcare services because they receive political recognition from the public, private, or non-profit bureaucracies that govern and administer such services. In effect, both groups often have some access to a right to health within their nation of residence.

Scholars point out that individuals with no legal nationality often have no venue in which to make claims to rights of health. Statelessness has been defined as the condition by which someone under national laws does not enjoy citizenship with any country. There are an estimated 11 million stateless people worldwide. Lack of nationality often creates obstacles related to documentation, the inability to access national healthcare, and challenges related to mobility that decrease a person's chances of arriving at a hospital. Many stateless people have shorter-than-average life-spans.

The UDHR addresses these stateless people by describing legal obligations to respect the right to health by refraining from denying or limiting equal access for all persons, including prisoners or detainees, minorities, asylum seekers, and illegal immigrants, to preventive, curative and palliative health services. Legal experts contend that these obligations are unbreakable and unenforceable , and the obligations are blocked at an individual level by a range of societal and political variables.

In response to concerns about indeterminacy and accountability, transnational actors have introduced new standards for advancing health as a human right and for specifying what this right confers. Advocates of health combine protections of the person (such as the right to refuse medical treatment or an occupying power's responsibility to allow healthcare for citizens and prisoners of war) with social rights (such as the right to be provided the highest level of care attainable within one's society). The World Health Organization (WHO), a public health organization, prepares a biennial list that outlines the core needs for a basic healthcare system and advocates for universal access to medications. Physicians for Human Rights recommends the highest attainable standard of health through access to skilled health workers and essential medications, as well as drawing attention to underlying determinants of health such as clean drinking water and health education.

This article was adapted from "Debate: Limitations on Universality: The "Right to Health" and the Necessity of Legal Nationality." Kingston LN, Cohen EF, Morely CP. *BMC International Health and Human Rights.* 2010. 10:11 doi: 10.1186/1472-698X-10-11 for use under the terms of the Creative Commons CC BY 3.0 license (http://creativecommons.org/licenses/by/3.0/legalcode).

Question 28

Based on the information in the passage, it can be inferred that those who currently receive their right to health:

- ○ **A.** can easily access their documentation.
- ○ **B.** have stronger health outcomes than those who do not receive this right.
- ○ **C.** enjoy adequate political support from their elected officials.
- ○ **D.** possess more economic wealth than people denied the right.

Question 29

The information in the passage suggests that stateless people suffer because:

   I. the politicians do not need their vote.

   II. legal obligations are not implemented.

   III. they lack adequate transportation services.

- ○ **A.** II only
- ○ **B.** III only
- ○ **C.** I and III only
- ○ **D.** II and III only

Question 30

Many industrialized countries have universal healthcare plans that even cover minor expenses for visiting tourists. In light of this information, the passage could add the clarification that the denial of the right to health only affects:

- ○ **A.** stateless people in countries without universal healthcare.
- ○ **B.** those who are unable to pay any fees.
- ○ **C.** individuals with specific social barriers.
- ○ **D.** patients seeking expensive health services.

Question 31

Which of the following findings would most undermine the argument that documented citizens have adequate access to healthcare?

- ○ **A.** It takes 2 weeks for newly immigrated citizens to apply for health insurance in the U.S.
- ○ **B.** Refugees from war torn countries are turned away from overfull hospitals in neighboring countries.
- ○ **C.** Illegal immigrants are supported by global non-profit agencies.
- ○ **D.** Much of the homeless population in industrialized countries dies from preventable diseases.

Question 32

Assume that a transgender prisoner is refused hormone therapy while incarcerated. According to the passage, this situation describes :

- ○ **A.** non-essential care, so it is not a denial of the right to health.
- ○ **B.** lawful responsibility to equal access of healthcare being ignored.
- ○ **C.** a violation of a stateless person's basic rights.
- ○ **D.** proof that the right to health is not enforceable.

Question 33

According to the passage, the role of public health organizations is to:

- ○ **A.** form cohesive international goals.
- ○ **B.** raise awareness about fundamental health necessities.
- ○ **C.** protect the rights of individuals worldwide.
- ○ **D.** implement guidelines that lead to better health outcomes.

Passage 7 (Questions 34-40)

To appreciate the significance of flat disc beads manufactured from ostrich eggshell, and their role in interpreting the cognitive evolution of humans, two factors need to be considered: the distribution of such finds, and the taphonomic explanation of these distributions.

Many archaeologists take the view that the appearance of beads and pendants coincides with and marks the advent of the Upper Paleolithic Period (40,000-10,000 years ago). It is true that the overwhelming majority of Pleistocene beads date to the Upper Paleolithic. Just three human inhumations at the Russian site Sungir (dating to about 28,000 years ago) contained more beads than have been found in all other Pleistocene sites combined. The three graves yielded 13,113 small ivory beads and over 250 perforated polar fox teeth. But the more than forty ostrich eggshell beads from the Libyan site El Greifa add an important dimension to the earliest beads we know about. They were recovered with stone tools from layers dated by uranium-series analysis to about 200,000 years ago (astride the dividing line between the Lower and Middle Paleolithic Periods). Initially, only three bead fragments were recovered, but another forty have been found subsequently.

The near-perfect rounded circumference and perforation of the El Greifa beads demonstrate that the society which produced them possessed the technology to work in this fragile medium with great confidence and skill. The first three beads found are preserved as fragments only, but they share a similar perforation diameter of about 1.7 mm, and even their external diameter is very consistent (5.8 - 6.2 mm). This consistency in size and the near-perfect rounding of all preserved edges indicate a conscious appreciation of an abstract, geometric form by the end of the Lower Paleolithic, at the latest.

A simple comparison of the El Greifa site to the Sungir site would suggest that beads were produced infrequently during the Lower and Middle Paleolithic Periods, and then became much more numerous with the advent of the Upper Paleolithic. While this is possible, disc beads such as those made from ostrich eggshell are not likely to have been made in very small numbers. To provide such symbolic objects with a social meaning it would have been essential that they were made in large numbers, because it is repeated and "structured" use which confers such meaning. Moreover, very small beads such as those made from ostrich eggshell were probably not worn singly: in later, intact specimens from the region they are strung in sets, to achieve a decorative effect.

This renders it necessary to explain why, wherever ostrich eggshell beads have been found in Pleistocene contexts, only extremely small numbers were recovered. Taphonomic logic offers the best explanation for this pattern of distribution. Ostrich eggshell is fragile, so the number of beads found is likely a tiny fraction of those produced: at some (theoretically identifiable) point, the vast majority of these beads would have succumbed to the ravages of time. The paucity of early Pleistocene finds can readily be explained by postulating that they survived only in minute numbers from beyond their "taphonomic threshold."

Next ▶

The hypothesis that humans of the Lower Paleolithic Period, by 200,000 years ago at the very latest but probably considerably earlier, possessed cultural systems involving bead production and use is at considerable odds with the currently dominant paradigm. But if the advent of the Upper Paleolithic does not indicate the advent of frequent bead manufacture, it is impossible to escape the deduction that Lower Paleolithic peoples must have been cognitively sophisticated, possessing a clear concept of the self. Without self-awareness, beads are entirely useless pieces of material.

This passage was adapted from "The Significance of the Earliest Beads." Bednarik, Robert. *Advances in Anthropology*. 2015. 5(2). doi: 10.4236/aa.2015.52006 for use under the terms of the Creative Commons CC BY 4.0 license (https://creativecommons.org/licenses/by/4.0/legalcode).

Question 34

What is at the Sungir site?

- **A.** Three graves, probably those of ancient Russian kings
- **B.** Over 13,000 eggshell beads
- **C.** Polar fox teeth, which suggests that high-status ancient Russians were buried with protector animals
- **D.** The largest discovered cache of Pleistocene beads in the world

Question 35

Based on the information in the passage, the society responsible for the El Greifa beads probably did not:

- **A.** bury their dead with bead adornments.
- **B.** have any means of assuring uniformity of bead size.
- **C.** carve beads from stone.
- **D.** wear beads in large numbers.

Question 36

From the information given in the passage, it can be inferred that taphonomy is:

- **A.** the study of ancient burial sites.
- **B.** the study of how artifacts change over time.
- **C.** the study of how prehistoric artifacts were actually used by their makers.
- **D.** the study of ancient production and manufacturing techniques.

Question 37

On what grounds does the author conclude that the beads found at the El Greifa site probably represent only a small fraction of the beads made in that location?

- I. Eggshell beads are tiny, and would not have been worn in small numbers.
- II. The beads are remarkably uniform, indicating that they were made by a skilled hand.
- III. Lower Paleolithic eggshell, unlike ivory from the same period, is not likely to have survived to the present day.

- **A.** I only
- **B.** I and II
- **C.** I and III
- **D.** III only

Question 38

Imagine that a dig elsewhere in Libya uncovers a cache of nearly 700 ostrich eggshell beads. Analysis reveals that they are at least 50,000 years older than the beads found at the El Greifa site. How would this discovery affect the author's conclusions?

- **A.** It would refute his contention that eggshell beads dating to the Lower Paleolithic Period are unlikely to be found in large numbers.
- **B.** It would strengthen his claim that Lower Paleolithic peoples possessed complex cultures and self-awareness.
- **C.** It would weaken both his contention that eggshell beads dating to the Lower Paleolithic are unlikely to be found in large numbers, and his claim that Lower Paleolithic peoples possessed complex cultures.
- **D.** It would strengthen his claim that bead production indicates complex culture and self-awareness.

Question 39

If the Sungir site also contained a large cache of goose eggshell beads, it would be most reasonable to conclude that:

- **A.** the chemical composition of the soil at the Sungir site is more conducive to the survival of eggshell than that of the soil at the El Greifa site.
- **B.** those interred at the Sungir site were very important, as they were buried with valuable ancient artifacts.
- **C.** eggshell was a popular medium for bead-making throughout the Pleistocene Era.
- **D.** ivory and goose eggshell can survive in the ground for approximately the same amount of time.

Question 40

The author's discussion of taphonomic logic suggests which of the following conclusions about Pleistocene bead-making?

○ **A.** Archaeologists may never know what the earliest beads were made from.

○ **B.** Pleistocene peoples were more likely to use durable materials like stone, only occasionally using fragile materials like eggshell.

○ **C.** We can pinpoint the advent of bead-making with some precision once we are certain of the taphonomic threshold for eggshell beads.

○ **D.** Ivory was favored for bead-making in the Upper Paleolithic because eggshell was thought to be too fragile.

Passage 8 (Questions 41-47)

Patient safety has become the cornerstone of health care. High-quality care ensuring patient safety requires high-quality professionals to care for patients. Competence in professional skills comes from practice, but it can be unethical to practice on live patients to gain proficiency. Simulations that use either newly dead cadavers or computer programs have been identified as a superior strategy to train health care providers in a controlled environment without causing any harm to patients.

Newly dead cadaver simulation is often justified as a necessary practice for developing professional competence. Cadaver simulation can be used to train health professionals in various invasive and non-invasive skills, such as intravenous insertions, intubation, and basic and advanced life support. Newly dead cadavers provide learners with accurate anatomical and physiological responses, which can facilitate technical success in practice. In response to critics of cadaver simulation, who often raise questions about respect for the dead, some ethicists have argued that by virtue of their state of being, cadavers cannot be harmed and no longer have the same rights that people do.

Opponents of newly dead cadaver simulation suggest that there is no difference between a computer-based simulation and a cadaver-based simulation. Novice practitioners who learn anatomy virtually gain experience in skills they would otherwise be unable to practice on a living patient. In fact, the realism associated with newly dead cadaver simulation lessens as the body ages. Moreover, the practice of cadaver simulation may drive learners to conceptualize patients as "objects" of analysis and manipulation.

A unique problem arises in the case of newly dead cadaver simulation that does not hinder computer simulations: concealment of practicing on cadavers is generally considered unethical and a disruption of public trust. While researchers have rationalized concealment by stating that mourning families would be further burdened by the news, the issue remains: as a living body, a patient's autonomy has to be respected. After death, do these same laws apply? (If so, then ethically, if the patient has not granted consent for practicing lifesaving skills post-mortem, families' permission has to be sought. Even then, if the patient has expressly forbidden the practice, families cannot undo those wishes.) An argument can be made two ways: (a) a dead body is incapable of making decisions, hence the concept of autonomy is no longer valid, and (b) a dead body is the physical remains of a living soul that had made autonomous decisions of how its physical remains are to be treated. In medicine, autonomy is defined as total responsibility in decision-making. These serious questions concerning the ethics of newly dead cadaver simulation make it a far more complicated practice than that of computer simulation, yet the educational advantages of visualizing and manipulating the human body are evident.

Antipaternalism believes strictly in "patient autonomy." Paternalism espouses the view that an individual's own stated preferences, choices, and actions are deemed unreasonable in light of other standards the person embraces, for example, safety for oneself and for others living in the same society. Based on a paternalistic view of this issue, the use of cadavers in medical learning is justified solely on the basis of how many lives will be saved because of the practice. Yet to submit wholly to this view is to ignore the rights of living patients. A patient's physical remains may not have "autonomy" as defined in health care, but a person's wish of how to be treated after death should be honored. Consent and a clear explanation on what type of cadaver simulations will be implemented should be initiated upon admission, when the patient is fully conscious, just as consent is garnered for each care intervention a patient is expected to undergo.

This passage was adapted from "Practicing on Newly Dead: A Type of Cadaver Simulation." Abraham J. *SAGE Open.* 2015. 1(5) doi: 10.1177/2158244015595270 for use under the terms of the Creative Commons CC BY 4.0 license (https://creativecommons.org/licenses/by/4.0/legalcode).

Question 41

Based on passage information about consent, with which of the following statements would the author be *least* likely to agree?

○ **A.** A comatose patient is unable to grant consent for any medical care.

○ **B.** Consent for care can be sought at any time throughout a patient's stay in the hospital.

○ **C.** Family members can serve as proxies of consent for patients who have died.

○ **D.** Professionals should expressly seek consent for each medical procedure a patient may have.

Question 42

Which of the following, if assumed to be true, would most *weaken* the author's arguments about cadaver simulation?

○ **A.** Newly dead cadaver simulation has been shown to be ineffective for teaching learners invasive medical skills.

○ **B.** Cadavers are unable to make decisions, and so they intrinsically lack the right to autonomy.

○ **C.** Religious authorities denounce the use of newly dead cadavers in medical simulation exercises as unethical.

○ **D.** No one, including the living patient, can dictate what should happen to a body after death.

Question 43

According to the passage, newly dead cadaver simulation has which of the following advantages?

   I. It provides students a way to practice techniques without risking harm to patients.

  II. It desensitizes students to death within a controlled setting.

 III. It provides more accurate exposure to human anatomy and physiology than do dissections with preserved cadavers.

○ **A.** I only

○ **B.** II only

○ **C.** I and II

○ **D.** I and III

Question 44

Based on passage information, which of the following situations best reflects the concept of medical paternalism?

○ **A.** A universal health care law requires every citizen to acquire health insurance, regardless of whether they want it, in order to prevent people from going bankrupt from medical bills.

○ **B.** A teenager's father takes away his cell phone privileges after he is caught sneaking out of the house.

○ **C.** A law mandates people to wear seatbelts when they are driving.

○ **D.** A patient and her physicians discuss her options after she learns she has a terminal illness.

Question 45

Which of the following criticisms of a military training program are most like those of critics of newly dead cadaver simulation, as the author presents their views?

○ **A.** Military training programs violate the autonomy of participating soldiers.

○ **B.** Computer-based simulations of combat cause soldiers to view civilians as collateral damage, rather than as humans.

○ **C.** As soldiers age, they increasingly view training simulators as unrealistic.

○ **D.** Soldiers acquire similar amounts of knowledge about combat strategies from war video games as from boot camp.

Question 46

Based on passage information, to what extent do cadavers have autonomy?

○ **A.** Cadavers completely lack autonomy.

○ **B.** A cadaver does not have autonomy unless the patient consented to that right while she was alive and conscious.

○ **C.** A cadaver does not have autonomy unless the physician caring for that patient indicates that it has the right.

○ **D.** Cadavers have autonomy because all patients had that right before they died.

Question 47

The information in this passage would likely be of most use to:

○ **A.** an ethicist considering how antipaternalistic views affect medical educational outcomes.

○ **B.** a physician deciding if she should donate her body to science after she dies.

○ **C.** a mortician determining how to dress a cadaver for a funeral.

○ **D.** a patient considering whether to consent to a surgical procedure.

Passage 9 (Questions 48-53)

Within the anthropology of dance, the term 'dance' is problematic as it carries preconceptions of what this activity engages with, which is rooted into a Western way of understanding the body in space and time, situating it in a particular relationship to a soundscape. Anthropologists Kaeppler and Williams, two key founders of the discipline, used terms such as *structured movement system* and *human action signs* to avoid unnecessary connotations. Similarly, the term aesthetics and art have been used with caution to deal with genres that are not rooted in European traditions. The categories human beings use are informative about how they engage with the world. The separation between dance and sport, or the classification of dance into art, social, folk, and so on says more about some Western views on class and race than about human movement.

The hegemony of ballet is undeniable given that most dance genres from around the world have been influenced by the ballet aesthetic when transformed into theatrical performances. For instance, the use of symmetry in staging a folk dance, even when in its original setting it is only performed on one side. The use of ballet terminology is commonly used to discuss non-ballet movement. Dance scholar Munsi, while discussing the south Indian Mohini Attam, referred to plié rather than an indigenous term to describe the same movement. Ballet is rarely perceived as being culturally rooted or implicated in cross-cultural transactions. Because ballet is now performed throughout the world, it is seen as somewhat 'neutral' and 'universal.' However, because the French court of Louis saw its 'birth,' one often forgets ballet's Italian origins. Dancers and ballet masters moving across borders were common in ballet's early years and the genre was multicultural from its inception. The French royal edict forbidding public representation of folk dances could also be significant in giving ballet its hegemonic position. In France, ballet training and terminology became standardized. This commoditization made the genre easier to export and become international.

The development of American modern dance also shows how the genre is embedded within the history of discrimination that was intrinsic to North America in the 20th century. Dance scholars like Thomas DeFrantz have written extensively on how early African American dancers and choreographers were discriminated against even by those who supported them. Many dancers of the Left encouraged black dancers as 'leftist culture was premised on a cross-class and cross-racial alliance.' However, African Americans were often still expected to work within a specific framework, drawing 'from black folk life.' As DeFrantz put it 'modern dance was ideologically and physically not only a gendered (female), but a racialized (white) affair.' A modern British choreographer, for example, has complained that bharatanatyam practitioners are 'valued as race relation officers, cultural ambassadors, experts in multiculturalism, anthropological exhibits – everything save dance technicians.'

Aside from cultural distinctions, dance is further characterized as a separate cultural domain from sport. One belongs to 'art', the other to 'competitor.' In this perspective, art is 'exalted', sport is not. In schools, dance was considered part of physical education, where it held a marginalized, 'feminine' status. A philosopher, David Best, distinguished between the 'purposive' sports, which

Next ▶

include games and track and field sports, and the 'aesthetic' sports, which include gymnastic, diving, and figure skating. Not only do some sports have aesthetic content, but in some instances it is largely the aesthetically minded observers who find an aesthetic quality in a beautifully executed move performed by a sportsperson in contrast to those sports where 'style' or 'artistic merit' are assessed under competitive conditions. In the former, the aesthetic qualities are largely by-products. In the latter, they count in the scoring and may indeed be significant in the performance of equally strong athletes, allowing one to win over the other.

Question 48

According to the passage, African American dancers in the early 20th century:

○ **A.** relied upon support from white, liberal colleagues for their success.

○ **B.** were welcomed as cultural ambassadors within the predominantly white American modern dance community.

○ **C.** faced limitations in the types of dance techniques they were encouraged to specialize in.

○ **D.** were discouraged from pursuing dance as a career because of modern dance's inescapable racialization.

Question 49

Which of the following is most analogous to the author's classification of dance forms in the first paragraph?

○ **A.** The distinction between physicians involved in medicine and those in surgery.

○ **B.** The division of medicine into a variety of sub-specialties.

○ **C.** The hierarchy of residents, interns, and attending physicians within a hospital.

○ **D.** The classification of a physicians as healthcare providers regardless of their specialty.

Question 50

In the passage, the author asserts that ballet has achieved its status in the world of dance because:

○ **A.** it provided an established model for theatrical dance performance.

○ **B.** its standardized structure allowed it to remain consistent as it spread around the globe.

○ **C.** the rise in its popularity occurred as a result of cross-cultural interactions and subsequently made the dance form appear "universal".

○ **D.** it was not altered by other concurrent dance forms during its crystallization into an established discipline.

Question 51

The phrase "structured movement system" as used by the author in the passage most closely refers to:

○ **A.** traditional western dance forms.

○ **B.** standardized body actions utilized for entertainment purposes.

○ **C.** ritualized dances that are multicultural in origin.

○ **D.** defined body movements derived from any cultural background.

Question 52

The author asserts that "the categories human beings use are informative about how they engage with the world." Which of the following pieces of evidence from the passage best supports this argument?

○ **A.** In schools, dance was considered part of physical education, where it held a marginalized, 'feminine' status.

○ **B.** Ballet is rarely perceived as being culturally rooted or having been historically implicated in cross-cultural transactions.

○ **C.** Many dancers of the Left encouraged black dancers as 'leftist culture was premised on a cross-class and cross-racial alliance'.

○ **D.** In France, ballet training and terminology became standardized; this commoditization made the genre easier to export and to become international.

Question 53

David Bests' distinction between different types of sports would be most weakened if which of the following statements were true?

○ **A.** Not only aesthetically minded observers find an aesthetic quality in a beautifully executed move by a sportsperson.

○ **B.** Athletes trained to intentionally emphasize the aesthetic qualities in games and track sports perform better than athletes trained otherwise.

○ **C.** "Artistic merit" is not awarded a point value in gymnastics, diving, or figure skating.

○ **D.** Style plays a large component in the perceived athleticism of sportsmen in sports Best would consider to be "purposive".

STOP. If you finish before time is called, check your work. You may go back to any question in this test.

ANSWERS & EXPLANATIONS for Test 3 can be found on p. 209.

TEST **4**

Number of Questions: 53
Time: 90 minutes

Passage 1 (Questions 1-7)

Parker McKenzie attended Rainy Mountain Boarding School from 1904 to 1914. One of several on-reservation boarding schools established by the federal government with the unstated goal of assimilating Native peoples to white American society, Rainy Mountain was located on the Kiowa-Comanche-Apache Reservation in southwest Oklahoma. Native students in photographs of these reservation schools stand posed and stoic in uniforms the Caucasian school administrators deemed "sensible." McKenzie kept one such propagandistic photograph, The Pie Club, depicting seven girls, including his little sister, Nellie, dressed in aprons and holding platters of desserts and standing outside a school building.

The Pie Club is one of the few Rainy Mountain school photographs retained by McKenzie that appears to be taken by an official school photographer. By the time this photograph was taken (ca. 1915), McKenzie had already advanced and transferred out of the school. Yet he held onto the photograph, and almost seventy-five years later, he was still able to name all of the people in the photograph and the tribes to which they belonged. Shortly after the picture was taken, his little sister would die of tuberculosis—an unfortunately common disease that plagued boarding schools. McKenzie had very few images of her, and although this is most likely the reason he kept the photograph, it can be read as much more than a wistful keepsake.

Creating a visual history is a question of ownership. By incorporating the Pie Club photograph into his personal archive and identifying the figures, McKenzie effectively claimed the picture as part of his family album. The image no longer functions as an anonymous group portrait like so many other Indian boarding school photographs have become. His preservation of this artifact is fundamentally an act of visual sovereignty, a rethinking of Native representations to counter the colonial imagery that has dominated the archives. This act of transference is possible because indigenous viewers look past the stereotypical way in which their relatives and ancestors have been portrayed; this is their way of honoring people who play a part in their family's history. That is not to imply that visual sovereignty is employed exclusively as a mnemonic device for the purposes of nostalgia. Visual sovereignty gives agency to Native peoples to combat decades of non-Native representations. Treating Native images as sentimental portraits reduces Native survival to a matter of nostalgia and precludes discussion of the political strategies that enabled Native survival.

For some students, surviving the boarding school experience meant taking ownership of their situation—some ran away, while others stayed on and carved out a space within the institution. The Pie Club image evinces the latter. Baking was not only encouraged but enforced by the domestic science curriculum that constituted half of the female students' coursework. The goal was the extinction of tribal cultures and the transformation of Native children into near copies of white children, with labor appropriate to "proper" gender roles. Regardless of the implications of baking as gendered work or its Anglo associations, the women pictured in the Pie Club appear to have enjoyed cooking enough to join an extracurricular club. Scholars rarely use notions of happiness and enjoyment to accompany the descriptions of Native boarding school photographs; if a student actually took pleasure in a school activity, these scholars have rushed to portray that student as a victim of brainwashing. Visual sovereignty shifts the dialogue of indigenous experience from a victimized narrative to a strategic one. Labeling these students as "victims" does little to explain how these people adjusted, endured, and maybe even enjoyed parts of their boarding school experience.

This passage was adapted from "Student Snapshots: An Alternative Approach to the Visual History of American Indian Boarding Schools." Strathman N. *Humanities.* 2015. 4(4) doi:10.3390/h4040726 for use under the terms of the Creative Commons CC BY 4.0 license (https://creativecommons.org/licenses/by/4.0/legalcode).

Question 1

It can be inferred from the passage that the author believes the academic literature concerning Native reservation school photographs has failed to:

- ○ **A.** impartially evaluate the memories these photographs evoke.
- ○ **B.** credit the federal government for positive experiences it gave Native students.
- ○ **C.** recognize multiple dimensions of the student experience.
- ○ **D.** empathize with Native Americans who cherish these photographs.

Question 2

Which of the following claims is LEAST supported by elaboration or evidence from the passage?

- ○ **A.** Enrollment at reservation schools put students' cultures and lives in jeopardy.
- ○ **B.** Portraits of Natives condemn their subjects to anonymity.
- ○ **C.** Natives retain boarding school photographs to subvert prevailing narratives about their experience.
- ○ **D.** Boarding school photographs are enduring testaments to the oppression of Native people.

Question 3

Suppose a white medical doctor displayed artifacts in her home to honor victims of the Tuskegee syphilis experiments, a notorious historical event in which poor black sharecroppers were denied needed medical care. The author's argument concerning visual sovereignty:

- ○ **A.** would extend to the doctor, because the artifacts remind the doctor about important events in her profession.
- ○ **B.** would extend to the doctor, because this gesture casts the sharecroppers in an empowering light.
- ○ **C.** would not extend to the doctor, because the doctor is unlikely to have familial ties to the sharecroppers.
- ○ **D.** would not extend to the doctor, because the doctor belongs to the profession that oppressed the sharecroppers.

Question 4

Which of the following findings, if true, would most seriously weaken the passage's argument that keeping photographs from their days at reservation schools allowed Natives to combat oppression?

- O **A.** Unlike Parker McKenzie, most Native families forgot the identities of people in the pictures.
- O **B.** These photos are of little historical or personal significance to non-Native people.
- O **C.** Native parents elected to send their children to these reservation boarding schools.
- O **D.** Graduates of these schools enjoyed far greater quality of life than others from their tribes.

Question 5

The author most probably uses the phrase "non-Native representations" (paragraph 3) to refer to depictions of Native people that:

- O **A.** portray them as victims of brainwash.
- O **B.** fail to convey the nuances of their culture.
- O **C.** attempt to invoke feelings of nostalgia.
- O **D.** parades the triumph of other cultures over theirs.

Question 6

The author includes a discussion of gender roles (paragraph 4) in order to:

- O **A.** provide an instance of scholars' excessive eagerness to classify people as victims.
- O **B.** argue that cultural norms varied widely between white people and Native Americans.
- O **C.** demonstrate that Native women endured constant psychological abuse at reservation schools.
- O **D.** dispute scholars' characterization of traditional gender roles as oppressive.

Question 7

On the basis of passage information, it can be inferred that the author would most likely agree with which of the following claims?

- O **A.** The reservation boarding schools never employed brainwash to assimilate Natives to Anglo society.
- O **B.** Despite their reputation for oppression, reservation boarding schools improved the lives of some students.
- O **C.** Oversimplification of the Native experience is itself a form of oppression.
- O **D.** Native Americans were not as helpless as the historical narrative has painted them to be.

Passage 2 (Questions 8-14)

First in Human (FIH) trials are studies where an investigational medical product (drug, vaccine, medical device, etc.), previously developed and assessed through in vitro or animal testing, or through mathematical modeling, is tested on human subjects for the first time.

Traditionally, these early phase trials have been conducted in high income countries. Low and middle income countries (LMICs) tend to lack the research and clinical infrastructure, institutional capacity, and regulatory agency strength needed to appropriately conduct such trials. Product developers—usually large multinational pharmaceutical companies—and local regulatory agencies have historically been unable to achieve the necessary clinical and scientific rigor and standards of safety for trial participants in LMICs. LMICs themselves have relied on regulatory authorities from developed countries such as the United States to ensure that necessary safety measures are met, yet these authorities often do not possess knowledge of endemic diseases and local conditions most prevalent in LMICs, making it possible that they will make judgments about investigational products based on inappropriate risk-benefit assessments.

Western companies, which currently develop most new and innovative products, have considered it risky to conduct FIH trials in LMICs for various reasons, including the inability to discriminate adverse events caused by the investigational product from the generally much higher frequency of all types of undiagnosed symptoms and untreated morbidities, the cultural obstacles to undertaking autopsies, and the fear that they may be perceived to be exploiting vulnerable persons in these countries. By definition, the risks in FIH trials are not known for sure. Some commentators argue that it is too risky to conduct FIH trials at all in LMICs, since the necessary conditions do not exist to ensure high technical standards and the well-being of research participants. However, FIH trials for diseases that present important public health challenges for LMICs may present an opportunity to address the relevant health conditions in these countries, if and only if participant safety and scientific rigor can be achieved.

The epidemiology, health services, social determinants of health, compliance patterns, comorbidities, and genetic make-up of any population have a bearing on the way in which health products will ultimately be used and hopefully achieve the desired outcomes. There is evidence that mutations in genes coding for drug-metabolizing enzymes may result in drugs and vaccines being metabolized differently in different populations. With the frequency of medication errors, differences in health literacy amongst distinct populations may similarly influence trial safety. Testing drugs and vaccines in developed countries, especially those that target diseases most prevalent in LMICs, may give misleading results about the efficacy of these products that will eventually be primarily used in LMICs.

Conducting FIH trials in low income countries in accordance with international regulatory standards should drive capacity building for local ethical review, facilitate health care infrastructure development, increase economic activity by encouraging research into more innovative products, and reduce the culture of dependency on developed countries. Clinical research in low income countries has a mixed history and in many instances has not enhanced equity. But this is true as well in some high income countries. Conducting more FIH trials in low income countries could call attention to deficiencies in health systems and regulatory capacity and help to improve clinical trial standards everywhere, particularly if LMICs take more ownership of trials and product development, rely less on developed countries, and become examples of safe clinical and scientific research .

Question 8

According to the passage, first in human trials require which of the following to be properly conducted?

    I. Protective measures for trial participants

    II. Support from international pharmaceutical companies

    III. Careful and accurate scientific research

○ **A.** I only

○ **B.** II only

○ **C.** I and II only

○ **D.** I and III only

Question 9

A new study finds that a FIH drug trial in a LMIC has resulted in a high number of deaths. The author would be *least* likely to recommend:

○ **A.** enacting stricter safety requirements in line with international standards.

○ **B.** providing more patient education to trial participants about drug dosage, usage, and side effects.

○ **C.** calling for assistance from regulatory authorities in other countries who have previously developed similar trials.

○ **D.** establishing a multidisciplinary organization to oversee physicians and scientists involved in the trial .

Question 10

Which of the following situations best reflects the author's argument about population-based characteristics (paragraph five)?

○ **A.** Most patients with diabetes and hyperlipidemia benefit from discussions with their physicians about therapeutic lifestyle changes.

○ **B.** One half of a group of older men who regularly attended yoga class lost more weight than the other half over the course of a trial membership.

○ **C.** People with mutations in a gene coding for a crucial immune cell protein respond similarly to a live polio vaccine as do people with the wild type gene.

○ **D.** Job search programs designed for college graduates are less effective when matching high school dropouts to potential employers.

Question 11

Based on passage information, what is a potential benefit of conducting trials in LMICs?

○ **A.** Regulatory authorities from more developed nations will become informed about local diseases and be better able to assess the risks and benefits of trial drugs.

○ **B.** LMICs will no longer need to rely on developed nations for assistance in conducting FIH trials.

○ **C.** More investigational products can be tested, and those that merit further research will reach people in need more quickly.

○ **D.** LMICs will improve their ability to regulate future FIH trials.

Question 12

Which of the following, if true, would most *weaken* the author's argument about the context in which investigational products should be tested?

- ○ **A.** Clinical trials for drugs that treat rare orphan diseases have largely produced successful medications, regardless of where the trials are conducted.
- ○ **B.** An antihypertensive drug tested and approved in the United States produces similar blood pressure-lowering effects in many residents of India.
- ○ **C.** Drugs and vaccines tested in high income countries have helped treat residents of those nations.
- ○ **D.** Studies show that FIH trials in LMICs do not have adequate safety and support measures for participants.

Question 13

Based on passage information, what is a risk that Western companies undertake when they conduct FIH trials in LMICs?

- ○ **A.** Difficulties assessing harm caused by the trial drug
- ○ **B.** Cultural and language barriers that lead to misunderstandings
- ○ **C.** Concerns over exploiting individuals in these countries
- ○ **D.** Significant financial investment in trials without guaranteed returns

Question 14

Suppose a number of lower and middle income countries recently began conducting clinical trials. A neighboring higher income nation subsequently tightens rules around enrolling individuals with disabilities into its trials. This is best explained by which of the following?

- ○ **A.** Based on years of its ethics committees' internal reviews, the higher income nation determined certain vulnerable individuals should be excluded from trials.
- ○ **B.** The neighboring LMICs created trials with strict criteria for eligible participants.
- ○ **C.** Pressure from other developed nations compelled the higher income country to adjust its regulatory and safety standards.
- ○ **D.** Competition for trial participants between the high income nation and its neighbors led to a reevaluation of participant criteria.

Passage 3 (Questions 15-21)

The controversy over the planned construction of an Islamic community center in lower Manhattan burst onto the public stage like a storm in late summer 2010. Journalists and pundits from both the political right and left offered views on the meanings and contexts of the debate. Should an Islamic organization be allowed to build near Ground Zero, the site of the terrorist attacks on the World Trade Center perpetrated by self-described Islamic jihadists so intent upon combating the United States that they murdered over 3,000 people in the trying?

Almost immediately after the attacks, the then-mayor of New York City publicly termed the site a "sacred space," and the phrase was repeated over and over in the press. But what did the term "sacred" mean with respect to this site? What is "sacred space"?

The concept of sacred space is not easy to pin down; it has been the focus of much debate among scholars of Religious Studies who advance a variety of understandings of it. Among the most prominent stems from the groundbreaking work of history of religions scholar Mircea Eliade, who proposed a "substantive" understanding of sacred space as that imbued with an extraordinary character through a direct connection with a divine source. Once a secular space has communed with the divine, its nature is forever changed.

A competing viewpoint on the nature of sacred spaces provides a clearer understanding of the debate about who may or may not occupy Ground Zero. Some, advocating a more instrumental perspective, have argued that space is made sacred through human endeavor. A product of human activity, "sacred space" is made sacred, or sacralized, by individuals and groups for specific purposes, be they social or political, through specific behaviors or practices. This viewpoint emphasizes the social character of the construction of sacred space and the related creation of prohibitions and taboos to separate it from profane space and to maintain its purity and sacred character. Those who ascribe to the instrumental perspective view the processes of sacralization as inherently social and political, rather than supernatural or substantive.

Nevertheless, it was an Eliadian-like understanding of the substantive character of sacred space that imbued dialogue surrounding the proposed Islamic community center with a radical tenor. The people of New York, the press, citizens of the United States understood the space as set apart, extraordinary–a site of death and unimaginable pain. Here the victims had breathed their last; here, many believers understood, the spirits of their loved ones had departed this world. Soon this understanding transitioned into an understanding of the site as a burial ground, but one of a unique character. Protecting the site from further desecration became paramount, a cause that united groups attempting to both appropriate the space and exclude others from it.

One seemingly miraculous survival further obscured the line between the sacred and the political: two still-joined I-beams in the shape of a cross discovered among the wreckage. Understood by some Christian believers as a powerful statement of God's presence among disruption and disorder, the space was made sacred through an eruption of the divine into ordinary space. For many, the image further underscored the notion of a divine and specifically Christian presence at the site. This powerful narrative of the cross was adopted nationwide, and even though the people who perished in the attacks represented a variety of religious and non-religious perspectives, the "miraculous" cross was seen to visually claim the space, fixing the site within the historically dominant Christian tradition.

This passage was adapted from "The Park 51/Ground Zero Controversy and Sacred Sites as Contested Space." Kilde JH. *Religions*. 2011. 2 doi:10.3390/rel2030297 for use under the terms of the Creative Commons CC BY 3.0 license (https://creativecommons.org/licenses/by/3.0/legalcode).

Question 15

Suppose that a legislature in a country that refuses to recognize a state religion erects a Christian monument on its public grounds. The author of the passage would likely interpret this initiative as a(n):

- ○ **A.** attempt to secure the blessings of a divine entity.
- ○ **B.** effort to solemnize the grounds as a sacred space.
- ○ **C.** statement about who is and is not welcome on the grounds.
- ○ **D.** move to suppress dialogue about the validity of other religions .

Question 16

A principal at a school officially unaffiliated with a religious doctrine decides to lead a Jewish prayer ritual of students and teachers each morning. Based on the passage's ideas, this gathering should be viewed as exclusionary:

- ○ **A.** unless all students and teachers are invited to attend.
- ○ **B.** unless speakers from all religions are brought to the school.
- ○ **C.** unless the group does not invoke a divine entity by name.
- ○ **D.** regardless of the stated intentions of the principal.

Question 17

The passage argues that the discovery of the I-beam cross was widely interpreted as a sign from the Christian God that hastened the classification of Ground Zero as a Christian space. This argument most strongly supports which conclusion?

- ○ **A.** If a group can manage to connect a space with a divine force, it will be easier for that group to lay claim to the space.
- ○ **B.** If a space holds significance to people of many faiths, the group belonging to the historically dominant religion will prevail in laying claim to it.
- ○ **C.** If a secular site becomes the location of a mass tragedy, that space will from then on be viewed as a sacred space.
- ○ **D.** If a politician invokes spirituality in designating a space as sacred, society will be more inclined to side with the politician's agenda.

Question 18

The passage describes the public's view of Ground Zero as a burial ground "of a unique character" (paragraph 5). This phrase emphasizes this site's distinction from other burial grounds in that:

- ○ **A.** it is embroiled in a political controversy.
- ○ **B.** evidence of a divine connection was discovered there.
- ○ **C.** the people laid to rest there also died there.
- ○ **D.** it has received more media attention.

Question 19

It can be inferred that the author sees the Eliadian viewpoint as:

- ○ **A.** unhelpful in the case of the Islamic center but not entirely without merit.
- ○ **B.** prone to depriving minority groups of their civil liberties.
- ○ **C.** dangerously misinterpreted by opponents of the Islamic community center.
- ○ **D.** a naïve philosophy that ignores political realities.

Question 20

Which of the following claims is LEAST supported by evidence or elaboration in the passage?

- ○ **A.** Secular sites can take on divine meaning.
- ○ **B.** The I-beam cross intensified anti-Islamic sentiment.
- ○ **C.** The public saw the Islamic center as a profane space.
- ○ **D.** Ground Zero was widely seen as a place for some and not for others.

Question 21

Which of the following arguments most seriously *weakens* the application of instrumentalist ideas to support the Islamic organization in its pursuit to build a community center near Ground Zero? In the instrumental view:

- ○ **A.** the drive to create taboos justifies the exercise of moral prerogatives and warrants a show of respect from the organization.
- ○ **B.** the Islamic organization, like its detractors, must have ulterior motives beyond the exercise of its members' spirituality.
- ○ **C.** those who seek to deny the Islamic organization a lease at Ground Zero have unspoken political intentions.
- ○ **D.** a power struggle between a dominant group and less powerful group will be won by the group that commands the most influence.

Passage 4 (Questions 22-27)

The complexity of conservative foreign policy needs careful examination. As a consequence of the Cold War, American conservatives developed the reputation for being hawkish, yet military adventurism is not, nor ever has been, a prerequisite conservative value in America .

Since the start of the Cold War, American conservatives have been successful when they have been able to build a "big tent." The "conservative big tent" referred to here is the coalition of various foreign policy preferences that have been welcome in the conservative movement from the Cold War era to the present.

The conservative, in any context and any culture, seeks to conserve a set of values and to limit the reach of government. To argue simply that conservatives in the arena of foreign policy are either "doves" or "hawks" would create a false dichotomy. This spectrum varies with other ideologies and political movements, but the conservative big tent can be effectively categorized into three groups. Nearly all self-identified conservatives in America fit somewhere into this spectrum. The two opposite ends of the spectrum are idealists in that they approach foreign policy with more normative values.

On the dovish extreme of the spectrum, the non-interventionist usually contends that enemies of the United States are so because they have been provoked. The cautious realists are often on the same side of foreign policy with the non-interventionists, but for very different reasons. Cautious realists will commonly reject the non-interventionist view that other people and other nations will only be a danger to us if we harm them. This would completely ignore the balance of power that is at the core of realist foreign policy. However, a cautious realist will usually avoid direct military intervention, believing that military adventurism is imprudent. Cautious realists certainly support a strong national defense, believing that enemies need not be provoked to wish us harm, but that they will not cause us harm if it is not in their best interest.

The neoconservatives, the most hawkish in the conservative big tent, have come to dominate conservative foreign policy over the last decade, despite the Cold War being long over. Whatever neoconservatives may say of President Woodrow Wilson, they seem to share his view that the might of the U.S. military *can* "make the world safe for democracy." Although neoconservatives share the realists' wariness of enemy states, they have the far more ambitious goal of maintaining an unrivaled U.S. global hegemony. However, the cost of constant military intervention clearly clashes with fiscal conservatism, as the U.S. budget over the last century has never been balanced during a full-scale war. The assumption of a universal desire for democracy articulated by neoconservatives is difficult to reconcile with the preference for tradition and global diversity held by most conservative intellectuals. Furthermore, military intervention has drastic consequences for the culture of the nation engaged, inevitably expands the size and scope of government, and thus clearly rattles the preference for status quo and gradual, incremental change preferred by more traditional conservatives.

The neoconservatives have certainly made a significant impact on the conservative big tent. However, neoconservatives now find it very difficult to convince the rest of the conservative big tent that fiscal responsibility, the American way of life, and constitutionally limited government are compatible with a one-size-fits-all democratic model for the world and the military industrial complex necessary to maintain American unipolarity.

Limited government at home is ever more difficult to reconcile with unlimited government abroad, and the youngest generation of conservatives, unclouded by the specter of the Cold War, can afford philosophical consistency in their efforts to limit the size of government and place greater faith in the innovation of free individuals and voluntary association.

Passage was adapted from "The Decline of Military Adventurism in the Conservative Big Tent: Why Grassroots Conservatives in the United States Are Embracing a More Cautious Foreign Policy." Wagner R. *SAGE Open*. 2015. doi: 10.1177/2158244015575556 for use under the terms of the Creative Commons CC BY 4.0 license (http://creativecommons.org/licenses/by/4.0/legalcode).

Question 22

Suppose that political scientists classify a fourth subcategory of conservatives, the hawkish realists, that lies on the ideological spectrum between cautious realists and neoconservatives. Which of the following positions might a hawkish realist assume?

- A. We should engage in frequent shows of military strength because enemy states might attack unprovoked.
- B. We should engage in frequent shows of military strength with little concern about expanding the scope of government.
- C. We should not engage in frequent shows of military strength because foreign powers will not attack unless provoked.
- D. We should not engage in frequent shows of military strength, in recognition of the autonomy of other states.

Question 23

It has been said that the best defense is a good offense. Which of the subgroups described in the passage would most likely share that sentiment?

    I. Non-interventionists

    II. Cautious realists

    III. Neoconservatives

○ **A.** I and II

○ **B.** III only

○ **C.** II and III

○ **D.** I and III

Question 24

The passage argues that neoconservatives and Woodrow Wilson are united in their desire to:

○ **A.** establish a global hegemony led by the U.S. military.

○ **B.** use the U.S. military to proliferate the ideals of American governance.

○ **C.** achieve world peace through military might so that foreign leaders can freely govern.

○ **D.** preserve the status quo and limit the scope of government.

Question 25

From the author's perspective, which of the following scenarios is LEAST similar to how neoconservatives developed their foreign policy?

○ **A.** A jurist relies on traditional constitutional principles to render a decision that is highly unpopular and otherwise impractical in its application.

○ **B.** A group of religious dissidents breaks from the national church and writes their own holy text that borrows liberally from the traditions of their former sect.

○ **C.** The local steelworkers' union votes democratically for new principles that many believe fly in the face of the union's charter.

○ **D.** A head of state declares a state of emergency in order to bypass legislative processes required by the country's constitution.

Question 26

From the author's perspective, neoconservatives are most vulnerable to the criticism that:

○ **A.** they are too skeptical about the actions of foreign powers.

○ **B.** their domestic policy is misaligned with their foreign policy.

○ **C.** their beliefs fly in the face of those held by conservative intellectuals.

○ **D.** they are too intent on maintaining a global hegemony rather than an oligarchy led by several major powers.

Question 27

Which of the following statements, if true, would most weaken the author's claim that neoconservative philosophy is in conflict with fundamental tenets of American conservativism?

○ **A.** Fundamental conservative beliefs are limited to domestic matters.

○ **B.** Foreign powers will only attack in retaliation to American military strikes.

○ **C.** A larger, more dynamic American government is necessary to secure domestic peace.

○ **D.** Democratic government cannot thrive in every country.

Passage 5 (Questions 28-32)

Though its industrial center is concentrated in Southern California, Hollywood maintains a global reach. A byword for the American dream, Hollywood serves to extol the virtues of the American way of life, promotes major industrial products, and builds and reinforces a positive national image. Hollywood movies idealize American conceptions of freedom, equality, and prosperity. These movies are key cultural artifacts, offering windows into American cultural and social history.

Indeed, Hollywood has succeeded in selling America to the world. It has planted an ideology in the subconscious of filmmakers and consumers that if a production falls short of Hollywood standards, it is simply not good enough. Beyond that, America is seen as a utopian society that is devoid of errors. Hollywood's projection of American values and products in bright colors has beguiled movie industries around the world into imitating American values on screen. Such Hollywoodization of the global film industry has been referred to as cultural imperialism.

This process of Hollywoodization is rampant. Hollywood has come to dominate the ways of thinking of filmmakers and audiences worldwide. Take the Nigerian film industry, for example. Nicknamed Nollywood, the Nigerian film industry is the third highest grossing moviemaking industry in the world. However, Nollywood movies are made on shoestring budgets of time and money: an average production takes just ten days and costs approximately $15,000. In order to remain profitable, the industry must put quantity before quality. Currently, some three hundred producers churn out between five hundred and one thousand movies a year. Nollywood films are commonplace in Nigeria and in households across the African continent. Even so, viewers use Hollywood as the standard for assessing the quality of Nollywood productions.

Even countries with laws meant to prevent Hollywood's encroachment are not entirely immune. China, via Hong Kong, welcomed a Disney theme park, with the Hollywoodization of Sino-communism being referred to as "the rise of Mouse Zedong." In addition, Hollywood enhances its penetration of the Chinese film industry through the production of remakes, transforming an existing storyline to suit the culture of another society. Given these interventions, it would seem that Hollywood's presence in China and its influence on the Chinese film industry is nothing short of a soft means of imperialism.

Hollywood's access to the world is America's access to the world. Some would consider this a good thing, the inevitable mixing of values and virtues by way of cultural exchange. But this exchange is by no means horizontal. Western ideologies, political beliefs, western science, western laws and social institutions, western moral concepts, sexual symbols, and ideals of beauty, have all become objectives, examples, and norms everywhere in the world. The representations of people and perspectives, places and politics are strongly skewed to one side. By watching Hollywood movies, people have come to see America as the ideal society where good always prevails over evil.

A more horizontal global film industry would benefit all parties involved. If not every movie had to hold up to the standards set by Hollywood, more diverse and artistic projections might be made on movie screens worldwide.

This passage was adapted from "Hollywood, The American Image and The Global Film Industry." Ibbi AA. CINEJ *Cinema Journal*. 2013. 3(1) doi: 10.5195/cinej.2013.81 for use under the terms of the Creative Commons CC BY 3.0 license (http://creativecommons.org/licenses/by/3.0/legalcode).

Question 28

The passage suggests that moviegoers in countries other than the United States do which of the following when they consider locally produced movies?

- ○ **A.** Evaluate them based on how accurately they portray local culture.
- ○ **B.** Prefer them because they are produced domestically.
- ○ **C.** Ignore them because they are produced domestically.
- ○ **D.** Dislike them if they do not resemble American movies in quality.

Question 29

The author would likely consider each of the following to be an example of cultural imperialism EXCEPT:

- ○ **A.** the opening of an American fast-food restaurant in China.
- ○ **B.** the airing of a French television show on a Moroccan network.
- ○ **C.** the popularity of American baseball teams in South Korea.
- ○ **D.** the casting of an American actor in a Nigerian film.

Question 30

The author's claim that "Hollywood's access to the world is America's access to the world" supports the idea that:

- ○ **A.** foreign audiences see unrealistic images of American society.
- ○ **B.** the United States government controls the production of Hollywood movies.
- ○ **C.** Hollywood movies spread the American way of life abroad.
- ○ **D.** American filmmakers have easy access to jobs in foreign movie industries.

Question 31

Which of the following trends, if assumed to be valid, would most support the idea that the global film industry is becoming increasingly horizontal?

○ **A.** Independently produced movies are grossing more each year.

○ **B.** Hollywood's gross annual revenue has diminished in recent years.

○ **C.** The most popular movie in China last year was produced in China.

○ **D.** Hollywood actors are increasingly taking roles in movies made outside the United States.

Question 32

The passage makes it clear that the author is:

    I. disdainful of Hollywood movies.

    II. partial to non-Western films.

    III. troubled by imperialism.

○ **A.** I only

○ **B.** II and III only

○ **C.** III only

○ **D.** I, II, and III

Passage 6 (Questions 33-36)

A profession is a calling requiring specialized knowledge and often long and intensive preparation and experience, including instruction in skills and methods, as well as in the scientific, historical, or scholarly principles underlying these techniques. A profession maintains high standards of achievement and conduct and commits its members to continued study and a kind of work which has for its prime purpose the rendering of a public service. Medicine is a profession. The attributes, behaviors, commitments, values, and goals that characterize a profession constitute professionalism.

Medical professionalism is a belief system about how best to organize and deliver health care. It calls on group members to jointly declare ("profess") what the public and individual patients can expect regarding shared competency standards and ethical values and to implement trustworthy means to ensure that all medical professionals live up to these promises. Society expects physicians to be competent, skillful, ethical, humanistic, altruistic, and trustworthy—professional—and the medical profession to promote individuals' and the public's health and well-being. In exchange, society allows the medical profession autonomy to admit, train, certify, and discipline its members, and it provides medicine with the means and infrastructure to meet its responsibilities. The medical profession and society have a "social contract," and professionalism is the foundation of that contract.

Training around these fundamental pillars of professionalism must begin in medical school and extend throughout the whole of training and into practice. Various methods for teaching professionalism are available. The didactic lecture is a popular and efficient means of summarizing large amounts of information, such as different codes of ethics and international views on professionalism. By emphasizing the importance of the "cognitive base" of professionalism, lectures improve knowledge and thereby change attitudes about professional behaviors. However, teaching programs that rely primarily on didactic lectures questionably improve patient outcomes and physician performance. Teaching and learning during didactic lectures can be enhanced with opportunities for interaction between students and teachers, for example by presenting a clinical ethical dilemma scenario and soliciting responses from the audience.

Web-based teaching modules are also growing in popularity. Like didactic lectures, they can incorporate a significant amount of information. Moreover, they have the advantage of convenience, as they can be accessed by learners at their will. They are also most effective when coupled with interactive assessments that determine whether learners have mastered necessary content. For instance, web-based teaching modules can include online discussions among teachers and learners or self-assessment questions that provide correct answers with explanations. Overall though, didactic lectures and web-based modules are relatively static methods of teaching professionalism.

A consensus is emerging that role modeling is an effective means of teaching professionalism. Ideal role models manifest clinical competence, excellent teaching skills, and desirable personal qualities. They are not only capable of providing students with necessary information, whether in a lecture- or discussion-based format, but they are also willing to leverage experiential teaching techniques. Role models demonstrate the attributes and behaviors of professionalism during interactions with patients, medical learners, colleagues, and teams, and then ask their students to simulate these same behaviors. Studies show that learners watch, embrace, and importantly, mimic role models' attitudes and actions. Students can also accomplish these goals when role models involve them in simulated situations and thereby place them in participatory, rather than passive, roles. These methods should be used in safe and structured environments, in other words facilitated by a respected faculty member.

Role modeling can be enhanced with reflection to motivate students to further engage with their professionalism experiences. For example, teachers may ask medical learners to actively reflect on meaningful events in patient care (e.g. difficult diagnoses, communication failures, adverse events, ethical dilemmas, etc .).

This passage was adapted from "Teaching and Assessing Professionalism in Medical Learners and Practicing Physicians." Mueller PS. *Rambam Maimonides Medical Journal*. 2015. 6(2) doi: 10.5041/RMMJ.10195 for use under the terms of the Creative Commons CC BY 4.0 license (https://creativecommons.org/licenses/by/4.0/legalcode).

Question 33

Based on information in the passage, with which of the following claims about medical professionalism would the author *least* likely agree?

- ○ **A.** Medical professionalism promotes patients' well-being in the form of strong clinical outcomes.
- ○ **B.** Practicing physicians should receive periodic training in medical professionalism.
- ○ **C.** Medical professionalism incorporates both concrete and abstract principles.
- ○ **D.** The tenets of medical professionalism represent a way to garner trust with the public.

Question 34

Which of the following, if assumed to be true, would most weaken the author's arguments about how to teach professionalism?

- ○ **A.** Students demonstrate greater knowledge of what constitutes professional behavior after listening to lectures on the topic, compared to after simulating those traits.
- ○ **B.** Self-assessment questions have been shown to be ineffective at teaching professionalism.
- ○ **C.** Patients consider health care providers who have not been taught professionalism as skillful as those who have received training.
- ○ **D.** Relying on role models to teach professionalism confuses students, who learn too many different ways of exhibiting professional behavior from their mentors.

Question 35

Suppose a new project intends to improve professionalism among medical students. The author would most likely support this project if:

- ○ **A.** Students shadow their role models and observe patient interactions silently.
- ○ **B.** Students form small groups and answer questions about a case study on professionalism.
- ○ **C.** Students pretend to be a care provider to a standardized patient and receive feedback from their peers about their performance.
- ○ **D.** Students listen to a series of seminars emphasizing the medical professional traits of altruism and humanity.

Question 36

The author mentions the "cognitive base" of professionalism in paragraph three most likely in order to:

- ○ **A.** emphasize the idea that didactic lectures are unable to teach professionalism effectively.
- ○ **B.** underscore the importance of educating health providers about medical professionalism.
- ○ **C.** describe the role that didactic lectures play in conveying information about professional behaviors.
- ○ **D.** comment on the need to provide medical students with a problem-based curriculum that is intellectually rigorous.

Passage 7 (Questions 37-41)

Academic studies of the role of repetition within narrative are numerous, encompassing countless cultures and language groups, written and oral traditions, literary and linguistic genres. Generalizing across these many and varied domains is exceedingly challenging: investigations can and do differ according to which elements of a narrative are repeated, where they are repeated, and how often. One characteristic common to this research is the focus on great works and classics. But this preference also limits generalization because it strongly favors in-depth analyses of a few texts over less detailed comparisons of multiple texts. That said, research in the above fields hold particular relevance for the cinematic arts.

Repetition is basic to our understanding of any film. For instance, we must be able to recall and identify characters and settings each time they reappear. More subtly, throughout any film we can observe repetitions of everything from lines of dialogue and bits of music to camera positions, characters' behavior, and story action.

Both in written and visual narrative, themes are repeated in different ways and places in a story. Words—both as dialogue and description—are invariably included among the ways that this repetition is manifested. However, it is rare to find more than anecdotal evidence offered in support of this point, let alone thoroughgoing theories. For example, Film Studies Professor Dudley Andrew made a compelling case for the in-depth and systematic study of narrative structure in transcribed "film scripts." The principal benefits he anticipated were the possibility of scrutinizing the sequence of events, cataloging of interrelationships between fragments scattered throughout the film, and an enhanced understanding of patterns in dialogue, narrative structure, and image clustering. Yet, he did not specify what form the sequences, fragments, patterns, and clusters could take, let alone what relationships, if any, they could or should bear to one another.

A second example comes from English Professor Kenneth Robson's study of the narrative structure of the film *Grey Gardens*. Repetition is essential to four recurrent themes that he says characterize the lives of the mother and daughter protagonists, Big Edie and Little Edie. Although Robson arranges the themes into several "clusters of antinomies", each of which is "linked with an often elaborate network of visual and verbal references," only two examples are provided. The most relevant one concerns how the subtheme of modesty and promiscuity is underscored by "repeated references to clothing." But beyond noting Little Edie's insistence upon wearing girdles, Robson does not place references to girdles within the context of other references to clothing, nor does he indicate what relationship those articles have to one another or to the four recurring themes.

There is also a lack of evidence and research regarding the linguistic repetition of motifs. These formal repetitions are defined as any significant repeated element in a film including, but not limited to, an object, a color, a place, a person, a sound, or even a character trait. While studies have offered several examples of the repetition of motifs, discussion of the relationship of words to the repetition of motifs is cursory. Throughout narrative studies, the repetition of words—whether as dialogue or description—is recognized as important, but evidence to support this claim is mostly anecdotal and largely atheoretical.

This passage was adapted from "Thematic and Lexical Repetition in a Contemporary Screenplay." Hunter S, Smith S. *Open Journal of Modern Linguistics*. 2013. 3(1) doi: 10.4236/ojml.2013.31002 for use under the terms of the Creative Commons CC BY 3.0 license (http://creativecommons.org/licenses/by/3.0/legalcode).

Question 37

Based on the passage, the attitude of the author towards "film scripts" (paragraph 3) could best be described as:

- A. apathetic, because Andrew's study did not provide strong results.
- B. favorable, because the author recognizes their potential use in research.
- C. ambivalent, because Andrew did not use them effectively.
- D. resentful, because they distracted Andrew during his study.

Question 38

Given the information in the passage, what advice would the author most likely give a film studies professor wanting to teach about repetition?

- A. Do not focus on this concept, since there is no evidence to support it.
- B. Cite recent studies only to convey the general concept of repetition.
- C. Teach the concept in relation to other forms of written text.
- D. Encourage the students to perform their own research with new techniques.

Question 39

Which of the following findings would most strengthen the hypothesis that repetition increases understanding of a film?

- A. Foreign films, even with subtitles, are the hardest genre to understand.
- B. Action films without much dialogue prove difficult to follow.
- C. Musical films are often easy to comprehend with their reiterative soundtracks.
- D. Romantic comedy is the easiest genre to understand, since all of the movies follow the same pattern.

Question 40

Based on information in the passage, which of the following is a reasonable conclusion about repetition?

- ○ **A.** Repetition is present in almost all narratives.
- ○ **B.** Repetition is too common in films.
- ○ **C.** Filmmakers might not even realize how many repetitive elements are in their films.
- ○ **D.** Motifs are difficult to study throughout a film.

Question 41

Assume a researcher has received funding to study repetition in film. According to information in the passage, the study should involve:

- ○ **A.** experienced researchers.
- ○ **B.** multiple films.
- ○ **C.** film scripts.
- ○ **D.** linguistic experts.

Passage 8 (Questions 42-46)

Is there an innate tendency in human nature to believe in something? Is there even a human nature? That tendency of believing something, call it a religion, a philosophy or something else, is an integral part of human beings; it is our innate tendency, so powerful that it affects our lives, so dominating that it has been prepossessing us for centuries and also so difficult to be solved. The question asked above is about ourselves, about all of us, who are in one sense so indefinite, ambiguous, and vague. We are the Man, The Unknown. On the other hand, we are also, in one sense, so definite, explicit and certain; we are like a battlefield where God and Devil try to beat each other, and even that definition creates its own vagueness.

Religion is something that reproduces itself in different shapes, always recreating itself in human life and mind. It can never be wiped out. It is not possible to say that all religions share the same characteristics but it is an undeniable fact that religion is found in all human societies. Even the earliest societies, that we know through archeological remains, have religious symbols and rituals. In that sense religion has remained the most important and crucial part of human history, explaining our existence, where we came from and how we should comprehend our environments and nature. Through the ages, religion has been telling us what science cannot, giving explanations about human existence when science has not given a clear answer . That is why religion has always been a central issue for societies, ranging from the earliest one to the most developed ones. That is why it can be said that religion plays an integral role in society.

Firstly, religion gives people individual support. During crises in their lives, such as war, death, and natural disasters, religion provides meaning and a source of comfort. In addition to that, religion not only gives individuals a sense of identity and security but also it provides a source of explanation, such as the meaning of life.

Secondly, religion guarantees social integration. Societies can only survive if people share common values about what is right and wrong. That is why religion helps to maintain cultural traditions. Religion is a kind of social glue, holding society together, integrating its people and making them accept basic social values. Scholar Emile Durkheim believes that religion has such a social function. For him, religion is a coherent set of beliefs and practices having sacred things, which collects every believer under a church (temple) and unites them into a moral community. By sacred, Durkheim means that "sacred is set apart from everyday experience and inspires awe and reverence." He contrasts sacred with the profane that is ordinary. Moreover, there is no religion that is wrong. Every single religion answers some questions in societies and nobody can give an exact date for when a religion started; there is not a starting point for Religion. Durkheim thinks that worshiping reinforces the sense of solidarity in social groups.

Thirdly, religion provides social control. The most distinguished supporter of this idea is Karl Marx. According to him, religion is "the opium of the people." It is not religion that created men, but it is men that created religion. Men are shaped by society, so religion must be too. The religious world is just a reflection of the real world. Although Marx thinks that religion is "the heart of a heartless world," it is never an illusion. It justifies existing social order and encourages people to accept their place in society. Religion shows inequalities as the will of God.

This passage was adapted from "Same Story But Different Cover: *The Substitution Principle in Religion* and Understanding It Through Watching Films." Ugur G. *CINEJ Cinema Journal*. 2013. 2(2) doi: 10.5195/cinej.2013.55 for use under the terms of the Creative Commons CC BY 3.0 license (http://creativecommons.org/licenses/by/3.0/legalcode).

Question 42

Which of the following findings, if assumed to be true, would most weaken the author's argument about religion?

- ○ **A.** A society without religious beliefs has existed for hundreds of years.
- ○ **B.** Societies with multiple religions tend to experience more violence than societies practicing one religion.
- ○ **C.** An atheistic family experiences less conflict than a deeply religious one.
- ○ **D.** Christians report a higher rate of security and identity than people who practice other religions.

Question 43

Suppose that a believer is feeling dissatisfied with his religion. Based on information in the passage, the author would be most likely to advise that he:

- ○ **A.** remain committed to his original religion.
- ○ **B.** go a few months without practicing a religion.
- ○ **C.** study scientific explanations of human existence.
- ○ **D.** try practicing a new religion.

Question 44

Karl Marx argues that religion provides social control (paragraph 5). This belief implies that:

- ○ **A.** without religion, the world would be in chaos.
- ○ **B.** ever since man has existed, so has religion.
- ○ **C.** social inequalities often have no worldly explanation.
- ○ **D.** religious leaders often have a powerful role in society.

Question 45

The author probably mentions the "earliest societies" (paragraph 2) in order to:

- ○ **A.** provide archeological evidence for his claims.
- ○ **B.** relate his argument to historians and scholars.
- ○ **C.** suggest that language is not needed to practice religion.
- ○ **D.** stress the universality of religion.

Question 46

Which of the following conclusions can be inferred from the passage?

- ○ **A.** Most individuals recognize the value of religion.
- ○ **B.** Man is the distinct middle ground between God and Devil.
- ○ **C.** Religion is valuable to skeptics.
- ○ **D.** All religions provide an understanding of a god's interactions with humans.

Next ▶

Passage 9 (Questions 47-53)

Social networking sites like Facebook have experienced an enormous growth in membership numbers in the last few years. These platforms allow people to present themselves and stay connected with their social contacts, even across long distances, time zones, and generations. In doing that they (can) satisfy a fundamental human need, the need to belong, which is a precondition of well-being. While in the early times of Internet communities and social networking sites a common assumption was that the new technologies will first and foremost be used to establish connections to strangers, it became apparent that social networking sites are predominantly used to electronically link to people one knows from offline life.

Online networks provide users with social capital, a currency of emotional, structural, and economic advantages derived from interpersonal networks. Social networking sites are well suited to establish and maintain social capital and, for this reason, have been shown to be able to positively influence well-being. Social capital comes in two strains, strong ties and weak ties. Strong ties such as family and close friends are assumed to predominantly provide emotional support. Weak ties like colleagues and acquaintances provide informational support because they overlap with less familiar networks and are better able to connect to other sources of information.

Some argue that weak ties have particular strengths that make them even more important than strong ties. Social networking sites are uniquely positioned to reinforce weak ties. One study demonstrated that searching for a job was not most positively affected by the number of strong ties to family and close friends but was dependent on weaker but more diverse relationships with acquaintances. Weak ties are not characterized by depth but by breadth in the sense that they provide information that might broaden horizons or worldviews. This is due to the fact that, usually, weak ties are people from different backgrounds connecting yet unlinked social networks, providing access to novel information. Cohesive strong-tie groups, by contrast, shelter members from outside opinions. Strong ties have little diversity in their backgrounds and tend to shun the ideas of outsiders.

The assumption that weak ties may be more important than strong ties has dominated studies of social capital and deserves closer scrutiny. One study demonstrated that first-year university students do not benefit from intense Facebook usage and its abundant opportunities to connect socially. For these students, the number of Facebook friends was negatively associated with emotional and academic adjustment. The number of Facebook friends was positively related to social adjustment and attachment to the institution only in upperclassmen, who had allowed time for their institutional relationships to mature offline. These findings corroborate the doubts of social networking skeptics, who argue that tie strength is the strongest predictor of feelings of emotional support; indeed, loose contacts might not be sufficient to increase social and emotional support.

A survey of Facebook users revealed their willingness to delete on average one third of their contacts. The more contacts people have, the more they are willing to delete some. A contact's status as a strong or weak tie did not affect users' propensity to remove him or her. When a user expects a contact to potentially provide a favor like help moving out of an apartment, the user will be less willing to delete the contact. This tendency points to the existence of forms of social support that go beyond emotional and informational support.

Passage was adapted from "Let the Weakest Link Go! Empirical Explorations on the Relative Importance of Weak and Strong Ties on Social Networking Sites." Kramer NC, Rosner L, Eimler SC, Winter S, Neubaum G. *Societies*. 2014. 4 doi:10.3390/soc4040785 for use under the terms of the Creative Commons CC BY 4.0 license (https://creativecommons.org/licenses/by/4.0/legalcode).

Question 47

The author's primary argument concerning weak ties is that they:

○ **A.** connect disparate acquaintances and information better than do strong ties.

○ **B.** are superior to strong ties in breadth but not in depth.

○ **C.** may be of proximate or lesser value than strong ties within social networks

○ **D.** do not actually offer social media users social capital or other advantages.

Question 48

The passage implies that strong ties principally differ from weak ties in that they:

○ **A.** homogenize the social experience and fortify pre-existing notions.

○ **B.** are actually responsible for providing the driving force behind social adjustment.

○ **C.** reinforce relationships of individuals with developed offline social networks.

○ **D.** are less prone to fading from an individual's social sphere than weak ties.

Question 49

In the author's view, if a social media user has very few contacts online, it can be concluded that that person:

○ **A.** maintains an online network composed primarily of strong ties.

○ **B.** is unlikely to delete any of those contacts.

○ **C.** will derive fewer benefits from weak ties.

○ **D.** has little need for social support that extends beyond the emotional and informational.

Question 50

A dean of an undergraduate institution wants to implement a policy to improve the social adjustment of the students. The author of the passage would see which policy as the LEAST effective means to this end?

- O **A.** Undergraduate students are required to live on campus in the course of their studies.
- O **B.** All online classes must schedule regular discussion-based meetings.
- O **C.** Each student must take a seminar-style class that challenges his or her worldview.
- O **D.** Underclassmen must join a silent weekly study hall with no internet access.

Question 51

Which of the following findings, if true, would *most* weaken the argument of the social networking skeptics described in the passage?

- O **A.** Online gamers tend to meet their closest friends online.
- O **B.** Online communities for grieving people help those users cope with loss.
- O **C.** People tend to lose weight faster when they share their progress in online forums.
- O **D.** Social media users report that these sites help them stay in contact with relatives and friends who live far away.

Question 52

Which of the following conclusions could most reasonably be drawn from ideas expressed in the passage?

- O **A.** Social media sites only enhance the social capital of those with strong existing interpersonal networks.
- O **B.** Contacts cannot be classified as strong or weak ties in the context of online social networks.
- O **C.** Online social networks cannot enhance a user's social capital.
- O **D.** Contacts on online social networks provide neither emotional wellbeing nor informational support.

Question 53

The author's views on using social networking sites as a means to derive social support might best be described as:

- O **A.** suspicious that this strategy has won nearly universal support without merit.
- O **B.** concerned that the implications of social media use have yet to be fully unearthed.
- O **C.** tentatively supportive because of its potential to increase the number of users' weak ties.
- O **D.** unconvinced that social networks go far enough to broaden users' worldviews.

STOP. If you finish before time is called, check your work. You may go back to any question in this test.

ANSWERS & EXPLANATIONS for Test 4 can be found on p. 225.

STOP

TEST 4

Number of Questions: 53
Time: 90 minutes

INSTRUCTIONS: Each passage is followed by associated questions. Read the passage, then select the best answer to each question. If you are unsure of the answer, rule out incorrect choices and select from the remaining options. Indicate your answer beside the option you choose.

Passage 1 (Questions 1-7)

The humanities scholar must be an eagle in the sky, surveying the landscape below for prey. Eagles cannot remain aloft in perpetuity; they have to plummet to the surface below, exchanging their distant two-dimensional perspective for a three-dimensional close-up rife with complexity. Likewise, scholars in the humanities survey the landscape and select concrete topics to probe their details and nuances. In the case of both the eagle and the humanities scholar, the two-dimensional view from above and the three-dimensional view on the ground mutually reinforce one another. The eagle can occupy neither the sky nor the ground permanently. Similarly, if the humanities scholar never looks at his or her subject matter from a distance, he or she will fail to discover meaningful research cases; however, if the scholar never studies cases in depth, his or her view of the global patterns risks stagnancy.

Unlike the oft-used opposition between the bird's eye view and the frog's perspective, the image of the eagle of humanities entails a unified, rather than dichotomous, enterprise. Instead of an opposition between two beings with totally different interests and worldviews, it presupposes a fruitful tension between two activities carried out by the same entity. This tension has always been a central challenge to the humanities and one of its principal charms. The recent digitization of both sources and research methods, however, has given an entirely new dimension to this tension. Most notably, it has dramatically enhanced the possibilities of the view from the sky. It seems as if digitization has helped to take away the fog which had hitherto prevented the eagle from sharply discerning patterns in the landscape below. Until the recent past, scholars in the humanities tried to reconstruct general patterns by assembling myriad pieces they had gathered through painstaking research requiring the combined effort of more than one lifetime. Today, some of these patterns reveal themselves with the click of the mouse.

But the scholarly community should not be tempted into unbridled optimism at the advent of digitization. Digital tools have the potential to democratize the informational landscape and present diverse viewpoints, but these are not absolutely truthful. The decision about whether or not a source is preserved for posterity has always been the province of archivists, librarians, and other scholars, and this selective conservation of sources has resulted in uneven accessibility to primary texts. The arrival of digital media has only exacerbated this tendency. Converting paper sources into digital sources requires technological means and manpower – and, therefore, money. Many historians have rightly warned that political willingness to provide these funds is more likely when a sense of urgency surrounds a certain issue and less likely when stakeholders have an interest in scuttling sources under the rug. Scholars are not the only ones guilty of conveniently omitting information that is not advantageous to publicize: politicians and financial executives have gone to great lengths to conceal information that does not cast them in a favorable light. The impulse to present one's best self is universal.

That being said, scholarly pursuits have been subject to these forces for centuries. Academic fashions come and go, often (though not always and seldom exclusively) determined by the demands of society. Subject matter that plumbs the depths of the latest research trends have always had the greatest odds of landing in the historical record. The digital age threatens to cloud the eagle's view of its prey below, but it also sharpens its talons for the hunt.

This passage was adapted from "Thick Description beyond the Digital Space." Beyen M. *Humanities*. 2015. 6(1) doi:10.3390/h5010002 for use under the terms of the Creative Commons CC BY 4.0 license (https://creativecommons.org/licenses/by/4.0/legalcode).

Question 1

The author's observation that "academic fashions come and go" (paragraph 4) functions within the passage to:

- ○ **A.** mitigate the severity of a criticism of digitization's impact on scholarly research.
- ○ **B.** introduce an alternative perspective on digitization that opposes the author's viewpoint.
- ○ **C.** substantiate the author's claim that research topics come from close inspection of the humanities.
- ○ **D.** rationalize scholars' drive to publish amid a flippant academic climate.

Question 2

The passage author most probably draws the analogy of the humanities scholar to the eagle in order to:

- ○ **A.** stress the role of interdisciplinary thought in advancing the frontiers of scholarly pursuits.
- ○ **B.** explain the scholar's obligation to develop scholarship from varying perspectives.
- ○ **C.** contrast the lofty vantage points of generalists with the narrow interests of scholars.
- ○ **D.** illuminate the contradictory nature of the scholar's academic responsibilities.

Question 3

The passage assertion that the "selective conservation of sources has resulted in uneven accessibility to primary texts" (paragraph 3) probably means that:

- ○ **A.** there is a delicate balance between overarching perspectives and detailed analysis.
- ○ **B.** the practice of culling some viewpoints from the historical record precedes the digital era.
- ○ **C.** the digitization process necessarily entails the filtering of some viewpoints.
- ○ **D.** technological research tools will probably make scholarship more readily available.

Question 4

The author's argument about digitization's impact on humanities research appears to assume that:

- ○ **A.** research topics can only be generated by broad inquiry into a discipline.
- ○ **B.** scholarship in the era preceding the digital age was less prone to political interference.
- ○ **C.** the costs of digitization far exceed the costs of archiving paper documents.
- ○ **D.** the most honest assessment of the humanities comes from the broadest vantage point.

Question 5

Suppose a physics professor makes groundbreaking discoveries in quantum mechanics but is unable to tutor high school physics, an introductory survey course. This information would appear to *challenge* which assertion made in the passage?

- ○ **A.** Digitization has influenced the scope of viewpoints to which scholars and the public are exposed.
- ○ **B.** The drive to publish and to satisfy stakeholders informs the research interests of many scholars.
- ○ **C.** Digitization has succeeded in narrowing the scope of scholars' research interests.
- ○ **D.** Scholars are most effective when they command mastery of both broad and narrow topics in their fields.

Question 6

A high school humanities teacher requires a final research project of his students but forbids them from using Internet sources. The author would most likely think that this constraint:

- ○ **A.** unequivocally improves the research skills of the students.
- ○ **B.** robs students of exposure to the spectrum of ideas in the humanities.
- ○ **C.** is a useful learning tool so long as sufficient time is allotted to explore the research question.
- ○ **D.** risks overloading the students with details when they should see the bigger picture.

Question 7

A technology entrepreneur launches a social media platform for humanities scholars to share ideas for specific research questions. The passage author would be most likely to raise which of the following objections to the software?

- ○ **A.** Scholars using this platform risk losing sight of broad trends in their discipline.
- ○ **B.** Circulating research questions is better left to libraries and archivists.
- ○ **C.** It enables modern scholars to sidestep the fruitful, painstaking research efforts of their predecessors.
- ○ **D.** The platform will distance its users from their areas of specialization.

Passage 2 (Questions 8-14)

Great art shows us the world as we were never able so clearly to see it before by leading us towards a more just, detailed, and refined understanding of human nature, or of the natural world which crowds upon our senses. For example, Rubens' painting of the Last Supper shows a dog sitting under the chair of Judas, the notorious traitor in the Christian faith. Their pairing invites viewers to see him not simply as the villain whose action led to the death of Christ but as a sinful human being with redeeming qualities—like other sinful human beings—and thus to conclude that human nature is never unambiguously good or bad.

Art not only reveals the true nature of reality, thereby pointing beyond itself towards a transcendent guiding principle of goodness; it also provides opportunities to consider morally relevant situations. It has been suggested that art is "a great hall of reflection where everything under the sun can be examined and considered." Literary works, in particular, allow for experimentation with different fictional situations in order to try to understand them and discover appropriate courses of action so that, when readers themselves are required to act, they act well. Although people may sometimes be able to gain the understanding they need by means of direct personal experience of a similar situation, or, perhaps, from the accounts of others whose life experiences differ from their own, no single person can gain all of their morally relevant knowledge in this way.

Art's ability to reveal the nature of reality may be limited because the significance of works of art is often ambiguous. For example, it is by no means clear that the dog under Judas' chair in the Rubens painting indicates a more than usually sympathetic treatment of Judas. Dogs were not well-regarded in the ancient world and the description "dog" was sometimes applied to nonbelievers and evildoers. One possible interpretation is suggested by a story in the Book of Matthew. In these verses, Jesus tells a woman that "it is not fair to take the children's food and throw it to the dogs," and she replies that "even the dogs eat the crumbs that fall from their master's table." It could be argued that Judas represents the children who reject the teachings they are offered and that the dog represents the nonbelievers who respond to the remaining "crumbs." In the light of this verse, Judas' association with a dog may be taken to indicate not his humanity but his sinfulness.

Such ambiguity may be viewed in a more positive light. The ambiguity of the moral significance of art and religion enables them to be appropriated by many individuals. Although moral philosophy may produce rules with the aim of achieving complete moral clarity, it is sometimes proper to stress the incomprehensibility of the world. Certain parables or stories owe their power to the fact that they incarnate a moral truth which is paradoxical, infinitely suggestive and open to continual reinterpretation. Such stories provide, precisely through their concreteness and consequent ambiguity, sources of moral inspiration that highly specific rules could not give. Religions gain adaptability from having as their center a person and not a set of rules.

This passage was adapted from "Images of Reality: Iris Murdoch's Five Ways from Art to Religion." Burns E. *Religions*. 2015. 6(3) doi:10.3390/rel6030875 for use under the terms of the Creative Commons CC BY 4.0 license (https://creativecommons.org/licenses/by/4.0/legalcode).

Question 8

Which of the following assertions is LEAST supported by evidence or elaboration within the passage?

- ○ **A.** Stories with characters are more helpful than sets of rules in achieving moral clarity.
- ○ **B.** Literature is more helpful than other art forms in achieving moral clarity.
- ○ **C.** The dog in the Judas painting may help to illustrate his sinful, reprobate character.
- ○ **D.** The dog in the Judas painting may have been included to underscore the many dimensions of his character.

Question 9

The author's apparent opinion about the Rubens painting's lack of a definitive, singular interpretation is that:

- ○ **A.** its ambiguity might be seen as an asset.
- ○ **B.** no conclusion about Judas can be drawn from it.
- ○ **C.** it demonstrates that human nature is multifaceted.
- ○ **D.** its ambiguity makes it more teachable than a painting with overt themes.

Question 10

In the biblical parable of the prodigal son, a son who brought dishonor on his family is welcomed warmly by his father. Which of the following perspectives on this parable might the author hold?

- ○ **A.** If this parable teaches no distinct lesson, then it is not intrinsically less valuable than other tales.
- ○ **B.** If the son lacks morals, then he is unlikely to use art to its full potential.
- ○ **C.** If the parable casts the son in a morally ambiguous light, then it is artistically superior to more straightforward stories.
- ○ **D.** If a dog features prominently in the parable, then those who hear it will think the son a sinner.

Question 11

Which of the following works is LEAST likely to accomplish the moral objectives of art, as described by the passage author?

- ○ **A.** A play about an ancient war with very clear symbolic overtones.
- ○ **B.** A song that recounts the valorous actions of a brave knight.
- ○ **C.** A painting that puts human cruelty on display in raw detail.
- ○ **D.** A book that elaborates on the central philosophies of a religion.

Question 12

Suppose a person used the parable from the Book of Matthew (paragraph 3) to interpret Judas in the Rubens painting. The viewer would likely consider Judas:

○ **A.** a complex, misguided man.

○ **B.** ignorant and insubordinate.

○ **C.** a nonbelieving vagrant.

○ **D.** intellectually deficient.

Question 13

Which of the following arguments, if true, most seriously weakens the passage's argument that art provides a more comprehensive vehicle for moral teaching than life experiences?

○ **A.** All works of art are inspired by the life experiences of the artists.

○ **B.** The meaning of art is more ambiguous than everyday experience.

○ **C.** Literary works are not the only art forms that allow for experimentation with fictional scenarios.

○ **D.** People can describe lessons from life experience better than they can lessons learned from art.

Question 14

In conveying the passage author's reasoning, the last paragraph serves to:

○ **A.** thwart a potential criticism of the thesis.

○ **B.** raise a new topic for future consideration.

○ **C.** undermine the author's initial argument.

○ **D.** conclude that parables provide more moral clarity than paintings.

Passage 3 (Questions 15-19)

A digital video recorder (DVR) enables viewers to pause, rewind, record, and playback selected programs at their convenience. Although video cassette recorder (VCR) also offered most of these features, the ease and significant recording capacity attracted users toward DVR. The practice of fast forwarding the commercials has led to serious concerns regarding the effectiveness of advertisements when fast forwarded by the viewers. Although various interesting studies have suggested that smart advertisements make an impact on TV viewers even when fast forwarded, these concerns have still persisted.

Some individuals highlight the claims made by early DVR users regarding the impact of new technology on television viewing and skipping the advertisements leading to an adverse impact on traditional television advertising. Nigel Hollis, a global analyst, opines that attractive features of DVRs such as time shifting, recording, pausing live TV and replaying where it was left, and saving time by fast forwarding boring advertisements will soon make it an indispensable home appliance. A recent study revealed that more than 50% of all DVR users identified fast forwarding through commercials as their favorite feature.

Hollis claims that these findings do not imply that the viewers would not see advertisements at all. The study indicated that even while fast forwarding, the viewers get to see rapid sequence of images with no sound, which still creates some impact. Therefore, fast forwarding may pose a threat to advertising business but cannot completely destroy the impact of ads on the viewers. Some researchers also state that fast forwarded ads bring back memories of the product in the viewers' mind. This argument is contradicted by others who assert that viewers fast forward all the ads without any selection or prior judgment.

Even if viewers fast forward ads, they can at least be engaged and not distracted by other technical gadgets. DVRs have the added advantage over VCRs that while fast forwarding through DVR, the viewers can see images and they can stop and replay the ad if something attracts them in terms of relevant information or enjoyable content.

TV viewers enjoy great choice and control through DVR. Communication analysts Ferguson and Perse make an interesting claim that DVR owners not only relish recorded television programs but also enjoy watching live programs, as this gives them greater control over their viewing habits. Hollis gives a ray of hope to the media planners by highlighting that not all viewers are Type "A" go-getters with busy schedules who consider their TV viewing a business task. Others, who may be categorized as Type "B," still like to utilize the TV viewing experience as time to relax and would not completely depend on time-shifted programming.

Some claim that increasing access to digital technologies has enhanced the consumers' control over media consumption, thus leading to lesser requirement for real-time broadcast. It has been predicted by forecasters that this rapid shift from "a world of linear TV to on-demand" would require a "radical rethink of advertising supported programming."

The advent of DVR is not the sole reason behind the change in the TV viewing environment. Other devices and technologies such as smart phones, tablets, social media, and TV viewing over the Internet pose more substantial challenges to TV advertising than DVRs. However, TV remains a formidable advertising vehicle and thus, it is important to discuss TV advertising, the challenges it faces, and the way advertisers can respond to those challenges.

This passage was adapted from "DVR and Its Impact on Indian Market: Now and in Future." Kalia S. *SAGE Open*. 2014. doi: 10.1177/2158244014560551 for use under the terms of the Creative Commons CC BY 3.0 license (http://creativecommons.org/licenses/by/3.0/legalcode).

Question 15

Assume that a family recently purchased a DVR. According to information in the passage, which feature will the family most enjoy?

- ○ **A.** Skipping through commercials
- ○ **B.** Rewinding live television
- ○ **C.** Pausing a program for a bathroom break
- ○ **D.** Recording different shows for each member of the family

Question 16

Suppose an advertising company is experiencing a drop in viewership. Based on information in the passage, what advice would the author most likely give ?

- ○ **A.** There is no need to be concerned, since every advertising company is experiencing the drop.
- ○ **B.** Focus on attention grabbing images.
- ○ **C.** Create advertisements for other devices instead of television.
- ○ **D.** Do not waste money on television advertisements.

Question 17

Which of the following conclusions about DVR can be inferred from the passage?

- ○ **A.** It has replaced the VCR.
- ○ **B.** It works alongside the VCR.
- ○ **C.** It was developed by the same engineers who created the VCR.
- ○ **D.** It is more expensive than the VCR.

Question 18

Which of the following claims, if valid, would most weaken the main passage argument regarding television advertising?

- ○ **A.** Companies have devoted more money to advertising in the last few years.
- ○ **B.** Focus groups have rated commercials more positively recently.
- ○ **C.** Americans with a DVR do not remember commercials the day after they aired.
- ○ **D.** Children are more likely to purchase toys they have seen on television.

Question 19

Suppose a study found that DVR sales have declined in the last year. Based on information provided in the passage, how would the author's argument be affected?

- ○ **A.** It would be weakened, because the argument would no longer apply.
- ○ **B.** It would be weakened, because the argument is based on the popularity of DVRs.
- ○ **C.** It would be strengthened, because the popularity of other devices might have increased.
- ○ **D.** It would remain unaffected, because the argument does not directly relate to the current sale of DVRs.

Passage 4 (Questions 20-26)

Historian David Miller's account of historical justice focuses on nations as the units of moral concern when discussing redress for historical injustices. Nations exist as ethical communities actively created by a body of persons who inhabit a common territory and continuously reinterpret and reshape their common identity. However, nations are distinct from states because nationals identify with the deeds of their ancestors as their own. It is because their members share a public culture, participate in the continuous reshaping of national identity and behave in a way that can be linked to their common membership that nations can be conceived as collective agents who are responsible for their actions. In particular, Miller conceives of a nation's inherited responsibility for its past wrongs as having intrinsic value: it is an obligation of justice, independent of the current conditions of those who suffered from such wrongs.

In order to establish what national responsibility for past injustices demands, Miller adopts a simple formula; he asks what the nature of the injustice under consideration is and, on this basis, he identifies a specific type of redress. According to his framework, known as the correspondence model, analysis of the form of injustice that occurred in the past is necessary in order to specify which type of redress is the most appropriate to repair that injustice and will thus fulfill national historical responsibility. For instance, in the case of wrongdoings for which there was no actual benefit to the wrongdoer, Miller prescribes financial compensation. This suggests how important it is for the form of redress to track the wrongness of the past injustice.

Colonialism should be understood mainly as a structural injustice because it was the result of a system of international structural processes and practices that legitimized and sustained colonial rule. However, historian Edward Said depicts colonialism as 'homogenizing and incorporating a world historical scheme that assimilated non-synchronous developments, histories, cultures, and peoples to it.' Even in the absence of instances involving the misappropriation of artifacts or the perpetuation of massacres, the injustice of colonialism occurred through a system of rules and social processes involving the continuous and day-to-day foreign subjection of the colonized. The colonial system was characterized by interconnected structures that reinforced each other, thus enabling and sustaining the subjection of the colonized over time. These structures included exploitation of the resources and labor of the colonized, political domination of the colonizers, coercively destroying or changing the culture of a place, and establishing new psychological structures in which the colonizers are perceived to be superior.

Miller is skeptical about drawing a strong enough connection between colonial injustice and present poverty to ground a remedial responsibility. Although Miller remains silent about colonialism, he does not consider national responsibility for historical injustice to be of the remedial type; rather than being triggered by present deprivation, national responsibility for historical injustice is grounded in the need to rectify a wrong that was brought about by a specific nation. However, colonialism was far from being a marginal or isolated phenomenon and this omission becomes particularly surprising in light of Miller's broader liberal nationalist account. Generally, liberal nationalism is non-xenophobic and values equality and individual rights. From within liberal nationalism, a concern for the injustice of colonialism is quite easily expressed as a concern for the denial of national self-determination that it entailed.

Perhaps Miller wanted to be parsimonious in developing his account of redress. His correspondence model is a rather simple formula that the case of colonial injustice would not seem to fit so easily into. Colonialism was constituted by interconnected structural processes and not merely by the instances of wrongs committed under colonial rule. Understanding colonialism in this way requires that the principle through which redress is established be sensitive to repairing both the single instances of wrongs as well as the structures under which these wrongs were justified.

This passage was adapted from "David Miller's theory of redress and the complexity of colonial injustice." Amighetti S, Nuti A. *Ethics and Global Politics*. 2015. 8 doi: 10.3402/egp.v8.26333. for use under the terms of the Creative Commons CC BY 4.0 license (https://creativecommons.org/licenses/by/4.0/legalcode).

Question 20

By discussing the injustices that occurred during colonialism, the author aims to:

○ **A.** reveal how colonialism resulted in the homogenization of distinct cultures.

○ **B.** demonstrate how misappropriation of artifacts and perpetuation of massacres were the most serious consequences of colonialism.

○ **C.** make the point that colonialism had lasting psychological effects on the oppressed that endured even after colonialism had ended.

○ **D.** illustrate the multifaceted factors that collectively oppressed people under colonialism.

Question 21

Miller's argument regarding redress for historical injustices is based upon the assumption that:

○ **A.** nations are composed of unified states.

○ **B.** a nation is a collective entity that can be held responsible for past actions.

○ **C.** members of a nation identify strongly with their collective ancestry and common identity.

○ **D.** nations necessarily act ethically due to their active creation by a body of persons.

Question 22

Which of the following examples is most analogous to the author's account of the structures characterizing colonialism?

- O **A.** A larger company purchases a smaller company which then undergoes a merger under the larger company's management.
- O **B.** A university hires a new dean to direct the school's trajectory.
- O **C.** A company under financial stress undergoes a downsizing process.
- O **D.** A newly-founded company begins promoting some entry-level employees to management positions.

Question 23

Which of the following passage statements best characterizes the author's opinion on why Miller's correspondence model does not specifically consider redress for colonial injustice?

- O **A.** Miller wanted to be parsimonious in developing his account of redress.
- O **B.** Miller does not consider national responsibility for historical injustice to be of the remedial type.
- O **C.** Miller's correspondence model is a rather simple formula into which the case of colonial injustice would not seem to fit so easily.
- O **D.** A concern for the injustice of colonialism is quite easily expressed as a concern for the denial of national self-determination that it entailed.

Question 24

White leaders of the South African Apartheid movement offered a collective formal apology for the injustices inflicted du ring Apartheid. This example supports the passage assertion that:

- O **A.** analysis of the form of injustice that occurred in the past is necessary in order to specify which type of redress is the most appropriate to repair that injustice.
- O **B.** colonialism was constituted by interconnected structural processes and not merely by the instances of wrongs committed under colonial rule.
- O **C.** nations can be conceived as collective agents who are responsible for their actions.
- O **D.** colonialism should be understood mainly as a structural injustice because it was the result of a system of international structural processes and practices.

Question 25

Information in the passage implies that the author would attempt to solve the issue of redress for colonialism by:

- O **A.** assigning each recorded instance of injustice a monetary value to be paid to the oppressed people in restitution.
- O **B.** requiring colonial nations to issue a formal apology for implementing an oppressive social structure in their colonies.
- O **C.** holding the citizens of former colonial nations responsible for mitigating their nation's past wrongs.
- O **D.** addressing institutional injustice and individual acts of injustice through different forms of restitution.

Question 26

The author's statement that it is "important for the form of redress to track the wrongness of the past injustice" (paragraph 2) most likely means that:

- O **A.** nations have to have redress that matches the magnitude of the injustice.
- O **B.** when implementing redress, nations must track all people the injustice affected.
- O **C.** nations should monitor the positive impact of their redress on people affected by injustice.
- O **D.** the form of redress should reverse the effects of the injustice.

Passage 5 (Questions 27-33)

In *The Old Law* (1618-1619), playwright Thomas Middleton addresses a nightmarish scenario that resonates in modern times. In the play, the Duke of Epire has determined that the elderly are unproductive, a burden to themselves, their heirs, and the state. Accordingly, men will be executed at age eighty and women at age sixty. Two sons debate the wisdom of the decree: one, eager to accelerate his inheritance, defends the expediency of terminating the lives of useless elders; the other, devoted to his father, criticizes the decree as monstrous and unnatural.

The Old Law envisions a world in which the elderly are put to death against their will because they represent a waste of resources. The justification may be financial, eugenic, or ecological – themes salient to an American public confronting a burgeoning national debt and strain on natural resources. As part of the perpetual debate concerning the equitable allocation of resources, the Western world is questioning whether affirmatively devoting the resources necessary to sustaining the elderly through expensive and heroic measures is justified. As the population ages and as medical technology improves, a tension has emerged between a humanist ethic that supports enhancing the lifespan of the elderly versus utilitarian arguments that would devote scarce dollars and therapies to younger and more productive members of society.

While geronticide might seem a far-fetched, dystopian nightmare, the question of whether and how to distribute healthcare resources as the population ages is, of course, a topic of extensive commentary. Advocates of the Fair Innings theory hold that if all else is held equal, one should devote the scarce resources to prolong the life of younger individuals who have not yet had their "fair innings." Its proponents suggest that older people should be given lower priority because they have already lived a long life, and other people should be given the opportunity to live as fully. They propose that government funding of eldercare should be limited to routine medical treatments that would relieve pain for patients who have lived a normal lifespan. In lieu of paying for life-extending care, proponents of the Fair Innings theory would restrict care to palliative treatments that allow for a "tolerable death." From their perspective, unless one is prepared to say that the elderly should have an unlimited right to taxpayer-subsidized healthcare regardless of cost and however marginal the benefits, then one has in principle opened the door for healthcare rationing.

Such rationing sends a message to the younger generation reinforcing prevalent notions about the negative social worth of the elderly. Explicit rationing according to age would threaten to fragment the ethical and social covenant binding different generations to each other at present, replacing interdependence with officially sanctioned age-group competition. Interdependence begins with dependence. It begins with the dependency of an infant and often ends with the dependency of a very ill or frail person close to dying. Americans have been able to fashion the pretense that we are independent—that the cooperation between persons that some insist is interdependence is simply the mutual (often voluntary) cooperation between essentially independent persons. Since all humans experience periods of dependency certain to occur in childhood and often occurring in illness and old age, generational interdependence is a biological reality and independence is a fiction.

This passage was adapted from "Forced Execution of the Elderly: *Old Law*, Dystopia, and the Utilitarian Argument." Schotland SD. *Humanities*. 2013. 2(2) doi:10.3390/h2020160 for use under the terms of the Creative Commons CC BY 3.0 license (https://creativecommons.org/licenses/by/3.0/legalcode).

Question 27

On the basis of information in the passage, it would be reasonable to conclude that advocates of the Fair Innings theory would support:

    I. changing existing approaches to end-of-life care.

    II. reducing government subsidies to federal programs.

    III. mandatory termination of the elderly.

○ **A.** I only

○ **B.** II only

○ **C.** I and II

○ **D.** I, II, and III

Question 28

The final sentence of Paragraph 3 justifies the Fair Innings theory by:

○ **A.** arguing that medical interventions do not extend life long enough to justify the cost.

○ **B.** implying that virtually everybody is in support of some form of healthcare rationing.

○ **C.** suggesting that those who pay the most taxes receive disproportionately small subsidies.

○ **D.** claiming that the benefits reaped from palliative care are too minimal to justify their cost.

Question 29

The "social covenant" (Paragraph 4) most likely refers to:

○ **A.** a belief that all persons contribute in some way to society.

○ **B.** an unwritten understanding that care will be reciprocated.

○ **C.** an agreement that people of all ages should receive the same standard of medical care.

○ **D.** a commitment to honor economic realities over familial ties.

Question 30

From the perspective of the Fair Innings theorists, which of the following findings would most strongly support the author's policy positions concerning healthcare expenditures?

○ **A.** Fewer retirees receive financial support from their families than in generations past.

○ **B.** Government subsidies increase the rates at which elderly people seek preventative care.

○ **C.** Palliative care tends to be more expensive than curative medical interventions.

○ **D.** Human beings are no more dependent on one another now than in the past.

Question 31

Suppose an American state legislature began the process of legalizing physician-assisted suicides. In response to this measure, the author would be most likely to:

○ **A.** campaign to promote awareness of alternative end-of-life treatments.

○ **B.** advocate for protections against coercion.

○ **C.** oppose legalization out of concern for individual choice.

○ **D.** support the measure to ensure access to a humane, tolerable death.

Question 32

The passage author answers all of the following questions EXCEPT:

○ **A.** does any human enjoy total autonomy?

○ **B.** should the elderly have access to unlimited healthcare resources?

○ **C.** do the elderly serve any productive purpose in society?

○ **D.** why has society engaged in a debate about the allocation of healthcare resources?

Question 33

Were the author's views on healthcare rationing shared by all U.S. citizens and policymakers, it is reasonable to conclude on the basis of information in the passage that:

○ **A.** the average life expectancy of American citizens would increase.

○ **B.** the issue of an ever-expanding national debt would go unresolved.

○ **C.** all citizens would enjoy access to free, universal healthcare.

○ **D.** research funding for palliative care would be reduced.

Passage 6 (Questions 34-37)

Language that seeks to go beyond the trivial can only be achieved through a high level of literacy, with the obvious corollary that if, for whatever reasons of circumstance and life experience, one is denied the ability to use language, then one is diminished. Without well-developed literacy skills, one cannot process narrative complexities, follow a dense argument, or attend to serious news sources reporting on complex situations.

This is not to deny that there are many realms of imagined and emotional experience that portend different kinds of truth, understanding and meaning, which are not language-based. Legendary painter Vincent Van Gogh commented that he did not paint what he saw, but what he felt. Music and art can take us to places of feeling that are as vital and necessary and important as any rationally apprehended, language-based sense of truth. But while art can deliver profound emotional experience, it is not all that useful if we are to have significant discussions about war, economic justice, or health care. Even Mahler or Aaron Copeland or Jay Z or Picasso or Constable would not be a great help there.

The eminent cultural critic Richard Hoggart has argued that "literacy is not enough." In his view, there is a hierarchy of literacy attainment, the highest level of which can round us out as citizens and evolved beings. At lower levels, we are less than we might be. He argued that basic literacy is critical for minimal functioning in contemporary society: without the ability to read street names, road signs, and transportation schedules, for instance, one can barely leave the house. He then states that we need to go beyond this basic literacy, to a kind of "critical" literacy which allows one to identify and dismiss propaganda, immunize oneself against the hard sell, and recognize the verbal cloaks that liars wear. But even that for him is still insufficient. The final step up, he argues, is to a condition of "cultivated literacy," in which one is sufficiently adept with a language and with conceptual schemes and cultural narratives to fully engage with the cultural, moral, and philosophical systems that define one's society. To achieve cultivated literacy is to embrace complexity, to eschew simplistic narratives and the simplistic judgments they engender. The vitality of a democracy depends on its citizens' ability to ascend the literacy hierarchy.

Hoggart's hierarchy of literacy—from a basic ability, to critical acuity, to the cultivated form of literacy—presupposes an equivalent hierarchy of cognitive abilities, with the related question of how those abilities do or do not get put in place. If there was a prescriptive element to Hoggart's commentary—and there manifestly was in that he wanted a culture defined by cultivated literacy—then he might well have asked a difficult question: how does that cognitive hierarchy come into being?

Reading studies have put much empirical flesh on the normative bone. It is clear that children who are talked to less and read to less, and who themselves read little—disproportionately, children from low-income families—are locked into a downward spiral of poor performance and disaffection. This phenomenon is labeled "the Matthew Effect," from Matthew 13:12: "For whomsoever hath, to him shall be given, and he shall have abundance, but whomsoever hath not, from him shall be taken, even that which he hath." If a child hears less language and reads fewer words, his or her cognitive abilities atrophy. Such a person is unlikely to achieve cultivated literacy, and a society with many such people is unlikely to have the conversations a mature democracy requires.

This passage was adapted from "The Language Desert: The Condition of Literacy and Reading in Contemporary America." Tracey, Michael. *Humanities*. 2015. 4(1). doi: 10.3390/h4010017 for use under the terms of the Creative Commons CC BY 4.0 license (http://creativecommons.org/licenses/by/4.0/legalcode).

Question 34

Hoggart's concept of critical literacy can best be described as:

○ **A.** the ability to read for information.

○ **B.** being responsive to complexity.

○ **C.** being sensitive to the ways that persuasive rhetoric operates.

○ **D.** the ability to intelligently critique those in power.

Question 35

What is the "Matthew Effect," according to the author?

○ **A.** It is the idea that children who hear fewer words when they are young will read fewer words later, compounding their weak language skills.

○ **B.** It is the idea that poor children are locked into a downward spiral of poor performance on reading and language comprehension tasks.

○ **C.** It is the claim that poor children cannot afford reading materials but need them more than the wealthy children who can afford them.

○ **D.** It is the claim that children who hear fewer words when they are young are more likely to be illiterate as adults.

Question 36

The author's attitude toward Richard Hoggart's views can best be described as:

○ **A.** uncertain.

○ **B.** ambivalent.

○ **C.** approving.

○ **D.** neutral .

Question 37

Which of the following, if true, would most undermine the author's claim that universal or near-universal cultivated literacy is essential to a mature democracy?

○ **A.** Most people vote for candidates who share their party affiliation.

○ **B.** Most political speeches are delivered using words comprehensible to the average 12-year-old child.

○ **C.** Some of the most highly literate societies are constitutional monarchies.

○ **D.** Regardless of education, people tend to make political decisions based on emotion.

Passage 7 (Questions 38-41)

The cause of a student dropping out of primary or secondary school is often termed the antecedent of dropout because it refers to the pivotal event which leads to dropout. This event, however, is the culmination of a much longer process of leaving school that occurs before the actual date that a student discontinues attendance. Even when multiple factors contribute to a student leaving, one can still be identified as the primary cause.

School completion rates have grown continually during much of the past century, a shift that has coincided with increased educational standards and benchmark assessments, as well as social and cultural changes, including the women's and civil rights movements, dual income families becoming the norm, and the strong impact of inflation on the need for employment. Secondary school completion guarantees a higher wage and opens doors to higher education. Still, the dropout problem has persisted; moreover, it is still found in alarming rates in many culturally and linguistically diverse groups, including African Americans, Hispanic Americans, and immigrants.

Students may drop out of school because they are pushed, pulled, or fall out. A student is pushed out when adverse situations within the school environment ultimately result in dropout. These include tests, attendance and discipline policies, and consequences of poor behavior. Students can be pulled out when factors intrinsic to the student divert them from completing school. These occur when factors such as financial worries, out-of-school employment, opportunities to explore an interest (including acting or athletics), or family needs or changes, like marriage or childbirth, pull students away from school. Illnesses can also cause students to put a greater value on something outside of school. Falling out of school occurs when a student does not show significant academic progress and becomes apathetic or disillusioned with school completion. It is not necessarily an active decision, but rather a side effect of students no longer feeling committed to their academic success. Although there seems to be similarities between pull and falling out factors, the definitive difference is that pull factors have a distinct object working as an attraction/distraction that students seek.

According to administrators, it is difficult to determine the exact cause of the dropout trend. Administrators state that students are largely affected by pull factors early in their schooling, though falling out factors also play a role in dropout later; jobs and family thus seem to have a stronger influence early on in school, whereas apathy and academic disengagement settle in during high school. Administrators may, however, report dropout reasons different than those identified by students themselves because of the two groups' distinct vantage points. Admitting that problems such as a lack of school support for students with financial or familial concerns contribute to dropout can reflect poorly on administrators.

Push factors, including a notable disliking for school, disciplinary problems, or poor academic performance/"poor grades," tend to affect male students more than female students. Conversely, pull factors, such as "got married" or "had to work", play a significant role in the dropout rates of young women because of the high rate of the antecedent, "became pregnant". Marital and familial responsibilities and child-bearing have a stronger impact on dropout for young mothers than for young fathers, although men are affected by the pull factor of needing to seek and maintain employment to support their families. This factor thus relates back to familial needs and household changes, suggesting that pull factors have a significant, albeit indirect, effect on dropout rates for young men. Additionally, both male and female students are impacted by having to care for relatives or having to cope with personal health issues, which can cause dropout before college. For interventions to offer the most help to young people, reasons for dropout must be clearly differentiated.

This passage was adapted from "Understanding Why Students Drop Out of High School, According to Their Own Reports: Are They Pushed or Pulled, or Do They Fall Out? A Comparative Analysis of Seven Nationally Representative Studies. " Doll JJ, Eslami Z, and Walters L. *SAGE Open*. 2013. 1(15) doi: 10.1177/2158244013503834 for use under the terms of the Creative Commons CC BY 3.0 license (http://creativecommons.org/licenses/by/3.0/legalcode).

Question 38

According to the passage, school completion rates have steadily increased for all of the following reasons *except*:

- ○ **A.** households becoming predominantly 'double income no kids' families.
- ○ **B.** greater empowerment of women.
- ○ **C.** the rising cost of goods and services.
- ○ **D.** an increased reliance on examinations to test students' academic achievement.

Question 39

Based on passage information, why might students and administrators report different causes of school dropout?

- ○ **A.** Administrators are not fully aware of all of the pressures in students' lives that contribute to dropout.
- ○ **B.** Administrators believe the primary reason for dropout changes over time, whereas students identify a consistent cause.
- ○ **C.** Administrators are concerned that they will be blamed for students dropping out.
- ○ **D.** Administrators find it difficult to pinpoint what induces students to drop out.

Question 40

Suppose a study shows that the majority of male students claim that pull factors lead them to leave school. Based on passage information, would this change the author's opinion about what causes young students to drop out?

- ○ **A.** Yes, because the author believes that young men drop out of school primarily because of push factors, including poor academic performance.
- ○ **B.** Yes, because according to prior studies, students report that the reasons they drop out change over the course of their schooling.
- ○ **C.** No, because the author states that reasons for dropout still need to be clearly differentiated.
- ○ **D.** No, because the author argues that pull factors primarily affect dropout rates for men and women.

Question 41

Which of the following statements about school dropout is most strongly implied by the author?

- ○ **A.** For most students who do not continue their education, familial obligations are to be blamed.
- ○ **B.** Language barriers and immigration policies contribute to school dropout rates.
- ○ **C.** Students who drop out do not realize the correlation between having a degree and earning higher wages.
- ○ **D.** School completion remains low among certain student populations.

Passage 8 (Questions 42-48)

Experience is defined as everything that is perceived by or perceptible to the senses, and, as such, is constantly informing our psyches about how it should be understood. Art, like all other experiences, is an "enclosing condition" that does not enjoy the same apparent external existence as every other experience. What is it that makes us identify one experience as different from another? Or, to narrow the discussion, what is it that leads us to identify some experiences as those of art?

When we experience a medium that has been organized with the intent of being meaningful, that is, when we are essentially manipulated into believing that its interrelations have meaning, we are likely to automatically regard the product as "art" and the experience of it as "aesthetic."

Poet Edgar Allen Poe understood that the manipulative potential of storytelling lies in making the central character one that the audience finds fascinating. Readers and listeners are then more likely to become suggestible to the story itself and so to react as if the story were real. The very process of organizing a certain medium wields a certain control over the way we think of the product of this process. Organizing sounds, for example, in a manner that is meant to be heard as music results in a creative product that is experienced in precisely that way. When we are experiencing music, we are doing so because that is how the sounds were intended by the composer or performer to be heard. This holds true even if what is beautifully harmonious and melodious to one listener elicits reactions of disgust in another: both may yet agree that the sounds have been arranged and played in order to create an effect. This is due to a quality that remains constant in spite of differences of taste that are not due to any difference within the art in itself.

Although our tastes may differ, the intentions of the artist, expressed in the way his or her art is created, exist independently of these differences, and are yet rife with signifiers that are analogous to hypnotic suggestions or commands. Despite subjectivity, the artist via the artwork is trying to tell people how to respond to it and what meanings may be derived from it. If this is not true, and none of these contextual influences are acting upon our experience of art, then creative activity is pointless. Art is saturated with both liminal and subliminal suggestions or commands that attempt to induce us to internalize these ideas that have been put into our minds, and to become what it would make of us.

Art is thereby no less a multidimensional phenomenon offering multidimensional experiences. Yet in a real and very important sense, all aesthetic experiences share the same thing in common: the deliberate introduction into the percipient's mind of that which causes him or her to identify art as art despite its innumerable forms and its susceptibility to personal interpretation. It is difficult to try to identify what that something is. Nevertheless, an attempt seems warranted because there is something in the mutual human experience of art that appears to be related to hypnosis. The Russian Formalists of the 1920s defined literature as a means of defamiliarizing, estranging, or alienating one from casual perception. "The technique of art", wrote one such observer, "is to make objects 'unfamiliar.'" Dream, delirium, hypnosis, and other altered states of consciousness would also seem to favor the dissolution of the normal states of being that keep us from genuine existential contact with things and the world.

This passage was adapted from "'Mesmeric Revelation': Art as Hypnosis." Gillespie Z. *Humanities*. 2015. 4(2) doi: for use under the terms of the Creative Commons CC BY 4.0 license (https://creativecommons.org/licenses/by/4.0/legalcode).

Question 42

The passage argues that an artist has the power to manipulate an audience. Later, the passage acknowledges that the reaction of two separate viewers to a work of art may vary greatly. On the basis of passage information, these claims:

- ○ **A.** are not at odds, because an artist's power does not extend to evoking specific emotions.
- ○ **B.** are not at odds, because art blurs the boundary between reality and fiction.
- ○ **C.** are at odds, because the power to create art differs from the power to control viewers.
- ○ **D.** are at odds, because the observation that viewers react differently sharply limits the artist's power.

Question 43

The author's argument that common to all artwork is its universal perception as art relies on the assumption that:

- ○ **A.** all artists are equally skilled giving their art meaning.
- ○ **B.** all viewers know how to recognize art.
- ○ **C.** all artwork has intrinsic value.
- ○ **D.** no artwork provokes the same reaction in all viewers.

Question 44

Which of the following findings most seriously *weakens* the author's assertion that all art retains "a quality that remains constant in spite of differences of taste" (paragraph 3)?

- ○ **A.** Modern readers scarcely read Poe and find his poems' protagonists dull.
- ○ **B.** The overwhelming majority of listeners misinterpret the major themes of the opera Carmen.
- ○ **C.** The unremarkable pieces hanging in a fast food chain were done by a classically trained artist.
- ○ **D.** Journals of art criticism refuse to publish any article about contemporary pop artists' music.

Question 45

Suppose that viewers are able to distinguish modern artists' work from amateur imitations in an overwhelming majority of cases. This finding supports the author's argument about the universal qualities of art so long as it is true that:

○ **A.** amateur imitations are not themselves art.

○ **B.** amateur artists are less skilled than professionals.

○ **C.** amateur artwork also has the ability to disrupt casual perception.

○ **D.** imitation artwork is similarly imbued with the original artist's meaning.

Question 46

Artist Pablo Picasso said, "Art is the lie that enables us to know the truth." His perspective undermines the passage author's argument that:

○ **A.** artists express their true convictions in their work.

○ **B.** audiences are influenced by the artist's perspective.

○ **C.** art blurs the boundary of the real and the imagined.

○ **D.** art facilitates the discovery of deeper truths.

Question 47

A sculptor erects a statue without any subjective purpose in mind. Were the passage author to look upon this statue, it could be inferred that he would:

○ **A.** consider the sculpture a waste of creative effort.

○ **B.** not consider this piece a work of art.

○ **C.** not expect this piece to elicit a wide range of reactions in its viewers.

○ **D.** insist that the author's experience is nevertheless present in the statue.

Question 48

Of the components of paintings listed below, which would the author LEAST likely consider a "liminal" (paragraph 4) element?

○ **A.** A general in a triumphant pose before an army

○ **B.** Two jealous suitors engaged in a duel

○ **C.** Ominous clouds drifting in the background

○ **D.** A bowl of fruit on a tabletop

Passage 9 (Questions 49-53)

There is a struggle occurring between public health advocates and commercial enterprises over the Human Papillomavirus (HPV) vaccine. Advocates believe that public awareness about the vaccine might facilitate both primary and secondary prevention of its spread by tackling issues such as embarrassment surrounding STIs, the public reception of HPV immunization, and the ability of HPV to reoccur. They think efforts to communicate and exchange information could promote acceptance and uptake. Commercial entities focus on industry marketing and how the entire range of stakeholders view the vaccine implementation. The administration of a vaccine is invasive, can be painful, and has potential for adverse events; the harms and benefits must be weighed. The HPV vaccine has become a contested object where industry advertising and profit motives have butted against its public health value.

Mandatory HPV immunization has been criticized as a violation of parental autonomy for the prevention of a non-casually transmitted infection, a misuse of taxpayers' money for a vaccine of unknown effectiveness at the expense of more pressing public health issues, an unnecessary addition to overloaded vaccine schedules, and a devaluation of abstinence messages. Mandatory immunization supporters argue that abstinence education is ineffective in protecting against STIs, that secondary prevention of cervical cancer has irremediable gaps, that there are already mandates for Hepatitis B Virus (HBV) immunization, and that socioeconomically vulnerable women must be protected against cervical cancer.

HPV vaccines are gallantly marketed as a woman's right, choice, and duty for health security, exemplified by the Gardasil "I choose" commercials. Socioeconomic realities pose barriers to access and choice for immunization and screening. Additionally, HPV and cervical cancer affect the families and social and economic networks of women who succumb to the disease because they lack access to both prevention and treatment. The advertising around HPV vaccines conflates HPV infection, which is widely prevalent and easily transmitted, with cervical cancer, which is a relatively rare consequence of a common infection. On occasion, the scientific literature equates HPV immunization with the end of cervical cancer.

Pharmaceutical advertising resonates with an operative dilemma for public health "social marketing:" Is the acceptability of the vaccine improved by presenting it as "anti-cancer" instead of "anti-STI?" Gardasil receives high acceptance from parents who wish to protect the health of their children, but parents worry that their children who have not previously been sexually active may interpret their acceptance of the vaccine as approval of sexual activity. Parents who reject the vaccine may believe that their children's 'safe' or 'moral' behavior is adequate protection against the STI. In the absence of balanced public health information, media reportage has stoked community concerns about the effects of HPV vaccines on teen behavior. The public profile of the HPV vaccine has been shaped by infomercials that create the impression of a personalized drug against risk, an object for commercial profit and consumer desire, separate from the public health considerations of the community.

The high cost of the vaccine has compelled public payers to ration its subsidization to unexposed adolescent females with the expectation that high uptake will build herd immunity. This has resulted in HPV being marked as 'women-only,' despite the fact that men also get and transmit the virus. The implication is that HPV is an exclusively heterosexual concern even though HPV also affects LGBT individuals. In a valiant effort to save money, HPV vaccine commercials and public health messages focus on cervical cancer, to the exclusion of throat, anal, and penile cancer. Even in many high-income countries, LGBT individuals may not seek sexual health advice or screening services due to fear of outing and its consequences.

This passage was adapted from "Global Challenges of Implemented Human Papillomavirus Vaccines." Graham JE, Mishra A. International Journal for Equity in Health. 2011. 10(27) doi: 10.1186/1475-9276-10-27 for use under the terms of the Creative Commons CC BY 2.0 license (http://creativecommons.org/licenses/by/2.0/legalcode).

Question 49

The information provided in the passage most strongly implies that public health education:

○ **A.** can be adequately conveyed by commercial ad campaigns.

○ **B.** is a paramount aspect of decision-making in healthcare.

○ **C.** might be intentionally undermined by profit-seeking stakeholders.

○ **D.** ultimately leads to rejection of colloquial health literacy.

Question 50

Which of the following situations is most similar to the parental dilemma described in the passage?

○ **A.** Permitting a former alcoholic teenager to drink one glass of red wine a night to promote heart health

○ **B.** Buying violent video games for introverted children to play with potential friends

○ **C.** Feeding children fast food twice a day because the family cannot afford other types of food

○ **D.** Allowing a teenaged cancer patient to smoke legalized marijuana for medical purposes

Question 51

Suppose the treatment of HPV became relatively inexpensive and effortless. How would this technology impact public health advocates?

○ **A.** The advocates would continue to support vaccine education and implementation.

○ **B.** The advocates would move on to a different task because the medical benefit and moral dilemma would vanish.

○ **C.** The advocates would shift their efforts to promote the more easily accessible treatment.

○ **D.** The advocates would increase their efforts to reach out to parents of non-sexually active preteens.

Question 52

With which of following statements would the commercial enterprises most likely agree?

○ **A.** Empowering women to make their own health choices is of utmost importance.

○ **B.** "Social marketing" is a way to snare potential customers who have not seen the ads.

○ **C.** Providing a list of side effects on a television commercial shows a commitment to ethics.

○ **D.** Mandatory HPV vaccination would be a good compromise between the enterprises and public health advocates.

Question 53

Which of the following marketing campaigns would be most in line with the author's argument?

○ **A.** A television ad that persuaded children to start smoking tobacco

○ **B.** An automated phone call about the benefits of supporting a racist organization

○ **C.** A radio ad about a yoga studio that replaced an ad for depression awareness

○ **D.** A door-to-door campaign to sell security systems in a community with a neighborhood watch

STOP. If you finish before time is called, check your work. You may go back to any question in this test.

ANSWERS & EXPLANATIONS for Test 5 can be found on p. 239.

TEST 6

Number of Questions: 53
Time: 90 minutes

Passage 1 (Questions 1-7)

In some discourses on sustainability, modernism in architecture is blamed for its technocratic beliefs that supposedly generated a lot of the social and environmental problems the world is facing today, but for today's high modernist architects, the new possibilities opened up by technology were a major source of inspiration for the environmental sustainability movement. At the same time, many architectural critics seem to be convinced that the present call for sustainability with its "green buildings" is but another screen behind which well-known old power structures hide.

In several schools of thought, modernism, the movement to align traditional practices with contemporary values, has acquired a bad reputation. Political scientist James C. Scott blames what he calls "high-modernist ideology" for a series of man-made tragedies, such as The Great Leap Forward in China, collectivization in Russia, and compulsory "villagization" in Tanzania, Mozambique, and Ethiopia. For Scott, high modernism relies upon a strong belief in science and technology as carriers of economic expansion, growing satisfaction of human needs, and a rational design of the social order. When combined with a strong administration, an authoritarian state, and a weak civil society, this high modernism gives rise to disastrous projects of social engineering that produce in the end much more human suffering than beneficial outcomes.

If modernism is seen as the body of intellectual and artistic movements that responded positively to the experience of modernity, is it correct to blame these movements for derailed ideological projects or for the ruthless exploitation of natural resources? Should we not be more careful in understanding modernism's complex relationship to the social and economic processes of modernization, rather than assume that modernism caused modernization or that it was responsible for modernization's worst effects? It might be possible to rather take up the legacy of modernism in order to deal with the inevitable tensions and contradictions that face us when we set out to embrace an ethos of sustainability.

There is much in modernism that is worth redeeming. Too many histories of modern architecture have been written that barely acknowledge modernism's rootedness in socio-political programs of justice and emancipation. Focusing on modernism's belief in science and technology leaves aside other aspects of its legacy, aspects that might be much more inspirational for the discussion of sustainability. For the Modern Movement in architecture certainly was not only about machines and technology. It was most of all about building a "rational" society—meaning a just society with opportunities for all.

One should not forget that modernism was one of the driving forces shaping the Welfare State, especially in Europe. When after the Second World War the social contract was renegotiated in Western European countries, this gave rise to a solidification of the social security system, which was underpinned not only by arrangements focusing on pension, child support, and unemployment benefits, but also by an effort to provide enough social housing to ban homelessness, ghettos, and slums as everyday occurrences. This effort has overall been hugely successful, even if its success has been overshadowed, in media representations, by stories about the problematic character of many housing estates.

Modernism was indeed about negotiating the constraints of nature, about using science and technology to arrive at a more just society. Rather than discrediting modernism, its legacy can be reimagined to further the emancipation of individuals and collectivities. Since sustainability has now become a main concern, this could then be interpreted as a shift of urgencies from providing a basic and equitable standard of living for everyone to preserving the natural resources needed to sustain it.

Passage was adapted from "Sustainable Development, Architecture and Modernism: Aspects of an Ongoing Controversy." Vandevyvere H, Heynen H. *Arts*. 2014. 3 doi: 10.3390/arts3040350 for use under the terms of the Creative Commons CC BY 4.0 license (https://creativecommons.org/licenses/by/4.0/legalcode).

Question 1

Which of the following passage assertions is most supported by examples or explanations?

○ **A.** Under the right circumstances, modernism can deteriorate human wellbeing.

○ **B.** The modernist movement was a proponent of technological innovation.

○ **C.** Most people think that the Welfare State did not improve standards of living in Europe.

○ **D.** Modernization is to blame for the environmental challenges that humanity faces today.

Question 2

Which of the following statements, if true, would most likely weaken the author's argument about modernism's role in the present movement for sustainability?

○ **A.** The use of natural resources will always improve human wellbeing in the short run and degrade it in the long run.

○ **B.** Failure to invest in research and development leading to advances in technology will have disastrous effects for human society.

○ **C.** Some blame the push to modernize for enriching oppressive power structures that only destabilize society.

○ **D.** Projects of social engineering and authoritarian regimes actually improve human standards of living, all effects considered.

Question 3

Which of the following is most similar to the activities of the "well-known old power structures," as defined by critics of modernization?

- ○ **A.** The Welfare State of Western Europe that provides expanded social services at the expense of creating dangerous neighborhoods
- ○ **B.** A corporation that publicly lobbies for business practices that threaten the environment
- ○ **C.** An advocacy group that calls for an expanded central governing body at the expense of the rights of individual voters
- ○ **D.** A business that contributes to the anti-smoking lobby while marketing an alternative to cigarettes that is even more harmful

Question 4

The passage argues that which of the following is most true concerning the "legacy" of modernism?

- ○ **A.** Modernism on balance has had deleterious effects on human society.
- ○ **B.** The push to preserve natural resources is the most urgent issue of our day.
- ○ **C.** The modernists, rather than causing modernization, expressed approval of some elements of modernization.
- ○ **D.** Modernist goals may suit the ends of today's sustainability efforts.

Question 5

Which of the following situations is most analogous to the author's recommendations for how society should treat the ideas of the modernists?

- ○ **A.** A daughter forgives her father for the meager means he could provide while she was growing up.
- ○ **B.** A developer builds a new apartment building on the sturdy foundation of what was once a dilapidated office building.
- ○ **C.** A university pulls down a statue of a controversial war figure and relocates it to a less conspicuous location on campus.
- ○ **D.** The president replaces a longstanding economic advisor with an individual trained in a more progressive school of economic theory.

Question 6

The "social contract" alluded to in the fifth paragraph most likely refers to:

- ○ **A.** the brokering of peace treaties among fractured nation-states following times of war.
- ○ **B.** the duty of young men to fight for the preservation of their way of life and their country's higher ideals during times of war.
- ○ **C.** an implicit understanding about what society owes its members and what, in turn, the collective owes to society.
- ○ **D.** the moral obligation of government to provide its citizens with the fundamentals needed to evade the harsh conditions of poverty.

Question 7

The author's attitude toward the views of critics of modernism can best be described as:

- ○ **A.** resolute opposition.
- ○ **B.** tentative approval.
- ○ **C.** polite disagreement.
- ○ **D.** mild offense .

Passage 2 (Questions 8-13)

In the United States alone, there are thousands of people every year whose lives could be saved by means of a liver or kidney transplant but who die because organs are unavailable. Even the tens of thousands who obtain a transplant often have to wait years for an operation, during which time their quality of life and post-operative prospects deteriorate. A sure way of increasing supply to meet the demand is to permit live donors to sell their organs in a competitive market. However, there is staunch opposition to permitting trade in human organs. It is argued that such trade would undermine altruism, coerce the poor, entice people to make decisions based on inadequate information, increase inequality, degrade the people who engage in it, be analogous to slavery, compel people to pay costs that they should not have to pay, and diminish the options available to third parties.

At the moment, the supply of these organs depends upon altruism or family pressure. Some people arrange that when they die their organs may be used for transplants. Some people offer themselves as a living donor for a family member. People who are sufficiently altruistic to want to offer an organ to a non-relative may be prevented from doing so because of official suspicion that money may be changing hands. If those in need of transplants could pay living donors for kidneys, livers, or liver-sections, the monetary incentive would call forth a greater supply.

More people would also be expected to donate their organs after death, since the payment received could be passed on to their heirs. However, this would not by itself be likely to increase substantially the supply of organs or their quality. Many dead donors do not have healthy, well-functioning organs free of infection. Also, the relatives of the deceased often resist the removal of organs, which causes delay and can make the organs unusable. Furthermore, the need to transfer an organ quickly from a dead donor to a recipient makes it difficult to secure a good match.

In less developed countries, the risks to organ donors are likely to be greater due to lower levels of hygiene and nutrition, as well as poorer quality of surgery, pre- and post-operative care. Surveys indicate that almost half of Indian and nearly two-thirds of Iranian kidney donors suffered bad health experiences afterwards, and almost four-fifths regretted the decision. Some of this dissatisfaction may be due to donors being given poor or misleading information about risks, especially since the Indian figures include some black-market organ sales. The situation would be improved by better regulation to ensure that donors are properly informed about risks and a "cooling off" period of a few weeks to reduce the likelihood of impulsive decisions. Even though the risks would remain greater than in the advanced countries, donors would be able to decide for themselves whether the payment is sufficient to compensate for the risks.

It is important that the market in organs should be competitive, with no significant barriers to entry. A monopolistic agency involved in the purchase or sale of organs, with little serious competition from rivals, would lack incentives to keep costs down and to improve quality of service, which would lead to inefficiency, waste, and poorer services to organ donors and recipients. A human organ market has the potential to save lives, but only if it is regulated, much like any other market.

This passage was adapted from "A Competitive Market in Human Organs." Frederick D. Libertarian Papers. 2010. 2(27) doi:10.1.1.364.8141 for use under the terms of the Creative Commons CC BY 3.0 license (http://creativecommons.org/licenses/by/3.0/legalcode).

Question 8

The author suggests that the characterization of a potential human organ market as unethical is:

- A. a completely unjustified classification.
- B. a potentially valid judgment.
- C. an antiquated belief.
- D. an unwarranted assumption.

Question 9

The author's most prominent concerns about a human organ market, as presented in the passage, point to:

    I. regulation.

    II. inequality.

    III. coercion.

- A. I only
- B. I and II
- C. II and III
- D. I and III

Question 10

Which of the following statements, if assumed to be true, would best support the author's argument regarding the creation of a human organ market?

- A. Increasing numbers of individuals are dying each year because organs are unavailable.
- B. Countries with black markets for human organs have lower rates of deaths that result from organ unavailability.
- C. Healthy individuals are more likely to participate in research studies if they receive compensation.
- D. Hospitals report that they have the resources to perform more organ transplants than they are currently.

Question 11

Which of the following criticisms of a proposed vacation is most similar to that of the author in regards to the current state of organ donation after death?

- A. The family is not inviting extended family members to join.
- B. The family is spending too much money on the vacation.
- C. No one in the family can agree about where to go on vacation.
- D. The family does not plan well and is rushed at the airport.

Question 12

The passage argument concerning a human organ market suggests that the author would likely *oppose* which of the following?

○ **A.** Legislation regulating the quality of organs eligible for donation

○ **B.** Government control of the price of organs

○ **C.** Legislation loosening regulations on health insurance

○ **D.** Reducing government expenditures on health care

Question 13

Which of the following findings would most *weaken* the author's claim that a human organ market could positively change the lives of many individuals?

○ **A.** Human organ donors often do not feel as fulfilled as they expected after their donation.

○ **B.** Most individuals report that they do not support the idea of a human organ market.

○ **C.** The more organ donations a hospital performs, the higher the death or complication rate.

○ **D.** Scientists are close to developing technology that can be used to create artificial organs.

Passage 3 (Questions 14-17)

The Soviet Union's achievement of being the first to transverse the space barrier with unmanned and manned vehicles could be considered one of the major defining moments in schooling for contemporary America. The Soviet's feat led to the belief that our nation's schools were deficient in math, science, and technology. Consequently, the National Defense Education Act (NDEA) was enacted in 1958 to fund and promote educational activities to advance the use of technology, teaching, and learning to strengthen national security. Similar to the NDEA's establishment to address the problem of technological readiness, the No Child Left Behind Act (NCLB) was established in 2002 to address the increasing problem of poor school performance in public schools. Its purpose was to initiate a launch sequence to boost the nation's sputtering schools out of the low orbit of failure for far too many children to a higher orbit encompassing success for all children. This time, with NCLB as the booster, public school principals were to be the thrusters that steered the ship.

Its mandate was driven, in part, by the need to address the failure of Black students. There is now a significant concern over the failure of male students (disproportionately Black male students), which is blamed on the feminization of schools. In the 2011-2012 school year, more than half of the nation's 89,810 public school principals were female. It is believed that as the power of U.S. female principals increased with their growing number, they were more likely to alter the gender composition of their schools' pedagogical staff to be increasingly female. Several other studies have reported that the success of female principals is dependent on access to resources that are more readily available to male principals within their androcentric network.

While some studies found no difference in how male and female principals ran their schools, one researcher reported that teachers and principals perceived differences in behavior between male and female principals. This researcher found that male principals exhibited leadership characteristics that were challenging in nature (i.e., nonsubmissive). Men were also aggressive, assertive, and domineering, which led teachers to prefer them as principals of high schools. The study reported that male principals were more successful at long-term planning, which is an important component of annual school performance indicators. Finally, the study found that more senior and higher ranked teachers worked more with male principals than female principals, and both male and female teachers expressed greater satisfaction working with male principals.

Female principals, on the contrary, were perceived as appealing to the heart, responsive, sensitive, and having a nurturing disposition—qualities more conducive to working with children and endearing to some teachers and parents. Furthermore, female principals were reported to have an affinity for students of lower socioeconomic status, to be more engaging with teachers, and to be more effective at day-to-day running of the school, resulting in better daily performance indicators, such as attendance. Students performed better and teachers were more involved, collegial, and cooperative with administration when the principals were females.

Even if there are individuals higher up in the power hierarchy, such as superintendents, principals are a critical factor in school success, and the characteristics related to their gender and race influence the achievement scores of urban schools. The significance of principal behavior is found in Associate Professor of Social Work Deneca Winfrey's study, which reports that student academic performance was found to be a function of teacher job satisfaction. Notwithstanding that principals do not regularly teach, they are held responsible for student and teacher performance.

This passage was adapted from "Effect of Principal and Student Gender on New York City High School Performance Outcome." Green R. *SAGE Open.* 2015. 5(3). doi: 10.1177/2158244015591707 for use under the terms of the Creative Commons CC BY 3.0 license (http://creativecommons.org/licenses/by/3.0/legalcode).

Question 14

A woman is looking for a new job as a principal. What advice would the author most likely give her?

- ○ **A.** Consider another career choice that does not take gender into account.
- ○ **B.** Look for schools with many female teachers.
- ○ **C.** Apply to positions serving specific populations.
- ○ **D.** Act assertively in an interview to compensate for gender stereotypes.

Question 15

The author suggests that the No Child Left Behind Act:

- ○ **A.** was inspired by the National Defense Education Act.
- ○ **B.** identified the cause of black students' struggles in school.
- ○ **C.** focused on administrators rather than students.
- ○ **D.** has successfully increased school performance.

Question 16

According to the passage, it is reasonable to conclude that:

- ○ **A.** female principals face discrimination.
- ○ **B.** principals are influential regardless of gender.
- ○ **C.** teachers aspire to become principals.
- ○ **D.** education reform aims to defeminize schools.

Question 17

Based on information in the passage, which of the following nautical roles is most similar to that of a school principal?

- ○ **A.** A captain who is in charge of the voyage
- ○ **B.** A first mate who carries out the captain's orders
- ○ **C.** A navigator who plans the route of the voyage
- ○ **D.** A crewman who assists in various tasks

Passage 4 (Questions 18-22)

Reginald Bibby, the most eminent sociology scholar researching the church in Canada, asserts that the church in Canada is in decline. In fact the Evangelical church in Canada has been in decline since the 1960s. The New York Times, in a front page article, highlights the difference between Canada and America by emphasizing the fact that 80% of Canadians agree that "you don't need to go to church in order to be a good Christian," whereas only roughly 50% of Americans would agree with that statement. Even more recent data highlight the idea that Canadian faith has become privatized, and show that while 84% of Canadians believe in God, 81% of Canadians agree that you do not need to go to church to be a good Christian.

There are many possible reasons for the decline in church attendance in Canada, but three key reasons are cited by researchers in the field of Canadian Evangelical Christianity. Some scholars believe that after 1960, Canada became a nation of believers, but not belongers. Today, Canadians do not go to church because they don't think they need to. They do not feel that attending a religious service is necessary to their own religious practices.

Another group of researchers argue that many Canadians believe that religion is not essential for guidance in their daily life. Canadians feel more independent and in charge of their daily decisions, and do not consult a higher being as often as in the past. Lastly, experts have found that many Canadians see all religions as equally true and good. For this reason, belief has moved from the realm of exclusivity and necessity in Christianity to a concept of a moral and privatized spirituality.

In contrast to the decline of Evangelical churches in Canada in the last sixty years, there has been a marked increase in Eastern non-Christian religions. In 1961, Eastern non-Christian religions comprised 0.1% of the Canadian population. In 2001, they comprised 5%. For the same period, those claiming to have no religion jumped from 1% to 16%. This increase in non-Christian religions has a twofold effect. First, it poses a spiritual alternative to those who are seeking spiritual guidance. Second, it strengthens the notion of pluralism and many paths to God. Many Canadians build close and meaningful relationships with immigrant people, and through that process come to see the religious perspectives of those immigrant people as both meaningful and sincere. For this reason, growing tolerance and inclusivity has most strongly influenced the decline of religious attendance.

Christianity in general, and Evangelical churches in particular, will increasingly find themselves relegated to the sidelines and marginalized within the emerging secular society that Canada is becoming. Evangelical church attendance is in decline, and new ways of being a part of the church and doing church ministry will need to be embraced. Churches will need to view themselves as communities on a mission with God. Instead of thinking how they might attract more people into the church building, they will need to creatively think of ways to go out into the community to act as servants, to live incarnationally among the people, and to back their message with the authenticity of their lives.

This passage was adapted from "A Missional Church Model." Elkington RL. SAGE Open. 2011. 1(3). doi: 10.1177/2158244011428086 for use under the terms of the Creative Commons CC BY 3.0 license (http://creativecommons.org/licenses/by/3.0/legalcode).

Question 18

According to the passage, Evangelical Canadian churches have experienced a decrease in attendance due to:

    I. the decline of meaningful social interactions at church.

    II. the change in lifestyle of many Canadians in the last sixty years.

    III. the decrease in Canadians attending any religious service.

○ **A.** I only

○ **B.** II only

○ **C.** I and III

○ **D.** II and III

Question 19

Based on information provided in the passage, the author would most likely liken the act of attending church to which of the following events?

○ **A.** Shopping even if one has a full wardrobe, since it is unnecessary

○ **B.** Cooking dinner with family, since it involves pleasant exchanges

○ **C.** Running a marathon, since some people view it as a priority

○ **D.** Going to school, since it is necessary for growth and becoming one's best self

Question 20

Which of the following beliefs best supports the information in the passage?

○ **A.** Religion is more individualized now than in the past.

○ **B.** Religion has lost some of its value in the last sixty years.

○ **C.** Religion does not fit into the secular world.

○ **D.** Religion is constantly expanding to fit new ideas.

Question 21

The passage implies that Christianity and Eastern non-Christian religions differ with respect to:

○ **A.** their religious services.

○ **B.** their tolerance of other beliefs.

○ **C.** their primary populations.

○ **D.** their acceptance in Canada.

Question 22

The author implies which of the following about Canadian Christians?

○ **A.** They are more likely to convert religions today than in the past.

○ **B.** They are more likely to practice faiths that look different from one another.

○ **C.** They are less likely to discuss religion in public.

○ **D.** They are less likely to believe strongly in their religion.

Passage 5 (Questions 23-28)

The rising incidence of diabetes in both developed and developing countries is generating a large humanitarian and financial burden. At least 93 million people are affected by diabetes in China alone. Especially worrying is the generalized fall in the age at onset of diabetes. With rapidly increasing globalization, lifestyles in low- and middle-income countries increasingly include high fat and calorie-dense diets and inadequate physical exercise, and are resulting in an increased worldwide burden of non-communicable diseases (NCDs).

Until recently there was much publicity for the view that diabetes and NCDs were largely manifest in adults as a result of the biblical sins of 'gluttony and sloth', so there was an urgent need both to get individuals to take more responsibility for their adult lifestyle and to discourage the food industry from producing the "unhealthy" foods which fueled this epidemic of disease. However, a substantial body of evidence makes it clear that early life influences also play an important part here, and that maternal (and, to a degree, paternal) lifestyle and conditions, such as gestational diabetes, affect not only prenatal and infant development but also the adequacy of responses to later challenges, such as an obesogenic lifestyle. This emphasizes the importance of NCD risk reduction starting with adolescents and young women before conception and during pregnancy.

The risk of NCDs such as diabetes is present for everyone and increases throughout life. Most interventions aimed at reducing overweight and obesity, and thus the risk of NCDs such as diabetes later in life, have focused on diet and lifestyle in adults. However, evidence suggests that interventions aimed at weight loss in adults or at preventing excessive weight gain during pregnancy and subsequent weight retention have had limited success. Weight loss and persistent changes in lifestyle are difficult to sustain in adults because the neuroendocrine changes that drive appetite remain unaltered. Additionally, recent evidence shows that risk factors for diabetes and cardiovascular disease are no greater in non-obese adults who had been obese children than they are in individuals who have never been obese, but are clearly lower than those in people who became obese as adults or who were obese both as children and as adults. This makes a strong case for focusing on earlier stages of life before appetite control, food preference, and fat cell number are established, and before obese children reach adulthood.

There has been much publicity on the 1000 Days Campaign launched by the First Lady of the USA to improve nutrition of mothers and children in developing countries. This period of life covers a woman's pregnancy and the first two years of her child's postnatal life, a time when the processes of developmental plasticity operate powerfully to influence offspring phenotype and when excessive growth is associated with later adiposity in childhood. Despite a unique window of opportunity to shape the healthy future of mothers and children during this period, findings are inconsistent in relation to which factors need to be targeted in interventions to reduce the risk of later NCDs such as diabetes. There is limited evidence of interventions to manage weight during this period being effective. Poor intervention effectiveness seems to be related to inadequately addressing social barriers that women experience in achieving healthy weight gain in pregnancy. These barriers include a perceived lack of control and contradictory or conflicting messages about nurturing behaviors during pregnancy. Pregnancy is a time when many influences operate on parents and it may not be the best time for messages to be delivered about preventing excessive weight gain in women.

This passage was adapted from "Early life opportunities for prevention of diabetes in low and middle income countries." Hanson M, Gluckman P, Ma R, Matzen P, Biesma R. *BMC Public Health.* 2012. 12 doi: 10.1186/1471-2458-12-1025 for use under the terms of the Creative Commons CC BY 3.0 license (http://creativecommons.org/licenses/by/3.0/legalcode).

Question 23

The passage implies that, until recently, NCDs were viewed as:

- ○ **A.** punishment.
- ○ **B.** unavoidable.
- ○ **C.** genetically driven.
- ○ **D.** location-based.

Question 24

According to the author, concluding that diabetes is a problem only of developed countries due to an overabundance of food would be:

- ○ **A.** a valid assessment.
- ○ **B.** assuming causation with correlation.
- ○ **C.** forgetting to consider a common cause.
- ○ **D.** forgetting to consider additional causes.

Question 25

The author mentions recent evidence regarding diabetes risk in obese/non-obese adults most likely in order to:

- ○ **A.** stress the importance of childhood factors in the development of diabetes.
- ○ **B.** suggest that adult body weight is determined at a young age.
- ○ **C.** argue that body weight is the primary risk factor for diabetes.
- ○ **D.** explain why people in developed and developing countries are at risk for diabetes.

Question 26

Which of the following, if assumed to be true, would most support the author's conclusion about the best way to prevent diabetes worldwide?

- ○ **A.** Brochures providing recommendations during pregnancy reach a wide audience.
- ○ **B.** Educating parents about the harms of tanning has reduced the occurrence of sunburns in children.
- ○ **C.** Medical trips to developing countries provide long-lasting improvements.
- ○ **D.** Shaming an individual induces them to act.

Question 27

Which of the following criticisms of a proposed road trip is most similar to the author's criticism of the biblical view of NCDs?

○ **A.** The driver does not consistently clean his car.

○ **B.** The driving route is not planned far enough in advance.

○ **C.** The car is comprised of old, worn down parts.

○ **D.** The driver has not spent enough money on his car.

Question 28

The author's argument about diabetes prevention implies that he or she would be likely to *oppose* which of the following?

○ **A.** A decrease in government regulation of elementary school lunches

○ **B.** Legislation limiting the amount of food one family can buy in a week

○ **C.** An increase in buffet halls at colleges or universities

○ **D.** Implementation of an online education program for parents of kindergarteners

Passage 6 (Questions 29-35)

For many literary critics, Samuel Beckett was above the hurly burly of the quotidian. His work was strictly universal, existing on the plane of the abstract and philosophical, rather than dealing with specific human foibles, particularly those peculiar to his native Ireland. In the era immediately following the Second World War, however, Beckett was not averse to exploring one of the most peculiar of the peculiarly Irish traits: begrudgery. A virulent combination of jealousy, spite, and festering resentment, begrudgery prevailed in epidemic proportions in the Ireland of Beckett's day.

Beckett himself was not untouched by Irish begrudgery. His character Moran, the protagonist and narrator of the second book of Beckett's Molloy, exhibits all of the characteristics of an archetypical Irish begrudger. To begin with, Moran is filled with an all-consuming and irrational spite and generalized resentment: "It's a strange thing, I don't like men and I don't like animals. As for God, he is beginning to disgust me." Throw in envy and Beckett's Moran emerges as a perfect example of Nietzsche's "creature of ressentiment," as philosopher Gilles Deleuze explains it in Nietzsche and Philosophy:

What is most striking in the man of ressentiment is not his nastiness but his disgusting malevolence, his capacity for disparagement. Nothing can resist it. He does not even respect his friends or even his enemies. He does not even respect misfortune or its causes. The creature of ressentiment, because of his faculty of forgetting nothing, is able to carry a grudge ad infinitum.

Moran vividly embodies all of the qualities of Nietzsche and Deleuze's creature of ressentiment.

Regarding Beckett's work, scholar Sean Kennedy observed that even though "Ireland has most often been read as a specter, a kind of afterthought or trace," the time has come when "that the ghostly presence of Ireland may need to be more carefully accounted for." For many decades, Beckett scholarship tended to shy away for the most part from such an accounting for various reasons. Indeed, for many years there was some question as to what nationality Beckett should be considered. Even when Beckett's nationality was not in question, many insisted that calling Beckett "an Irish writer involves some semantic sleight of hand." As a result, Beckett was often consigned to a nationless universality, a "Nayman from Noland," rather than being fully embraced as an Irish author.

More recently, it has been demonstrated that the Irish detail in Beckett's work has been repeatedly underestimated. In what was an unspoken, and sometimes spoken, critical orthodoxy, Beckett critics did overlook or underestimate Irish details in Beckett's work for decades.

Beckett's use of Irish details is not limited to his language or to historical references; Beckett also makes use of sociological aspects of the Irish character, such as begrudgery, that might escape the notice of a non-Irish audience. Even after leaving Ireland in 1937, the Irish particularities of Beckett's writing remained in his work. Indeed, Ireland continued to influence Beckett's writing long after he permanently relocated to France, not only in setting but in other, more minute aspects of literary form as well. Even while Beckett's writing transcends many linguistic and cultural boundaries, it remains informed by the sociology of its time.

Question 29

Based on information in the passage, Samuel Beckett's writing following World War II can best be characterized as:

○ **A.** firmly grounded in experiences of daily life.

○ **B.** universally acclaimed for its literary worth.

○ **C.** exemplary of Irish literature during that era.

○ **D.** containing a few subtly Irish elements.

Question 30

The author suggests that attitudes of *ressentiment* were:

○ **A.** more common in Ireland than elsewhere in the years following World War II.

○ **B.** unique to Ireland during Samuel Beckett's life.

○ **C.** overlooked in their relevance to Samuel Beckett's work.

○ **D.** the defining element of Samuel Beckett's writing style.

Question 31

The passage suggests that the author's main point of contention with the "critical orthodoxy" (paragraph 4) is:

   I. whether or not Moran can be called a begrudger.

   II. the extent to which Beckett's writings should be considered Irish.

   III. the influence of begrudgery on Beckett's work.

○ **A.** I and II only

○ **B.** II and III only

○ **C.** II only

○ **D.** III only

Question 32

In *Molloy*, Moran states: "A man like me cannot forget." What information from the passage best explains the aspect of Moran's character that would compel him to make this claim?

○ **A.** Moran is an archetypical Irish character.

○ **B.** Moran is resentful throughout *Molloy*.

○ **C.** Feelings of begrudgery consume Moran.

○ **D.** Moran embodies the characteristics of a "creature of *ressentiment*."

Question 33

Which of the following statements, if true, would most contradict the author's claim that "Ireland continued to influence Beckett's writing long after he permanently relocated to France" (paragraph 5)?

○ **A.** Beckett wrote very few envious characters in his later works.

○ **B.** Beckett wrote the majority of his later works in French.

○ **C.** Beckett used Irish names for many of the characters in his novels.

○ **D.** Beckett thought of himself as a strictly universalist writer.

Question 34

The author thinks that, relative to literature, sociology is:

○ **A.** irrelevant, and therefore unnecessary to consider.

○ **B.** important to a thorough understanding of an author's work.

○ **C.** central to any understanding of a text.

○ **D.** only important to understanding Beckett's work.

Question 35

Based on the passage, a movie employing begrudgery as a stylistic trait would most likely have:

○ **A.** central characters who are jealous of one another.

○ **B.** sparse and unemotional dialogue.

○ **C.** highly abstract and philosophical imagery.

○ **D.** themes specific to Irish history.

Passage 7 (Questions 36-41)

The brain is a mysterious canvas of actualized and unrealized possibilities. As Diane Ackerman notes, "…each person carries around atop the body a complete universe in which trillions of sensations, thoughts, and desires stream." Brain science remains uncharted territory despite the significant efforts that have been and are being realized to better understand brain and behavior. More than mere coincidence or happenstance, plays like Shakespeare's famous Romeo and Juliet, with great storylines, brilliant costumes, and emotional stimulation, continue to survive for ages based upon pure artistic excellence that engages the audience in a unique manner. There is a need to more fully understand how our brains process drama and the manner in which like versus dislike is decided. Most important is the factor of longevity and what makes the appealing quality of drama survive over years across cultural and generational shifts.

Humans interact with one another, but the way in which each individual interacts differs greatly. The way people live their lives differs in this way as well. This is primarily due to a combination of variable brain compositions, personality traits, and cultural-environmental conditions. As Steven Pinker stated, "Intelligence…is the ability to attain goals in the face of obstacles by means of decisions based on rational (truth-obeying) rules." However, intelligence is different from thought, as "[h]umans… emit a response to a stimulus either because it was earlier paired with a reflexive trigger for that response…or because the response was rewarded in the presence of that stimulus." Stimuli trigger responses that include action, non-action, covert, and overt behavior.

As humans age and accumulate more life experiences, they learn how to more efficiently react to stimuli under different conditions. This is especially true with the prefrontal cortex. This part of the brain deals with executive functioning and is not fully developed until at least 21 years of age. Until then adolescents rely on "fight or flight" hormones, neurotransmitters, and the amygdala (the emotional control center of the brain) to react with their world, while adults can more efficiently sort out stimuli.

At the University of Liverpool, research has shown that reading William Shakespeare's works stimulates the brain. Shakespeare's works create functional shifts for the brain, which allow the brain to "understand what a word means before [the brain] understands the function of the word within a sentence… [This causes] …a sudden peak in brain activity and forces the brain to work backwards in order to fully understand what Shakespeare is trying to say." This brain function does not happen easily and because of this, the brain is affected greatly in an effort to adapt to this new and exciting environment. Drama represents to the brain a challenge which must be managed. Shakespeare's way of "…throwing odd words into seemingly normal sentences, surprises the brain and catches it off guard in a manner that produces a sudden burst of [positive] activity—a sense of drama created out of the simplest of things."

This is paramount to the understanding of how the mind works. Through knowing what creates positive brain waves in the brain, drama could act as a medium for alleviating depression while allowing individuals to develop happy dispositions. To keep the brain "fit" has become a cliché nowadays, as businesses have attempted to mass-produce brain games/puzzles/activities that are advertised to keep the brain functioning efficiently and clearly for longer periods of time than nature would allow. However, Dave Munger argues that theater and drama may be the best activity for brain health, while also being enjoyable.

This passage was adapted from "The Play Was Always the Thing: Drama's Effects on Brain Function." Hough B, Hough S. Psychology. 2012. 3(6) doi:10.4236/psych.2012.36064 for use under the terms of the Creative Commons CC BY 3.0 license (http://creativecommons.org/licenses/by/3.0/legalcode).

Question 36

An experiment found that Shakespearean actors reported feeling happier more often than other actors. Based on the passage, this finding is probably explained by:

○ **A.** their love of their profession.

○ **B.** their more successful careers.

○ **C.** their higher intelligence levels.

○ **D.** their stimulating rehearsals.

Question 37

Which of the following findings would most weaken the author's claim about the longevity of Romeo and Juliet?

○ **A.** Adolescents no longer relate to the main characters.

○ **B.** It is rarely taught in high schools anymore.

○ **C.** It is no more engaging than other plays.

○ **D.** Readers have trouble understanding it at first.

Question 38

It has been said that professionals associated with Shakespearean performances tend to live adventurous lives. Which of the following points from the passage would best explain this claim?

○ **A.** People live their lives differently due to cultural-environmental conditions.

○ **B.** Older humans can more efficiently react to different stimuli.

○ **C.** Drama challenges the brain with new and exciting situations.

○ **D.** Adventure helps alleviate depression.

Question 39

In the first paragraph, Ackerman discusses all that is possible in human life due to the structure "atop the body." Ackerman's point is that:

○ **A.** the brain's complexity is easy to take for granted.

○ **B.** the body must be able to act on the brain's wishes.

○ **C.** each body is different but the brains are similar.

○ **D.** more research is needed in brain science.

Question 40

Based on the passage, it is reasonable to conclude that the author thinks the puzzles designed to keep the brain "fit" (paragraph 5) are:

○ **A.** supported by research.

○ **B.** consumer-driven.

○ **C.** successful for only some individuals.

○ **D.** fun regardless of their success.

Question 41

Suppose a theatre company wants to prepare a performance of *Romeo and Juliet* in 24 hours. What advice would the author most likely give?

○ **A.** Focus on captivating costumes.

○ **B.** Cast actors with the most experience.

○ **C.** Make sure the physical actions explain the text.

○ **D.** Enunciate each phrase.

Passage 8 (Questions 42-46)

As one of the outstanding British novelists of his generation, Ian McEwan has won several awards. Those honors and awards have confirmed his position at the forefront of the contemporary British literary world, and have ensured him a niche in the British literary pantheon. The contemporary literary field is permeated with all kinds of experimental genres of novels; the postmodern novel is one of the most influential ones, with the unique techniques of postmodern narration. Like many writers of this age, McEwan was strongly influenced by the postmodernist techniques of contemporary novelists such as Iris Murdoch and John Fowles in England.

Many postmodern novelists feature metafiction or "historiographic metafiction" and intertextuality in their writings. Ian McEwan is of no exception. The settings of McEwan's The Innocent, Atonement, and Black Dogs carry postmodern features, which have confirmed his position as a postmodern experimentalist. With self-conscious language, the issues of imagination, fabrication, and history are closely connected with these novels. Metafiction allows authors to turn a mirror on the readers who, in that moment, are combining their reality with fantasy. McEwan's recent novels always carry the features of metafiction and using such kind of devices can consciously or unconsciously influence how a reader interprets the novel. It is without doubt that McEwan is an experimentalist in his exploration of metafiction in the framework of the historical novel. While other authors may tentatively allude to their writing's status as a work of writing in metafiction, McEwan takes it one step further by mixing the lines of fictional storytelling and real life in his character's trajectories.

McEwan seems to be interested in the relationship between imagination and reality (fiction and reality) in the process of writing, which is generally considered to be one of the themes related to metafiction writing. In his novels, McEwan lays great emphasis on the constructive power of imagination on reality and fiction writing, discussing fictionality inexplicitly in the first chapter. The relationship between art and fiction is complex, as the theory of writing is developing with the time. On one hand, the gap between imagination and fiction is hard to overstep. On the other hand, "reality" is to some extent "fictional" or "imagined" and can be understood through an appropriate "reading" process, so there is concord between them. Thus, metafiction does not give up the "real world" for the mere pleasure of the imagination. By showing us how imagination creates a new world, the metafictionist is indicating that composing a novel is no different from composing "one's reality."

McEwan's *Atonement* is a novel about storytelling. The writer focuses on issues like writing, imagination, history, and the nature of truth. Thus, imagination plays a vital role in this novel, helping the story develop into the final incident. The issue of imagination is best represented by the protagonist and underlying writer, Briony,

Next ▶

a 13-year-old girl embedded with a wild imagination. The twisting of life by Briony's imagination leads to a terrible disaster which changes the destiny of the other characters Robbie, Cecilia, and even herself, and which makes her atone for the rest of her life. Briony interprets events according to her own will, and sees what she expects to see. She believes in symmetry, forbidding any stories being violated in real life. She composes stories out of scenes she witnesses in real life, not realizing the serious consequences she will bring about. By relating Briony's fantasy and imagination and the series of misunderstandings resulting from them, this novel explores the problematic relationship between life and fiction. Briony misunderstands, misinterprets, and misconceives the life of others through imagination, and blurs the line between fact and fiction.

This passage was adapted from "Postmodern Strategies in Ian McEwan's Major Novels." Han J, Wang Z. Advances in Literary Studies. 2014. 2. doi:10.4236/als.2014.24020 for use under the terms of the Creative Commons CC BY 4.0 license (https://creativecommons.org/licenses/by/4.0/legalcode).

Question 42

According to the passage, one societal critique presented by *Atonement* concerns:

○ **A.** honesty.

○ **B.** bias.

○ **C.** imagination.

○ **D.** storytelling.

Question 43

Based on information in the passage, postmodern writers utilize metafiction in order to:

○ **A.** join the ranks of respected authors.

○ **B.** write in an influential genre.

○ **C.** inspire readers to self-reflect.

○ **D.** question man's existence.

Question 44

According to passage information, which of the following artists would be most likely to "compose one's reality" (paragraph 3)?

○ **A.** A dancer working her own style into a classic piece

○ **B.** A director in charge of a new alien movie

○ **C.** An actor reprising a role after many years

○ **D.** A screenwriter adapting an old movie about Hollywood

Question 45

Female readers generally have more sympathy for Briony than do male readers. According to the passage, this is likely true because, compared to men, women:

○ **A.** have more active imaginations.

○ **B.** read metafiction more often.

○ **C.** are more likely to become writers themselves.

○ **D.** are more sympathetic in general.

Question 46

Which of the following passage assertions is LEAST supported by evidence in the passage?

○ **A.** Ian McEwan is one of the outstanding British novelists of his generation.

○ **B.** The issues of imagination, fabrication, and history are closely connected with metafictional novels.

○ **C.** The relationship between art and fiction is complex, and the theory of writing is still developing.

○ **D.** Metafiction does not give up the real world in exchange for imagination.

Passage 9 (Questions 47-53)

Traditional evolutionary psychological theory stipulates that men and women face different challenges to reproductive success, such as paternity uncertainty, and therefore would prioritize different qualities in romantic mates. In the context of heterosexual mating, men are theorized to favor young partners with higher levels of physical attractiveness because youth and attractiveness convey information about a woman's reproductive fitness. In contrast, women are thought to favor partners with higher levels of social status and economic/material resources because a stronger commitment of resources from a male partner will increase the odds that her children will survive to adulthood. These hypotheses rely greatly on parental investment theory, which proposes that women are more selective in their mates because the amount of investment they must put into caring for offspring has been much greater throughout evolutionary history.

Research using hypothetical mate preference surveys has tended to support evolutionary theory, finding that men place higher value on vitality-attractiveness, women place higher value on status-resources, and men and women value warmth-trustworthiness about equally. However, in a face-to-face setting, it is not clear that men and women would display such differences in the live experience of romantic attraction. Indeed, some studies have suggested that the gendered mate preferences predicted by evolutionary theory might not hold when potential mates actually interact with one another. Studies have shown women being more choosy or selective than men, women valuing earning prospects and men valuing attractiveness more than their counterparts, women valuing intelligence more than men, and men valuing attractiveness more than women. However, a recent meta-analysis compiling live-attraction data from multiple studies suggested that these gendered mate preferences do not hold when analyzed in aggregate. Based on the studies to date utilizing live-attraction methods, the findings are mixed with evidence leaning toward no gender differences in short-term, face-to-face dating contexts. When men and women meet face to face, the associations between partner traits and romantic interest are statistically equivalent across genders.

This is consistent with a more recent theory about the nature of romantic attraction. Specifically, construal-level theory predicts that people tend to evaluate specific stimuli (in this case, when meeting potential romantic partners in person) differently than they would conceptualize abstract ideas (in this case, general preferences for what they would prefer in an ideal romantic partner), thus accounting for the divergent results when examining hypothetical and actual dating experiences.

Furthermore, although explicit preferences tend to be poorer predictors of face-to-face romantic attraction, implicit "gut-level" preferences provide better predictors of face-to-face romantic attraction. This does not mean that explicit preferences are completely without predictive value. Explicit reports of ideal partner preferences significantly predict divorce rates when examined as patterns (e.g., preferring warmth over ambition in potential partners) but not as levels (e.g., preferring high amounts of warmth or ambition in potential partners). Similarly, studies that have examined long-term relationship outcomes have found support for the idea that spousal partner selection is driven by sex-specific preferences consistent with parental investment theory. For men, the physical attractiveness of their spouses significantly predicted their marital satisfaction over a 4-year period—a pattern not found in women. Explicit preferences may play a larger role in predicting other dating/relationship outcomes, rather than initial feelings of romantic attraction.

This passage was adapted from "Do Men and Women Exhibit Different Preferences for Mates? A Replication of Eastwick and Finkel (2008)." Selterman DF, Chagnon E, Mackinnon SP. *SAGE Open.* 2015. 5(3) doi:10.1177/2158244015605160 for use under the terms of the Creative Commons CC BY 4.0 license (https://creativecommons.org/licenses/by/4.0/legalcode).

Question 47

Which of the following describes an assumption made by the author in the passage?

- O **A.** Parental investment theory applies only to heterosexual couples.
- O **B.** Long-term romantic attraction is difficult to predict.
- O **C.** Men value attractiveness above all other traits.
- O **D.** Individual attraction preferences are apparent in live settings.

Question 48

Which of the following statements about parental investment theory is most strongly implied by information in the first paragraph?

- O **A.** A father's greatest contribution to his child's life is material goods.
- O **B.** A father must put his child's needs before his own.
- O **C.** A mother passes on her attractiveness to her child.
- O **D.** A mother can receive more financial support if there is uncertainty about paternity.

Question 49

In which of the following pairs could the author best predict the chances of divorce based on learning explicit partner preferences?

- O **A.** A same-sex couple visiting a therapist after five years together
- O **B.** A same-sex couple meeting for a third date
- O **C.** A heterosexual couple being introduced by friends
- O **D.** A heterosexual couple moving in together

Question 50

Which of the following findings would most strengthen the argument made for the validity of parental investment theory?

- ○ **A.** Initial feelings of attraction can be predicted by explicit partner preferences.
- ○ **B.** Women take longer than men to decide if an individual can be a potential partner.
- ○ **C.** Men are more likely than women to desert a child.
- ○ **D.** Mothers and fathers are not equally invested in parenting.

Question 51

Which of the following passage assertions is LEAST supported by evidence?

- ○ **A.** Men and women face different challenges to reproductive success.
- ○ **B.** Youth and attractiveness convey information about reproductive fitness.
- ○ **C.** Women favor partners with higher levels of social status and economic resources.
- ○ **D.** Partner traits and romantic interest are statistically equivalent across gender in live settings.

Question 52

Which of the following situations is most analogous to face-to-face meetings between men and women as described in the third paragraph?

- ○ **A.** A woman who always wanted a cat but adopts a dog when she visits a shelter
- ○ **B.** A baseball fan who is disappointed by his team when he attends a game
- ○ **C.** A coffee drinker who changes her order one day
- ○ **D.** A college student who cannot choose a major area of study

Question 53

On a recent reality television show, a woman chose to marry a man that many people described as attractive. Based on the parental investment theory, this selection was probably influenced by:

- ○ **A.** the woman's expectation that the marriage will not last long.
- ○ **B.** the woman's own appearance and attractiveness.
- ○ **C.** the man's employment at a successful business.
- ○ **D.** the man's promise of love and commitment to the woman.

STOP. If you finish before time is called, check your work. You may go back to any question in this test.

ANSWERS & EXPLANATIONS for Test 6 can be found on p. 255.

TEST 7

Number of Questions: 53
Time: 90 minutes

INSTRUCTIONS: Each passage is followed by associated questions. Read the passage, then select the best answer to each question. If you are unsure of the answer, rule out incorrect choices and select from the remaining options. Indicate your answer beside the option you choose.

Passage 1 (Questions 1-5)

Multimodal social semiotics focuses on situated social and material resources through which meaning is made. These materials and modes (verbal linguistics, audio, gestural and spatial relations, mimetic or technological, and visual modes) are ways to use culturally available resources based on young children's interests to assist in communication of meaning. Children negotiate their own identities and pathways by remaking texts and representations. They participate in learning processes by capturing through texts the essence of the alterations, transformations, and re-makings of social arrangements and practices. Children constantly use representations—ways of framing an aspect of their world—throughout the learning process. Drawings, verbal linguistic communication, pauses, gestures, videos and music, and written texts are examples of these representations. Children use them to explore and make meaning of their world, to frame it, to discuss ideas, and to reflect on what they have learned.

Motivated by interest, children are known to make selections of vocal sound resources and reorganize these in the audio-linguistic mode. This is known as invented song. They also substitute specific concrete speech actions with abstractions such as sounds and non-verbal processes. Visual symbols and spatial design elements have also become recognized as important representational and communicational resources in the written linguistic mode. As part of this multimodal ensemble of meaning making, sound significantly shapes the communicational landscape of children. While exploring potentials of sound to convey meaning, they develop conceptual understanding in music. This is not just evident in audio linguistics of shared and invented song in early childhood settings. Children make decisions based on movement vocabulary and play potentials of instruments, such as Orff xylophones, to create accumulative sequences of sound. In transformative music invention, they are agentive in redesigning or reordering elements of music, knowing when to focus on phrasing, dynamics, melody, or rhythm, similar to the concept of turn-taking. These young children are problem solving in a way that can improve classroom interactions later.

The range of responses children demonstrate during inventive music making, listening, and valuing can be connected to their sociocultural experiences. This is known as music praxis. Literacy has been examined as a social and cultural practice in family life, and researchers now view children's acquisition of literacy, their text-making practices, through an active engagement in their social and cultural worlds. It is recognized that learning occurs informally from an early age: children progress from unconventional to conventional literacy practices over time. Within early childhood learning programs, there is a need to plan for creative music invention tasks that support children by validating their experiences and competencies, their cultural dispositions and identities. Children's dispositional and creative approaches to learning, their transformation of prior knowledge, and an enriched conceptual understanding should emerge through study of a variety of multimodal redesigns in music invention and literacy in early learning settings. If such tasks are approached through play-based learning and investigations in context, children will be intrinsically motivated to apply imagination and organizational skills, building on musical ideas, co-constructing music, negotiating new ideas, and developing confidence in their ownership and expression of music.

This passage was adapted from "Literacy and Music in Early Childhood: Multimodal Learning and Design." Tomlinson M. *SAGE Open*. 2013. 3(3) doi:10.1177/2158244013502498 for use under the terms of the Creative Commons CC BY 3.0 license (http://creativecommons.org/licenses/by/3.0/legalcode).

Question 1

Which of the following assertions is supported by information in the passage?

○ **A.** Music is most educational during early years of development.

○ **B.** Children benefit from music the most when creating their own songs.

○ **C.** Children who engage in music making perform better in school.

○ **D.** Music can improve social skills in developing children.

Question 2

The author's apparent attitude towards music education is that it is:

○ **A.** underrated.

○ **B.** necessary.

○ **C.** overvalued.

○ **D.** comparable to art education.

Question 3

Fundraisers for low-income communities often gather musical instruments for children of all ages. Which of the following is information from the passage that LEAST explains why they focus on these toys?

○ **A.** Music is a resource through which meaning is made.

○ **B.** Sound can influence the communicational abilities of children.

○ **C.** The process of making music fosters creativity.

○ **D.** Music can enhance social interactions.

Question 4

Which of the following would provide the best evidence to support the author's conclusion regarding music education?

- ○ **A.** Preschools that encourage learning through play have less conflict than other preschools.
- ○ **B.** Elementary schools with musical instruments have higher test scores than average schools.
- ○ **C.** Middle schools students who play an instrument are more mature than other students.
- ○ **D.** High schools with music education programs have more confident students than schools without such programs.

Question 5

The ideas discussed in this passage would likely be of most use to:

- ○ **A.** teachers in charge of the music curriculum.
- ○ **B.** principals who run the daily activities at a school.
- ○ **C.** administrators who make schedules for the students at a school.
- ○ **D.** parents deciding where to send their child to school.

Passage 2 (Questions 6-12)

Many studies have analyzed the relationship between general intelligence and chess abilities. In particular, some studies have investigated the correlation between these two variables, suggesting that the population of chess players (both adults and children) is more intelligent than the general population. This evidence, however, does not necessarily lead to the conclusion that chess improves intelligence because the direction of causality is uncertain. In fact, there are several possible alternative explanations: a high IQ (intelligence quotient) could be the cause of a high chess ability (and not vice versa). In other words, an intelligent individual could achieve a high chess ability because chess requires a high degree of intelligence, rather than because the game increases it. Alternatively, people with high IQs could be "selected by the game" much more easily than others: subjects playing chess can find out that they are good at the game, so they are encouraged to continue playing it. However, whoever turns out to be not so good at chess may be discouraged from playing it again. In this case, chess "selects" motivated people with high IQs who are able to play well.

Beyond the question of direction of causality, the more general problem of the transfer of skills must be held in consideration. If the former problem is addressable by using a proper experimental design (experimental and control groups; pre- and post-tests), the latter represents a theoretical problem. The theory of identical elements states that the transfer of cognitive abilities from one domain to another occurs only when the domains share common elements. This implies that the transfer of skills is quite rare and limited to the extent that there is an overlap between the domains.

Some studies have shown that this limited transfer of skills applies to the game of chess as well. In her classic study, education professor Michelene Chi demonstrated that chess players' memory skill for chess positions did not extend to recall of numerical digits. Many other researchers have replicated the study and obtained the same outcome. More recently, studies have found that chess players' planning abilities did not transfer to the Tower of London, a test assessing executive function and planning skills. Chess players' perceptual skills also did not transfer to visual memory of shapes, nor did chess abilities correlate with performance in a beauty contest experiment. All of these studies have suggested that transfer is, at best, improbable, and that chess players' special abilities are context-dependent.

The more specific a skill is, the less that skill is transferable to another domain. Nevertheless, it is reasonable to suppose that a game requiring attention, logical thinking, planning, and calculation abilities would be able to improve at least some of the aforementioned cognitive abilities, like memory and executive functioning, which are linked to problem-solving competence and, overall, to general intelligence, at the beginning of their development. Put simply, even if chess players' abilities do not transfer to other domains, it is not impossible that chess helps children to develop the above abilities, especially when these latter are yet to be fully developed, and still general enough to allow the transfer.

This passage was adapted from "Mathematical Problem-Solving Abilities and Chess: An Experimental Study on Young Pupils." Sala G, Gorini A, Pravettoni G. *SAGE Open.* 2015. 5(3) doi: 10.1177/2158244015596050 for use under the terms of the Creative Commons CC BY 4.0 license (http://creativecommons.org/licenses/by/4.0/legalcode).

Question 6

According to the passage, which of the following skills is common to most chess players?

- ○ **A.** Memorizing patterns easily
- ○ **B.** Planning actions in advance
- ○ **C.** Learning from each game of chess
- ○ **D.** Scoring high on intelligence tests

Question 7

The passage suggests that chess players may have a high IQ for all of the following reasons EXCEPT:

- ○ **A.** they have been playing chess for many years.
- ○ **B.** the game of chess is more likely to be taught to smart individuals.
- ○ **C.** they win games easily, so they continue playing.
- ○ **D.** the game of chess requires intellect.

Question 8

A teacher wants to start a chess club at her school to inculcate cognitive skills related to the game. Based on information in the passage, which group of students should the teacher recruit for this club?

- ○ **A.** High school students who are quick learners
- ○ **B.** Students who already know how to play chess
- ○ **C.** Students in elementary school
- ○ **D.** Children whose parents have high IQs

Question 9

According to the passage, chess skills do not easily transfer to other skill sets. Which of the following passage assertions provides the best evidence for this statement?

- ○ **A.** The direction of causality between chess ability and general intelligence is uncertain.
- ○ **B.** The transfer of skills is limited to the extent of overlap between two domains.
- ○ **C.** Studies have found that chess players' planning abilities and memory skills did not transfer to other tasks.
- ○ **D.** The more specific a skill is, the less likely it can be transferred to another domain.

Question 10

Given the information provided by the passage, if a high school student who plays chess regularly performs poorly on an academic test, the most likely explanation is that:

- ○ **A.** the student devoted more time to playing chess than studying.
- ○ **B.** the student may not have as high of an IQ score as the average chess player.
- ○ **C.** the subject required different skills than the student normally employs.
- ○ **D.** the subject was unrelated to chess.

Question 11

Which of the following discoveries would most *weaken* the author's argument regarding the transfer of chess skills?

- ○ **A.** Children cannot proficiently develop skills in the game of chess.
- ○ **B.** Recent studies failed to find a correlation between chess ability and IQ.
- ○ **C.** More adults than children play chess.
- ○ **D.** Chess does not requires as high a level of intellect as previously believed.

Question 12

Suppose a new study found that a small sample of adult chess players can transfer the memory skills that they demonstrate in chess to other domains, but the same could not be said for other skills. How would the author likely explain this finding?

- ○ **A.** The chess players probably started playing the game very early in life.
- ○ **B.** The chess players probably shared another commonality affecting memory skills.
- ○ **C.** The chess players probably played each other to develop this specific skill.
- ○ **D.** The chess players probably got lucky when performing the tasks in the study.

Next ▶

Passage 3 (Questions 13-18)

We have seen that people live in a more and more complicated, post-modern and globalized world. This tendency of modernization and post-modernization still presents growing challenges for leaders in organizations. The dilemma of narcissism is one of the most acute problems in leadership behavior in the Western world. Why do bad and destructive leaders with or without charisma exist? How is this evilness produced and reproduced in organizational behavior? The culture of trust is said to be the most important factor behind wellness and wellbeing in organizations. Commitment is an inevitable part of this culture. Good management and leadership are also central factors influencing these processes. Destructive and narcissistic leaders are, on the other hand, negative dark forces causing damage and harm in organizations.

Charisma, in the sense used by Max Weber, literally means "the gift of grace." It is used by Weber to characterize self-appointed leaders followed by people who are in distress and who need to follow the leader because they believe him to be extraordinarily qualified. The actions of charismatic leaders are enthusiastic, and with such extraordinary enthusiasm, fraternization and exuberant community sentiments can be pursued. For this reason, charismatic heroes and prophets are viewed as truly revolutionary forces in history. Weber characterized charisma as "specifically outside the realm of everyday routine and the profane sphere, a direct antithesis of rational and traditional authority. Inherently transient, volatile, and evanescent, charisma in its pure form exist(s) only in the process of originating." It cannot remain stable, but becomes either traditionalized or rationalized, or a combination of both.

For the narcissistic leader, the world revolves on the axis of self, and all other people and issues closely orbit them. They present various combinations of intense ambitiousness, grandiose fantasies, feelings of inferiority and overdependence on external admiration and acclaim. Narcissistic leaders also tend to overestimate their own achievements and abilities while stubbornly refusing to recognize the quality and value of the same in others. Another characteristic is their tendency to exploit in interpersonal contexts, in which others are taken advantage of in order to indulge their own desires. Because narcissistic leaders tend to use others to advance their own goals, they are notorious for being unable to empathize with those they lead. This enables them to pursue their own ends without restraint.

Incompetent leaders are the least problematic (damaging) while unethical leaders are the most problematic (damaging). One must also consider both means and ends. Ineffective leaders fail to achieve the desired results or to bring about positive changes due to a shortfall in means. Unethical leaders fail to distinguish between right and wrong. Ethical leaders put followers' needs before their own, exhibit private virtues (courage, temperance), and serve the interests of the common good.

Fear, threats, egoism, narcissism, brutality, and cultism are such things that will cause fatal damage to organizational trust and commitment. Leaders who betray their followers may miss out on opportunities to be trustworthy forever. Leaders can lose trust only once. However, in work-organizations employees act to earn their living, and thus affective or emotional commitment may lay more in the background compared with other social or private life organizations, such as in the family. Humans are social beings, and trust in their companions is fundamental to survival.

This passage was adapted from "Dark Leadership, Charisma and Trust." Takala T. Psychology. 2010. 1 doi: 10.4236/psych.2010.11009 for use under the terms of the Creative Commons CC BY 3.0 license (http://creativecommons.org/licenses/by/3.0/legalcode).

Question 13

According to the passage, one drawback of charismatic leadership is that it is:

- ○ **A.** temporary.
- ○ **B.** exploitive.
- ○ **C.** ineffective.
- ○ **D.** rare.

Question 14

Based on information in the passage, narcissistic leaders tend to surround themselves with people because:

- ○ **A.** they want to exert their dominance over the greatest number of people.
- ○ **B.** they can effect the most change that way.
- ○ **C.** they are very popular in social settings.
- ○ **D.** they need social support.

Question 15

Which of the following situations would most strengthen the author's argument?

- ○ **A.** A CEO caught embezzling is forgiven as long as he does not do it again.
- ○ **B.** A mayor with no background knowledge or experience ruins a city's economy.
- ○ **C.** A charismatic commander has not been able to control her soldiers ever since she lied about the risks of a mission.
- ○ **D.** A narcissistic actor learns that his selfishness pushes others away and leads to a lonely life.

Question 16

A politician wants to be viewed as a charismatic leader. Based on the passage, the author would most likely recommend what advice?

○ **A.** Become an expert on domestic policy.

○ **B.** Step up in difficult situations.

○ **C.** Make decisions with confidence.

○ **D.** Never let the voters see a sad moment.

Question 17

According to the passage, an egotistical leader may be tolerated best in which setting?

○ **A.** Politics

○ **B.** Entertainment Industry

○ **C.** Their household

○ **D.** Workplace

Question 18

Based on information in the passage, one could most reasonably conclude that destructive leaders:

○ **A.** are usually charismatic.

○ **B.** often come from the Western world.

○ **C.** can harm an individual or organization.

○ **D.** lack a moral compass.

Passage 4 (Questions 19-22)

Middle school educators believe that young adolescents learn in ways that are developmentally different from older adolescents, and that the middle years are among the most significant periods of cognitive, socio-emotional, and biological growth. Yet research shows that most experienced teachers do not feel prepared to apply knowledge of adolescent development to teaching. Even recent efforts to improve achievement outcomes through the implementation of a common core of academic standards have not taken the developmental sciences into account. To hold students to higher standards and build those standards from grade to grade may do little to improve student achievement without teachers' understanding of the socio-emotional and instructional climates that support growth at different developmental stages.

Along with strengthening teachers' subject matter knowledge and pedagogical expertise, it is important to improve teachers' ability to apply a developmental perspective whereby age-based characteristics of students are used to design instruction. For teachers of middle-grade students, understanding the importance of active learning strategies and knowing how and when to implement them is essential.

Play has been described by neuroscientists Leong and Carlson as a mechanism that allows our brains to practice flexibility and learn the self-regulatory skills necessary in life and work. Psychologist David Elkind maintains that play experiences are especially critical in the middle grades because they reinforce the central task of early adolescence: learning to persist in work. Play, simply stated, makes work more fun. While playing games, adolescents must sustain their focus. They engage in planning, initiating, shifting, prioritizing, and sequencing to master the objectives of the game, often without realizing that these same executive skills are important to college and career readiness. In today's world, in fact, educators believe that successful math-related careers require the executive skills that are practiced in games.

Despite growing interest in the potential of games to teach skills and concepts, solid research that tests the effects of different types of games on development and learning is limited. Research does suggest that middle school students' motivation and attitudes toward math are positively influenced by games, and that using games and imaginative play can help struggling secondary students learn to regulate their behavior. Empirical evidence has shown that playing games improves middle school students' math fluency, increases their interest in and enjoyment of math, and leads to the adoption of a mastery goal orientation. It appears that, when games provide opportunities for learners to integrate new knowledge with previous understanding and to verbalize their thought processes, students pay closer attention and are likely to retain what they learned. A recent report from the National Research Council on simulations and games in science supports these findings, concluding that learning through games increases student interest and engagement in science and therefore should be further investigated as an instructional strategy.

Although play is considered an integral part of early childhood education, the further up in grades a student progresses, the less likely teachers are to use game-based activities as an instructional strategy. Accountability pressures and lack of professional development may undermine middle-grade teachers' willingness to replace more traditional lecture and paper–pencil exercises in favor of games and simulations. Simply put, solid research on the impact of games and simulations on achievement outcomes is limited, and teachers' beliefs about the efficacy of games to promote learning are unclear.

This passage was adapted from "Playing to Learn: How After-School Clubs Influence Teachers' Beliefs About Instruction." Schlosser L, Balzano B. SAGE Open. 2014. doi: 10.1177/2158244014558031 for use under the terms of the Creative Commons CC BY 3.0 license (http://creativecommons.org/licenses/by/3.0/legalcode).

Question 19

Which information from the passage provides the greatest support for the claim that middle school educators do NOT know how to teach their students in the most effective manner?

- **A.** Middle school educators believe that young adolescents learn in ways that are developmentally different from older adolescents.
- **B.** Middle school educators have not engaged in play for many years and have forgotten its benefits.
- **C.** There is pressure to focus on professional development during middle school.
- **D.** Teachers' beliefs about the efficacy of games to promote learning are unclear.

Question 20

The author of this passage would most likely stress the real-world importance of which of the following skills developed from play?

- **A.** Social interactions
- **B.** Flexibility
- **C.** Perseverance
- **D.** Motivation

Question 21

Which of the following professionals would most likely be a "pedagogical" (paragraph 2) expert?

- **A.** A developmental psychologist
- **B.** A martial arts instructor
- **C.** A sociologist
- **D.** A school counselor

Question 22

Which of the following claims would most *weaken* the author's argument?

- **A.** Students only benefit from educational games if they engaged in play during childhood.
- **B.** Students are graduating from high schools with higher GPAs than in previous years.
- **C.** High school drop-out rates have increased in the last ten years.
- **D.** More students are attending college than in the past.

Passage 5 (Questions 23-29)

In recent years, there has been significant interest in the writings of Voltairine de Cleyre, a poet, anarchist, atheist, and potential feminist. De Cleyre's literary writings were proficient, although they never concealed her political motives. One of the purposes of her stanzas was to show her support of those who have used violence, and her desire to memorialize and celebrate their courage.

De Cleyre's anarchism lies in her sympathies with Peter Kropotkin, a Russian anarcho-communist thinker. De Cleyre reflected the same profound grasp of the power of ethical thought as did Kropotkin, and had no illusions that anarchism might be actually implemented in her lifetime—or ever, for that matter. Both anarchists ultimately saw the solution to women's exploitation by men as residing in a future utopia where it would be unnecessary for people to work very many hours each week. De Cleyre was the natural enemy of an economic system that reduced labor to sheer drudgery while starving the workers. She also believed that the state is by nature violent and exists to protect a minority's appropriation, by force, of the earth's resources, of technological resources, and of human labor.

De Cleyre's active exploration of the Woman Question manifested both in her published work and in private correspondence. She demanded the freedom to make her choices as a human being without the hindrance of feminine constraints. In one of her stories, an anarchist couple's relationship is undermined by the woman's need to perform domestic labor. The story is a vehicle for the writer's feminist ideas, allowing her to present women's work in the home as a form of labor exploitation.

The influence of individualistic anarchism can be seen in de Cleyre's ardent defense of "the sanctity of the individual," a passion that traces back to the asceticism of her Catholic school training. She opposed authority and the compulsion that it invoked, including loyalty to any particular strain of anarchism itself. Her time at a convent school led her to resist the oppression of dogma, and, later in life, advocate for complete individuality of woman.

De Cleyre wanted women to challenge traditional feminine expectations, to refuse to marry or to fulfill wifely duties. In effect, she advocated a leaderless general strike against marriage. She also lived in conformity with her feminist principles, which forced those who came into contact with her to confront her philosophy in the particular as well as in the abstract. However, her viewpoint does not resemble those of most feminists. De Cleyre was an outstanding political thinker who valued liberty and sought equality for men and women within an anarchist framework of social justice that would watch over the needs of all people, regardless of gender. To that end, she advocated the abolition of marriage, which she considered a repressive and unnecessary institution. Such a program is compatible with many feminist goals, but the attribution of the adjective "feminist" often substantially distorts the record of her many intellectual achievements.

Scholars have noted the imbrication of gender oppression with other forms of oppression in de Cleyre's feminist theory, commenting that de Cleyre may not really have a feminist theory at all, but, rather, an anarchist theory that, quite naturally, rejects the oppression of women. De Cleyre's analysis of power relations in general is deeply intertwined with a more specific analysis of women's subordination, indicating that anarchism's desire for liberty includes women too.

This passage was adapted from "Voltairine de Cleyre: More of an Anarchist than a Feminist?" Shone S. *Libertarian Papers*. 2010. 2(8). Online at libertarianpapers.org for use under the terms of the Creative Commons CC BY 3.0 license (http://creativecommons.org/licenses/by/3.0/legalcode).

Question 23

The author suggests that concluding that de Cleyre is a feminist:

- **A.** shows a blatant misunderstanding of her motives.
- **B.** is a definitive interpretation of her writings.
- **C.** adequately classifies her pro-woman sentiment.
- **D.** neglects to factor in certain ideals that she supported.

Question 24

Anarchism, as presented in the passage, can best be described as:

- **A.** an unattainable ideal.
- **B.** a violent political movement.
- **C.** an anti-authoritarian campaign.
- **D.** an emphasis on the individual.

Question 25

Which of the following statements would most *weaken* the author's conclusion that de Cleyre's Catholic school education led to her individualism?

- **A.** None of de Cleyre's writings date from before her Catholic education.
- **B.** De Cleyre remained a devout Catholic throughout her adult life.
- **C.** De Cleyre's father championed freedom of expression and religion.
- **D.** Biographers have noted eccentric tendencies in de Cleyre's childhood.

Question 26

The passage suggests that de Cleyre's similarities with Kropotkin lies in their perceived:

- I. role of anarchism in society.
- II. role of women in society.
- III. role of labor in society.

- **A.** I only
- **B.** III only
- **C.** I and III
- **D.** II and III

Question 27

Which of the following descriptions of advocacy is most similar to the author's description of de Cleyre as a feminist?

- **A.** A carnival worker on strike for equal pay for side show performers and ride operators
- **B.** A gay man campaigning for marriage equality for the LGBTQ community
- **C.** A black medical student supporting a patient advocate movement motivated by racial health disparities
- **D.** A first generation American writing editorials that support female immigrants

Question 28

De Cleyre had a child out of wedlock during the peak of her writing career. How does the birth of this child affect the author's argument that de Cleyre lived her feminist ideals?

- **A.** It supports the argument, because she did not submit herself to the societal norms around childbearing.
- **B.** It opposes the argument, because having a child perpetuates the traditional expectations of females.
- **C.** It fortifies the argument, because she chose her own path for her personal life.
- **D.** It undermines the argument, because the dependence of the child would remove some of her individuality.

Question 29

Based on the information provided in the passage, with which of the following statements would the author most agree?

- **A.** Feminism and anarchism are undeniably linked.
- **B.** De Cleyre is an anarchist, not a feminist.
- **C.** Atheism contributed to de Cleyre's anarchism.
- **D.** De Cleyre's disregard of constraints aligns with traditional feminism.

Passage 6 (Questions 30-34)

Even though women earning wages in the workforce are part of an established modern phenomenon, many of the biggest workplace challenges facing working women worldwide orbit around gender. Specifically, gender inequality in the workplace presents women with stubbornly persistent challenges with respect to scale and form of employment and remuneration. Links between symbolic patriarchy and gendered privileges must be examined in order to better understand the ways in which gender inequality and patriarchal ideologies in a given society are perpetuated within historical periods.

A look at gender discourse considers "masculinity" or the symbols of manhood as socially produced subject positions, while the rewards derived from this status indicate the ways in which male-constructed stereotypes discriminate against women. Symbols of patriarchy include objects, people, and events in the so-called "gendered world," serving to classify and organize the world into meaningful categories. But symbols of patriarchy can also reference imaginary things and fantasy worlds, or abstract ideas that are not in any obvious sense part of our material world.

Gender inequalities in occupational divisions of labor are best understood in reference to the concept of symbolic patriarchy, which shifts from the dichotomized vision of gendered individuals of women and men, and instead focuses on the intra-familial power relations of father or oldest male as "symbolic fathers" and "father figures." By extension, the term symbolic patriarchy also refers to a system of government by males, and to the dominance of men in social or cultural systems. In this way, patriarchy imposes masculinity and femininity character stereotypes in society, which strengthen unfair power relations between men and women. Imposing male-dominated stereotypes illustrates the mental frames of metaphoric structures and the deep-seated psyche of mindscapes that pervade the symbolisms of gendered patriarchal privilege and its influence on the social order. The concept of patriarchy can be directed toward social relations rather than individual men or fathers who are motivated to dominate.

The historical nature of patriarchy is complex, and patriarchies have a number of interrelated dimensions that vary across time, place, material context, and borders. These varieties are constantly shifting as power relations change in concert with other key changes. Symbolic patriarchy opens up spaces to examine privilege and benefit infringements in normalized places (outside individual men and women). The effects of symbolic patriarchy sometimes benefit one gender and estrange the other, and other times happen in the form of "patriarchal bargain" as in the case of female submissiveness in exchange for protection.

The concept of patriarchy evokes images of gender hierarchies, dominance, and power arrangements in a fatherless working environment. Symbolic patriarchy is increasingly becoming dominant in society and social institutions, and permeates, complete with its attendant symbols and metaphors, the institutions of civil society both ideologically and even practically. For these reasons, symbolic patriarchy must be examined further in the social conditions within which it operates and normatively manifests itself. The main objective must be to probe the gaps in the belief systems and raise questions about how power is gendered. The underlying assumption of this method of analysis is to direct attention to the varieties of patriarchy that retain gender as a central organizing feature, maintaining a hierarchical emphasis and allowing the discussion to focus on social systems and social arrangements that reinforce or permit domination.

This passage was adapted from "Rethinking Mindscapes and Symbols of Patriarchy in the Workplace to Explain Gendered Privileges and Rewards." Semali L, Shakespeare E. *International Education Studies.* 2014. 7(2) doi: 10.5539/ies.v7n2p37 for use under the terms of the Creative Commons CC BY 4.0 license (https://creativecommons.org/licenses/by/4.0/legalcode).

Question 30

Why does the author likely use quotations to describe a "gendered world" in the second paragraph?

- O **A.** To cite another author's beliefs
- O **B.** To suggest skepticism
- O **C.** To draw attention to gender inequality
- O **D.** To propose a new term

Question 31

According to the passage, which of the following characteristics is common to all forms of symbolic patriarchy?

- O **A.** Familial relations
- O **B.** Dichotomized gender views
- O **C.** Bargaining for protection
- O **D.** Specific power arrangements

Question 32

Which of the following assertions is LEAST supported by evidence or explanation in the passage?

- O **A.** Gender inequality in the workplace presents women with many challenges.
- O **B.** Symbolic patriarchy can be described as the dominance of men in social systems.
- O **C.** Symbolic patriarchy can vary across time and situations.
- O **D.** Further research must be conducted regarding symbolic patriarchy.

Question 33

According to the passage, if a female employee earns lower wages than a male employee in the same role, the most likely explanation would be that:

○ **A.** the male employee has worked at the company longer.

○ **B.** the male employee is more well-liked by the male boss.

○ **C.** the company is operating under outdated standards.

○ **D.** the company rewards stereotypes of masculinity.

Question 34

A study found that men with younger siblings were more likely to have dominating personalities. Does this finding support the author's argument about the origins of the patriarchy?

○ **A.** Yes, because they are more likely to have experienced a "fatherly" role.

○ **B.** Yes, because men enjoy placing themselves in dominating positions.

○ **C.** No, because symbolic patriarchy is not confined to familial relations.

○ **D.** No, because this information does not relate to the author's argument.

Passage 7 (Questions 35-40)

According to Joseph Needham, probably the mostly renowned scientist and sinologist studying the history of Chinese science, ancient Chinese interest was in combinatorial analysis, or the construction of magic figures. Numbers were arranged in such a way that logistic operations could be performed by referencing how the numbers were arranged in a chart. 18 standard charts, including the most well-known, Luo Shu, are popularly used by contemporary Feng Shui masters of the Compass School. In some schools of Feng Shui, 18 more charts are used, resulting in a total of 36 standard charts. One immediate observation of the original Luo Shu is that any three numbers along a row, a column, or a diagonal, when added together, give a sum of "15." This fact was also well known in the Western world, which is why Feng Shui is appreciated in other cultures as well.

The idea of the Luo Shu was not unique to ancient China. Magic squares were found in old Persia around the 10th century CE from the manuscript of Buzjani, a mathematician. They were also known to Islamic mathematicians in Arabia as early as the 7th century CE. However, it seems that there was no special application in terms of divination of such magic squares outside China in ancient times. In fact, there are 35 additional variations of Luo Shu, and all 36 variations are useful in Feng Shui study (though 18 of them are more popular today). No such variation was found anywhere other than ancient China. Once the Luo Shu is varied, the characteristic of "added together equals 15" immediately disappears. This finding may explain why variations were not common outside China, and why the Chinese still remain the most informed regarding the practice of Feng Shui.

The practice of Feng Shui could roughly be categorized into two schools, namely the Form School and the Compass School. The Form School studies landscape and water flow. Mountains and ridges are believed to be the source of Qi, the name of energy or natural force in all schools of Chinese studies, including medicine, martial arts, and meta-physics. The Qi flows down from high mountains and is dispersed by wind and stopped by water. A good site, according to the Form School, should have tall mountains at the back and flowing river in the front. By the two sides, there should be low ridges, called azure dragon on the left and white tiger on the right. Air movement is necessary at the site, and the river should be concave to the site with flowing water. In other words, a dead pond of water is not favorable. The Form School deals with the form only, and therefore has no temporal concern.

The Compass School concerns both space, in terms of directions, and time. After a good site is selected, the Compass School directs Feng Shui masters to determine the orientation or facing direction of the building as well as the best time to erect the building. It therefore involves the extensive use of the compass, as the name suggests, which is professionally called "Luo Pan" in Feng Shui study. The whole circle of 360 degrees is divided into 24 sectors, called mountains. Each mountain has a span of 15 degrees.

To dwell in a house, it is essential to determine the best locations for all doors and the allocation of main rooms to harness the beneficial distribution of Qi. Whether determined by the Form School or the Compass School, the practice of Feng Shui can greatly benefit residents of all geographic locations and backgrounds.

This passage was adapted from "Luo Shu: Ancient Chinese Magic Square on Linear Algebra." So ATP, Lee E, Li KL, Leung DKS. *SAGE Open.* 2015. doi: 10.1177/2158244015585828 for use under the terms of the Creative Commons CC BY 4.0 license (https://creativecommons. org/licenses/by/4.0/legalcode).

Question 35

The author claims that on the subject of variations of the Luo Shu, the Western world is:

○ **A.** generally supportive.

○ **B.** generally opposed.

○ **C.** mostly unaware.

○ **D.** uninterested in new ideas.

Question 36

Based on the passage, ancient foreign scholars believed that magic squares were:

○ **A.** useful concepts that could be applied to all aspects of life.

○ **B.** confusing topics not worth investigating.

○ **C.** related only to Chinese culture instead of their own.

○ **D.** interesting in theory but lacking in practical applications.

Question 37

The author discusses the two schools of Feng Shui with a tone that could best be described as:

○ **A.** detached, since the author writes objectively.

○ **B.** respectful, since the author values the two schools.

○ **C.** curious, since the author seems eager to learn more.

○ **D.** enthusiastic, since the author supports Feng Shui so strongly.

Question 38

Based on the passage, Feng Shui masters from the Compass School would most likely recommend which of the following to construction workers erecting a new building quickly in a city environment?

○ **A.** Find an area that is closest to nature.

○ **B.** Wait until the time seems right.

○ **C.** Pay attention to the orientation of the rooms.

○ **D.** Construct a compass-shaped building.

Question 39

The passage suggests that Feng Shui masters from the Form School can help with:

   I.   harnessing the beneficial distribution of Qi.

  II. planning the location of any building.

 III. determining the best time for construction.

○ **A.** I only

○ **B.** I and II

○ **C.** I and III

○ **D.** II and III

Question 40

Which of the following findings would most support the author's argument regarding the value of Feng Shui in various countries?

○ **A.** Feng Shui is practiced more often in Chinese cultures than any other countries.

○ **B.** Foreigners who adopt Feng Shui practices are as satisfied as Chinese citizens.

○ **C.** Foreign citizens report doubt regarding the success of Feng Shui.

○ **D.** Ancient cultures also discovered Feng Shui but gave it a different name.

Passage 8 (Questions 41-46)

The concepts of *climate change skepticism* and *climate change skeptic* are in wide use and refer to a fairly consistent family of arguments and pool of individuals that reject, dispute, or question the mainstream thesis that the global climate is changing primarily due to human activities and that these changes will affect severely both ecosystems and human populations if left unarrested. Climate change skepticism has a strong negative connotation because non-acceptance of the standard thesis is generally considered indefensible given the established nature of the science and the gravity of the problem. The concept is often used as a means to isolate and delegitimize arguments and individuals assigned to the category. Mainstream exponents have little difficulty labeling critics of the orthodoxy as "skeptics" or "deniers." For many mainstream adherents, it does not matter if one positively rejects, disputes, or is merely unconvinced, ambivalent, or agnostic about the core climate claims. The net effect is the same: non-acceptance of a thesis about which no doubt should exist.

It is noted that skeptics from different walks of life and with different levels of expertise deliver a wide array of critiques toward the mainstream thesis and display a wide range of intensities of belief (or nonbelief). Some act as vocal public champions of the skeptic cause while others reservedly express unease about the reliability of the science. Some evidently exploit the issue for personal gain and others are seen to raise their critiques as concerned and responsible citizens. These shades of the phenomenon are largely lost in both the public and scholarly discourse where the blanket labels climate change skepticism/denial and climate change skeptic/denier still dominate. On occasions where the concept is being disentangled, some contestation of the concept and its labels remains evident.

Some observers have tried to distinguish between skeptics on the basis of their motivations and, consequently, the modes they have chosen for airing their views. Most of these attempts are premised on the argument that some skeptics are merely using their climate views to advance their material or ideological interests, and because of this deception, they should be considered qualitatively different from those who are truly mistaken or misguided about the climate issue.

James Painter thinks it is useful to distinguish between organized skepticism linked to well-funded bodies and individual skeptics with no such links. James Powell distinguishes between professional science deniers who do it for money or ideological reasons and scientists who are "contrarian by nature," who revel in being different and provocative and seriously believe they are advancing the science by questioning the orthodoxies. Stefan Rahmstorf proposes three skeptic archetypes: paid lobbyists (those in the pay of fossil fuel interests), Don Quixotists (those who are "emotionally committed"), and eccentrics (scholars from other scientific disciplines).

Much of the mainstream response to climate change skepticism fails to convince skeptics precisely because the science is skirted for the sake of a grand theory that casts skeptics as ill-intentioned rather than ill-informed. Once the motivations of a participant are questioned, there could hardly be any chance of constructive dialogue and critique that might improve the quality of the science, the articulation of the science, or the debate in general. The right–wrong, serious–disingenuous dichotomies that dominate so much of the debate has made it difficult to engage skeptics in a discerning fashion, to direct chagrin at the egregious skeptic arguments, and give leeway and credit to those skeptic arguments made in good faith. Pigeonholing skeptics who are sincerely concerned about aspects of the science with those who are egregious and entrenched in their skepticism has an unnecessarily polarizing and politicizing effect on the participants in the debate and their followers.

This passage was adapted from "Climate Change Skepticism: A Conceptual Re-Evaluation." Van Rensburg, W. *SAGE Open.* 2015. doi: 10.1177/2158244015579723 for use under the terms of the Creative Commons CC BY 3.0 license (http://creativecommons.org/licenses/by/3.0/legalcode).

Question 41

The passage suggests which of the following assumptions about climate change?

- O **A.** It was unavoidable in the past.
- O **B.** It can be reversed if humans act swiftly.
- O **C.** Skeptical scientists hurt the cause the most.
- O **D.** Skeptic arguments should not be ignored.

Question 42

Based on the passage, it is reasonable to conclude that a skeptic's motivation could be influenced by all of the following EXCEPT:

- O **A.** morality.
- O **B.** stubbornness.
- O **C.** animosity.
- O **D.** responsibility.

Question 43

According to the passage, most climate change skeptics:

- I. refute a thesis that should not be doubted.
- II. do not like having their motivations questioned.
- III. eventually change their tune.

- O **A.** I only
- O **B.** II only
- O **C.** III only
- O **D.** I and II

Question 44

Which of the following statements is most supported by evidence in the passage?

- ○ **A.** The government should regulate lobbyists' influence over scientific issues.
- ○ **B.** With the proper approach, anyone can be convinced of the climate change thesis.
- ○ **C.** Skepticism is often not characterized by one belief.
- ○ **D.** Climate change should be taken more seriously.

Question 45

A grandfather believes cheerleading is not a sport. Based on the passage, what would be the most effective response from the granddaughter?

- ○ **A.** Stop talking to her grandfather about the topic and agree to disagree.
- ○ **B.** Bring him to a practice or competition.
- ○ **C.** List all the reasons why cheerleading is a sport without letting her grandfather present his case.
- ○ **D.** Argue that she does not think golf, her grandfather's favorite activity, is a sport.

Question 46

A new study found that most climate change is not caused by human activities. How would the author's argument be affected?

- ○ **A.** It would be strengthened because the author suggests considering all explanations.
- ○ **B.** It would be strengthened because the author questions the mainstream thesis throughout the passage.
- ○ **C.** It would be weakened because the mainstream thesis would be disproved.
- ○ **D.** It would remain unchanged since the author's argument does not relate specifically to the validity of the mainstream thesis.

Passage 9 (Questions 47-53)

In the United States, approximately 13% of children are clinically obese. Of those children who are obese, 40% to 70% will continue to be obese as adults. Obese children are at risk for health problems that usually affect only adults, including type 2 diabetes and cardiovascular disease. Furthermore, obese children have higher mortality rates than lean children of similar age. The societal and economic burden of childhood obesity is enormous, with approximately 14 billion dollars in direct medical costs attributed to obesity in children in the United States alone. Reducing the prevalence and alleviating the burden of childhood obesity is a global priority.

With regard to obesity, a comparison is drawn to addiction, whereby thoughts and feelings about food create disordered eating behaviors. Parents describe their children as craving, desiring, and/or working to get food in varying degrees and along different dimensions. Food addiction has been demonstrated in obese adults, and evidence suggests that food addiction may be present in obese children. One study found that 29% of 8- to 21-year-old individuals who participated in an interactive website for overweight teens and preteens reported being addicted to food and 37% reported being addicted to certain foods. Obese children who exhibit more addiction-like eating behaviors are more likely to report other disordered eating-related attitudes and behaviors. Addiction-like eating may be a problem for a subset of obese children, share features with other disordered eating behaviors, and pose greater barriers for parents and health care providers to adequately promote weight loss and achieve optimal weight.

For many parents, attempts at modifying desirable food quality and food access are met with resistance, persistence, and, in some instances, clandestine eating behaviors. Restrictive practices and increasing levels of parent control have been shown to increase disordered eating behaviors, such as eating in the absence of hunger, and have been associated with higher levels of adiposity. The standard of treatment for overweight and obese children and adolescents focuses on maximizing physical activity, decreasing sedentary behaviors, and improving dietary habits. In the short term, such programs have been shown to assist in weight maintenance and/or weight loss. Yet anywhere from 50% to 80% of children regain their weight in as little as 18 months. Weight loss interventions in the home setting are even less successful, with approximately 10% of children maintaining their weight beyond 2 years.

There are likely several reasons for unsuccessful weight control. One plausible reason, however, is that parents are unaware of or do not understand the emotional susceptibility of their child in relationship to food in times of stress or discomfort, and do not recognize the early compensatory response of emotional eating until noticeable weight gain is evident. In addition, children and adolescents may not be screened effectively for subclinical disordered eating behaviors by health clinicians. Adequate screening at child health care visits for disordered eating behaviors and emotional attachments to food may facilitate optimal and alternative approaches to weight management for affected children and adolescents. Emotion-focused family therapy (EFFT) has been found to be effective in children and adolescents with clinical eating disorders. Most promising is an EFFT approach that assists parents in becoming emotional coaches for their children with the aim of increasing parental awareness of their children's emotional vulnerabilities and providing adaptive strategies to reduce emotional eating. Such approaches may be more efficacious in weight control as well as weight maintenance in adolescence than standard interventions alone.

This passage was adapted from "Food Intimacy: A Parental Perspective of Eating Behaviors in Obese Youth." Laurent J. *SAGE Open.* 2015. doi: 10.1177/2158244015604688 for use under the terms of the Creative Commons CC BY 4.0 license (https://creativecommons.org/licenses/by/4.0/legalcode).

Question 47

A group of obese children were assigned physical trainers for a year and did not experience significant weight loss in that time. The author's comments suggest that this could be interpreted as evidence that obese children:

○ **A.** cannot focus on exercising when they are experiencing food addiction.

○ **B.** have already established bad habits that cannot be broken.

○ **C.** could benefit from psychological treatment.

○ **D.** need a strict lifestyle change in order to lose weight.

Question 48

A child's parents notice that he is snacking more than usual. The passage author would be most likely to advise:

○ **A.** waiting to see if this is a new habit.

○ **B.** buying healthier foods for snacks.

○ **C.** consulting with an addiction specialist.

○ **D.** asking the child about his motives for eating.

Question 49

The author argues that standard interventions for weight loss and maintenance in obese children are often not successful because they do not address underlying food addiction. These beliefs imply that:

○ **A.** children who cannot maintain a healthy body weight should be diagnosed with food addiction.

○ **B.** obese children who cannot lose weight might need further intervention.

○ **C.** obese children who do not receive proper treatment will grow up to be obese adults.

○ **D.** obese children who develop substance addiction are likely to suffer from food addiction as well.

Question 50

"The burden of childhood obesity" (paragraph 1) most likely refers to:

○ **A.** buying more food to satisfy cravings.

○ **B.** public health concerns.

○ **C.** the strain on familial relationships.

○ **D.** bullying experienced in childhood.

Question 51

Which of the following conclusions about childhood obesity can be inferred from the passage?

○ **A.** It is more likely to occur in unstable home environments.

○ **B.** It is especially important to address in children with other medical conditions.

○ **C.** It requires long-term treatment past childhood.

○ **D.** It needs to be addressed globally due to its increasing prevalence.

Question 52

Which of the following findings would most *weaken* the argument in favor of the psychological treatment for childhood obesity?

○ **A.** Children are too young to benefit from professional counseling.

○ **B.** Children with food addictions believe that their habits are out of their control.

○ **C.** Most obese children do not have a food addiction.

○ **D.** Adults can also develop food addictions.

Question 53

Which of the following individuals would the passage author most likely consider to have an addiction, as the concept is described in the second paragraph?

○ **A.** Someone who drinks coffee every morning

○ **B.** Someone who eats chocolate after completing a task for work

○ **C.** Someone who looks forward to eating lunch hours in advance

○ **D.** An overweight person who still eats excessively

STOP. If you finish before time is called, check your work. You may go back to any question in this test.

ANSWERS & EXPLANATIONS for Test 7 can be found on p. 267.

TEST 7

TEST 8

Number of Questions: 53
Time: 90 minutes

INSTRUCTIONS: Each passage is followed by associated questions. Read the passage, then select the best answer to each question. If you are unsure of the answer, rule out incorrect choices and select from the remaining options. Indicate your answer beside the option you choose.

Passage 1 (Questions 1-6)

Philosophers of language believe that each word used in our language must be distinctively defined. The meaning of a word must be established prior to discussing it. Words can be either concrete or abstract: concrete concepts are those which can be touched and defined, while abstract concepts are words unattached to anything real or tangible.

Throughout history, philosophers of language have debated the abstract concept of love. This investigation has included the tasks of distinguishing between the kinds of personal love, asking if and how love is or can be justified, and inquiring about its value. Specifically, those who have studied love extensively have assessed the role that love plays in improving physical and emotional wellbeing, in part through providing the social infrastructure needed to build relationship networks. Love may be interpersonal—a potent sentiment where both lover and beloved are human beings—or impersonal—love of an object, idea, or goal, such as volunteers' love for and deep commitment to a cause. In his famous book "Symposium," Plato discussed love in a dialogic form, concluding that the most qualified form of love is platonic (love without sexual attraction). Throughout the twentieth century, as the empirical sciences of biology, psychology, and sociology have developed, arguments around the definition of love have found their way into these fields. Empirical studies of love have relied on quantitative and qualitative methodology to broaden understanding of this concept.

Everyone has a conceptual image of love. Generally speaking, the general public understands love to be an intense feeling of affection and care toward another person; some people may construe it as a deep or abiding liking for somebody or something. People's definitions of love often vary wildly based on personal experiences and relationships. As a result, many believe that love cannot be sequestered to any single definition. Because of the complex nature of feelings and motivations that produce the sentiment of love, this emotional state—far above others—is viewed as consistently difficult to pin to one definition.

This mode of thinking about and defining love, which has been used throughout history, is not comprehensive or precise. Abstract concepts can be defined strictly. To do so, the common features of all forms of the concept must be determined, if possible, and then these features can be used to construct a pattern that forms the basis of the definition.

Suppose there is a concept, A, and that the possible forms of A are A1, A2, and A3. Given that the features of A1 are b, c, x, y, and z, the features of A2 are c, d, k, y, r, and z, and the features of A3 are c, d, t, h, z, and s, then the common features of A1, A2, and A3 are c and z. A can be defined as something that has two features: c and z. In order to establish a comprehensive definition of love, the common features of all forms of love must be determined. To do so, all theories and types of love must be taken into account.

The triangular theory of love states that the three fixed components of love are intimacy, passion, and decision/commitment. Intimacy encompasses feelings of attachment, closeness, affection, and connectedness, where people share confidences and various details of their personal lives. Passion encompasses drives connected to emotional and sexual attraction and limerence, the state of being infatuated with someone else, usually involuntarily. Commitment encompasses the decision to remain with another, and in the long term, to make plans with that other on the expectation that the relationship is permanent.

Aside from the triangular theory, other types of love encompass different components. For example, erotic love includes affection, passion, and physical and sensual desire, while altruism includes intimacy, care, commitment, and sacrifice.

Taken altogether, with current knowledge of all forms of love, the conclusion can be drawn that love is a strong feeling of affection for somebody or something that induces attraction, either sexual or emotional.

This passage was adapted from "The Concept of Love in Dostoevsky's 'White Nights'." Yousefvand M and Tatari H. *International Journal of Applied Linguistics & English Literature.* 2015. 4(4) doi: 10.7575/aiac.ijalel.v.4n.4p.23 for use under the terms of the Creative Commons CC BY 4.0 license (https://creativecommons.org/licenses/by/4.0/legalcode).

Question 1

Based on passage information, love has been defined by all of the following EXCEPT:

O **A.** moral philosophers.

O **B.** psychologists.

O **C.** individuals reflecting on their past experiences with love.

O **D.** those who study language.

Question 2

Which of the following, if true, would most *weaken* the author's argument about how to define love?

O **A.** Not everyone has a conceptual image of love.

O **B.** A new form of love is found such that the author's definition should now include an aspect of commitment.

O **C.** Taken together, individuals' own conceptions of love form a complete definition for love.

O **D.** Philosophers have long ceased to debate the definition of love.

Question 3

Based on his experiences with love, a philosopher concludes that love includes the components of intimacy, passion, and commitment. According to passage information, would the author agree with this finding?

O **A.** Yes, because the author presents the triangular theory as one form of love.

O **B.** Yes, because philosophers have concluded that intimacy and passion are common features of love.

O **C.** No, because the triangular theory is just one element of the model used to define love, and other types of love also exist.

O **D.** No, because the author argues against using personal experience to inform definitions.

Question 4

Based on passage information about abstract concepts, which of the following situations is most likely?

- ○ **A.** A biologist finds that people's abstract conceptions of 'friendship' fail to align with the quality of their actual friendships.
- ○ **B.** A philosopher of language presents her ideas on the abstract concept of loyalty and its value. She concludes her talk by discussing the meaning of the word.
- ○ **C.** A city mural can be defined as the resulting product of artistry, dedication, and collaboration.
- ○ **D.** Because the abstract concept of 'the mind' can be described as sentience and willfulness, sentience and willfulness share certain characteristics.

Question 5

Which of the following situations best reflects the author's argument about the general public's conceptions of love?

- ○ **A.** After reading a philosophy article, a man determines that based on the theories presented in the text, he should reconsider love as a product of intense affection.
- ○ **B.** Depending on the status of her marriage, a woman alternately views love as a necessary burden and the epitome of happiness.
- ○ **C.** A teenager changes her definition of love after every romance novel she reads.
- ○ **D.** A mathematician assigns variables with different abstract meanings to those in his life with whom he has loving relationships.

Question 6

According to the passage, how has the study of love changed throughout time?

- ○ **A.** Philosophers' arguments about love have shifted depending on which questions they are interested in answering.
- ○ **B.** Debates about love have evolved from being purely philosophical to incorporating experimental findings.
- ○ **C.** With the advent of new theories, love as a concept may now be considered a combination of abstract and concrete.
- ○ **D.** Philosophers of language have been replaced by empirical researchers as the major investigators of love.

Passage 2 (Questions 7-13)

With such dependence on mobile technology in all aspects of our lives, it is difficult to imagine that educators would not fully embrace and incorporate these devices into learning environments, especially given the implications for student learning and teacher training. Apple, Inc.'s recent announcement that they will "offer a series of software tools to make it possible to move education from textbooks to interactive digital lessons easily prepared by publishers, teachers, or others interested in creating learning materials" suggests the direction resources in education will take: digital and interactive.

Rapidly-evolving mobile technology has created opportunities and challenges for teachers and students. With the advent of iPads and other mobile devices came the ability to find, evaluate, and use information nearly instantaneously at any time and place. However, very little research has been reported in professional journals that describes ways in which educators can integrate the technology into teaching and learning in order to capitalize on the opportunities or overcome the challenges they will likely encounter as they move to integrate mobile devices into university coursework.

In one recent study, a professor was able to successfully implement iPads into a university-level course. Instead of the traditional paper-based classroom, this transitional classroom was paperless, focused on problem-solving, and emphasized teacher and student collaboration rather than the all-knowing professor. Because of the positive and collaborative environment that the professor created, the students responded positively and acknowledged this course as meaningful, engaging, and challenging.

The solutions to the challenges of mobile technology integration into all levels of classroom teaching and learning are complex. The one definite is that mobile technology is ubiquitous and will continue to change both teachers and learners as it is implemented in classrooms. Meeting the challenges will require more large-scale research to determine the effects of mobile learning on student outcomes. This will provide educators with insight into how exactly technology should be used, which will affect what technology will be purchased by school districts and universities and in what quantity. Mobile learning research must be more readily available for educators so that they know the best uses of mobile devices, and teachers and students must become better problem-solvers as the applications to educational learning rapidly multiply and change. Universities must also make the commitment to technology integration and must keep it on a level playing field so that all teachers and students are provided with equal teaching and learning opportunities.

With each technological innovation are questions about whether it is better than what was previously used or currently exists, and how we as educators should integrate each new innovation into the classroom. Historically, educators have relied on research-based instruction to guide the direction of learning. However, with ever-evolving technology, it is difficult to rely on the slower accumulation of research. Educators must become experiential researchers who constantly search for answers, evolve their instruction and become adaptable to the constantly evolving mobile technology. The idea of mobile learning and the ability to equalize learning experiences have significant implications for the future of teaching and learning. If the adage, "teachers teach the way they've been taught" has any traction in teacher preparation programs, then more research related to mobile learning will facilitate the advancement of using technology in teaching and learning. There are multiple points of "tension" for both teachers and learners as educators navigate the changes from Socrates to satellites.

This passage was adapted from "From Socrates to Satellites: iPad Learning in an Undergraduate Course." Wakefield J, Smith D. *Creative Education.* 2012. 3(5) doi: 10.4236/ce.2012.35094 for use under the terms of the Creative Commons CC BY 3.0 license (http://creativecommons.org/licenses/by/3.0/legalcode).

Question 7

The passage suggests that teachers who do not implement new technology in the classroom will:

○ **A.** eventually be forced to adapt.

○ **B.** have trouble finding jobs in the future.

○ **C.** struggle to teach students effectively.

○ **D.** be excused if they were taught without technology.

Question 8

According to the passage, the professor (paragraph 3) assumed he was successful in implementing iPads into a college course because:

○ **A.** each student earned a passing grade.

○ **B.** his course was entirely paperless.

○ **C.** students gave his course a good review.

○ **D.** his course rose in popularity.

Question 9

According to the passage, Apple is likely to offer which products in the future?

    I. Online textbooks

    II. Educational games

    III. Applications that budget time for each task

○ **A.** I only

○ **B.** II only

○ **C.** III only

○ **D.** I and II

Question 10

Which of the following conclusions would be most in agreement with a theme of the passage?

○ **A.** Technology has direct benefits on education.

○ **B.** Technological innovations are always an improvement.

○ **C.** It is up to teachers to integrate technology into the classroom.

○ **D.** Rapidly-evolving technology poses many challenges.

Question 11

A new study found that students were more distracted than productive from using technology during the school day. The author would be LEAST likely to recommend:

○ **A.** setting up parental locks on iPads.

○ **B.** giving the students time to adjust.

○ **C.** abandoning the effort and trying again with older students.

○ **D.** meeting with the students to discuss their behavior.

Question 12

Based on the passage, it is reasonable to conclude that educational technology's success can be affected by:

○ **A.** students' intelligence.

○ **B.** institutional support.

○ **C.** teachers' subjects.

○ **D.** which mobile programs schools implement.

Question 13

A college student plans to become a high school teacher. What advice would the author be most likely to give to the student?

○ **A.** Take a computer coding class to stay ahead of the game.

○ **B.** Study books about teaching that were published in the last twenty years.

○ **C.** Never take classes from older professors who may not have adapted to technological innovations.

○ **D.** Familiarize yourself with educational applications during free time.

Passage 3 (Questions 14-18)

Søren Kierkegaard was once asked by the Danish king if he needed solitude to write. In his diary he noted that he responded affirmatively. When the king asked if Kierkegaard would then seek the most remote part of the country, Kierkegaard answered: No, he intended to go to Berlin—"There I am totally alone and can work harder than ever." Seeing the king's amazement, he continued that even in the smallest hamlet "and incognito, I would not be able to find a hideout of 400,000 people."

It is customary to think of solitude primarily in spatial terms. On this view, solitude is achieved by occupying an extraordinary spatial position. Many ancient heroes and their modern counterparts have sought it, or had it thrust upon them, through adventurous travels to parts remote and unknown: think of Orpheus' descent into Hades, Gilgamesh walking the Road of the Sun, Crusoe alone on his island, Ahab's pursuit of Moby Dick, Marlow confronting the heart of darkness, Dr. David Bowman's space odyssey.

But Kierkegaard clearly had a different take on solitude. By placing solitude in the crowded city and within the limits of everyday life instead of in a remote location where events of potentially cosmic proportions are staged, Kierkegaard theorized solitude as an imaginary space, a self-invented Archimedean point from which to consider the limits and the potentialities of humanity. Because it requires no boat or starship, no island or mountain, it is available to everyone and, according to Kierkegaard, is also necessary for everyone. On his view, this imagined solitude enables a process of creative contemplation that allows us to see ourselves and the entire human life-world around us with greater clarity and compassion. Spatial solitude, in Kierkegaard's view, is spiritually arid, necessarily self-involved, nothing more than apartness from other people. But to imagine oneself alone in the midst of crowded, modern urban life is to embrace the tumult of humanity, connecting oneself, he believed, more deeply with others.

How differently solitude is portrayed in Shakespeare's *King Lear.* In the first act, Lear disinherits his daughter Cordelia, who loves him but refuses to flatter him. Lear's attempt to isolate Cordelia, to place her outside the natural and recognizable order of the family relationship, reverberates throughout the drama and culminates in cataclysm: war, murder, suicide. In disinheriting his loving daughter, Lear brings upon himself an infernal curse: he grows, by stages, more and more isolated as he realizes that he has badly misjudged his daughters. His daughter Goneril throws him out into the night when his retinue annoys her. Later, she plots with her sister Regan to murder him. Upon learning of the murder plot, Lear wanders the stormy heath, mad with rage and grief. His recognition of Cordelia as his one loyal daughter comes too late to rescue her from hanging. Having truly lost all three daughters, Lear despairs and dies. On this view, the solitary individual is one who has been abandoned by his or her fellow human beings—perhaps because he or she has abandoned them first. Solitude is the wage of disloyalty.

Paradoxically, the spatial solitude of the adventurer may point to a commonality between the disparate visions of Kierkegaard and Shakespeare. To leave (or to be cast from) the company of other people is to enter the wilderness, to walk in nature among beasts, gods, and monsters. Inevitably, the isolated person takes on the wild character of the creature he stalks, the storm that lashes him, the deity who thwarts his progress. It is only among other people that we are fully human.

This passage was adapted from "Into the Desert: Solitude in Culture and Literature." Larsen S. *Advances in Literary Study.* 2013. 1(3); doi: 10.4236/als.2013.13007 for use under the terms of the Creative Commons CC BY 3.0 license (http://creativecommons.org/licenses/by/3.0/legalcode).

Question 14

According to the author, the visions of solitude presented by Kierkegaard and *King Lear* differ in which of the following respects?

○ **A.** Kierkegaard's vision of solitude requires spatial isolation in order to facilitate contemplation, while *Lear*'s treats spatial isolation as a kind of punishment.

○ **B.** *Lear's* conception of solitude does not require spatial isolation, while Kierkegaard's does.

○ **C.** Kierkegaard's conception of solitude views spatial isolation negatively, and so does *Lear*'s.

○ **D.** *Lear* views solitude as a kind of punishment, while Kierkegaard's conception of solitude is positive.

Question 15

Imagine that another scholar believes that the author has misunderstood Kierkegaard. Which of the following objections, if true, would most damage the author's presentation of Kierkegaard's views on solitude?

○ **A.** In speaking of a "hideout of 400,000 people," Kierkegaard meant that no one is truly alone in a large city like Berlin.

○ **B.** Kierkegaard was devoutly Christian and believed that communion with God was the most important human activity.

○ **C.** In speaking of a "hideout of 400,000 people," Kierkegaard meant only that the crowded city allows for anonymity.

○ **D.** Kierkegaard spent a lot more time developing his views on the nature of God and the universe than on developing his views on solitude.

Question 16

The phrase "solitude is the wage of disloyalty" (paragraph 4) is intended to convey:

   I. that King Lear earned his fate through his actions.

   II. that others may perceive our desire for solitude as rejection and betrayal.

   III. that Kierkegaard's view of solitude is incorrect.

○ **A.** I only

○ **B.** II only

○ **C.** I and III

○ **D.** II and III

Question 17

The author would *most disagree* with which of the following descriptions of *King Lear*?

○ **A.** *King Lear* tells the story of a father betrayed by his children.

○ **B.** *King Lear* is about a disinherited daughter's revenge on her father.

○ **C.** *King Lear* is about the importance of showing loyalty to those who merit it.

○ **D.** *King Lear* tells the story of the downfall of a king.

Question 18

Which of the following would be the most effective criticism of the author's comparison of the differing visions of solitude presented by Kierkegaard and *King Lear*?

○ **A.** Kierkegaard and Shakespeare are not talking about the same concept.

○ **B.** The author has misunderstood Kierkegaard's view.

○ **C.** It is not possible to compare the views of a philosopher, who states ideas outright, with the views of a playwright, who explores ideas through stories.

○ **D.** The author has left important plot points out of his description of *King Lear*.

Passage 4 (Questions 19-24)

It has been 35 years since the Chinese one-child policy was launched. The root cause of this policy lies in an ideology that a falling birthrate offers a demographic dividend, as the economically productive proportion of the population grows more rapidly than the general population. However, one aspect of the policy that has been alarming has been the "little emperors" syndrome. Ungratefulness has become a serious social issue in China.

The implementation of the one-child policy has engrained the notion of "all for the child" in the minds of most Chinese parents of one-child generations. However, their self-sacrifice is often taken for granted by the child as the parents' obligation. In the publicized views of the Chinese Communist Party, much of the responsibility for this problem is attributed to "selfishness arising from economic marketization" or "bourgeois liberalization," in which, they claim, people are apt to lose themselves while trying to maximize personal gain. Based on its own self-interested, politically-charged interpretations, the Party has had recourse to apply a traditional means of ideological work to this social problem—campaigns. Recently, widespread gratitude campaigns have been launched by the Chinese government at all levels of education and across the nation.

Gratitude should be seen not just as the positive recognition of benefits received, but more importantly, as the act of returning kindness. Gratitude education campaigns focus on raising awareness of gratitude through activities such as writing articles in praise of parental love, sharing in family housework, and listening to parents' stories. By involving parents in these demonstrations of gratitude, the Chinese government expects that families will play a major role in gratitude education. Yet as important as children's consciousness of gratitude is, it is also crucial to develop in them the habit of undertaking acts to repay the dedicated contributions of others. The difficulty with gratitude campaigns is that they do not realize gratitude needs to be trained.

Gratitude, as a moral agent associated with personality traits, conforms to the rules of moral development. The American psychologist Kohlberg states that in order for moral values, including gratitude, to develop, a sense of justice is fundamental. In his three-staged moral development theory, he argues that children come to understand justice by following rules and practicing obedience. Authority and discipline function first and foremost to imbed in children a strong sense of justice. Past the stage of grasping justice, children move into a second level of mutual understanding and social conscience, which lays groundwork for the third level of moral development, autonomy.

A strong sense of justice crucially underpins the notion of responsibility, a product of human socialization and interdependence. Human nature tends to pursue and maximize material and spiritual comfort for itself. It is the sense of responsibility, unrelated to personal affection, which mostly drives people away from self-indulgence and to sacrifice—casting away considerations of personal gain in the form of material goods or spiritual acclamation—in order to repay kindnesses.

In contemporary China, there is little training on justice by schools or parents in one-child families, both of which the Chinese government expects to play a major role in gratitude education campaigns. Yet there has been no emphasis on the need for such training in the home or at school. What exacerbates this issue is that familial education on gratitude originates from parents who, born between the 1950s and 1970s, experienced authoritarian upheavals such as the Cultural Revolution. They learned the skills necessary to survive and flourish. These parents will do everything they can to provide for their families and prevent what they suffered from occurring to their children. Consequently, they rarely discipline their children. Without any kind of adjustment for misbehavior, young children fail to develop a sense of justice or, consequently, responsibility.

This passage was adapted from "How to Make a Grateful Child? Reflection on Gratitude Campaigns in China in Recent Years." Li S. *SAGE Open.* 2014. 1(7) doi: 10.1177/2158244014559017 for use under the terms of the Creative Commons CC BY 4.0 license (https://creativecommons.org/licenses/by/4.0/legalcode).

Question 19

According to the passage, Kohlberg's theory of moral development involves which of the following?

    I. A stage of collective understanding and social con-science, without which a strong sense of justice cannot be instilled

    II. The idea that without staunch moral values, there can be no justice

    III. An emphasis on the role of discipline in moral development

○ **A.** I only

○ **B.** III only

○ **C.** I and II

○ **D.** II and III

Question 20

The central thesis of the passage is that:

○ **A.** the one-child policy has produced Chinese children who are inherently ungrateful for their parents' sacrifices.

○ **B.** gratitude education campaigns are ineffective because they do not instill in children a strong sense of justice.

○ **C.** disciplinary practices directly create feelings of gratitude in individuals, such that they actively seek to repay kindnesses.

○ **D.** Chinese parents' failure to teach thankfulness is entirely to blame for the ingratitude displayed by Chinese children of the one-child era.

Question 21

The author believes that the function of gratitude education campaigns is most like which of the following?

○ **A.** Parent-teacher conferences, which incorporate family members into discussion about how to promote students' well-being

○ **B.** Educational reform, which incorporates empirical findings on how students learn best to improve academic achievement

○ **C.** Propaganda, which advocates for a beneficial social ideal while also endorsing an underlying agenda

○ **D.** Social media campaigns, which make the general public aware of an existing problem but do not engender much of a collective effort to resolve the issue

Question 22

Based on passage information, which of the following best reflects the author's depiction of a strong sense of responsibility?

○ **A.** Despite financial hardships, a couple buys a holiday gift for their neighborhood mailman in recognition of his service.

○ **B.** Out of love, a woman spends every night by her sick grandmother's bedside.

○ **C.** A child shares a piece of candy with his sister because he knows he will be applauded for doing so.

○ **D.** A teenager dutifully completes her chores every night because she understands she is obligated to contribute to her household.

Question 23

Which of the following, if assumed to be true, would most *weaken* the author's claims about Chinese parents?

- ○ **A.** Chinese parents who have had children under the one-child policy reprimand their kids only when they feel their children have made mistakes.
- ○ **B.** Chinese parents born in the last two decades of the 20th century have children who exhibit a strong sense of responsibility and desire to act gratefully.
- ○ **C.** Chinese parents believe their children should not be sheltered from life's failures because children who overcome obstacles are more likely to flourish.
- ○ **D.** Children in China feel stifled by their parents' stringent rules about what they can and cannot do.

Question 24

Given passage information, the best way to instill a sense of justice in children is to:

- ○ **A.** commend them when they repay kindnesses.
- ○ **B.** tell them morality stories about the importance of justice.
- ○ **C.** correct their actions when they have erred.
- ○ **D.** make their teachers aware of their wrongdoings.

TEST 8

Passage 5 (Questions 25-30)

While laws that permit or prohibit assistance to hasten death are evident in most jurisdictions around the world, the ethical dimensions associated with them remain deeply contentious. Assisting an individual in dying is unethical for some because of the inherent value and sanctity of all human life. For others, concerns about the authenticity of a patient's consent, the potential for widespread abuse of society's most vulnerable persons, and disagreement about the need for assisted dying in light of other avenues such as palliative or hospice care, raise resistance among some healthcare practitioners. Some commentators indicate that denying terminally-ill individuals an assisted death who wish it is perhaps cruel and unfair. Healthcare practitioners may thus encounter a tension between balancing the self-determined interests of the patient with their own autonomy, and the broader socially accepted duty of care by practitioners to patients at the end of life.

Respect for the autonomy of patients now underpins most professional codes of practice and also patient codes of rights. The dilemma now is that fear of losing autonomy or dignity during the dying process could lead some patients to request a hastened death. Evidence from Oregon's first year of legalized physician-assisted suicide (PAS) shows many terminally-ill patients worried about their loss of autonomy and loss of bodily functions, leading scholars to suggest that controlling the time of death was important to them. The scholars further concluded that the decision to request and use a prescription for lethal medications was associated with views on autonomy and control, not with fear of intractable pain or concern about financial loss.

Other experts argue that PAS is in fact an impediment to an individual's autonomy. These experts claim that PAS ultimately extends the power of physicians in regulating death. They say that a person's right to do with their bodies what they will is relevantly different from a right to demand hastened-death assistance from others. Even where a right to die is recognized in a country, it does not oblige someone to assist another person to die. The healthcare practitioner is an autonomous agent. Some have argued that respecting healthcare professionals' autonomy necessitates that they cannot be required – against their will - to assist patients to die, an argument that obliges some practitioners to refer patients to someone else who will help them achieve a hastened death.

The role of healthcare providers near the end of life has shifted over time from that of healer and decision-maker to one that may be better articulated as a chaperone or companion through a highly normal but often difficult life process. Some claim that if doctors were to engage in assisted suicide or euthanasia, the fundamental distinction between the physician as healer and the physician as killer would be vaporized: morality would be severed from mortality. Others argue that doctors are educated to preserve life, not to take it. They claim that PAS does not fall within the remit of treatments or healthcare interventions and so PAS cannot be in a patient's best interest.

Other clinicians and academics have argued that the role of the doctor may extend to assisting a competent patient to die when that person's life has become unbearable for them. They also stated that this assistance must be a practice of last resort. One general

Next ▶

practice physician stated: "If somebody did make that autonomous choice for PAS, I wouldn't wish to disengage myself from it and actually it is probably the last service you can render to somebody in that situation."

Question 25

Suppose that a physician who believes in the sanctity of life is asked by a patient to hasten that patient's death. Information from the passage suggests that:

○ **A.** the physician is required to administer PAS to preserve the patient's autonomy.

○ **B.** the physician is not required to perform PAS because it is not a duty of a physician.

○ **C.** the physician can choose not to perform PAS for personal reasons.

○ **D.** the physician must perform PAS if the patient gives informed consent.

Question 26

Which of the following conclusions about the role of health care practitioners can be inferred from the passage?

○ **A.** Physicians are meant to provide care, not to harm their patients.

○ **B.** Physicians guide patients to the decisions that they think are best for the patient.

○ **C.** The role of a physician is to give their patients the care they desire.

○ **D.** The role of a physician is changing due to a changing climate of health care.

Question 27

The phrase "vulnerable persons" in paragraph 1 most likely refers to:

○ **A.** the patients, because people at the end of life are often dependent on others.

○ **B.** the patients, because people on the edge of death are susceptible to rash decision-making.

○ **C.** the doctors, because their profession puts them at risk of dire consequences with failure.

○ **D.** the doctors, because they are at risk of malpractice lawsuits every time they perform PAS.

Question 28

Assume that a hospital without a legal policy prohibiting or allowing physician-assisted suicide refused to assist in a patient's death. Information in the passage suggests that this situation could reasonably be interpreted as evidence that:

○ **A.** the autonomy of the physician is greater than the autonomy of the patient.

○ **B.** the hospital has determined that PAS ultimately harms patients.

○ **C.** the physicians at the hospital are permitted to make independent decisions.

○ **D.** the sanctity of life is valued over relieving the patient from prolonged pain.

Question 29

Which of the following statements most closely describes an assumption made by the "other experts" in paragraph 3?

○ **A.** Patient autonomy is one of the most important considerations in discussing end-of-life care.

○ **B.** Society believes that people have a right to make their own decisions about their bodies.

○ **C.** If physician-assisted suicide were legalized, physicians would be given considerable leeway in distributing their services.

○ **D.** Healthcare has become a commodity in which its customers can ask for the services they would like rendered.

Question 30

In paragraph 4, the author discusses the line crossed when a physician becomes a killer. Which of the following situations is most analogous to this breach?

○ **A.** A banker becoming a bank robber because of his wife's medical bills

○ **B.** A superhero becoming a supervillain because she was betrayed by her allies

○ **C.** An artist becoming a forger because a curator needed a specific piece

○ **D.** A computer specialist becoming a hacker because she was promoted to electronic security

Passage 6 (Questions 31-35)

In the early stages of literacy growth and development, young children make critical decisions about what they like and do not like to read, view, or listen to when it comes to literature. Babies, by 6 months, already have the fine motor, visual, language, and hearing capacities to enjoy listening to literature. To think that critical taste in reading material only develops over time or is dependent on the child being able to read ignores what we have experienced firsthand as parents and teachers. Children use all of their senses, where emotion and intellect unite to make meaning of the world around them. Personal interest in literature is determined in large part by the personality of the reader, the characteristics of the text, and the interaction between the two, as well as background knowledge. Some research has demonstrated that students select their favorite literature based on psychological factors such as novelty, surprise, and the unexpectedness of events or ideas, whereas other research has indicated that students' personal choices in literature relate more to the genre and format of the text.

What happens so often within the context of literature selection is that there is a contradiction between what students view as literature worthy of reading for enjoyment and what teachers view as important and necessary to read for the sake of learning. Many teachers feel pressured to restrict students' choices to reading books that they consider challenging, presenting new information or vocabulary, or books from an approved reading list, for the sake of making the reading count.

Past research has confirmed that students who are allowed to choose their own reading materials are more motivated to read, expend more effort, and gain better understanding of the text. Shirley Brice Heath contended that students' special interests often lead them into reading a broad range of texts, including more genres than students read in previous decades.

We know that when students are excited about what they are reading, they quite naturally want to share their experiences with others. It is through this social interaction or communication with others that students find out about interesting literature, thereby piquing their curiosity and increasing their confidence in their ability to succeed in reading. Researchers have found that instruction that incorporates social interaction about texts increases students' motivation to read and reading comprehension achievement. Students sought out each other in relation to their shared literacy interests, and friendships grew based on the amount of time any chosen friend was willing to put into exploring expertise with different forms of literacy.

Reading achievement and positive student attitudes about reading have both been linked to time spent reading self-selected reading materials during school. However, instructional programs such as Sustained Silent Reading, Drop Everything and Read, and Free Voluntary Reading have been pushed aside and replaced with skills instruction and test preparations. Teachers are being pressured to demonstrate student achievement through high-stakes tests. Therefore, teachers are preparing their students to take these tests rather than building lifelong aspects of reading enjoyment within their students. To highlight this quandary, Frank Serafini so aptly said, "Lifelong readers do not pick up books to get better at reading."

This passage was adapted from "Revealing Relationships: First Graders Share Personal Literature." Weih T. *SAGE Open.* 2014. doi: 10.1177/2158244014529438 for use under the terms of the Creative Commons CC BY 4.0 license (https://creativecommons.org/licenses/by/4.0/legalcode).

Question 31

According to the passage, valuable literature that increases reading skills:

○ **A.** is read in the context of the classroom, but never chosen independently.

○ **B.** can be read either in the context of the classroom or chosen independently.

○ **C.** is chosen independently, but never read in the context of the classroom.

○ **D.** is neither read in the context of the classroom nor chosen independently.

Question 32

An experiment found that avid readers tend to form friendships with one another in school. Based on the passage, the most likely explanation for this finding is that:

○ **A.** readers like to discuss literature together.

○ **B.** readers are often more social than non-readers.

○ **C.** students with similar reading skills are grouped together on assignments.

○ **D.** students who enjoy reading possess a similar set of values in other aspects of life.

Question 33

The author quotes Frank Serafini's claim that avid readers "do not pick up books to get better at reading" (paragraph 5). Serafini's point is most likely that:

○ **A.** an individual must put in effort to become a strong reader.

○ **B.** strong readers are born, not bred.

○ **C.** specific reading material can affect the development of reading skills.

○ **D.** reading skills develop naturally while reading.

Question 34

Based on information in the passage, which of the following conclusions is most likely to be true?

○ **A.** Fiction novels are the most popular choice for children reading for pleasure.

○ **B.** Children with similar personalities may enjoy vastly different books.

○ **C.** Book sales have declined with the increased focus on standardized testing in schools.

○ **D.** Children must reach a certain age in order to enjoy reading.

Question 35

Suppose a child wants to read a book of her choice with her father. According to the passage, how should her father respond to most increase her reading skills?

○ **A.** Agree to read the book alongside her

○ **B.** Encourage her to read alone

○ **C.** Suggest a more challenging novel

○ **D.** Offer to read his own book beside her

Passage 7 (Questions 36-41)

At the United Nations' Vienna Convention, ninety-two nations created a treaty that standardized consular law, that is, the legal abilities of a consul or ambassador residing in a host country, including consular rights, privileges, and duties. The United States Senate ratified this treaty, which ensures communication and contact with foreign nationals in the receiving state and requires that the receiving state notify a detained or imprisoned foreign national of his right to contact his consular post without delay. Mexico has an extensive and increasingly sophisticated program of consular assistance to Mexican nationals residing in the U.S. due to the high number of Mexican nationals facing U.S. death sentences.

Mexican government officials claim that the U.S. repeatedly violates the Vienna Convention, yet the U.S. has remained impervious to international pressure, demonstrating federal unwillingness to control state action because it values their states' rights to uphold their own criminal laws. The U.S. argues that their liberty and democracy should have no constraints, not even by the United Nations (UN), and this individualistic spirit has led the country to become increasingly isolated from other industrialized countries as a death penalty hold out.

The International Court of Justice heard *Mexico v. United States of America* and found that the U.S. had breached its obligations by failing to notify Mexican nationals of their rights, and continued to violate these rights by not reviewing and reconsidering the nationals' sentences in light of the breaches.

The U.S. argues that it has made sufficient efforts to educate law enforcement officers about the Vienna Convention, pointing out the 100,000 copies of a compliance manual and 600,000 pocket cards now in circulation. It appears that law enforcement agencies in major metropolitan areas are not convinced of the need to secure the consular rights of foreign nationals. A host of solutions has been suggested, including improving educational measures at all levels of law enforcement and incorporating the right to consular assistance into the Miranda warning given at the time of arrest, though this addition may be met with resistance. The district attorney is responsible for ensuring consular rights in lieu of the police force, but the defendant may already be prejudiced by a confession or some other action that could be used as evidence of his guilt. To ensure that the justice system enforces treaty rights, cases could be dismissed or evidence thrown out when officers fail to comply with consular rights.

Some argue that despite attention to violations of the Vienna Convention and subsequent protest from the International Court of Justice, the strength of the evidence in these foreign nationals' cases is overwhelming, and there is little to suggest that their cases were somehow prejudiced. When a Mexican national murdered a sixteen-year-old in San Antonio, the evidence was undeniable. After his conviction, he exhausted his appeals as he sought both state and federal collateral relief in the same manner as a U.S. citizen. As such, the issues in these cases with respect to the Vienna Convention are not a violation of constitutional rights, but merely violations of a treaty.

Others argue that, had they been notified, the Mexican consulate could have provided experienced and highly qualified attorneys who would have at least presented powerful mitigating evidence at the penalty phase, such as information about the accused's personal history and past traumas. These advocates argue that the U.S. regularly assigns Mexican defendants public defenders who speak little Spanish and have no experience in death penalty cases. If the United States would follow the treaty, Mexican consulates would have the opportunity to provide defendants with Spanish-speaking lawyers who are well versed in U.S. capital cases.

This passage was adapted from "The Imposition of the Death Penalty on Mexican Nationals in the United States and the Cultural, Legal and Political context." Olivero JM. *Laws*. 2013. 2 doi: 10.3390/laws2010033 for use under the terms of the Creative Commons CC BY 3.0 license (http://creativecommons.org/licenses/by/3.0/legalcode).

Question 36

Which of the following policies is most similar to the provisions required by the treaty signed at the Vienna Convention, as described in the passage?

- **A.** Research students are allowed to bring fellow citizens as interpreters in foreign countries.
- **B.** Tourists are only able to use currency from their country of origin when traveling.
- **C.** Children in detention are given written instructions on what is allowed in the detention room.
- **D.** Transfer students are permitted to transfer all of their previous credits to their new school.

Question 37

Which of the following statements about U.S. law enforcement best illustrates an assumption made by the author in paragraph 4?

- **A.** Law enforcement officials are generally averse to mandated change.
- **B.** Officers of the law often disregard written instructional materials.
- **C.** The lowest level of law enforcement is facilitating the brunt of Vienna Convention violations.
- **D.** Police officers intentionally use tactics to intimidate and procure false confessions.

Question 38

Which of the following situations would the author consider most similar to the United States' actions as described in the passage?

- **A.** A soccer coach who encourages her players to sneakily trip players from the other team.
- **B.** A mother who chastises a child for being too loud while her own child is screaming.
- **C.** A teacher who refuses to give up years of lesson plans to teach for a standardized test.
- **D.** A doctor goes outside to smoke a cigarette after lecturing a patient about healthy living choices.

Question 39

Which of the following opinions about the United States is most strongly implied by the author?

- **A.** The United States cares less about its international reputation than its domestic reputation.
- **B.** The United States has no intention of keeping its promises.
- **C.** The United States is disrespectful toward foreign visitors.
- **D.** The United States is selfish in its policy making.

Question 40

Suppose a U.S. national is detained in Mexico without learning about her consular rights. Based on the information in passage, which of the following is likely to occur?

- **A.** The U.S. would retaliate and demand that their citizens be sent back to country of origin.
- **B.** Mexico would apologize and rectify the situation immediately.
- **C.** The national would be unfairly tried in Mexico because of a lack of adequate representation.
- **D.** Mexico would reprimand the arresting officers for failure to adhere to protocol.

Question 41

Which of the following claims from the passage is LEAST supported by evidence or explanations?

- **A.** The U.S. ignores the Vienna Convention in their proceedings with detained foreign nationals.
- **B.** Adequate information about consular rights has been provided to U.S. law enforcement officials.
- **C.** Violating the treaty is not as severe as violating constitutional rights.
- **D.** Information about a detainee's past could influence their fate in the court system.

Passage 8 (Questions 42-48)

The modern-day pandemic of obesity, with its spectrum of non-communicable disease (NCD) sequelae, is a truly new phenomenon, a transformation that can be charted across only a few decades; the World Health Organization estimates that since 1980 obesity has nearly doubled worldwide. The early harbingers of rising diabetes, heart disease, cancer, and, more recently, even dementia, are being vindicated with surprising rapidity. The unprecedented scenario of up to one in three members of the human race in the grip of a seemingly relentless obesity epidemic begs the question – is this epidemic caused by intrinsic or extrinsic factors?

Paleolithic artifacts, some almost 35,000 years old, depict obesity in its classical gynoid form, suggesting that early hunter-gathers were not entirely safeguarded by the assumed Stone Age diet. It has been convincingly argued that the 21st century epidemic of NCDs, including obesity, is attributable to mankind no longer enjoying the diet of our ancestors for which we remain genetically and metabolically programmed. Our Stone Age forebears were in no position to take nutritional advice or make the right "lifestyle choices," so given the apparent female propensity towards obesity, it would seem that nowadays the human race must be even more vulnerable, given what has been widely regarded by many experts as today's "toxic" food environment.

Social, economic, and environmental changes have marked the second half of the 20th century. Not least among the fundamental shifts is the altered nature of the human diet itself due to the radical transformation of the food chain. This may not be the result of dissimilar personal preferences or individuals' lack of understanding of "healthy choices," but is marked by the rise and dominance of agribusiness conglomerates. Global corporations have spurred monoculture, modification of the genes of staple foods, globalized production and distribution systems which eliminate seasonal variation, and cunningly contrived mass marketing strategies, which in turn have stimulated and sustained mass consumption.

Other outside factors range from the obvious, like the population's ubiquitous decline in physical activity, to less immediately transparent elements such as in utero conditioning and hormones mimicking environmental pollutants. The mantra of the global industries seeks to shift responsibility onto the consumer to make healthy choices while enjoying their unhealthy products "as part of a balanced diet."

Despite the over-simplistic cliché that excessive weight gain is simply the result of eating too much and exercising too little, there is much more to becoming obese than the old "greed and sloth" charge. Research has done a great deal to confirm that the etiology of obesity lies far deeper in the complex interaction of human genetics, metabolism, and environment. No longer is it scientifically acceptable to simply point an accusing finger of blame at the obese.

It has been argued for some time that there may be an association between rising levels of obesity and eating disorders. While it is clear that obesity is multifactorial and that in many cases internal psychological factors do play a role, the extent of the obesity problem across a large section of the population confounds any attempt at generalization beyond the recognition that obesity involves mental health concerns.

What is clear is that the failure to implement effective commercial measures to improve dietary health makes it certain that the obesity epidemic will remain one of the biggest threats to health in the 21st century. Whether or not it is too late to overcome the challenge, only time will tell.

This passage was adapted from "Eating and Obesity – The New World Disorder." Rigby N. *Nutrients.* 2013. 5 doi: 10.3390/nu5104206 for use under the terms of the Creative Commons CC BY 3.0 license (http://creativecommons.org/licenses/by/3.0/legalcode).

Question 42

Based on the information provided in the passage, the attitude of current scientific researchers is that obesity:

○ **A.** is a problem curable with gene therapy.

○ **B.** is an example of the nature versus nurture debate.

○ **C.** is not at all the fault of obese people.

○ **D.** may be treatable after further metabolism research.

Question 43

The passage suggests that our Paleolithic ancestors:

○ **A.** honored the obese, as they were inscribed in recovered artifacts.

○ **B.** ate healthier than the current global population.

○ **C.** had obese people because they were not affected by agribusiness.

○ **D.** were more adequately fed than the current population, based on their gynoid form.

Question 44

The passage suggests that corporations influence eating habits by:

    I. changing food composition.

    II. circulating global produce.

    III. promoting particular portion sizes.

○ **A.** I only

○ **B.** II only

○ **C.** I and II

○ **D.** I, II, and III

Question 45

Which of the following claims from the passage most *weakens* the argument that obesity arises primarily from extrinsic factors?

○ **A.** The Paleolithic population had obese members.

○ **B.** Global corporations allow people to eat out-of-season food.

○ **C.** Obesity and mental health are conclusively linked.

○ **D.** Physical activity is less prevalent now than ever before.

Question 46

Many extreme weight loss reality TV shows force their obese "stars" to blame themselves for their inability to lose weight. Based on the information in the passage, how would the author likely react to these shows?

○ **A.** There is a clear genetic component, so it is unfair to blame obese people for their size.

○ **B.** The blame is undeserved due to the abundance of commercial and socioeconomic pressures.

○ **C.** The blame is well-founded, as the stars make their own lifestyle choices and eating habits.

○ **D.** These people may have mental illnesses, so the obesity is at least partially their fault.

Question 47

In which of the following populations would the author be most likely to predict a high obesity rate?

○ **A.** An aboriginal population recently infiltrated by Western tourists.

○ **B.** A growing Third World country with an expanding economy.

○ **C.** A group of computer programmers with unlimited Internet access.

○ **D.** A future Western population with failed genetics research.

Question 48

According to the passage, the role of psychological health is:

○ **A.** paramount to finding a solution for the obesity epidemic.

○ **B.** not a factor in the rising obesity epidemic.

○ **C.** easily rectifiable in the quest to end the obesity epidemic.

○ **D.** a player of unknown significance in the obesity epidemic.

Passage 9 (Questions 49-53)

Some academics believe in a definitive understanding of historical events—they think they know the objective truth. Postmodern theory, on the other hand, suggests a different view of history than that of the nineteenth century. According to this historical perspective, the relationship between history and fiction is blurred. What lies beneath this change can be taken as the altered view of language. By the poststructuralists' arguments that result in the split between the signifier and the signified, language no longer carries the full and total meaning. When it is applied to the field of history and viewed through the lens of French philosopher Jean-Francois Lyotard's idea of legitimization, that which is accepted as "historical truth" is subverted. Lyotard suggests that his questioning of legitimatization undergirds his investigation into the status of knowledge. The availability of objective truth free from subjective dimensions is suspect.

This new tendency has infiltrated postmodern literary works, which has led to the creation of historiographic metafiction. *The Passion* by Jeanette Winterson is one of the best examples of historiographic metafictions, innovatively reflecting the tense connection between history and fiction. In *The Passion*, Winterson's treatment of the subject is exemplified by her use of multiple narratives, parody, and fantasy.

Rather than providing the historical events, seemingly unnecessary details are presented by means of the first narrator to emphasize the subjectivity. Moreover, the primary narrator Henri's diary is the metafictional vehicle in *The Passion*, which helps him to change his views on past. This is the primary feature of historiographic metafiction—combining fiction and history. The second narrator, Vilanelle, brings attention to the use of fantasy and parody in the novel. She is supernatural, passionate and free. The novel is one of the best examples of historiographic metafiction because it melds the disparate elements of history, fiction, parody, and fantasy into a semi-cohesive whole. As one literary critic said, Winterson enjoys "putting new wine in old bottles – especially if the pressure of the new wine makes the old bottles explode."

The rise of the postmodern historiographic metafiction has its roots in the changing views of both the concept of history and the concept of fiction. As Canadian professor Linda Hutcheon claims, both history and fiction are discourses that constitute systems of "signification by which we make sense of the past. In other words, the meaning and shape are not in the events, but in the systems which make those past 'events' into present historical 'facts.'" History and fiction are seen as constructed systems that reflect subjective points of view. Hutcheon's analysis also emphasizes that in the postmodern era the meaning underlying "the historical" and "the fictional" has gained another dimension. According to this perspective, meaning, in general, is constructed within an already existent system.

A skeptical view of these ideas has arisen in academia, and the idea that there can be no single, transcendent concept of history is becoming widely accepted. This understanding of history is reflected in Hutcheon's belief that scholars "can no longer assume that [they] have the capacity to make value-free statements about history." The interpretation of history is no less a subjective construct as history itself.

Writers of historiographic metafiction have an understanding of history and fiction as a combination. This combination has its own standards, such as the complex linguistic construction of the historical and the fictional, the subjective nature of this construct and the relative approach to truth and knowledge. Hence history is reconstructed and rewritten in historiographic metafiction. Postmodern fiction suggests that to rewrite or to represent the past in fiction and in history is, in both cases, to open it up to the present and to prevent it from being conclusive.

This passage was adapted from "History Rewritten in a Postmodern Novel: Opposed Views on History in Jeanette Winterson's *The Passion*." Esberk H. *International Journal of Applied Linguistics & English Literature.* 2015. 4(4) doi: 10.7575/aiac.ijalel.v.4n.4p.26 for use under the terms of the Creative Commons CC BY 4.0 license (https://creativecommons.org/licenses/by/4.0/legalcode).

Question 49

Suppose an English professor wishes to learn more about postmodern theory. Passage information suggests that the author would likely recommend which of the following actions?

- ○ **A.** Reading history textbooks to better understand past events
- ○ **B.** Interviewing historians to hear expert opinions
- ○ **C.** Using works of fiction to compare accounts of historical events
- ○ **D.** Treating fictional accounts of history as literal documentation

Question 50

The author argues that postmodern theory is valuable when interpreting past events. This belief implies that:

- ○ **A.** postmodern theory is the most accurate of historical theories.
- ○ **B.** postmodern theory involves questioning ideas.
- ○ **C.** theorists are more valuable than historians.
- ○ **D.** theorists do not need to propose new theories anymore.

Question 51

With respect to *The Passion*, "seemingly unnecessary details" (paragraph 3) probably refers to:

- ○ **A.** a description of the setting.
- ○ **B.** intricate character networks.
- ○ **C.** recounting historical events up until that point.
- ○ **D.** constant updates of the narrator's feelings.

Question 52

Which of the following conclusions about truthfulness can be inferred from the passage?

- ○ **A.** Concepts can rarely be considered facts.
- ○ **B.** Historical accounts are often inaccurate.
- ○ **C.** Skepticism can be a valuable tool.
- ○ **D.** Multiple accounts are needed to verify honesty.

Question 53

Which of the following findings would most *weaken* the argument made for the value of fiction when assessing historical events?

- ○ **A.** Historical textbooks propose multiple theories regarding the past.
- ○ **B.** Historical textbooks are often reprinted with new information.
- ○ **C.** Fictional works present biased views on historical events.
- ○ **D.** Fiction authors are not biased when they devise characters.

STOP. If you finish before time is called, check your work. You may go back to any question in this test.

ANSWERS & EXPLANATIONS for Test 8 can be found on p. 279.

TEST 8

TEST **9**

Number of Questions: 53
Time: 90 minutes

INSTRUCTIONS: Each passage is followed by associated questions. Read the passage, then select the best answer to each question. If you are unsure of the answer, rule out incorrect choices and select from the remaining options. Indicate your answer beside the option you choose.

Passage 1 (Questions 1-7)

In the September of 1921, 66-year-old Alfred Watkins delivered a talk to the Woolhope Naturalist's Field Club presenting his thesis that the landscape could be mapped as a series of straight lines or "alignments" that "connected ancient burial mounds, monuments, barrows, ditches, castles, ponds and trackways." Watkins went on to name such alignments "leylines." Already well published in the fields of photography and local history, Watkins' long walks across the undulating Herefordshire countryside had generated a huge amount of data, both written and photographic; his work indicated the age and locations of ancient monuments, hill forts, pre-Roman villages, churches, trees, follies and more. Watkins noticed that these objects and their places appeared to be aligned in an unmistakably intentional fashion: long, straight trackways appeared to etch their way across the landscape and Watkins attributed the causation of these lines as matching the age of the monuments that marked them: early man.

According to Watkins what he was describing was not, then, an enchanted genealogy, but rather simply a diagnosis of the facts as they presented themselves to him. For Watkins, leys indicate a forgotten and ancient knowledge, or rather a composite of knowledge; lost, historic and immanent. Watkins insisted that such an understanding was embedded within the landscape, left for us to uncover. Knowledge is only to be gleaned from three types of evidence. Firstly and chiefly, from what exists or is recorded on or in the earth of the work or remains of man of that period. Secondly, from what can be gleaned and surmised in place-names and words, for it is often forgotten that words were spoken in Britain for more centuries before they were written down than there have been centuries of written record, and there are indications that many words elements come down through both periods. Thirdly, from folkloric legends; lingering fragments of fact disguised by an overlay of generations of imaginings. In its Watkinsian form then, ley hunting is a way of retracing history: uncovering site narratives and reimagining the landscape, it is a particular way of knowing place, of developing a biography for and of place.

Leys belong to that classification where lines are engendered through a process of production; they trace connections between and bind ancient objects to the landscape, and as such, are valorized by something far more than just the provision of scale, distance, direction or destination. As lines, leys provide meaning; they suggest that our ancestors knew the land around them in a manner that many believe has been lost in the contemporary urban existence. Leylines enrich history through a deepening of our interrelation with the natural world and of greater import still, they provide a way of getting back into the landscape, of mapping, retracing, reimaging and resurrecting our position within and amongst places.

Leylines imply a meaning between places; they indicate a movement between spheres, areas that might once have appeared as the hostile milieu of otherwise abstract space. Watkins' leys, then, can be seen to make sense of things, to provide clarity through the making of lines and a close or "deep" mapping of landscape. Stephen Daniels explains Watkins' thesis not so much as a theory but as "a sorting out of previously unrelated and unnoticed information 'embedded' in the mind and on the ground." Daniels may be right, but the ramifications of this "sorting out"

have remained unexplored almost ninety years on. To be sure, when discovering leys, we are unveiling our surroundings as a "topography of generosity"; a space that creates and offers us a multitude of places in its very unfolding, providing new routes into and across the landscape. Through leylines, the landscape affords us possibilities for the (deep) mapping and reimagining of the world around us, ones that might not ordinarily have come to our attention.

This passage was adapted from "A Strange Cartography: Leylines, Landscape and "Deep Mapping" in the Works of Alfred Watkins." Thurgill J. *MDPI.* 2015. doi:10.3390/h4040637 for use under the terms of the Creative Commons CC BY 4.0 license (http://creativecommons.org/licenses/by/4.0/legalcode).

Question 1

The author's claim that Watkins' leylines creates "a biography for and of place" (paragraph 2) most nearly means that Watkins's approach:

○ **A.** allows a landscape to reveal its own history.

○ **B.** provides better connections between place and noteworthy historical people.

○ **C.** offers a personalized account of Watkins' own relationship to historical events.

○ **D.** provides an alternative to other mapping techniques from the same period.

Question 2

The author's primary purpose in writing the passage is to:

○ **A.** critique the intellectual premise of leylines.

○ **B.** encourage other scholars to explore the implications of Watkins' ideas about landscape.

○ **C.** provide a general introduction to the history of English cartography.

○ **D.** open a debate about the historical legitimacy of leylines.

Question 3

If the author convened a panel of experts to discuss Watkins' leylines, experts from which discipline(s) would most likely be invited?

    I. Urban Design

    II. Cartography

    III. History

○ **A.** II only

○ **B.** I and II

○ **C.** II and III

○ **D.** I, II, and III

Question 4

If another scholar were to observe that various historical events that happened hundreds of years apart are probably unrelated, how would the author of the passage respond?

○ **A.** Leylines can uncover unrecognized cause-and-effect relationships between events from various eras.

○ **B.** Watkins' project was not historical, but in fact an autobiographical account of his own travels.

○ **C.** Leylines provide an alternative and enriching way of studying history through landscape.

○ **D.** Watkins' approach is the only historical approach that accounts for all existing historical evidence.

Question 5

What is the author's primary purpose in quoting the scholar Stephen Daniels in the conclusion of the passage?

○ **A.** To direct attention to the fact that Watkins' scholarship has been neglected by recent scholars

○ **B.** To offer a subtle refinement in interpreting Watkins' ideas as something other than a theory

○ **C.** To offer the reader a more skeptical interpretation of Watkins' accomplishment

○ **D.** To draw attention to Watkins' idea that one space may in fact contain many spaces

Question 6

If a document were discovered in which one of Watkins's contemporaries describes the identification of leylines as an opportunity for personal creativity, Watkins would probably:

○ **A.** agree, because Watkins considered a variety of options before establishing his own leylines.

○ **B.** agree, because his extensive notes often digress into personal matters.

○ **C.** disagree, because ley lines are supposed to be an objective investigation of one's surroundings.

○ **D.** disagree, because Watkins viewed creativity as a historical rather than a personal force.

Question 7

Which of the following pieces of contemporary research would be most consistent with Watkins' approach?

○ **A.** An analysis of all the materials printed in a single 18th century English printing house

○ **B.** An annotated map of Park Avenue in New York City discussing all the writers who ever lived there

○ **C.** An anthology all authors who lost draft materials during the Chicago fire

○ **D.** A published study of folk music and illiteracy at varying distances from London

Passage 2 (Questions 8-13)

Some would argue that the term "building failure" applies only to major collapses of an entire building or structure. Others—particularly many forensic engineers—are of the belief that a failure is any component or system that does not perform as intended. This broader definition in the context of the building industry would include myriad building performance problems associated with roofs, facades, mechanical, electrical, and plumbing system balancing and control, and structural serviceability.

Failures do not discriminate or target specific projects. Buildings of all types can experience a variety of failures. Even on a large project the smallest of items can lead to an unanticipated and catastrophic event. In 2006, the failure of a grouted anchor caused the collapse of a concrete ceiling panel on an Interstate 90 connector tunnel, resulting in one fatality. On the same project, a more recent failure caused by something as simple as the anchorage for the light fixtures led to that fixture crashing down onto a travel lane. This failure created the need to temporarily stabilize a vast number of light fixtures, pending confirmation of the cause, and determination of a more permanent fix or replacement program. Galvanic corrosion has been blamed for this failure, a design condition that many professionals would not think to consider as a typical part of their projects.

A number of recent events point to inadequate design, planning, and construction of temporary structures as areas that need attention by the architecture profession. Fatalities, injuries, and, to a lesser degree, economic damages are stark reminders that these structures need increased attention from seasoned architects. Unfortunately, clear and conclusive standards for these types of structures do not exist and are resisted in most jurisdictions.

Most practitioners learn from their past mistakes and tend not to repeat them, but similar building failures continue to happen. A new Google Feed monitors reported industry failures and provides a constant stream of reports related to collapsed decks and balconies due to inadequate design, construction, and maintenance; inadequate temporary braced metal-plated wood trusses that fail in relatively light winds during construction; and façade failures of virtually all material types and sizes.

A sizable factor in contemporary building failures is education – not continuing education, but the process of "continuous education." As an industry, architects have limited institutional memory. What one person learns is seldom passed on to others. Continuing education addresses one individual at a time, while the next new hire or generation of building designers has to start all over learning from their own mistakes. Institutionally, some of the lessons learned from major failures and collapses have been incorporated into our codes and standards over the years, but even then, the origin of the lesson and context of the problems are often lost, making it difficult to apply the lesson to future situations.

The full details of many failure examples and lessons are not made public. Fear of blame, lawsuits, damaged business opportunities, and ruined reputations are all often cited as reasons for keeping failure cases under legal non-disclosure agreements and in insurance company files. Finding a way to at least generically share the lessons through more comprehensive failure dissemination methods and educational repositories should be made a priority.

As an industry, architects seem to be making progress on some fronts but regressing or stagnating on others. Every practitioner needs to make the effort to educate themselves and mentor students so they can learn from others' mistakes. The industry and the public in general will be better for it if we take up the challenge.

This passage was adapted from "Why Buildings Fail: Are We Learning from Our Mistakes?" Parfitt KM. *Buildings.* 2012. 2 doi: 10.3390/buildings2030326 for use under the terms of the Creative Commons CC BY 3.0 license (http://creativecommons.org/licenses/by/3.0/legalcode).

Question 8

Based on the information in the passage, a building failure is an occurrence that:

○ **A.** happens all the time.

○ **B.** signifies a lack of attention to detail.

○ **C.** is a new threat to the architecture industry.

○ **D.** highlights a vulnerability in architecture education.

Question 9

A recently built solar panel field fell apart because the couplings could not withstand extreme heat. Based on information from the passage, this situation can most likely be explained by the fact that:

○ **A.** the architect had never before worked with solar fields.

○ **B.** solar panels are not the focus of an architect's training.

○ **C.** the architect did not have a mentor.

○ **D.** the guidelines for building solar fields are flawed.

Question 10

Which of the following discoveries would most *weaken* the contention that mentoring students will lead to fewer mistakes?

○ **A.** Sculpture students learn more from viewing famous sculptors' works than from lectures.

○ **B.** Electrical students are more likely to wire poor circuits on their apprenticeships than in classrooms.

○ **C.** Medical students gain less basic science knowledge on clinical rotations than through the core curriculum.

○ **D.** Physical therapy students practice information gathering in controlled scenarios better than when interacting with actual patients.

Question 11

When the author notes that architects do not need continuing education but continuous education, the author's point is that:

○ **A.** architects should always learn new information, not just during designated continuing education sessions.

○ **B.** architects should find resources outside of the required curriculum to make the best building choices.

○ **C.** the current education system does not provide appropriate avenues for learning about building mistakes.

○ **D.** continually sharing information will ultimately lead to better architectural outcomes.

Question 12

Which of the following situations has the most similar purpose to that of the new Google Feed described in the passage?

○ **A.** A security camera that allows a manager to watch for protocol infractions among employees

○ **B.** A teleconference where biologists around the world can share their current research projects

○ **C.** An annual meeting of neighboring hospital administrators to review quality improvement plans

○ **D.** A telephone hotline that can share current traffic conditions with callers

Question 13

Imagine that an entirely new system for training architects were being devised. Based on the information in the passage, which of the following items would the author most want to include in the new curriculum?

○ **A.** An overview of the specifics of the most catastrophic building mistakes in history

○ **B.** A networking event to meet fellow architect students

○ **C.** A workshop on how to access information about new projects

○ **D.** A lecture on the need to provide better standards and protocols

Passage 3 (Questions 14-19)

The chariot, a straightforward application of the wheel and axle, might be said to represent humankind's first sophisticated mechanical technology, as opposed to simple machines such as the hand axe (i.e., the wedge) and the digging stick (i.e., the lever). Given the cultural conservatism which often distances itself from the new and sophisticated, it is remarkable that the chariot appears nearly everywhere in early Indo-European art and literature, whether Vedic, Hellenic, Celtic, or Germanic. Equally remarkable—given the ironclad physics of the wheel and axle— is the fact that the chariot has taken on the role of mystical conveyance, and has been so apotheosized in the famous African-American spiritual. The key point, in respect to Western culture, is that, from almost the advent of human technology, we find the arts engaged with it, and to the benefit of both—art finds fresh stimulation, and the technology itself is integrated into the landscape of the human psyche.

This virtuous cycle appears, at present, to be inoperative. On the one hand, there is a universal unease with the ever-increasing degree to which our lives seem to revolve about technology, but which technology seems to do little to ease our burdens. The visual arts, on the other hand—as per the example of the Renaissance, that sector of the arts most capable of assimilating and entering into a fruitful dialogue with science and technology—are currently preoccupied, under the aegis of "Postmodernism," with that which is difficult to characterize as anything other than ephemeral. At the very moment when we are depending upon the visual arts to create a mature vision of man and machine—and here we think of Monet setting up his easel at the Gare St. Lazare, or Rivera laboring over his Man at the Crossroads—we are offered ball bearings and slabs of black felt strewn petulantly across the floors of the Whitney Museum, or a cargo cult tribute to the Apollo missions at the Park Avenue Armory.

The fact of the matter is that no can one predict the outcome of our ever-accelerating rush into the embrace of technocentrism—Teilhard de Chardin used the analogy of a whirlpool into which we are being swept, and so I am not suggesting that we relax our vigilance. At the same time it is worth remembering that humankind—Homo Faber—is a technological species; that the machine, though perhaps now emerging as a threat, can also be a marvelous and inspiring thing, as exemplified by those rovers on the Martian surface; and that our virtuous cycle is one of the most definite and characteristic features of Western culture, and one in which art plays a critical and complementary role in respect to technology. The operative term is assimilation: not the mere referencing of science and technology, but their complete transubstantiation.

Hence it is that we welcome two new and related artistic movements—"Techno Art" and "Sci Art", respectively—which show great promise in restoring to the aesthetic realm not only a substantive engagement with science and technology, but also a focus on the visual as opposed to the anecdotal. This the former accomplishes by taking advantage of the incredible power of electronic/computer media (and thus also known as "new media art"), and the latter by realizing the incredible expressive power of the latest scientific imagery. Nor are these initiatives unaccompanied by that which is the sine qua non of a revolutionary art—i.e., the brash, new journal. In short, with Impressionism and Cubism and Constructivism towering behind us, do not many of us sense that there is something missing at the very core of our own endeavors? Must we not also suspect that this missing element might have been in part responsible for the futility of Postmodernism and Conceptualism? The visual arts may well be suffering under the effects of an evolutionary misadventure that occurred at a precise point in the 20th century—and the possibility of which misadventure has not to this day been widely acknowledged, much less addressed.

This passage was adapted from "Swing Low Sweet Chariot: Kinetic Sculpture and the Crisis of Western Technocentrism." Smith GW. *MDPI*. 2014. doi: 10.3390/arts4030075 for use under the terms of the Creative Commons CC BY 4.0 license (http://creativecommons.org/licenses/by/4.0/legalcode).

Question 14

The author's view of Postmodern art can best be described as:

○ **A.** enthusiastic.

○ **B.** inhibited.

○ **C.** dismissive.

○ **D.** unimpressed.

Question 15

Based on the information in the passage, which of the following pieces would the author be most excited to find in a contemporary art museum?

○ **A.** A collage of images generated by x-ray crystallography

○ **B.** An ink drawing of a water wheel from medieval China

○ **C.** A life-size reproduction of the Apollo 13 lander

○ **D.** A series of full-life scarecrows inspired by Bedouin cloth children's dolls

Question 16

Which of the following, if true, would most *weaken* the author's primary argument?

○ **A.** Chariots were no longer new technology by the time African-American spirituals were being composed.

○ **B.** Most post-modern exhibits make use of new imaging techniques.

○ **C.** Other scholars have argued that "Techno Art" relies heavily on abstraction.

○ **D.** Newer artists rarely understand how the machines they depict actually function.

Question 17

Which of the following best explains why the author mentions the artists Monet and Rivera?

○ **A.** To introduce two current artists that are part of the new artistic movements described in the passage

○ **B.** To provide an example of past painters who properly engaged the question of technology

○ **C.** To suggest that what artists painted before technology was a worthwhile subject

○ **D.** To show how Renaissance artists celebrated technological achievements

Question 18

The Italian artistic movement known as Futurism expressed complete enthusiasm for the power of technology. Would it be appropriate to call the author of the passage a Futurist?

○ **A.** Yes, because the author also sees the future of art in the effective integration of new machines and images

○ **B.** Yes, because the author shows enthusiasm for Cubism, which contributed to Futurist forms of expression

○ **C.** No, because the author is skeptical that technology is entirely good

○ **D.** No, because the author views new art as transcending nationalistic artistic views

Question 19

If a visual artist were to transfer images taken by the Mars Rover onto paper and publish it as a book, the author of the passage would probably find this artwork to be:

○ **A.** meaningful, because it draws upon the newest forms of human technology.

○ **B.** meaningful, because it brings the average human into contact with the power of technology.

○ **C.** not meaningful, because it would be better characterized as literature.

○ **D.** not meaningful, because the artist is not creatively engaging with the images.

Passage 4 (Questions 20-24)

To date, sports psychologists have had a mostly psycho-physiological or cognitive interest in studying the athlete from an individual point of view. Although groups are the basis of team sports, they have certainly received less attention as specific social phenomena. The majority of studies on sports teams use "individual" instruments such as questionnaires or measurement scales of attitudes and behaviors of athletes or coaches.

Identity in sports teams has been studied from two main perspectives: the first, an individual perspective, most widespread among sports and exercise psychologists, which focuses on identity as a cognitive and stable dimension of the individual using standardized scales, tests, and interviews to "measure" such an identity; and the second, a social perspective, most widespread among sports sociologists and anthropologists, which focuses on wider social variables and contextual features (such as cultural, national, and political issues) using narrative and ethnographic methodology. It is high time for a third perspective encompassing cultural and discursive psychology to be adopted. Individual psychological functioning is considered to be built in and affected through social interactions within groups.

Cultural psychology, particularly in its discursive thread, has laid the foundations for the contextual and rhetorical study of psychological constructs. It emphasizes the importance of the social and discursive context of interaction as the locus for the construction and negotiation of individual and social identity. This perspective utilizes communities of practice and natural interactive situations, in which the construction and negotiation of shared meanings about identity can be identified.

"Discursive" is used here to mean varying from person to person. The discursive manipulation of one's own identity or those of others appears to be functional to the achievement of specific rhetorical objectives. These rhetorical strategies highlight the fact that identities can be altered among members of a group rather than being a stable characteristic of the members' individuality. Consequently, identity should not be considered as a pure and stable unit but as a sum of acts of participation.

In pursuit of their rhetorical goals, members of a team segment their social world by allocating themselves and others to identity groups or categories functional to the presentation and sharing of a particular representation or interpretation of past, present, and future events. Examples are provided by the coach, who "taught" a certain attitude by discursively creating a group of older players (as opposed to the younger ones); by the player who gave salience to a group corresponding to a section of the team in order to emphasize its responsibility for errors; by the manager, who took note of characteristics of specific players in order to imagine their role in forthcoming matches; and by the team, which analyzed itself in order to determine its strengths and weaknesses.

One of the primary demands of social—and individual—life is to ensure the continuity of identities and interpretations of reality while also being able to introduce novelties and to cope with desired or imposed changes. For groups, and sports teams as well, this entails the constant sharing of information about the past and the planning of new courses of action, while respecting the complex array of roles, responsibilities, and specialist practices unevenly distributed among the various team members and in the socio-physical setting in which they function.

This passage was adapted from "Identity in Sports Teams." Zucchermaglio C, Alby F. *Psychology.* 2011. 2(3) doi: 10.4236/psych.2011.23031 for use under the terms of the Creative Commons CC BY 3.0 license (http://creativecommons.org/licenses/by/3.0/legalcode).

Question 20

If a World Cup-winning soccer team were participating in a research study, the author would most likely suggest studying the team members:

- ○ **A.** in individual sessions.
- ○ **B.** over a long period of time.
- ○ **C.** during training sessions.
- ○ **D.** while interacting with their coach.

Question 21

Which of the following opinions is most *contrary* to that of the author regarding the psychology of sports?

- ○ **A.** Past research has identified the most accurate theories.
- ○ **B.** Team members should not be studied individually.
- ○ **C.** Every sports team has the same group dynamic.
- ○ **D.** A sports team's identity never changes.

Question 22

Assume that a volleyball team gives an interview regarding identity negotiation. Based on information in the passage, which of the following statements about the interview is most likely to be true?

- ○ **A.** The athletes acknowledge how their identities have changed over their lifetimes.
- ○ **B.** Individuals discuss how other team members have tried to change one another.
- ○ **C.** The athletes describe themselves before and after joining the team.
- ○ **D.** Individuals list ways in which the team identity changed in the last year.

Question 23

Which of the following findings would most *weaken* the author's argument about studying identity change in team interactions?

- ○ **A.** Athletes prefer to participate in research studies individually.
- ○ **B.** Individuals experience identity changes whether or not they participate in team sports.
- ○ **C.** Athletes on a sports team tend to have similar personal identities.
- ○ **D.** Team dynamics are often not affected by individual identity changes.

Question 24

Which of the following conclusions would most agree with a theme of the passage?

- ○ **A.** Team sports build character.
- ○ **B.** Leadership roles often alter an individual's personality.
- ○ **C.** Social interactions are necessary for self-development.
- ○ **D.** Identities of team members are often in flux.

Passage 5 (Questions 25-31)

Buddhism is often looked upon to defend the reality of mind and consciousness from the reductions of scientific materialism, in which causal reductions of mind to brain affirm matter as the fundamental entity or property. Classic Buddhist thought understands the mind as arising in a way that depends on the body. While this may seem outwardly similar to scientific materialism, the Buddhist relation between mind and body is a purely phenomenological description that rejects both "mind" and "matter" as entities possessing substance or essential natures. The current Dalai Lama—perhaps the most eloquent and influential spokesman for what Buddhism has to offer science—makes an observation that is compelling to many: "Given that one of the primary characteristics of consciousness is its subjective and experiential nature, any systematic study of it must adopt a method that will give access to the dimensions of subjectivity and experience." This view questions the presumption that matter is external, real, and scientifically accessible, whereas mind is internal, subjective, and harder to empirically observe. Instead, perceptions of mind and matter are understood to be different kinds of experiences of equal phenomenological reality.

Appeals for non-reductive scientific studies of consciousness can reinforce a strong cultural assumption, in that they reinforce the conceit that the physical world—in contrast to the mental one—is the entity that is much easier to access. It is assumed that matter is "out there" for all to observe, unlike someone's consciousness, which is internal and difficult to empirically see. This is why the study of consciousness as consciousness, rather than as the brain, is approached in the manner of an apology. However, the Buddhist tradition of phenomenological observation has led it to note that all categories—including matter—are ultimately internal rather than external to consciousness. This recognition tempers the idea that the physical world is plainly "out there" for all to see with the observation that the dualism of "inner" and "outer" worlds is itself a mental discrimination. The result of this observation is not philosophical mentalism, or some assertion that mind is the only thing that exists. On the contrary, Buddhist thought exhibits its own brand of materialism, which confirms that consciousness is rooted in and dependent upon the body. But just as it rejects the idea of a soul-entity, Buddhist materialism does not treat matter like a real substance. Instead, matter is one kind of phenomenological event, which is to say, a way in which things appear to us in experience.

There are at least two benefits to exploring and understanding this Buddhist materialism. First, it offers a new and non-reductionist paradigm for using the language of "mind" and "matter". When scientists and philosophers deploy such language, the default Western philosophical framework encourages a view of matter in terms of a substance-essence ontology. Although substance dualism is now commonly rejected in favor of "property dualism," the logical and explanatory dilemmas both create are essentially the same. Buddhist discussions of matter, in contrast, understand it as a range of sensory experiences rather than as a constitutive substance or causal force. This avoids matter-only reductionism and remains consistent with the doctrine of *anaatman*, which not only rejects a soul-substance but also a substance or essence behind any and all "things."

Second, the Buddhist materialism I articulate here helps to clarify common misunderstandings of Buddhism. Buddhism is often described as consonant with science because it rejects the idea of a soul. This sometimes leads people to mistake Buddhism for a form of matter monism. The biologist David Barash, for example, thinks Buddhism agrees "that dualism is nonsense—[and] our minds are nothing but the result of mechanical processes occurring within our brains." Such confusions need to be eliminated. On the other hand, the Buddhist emphasis on the importance of the mind lead others to conclude that Buddhism is a form of dualism that asserts a "spooky" and non-naturalistic form of causation. This too is confused. Buddhist views confirm neither a monist nor dualist view of the mind-body complex. Instead, they operate entirely outside the long shadow cast by Cartesianism. Buddhist thought functions with an entirely different paradigm and thereby calls attention to a different way that one might understand modern scientific discussions of matter.

This passage was adapted from "Buddhist Mind and Matter." Cho F. *MDPI*. 2014. doi:10.3390/rel5020422 for use under the terms of the Creative Commons CC BY 4.0 license (http://creativecommons.org/licenses/by/4.0/legalcode).

Question 25

According to information presented in the passage, a Buddhist would not approve of the power of neuroscience to explain consciousness because the Buddhist:

○ **A.** would be reluctant to say that physical matter has an essential nature that can be studied.

○ **B.** believes that the mind is entirely dependent on the brain.

○ **C.** feels that neuroscience views matter as a phenomenological event.

○ **D.** supports a monist, rather than a dualist, view of the relationship between mind and body.

Question 26

Based on the passage, the term "phenomenological" (paragraph 2) most probably describes:

○ **A.** extraordinary appearances, like supernovae, that warrant the attention of both science and religion.

○ **B.** the apparent reality of experiences vividly imagined in the mind.

○ **C.** internal or external events that affect human experience.

○ **D.** encounters with the outer world that shape the inner soul of the observer.

Question 27

When confronted with the question, "When a tree falls in the forest, and nobody is around to hear it, does it make a sound?" a Buddhist would most likely:

○ **A.** agree, because events in the outer world always have the power to bear directly on individual experience.

○ **B.** agree, because no truth can be approached without a clearly defined question.

○ **C.** disagree, because knowledge of the tree falling does not qualify as a legitimate experience.

○ **D.** disagree, because physical events lack an essential nature outside of experience.

Question 28

Which aspect of the field of psychology would contrast most sharply with Buddhist thought?

○ **A.** The notion that inquiry into the varied nature of individual experiences is worthwhile.

○ **B.** The field's willingness to seek causal relationships between external events and internal states.

○ **C.** A lack of replicability in famous psychological experiments.

○ **D.** Psychology's indebtedness to psychoanalytic attitudes and methods.

Question 29

According to information presented in the passage, which of the following movie premises would most effectively dramatize a Buddhist worldview?

○ **A.** One journalist's realization that reality is nothing more than the dream of a child in a coma

○ **B.** The quest of French chemist Antoine Lavoisier to prove the existence of oxygen gas, despite the resistance of his contemporaries

○ **C.** The story of a bricklayer whose moods affect weather patterns

○ **D.** A tale of a detective who must relive the same hour until he solves a crime

Question 30

Which of the following statements best captures the author's objection to the understanding of Buddhism by scientists like David Barash?

○ **A.** In their inquiries into the physical world, scientists diminish the essential nature of the soul.

○ **B.** While the mind and body are both crucial to experience, it would be unwise to assume that one is entirely determined by the other.

○ **C.** Religion and science depart from the separate principles of spirit and matter, which are impossible to reconcile.

○ **D.** Science applies Cartesianism in a one-sided way that favors physical phenomena.

Question 31

With which of the following statements would both scientists and Buddhists likely agree?

○ **A.** It is possible to make legitimate claims about the world based only on the observation of matter.

○ **B.** Internal and external phenomena are best explored through causal relationships.

○ **C.** While the world is comprised of only individual mental states, science is at least able to offer a provisional understanding of common experiences.

○ **D.** Consciousness can only be understood in the context of the body.

Passage 6 (Questions 32-36)

Physical activity (PA) is associated with lower levels of cardiovascular risk and type 2 diabetes among children, and is linked with improved psychological health including emotional well-being, self-esteem, and confidence. Despite this, many young people do not meet PA guidelines of 60 minutes of moderate-to-vigorous PA per day. There is an age-related decline in PA during childhood, particularly among girls during the transition from primary (elementary) to secondary (high) school. Therefore, childhood and adolescence are key periods to promote PA and the development and evaluation of interventions to target PA during youth is a priority.

Schools are a popular setting for the implementation of interventions, due to their frequent contact with most children. However, many school-based interventions have not yielded increases in youth PA. Due to pressures to raise academic standards and improve test scores, curriculum time devoted to PA and physical education (PE) is limited. There is a need for interventions delivered at school, but outside of curriculum time.

Dance is a highly favored form of PA among UK secondary school-aged girls. Dance does not require exceptional abilities or equipment and can motivate and excite young people, not to mention its capacity to develop teamwork and creative thinking. Importantly, participating in dance contributes to moderate-to-vigorous PA among 11-18 year old girls.

In terms of dance program content, dance teachers' knowledge and experience can help to create a relevant, fun, and enjoyable dance intervention, while fostering a supportive relationship with and between the pupils. Dance teachers can enhance personal motivation and enjoyment by being autonomy-supportive (giving choice during dance sessions), providing structure (clear expectations guidelines and rules), and being interpersonally involved (showing interest and understanding pupils). These empowering strategies have positive effects on the motivation, needs and psychological well-being of dancers.

Although dance is part of the UK PE national curriculum, it is usually only taught during one term for six weeks. Furthermore, an audit conducted by the Youth Sports Trust raised concerns about the quality and equality of school-based dance provision. It was identified that only 8% of teachers had a dance specialism and 60% of PE teachers were generalists without dance qualifications. Limited curriculum time as well as the skills and expertise needed to teach dance suggest that current extra-curricular dance programs may not succeed in motivating adolescent girls. Rather, a program delivered by dance specialists who have adequate time to share their passion may provide an alternative way to increase PA amongst young women.

Guidance for the design and implementation of school-based dance programs is not available. However it is crucial to conduct and disseminate formative and feasibility research so that interventions can be developed that align with best practice and user group experience. Developers of extracurricular interventions need to respond to logistical challenges posed in school settings. A dance intervention can be grounded in behavioral theory and run by specialist dance teachers using a combination of teacher-led tasks and student-directed time with the aim of increasing PA. The intervention should focus on being fun, energetic and encouraging, work towards a dance performance element and developing pupils' skills and confidence to engage in dance and PA more broadly.

This passage was adapted from "Designing extra-curricular dance programs: UK physical education and dance teachers' perspectives." Sebire JS, McNeill J, Pool L, Haase A, Powell J, and Jago R. Open Journal of Preventive Medicine. 2013. 3(1) doi: 10.4236/ojpm.2013.31014 for use under the terms of the Creative Commons CC BY 3.0 license (http://creativecommons.org/licenses/by/3.0/legalcode).

Question 32

According to the passage, UK schools successfully use dance programs to do which of the following?

   I. Satisfy physical activity requirements

   II. Strengthen teamwork skills

   III. Motivate young women and build confidence

○ **A.** I only

○ **B.** II only

○ **C.** I and III only

○ **D.** II and III only

Question 33

Which of the following statements best supports the information given in the passage?

○ **A.** Dance programs in the UK are unsuccessful.

○ **B.** Dance programs require more funding from the UK school system.

○ **C.** Dance teachers often do not apply to work at school-based programs.

○ **D.** Dance teachers need to be passionate to be effective.

Question 34

The passage suggests that for girls, dance serves as:

○ **A.** an outlet.

○ **B.** a social connection.

○ **C.** a lifestyle.

○ **D.** a form of relaxation.

Question 35

Studies have found that the younger a child starts to play a sport, the more likely he or she is to keep playing that sport throughout secondary school. How does this statement affect the author's claims?

- ○ **A.** It supports the author's argument for stronger school-based dance programs.
- ○ **B.** It questions the author's argument for stronger school-based dance programs.
- ○ **C.** It is irrelevant to the author's argument.
- ○ **D.** It repeats earlier points about school-based dance programs.

Question 36

The author implies which of the following about adolescent women?

- ○ **A.** They are at greater risk for type 2 diabetes than adolescent men.
- ○ **B.** They do not participate in sports as much as men as they grow up.
- ○ **C.** They are disappointed in current school-based PA.
- ○ **D.** They recognize the value of dance.

Passage 7 (Questions 37-41)

Jackie Kay, one of the most important Scottish writers of today, was born to a Nigerian father and a Scottish mother in 1961, and was adopted by a Scottish couple. Kay's adoption places her in a trans-cultural environment; literature on "transculturality" describes it as oscillating "between hybridity and purity, fluidity and fixation, globalization and localization." This oscillation in theory may become a symbiosis in practice, with the person living in a transcultural community moving between the poles of such dichotomies. Kay's titular poetic sequence of The Adoption Papers foregrounds the interrelated issues of identity. This sequence represents identity as a riddle that engages Kay in a long-term quest for a solution that is never reached, or rather that does not take a stable form.

Although the daughter's potential sources of ethnic belonging – her birth mother and her Nigerian father – are not present, she shares the ethnic identity of her adoptive mother. The first step to the actualization of this identity is language. Her use of Scottish language in this poem implies that she has the ability to move freely across the boundaries between different aspects or concepts of identity. The daughter's natural use of Scottish in the poem attests to the fact that she linguistically regards herself as having a Scottish identity. She implies that parenthood is a concept that transcends the barrier of blood; biology does not play a decisive role in her sense of familial and social identity.

The daughter expresses her longing for information about her matrilineal relatives. She realizes that the family plays a role in the construction of her identity represented in "the soil in my blood" and "the land I come from." Both soil and land imply roots, a fact which suggests that familial construction of identity is as important as the biological one. She feels that biology is part of her identity, but she searches for her biological roots just because she wants to acquire knowledge about the multifaceted manifestations of her identity. While Kay recognizes in her writing the fictional nature of our identities, she is also aware of the need for those fictions to give us a sense of ontological security.

Her quest for her mother is for the sake of mere knowledge, knowledge which cannot alter the status quo. This may suggest that biological identity is less important than the familial and socially constructed ones. For the former is portrayed here as a mere idiosyncratic formulation or fabrication on the part of the daughter.

The act of fantasizing at the very end of the poem symbolizes the continuity of the quest and the willful and fluctuating formation of self-identity. The end of the poem does not resolve the questions that the daughter poses throughout it. Kay does not regard black or ethnic identity as essentialist; it is a marker derived from socialization and personal relationships. The same can be said about biological identity. In her imagined meeting with her mother, the daughter does not feel intimacy with her, and sees her as a strange person she does not know. The anxiety and boredom felt by both daughter and birth mother during this meeting shows that her familial identity does not relate to the biological one; she instead locates her true familial identity in her adoptive family.

Question 37

The passage implies that the daughter's feelings about her own identity would be different if:

○ **A.** she had grown up in a place other than Scotland.

○ **B.** she were not a mixed race individual.

○ **C.** she were aware of the fictional nature of identities.

○ **D.** she did not identify with her adoptive mother.

Question 38

According to the passage, Kay's use of Scottish language in the poem is significant because:

○ **A.** it demonstrates the daughter's affinity toward her biological mother.

○ **B.** it indicates that the daughter overcame her personal struggles and succeeded academically.

○ **C.** it expresses the daughter's identification with the cultural identity of her adoptive mother.

○ **D.** biological identity is less important than socially constructed identity.

Question 39

Based on the passage information, which of the following are accurate statements?

   I. The daughter feels that her identity is dominated by her adoptive mother.

  II. The daughter has thoroughly internalized her biological identity.

 III. The daughter feels a strong curiosity toward her biological heritage.

○ **A.** III only

○ **B.** I, II, and III

○ **C.** II only

○ **D.** I and II

Question 40

Which of the following statements is most in agreement with the overall theme of this passage?

○ **A.** Adopted children will not necessarily feel emotionally conflicted.

○ **B.** An individual's identity is not static.

○ **C.** A person's identity is the product of many influences.

○ **D.** Many scholars agree that language is a powerful expression of cultural identity.

Question 41

Based on the passage, the author defines identity as:

○ **A.** something that is fluid and ever-changing.

○ **B.** a set of values adopted from a significant figure in an individual's life.

○ **C.** something that is learned from one's environment.

○ **D.** completely fictional.

TEST 9

Passage 8 (Questions 42-47)

An early attempt to make creationism visibly scientific so it would be taught in public schools was creation science such as Intelligent Design (ID). According to the Discovery Institute, the theory of ID holds that certain features of the universe are best explained by an intelligent cause, not an undirected process such as natural selection. The Discovery Institute's website has almost 70 links to websites that disprove the validity of Darwin's theory of evolution by such scientific research as blogging.

Creationists often call evolution just a theory. Biologists do not claim to understand all of the details about how evolution works; they do claim that there is enough evidence to remove significant doubt about the existence of the overall process, and there is currently no debate in the peer-reviewed biological community about whether evolution has taken and is taking place. However, there are biologists who have taken an unusually anti-evolution stance, arguing through biochemistry that evolution cannot explain the origins of many biological processes. They also argue that while Darwin was partially correct, biologists often treat as infallible his flawed theory.

While many evolutionists believe in God, some do not. The most extreme group includes atheists, who tend to write in ways that antagonize religious people. Richard Dawkins points out that Earth's age according to religious teachings is incompatible with biological and geological evidence. He goes on to admit that God's role in evolution cannot be disproven. To him, the problem with religion is that it does not provide a basis grounded in evidence in support of its origin theory. If Dawkins had stopped there, his book would have been much less antagonistic to the many religious people, but he finishes his book by concluding that the only logical choice is to reject creationism and religion in general.

Because of people like Dawkins, researchers have pointed out that scientists treat evolution as a secular religion. Scientists get overenthusiastic in their claims, a fact not only observed by religious groups and political parities, but by the public as well. The number of U.S. citizens who embrace the theory of evolution has decreased by 5% in the last twenty years, and belief in the original tenet of "natural selection" becomes shakier with each passing decade.

Controversies in scientific disciplines and controversies in science education vary greatly from each other. While scientific controversy originates in the scientific community, controversies in science education usually originates with parents, community members, and administrators with little scientific or educational research background. Scientific controversies are usually caused by new data, while science education controversies usually grow out of non-scientific considerations. Just before the 1925 Scopes "Monkey trial," John Dewey wrote that the establishment of the public's right to vote on issues did not necessarily allow them to discriminate between scientific and unscientific arguments. In other words, people are often asked to vote on matters they do not understand well, and thus public policy is swayed by preaching to an uninformed choir.

The evolution vs. creationism debate has long been primarily between the vocal extremists on both ends of the spectrum, with those in the middle trying to compromise. In 1925, the scientific journal *Nature* published a letter attributing the debate to the tendency of both secular and religious teachers to pour equal amounts of scorn upon the other. In the relative absence of such moderate voices, the controversy of whether to teach evolution in public schools does not seem to be ending as quickly as most biologists would wish. Science and religion can both serve legitimate functions in human lives, but they are not one in the same. It is important for everyone to remember the common goal: a quality education for children.

This article was adapted from "Evolution in the Science Curriculum: The Need for a Middle Ground." Diamond BS. *Journal of Education and Training Studies.* 2014. 2(4) doi: 10.11114/jets.v2i4.488 for use under the terms of the Creative Commons CC BY 3.0 license (http://creativecommons.org/licenses/by/3.0/legalcode).

Question 42

The passage suggests that evolutionists and creationists differ mostly in respect to:

- O **A.** their choice to align with either God or Darwin.
- O **B.** their sources of evidence.
- O **C.** their interactions with each other.
- O **D.** their belief in the validity of science.

Question 43

Which of the following does the author imply about evolutionists?

- O **A.** They are all intentionally antagonistic towards creationists.
- O **B.** They only believe in factual and observable phenomena.
- O **C.** They should be in charge of science curricula.
- O **D.** They have a solid foundation for their argument.

Question 44

The author cites John Dewey because:

- O **A.** Dewey's statement is applicable to the controversy today.
- O **B.** the Scopes Trial was an important moment in the creationism vs. evolution debate.
- O **C.** the example emphasizes the low education level of the general population.
- O **D.** Dewey highlights the dichotomy between scientists and nonscientists.

Question 45

According to the information provided in the passage, with which of the following statements are many creationists likely to agree?

- O **A.** Dinosaurs and humans lived together because the earth was created in seven days.
- O **B.** Prayer should be allowed in schools so that students can exercise religious freedom.
- O **C.** The theory that the single continent of Pangea later split into the modern continents is overreaching.
- O **D.** Genetically modified plants should be banned because they meddle with God's plan.

Question 46

The author suggests that the problem in the creation vs. evolution controversy is that:

- O **A.** creationists have an inappropriate understanding of valid evidence.
- O **B.** evolutionists are too pedantic and creationists are too didactic.
- O **C.** the focus of the problem is not where it should be.
- O **D.** extremists are always combative and uncooperative.

Question 47

Assume a study finds that creationists are more likely than evolutionists to insist on keeping the phrase "Under God" in the pledge of allegiance at schools. How would this study affect the author's argument?

- O **A.** It supports the author's claims about the current state of public education.
- O **B.** It negates the author's claims about the current state of public education.
- O **C.** It reiterates other points made about the current state of public education.
- O **D.** It is irrelevant to the author's claims about the current state of public education.

Passage 9 (Questions 48-53)

In basket divination, a highly respected fortune-telling technique practiced in Zambia, Angola, and the Democratic Republic of the Congo, the diviner tosses symbolic objects of different sizes, shapes and materials into a woven basket. Those who have had the good fortune of observing a basket diviner at work often describe basket divination as a rational, analytical, and detached way of knowing.

Truthful knowledge in basket divination is not delivered as a set of abstract propositions flushed out of the diviner's mind. Instead, divinatory knowledge is delivered by an ancestral spirit that becomes objectified in three forms: the bodily pain felt by the diviner in his heart, the material configurations of small symbolic articles contained in the diviner's basket, and the diviner's translation of those meaningful configurations into words. In this liminal universe defined by spirit possession, knowledge is imputed to an ancestral spirit; this spirit, however, manifests itself through a human body that feels pain and operates the oracle by shaking it. Basket divination is the story of birthing knowledge to the world, and a part is played in this delivery by the mind, the body, and the spirit.

In comparison with shamanic séances and other types of mediumistic divination, basket divination seems awkwardly secular and deprived of emotion and spectacle. The picture of a diviner, always a man, shaking his basket with brisk, up and down motions and interpreting successive configurations of divinatory articles as these articles land inside the basket seems more like of an act of reading and interpretation than of a ritual. The expert diviner observes the patterns of articles and interprets their meaning for his clients, who do their best to follow. His clients sit across from him with deadpan faces and observant eyes, hiding their feelings of worry and apprehension. The ambience evokes seriousness, reflection, and resolve.

In light of this brief sketch, it is hardly surprising that basket divination has appeared to the eyes of foreign observers as a highly rational undertaking. Because each article has different meanings, diviners have to determine what meaning of an article relates to what meanings of selected contiguous articles, both in one configuration and across configurations. This difficult work is particularly impressive because the diviner must deliver his pronouncements without delay in between basket shakings.

This redeeming combination of epistemological and ideological factors has led, more recently, to the famed analogy in African studies between divination systems and Positivist social science. In some ways, these are well-intentioned and thought-provoking approaches that successfully highlight the intellectual and analytical aspects of divination systems. Scholars say that diviners are scientists, placing divination and science on the same footing, but they also say that diviners are Positivist social scientists because they value objectivity and detachment. Purportedly, diviners also lack a developed unawareness of alternatives in comparison with so-called "true" science, as historian Evan Horton said of African religion in general. Whereas Western science is open, African religions are closed. In this way, scientists promote and demote African diviners with one and the same stroke.

Portraying diviners as Positivist scientists does little justice to divination as a way of knowing. It is a generous, and bold, interpretive gesture, but it is also a glaring misrepresentation. Cognizant of this problem, some of the same authors who promote diviners to Positivist social scientists also show that divination knowledge, far from being an abstract intellectual exercise exclusively concerned with questions of veracity, is part and parcel of the clients' coping strategies and desperate attempts to assuage suffering. Positivist social scientists may believe that their work as scientists is disconnected from their daily struggles and concerns, but basket diviners know better. For them and their clients, divination is not simply a way of knowing, Positivist or not; divination is also a way of coping with suffering and misfortune by seeking help and taking action in a culturally accepted and spiritually sanctioned way.

This passage was adapted from "Mind, Body and Spirit in Basket Divination: An Integrative Way of Knowing." Silva S. *MDPI*. 2014. doi:10.3390/rel5041175 for use under the terms of the Creative Commons CC BY 4.0 license (http://creativecommons.org/licenses/by/4.0/legalcode).

Question 48

According to the author, what distinguishes basket divination from other forms of fortune telling?

- ○ **A.** The power of basket divination to make accurate predictions.
- ○ **B.** The high esteem in which basket diviners are held.
- ○ **C.** The sense of mystery that attends a basket divination.
- ○ **D.** The straightforward manner of the basket diviner.

Question 49

The interaction between the basket diviner and his clients is most similar to which of the following Western social practices?

- ○ **A.** A couple receiving news of important test results from a physician.
- ○ **B.** A therapy session between a psychologist and a client.
- ○ **C.** A family meeting with a bank lender about a loan.
- ○ **D.** A pair of suspects being questioned by the police.

Question 50

Based on the passage, the author finds the outlook of Positivistic science to be:

- ○ **A.** a useful model to study contemporary basket divination.
- ○ **B.** an emotionally limited form of pursuing knowledge.
- ○ **C.** indebted to the analytic tradition started by basket divination.
- ○ **D.** somewhat compatible with a basket diviner's worldview.

Question 51

How would the author's argument be affected if a study were released that indicated that some contemporary basket diviners had pursued and abandoned formal training in Western sciences?

- ○ **A.** It would be strengthened, because it would show that basket diviners are aware of other ways of understanding the world.
- ○ **B.** It would be strengthened, because it establishes a clear link between basket divination and Positivist social science.
- ○ **C.** It would be weakened, because it would discredit the notion that basket diviners are rational scientists.
- ○ **D.** It would be unaffected, because basket divination is a separate way of understanding the world than Western science.

Question 52

According to the passage, which of the following events would be LEAST likely to occur during a basket divination?

- ○ **A.** The diviner proceeds without pause through his interpretations.
- ○ **B.** The diviner consoles a client who weeps openly.
- ○ **C.** The diviner's clients sit silently and sometimes appear confused.
- ○ **D.** The diviner counsels a woman unaccompanied by a man.

Question 53

It can be inferred from the passage that the author thinks those scholars who compare basket divination to Positivist social science:

- ○ **A.** understand the limitations of the comparison.
- ○ **B.** have a narrow view of basket divination.
- ○ **C.** accurately draw a connection between the disciplines.
- ○ **D.** are disconnected from daily struggles and concerns.

STOP. If you finish before time is called, check your work. You may go back to any question in this test.

ANSWERS & EXPLANATIONS for Test 9 can be found on p. 293.

Passage 1 (Questions 1-6)

A comedy show may provide laughter and entertainment for audience members for only a few hours, but for a comedian, the show serves as an expression of their tireless hours working for a living. While some individuals may tell jokes for fun or perform comedy without compensation, this is not the norm for a comedy show. Comedy writing is characterized effectively by actor and comedian David Schneider: "It takes a lot of work to make a good joke. I know it's not work in the sense of a seven-year old child down an Angolan tin mine, and I also know some jokes just pop out spontaneously. But more often than not, the birth of a joke is a long, painful process, without gas and air, or epidural."

Comedians have said it might take them two hours to generate two minutes of material. Stand-up comedian Bethany Black describes similar levels of work. Using her own life and observations as her primary sources, she sometimes finds that ready-made jokes emerge. Her experience is that these tend not to be as good as those that require work. She aims to devote at least 3 hours per day to writing and tests material via social media, reckoning that about 20 favorable responses indicate that a joke will work. A comedian such as Gary Delaney, whose material consists of those tiny comic units we call "one liners," has to generate enormous numbers of jokes. Delaney records them on his phone as they occur to him. He calculates that only about 1 in 20 is worth persisting with for his own routines (though he may use the best of the rest in scripts for other comedians).

The nature of this persistence, which turns a comic idea into a well-formed joke, naturally varies from comedian to comedian. Even though critics and TV Commissioners always talk about the art form in terms of its content, it is the rhythm, pitch, tone, and pace—the non-verbal cues—that are arguably more important. Imagine the work as first identifying or creating content and then giving that content the form in which it can be performed successfully. Bethany Black identifies a threefold formula: writing skills, turnover of content, and a comic persona. Turnover might merely be based on the resolution to perform fresh material for the artist, but skills include both the writing of jokes and embedding them in a persona. The persona tends to be presented to an audience as if it is a truthful representation of the comedian's attitudes, beliefs, and behavior, but in fact it is always more or less artificial. This combination is intensely personal and, indeed, authentic even if it only represents part of the comedian's personality and natural voice.

On the other hand, there are comedians who describe their creative process as easy and natural. They pride themselves on their inherent humor and ability to convey that to others. Comedians should be able to react to situations with humor, rather than construct it in careful and refined writing sessions. Just as not every individual is cut out for certain professions, maybe not every struggling artist is cut out for performing comedy.

There is, in Britain and the United States and to a lesser extent in other countries, a content producing community that creates the thousands of small, often ephemeral, works of commentary on human life that we call jokes. In response to the demands of societal expectations, the writing of jokes has become a painstaking process, despite its essential playfulness. On every night of every year, comedians in pubs, clubs, and small theatres try out new material which they themselves have created in their own authentic voice, but this is only part of the story. The extent to which this material has already withstood the test of the creative writing process and time-consuming revisions attests to the validity of the profession of the comedian.

This passage was adapted from "The Production of Comedy: The Joke in the Age of Social Media." Sturges P. *SAGE Open*. 2015. doi: 10.1177/2158244015612521 for use under the terms of the Creative Commons CC BY 4.0 license (https://creativecommons.org/licenses/by/4.0/legalcode).

Question 1

The author's analysis of a comic persona rests on the assumption that the audience values:

- ○ **A.** uniqueness.
- ○ **B.** identifiability.
- ○ **C.** authenticity.
- ○ **D.** hard work.

Question 2

Which of the following passage assertions suggests most strongly that the author is critical of society's view towards comedians?

- ○ **A.** A comedy show may provide laughter and entertainment for audience members for only a few hours.
- ○ **B.** Some individuals tell jokes for fun or perform comedy without compensation.
- ○ **C.** Critics and TV Commissioners always talk about the comedic art form in terms of content only.
- ○ **D.** Comedians create thousands of small works of commentary on human life that we call jokes.

Question 3

Suppose one comedian is able to improvise her entire performance and garner successful reviews. This situation most *challenges* the passage assertion that:

- ○ **A.** professional comedy requires hard work.
- ○ **B.** professional comedy takes up an individual's time.
- ○ **C.** comedians must create a comic persona.
- ○ **D.** jokes are better received after social media approval.

Question 4

Based on the passage, which of the following would be the most likely reason for Bethany Black's threefold formula?

○ **A.** Comedians with dark personalities are not received well by audiences.

○ **B.** Comedians who steal jokes from other comedians are not received well by audiences.

○ **C.** Comedians who have not practiced their routines are not received well by audiences.

○ **D.** Comedians who do not write their own material are not received well by audiences.

Question 5

The author's main purpose in exploring the comedic writing process is to suggest that comedians must:

○ **A.** be prepared to cut jokes they have written.

○ **B.** devote adequate time to writing each day.

○ **C.** be strong writers, as they create their own material.

○ **D.** test new material online before performing it.

Question 6

Which of the following is most comparable to writing jokes for a comedy routine consisting mainly of one-liners?

○ **A.** Painting more landscapes than necessary for an art show

○ **B.** Filming multiple takes of one scene and discarding the worst ones

○ **C.** Writing short songs for a pop music album

○ **D.** Designing the sets for a play involving many short stories

Passage 2 (Questions 7-12)

Human beings desire to be happy. Most of our daily thoughts and actions have the end goal of achieving, maintaining, or salvaging our happiness. Yet despite the species clamoring toward these goals since antiquity, a formula offering a consistent, reliable path toward their realization remains elusive. People turn to myriad ways to achieve happiness, such as physical pleasures, relationships, or the achievement of goals. Success in these endeavors varies, however, and may not be sustainable. As Adler has pointed out, the framers of the Constitution of the United States could only guarantee the right to pursue happiness. They were wise enough to realize they could not assure that it would be attained.

Throughout history, philosophers, priests, playwrights, self-help gurus, and now researchers have struggled to understand what happiness is and how we can have more of it in our lives. Yet each of these approaches offers a perspective that yields different advice. Aristotle, in the Nicomachean Ethics, describes a happy life as a good life. He claims that we can judge whether a life was happy only after it is over. The Bible tells us something different. In the Gospels, we are told that happiness must wait until we are in heaven: "How happy you are when men hate you and turn you out of their company…Be glad when that happens and jump for joy—your reward in Heaven is magnificent." In Buddhism the Karmic cycle of cause and effect returns the soul to this life to continually rid the mind of delusions and desires. When this is accomplished, and a soul also becomes free of its aversions, the mind becomes still and the soul reaches a state called Nirvana. This can take several lifetimes.

Is there something we can do now without having to wait? What about being happy in this life? Waiting for others to evaluate our life when it is over, waiting until we get to heaven, or reincarnating until we get it right makes it seem like happiness is being put on hold.

Recent advances in scientific research may be able to help, with a number of studies suggesting that people have the power to increase happiness through intentional activities. The new science of positive psychology is devoted to researching how people thrive and flourish. Historically, psychology has emphasized what is wrong with human beings and ways to help people cope with mental illness. This focus on alleviating suffering did not look much past getting people out of pain. Positive psychology adds something beyond recovery. It seeks to move toward happiness and wellbeing, not simply away from suffering.

Martin Seligman, former president of the American Psychological Association, made his 1998 presidential term a clear platform for the development of positive psychology. The creation of positive interventions that can be tested for effectiveness is central to this effort and focus. A positive intervention is an intentional act that has the goal of increasing happiness. The application of positive interventions is important because among other benefits, research shows happier people live longer, are kinder and more successful, and have better relationships.

Seligman has set a goal for fifty-one percent of the world to be flourishing by the year 2051. To achieve this, people will need to be educated and inspire other people to use positive interventions.

Stories seem a natural means for promoting this effort. Storytelling is woven into the human psyche through our cultures and development. Stories are embedded into the facilitation of positive interventions, and the personal narrative can provide a vehicle for recovery from negative emotions while helping to integrate meaning into our lives.

This passage was adapted from "Happily Ever After: The Use of Stories to Promote Positive Interventions." Tomasulo D, Pawelski J. *Psychology.* 2012. 3(12A) doi: 10.4236/psych.2012.312A76 for use under the terms of the Creative Commons CC BY 3.0 license (http://creativecommons.org/licenses/by/3.0/legalcode).

Question 7

Which of the following is an assertion supported by evidence in the passage?

- ○ **A.** Only individuals practicing positive psychology can be happy.
- ○ **B.** Surrendering to a higher power results in the most happiness.
- ○ **C.** The longest living individuals are the happiest.
- ○ **D.** Happiness is often not attained in a lifetime.

Question 8

Which of the following would most reasonably be considered a positive intervention?

- ○ **A.** Taking blood pressure medication after a heart attack
- ○ **B.** Training for a marathon because a doctor recommends it
- ○ **C.** Joining an intramural sports team after having played that sport in high school
- ○ **D.** Drinking fewer soft drinks because a boss bans them from the workplace

Question 9

The author's apparent attitude toward religious views on happiness is:

- ○ **A.** supportive.
- ○ **B.** skeptical.
- ○ **C.** outraged.
- ○ **D.** ambivalent.

Question 10

A study found that avid readers tend to live longer than non-readers. Does this finding strengthen the author's argument?

- ○ **A.** Yes, because the individuals must be reading stories with happy endings.
- ○ **B.** Yes, because the presence of storytelling in their lives has increased their level of happiness.
- ○ **C.** No, because the finding is merely a correlation.
- ○ **D.** No, because the finding is unrelated to the authors' argument.

Question 11

Why is positive psychology being investigated as a method for increasing happiness?

- ○ **A.** Physical pleasures, relationships, and achievement of goals do not result in true happiness.
- ○ **B.** Positive psychology is a reliable method that individuals of diverse backgrounds can use to achieve happiness.
- ○ **C.** Current methods for achieving happiness are inadequate.
- ○ **D.** Fewer Americans report feeling happy these days than ever before.

Question 12

A new researcher develops a method for implementing positive psychology in schools, but it would be a huge expense for the government. The author would most likely react by:

- ○ **A.** supporting its implementation because the benefits outweigh the costs.
- ○ **B.** rejecting such extravagant expenses.
- ○ **C.** attempting to develop a method that is less expensive.
- ○ **D.** waiting to draw conclusions until more research has been performed.

Passage 3 (Questions 13-19)

The pioneers of tobacco research in the 1960s and 1970s could not know how tobacco addiction developed because the first study of this issue was circulated in the year 2000. However, they did recognize that heavy daily smokers were addicted to tobacco. Starting in the early 1970s, a series of articles in prominent medical journals equated tobacco addiction with a high frequency of smoking. By today's standards, these articles are notable for their many pages of detailed assertions regarding the nature of tobacco addiction, which are unsupported by a single reference. These articles formed the foundation for what would become the accepted wisdom among tobacco researchers for the next four decades: the threshold model.

The threshold model maintains that until tobacco consumption is maintained above a threshold of 5-10 cigarettes per day for a prolonged period, smokers are free of all symptoms of tobacco addiction. It holds that declining blood nicotine levels trigger withdrawal symptoms so quickly that addicted smokers must protect their nicotine levels by smoking at least five cigarettes per day.

A series of studies on "chippers," atypical individuals who smoke fewer than five cigarettes per day over many years and who were reported to have no symptoms of addiction, has reinforced the idea that moderate daily smoking is a prerequisite for nicotine dependence. The assertion that adult chippers had no symptoms of addiction was generalized to indicate that all light smokers are free of addiction. Recent studies, however, have shown that many individuals develop symptoms of addiction without smoking daily and quite soon after the onset of intermittent tobacco use. Even in the largest chipper study, slightly less than half of the chipper participants reported that it would be difficult to go without smoking for a week, and smaller proportions experienced withdrawal symptoms. Research has shown that until addiction is established, smoking is motivated and maintained by peer pressure, pleasure seeking, or loneliness.

The Diagnostic and Statistical Manual (DSM), which provides standard classification criteria for mental disorders, including addiction, does not reference the threshold model, but restates many of its speculations as fact. The DSM is used by healthcare professionals worldwide as the definitive guide to the diagnosis of mental illness. For the past 30 years, the DSM has stated that moderate daily smoking is a prerequisite for addiction. The DSM has asserted that tobacco withdrawal symptoms can be diagnosed only in individuals who use tobacco for at least several weeks at a level equivalent to more than ten cigarettes per day. It also states that daily use of nicotine for at least several weeks is required for nicotine withdrawal.

It may not be surprising that none of the DSM's assertions about the threshold model are supported by references. The appearance of factual errors in the DSM reveals that it is not an entirely evidence-based document. What few people realize is that the DSM represents suggested nomenclatures, a set of definitions intended to foster clearer communication among researchers and practitioners. The criteria encourage a common usage of language, but the definitions do not necessarily reflect the outcome of scientific studies that establish the true nature of mental conditions, including tobacco addiction. They are not a distillation of all human knowledge about individuals with these disorders; instead, they represent a gentlemen's agreement on vocabulary. Some researchers may accept that tobacco addiction is whatever the American Psychiatric Association or the World Health Organization say it is. But the DSM cannot "define" the characteristics of tobacco addiction; nature defines the characteristics of tobacco addiction. At best, mankind can only accurately describe what nature produces.

This passage was adapted from "Thwarting Science by Protecting the Received Wisdom on Tobacco Addiction from the Scientific Method." DiFranza JR. *Harm Reduction Journal.* 2010. 7(26) doi: 10.1186/1477-7517-7-26 for use under the terms of the Creative Commons CC BY 3.0 license (http://creativecommons.org/licenses/by/3.0/legalcode).

Question 13

The author claims that the threshold model emerged from:

- O **A.** research that was erroneous.
- O **B.** articles that found correlations between tobacco addiction and light daily smoking.
- O **C.** publications that were not corroborated by data.
- O **D.** studies that described a theory about the progression of tobacco addiction.

Question 14

Based on information in the passage, one could reasonably draw which of the following conclusions about tobacco consumption?

- O **A.** After an individual becomes addicted to tobacco, social influences play a role in continued addiction.
- O **B.** Individuals who are addicted to tobacco undergo withdrawal symptoms including restlessness, fatigue, and difficulty concentrating.
- O **C.** People who smoke fewer than five cigarettes each day become addicted to tobacco at a slower rate than people who smoke more frequently.
- O **D.** The pattern of addiction experienced by chippers is similar to that of smokers in general.

Question 15

Which of the following statements, if assumed to be true, would most *weaken* the author's assertions about the DSM?

- O **A.** The DSM contains references to studies on tobacco addiction that support the threshold model.
- O **B.** The DSM incorporates clinical studies of individuals with mental disorders in its descriptions of those conditions.
- O **C.** The newest version of the DSM states that non-daily use of nicotine over the course of several weeks can cause nicotine withdrawal symptoms.
- O **D.** The DSM is written only in English, which fails to encourage a common usage of language for researchers from different countries.

Question 16

Suppose a new document intended to improve adults' communication with teenagers is circulated among organizations providing social services to adolescents. The author would most likely support this project if:

○ **A.** it was created based on findings from one of many research studies about how teenagers interact with adults.

○ **B.** it received support from major youth organizations like Big Brothers Big Sisters.

○ **C.** it included standard definitions of current slang.

○ **D.** it was fact-checked extensively.

Question 17

According to passage information about addiction, which of the following is most likely to be true?

○ **A.** Researchers have demonstrated that nicotine has a long half-life because withdrawal symptoms do not appear for some time after an addicted individual stops smoking.

○ **B.** According to new research, a threshold model for alcohol indicates that no addictive symptoms are seen when people have three or fewer drinks per day.

○ **C.** An effective smoking cessation program used cigarettes with reduced nicotine levels such that individuals could not obtain as much nicotine from smoking these cigarettes as normal cigarettes.

○ **D.** Scientists have shown that providing healthy community engagement for individuals who have begun using cocaine decreases the number who later become addicted.

Question 18

Assume a new clinical study finds that a group of individuals can smoke up to five cigarettes a day for a prolonged period without developing symptoms of tobacco addiction. How would this study affect the author's arguments?

○ **A.** It supports the author's claim that the threshold model is a reasonable way of studying tobacco addiction.

○ **B.** It negates the author's claim that there are individuals who develop addiction symptoms without smoking daily.

○ **C.** It negates the author's claim that the DSM's assertions about the threshold model are not supported by references.

○ **D.** It is irrelevant to the author's claim that the DSM is not an entirely evidence-based document.

Question 19

Based on information in the passage, with which of the following statements about research into mental disorders would the author most likely agree?

   I. Researchers can adequately describe patients' experiences struggling with mental disorders if they inform these descriptions with evidence.

  II. The DSM should not be consulted when conducting research into mental conditions.

 III. The threshold model garnered initial credibility because it was directly referenced in the DSM.

○ **A.** I only

○ **B.** III only

○ **C.** I and II

○ **D.** II and III

Passage 4 (Questions 20-25)

Highly active antiretroviral therapy (ART) has transformed HIV/AIDS from a death sentence into a manageable chronic disease. Today, an adult 20 years of age diagnosed with HIV/AIDS in the developed world can expect to live at least 23 more years. In the developing world, fewer therapeutic options are available for patients. Nevertheless, current treatment approaches are effective at reducing mortality, with studies demonstrating similar survival outcomes compared to Western countries, at least in the short term.

The question of when to initiate ART in resource-limited settings is gaining attention. Early initiation results in substantial improvement in rates of survival and reduced incidence of opportunistic infection. On the other hand, allowing people with HIV to develop symptoms may increase their risk of being stigmatized, and stigma can act as a barrier to later uptake of HIV services. However, a number of concerns have been put forward against starting treatment earlier, namely increased costs, potential toxicity of treating more patients longer, and increased burden on health systems.

The decision of when to start ART is generally made according to clinical or immunological criteria, though decisions based on clinical criteria alone are generally only used in resource-limited settings where laboratory capacity is limited. More commonly, the decision to start ART is based on immunological criteria, as defined by the level of CD4 cells.

Guidelines for developing countries have recently been revised to match developed world recommendations relating to CD4 levels. The International AIDS Society stated that the core principle underlying these guidelines, namely pathogenesis-directed therapy with regimens designed to achieve full virologic suppression with minimal toxicity and maximal simplicity, is applicable to the developing world, and the latest WHO antiretroviral treatment guidelines for resource-limited settings recommend a move towards earlier initiation.

These recommendations have for the most part yet to be translated into country-level policy, and most national guidelines in developing countries continue to recommend "deferred" ART initiation. The main concern for developing countries is that providing treatment earlier, for longer, would increase overall drug expenditure costs as well as other significant costs to health systems. Given that most people present at ART services with an even lower CD4 count than that recommended for ART initiation, the issue of early initiation has been called a moot point.

From a human rights perspective, rationing ART regimens could bring a benefit if it resulted in broader access, and thus to greater overall implementation of the rights to life, access to healthcare, and access to medicine, if limiting indications enabled health systems to provide access more extensively to persons who would otherwise be deprived of it. This could apply if rationing was required to make ART available to everyone who met a lower CD4 threshold, even in rural areas, rather than to all who presented with the higher threshold, but exclusively at urban centers. Such a benefit could only ever be said to exist in circumstances where full access for all was not feasible.

There is a concern regarding the fact that eligibility based on laboratory investigations requires access to those investigations, which varies by location. Those who would be eligible on immunological but not clinical grounds would be denied care due to lack of laboratory facilities. This logic applies equally to any CD4-based initiation strategy, whether early or deferred. Higher CD4 count at treatment initiation gives a greater chance of escaping symptomatic disease. However, the main human rights burden of limiting ART is that it denies treatment to people who, in other parts of the world, would be considered eligible. If the latest evidence suggests that ART should be provided earlier, then from a human rights perspective every effort should be made to ensure this happens and happens for all.

This passage was adapted from "When to Start Antiretroviral Therapy in Resource-Limited Settings: A Human Rights Analysis." Ford N, Calmy A, and Hurst S. *BMC International Health and Human Rights*. 2010. 10(6) doi: 1472-698X.10.6 for use under the terms of the Creative Commons CC BY 2.0 license (http://creativecommons.org/licenses/by/2.0/legalcode).

Question 20

Which of the following findings would most support the argument that rationing ART has positive results?

- ○ **A.** HIV patients who receive ART therapy earlier have a lower chance of virus transmission.
- ○ **B.** Rural populations are less likely than urban areas to receive staff, funding, and laboratory materials.
- ○ **C.** Overuse of ART causes some populations to use fewer HIV precautions because the treatment is accessible.
- ○ **D.** Increasing resources in rural areas by 50% leads to a 65% lower rate of HIV contraction.

Question 21

Which of the following situations most closely matches the interplay of clinical and laboratory HIV diagnoses as described in the passage?

- ○ **A.** Beauty pageant contestants are more likely to win based on their swimsuit score than their talent score.
- ○ **B.** People with a good sense of smell are less likely to drink sour milk than people who only refer to the sell-by date.
- ○ **C.** Donuts with cream filling sell better than those without only when the cream filling donuts are a different color.
- ○ **D.** Contestants on game shows are more likely to pick suitcases that glitter than those that are plain regardless of a previous glittery suitcase's contents.

Question 22

Which of the following ideas presented in the passage provides the most support in favor of initiating ART early?

○ **A.** Patients in both developed and developing countries have similar survival rates with ART.

○ **B.** Presenting HIV symptoms leads to a low quality of social life in developing nations.

○ **C.** Antiretroviral therapy boosts HIV patients' immune systems.

○ **D.** The World Health Organization suggests early ART initiation for all.

Question 23

Suppose a study found that earlier initiation of ART leads to more frequent diagnosis of cancer. Believers in the human rights perspective of providing ART to all would be likely to respond to this study by:

○ **A.** disregarding the study and continuing to advocate for medication equity.

○ **B.** supporting research for therapy that causes less harm to patients.

○ **C.** using the study as evidence that ART is allowing patients to live long enough to develop cancer.

○ **D.** rejoicing that there are enough resources available to diagnose cancer.

Question 24

Assume that inconsistent use of ART leads to the development of drug-resistant HIV strains. How would this information affect the argument for early ART initiation?

○ **A.** It would support the argument by providing motivation for earlier education with initiation.

○ **B.** It would reiterate the idea that poor access can lead to poor outcomes.

○ **C.** It would oppose the argument that higher CD4 count treatment can lead to lower symptom rates.

○ **D.** It would undermine the idea that a reduced chance of symptoms and stigma is a major benefit to HIV patients.

Question 25

Based on the information presented in the passage, with which of the following statements would the author most agree?

○ **A.** ART therapy should be given to every clinically diagnosed patient in developing countries.

○ **B.** Public health organizations have a responsibility to implement their proposed guidelines.

○ **C.** Developing countries should develop a system for ART initiation based on their specific resources and needs.

○ **D.** Drug companies need to reduce the cost of ART to uncomplicate the worldwide issue of initiation.

Passage 5 (Questions 26-30)

In the past few years, several attempts have been made to account for value in online video gaming. Whether value is judged according to economic, social or psychological systems, these studies have theorized how online gaming functions as a discrete space in which something (an experience, the quality of time spent, the economic structures at work in the online world, etc.) is intrinsically and extrinsically valued. Often, the objects of study are capitalist concepts that are either figurative (skills, levels of accomplishment, etc.) or concrete (weapons, property, etc.) factors that are either exchanged or produced in the world of the game, with a corresponding value based on the expense and difficulty of production in the real world. These studies are important because they establish that systems of exchange, pleasure, and desire operate similarly to systems in the real world and are usually based on a reciprocal value exchange rate. Games researchers, and those interested in online worlds in general, should be familiar with the media attention in recent years on sweatshops across the globe where workers punch keys for hours on end in order to complete mundane tasks so that gamers can purchase these products and skill sets for use in the games without having to actually complete the tasks themselves. As far as advanced capitalism goes, this is hardly surprising.

The Dutch cultural historian Johan Huizinga originally theorized value as a quality in gaming. In his novel *Homo Ludens*, Huizinga finds four identifiable structures inherent to all forms of play: 1) play happens for its own sake, with no external goal; 2) play exists outside the scope of ordinary life; 3) play operates within fixed boundaries of space and time, with its own set of rules; and 4) play is labile. Additionally, oftentimes play and life are constantly and universally antagonistic to each other. Huizinga clearly devalues games in the face of more important pursuits, such as labor. While he finds that the playspace is a culturally significant arena with its own rules and logic, he writes from a clearly Modernist position, so that the divide between high and low culture must be necessarily maintained. The view that play and games clearly possess cultural value found a historical home in Postmodernism, and in the academy in the areas of sports studies, performance studies, and queer and gender studies. With the birth of digital games studies, a de facto sense that games and play have value was established by the quick growth of the field and the rise of research centers and departments devoted to the field.

Two recent studies, both published in the same issue of *Games and Culture*, deal with value, although they do not address actual player experience. Anthropology professor Thomas Malaby theorizes the structure of capital in virtual worlds, showing that a third category of value (other than market value for commodities and the social value of networks in the virtual), cultural capital, if studied properly, can explain how all three forms of capital operate in virtual worlds. While his analysis is excellent, it is not distinctly concerned with what actual players consider valuable—in concrete and abstract terms—and how this value relates to value orientation outside the virtual. This is a trenchant analysis but does not seek to establish individual players' notions of value.

In *The Sublime Object of Ideology*, Slovenian philosopher Slavoj Zizek writes, "The notion of social fantasy is a necessary counterpart to the concept of antagonism: fantasy is precisely the way the antagonistic fissure is masked. In other words, fantasy is a means for an ideology to take its own failure into account in advance." It seems clear that online gaming, in a similar fashion, functions as a fantasy-machine so that the players need not formally establish value in gaming, but instead they manufacture value in gaming in relation to the real. Through the gaming experience, the player enters into a transaction where other pursuits become naturally tinged with less value, or, potentially, more failure. Online gaming serves as a powerful system of desire and longing for the odd, the other, and the inescapable pursuit (and unavoidable failure) to achieve the most slippery of negotiations in postmodern capitalism—the total integration of the internal and external, the self and surrounding culture.

This passage was adapted from "Value Theory and Online Video Gaming." Burrill D. *Advances in Journalism and Communication.* 2014. 2 doi: 10.4236/ajc.2014.23010 for use under the terms of the Creative Commons CC BY 4.0 license (https://creativecommons.org/licenses/by/4.0/legalcode).

Question 26

What does the passage suggest about the cultural capital theory of value in gaming?

- ○ **A.** It is the most recent theory proposed regarding the value of gaming.
- ○ **B.** It is too detailed to encompass the experience of every individual playing a game.
- ○ **C.** It focuses too much on experiences and values held in virtual reality.
- ○ **D.** It does not emphasize social values as much as it should.

Question 27

Which of the following best describes the author's attitude toward a strictly capitalist value in gaming, as described in the first paragraph?

- ○ **A.** It does not account for all of the value in playing video games.
- ○ **B.** Only certain individuals playing video games hold this value.
- ○ **C.** It is not a value that game researchers should encourage.
- ○ **D.** It is not necessarily valuable to game developers and technicians.

Question 28

Why does the author quote the philosopher Slovaj Zizek (paragraph 4) in reference to fantasy?

○ **A.** To emphasize a point made earlier in the passage

○ **B.** To suggest a new approach to value theory

○ **C.** To question the theory just previously discussed

○ **D.** To admit defeat in determining value

Question 29

Which of the following adjectives to describe video game players would the author most likely support?

○ **A.** Aggressive

○ **B.** Introspective

○ **C.** Escapist

○ **D.** Friendly

Question 30

The change to an aspect of video games that would most *weaken* the author's argument regarding value would be:

○ **A.** the plot of the video game.

○ **B.** the individual playing the game.

○ **C.** the motivation for playing the game.

○ **D.** the location of individuals playing the game.

Passage 6 (Questions 31-36)

The concept of Cognitive Mobilization (CM) put forward by Inglehart, a political scientist and director of the World Values Survey, states that in postindustrial societies, citizens' political participation is influenced by their level of education and access to information. Inglehart studies the evolution of CM under the premise that levels of education and access to information are on the rise.

Inglehart sees CM as a central aspect within a broader process: the modernization and development of Western societies. In his work, *The Silent Revolution*, he defines it as follows:

Social mobilization is a broad process. Western countries have long since completed many of its most important stages, such as urbanization, basic industrialization, widespread literacy, mass military service, and universal suffrage. Nevertheless, an essential aspect continues –the very core of the process: the increasingly wide dissemination of the skills necessary to cope with an extensive political community. We use the term "Cognitive Mobilization" to refer to this central aspect of the broader process.

Much of the literature on CM has focused on the link to political parties. The oldest precursors of these organizations reflect on the phenomenon of party identification. For these authors, the phenomenon is psychological and it has emotional components that are formed during the process of socialization, the main source of which is the family. They are interested in how attitudes are formed and how people participate in government through political parties that enhance accessibility. However, Campbell and Converse, political scientists representing an opposing school of thought, draw the conclusion that the political party acts as a funnel. As an agent of political socialization, this funnel model determines the attitudes and votes of citizens, who develop a feeling of emotional identification toward a party's "label." This theory posits that political parties translate abstract political concepts for citizens and offer them an interpretation of reality.

Another concept closely linked to CM is "political sophistication," as discussed by Converse, who studies the degree of influence of ideology and beliefs on political behavior. The author's aim is to determine the degree of coherence of citizens' ideological constructs and to measure their ability to understand and apply political information when assessing certain issues or deciding how to vote. The relationship between interpretation, belief systems, and education underlies the concept of "political sophistication." For Converse, the most politically sophisticated are those who are most highly educated, politically involved, and well informed, while political party identification preferably facilitates the decision-making process for voting in less politically sophisticated voters. Another important contribution is simply functional: political parties translate political information for citizens and make it easier to access. This is because party identification is a time-saving device in the decision-making process of which party to vote for. With higher levels of education, there is less need for party guidance.

Next ▶

Due to the effect of disassociation with parties, the rise in information, and the change in priority in terms of young people's values, electoral participation is not the only form of political expression. Unconventional forms of political action and the formation of ad hoc structures as a way of making demands are more likely in societies with a higher level of CM. Due to the effects of increased education, the generational change means an increase in "potential" political participation and, more importantly, a drop in the importance of suffrage. For a population that has moved beyond materialist values, the vote is no longer as important. There are other priority interests (environment, solidarity, identity) where unconventional forms of political expression can be used, relegating the vote to a secondary plane. Votes will be used to the extent that the issues at stake in the ballot box will affect what is hoped to be achieved according to these new values.

This passage was adapted from "The Cognitive Mobilization Index: Crises and Political Generations." Alaminos A, Penalva C. *SAGE Open*. 2012. 2(1) doi:10.1177/2158244012440437 for use under the terms of the Creative Commons CC BY 3.0 license (https://creativecommons.org/licenses/by/3.0/legalcode).

Question 31

Which of the following, if true, would most support the author's argument?

- **A.** Recent developments in CM explain the significant moves by political parties to reorient and rebrand for younger voters.
- **B.** Statistics indicate that the rate of electoral participation among younger generations is directly proportional to their interest in the issues under discussion.
- **C.** More young people are informed and passionate about issues than in the past but are unable to find candidates that represent their views.
- **D.** Individuals in the current generation are the best informed but least politically active in history.

Question 32

According to Converse, political parties:

- **A.** are a relic of a previous era of political participation.
- **B.** represent an organic motion toward organization by individuals who share a common set of goals.
- **C.** appeal to people because they allow for a more manageable interpretation of political realities.
- **D.** allow average individuals to engage with the cognitive dissonance of the political arena more readily.

Question 33

The author would most likely agree with which of the following statements?

- **A.** Political sophistication has evolved to the extent that CM has become less relevant.
- **B.** In developed countries with mature political systems, voting no longer necessarily represents the interests of the people.
- **C.** The development of CM has brought with it a large-scale sense of cynicism toward the political system.
- **D.** The age of representative democracy has passed because technology, political sophistication, and CM have progressed to the point where representatives are unnecessary.

Question 34

According to the information in the passage, the importance of political sophistication is that:

- **A.** it allows for a more nuanced and cynical interpretation of political realities.
- **B.** it allows for individuals to transcend simple adherence to political parties.
- **C.** it recognizes a new and distinct development in the factors influencing CM.
- **D.** it is the most significant paradigm for considering and contextualizing the modern political landscape.

Question 35

Which of the following would contribute the LEAST to CM?

- **A.** Political activism on blogs
- **B.** Greater education on governmental structure and policy
- **C.** The deployment of political advertising campaigns
- **D.** The resurrection of the political salon discussion forum

Question 36

A higher level of CM would be most directly associated with:

- **A.** increased voting rates.
- **B.** greater interest in politics.
- **C.** a more personal and less partisan model of participation.
- **D.** a citizenry's efficient communication of its concerns to the government.

Passage 7 (Questions 37-43)

In November 1972, in the midst of the North Sea oil and gas exploration boom, the British Gas Council and Total announced plans to construct a gas reception terminal on a disused airfield. At this stage, the developers were not forthcoming with details of their proposals: all that they would reveal was that the terminal would be built on a 500-acre site, would cost several hundred million pounds, and would result in around 50-60 permanent jobs, although the pipelaying and construction stages would employ hundreds of workers.

The proposed site was adjacent to Britain's largest coastal dune lake, the Loch of Strathbeg, which had long been recognized as an internationally important site for wintering geese and ducks, and was in the process of becoming a nature reserve. The situation was further complicated by the fact that the Ministry of Defense (MOD) had already received clearance to build an important Royal Naval radio station on the same airfield site.

The Northeast Environmental Liaison Group (ELG), which consisted of academics and representatives of various conservation groups, sought not only to prevent the terminal being built on the airfield site, but also to appeal for a more careful planning approach to industrial development in general. The ELG came to play a crucial role in disseminating information and advice through sympathetic newspapers and the journal *Nature*, ensuring that the story reached an international, scientific audience.

This unsystematic approach to public engagement was evident during the initial public consultation period, where a copy of the terminal site plan could be inspected at the offices of the local planning authority. The lack of detail on the plan, and the short timeframe in which representations could be made, angered local environmental opponents. They questioned how anyone could be expected to make sensible decisions on the basis of such meager information and how any responsible planning authority could give planning permission on such data.

Individuals in another protest group organized a public meeting, at which representatives of the Gas Council and Total appeared in order to explain their choice of the airfield site. They stressed the certain influx of jobs and revenue to the area, and charted the projected improvements to the local economy. Yet opponents remained critical of the lack of detail from the developers.

In April 1973, the Gas Council and Total announced that they had found an alternative site for the terminal in a far less environmentally sensitive area. The developers refused to concede victory to the conservationists, insisting that the decision to change sites was driven solely by the MOD's need for the airfield site. Although further concerns were expressed by the conservation lobby about a lack of detailed information on the new site proposals, planning permission was granted.

Early assessments of the construction and subsequent expansion of the new terminal indicated that the landform and hydrology had been restored satisfactorily, although efforts at re-vegetation had met with mixed success. There have been no public or local inquiries, no complaints of substance by local or national regulatory bodies, and no controversies as engendered by official or voluntary environmental or ecological bodies. The terminal itself became something of a haven for birdlife. A flat-roofed building on the site housed Britain's first roof-nesting common terns, and security fences protected against four-legged predators, allowing ground-nesting birds to flourish. The terminal operators have won a number of environmental awards, and they continue to make information on their environmental policies, systems, and performance publicly available.

This passage was adapted from "Rough Justice? Exploring the Relationship between Information Access and Environmental and Ecological Justice Pertaining to Two Controversial Coastal Developments in North-East Scotland." Baxter G. *Cosmopolitan Civil Societies.* 2014. 6(2) doi: 10.5130/ccs.v6i2.3914 for use under the terms of the Creative Commons CC BY 4.0 license (https://creativecommons.org/licenses/by/4.0/legalcode).

Question 37

Based on the information provided in the passage, it is reasonable to conclude that the developers did not acknowledge the conservationists' victory because:

- ○ **A.** the military truly does have more pull than groups of academics.
- ○ **B.** the developers did not want to surrender their ideology.
- ○ **C.** permission was granted for an alternative site without the conservationists' approval.
- ○ **D.** the developers did not want to set a poor precedent.

Question 38

Assume that environmentalists disapproved of the construction of a hydroelectric power plant. From the information provided in the passage, the environmentalists' opposing argument would include all of the following points EXCEPT:

- ○ **A.** an emphasis on the potential dislocation of local animal species.
- ○ **B.** a demand to access the hydroelectric company's projected construction time.
- ○ **C.** an overview of the plant life in the affected area.
- ○ **D.** a requirement for the hydroelectric company to be totally transparent.

Question 39

Which of the following findings would most strengthen an argument that the construction of a new industrial site can involve insurmountable environmental costs?

- ○ **A.** Endangered bears are no longer sighted after the construction of a coal plant.
- ○ **B.** A new solar field destroys the grass below the solar panels.
- ○ **C.** A recently built gas pipeline drips petroleum onto unsuspecting squirrels.
- ○ **D.** A new wind turbine field prevents a flock of rare birds from finding their mating ground.

Next ▶

Question 40

Based on the information provided in the passage, with which of the following statements would the author most likely agree?

- O **A.** Generating livelihoods for local communities is a valid reason to consider altering the environment.
- O **B.** Local ecosystems are limited resources that should be protected and maintained unchanged.
- O **C.** Commercialism and expansion are necessary evils in an increasingly globalized society.
- O **D.** Local wildlife will always find a way to cope with human interference.

Question 41

The passage assumes that giving a short amount of time to review development plans:

- O **A.** is necessary to move along a large project.
- O **B.** disallows the public from gathering adequate information.
- O **C.** was a strategy intentionally used by Gas Council and Total.
- O **D.** should not be a mainstay of industrial developments.

Question 42

Based on the information in the passage, if a confusion (that is, a group) of weasels moved to a proposed terminal site, the author would suggest:

- O **A.** terminating construction of the new terminal site to avoid displacing the new weasels.
- O **B.** making this information available so that developers can act according to public opinion.
- O **C.** asking conservationist groups for advice on how to proceed.
- O **D.** researching weasels' habitat preferences to assess the prospect of the weasels and the terminal coexisting.

Question 43

According to the passage, the conservationists appeal to Nature in order to:

- O **A.** garner support from an academic following.
- O **B.** convey the subtleties of the plan to a national audience.
- O **C.** gain legitimacy through the use of a peer-reviewed journal.
- O **D.** oppose a private company through public awareness.

Passage 8 (Questions 44-48)

The Victorian era has inspired a wealth of literary genres, from gothic horror to early detective stories. Contemporary writers are still drawing inspiration from that period. Among the many fictions inspired by the Victorian period in the late 20th and early 21st century, steampunk holds a special place. Steampunk works stage a reimagining of the Victorian era, strongly influenced by science fiction and fantasy, where technical feats and outright miracles exist in tandem with a setting inspired by 19th century aesthetics. Since the appearance of the first steampunk works in the 1970s and 1980s, its popularity has grown steadily.

As a genre, steampunk is essentially transfictional: in addition to frequently showcasing historical characters, many works give a new life to famous fictional figures from 19th century literature, each time reasserting the ties between the literature of the Victorian era and steampunk. Therefore, steampunk is grounded in contemporary imaginings of past tropes and technologies. Inspired by proto-science fiction authors such as Jules Verne or H. G. Wells, pulp magazines, Victorian imagery as well as science fiction and fantasy in general, steampunk has nonetheless, in its thirty years of existence, built its own specific figures. Among them, the steampunk doctor holds an intriguing place.

In popular imagery, the doctor—or healer—is a benevolent figure of both knowledge and power. In steampunk fiction, the doctor becomes a more shadowy figure, in which both characteristics are taken to the extreme and supersede the exercise of medicine itself in importance. In the particular context of the Victorian era, the doctor is, first and foremost, an embodiment of dizzying scientific progress. The steampunk doctor has ties to the figure of the isolated genius scientist, while retaining the mysterious and disquieting quality of the medieval plague doctor. They are often pioneers in medicine, having created their own groundbreaking medical techniques. However, the power thus acquired lends them a large measure of ethical ambiguity: the steampunk doctor can affect the human body in almost unlimited ways, hybridizing it with machines or animals and turning death and illness into secondary concerns, at the potential cost of a number of moral violations.

While this initial description could fit a number of 19th century characters like Dr. Frankenstein, Dr. Jekyll, and Dr. Moreau, the steampunk doctor is fundamentally different. *Frankenstein*, *The Strange Case of Dr. Jekyll and Mr. Hyde,* and *The Island of Dr. Moreau* were all, on a certain level, cautionary tales. Their heroes bring about their own doom through their experiments, and the moral violations committed in the name of science – attempting to substitute oneself to God, creating monsters, inflicting terrible pain on innocent beings – eventually trigger their demise. Importantly, their science dies with them: Frankenstein gives up his attempts to create a human being and embarks upon a solitary quest to find his creature before dying in a remote place; the ingredients of Jekyll's salts run out, ensuring that with his suicide, the chemicals that enabled him to turn into Hyde will be impossible to find again; Moreau's island remains isolated and its denizens revert to bestiality, thus cancelling the effects of the original experiments. The hubris of those characters only results in the destruction of their own lives and works, purging society of their legacies.

The opposite happens with the steampunk doctor. Steampunk cannot, indeed, be solely described as a resurrection of 19th century science fiction. It is instead a complete reimagining of what society could have been if the evolution of technology had been radically different from the beginning, and it usually includes a more than liberal sprinkling of magical possibilities, often presented as fantastical science. In steampunk, the limits of science are more flexible than in traditional science fiction. Additionally, authors rarely adopt the condemning stance 19th century literature has used. As a result, steampunk doctors push back the boundaries of science, with varying, often positive, consequences.

This passage was adapted from "The Steampunk Doctor: Practicing Medicine in a Mechanical Age." Cristofari C, Guitton M. *Advances in Anthropology.* 2014. 4 doi:10.4236/aa.2014.42012 for use under the terms of the Creative Commons CC BY 4.0 license (https://creativecommons.org/licenses/by/4.0/legalcode).

Question 44

The single change to a steampunk novel that would most *weaken* the author's distinction between contemporary imagery and steampunk doctors would be:

○ **A.** publishing the work at a later date.

○ **B.** changing the tone throughout the novel.

○ **C.** specifying the doctor's motivations.

○ **D.** allowing the doctor to have an effect on society.

Question 45

The author uses the term "transfictional" (paragraph 2) to characterize which aspect of steampunk literature?

    I. The genre's reimagining of historical characters

    II. The genre's reimagining of famous fictional characters

    III. The genre's relation to previous works of literature

○ **A.** I only

○ **B.** III only

○ **C.** I and II

○ **D.** II and III

Question 46

The passage offers *no* information about 19th century characters':

○ **A.** original experiments.

○ **B.** professional attitudes.

○ **C.** moral offenses.

○ **D.** ethical dilemmas.

Question 47

The passage describes a juxtaposition of Victorian era-inspired steampunk literature, namely that:

○ **A.** such realistic actions exist in unrealistic settings.

○ **B.** such unrealistic actions exist in realistic settings.

○ **C.** such realistic characters exist in unrealistic settings.

○ **D.** such unrealistic characters exist in realistic settings.

Question 48

The author's primary purpose is to:

○ **A.** argue for the value of steampunk literature.

○ **B.** critique 19th century works' cautionary tones.

○ **C.** provide advice for readers analyzing steampunk literature.

○ **D.** discuss steampunk literature in the context of other genres.

Passage 9 (Questions 49-53)

Is music fandom a realm of spiritual practice? Do fans use their connections with heroes to adopt practices like veneration, sanctification or idolatry? Contemporary religious studies scholarship has a tendency to gloss over the distinction between paying attention to one's hero and relinquishing one's individuality, otherwise known as "submitting." In his book *Sacred Matters: Celebrity Worship, Sexual Ecstacies, The Living Dead and Other Signs of Religious Life in the United States*, Professor Gary Laderman claims that the Elvis Presley phenomenon is "seemingly secular but abundant with religious meanings" and its star "saves… the masses." His work takes it as self-evident Elvis' fans think of him as a deity. Laderman is not the only scholar to propose that spiritual identification shapes the Elvis phenomenon. His work comes in the wake of a range of scholars who hold similar views. Slyvan, for instance, claims that Elvis and Beatles fan cultures "had powerful but unconscious religious dimensions" not just because of "West African spirituality implicit in the music, but also because they were deifying their musical heroes and engaging in what might be described as a form of worship."

Elvis' fans tend to say that his magnetic appeal is either solely based on him as an individual or is inexplicable. This understanding of personality as a source of charisma is not the same as deification, which is the attribution of metaphysical divinity. Fans become emotionally moved when paying attention to their heroes, but that does not mean that they sacralize, venerate, transfigure, sanctify, or worship them.

Neo-religiosity scholarship has a significant central problem. One of the problems with liberal definitions of spirituality and the sacred is that they stretch almost *ad infinitum*, or infinitely. Scholars who study religiosity constantly run the risk of empire-building beyond notions of the sacred that can be offered with any degree of precision. In scholar Christopher Partridge's work, for example, the sacred is applied to anything set apart from daily life. In his view, high culture and art are sacred because they require cultivation to appreciate. The profane is seen as a variant because it transgresses the absolutely sacred and thus reinforces its importance as a category. Loud music is seen as sacred because it immerses us in an experience that is different from daily life. Celebrity-following is seen as a sacred practice because fans supposedly sacralize anything touched by heroes who are set apart from daily life. Through such acrobatic semiotic feats, Partridge's use of the term encompasses almost every popular music-related experience.

The idea that spirituality nebulously impregnates and interpenetrates everyday life mystifies the term itself. The argument that religious faith is like some kind of gothic mist falling on individuals and cultures mistakes a process that mediates between social activities and personal convictions. Contrary to the claims made that sacredness is everywhere, spirituality can be understood as a perspective from which daily life can be seen as miraculous. The issue is that anything and everything can be seen as spiritual if it is framed that way: even science and materialism, for example, can arguably be construed as alerting us to the magnificence of God's creation. If a star signs an autograph, it has value in the fan community not because it has radiated out as something contagiously sacred, but precisely the other way round: being a

personally inscribed endorsement, it draws us closer toward (and makes us more intimate with) him or her. The process is a pull, not a push. We are not drawn to Elvis—or contemporary boy bands for that matter—because they are intrinsically sacred (or socially sacralized); if we are drawn to them, it is because we recognize their popularity and feel an emotional investment in their performance. In contemporary society, neither of those aspects are sacred or spiritual things.

This passage was adapted from "Elvis' Gospel Music: Between the Secular and Spiritual?" Duffett M. *Religions.* 2015. 6 doi: 10.3390/rel6010182 for use under the terms of the Creative Commons CC BY 4.0 license (https://creativecommons.org/licenses/by/4.0/legalcode).

Question 49

According to the author's argument in the passage, spirituality:

○ **A.** can distance people from God.

○ **B.** recognizes divergence from everyday life.

○ **C.** can involve worshipping individuals other than God.

○ **D.** can be found in West African music.

Question 50

Which of the following findings would most *weaken* the claim that musical fandom is not a spiritual practice?

○ **A.** Music fans often identify as very religious individuals.

○ **B.** Music is frequently used in worship settings.

○ **C.** Famous singers have been asked to bless fans at concerts.

○ **D.** Individuals enter a trance when listening to their favorite music.

Question 51

To provide an example of celebrity worship, Laderman noted in paragraph 1 that the Elvis Presley phenomenon is "seemingly secular but abundant with religious meanings." Laderman's point is that:

○ **A.** Presley's fandom was more religious than he intended.

○ **B.** Presley inadvertently provided spiritual inspiration for his fans..

○ **C.** the lyrics of Presley's songs had religious undertones.

○ **D.** fans wanted to believe that their admiration was secular.

Question 52

Which of the following would provide the best evidence to support the author's conclusion regarding spirituality in contemporary society?

○ **A.** Celebrities are treated like regular citizens in most societies.

○ **B.** Celebrities feel infallible and as though they can do no wrong.

○ **C.** The general public has differing views regarding that which is spiritual.

○ **D.** The general public believes that spirituality has changed since Presley's time.

Question 53

In the context of the passage, the central problem of neo-religiosity scholarship is most likely discussed to suggest that:

○ **A.** religion is too complex to define.

○ **B.** the term "sacred" encompasses too many concepts.

○ **C.** no event is truly sacred anymore.

○ **D.** religion and scholarship are unrelated.

STOP. If you finish before time is called, check your work. You may go back to any question in this test.

ANSWERS & EXPLANATIONS for Test 10 can be found on p. 307.

TEST 10

STOP

TEST 11

Number of Questions: 53

Time: 90 minutes

INSTRUCTIONS: Each passage is followed by associated questions. Read the passage, then select the best answer to each question. If you are unsure of the answer, rule out incorrect choices and select from the remaining options. Indicate your answer beside the option you choose.

Passage 1 (Questions 1-7)

Our society is well-served when schools function at their highest level. Students develop the skills, values, and habits of mind that will allow them to become productive and engaged citizens of our democracy. The well-being of our society suffers when schools fail to adequately fulfill our hopes for them.

Trust is increasingly recognized as an essential element in vibrant, well-performing schools. This is in part because trust undergirds the cooperative behavior necessary for cultivating high performance. Trust becomes salient when people enter into relationships of interdependence. Although trust occurs between individuals, it also occurs among individuals within complex human organizations, such as schools. Schools present a unique setting in which trust is exercised both in an administrative and educational capacity, as principals interact with faculty and faculty interact with students.

There are myriad responsibilities placed on the shoulders of principals in order to foster the kinds of learning environments we hope for. Like all leaders, school principals are responsible for the development of a shared vision and stewardship of that vision, engaging members of the community, managing the organization, and ensuring the effectiveness of employees. While withholding important information is a tactic some leaders use to maintain power or manipulate employees, trustworthy principals produce conditions that inspire teachers to be open about challenges in the classroom and to address them.

In a study that included elementary, middle, and high school levels in both urban and suburban settings, the level of trust that teachers held for the principal set a tone for the building. Faculty trust in the principal was related to their trust in colleagues, students, and parents, as well as the level of parent trust in the school. Student trust in teachers was not directly related to faculty trust in the principal, but was indirectly related to the overall climate of trust in the schools through intercorrelations with the above faculty and parent trust measures. Each of these types of trusting relationships in schools was moderately to strongly related to student achievement.

Numerous mediators exist between leadership actions and student experience. Beyond administrative trust, interactions between teachers and students play a significant role in the development of a high-functioning school. The construct of academic press, or the degree to which teachers believe that students are capable of succeeding academically and help them meet academic expectations, has persistently been identified as a variable in student achievement. Strong academic press motivates students to work hard and respect others who are academically oriented. Academic press may be leveraged by school policies and practices, but it is also dependent upon norms of behavior exhibited and modeled by leaders of a school community. Various studies have found that instructional leadership is positively correlated with academic achievement, even when controlling for the effects of socioeconomic status.

Another concept, collective teacher efficacy, is based on the shared perceptions of teachers that the efforts of the faculty will have positive effects on students. These beliefs can powerfully shape group behavior and group outcomes through the goals, effort, perseverance, and resilience that flow from them. In schools where teachers were willing to acknowledge their pitfalls and then improve their educational practices, they were rewarded with higher student achievement, which directly increased teachers' sense of being able to help even their most disadvantaged students. Like academic press, collective teacher efficacy has been linked to student achievement even when taking into account the impact of students' socioeconomic status.

This passage was adapted from "Principals, Trust, and Cultivating Vibrant Schools." Tschannen-Moran M, Gareis CR. *Societies*. 2015. 5 doi: 10.3390/soc5020256 for use under the terms of the Creative Commons CC BY 4.0 license (https://creativecommons.org/licenses/by/4.0/legalcode).

Question 1

According to the passage, which of the following factors directly influences student achievement?

- ○ **A.** Parental involvement in students' academics
- ○ **B.** The financial status of a student's family
- ○ **C.** Student trust in the principal of the school
- ○ **D.** A student's inherent motivation to succeed

Question 2

Based on the passage, it is reasonable to conclude that a school's climate:

- ○ **A.** encourages students to become politically active citizens.
- ○ **B.** is always determined by the level of trust faculty have in their principal.
- ○ **C.** reflects the behavior of school principals.
- ○ **D.** is shaped by school policies and practices.

Question 3

According to passage information about effective leadership, which of the following situations would be most likely?

- ○ **A.** By making information about company progress available, the CEO inspires employees to recognize and resolve their own weaknesses.
- ○ **B.** To ensure the safety of the nation, the president of a country keeps military tactics secret, even from cabinet staff.
- ○ **C.** To engage members of the school community, a principal organizes parent-principal conferences.
- ○ **D.** A medical school dean reviews the academic records of her medical students and meets with anyone who is struggling.

Question 4

Which of the following best represents a loss of "collective teacher efficacy" as described in paragraph six?

- ○ **A.** An artist is negatively critiqued on his work by colleagues and he subsequently loses confidence in his aesthetic ability.
- ○ **B.** After a group of physicians successfully resuscitates a patient who has coded, they collectively agree that they need a break from difficult cases.
- ○ **C.** The teachers at one high school do not push their students to apply to college.
- ○ **D.** After a team of superheroes is unable to rescue people from a burning building, they resign from their positions.

Question 5

Which conclusion about principals can be inferred from the passage?

- ○ **A.** Teachers and students act in ways that match the conduct of their principal.
- ○ **B.** Studies using intercorrelational measures have found that the quality of school leadership is related to faculty achievement.
- ○ **C.** Principals who emphasize self-reliance lead schools that achieve academic success.
- ○ **D.** Principals who do not establish trusting relationships with other members of the school community do not deserve respect because their schools do not produce engaged citizens.

Question 6

Which of the following, if true, would most weaken the author's argument about student achievement?

- ○ **A.** Teachers who do not believe in the benefits of academic press have more A students than teachers who do.
- ○ **B.** Principals who do not often interact with students, but who are trusted by their teachers, lead schools that perform above average on standardized tests.
- ○ **C.** Disadvantaged students demonstrate academic achievement that is comparable to that of their more advantaged peers.
- ○ **D.** Students educated in a trusting school environment feel so comfortable that they do not strive academically.

Question 7

Which of the following passage assertions is LEAST supported by the passage?

- ○ **A.** "Schools with a climate of tension and fear interfere with educational advancement."
- ○ **B.** "Where the principal has established high trust relationships, teachers are more likely to perceive that they can trust their colleagues as well."
- ○ **C.** "Principals have both a direct and indirect influence on student learning."
- ○ **D.** "When teachers and principals do not trust one another, each seeks to minimize their vulnerability and risk by adopting self-protective stances."

Passage 2 (Questions 8-12)

Complaints about the ethics of medical ghostwriting have increased in the last decade, but little has changed. Corruption of the scientific literature through ghostwriting persists in medicine due to the enormous profits for all stakeholders, including the pharmaceutical industry that creates the publication strategy, academic researchers acting as key opinion leaders (KOLs) for industry, universities employing KOLs, medical journals and their proprietors (including medical societies and publishers), and medical communication companies employing ghostwriters.

Ghostwriting openly infringes academic standards and, in many cases, as recently argued by Stern and Lemmens in PLoS Medicine, contributes to fraud. Typically, the practice involves industry-financed writers generating articles that either promote the sponsor company's products or discredit competing ones, with eventual authorship credited to academic researchers who provide little or no input, thereby concealing industry involvement and contributing to distorted drug profiles.

Although some journals, most notably PLoS Medicine, and several editors' associations have produced policies against the practice, in some cases adopting clear and visible positions, articles with ghostwriting are still being published. This could be due to the predicament in which editors find themselves: questioning the validity of an article technically authored by a scholar. Additionally, despite efforts to reinforce authorship and publication requirements, journals' responses to ghost-writing remain unsatisfactory, as shown by a recent study of 630 articles from six high-impact medical journals. In 2008, the overall prevalence of articles with honorary authorship, ghost authorship, or both was 21.0%, which represented a decline from 29.1% in 1996. Although the prevalence of ghost authorship showed a significant decline, there was no change in the prevalence of honorary authors relative to 1996. This study concluded that inappropriate authorship remains a significant problem in high impact biomedical publications.

Indeed, even the policies adopted by the International Committee of Medical Journal Editors have failed to clarify how the corruption of medical literature could be curtailed. Substantial contribution to manuscript design or drafting is of little significance when marketing messages are planted in the ghostwriter's first draft well before a nominal author is selected. Authors may give approval when the paper is submitted for publication, but this occurs only after the sponsor company has ensured that the manuscript meets its marketing goals and the legal department has transferred ownership to the submitting author. The manuscript and message are therefore controlled by the company rather than the nominal authors.

Since self-regulation has not produced results and the government has failed to have any significant impact, the only remaining option is the legal system. Stern and Lemmens recently advanced various legal theories under which "guest authors" can be held accountable, including filing an action under the Racketeer Influenced and Corrupt Organizations Act (RICO).

They opined that monetary damages could include a reduction in the subscription value of the journal publishing ghostwritten articles. They concede that individual damages would be nominal but suggest that potential liability and reputational harm may curb ghostwriting.

This passage was adapted from "Challenging Medical Ghost Writing in US Courts." Bosch X, Esfandiari B, and McHenry L. *PLoS Medicine*. 2012. 9(1) doi: 10.1371/journal.pmed.1001163 for use under the terms of the Creative Commons CC BY 3.0 license (http://creativecommons.org/licenses/by/3.0/legalcode).

Question 8

In the past few years, more journals have adopted a policy of refusing to publish articles with ghostwriters but a study found that the prevalence of ghostwritten articles did not change. Which of the following is a reasonable explanation for this finding?

- ○ **A.** Editors are not enforcing the new policies.
- ○ **B.** Pharmaceutical companies are submitting more articles to increase the likelihood of being published.
- ○ **C.** Editors have difficulty determining the authorship of articles.
- ○ **D.** Articles with ghostwriting are published in more unique outlets.

Question 9

Suppose a nominal author reveals that he was able to make slight edits to a ghostwritten article before submitting it for publication. When in the writing process could he most likely edit the article?

- ○ **A.** As soon as he was selected as the author
- ○ **B.** When he legally owned the article
- ○ **C.** While the marketing goals are being developed
- ○ **D.** Anytime, since he is involved in the entire process

Next ▶

Question 10

In the first paragraph, "enormous profits" could refer to all of the following EXCEPT:

○ **A.** knowledge.

○ **B.** money.

○ **C.** prestige.

○ **D.** popularity.

Question 11

Which of the following conclusions about proposed legal punishments for ghostwriting can be inferred from the passage?

○ **A.** Individuals would have to pay large fines.

○ **B.** Government regulation would be very strict.

○ **C.** Pharmaceutical companies would be shut down.

○ **D.** Guilty journals would make less money from individual consumers.

Question 12

Which of the following statements, if true, would most weaken the author's argument about ghostwriting?

○ **A.** Medical journals are publishing fewer editions per year.

○ **B.** Pharmaceutical companies are designating less money each year for marketing.

○ **C.** Pharmaceutical companies that employ the most ghostwriters produce the most effective drugs.

○ **D.** Journal editors are often close friends with pharmaceutical representatives.

Passage 3 (Questions 13-18)

On his frequent tours, the Dalai Lama makes headlines the world over, drawing crowds and media wherever he goes. As the figurehead of Tibetan Buddhism and a Nobel laureate, he converses with prime ministers, presidents, popes, and kings, and shares the stage with eminent scientists and religious leaders of all denominations. Over the past decades, the Dalai Lama has achieved iconic status in the West. Images of the Dalai Lama's famed openness and tolerance often precede him, effectively blocking a view of the robust and resilient nature of some of his established ideas. Public understanding of the nature and scope of the Dalai Lama's thought suffers from a definite lack of critical analysis. Very little has been written in the West exploring the influence of the current Dalai Lama's epistemology and philosophy on relations between contemporary science and Tibetan Buddhist thinking. Consequently, little light has been shed on the vested religious, philosophical, and institutional interests that at least partially govern the Dalai Lama's relationship to scientific knowledge. Teasing out the Dalai Lama's catalogue of philosophical positions, religious beliefs, and epistemic resources opens a window on the way he understands science and scientists.

The thrust of the Dalai Lama's argument goes well beyond hypothesizing what can or cannot be thought to be scientifically established. Scientific progress ought to be subservient to the wellbeing of sentient life, the Dalai Lama believes. Besides their scientific tenability, the new realities that scientific discoveries create ought to be considered. Likewise, beside their cogency and merit, the soteriological efficacy of Buddhist doctrines such as rebirth ought to be factored into the appraisal of scientific findings. In his view, at any given moment of assessment, Buddhists' ontological, epistemological, and moral commitments may pull in different directions. The reciprocal exchange of ideas between the Dalai Lama and scientists is governed as much by rhetoric, contestation, and ethics as by empiricism and logic.

The Dalai Lama regularly exhorts the Tibetan monastic community to recognize that a working knowledge of fundamental scientific principles, valuable in its own right, has added value in propounding Buddhist thought. At the same time, he champions Buddhists' right to a measured, critical reception of science. From his perspective, Tibetan Buddhist thinkers ought to engage scientific thought on their own terms, breaking into their own traditional rhetorical and epistemological repertoire. Leading by confident example, the Dalai Lama himself occasionally deflects the burden of proof through the application of age-old Tibetan Buddhist rhetoric.

The Dalai Lama believes that the course of science ought to be governed by ethical understandings and concerns. The doctrine of reincarnation, for instance, serves as a cornerstone for Tibetan Buddhist morality. The Dalai Lama, lacking ready-made alternatives, may be unwilling to give it up prematurely, before irrefutable scientific proof has been submitted. In this case, for him, soteriological expediency and moral responsibility may supersede "taking the growth of knowledge seriously" or "being epistemically responsible." Together, these and other critical perspectives on the Dalai Lama's way of thinking illustrate that any one putative hierarchy between Buddhists' epistemological, ontological, and moral commitments is not self-evident. Reductive views of the Dalai Lama's relation to science, so often informed by the popular images that precede him, serve only to hinder the interaction of Buddhism and science, which otherwise entail similar pursuits: the methodical formation, exchange, and testing of human ideas.

This passage was adapted from "Caveat Emptor: The Dalai Lama's Proviso and the Burden of (Scientific) Proof." Hogendoorn R. *Religions*. 2014. 5 doi:10.3390/rel5030522 for use under the terms of the Creative Commons CC BY 3.0 license (http://creativecommons.org/licenses/by/3.0/legalcode).

Question 13

Which of the following most *contradicts* the author's view of how the Dalai Lama approaches scientific ideas within the Tibetan Buddhist monastic community?

O **A.** The Dalai Lama wants to see scientific principles adopted into Tibetan Buddhist theology.

O **B.** The Dalai Lama considers scientific thought important to furthering Buddhist thought.

O **C.** The Dalai Lama refuses to accept scientifically drawn conclusions about nature.

O **D.** The Dalai Lama takes a guarded approach to science.

Question 14

Given the information in the passage concerning the Dalai Lama's approach to scientific knowledge, the Dalai Lama would most likely embrace a scientific discovery that:

O **A.** does not contradict Tibetan Buddhist beliefs.

O **B.** demonstrates the existence of intangible matter.

O **C.** furthers the development of technology.

O **D.** helps people live more comfortably.

Question 15

Based on the information in the passage, research at a contemporary Tibetan Buddhist scientific academy would most likely be guided by which of the following principles?

O **A.** The growth of knowledge is paramount.

O **B.** Science is worthwhile in developing Buddhist thought.

O **C.** Scientific discovery is secondary to moral responsibility.

O **D.** Buddhist ontology benefits from scientific principles.

Question 16

Imagine the Pope, as leader of the Roman Catholic Church, publicly endorsed researchers working to lessen the effects of human-generated climate change. The author would most likely argue that the Pope:

O **A.** made a theological concession to science.

O **B.** thought the researchers' work would yield .

O **C.** felt compelled to be epistemically responsible.

O **D.** was influenced by Tibetan Buddhist thinking.

Question 17

According to the author, a scientist who believes in reincarnation would most likely agree with which of the following statements?

O **A.** There are limits to what science can explain.

O **B.** Scientific progress affects the quality of human life.

O **C.** Moral conclusions should be drawn based on empirical evidence.

O **D.** Theological beliefs are irrelevant to scientific pursuits.

Question 18

Which of the following claims most *weakens* the author's argument about the Dalai Lama's approach to scientific thinking?

O **A.** Scientific thinking cannot fulfill human needs.

O **B.** The Tibetan Buddhist doctrine of reincarnation has no scientific basis.

O **C.** The current Dalai Lama's openness to scientific thinking is anomalous in Tibetan Buddhist philosophy.

O **D.** Ethical decisions can only be reached through scientific thinking.

Passage 4 (Questions 19-24)

Defining psychogeography is a difficult task to accomplish. Guy Debord, one of its founding fathers and most outspoken proponents, describes it as the "study of the specific effects of the geographical environment, consciously organized or not, on the emotions and behavior of individuals." This definition poses further questions, particularly those concerning the very nature of the enterprise. As Merlin Coverley suggests, psychogeography keeps "resisting definition through a shifting series of interwoven themes and is constantly being reshaped by its practitioners." As a result, the term has become so widely appropriated and has been used in support of such a bewildering array of ideas that it has lost much of its original significance.

No matter how ambiguous, psychogeography possesses several predominant characteristic features: urban walking, the spirit of political subversion and radicalism, the focus on the mysterious and occult, and the preoccupation with rediscovering the past as a means of casting light on the present. It is a moving or travelling in which the physical dimension is intrinsically interwoven with the mental, one in which thorough planning of the journey gives way to haphazard randomness.

Iain Sinclair is responsible for the current revival of psychogeography as a literary form. For Sinclair, walking the streets becomes continuous research into the hidden layers of modern urban experience carried out through the ultimate immersion into the gravity field of its lines of force. The output of such undertakings is inevitably fragmentary and inconsistent, transforming the city into a puzzle whose bits often do not fit together. Dealing with themes such as fragmentation and multiplicity is a project destined to remain inconclusive, based on the practitioner's subjectivity rather than on his unbiased observation, and Sinclair uses this poetic license to construct progressive and reformist commentary.

Although Petr Ackroyd would definitely not label his writing as psychogeographic, the publication of his *London: The Biography* has been hailed by some as the moment when psychogeography entered the mainstream. Ackroyd invites his readers to accompany him on his roaming around London and across its history. His image of London and its history corresponds with the ambivalent view of the metropolis shared by its many current inhabitants—it seems fragmentary and often chaotic. Ackroyd's approach to London sees the aspects of its "unofficial" history as being as, or even more, important than the "official" ones, yet his interpretations of this history often coincides with the established philosophical climate. His position is one of inherent conservatism in which all change is subsumed within this unending historical overview.

There are two major similarities between Sinclair and Ackroyd: an obsessive focus on the repressed history of the contemporary landscape, and the vision of the city as a text that is endlessly recomposed. Ackroyd is also convinced of the underlying forces operating within certain areas of London, which have managed to retain their particular spirit and atmosphere across centuries until the present day.

Ackroyd is by no means a prototypical representative of contemporary psychogeographic tradition. Although he is a keen London walker, his writing lacks the overtly documentary form and narrative perspective, employing instead visionary projections of a timeless and everlasting city. Regardless of Ackroyd's occasional tendency to espouse and promote certain unorthodox phenomena, his concept of London is generally traditionalist and lacks any undertones of a revolutionary agenda. Ackroyd's, perambulations are far from politically motivated and subversive, as he is primarily interested in the intricate and often contradictory relationship between personal and official histories. His is a fundamentally idealistic vision of the city, one which is based on reconciliation rather than discord, integration rather than incongruity.

This passage was adapted from "London of the Mind – The Narrative of Psychogeographic Antiquarianism in Selected London Novels of Peter Ackroyd." Chalupsky P. *English Language and Literature Studies.* 2014. 4(1) doi: 10.5539/ells.v4n1p10 for use under the terms of the Creative Commons CC BY 3.0 license (http://creativecommons.org/licenses/by/3.0/legalcode).

Question 19

The nature of psychogeography can most accurately be described as:

    I. an artistic movement.

    II. a narrative strategy.

    III. a rebellious political act.

- **A.** I and II
- **B.** I and III
- **C.** II and III
- **D.** I, II, and III

Question 20

With which of the following statements about London would Ackroyd most agree?

- **A.** The eclectic communities of London lead separate and inharmonious lives.
- **B.** London is not a stagnant and predictable city filled with disjointed characters.
- **C.** Small pieces of the city change from day to day but the soul remains the same.
- **D.** Changes in the city of London are made by radical visionaries.

Question 21

Sinclair most differs from Ackroyd in that Sinclair:

- **A.** relays a factual account of his wanderings.
- **B.** is a true psychogeographic writer.
- **C.** writes subjectively rather than objectively.
- **D.** only finds pieces instead of the full puzzle.

Question 22

According to the information provided in the passage, which of the following situations would most likely occur in a traditional psychogeographic writing?

- **A.** The author accidently participates in a march against artificial intelligence.
- **B.** The author meets several mysterious people who turn out to have intricately connected pasts.
- **C.** A character stumbles upon a clan descended from gypsies that cannot get government aid.
- **D.** A character finds an underground tunnel housing a multigenerational family.

Question 23

If Ackroyd wrote a piece about the resolution of a political riot he witnessed on his wanderings, would the author of the passage be likely to consider Ackroyd a prototypical psychogeographic writer?

- **A.** Yes, because it was his lack of political motivation that made him a non-quintessential psychogeographer.
- **B.** Yes, because a narrative of urban walking is the norm for psychogeography.
- **C.** No, because the resolution of chaos would separate him further from psychogeography ideals.
- **D.** No, because his account of reconciliation might not be subversively motivated.

Question 24

Which of the following statements is most supported by the information provided in the passage?

- **A.** Peter Ackroyd is a fantasist who finds promise and hope in the cities through which he wanders.
- **B.** Psychogeography is an amorphous literary movement with multiple practitioners and manifestations.
- **C.** Iain Sinclair is a pragmatist whose conclusive accounts support the government's adversaries.
- **D.** Psychogeography links people together through their connection to certain locales.

Passage 5 (Questions 25-30)

With significant improvements in healthcare over recent decades, the life expectancy of people with Intellectual Disabilites (ID) has increased, and they now form an aging—and uniquely vulnerable—population. This epidemiological development is connected with growing incidences of life-limiting illnesses, such as progressive cancer, chronic cardiovascular diseases, and dementia. As a result, people with ID increasingly need end-of-life care.

End-of-life care may start early on in the trajectory of a life-threatening illness. It can be typified as multidisciplinary care aimed at enhancing the quality of life by assessing and relieving pain and other distressing symptoms. This standard of care takes into account the physical, psychological, and spiritual needs of patients, all of which are addressed by professionals who specialize in those fields. End-of-life care for people with ID is particularly challenging due to their limited level of understanding of the implications of end-of-life care.

When death is imminent, people with ID need an approach covering all aspects of end-of-life care, an approach that may not be naturally rooted in ID care services. Several studies have indicated that ID care professionals have a lack of knowledge and expertise in end-of-life care, such as in pain and symptom management. Symptom relief especially can often be a challenge in people with severe ID, as health providers must identify pain, anxiety, and other signals of distress without many cues. Often these symptoms only become visible through small changes in behavior or signals such as grimaces or a stretching of the neck. Physicians must rely heavily on information from people closely involved with the patient, such as relatives. Relatives who have had a lifelong relationship with the person are often best equipped to interpret the patient's signals and expressions of needs, distress, and pain.

Yet joint efforts between ID care providers and family members can be problematic, as both parties may not always proactively seek contact or find a common language to talk about the patient's condition. Many medical decisions need to be made during end-of-life care, including about life-prolonging treatments, tube feeding, and the provision of oxygen and pain medication. Relatives often feel overwhelmed by the dependency of the person with ID, a feeling that is magnified during end-of-life care. It may not always be easy for relatives to deal with professionals during this emotional period, and they can feel that even the presence of the provider, let alone her advice, is an infringement of their privacy and rights as representatives. If perceptions of what constitutes good care differ and communication fails, the good intentions to provide joint care may turn into a burden and source of distress for the dying person. Doctors often feel they have a duty to provide the best possible care for their patients based on their extensive training and expertise, and so in these times of conflict, may believe it more efficient to make care decisions without input from family members. Problems in the joint provision of end-of-life care between relatives and care staff are not exclusive to ID care: they are also found in nursing homes and care homes for a variety of patients, especially those who are elderly.

However, having "two families" comprised of relatives and ID care staff come together and jointly provide for a patient with ID can lead to warm, loving care in the proximity of the people who know the patient's needs best. Intensified cooperation both among professionals and also between relatives and professionals can seem burdensome even while it is the epitome of patient-centered care. This cooperation entails being able to communicate adequately about the person's signals and needs, facilitating an openness required to make joint medical decisions. Care for people with ID, especially at the end of life, is premised on relationships. As much as professionals need information from relatives to provide good patient-centered care, relatives need the support of professionals as they prepare to let go.

This passage was adapted from "'From activating towards caring': shifts in care approaches at the end of life of people with intellectual disabilities; a qualitative study of the perspectives of relatives, care-staff and physicians." Bekkema N, de Veer AJE, Hertogh CMPM, and Francke AL. *BMC Palliative Care.* 2015. 14(33) doi: 10.1186/s12904-015-0030-2 for use under the terms of the Creative Commons CC BY 4.0 license (https://creativecommons.org/licenses/by/4.0/legalcode).

Question 25

Which of the following objections to a guidance counselor's recommendations for a student are most similar to those of ID patients' relatives (paragraph 4), as the author presents their views?

- ○ **A.** Guidance counselors do not spend enough time with each of their individual students to make student-centered recommendations.
- ○ **B.** Students may feel unnecessary stress due to the conflicts that arise between educators and parents due to these recommendations.
- ○ **C.** Guidance counselors do not have the necessary expertise to provide advice.
- ○ **D.** School staff opinions are intrusive and imply that educators know better than parents how their children learn.

Question 26

The passage implies that one of the reasons providing end-of-life care specifically for people with ID is difficult is that:

- ○ **A.** they are unable to communicate that they are experiencing pain.
- ○ **B.** they may not comprehend that they are dying.
- ○ **C.** physicians and family members may experience conflicts when they try to jointly provide care.
- ○ **D.** they make up a uniquely vulnerable patient population.

Question 27

According to passage information, which of the following situations best reflects the concept of "two families" (paragraph 5)?

- ○ **A.** A school nurse calls a conference with a failing student's mother to discuss behavioral strategies they can implement at home and at school.
- ○ **B.** A future bride enlists a wedding consultant and her friends to help her select a dress.
- ○ **C.** A patient stresses the importance of his physicians and his case manager working together to ensure that he receives care that meets his needs.
- ○ **D.** A homeowner renovates her house with assistance from her husband and from online videos.

Question 28

According to the passage, which of the following is NOT a problem that health professionals and family members encounter about working together to provide end-of-life care?

- ○ **A.** Distinct sets of vocabulary used to describe a patient's disease
- ○ **B.** Differentials in knowledge about how a patient's symptoms present
- ○ **C.** An unwillingness to communicate about a patient's condition to each other
- ○ **D.** The feeling that a provider is intruding on the family

Question 29

The author' arguments about end-of-life care for people with ID imply that she would most likely *oppose* which of the following arrangements?

- ○ **A.** An ID care professional who lacks expertise in end-of-life care serves as the primary provider for one of her dying patients.
- ○ **B.** A patient's family members spend many hours consulting his doctors about how to administer oxygen at home.
- ○ **C.** Because he is pressed for time, a physician decides to provide pain medication to his patient independently from family input.
- ○ **D.** A doctor who disagrees with the tenets of end-of-life care argues strongly to his patients that they should continue cure-directed treatment, rather than "giving up."

Question 30

Which of the following, if assumed to be true, would most *weaken* the author's conclusion about the role of relatives?

○ **A.** Research shows that when people with ID are dying, the majority of family members who provide care for them have been estranged for decades.

○ **B.** Relatives of people with ID experience significant stress when they disagree with physicians about what constitutes the best care.

○ **C.** Studies show that family members cannot explain why they are aware of the small changes in a patient's behavior that signal distress.

○ **D.** Some patients with ID do not have many relatives who are willing to visit them at the end of their lives.

Passage 6 (Questions 31-35)

Adults represent one of the fastest growing sports cohorts in many Westernized countries. Adult sportspersons are referred to as Master athletes, particularly when they are above 35 years of age and registered to compete in sports, and when they acknowledge they "prepare in order to participate." Master athletes are often characterized by physical activity that includes formal registration to a sports club with a dedicated coach.

Coaches structure participants' training and establish the tone of the sports environment. Furthermore, coaches can make sports more enjoyable for athletes, with athlete satisfaction being greatest when coaches' actions are congruent with athletes' preferences. However, coaches' impact on adults' experiences in sports is unclear, and there is very little empirical evidence describing adult athletes' unique psycho-social coaching needs. At present, a paucity of research exists regarding how adult athletes perceive their interactions with coaches, whether they value coaches, and what they want from coaches.

The potential importance of Master coaches can be gleaned from various sources. First, more than 70% of serious Master swimmers report having a personal coach. Second, Master athletes report strategically using coaches to motivate themselves. Third, coached Master athletes report more self-determined profiles beneficial to overall psychological wellbeing and persistence than do athletes without a coach. These athletes often turn to their coaches as a source of internal determination. Coaches appear to be an instrumental resource for Master athletes, yet we know little about how Master athletes perceive their experiences with coaches, and what their preferences are during these experiences.

The need to understand Master athletes' interests is evidenced by a gap in knowledge relating to the structure of coaching education programs. In Canada, for instance, programs spell out age-specific needs distinguishing children, adolescents, and athletes in early adulthood, but no coach education work discriminating athletes' needs exists for older adults engaged in sport. The Coaching Association of Canada (CAC) has produced a resource booklet pertaining to biophysical considerations of coaching Master athletes; however, psychosocial aspects of coaching this age cohort are less developed. For example, the following lines are included in the CAC booklet for Master coaches: "What's different about coaching Master athletes? And the answer is, probably not much. As long as they're healthy, there's no real difference between coaching them and coaching younger athletes." These statements reflect an implicit assumption that coaching approaches for Master athletes need not vary from those who coach younger athletes. In general, athlete development models, such as the internationally recognized Long Term Athlete Development Model or empirically based models of talent development, also do not elaborate on how coaches might work specifically with adult athletes. Currently, competitive but non-elite adult athlete coaching requirements are simply conceptualized as the same as those for younger athletes. This situation needs to be addressed by research that asks Master athletes to explicitly describe nuanced aspects of their experiences with coaches.

Next ▶

Coaches learn largely from experience in coaching practice, so understanding athletes' experiences and preferences with coaches is an important first step in considering what coaches can do (or should refrain from doing) to accommodate the needs of Master athletes. Indeed, certain elements of coaching, such as how one empowers or motivates, the manner of exchange with athletes, and styles of instruction and feedback delivery may be unique when coaching Master athletes. Pedagogical models of coaching and adult learning indicate that learning variables should be understood with a particular eye to individual characteristics of the person/social situation of the cohort in question, which suggests that approaches prevailing in younger sports cohorts may not hold for Master athletes.

This passage was adapted from "Masters Swimmers' Experience with Coaches: What They Want, What they Need, What they Get." Callery B, Rathwell S, Young B. *SAGE Open.* 2015. doi: 10.1177/2158244015588960 for use under the terms of the Creative Commons CC BY 4.0 license (http://creativecommons.org/licenses/by/4.0/legalcode).

Question 31

According to the passage, Master athletes utilize coaches in order to:

    I. enjoy sports participation.
    II. increase their motivation.
    III. improve their self-determination.

- **A.** I and II
- **B.** I and III
- **C.** II and III
- **D.** III only

Question 32

Which of the following best describes a point made in the passage that supports the author's argument about studying the influence of coaches?

- **A.** Master athletes do not benefit from coaching.
- **B.** Master athletes are increasing in prevalence.
- **C.** Coaches are more important for younger athletes.
- **D.** Coaches should focus on instructing one age group.

Question 33

The passage implies that coaching Master athletes versus younger athletes differs with respect to:

- **A.** physicality.
- **B.** psychology.
- **C.** teamwork.
- **D.** motivation.

Question 34

Suppose a coaching association advises different coaching styles for lifelong athletes and athletes new to a sport. Would the author be likely to agree with this advice?

- **A.** Yes, because it would recognize the distinct psychological needs of two groups.
- **B.** Yes, because it would acknowledge differing levels of experience.
- **C.** No, because this advice could worsen coaching for Master athletes.
- **D.** No, because the advice does not explicitly take age into account.

Question 35

Athletes' performance tends to decline with age. How does this finding affect the author's argument presented in the passage?

- **A.** It supports the author's claim that coaching for Master athletes needs to be adjusted.
- **B.** It questions the importance of a coach for Master athletes.
- **C.** It does not affect the author's argument.
- **D.** It repeats claims already suggested in the passage.

Passage 7 (Questions 36-40)

Yoruba is the name given to represent the ethnic group and language of those living in South-West Nigeria. The Yorubas have a very rich culture with a strong spiritual background. These cultural and spiritual beliefs are exhibited during their festive periods. Although there are festivals celebrated in all the Yoruba communities, some are specific to certain Yoruba communities. These festivals are often staged on an annual basis. One of the most popular festivals, the Ojude Oba festival, is in the Ijebu-speaking community, a subgroup of the Yoruba ethnic group. The festival celebrates the uniqueness of the community, such as their aesthetic taste in clothes, music, costumes, food, and so on.

Ojude Oba, which means "the king's forecourt or frontage," could also be translated as "majestic outing." The native age groups (regberegbe), indigenes, their friends, and associates from near and far gather at the palace of the Awujale of Ijebuland for the carnival-like celebration. Ojude Oba is one of the most glamorous cultural and spiritual festivals in Ijebuland, and has been celebrated for more than 100 years. While the celebration was founded in religious beliefs, it now has traditional, social, military, and, most importantly, social significance.

The Ojude Oba festival normally begins with prayers by the Imam of Ijebuland, or Islamic leadership, followed by the National Anthem, Ogun state Anthem, and the Awujale Anthem—ending with the lineage praise of the Ijebus. These aspects pay tribute to the religious origin of the festival, but are not necessarily appreciated by all attendants of the festival. During the one day event are the glowing tributes of a festival that is responsive to social trends, while retaining the tradition of having different age groups to entertain and renew their allegiance to the traditional ruler. It is usually a dance, but more importantly, a dance with meaning. Each age group performs at the expansive lawn that separates the king and his guests from the crowd.

The Ojude Oba festival has always had enough visual pleasantries for visitors, who seem to frequent the area more during the celebration, regardless of their religious beliefs. One of the attractions is the beauty of a group of people in the same age group coming together in service of their motherland. Many of the regberegbe's names are related to the king such as Obafuwaji, Bobakeye, Gbobayo, Gbobaniyi, and Gbobalaye. Each of these groups has its uniqueness, either in the manner of appearance, style of dressing, or dance style.

A festival like Ojude Oba is an aspect of African culture imported from Islam. Primarily, the spiritual significance is derived from the origin and initial aims of the festival. It was started by Muslims during their *Eid-l-Adha*, after settling into the area. The festival is seen as a continuation of the *Eid-l-Adha* celebration by the Muslims in the community, as it is held on the third day of *Eid*. The festival today is not only celebrated by Muslims; Christians, as well as people from other faiths, join the Muslims in this celebration. They often travel from long distances, bringing their own beliefs with them. The Ojude Oba festival encourages peaceful co-existence of people of different faiths, celebrating cultural communities rather than one religion.

The festival also promotes cultural contact, as it is usually graced by people from all works of life. Other ethnic groups in Nigeria also participate in the festival, so people from neighboring areas are not left out. Ojude Oba has promoted peace, tranquility, and harmony, which contribute to socioeconomic and cultural development of Ijebuland.

This passage was adapted from "Ijebu Ode's Ojude Oba Festival: Cultural and Spiritual Significance." Fahm AO. *SAGE Open.* 2015. doi: 10.1177/2158244015574640 for use under the terms of the Creative Commons CC BY 4.0 license (https://creativecommons.org/licenses/by/4.0/legalcode).

Question 36

According to the passage, which of the following activities is common to each regberegbe?

- ○ **A.** Dancing for the king
- ○ **B.** Renewing their allegiance
- ○ **C.** Discussing age-specific activities
- ○ **D.** Praying for the king

Question 37

The passage suggests that the festival's positive impact on the community stems from:

- ○ **A.** its renewal of beliefs.
- ○ **B.** its recognition of Ijebu history.
- ○ **C.** its tolerant message.
- ○ **D.** its economic impact.

Question 38

Assume that a new festival was discovered in a location founded by the settlers of the Ijebu community. On the basis of information presented in the passage, this festival would most likely contain which of the following?

- ○ **A.** Singing of the national anthem
- ○ **B.** Prayer from the imam
- ○ **C.** Performing for the king
- ○ **D.** Welcoming of Christians

Question 39

Given the information contained in the passage, if a visitor attends a different Ijebu celebration and it does not include a prayer, then it most likely:

- O **A.** is a relatively new festival.
- O **B.** is a festival imported from a nearby region.
- O **C.** is rooted in a cultural origin.
- O **D.** unites the members of the Ijebu community.

Question 40

Which of the following discoveries would most strengthen the proposal that Ojude Oba has both cultural and spiritual significance today in the Ijebu community?

- O **A.** Ijebus report this festival as their favorite of the year.
- O **B.** Ijebus feel most unified as a community during this festival.
- O **C.** Ijebus report feeling closest to Allah during this festival.
- O **D.** Ijebus bond with one another and visitors during the festival.

Passage 8 (Questions 41-46)

Saharan massifs are dotted by thousands of paintings and engravings; vanishing traces of humans that inhabited the region at least since the beginnings of the Holocene. The region is one of the warmest arid lands in the world, hard to cross and to live in, today almost completely uninhabited, but for a few resilient nomadic groups. For these reasons, the artworks remained unknown until the late 19th century, when the first exploration of the Great desert by western travelers started and rock art began to capture the imagination of scholars. However, after more than two centuries, rock art is still scarcely known and understood.

Tadrart Acacus—a massif in the western region of contemporary Libya—represents the emblematic context for the study of the Saharan rock art. Discovered later relative to other important rock art galleries, Tadrart Acacus rapidly became the key area of the Saharan rock art. The massif in fact hosts an impressive amount of real masterpieces of prehistoric rock art and, since it was first discovered, has been the object of research that changed aims and methods, reacting to the wider scientific framework.

The 1950s and 1960s have been repeatedly defined as the time of 'pioneering' research, when the massif was explored and the rock art discovered. The researchers in this first period aimed to reveal this rock art to the Western world, leading to its acknowledgment by the international community as a site of outstanding universal value. These years were completely devoted to the first survey of the rock art contexts and to their reproduction by master painters. Even if this research is today highly disputed for the damaging impact that the recording procedures had on the paintings and for its analytical and methodological shortcomings, it marked the beginning of rock art study in the area and produced the official documentation of the rock art until recent times.

Multidisciplinary research carried out in the region since the 1960s laid the foundations for the main questions about chronology, which still constitute part of the contemporary debate. The chronological debate developed around two proposals both based on stylistic assumptions, superimpositions, studies of varnish, environmental conditions, and represented subjects. A 'long' chronology identified the earliest rock art as a late Pleistocene/early Holocene production, due to hunter-gatherers, whereas a 'short' proposal referred all the rock art evidence to the Holocene, starting with pastoralists. A consensus on chronology is still to be gained as definitions of styles, as well as what they indicate about chronology, remain contested.

Wild Fauna style is the most debated phase. It has been traditionally defined and described as a style including only engravings representing wild animals. On the basis of the type of subjects they represent, these engravings have been thought to be the earliest form of Saharan rock art, and a possible cultural framework has been identified in the early Acacus hunter-gatherer culture. However, stylistic, chronological, and cultural attribution is still problematic. The unsolved problem of the dynamics and timing of repopulation of the central Sahara, and the presence of rock art at sites inconsistent with hunter-gatherer settlement, suggest that scholars should reconsider the available data, and develop the research with analytical and methodological improvements.

The Tadrart Acacus massif is an ideal context to further these debates, for the richness and variability of artworks, as well as for the huge archaeological data known. While early research remains an important part of the debate about chronology, sounder conclusions could stem from the huge amount of now available data, if properly re-analyzed thanks to the use of advanced methodologies.

This passage was adapted from "Saharan Rock Art: Local Dynamics and Wider Perspectives." Gallinaro M. Arts. 2013. 2(4) doi: 10.3390/arts2040350 for use under the terms of the Creative Commons CC BY 3.0 license (http://creativecommons.org/licenses/by/3.0/legalcode).

Question 41

Which of the following best describes the author's view on research conducted at Tadrart Acacus during the 1950s and 1960s?

○ **A.** Methodologically sound

○ **B.** Influential, but inconclusive

○ **C.** Damaging and invalid

○ **D.** Analytically conclusive

Question 42

A team of researchers proposes a new research project on rock art at Tadrart Acacus. The author would most likely support this project if it:

○ **A.** included methods for replicating the artworks.

○ **B.** drew support from Western countries.

○ **C.** intended to analyze paint from diverse rock art styles.

○ **D.** utilized newly available techniques.

Question 43

Which of the following, if assumed to be true, would most *weaken* the "long chronology" discussed in paragraph five?

○ **A.** Pastoral societies had larger populations than hunter-gatherer societies during the early Holocene.

○ **B.** Pastoral societies did not come about in the Sahara until well into the Holocene.

○ **C.** Pastoral societies quickly transformed into sedentary, agricultural societies in the Sahara early in the Holocene.

○ **D.** Pastoral societies were the only societies in the Sahara from the late Pleistocene through the early Holocene.

Question 44

The passage suggests that research on the Tadrart Acacus massif in the 1950s and 1960s was:

○ **A.** problematized by later analysis.

○ **B.** immediately rejected on the basis of its methodology.

○ **C.** authoritative during the following decades.

○ **D.** foundational in the field of rock art studies.

Question 45

Based on information in the passage, with which of the following statements about rock art chronology would the author be most likely to agree?

    I. Lack of data makes establishing a chronology impossible.

    II. Wild Fauna is the earliest rock art at Tadrart Acacus.

    III. A consensus on chronology could be reached based on available data.

○ **A.** I only

○ **B.** II only

○ **C.** II and III

○ **D.** III only

Question 46

According to the passage, the Tadrart Acacus massif provides an excellent location for the study of rock art in the Sahara. Based on claims made in the passage, which of the following best supports this statement?

○ **A.** The massif was discovered more recently than other important rock art sites.

○ **B.** The massif contains a wide array of artworks.

○ **C.** The massif is located in an easily accessible region.

○ **D.** The massif contains extremely well-preserved artworks.

Passage 9 (Questions 47-53)

Concerns about participation in public life have long been central to sociology. In *Democracy in America*, Alexis de Tocqueville (1847) remarked that "almost the only pleasure of which an American has any idea, is to take a part in the government, and to discuss the part he has taken . . . if an American were condemned to confine his activity to his own affairs, he would be robbed of one half of his existence."

Tocqueville did not use the term *public sphere*, but his description of American civic life anticipated the more recent formulation of the public sphere as "a common space in which the members of society are deemed to meet through a variety of media . . . to discuss matters of common interest;

and thus to be able to form a common mind about these." For Tocqueville, as for many scholars of democracy since, participation in the common space of the public sphere through public political talk is a crucial part of self-governance, citizenship, and the formation of political will.

Yet an abundance of social science research documents a serious participation deficit in American public life. Robert Putnam suggests that the rich associational life that characterized the America of Tocqueville's time has unraveled, loosening the social connections that support the public sphere. As a recent *Contexts* article put it, "The ties that bind are fraying." Similarly, Fung and Wright claim that efforts to shrink the "affirmative state" have constrained representative institutions and limited opportunities for egalitarian participation in public life. And Lichterman shows how existing civic organizations (such as church groups) sometimes limit, rather than enable, participation in the public sphere.

The Tocquevillian concern about a general participation deficit is reinforced by studies focusing on how persons engage (or not) in public political talk. Eliasoph shows that even persons who are already members of civic organizations nevertheless actively practice "avoiding politics." Overwhelmed by the scale of political problems, and discouraged by the confrontation and division on display in public debate, members avoid "political" talk to preserve "civic etiquette" in their associational groups. Similarly, Mutz finds that participation decreases when exposure to alternative political perspectives increases, as people solve the problem of "mixed political company" by avoiding confrontation altogether. Americans seem to respond to problems of public debate by "producing apathy" and moving political talk to private life.

At the same time, a growing interdisciplinary literature in empirical public sphere studies suggests that the Tocquevillian concern may be misplaced. In contrast to the Tocquevillian account, which treats participation universally as public talk about political issues, the alternative account suggests that there is no standard set of activities called "participation" that people do (or not). To take a recent example, Perrin includes "thinking and talking" as "citizenship activities" along with "voting, running for office, demonstrating, or signing petitions." But, obviously, sometimes "thinking and talking" are not actually "citizenship activities." Rather, thinking and talking, like many of the things that people already do, are variably directed toward political ends. Likewise, the different activities in which people engage are

variably public. And in practice, activities of all sorts are variably treated as "participation" by social scientists, by political elites, and by the alleged participants themselves. From this perspective, there cannot be an overarching participation deficit, because there is no consistent version of "participation" to be evaluated across all cases.

For the Tocquevillians, increasing "participation" in the form of public political talk is important for creating durable trust relations that extend into other domains and foster development of valuable social capital in communities. However, if "participation" describes a contingent and variable configuration of activities, conditions, and descriptions that reflect relations of power in a particular time and place, then efforts toward increasing public political talk may reinforce existing inequalities of access and power, provide opportunities for private interests to capture the processes of public political talk for their own purposes, and ignore possibilities to foster democracy as it is actually practiced by citizens.

This passage was adapted from "Speaking of Participation: A Qualitative Research Note." Evans, MS. *SAGE Open.* 2014. 4(4) doi:10.1177/2158244014563520 for use under the terms of the Creative Commons CC BY 4.0 license (https://creativecommons.org/licenses/by/4.0/legalcode).

Question 47

If a study found that modern political participation occurs primarily online, the anti-Tocquevillian argument:

○ **A.** would be weakened as the study provides a strong counter argument to the claims of social scientists, political elites, and even participants.

○ **B.** would be strengthened because the Tocquevillian model focuses on public political discussion.

○ **C.** would be weakened, as the study illustrates that interpersonal relations have extended into other domains, developing new social capital.

○ **D.** would be strengthened, because the study indicates that the Tocquevillian goal of participation is still alive in a different form.

Question 48

According to current research, through digital media, people are now better informed about political issues than at any time in history. How would the author respond to this trend?

○ **A.** This development best supports the claims of those who contend that the Tocquevillian crisis is overstated.

○ **B.** This development would likely be ignored by the Tocquevillian camp as with the other studies described.

○ **C.** This information is irrelevant as the issue under discussion is participation.

○ **D.** This raises a complex issue as the original purpose of political speech is to inform people about politics.

Question 49

Based on the passage, which of the following is closest to the passage definition of "affirmative state" (paragraph 3)?

- A. A state of general acceptance by citizens of authority and government.
- B. A state that plays an influential and active role in public life.
- C. A state where the public plays a large and active role in deciding policy.
- D. A state subscribing to Tocquevillian ideals of participation.

Question 50

Based on the passage, which of the following conclusions can be inferred?

- A. Political talk in the public sphere is an essential prerequisite for engaging in democracy for the Tocquevillians.
- B. The role of thinking and talking is extremely difficult to quantify.
- C. The role of thinking and talking has an undetermined impact on the participatory system.
- D. According to those with Tocquevillian concerns, the traditional nucleation points of political discourse are disappearing.

Question 51

Based on the information in the passage, with which of the following statements would the author be most likely to agree?

- A. There should be a major investment in attempting to reignite the political debate in American life.
- B. While an informed populace engaging in meaningful discourse is attractive, increasing participation may actually cause more harm than good.
- C. The status quo offers a balance between the outmoded Tocquevillian position and the potentially dangerous one that could develop.
- D. Participation describes a wide range of activities, so reducing it to either the Tocquevillian or non-Tocquevillian perspective is no longer viable.

Question 52

Which of the following is an assumption made by the author of the passage?

- A. Americans historically took part in vigorous participatory debate.
- B. Discussing politics leads to a breakdown in civility
- C. Participating actively in organizations may lower political participation.
- D. A new definition of participation needs to be developed.

Question 53

Which of the following, if true, would most weaken the author's argument?

- A. Those who espouse the Tocquevillian perspective and those who do not tend to agree on most practical issues.
- B. The disputed nature of 'thinking and talking' in participation is hard to define but is readily identified by those who see it.
- C. There are very few people who identify themselves as Tocquevillians.
- D. The development of grass roots discourse and collegial debate creates natural resistance to misappropriation.

STOP. If you finish before time is called, check your work. You may go back to any question in this test.

ANSWERS & EXPLANATIONS for Test 11 can be found on p. 321.

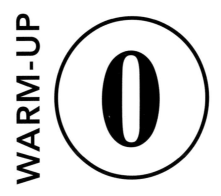

WARM-UP

ANSWERS & EXPLANATIONS
Questions 1–8

ANSWER KEY	
1. A	5. B
2. C	6. C
3. A	7. A
4. D	8. D

EXPLANATIONS FOR WARM-UP

Passage 1 (Questions 1-4)

1. **A is the best answer.** The main idea of the passage is that hunger encompasses both undernourishment and food insecurity because individuals who do not have healthy food options available to them also experience hunger-related health problems. The author describes this definition of hunger as a stepwise process, in which an individual first becomes food insecure and then becomes undernourished. It is reasonable to assume that an individual who is food secure has not experienced this progression, so they are likely to be well-nourished. Choice A is a strong answer. Although this stepwise process begins with food insecurity and advances to undernourishment, the author also suggests that every individual continues on this path once it has started. Because they point out that there are more food insecure individuals than undernourished individuals, it is reasonable to conclude that not every food insecure individual becomes undernourished. Choice B can be eliminated. Because the author emphasizes that hunger progresses in this order, it is unlikely that an undernourished individual is food secure. Choice C is not a strong answer. The author points out that while many individuals may receive adequate caloric intake, meeting the minimum energy requirement of nourishment, they may still experience food insecurity if they do not have nutritious foods available to them. Well-nourished individuals may be experiencing food insecurity but still receiving sufficient calories. Choice D is not as strong as choice A.

2. **C is the best answer.** This passage argues that the definition of hunger should include both caloric intake and nutritional availability. The author presents a definition of hunger primarily based on caloric intake as a misconception, but does not present evidence for why this is the greatest misconception about hunger. Choice A can be eliminated. While many individuals would understand how undernourished individuals are suffering, the author does not describe or list these struggles. Remember not to bring in outside information when answering CARS questions. Choice B can also be eliminated. When defining food insecurity, the author points out that this condition affects more individuals than does undernourishment. They proceed to discuss the prevalence of food insecurity in America, as many individuals who would not be considered undernourished have lacked access to healthy foods at some point. Choice C is a strong answer. While choice D is another statement that inherently makes sense, it is not discussed in detail by the author. They do not propose a situation in which an individual has sufficient food, but insufficient nutrition for a healthy life. Do not make assumptions based on personal knowledge. Choice D is not as strong as choice C.

3. **A is the best answer.** The author argues that famine is not caused simply by lack of food, but rather by a lack of equal distribution of food. There may be plenty of food in a given area, but certain individuals lack the opportunity or funds to acquire it, so the word "receive" in choice A makes it a promising answer. The author does not suggest that these individuals failed to look hard enough for food, but rather could not control their access to it. Choice B is not as strong as choice A. The author also does not discuss the production of food, but does say that there is food available in areas where people die of hunger. This suggests the issue is not one of production, so choice C can be eliminated. The author does not discuss excess consumption of food, so choice D is not a strong answer. Choice A is the best answer.

4. **D is the best answer.** The author emphasizes the relationship between power and food security, and points out that, globally, women tend to have less power and more food insecurity. The author does not suggest that transferring power to a man would fix their food insecurity, as one-fourth of male-headed households are also food insecure. Choice A is not a strong answer. The author discusses this gender discrepancy as a global issue, so relocating to another area would not necessarily solve the problem either. Choice B can be eliminated. Applying for help from the government may expand the household's access to nutritious foods, but this is not suggested in or supported by the passage. Choice C is possible, but likely not the strongest answer. The author emphasizes that women are more likely to experience food insecurity due to their lack of power. By becoming more powerful in the community, they may be more likely to gain access to food. Choice D is stronger than choices A and C because it aligns more closely with the main argument of the passage, which connects power and food security.

Passage 2 (Questions 5-8)

5. **B is the best answer.** This question is tricky and requires a deeper reading of the third paragraph to understand the author's opinion about the subject. The author points out that "Miss" and "Mrs." denote marital status, while "Mr." is ambiguous. By emphasizing a woman's marital status, these terms suggest that women are subordinate to their husbands, and that everyone needs to know whether or not they are married. The author does not believe that women are subordinate or that their marital status affects their professional role, so choices A and C can be eliminated. The title of "Ms." leaves the martial status ambiguous and keeps the focus on the applicant, so choice B is the best answer. In the fourth paragraph, the author argues that by placing a "lady" or "female" in front of a job title, it suggests that the job is not normally held by a female. Since this phrasing is also not empowering for woman, choice D is not as likely as choice B.

6. **C is the best answer.** This passage discusses terminology that has become popular in today's society that is offensive to women without most people realizing it. Because these terms and phrases are still used by the media, females have to struggle with sexism more than males. Choice C is the best answer. The author does not discuss the individuals who are writing or reporting these articles. They do not mention whether they can identify with the subjects they are writing about, or if they realize they are using sexist terms, so choice A cannot be assumed to be true. The author similarly does not discuss female politicians as a whole, but rather a few particular examples, so it cannot be assumed from the passage text that there are fewer females than males in politics. Remember not to bring in outside knowledge when answering questions in the CARS section. Choice B can be eliminated. In the fourth paragraph, the author discusses how terminology makes it seem like some professions are usually held by men, but they do not report statistics about gender in each profession, so choice D is not the best answer.

7. **A is the best answer.** The author argues that language sexism can unconsciously affect portrayals of women and what readers/viewers think of them. If a newspaper used sexist terminology frequently, then the author would expect readers to unconsciously carry a negative image of the female candidate. The finding that readers still voted for that female undermines the author's argument, so choice A is the best answer. The author's argument never discusses how females feel about sexist language or how they react to it. Choices B and C can be eliminated because they go beyond the scope of the passage text. The author's argument would not be weakened by men experiencing sexist language, because it would reinforce the power and influence that the language sexism can have on readers. Choice D is not as strong as choice A.

8. **D is the best answer.** In the second paragraph, the author states that Hillary Clinton, Margaret Thatcher, and Angela Merkel are often described as mothers, wives, and daughters. These women are classified in roles other than their occupation as politicians, while male politicians do not face the same alternative classification. For this reason, choice D is the best answer. Choices A, B, and C could all be true, but none of those situations are mentioned or suggested in the passage text. Be careful not to carry in assumptions about sexism in the media from personal experience.

TEST **1**

ANSWERS & EXPLANATIONS
Questions 1–53

ANSWER KEY					
1. D	10. A	19. A	28. B	37. A	46. B
2. A	11. A	20. A	29. B	38. C	47. D
3. B	12. C	21. D	30. B	39. D	48. D
4. B	13. C	22. C	31. D	40. A	49. B
5. D	14. A	23. D	32. B	41. C	50. C
6. A	15. D	24. A	33. B	42. D	51. C
7. B	16. C	25. B	34. C	43. A	52. B
8. B	17. D	26. C	35. A	44. B	53. A
9. B	18. B	27. C	36. C	45. C	

EXPLANATIONS FOR TEST 1

Passage 1 (Questions 1-6)

1. **D is the best answer.** The main idea of the passage is that an adequate history curriculum in England would include aspects of both the new and old curriculums, as both have their own strengths and weaknesses. The author argues against the idea of nationalism in education and promotes the concept that students should be able to interpret information in various ways. On a spectrum from traditional nationalist history to more modern approaches to history focusing on critical analysis, the author leans more toward the latter while still acknowledging the problems of that side. There is no information to suggest that the author believes history is the most important aspect of education and should be integrated into all things. Choice A can be eliminated. Choice B also emphasizes history in science, but goes further to integrate nationalism, so it is not in line with the author's arguments and is a weak answer. The scientific method allows students to come up with their own conclusions, so choice C seems to correlate with the author's arguments. Interactive experiments and models would also allow students to interact with the scientific story they are being told, making choice D a strong answer. Choice D is better than choice C because the interactive models would be more likely to spur interest in the subject, an aspect of the National Curriculum that the author values, and a brief, non-active overview of the scientific method would be less likely to thoroughly engage the students in creating their own conclusions.

2. **A is the best answer.** The answer to this question must both be an opinion discussed in the passage and be accompanied by less evidence than the opinions in the other answer choices. The main idea of the passage is that the appropriate course of action for the history curriculum in England is not to go back to a traditional nationalistic ethos, but to improve upon the flaws of the National Curriculum to further engage modern day students and promote free thinking in education. The author claims that officials believe that youth in England have a weaker national identity under the National Curriculum, but the author provides no specific evidence for or against those claims. Choice A is a strong answer. In the passage the author notes that an event known as the 7/7 bombings could have created the need for increased nationalism. While there is no way to compare this new need for nationalism with the need for patriotism in the past, choice B is still not as strong as choice A. The author provides statistics to oppose the idea that students are losing interest in history, so choice C can be eliminated. The National Curriculum opponents believe that the new curriculum is causing the country to disintegrate, so they are likely to agree with the opinion in choice D. The author also likely agrees with this statement as they seem particularly invested in history in public education. However, the claim in choice D was never explicitly stated in the passage, and so can be eliminated. Choice A is better than choice D because the latter choice is not a focus of the passage.

3. **B is the best answer.** The main purpose of the passage is to argue for a new history curriculum that fixes the flaws in both the traditional and current history curricula. The author argues that the old curriculum is outdated and misused to unsuccessfully promote nationalism, while the new curriculum has more practical flaws than ideological deficiencies. The author believes the new curriculum could use improvement, but not in a direction that would bring it back to the traditional curriculum. While flaws in the new curriculum are briefly identified, this is not the main purpose of the passage, so choice A is not a strong answer. As the author clearly states that there are deficiencies in the new National Curriculum, it is not completely accurate to say that the author would defend the curriculum. Choice B is not a compelling answer. While the author criticizes the indoctrination of students with nationalism via the public education system, they never directly criticize the idea of nationalism, so choice C can be eliminated. The author states that the former and current modes of history education are inadequate, but does not offer any concrete solutions, so choice D can also be eliminated. Neither choice A or choice B seem particularly strong, but choice B is better than A because the author seems to support the ideology of the National curriculum – especially its empowerment of free thinking in students – and merely concedes its flaws instead of dwelling on them.

4. **B is the best answer.** The author mentions cultural restorationism as a method the government uses to indoctrinate history students with nationalism, and defines it as the use of the education system to publicize and advocate for a certain ideology. To employ such a concept, it seems reasonable that all the students would receive a similar education, so choice A is a possible answer. Members of a political party have similar ideologies, so choice B is convincing as well. Choice C focuses on a single ideological point that could be encouraged through cultural restorationism. It would be true only if the schools explicitly promoted anti-terrorism legislature, which cannot be concluded from the passage or the question stem. Choice C can be eliminated. Churches promote certain ideologies, but religious leaders have special training according to the ideology of their particular denomination, meaning it is less likely that popular sentiment would leak into the church. Choice D a weak answer. Choice B is a better answer than choice A because students would not necessarily have to receive a uniform education, but could develop the same ideals if educated according to the same themes. A good approach for the MCAT® is to be wary of answers that use absolutes such as "all," since the MCAT® usually prioritizes more moderate answer choices. Choice B is the strongest answer.

5.   **D is the best answer.** The passage presents a spectrum of ideas about how history should be taught in the public education system in England. One end of the spectrum houses proponents of the traditional curriculum and argues that England should move back towards the curriculum used prior to the 1970s. The other end of the spectrum believes that the new National Curriculum is the best choice for England. The author lies somewhere in the middle of this spectrum, but leans towards the new National Curriculum because it includes ideological improvements, such as allowing for more than one story to be told about an historical event, and its flaws are largely practical, such as how to assess learning. While the author believes that the government's need for nationalism via history curriculum is flawed, the author would probably think it is too extreme to call this "propaganda," so choice A is an extreme distractor. The author argues that the new curriculum does not cater to the modern generation, but the older generation may have had distinct needs, making choice B a possible answer. The author takes issue not with the facts of history education but with how those facts are interpreted, so choice C can be eliminated. The traditional curriculum's lack of concordance with today's knowledge and ability to access information is one of the main flaws noted by the author, making choice D a strong answer. Choice D is stronger than choice B because it is more in line with the author's main idea that the traditional curriculum is flawed.

6.   **A is the best answer.** The main argument of the passage is that while the National Curriculum is flawed, England should fix the National Curriculum's deficiencies rather than return to the traditional curriculum. The increase in newly awarded master's degrees could indicate a newfound interest in history, so choice A is a possible answer. Students who attain master's degrees in history presumably kept taking courses in history after they could opt out, making choice B a contrary distractor. The increase in master's degrees does not provide any information about how many people were getting degrees before the change, so the interest level of previous students cannot be determined. Choice C can be eliminated. The idea that the curriculum is gaining interest does not mean the new curriculum is without flaws, so choice D can be eliminated. Choice A is the best answer.

Passage 2 (Questions 7-12)

7.   **B is the best answer.** The major theme of this passage is that, to AA and its participants, alcohol represents the externalized embodiment of an evil force that is not entirely within some individuals' power to deny. This passage is largely a *comparison* of AA's ideas to those of Christians because it repeatedly references ways in which AA philosophies harken back to ancient questions. The best answer may rely on this theme, or the theme can be used to eliminate answer choices. Choice A alludes to alcohol as an evil force that can circumvent human willpower, but notice that this is slightly overstated. The last paragraph notes that, in AA's view, temptation can be avoided through total abstinence. It also notes that the temptation of alcohol does not affect everyone. Choice A is a beyond distractor and can be eliminated. That AA gave form to a symbolic enemy is true according to the passage. This argument speaks to the nature of AA's spiritual adversary and less directly about its impact on the human will. In the last paragraph, the passage argues that giving form to the spiritual threat allows it to be denied, so the reasoning in choice B has implications for human willpower. Keep it for now. The passage references biological determinism in the third paragraph and states that AA explicitly rejects the notion that humans can choose to be good or evil. Choice C is a mischaracterization and can be eliminated. Once again consider the main idea of the passage. AA is like Christianity in that it views sin not entirely as a function of human will. That is why alcohol affects some people more than others. For that reason, choice D actually supports a comparison between the two philosophies and can be eliminated. Even though choice B does not directly speak to multiple understandings of willpower, it is the only choice that highlights a difference between the two philosophies. Choice B is the strongest answer.

8.   **B is the best answer.** If addiction were more of a moral evil than a radical evil, resisting it would be strongly within the power of an individual to control. The passage attributes the success of AA's message to its recognition of alcohol's ability to dominate human will, freeing the addicted individual from blame and judgment. Choice A mischaracterizes the argument of the passage, so it is unlikely that the author would support it. Choice A can be eliminated. Although the author argues that addiction can strike in a seemingly random way and can affect some more than others, the last paragraph muses that addiction can assume many forms in nearly everyone. Choice B is similar to that idea, so it is a strong answer. Although AA is described as moving away from a moralistic assessment of human addiction that judges their goodness, the passage never describes whether one viewpoint is more likely than another to free someone from addiction. Choice C can be eliminated. The passage describes AA as departing from biological determinism, the idea that genes control destiny, but the author never evaluates the contribution of genes to addictive behavior. Choice D can be eliminated. Choice B is the best answer.

9. **B is the best answer.** This passage contrasts the philosophies of AA and Christianity lightly, but the bulk of the text is a comparison between the two in their tendency to present evil forces and actions as external to the individual. The best answer will cite a comparison made in the passage. The passage does make what appears to be a slight criticism of science, but it is very indirect. The passage does not provide sufficient evidence to support choice A, which can be eliminated. To convey its main idea, the passage makes several points to argue that Christianity and AA externalize evil: externalizing allows for judgment-free reflections on sin, evil is a force outside the body rather than something chosen by the sinner, etc. Several paragraphs argue this theme, so choice B is a strong answer. Remember that AA does not argue that humans have complete free will – some are more prone to alcohol addiction than others, so it must be that will alone is insufficient for all humans to bypass addiction. Choice C can be eliminated. The reference to food in the final paragraph is meant to illustrate that all humans, by engaging in normal processes like eating, have the potential to become addicted. Addiction is not limited to a subset of the population, as suggested in choice D. The passage also makes it unclear whether Christianity, AA, or both has this perspective on food. Choice D can be eliminated. Choice B is the best answer.

10. **A is the best answer.** The passage defines radical evil as a sin committed without personal wrongdoing, and says that AA's conception of alcohol comes *close* to this definition. The author states that the temptation of alcohol can be eluded through total abstinence, implying that human willpower can overcome alcohol's influence. It follows that AA views alcohol abuse as at least somewhat tied to personal wrongdoing. Choice A is a strong answer. It is true that AA believes alcohol addiction has deleterious effects, but those effects are not discussed in the passage. Choice B is also unrelated to the definition of radical evil presented in the passage, so it is a weak answer. Notice that choice C presents the definition of radical evil from the passage – a sin unrelated to the force of a person's willpower – but does not answer the question. If choice C were true, the author would likely describe alcohol as a textbook example of radical evil, but this answer choice mischaracterizes the author's argument. Choice C can be eliminated. While the passage concludes by acknowledging the various manifestations of human dysfunction, it does not discuss whether those are forms of radical evil, much less whether they should preclude singling out alcohol. Choice D can be eliminated. Choice A is the best answer.

11. **A is the best answer.** Consider what the passage and question stem mean by the adjective "externalized." What is it that is exterior to the self? While some sins might be attributed to an individual's desire to commit evil acts, the passage argues that alcohol tempts people by circumventing their willpower. The sin of alcohol abuse is not totally the fault of the individual because the demon is not from within. The best answer choice will likely contradict that argument by providing a reason to believe that alcohol abuse is a chosen behavior. If alcoholism were a predominantly genetic condition, that would support AA's argument that consumption is not entirely a choice. If instead alcohol abuse developed from habit, then that appears to be more within the individual's locus of control. Choice A seems like a strong choice. Notice that choice B is very similar. Binge drinking, which may be the result of habit, is related to addiction. The difference between the first two choices is that choice A speaks to causality whereas choice B merely speaks to correlation. For that reason, choice B is weaker than choice A and can be eliminated. Choice C presents a finding that withdrawal is excruciating. If that is the case, then this characteristic of alcohol is another external factor that would contribute to alcoholism, strengthening the argument. Choice C can be eliminated. If most of those who complete rehabilitation relapse, as in choice D, then this would *strengthen* the passage's argument because even after rehabilitation, alcohol manages to tempt individuals. Choice D is a contrary distractor and can be eliminated. Choice A is the best answer.

12. **C is the best answer.** The author defines radical evil as an act that is beyond the individual's ability to control. Since the question asks for a weak example of radical evil, look for an act that is well within the power of an individual to control. If a flood were to destroy a village, the fight for survival would likely explain theft from neighbors. The villagers in the scenario in choice A were compelled to this behavior by external factors, so choice A can be eliminated. The man in choice B breaks the law in order to rush his wife to the hospital to receive medical attention. In this situation that is beyond the couple's control, speed is of the essence, so this seems like a solid example of radical evil. Choice B can be eliminated. Choice C presents a dire situation in which a mother intervenes to prevent her son from going to jail, falsely implicating someone else in the process. While some might see this as an act of love, the woman was not compelled to lie on behalf of her son. The woman was also not compelled to implicate a neighbor. The illegal behavior in the previous two choices seemed much more forced than this situation, so choice C appears to be a strong answer. Choice D describes a situation in which a father berates his partner and children as a symptom of his mental illness. The implication is that this illness, rather than his own willpower, is to blame for causing his family emotional distress. Even though choice D requires an inference, it is still a weaker choice than choice C because it presents an external factor beyond individual choice that compels objectionable behavior. Choice C is the best answer.

Passage 3 (Questions 13-18)

13. **C is the best answer.** This passage presents the aggression catharsis hypothesis, which argues that engaging in violent media, such as video games, movies, and TV, allows people to vent their aggression and thereafter behave less aggressively (the aggression catharsis hypothesis). The main idea of the passage is that this hypothesis does not hold. The author argues that people may interpret their emotional and physical reactions after partaking in violent media as "aggression catharsis," but that these reactions are not truly cathartic. Instead, people are likely to behave more aggressively after experiencing violent media. While the author states that experiencing media violence can serve as a distraction and reduce the immediate desire to behave aggressively, this argument is part of the larger point that angry people misinterpret their feelings as cathartic. The author implies that while the short-term risk is allayed, the tendency to respond aggressively has not been diminished. Choice A can be eliminated. The author brings in empirical evidence—a study demonstrating that people's belief in catharsis impacts their behaviors—as a lead-in to their main argument that people can believe they are experiencing catharsis when they actually are not. Choice B is a weak answer both because it does not address the main idea and because it does not really say anything—it is a *round-about* distractor. The end of the passage indicates that the author believes that angry people who engage in media violence perceive their reactions afterwards as cathartic, when actually they are primed to act aggressively. Choice C is a strong answer. While the passage states that playing violent video games can cause a stress response to be active for hours, it does not further argue that this chronic stress undoubtedly causes people to become aggressive. In general, avoid extreme answer choices, such as those that say media violence definitely does or does not cause people to be more aggressive. The author is more interested in the idea that individuals can mistakenly believe they have experienced catharsis when they are angry and have turned to media violence as an outlet. Choice D can be eliminated, and choice C is the best answer.

14. **A is the best answer.** One of the major differences between "aggression catharsis" and "therapeutic catharsis" is that aggression catharsis can derive from a passive act, such as watching a movie where people are behaving violently. According to the author, the aggression catharsis hypothesis stems from the idea that engaging in violent media allows individuals to vent their anger and lessen their aggression. On the other hand, therapeutic catharsis is more active: the author says that expressing one's emotions, including anger, helps modulate those emotions and prevent conflict. The author compares these two concepts to reinforce the idea that the aggression catharsis hypothesis is not clinically beneficial. In their opinion, people do not achieve true catharsis and relief from anger when they watch violent media. Choice A is a strong answer because it describes a situation in which an individual allows herself to feel her frustration and acts out that frustration—the definition of therapeutic catharsis. Burying one's feelings is the opposite of expressing one's emotions, so choice B is not consistent with therapeutic catharsis and can be eliminated. Watching a comedy is more of a diversion than it is a means of allowing oneself to fully feel emotions, so choice C can be eliminated based on the author's view that distraction does not produce lasting catharsis. Choice D better describes the concept of aggression catharsis, or the idea that watching something violent will lower one's desire to act aggressively. Choice D can be eliminated, and choice A is the best answer.

15. **D is the best answer.** According to the author, people commonly believe that engaging in violent media when angry reduces their tendency to behave aggressively afterwards, because they have experienced catharsis. However, the author argues that violent media does not allow people to actually vent their feelings, so their drive to act aggressively in the long-term has not in fact been ameliorated. The passage states that media may produce a variety of emotions in individuals, including aggression, pleasure, and excitement, so choice A is true and can be eliminated. The author states that media can serve as a short-term coping strategy and can distract people from difficult feelings they may have at the time, and that this is one reason people mistakenly believe violent media has a cathartic effect. Choice B can be eliminated. The author writes that media includes video games, TV, movies, and even prize fights, so choice C can be eliminated. They do not believe that media presented in the context of the passage can be therapeutic. The author juxtaposes the concept of violent media and aggression catharsis with therapeutic catharsis. In fact, they state that playing violent video games creates stress. Choice D is the best answer.

16. **C is the best answer.** The author disproves the aggression catharsis hypothesis on the basis that engaging in violent media does not allow individuals to vent their anger, and as a result they do not experience true catharsis. Violent media may produce emotional and physical reactions that resemble catharsis though, and as a result people believe the media has helped them lower their aggressive drive. In comparison, therapeutic catharsis occurs when people are encouraged to feel and express their emotions. The author says there is empirical support for the impact of therapeutic catharsis on conflict resolution. The research described in the question stem found that people who are able to express their emotions when they are angry are less likely to behave aggressively. These results are in line with the author's main idea. The author would not change their opinion that the aggression catharsis hypothesis is faulty. While speaking to a therapist can be viewed as a coping strategy, the author says that distractions can reduce the immediate risk of acting aggressively. The reason given in choice A for why the author would change their opinion is a statement the author already agrees with. Choice A can be eliminated. Choice B is a similarly weak answer because the author would not change his mind. The author does not believe people are unable to vent their anger, just that they are unable to vent via violent media. They present therapeutic catharsis as one way in which people can achieve true catharsis. Choice B can be eliminated. Choice C is a strong answer because the new research findings support the idea of therapeutic catharsis. The author states that therapeutic catharsis, which is achieved through emotional expression, has already been shown to reduce aggression. Throughout the passage, the author argues that the aggression catharsis hypothesis should be rejected, in part because they believe there is no clinical benefit to it, so choice D can be eliminated. Choice C is the best answer.

17. **D is the best answer.** In their explanation of why people believe they are able to vent their aggression when they engage in violent media, the author explains that the stress produced from playing video games can produce a feeling of exhaustion similar to—but not the same as—catharsis. They use this reaction to the stress response as an example of how people misinterpret their feelings after experiencing violent media. While they think they have vented their frustrations and are now less aggressive, they are actually only tired from the prolonged stress and are likely to have the same or a greater aggressive drive. According to the author, while chronic stress is possible, the stress response is meant to be acute and was not designed to last many hours at a time. Choice A is a weak answer. While they describe a few of the physiological symptoms of stress, including increased heart rate and blood pressure, they do not say any of these symptoms can be dangerous. As with the other answer choices, consider choice B only in the context of information provided in the passage. Distractors that incorporate outside knowledge but are not substantiated by the passage can be eliminated. Choice B can be eliminated. The passage states that the symptoms of stress are reasons why media violence is exciting. Stress, at least in the short term, can be fun—it does not only promote further feelings of aggression. Choice C can be eliminated. The author writes that violent media, including video games, can induce the stress response. According to passage information, even if an individual recognizes that she is playing a game, her body reacts as if she were facing true danger. Choice D is stronger than choice A because it is better supported by the main idea. Choice D is the best answer.

18. **B is the best answer.** The author believes that people often misinterpret their feelings and reactions and subsequently believe that they have experienced something when they have not. In the passage, the author describes this idea in the context of the aggression catharsis hypothesis: after engaging in violent media, people may feel physically spent and less aggressive in the short-term. As a result they mistakenly think they have vented their frustrations, when in fact they have not achieved true catharsis and instead have the same or higher drive to behave aggressively. Choice A does not describe a situation where an individual misattributes their feelings or physiological reactions. It is a tricky choice because it employs distracting key words like "psychiatry" and "anger" that are familiar the passage. Choice does not correspond to the main idea, though, so it can be eliminated. Choice B presents a scenario in which students who believe they are happy are inaccurately judging their emotions. This choice aligns with the author's central point that individuals can be mistaken about their current feelings and future behaviors, so it is a strong answer. Choice C describes a situation that opposes the main idea, as the actors would be successfully interpreting their own emotions in order to behave more convincingly as their assumed characters. Choice C can be eliminated. While the author addresses the stress response, there is not enough information about stress for this passage to be useful for the research described in choice D. The author refers briefly to the stress response as an example of how people misinterpret their exhaustion after playing violent video games. Choice D is not as strong as choice B and can be eliminated. Choice B is the best answer.

Passage 4 (Questions 19-24)

19. **A is the best answer.** Consider each option in turn. Option I is true of the networks of newer actors rather than more established actors, whose networks are expansive social webs that have grown with industry experience. Option I is not true, so choices B and C can be eliminated. The passage stated that option II is one of the few advantages a broader network confers on musical actors, so the best answer will contain this option. In deciding between choices A and D, determine whether option III is true. Consider the passage carefully. The author's main argument is that it takes a long time to build a broad network, and that networks turn out not to be as useful to the audition process as older actors may have expected. Option III is contrary to the author's main argument about the relative efficacy of adaptive and adaptable strategies, so it can be eliminated, leaving choice A as the best answer.

20. **A is the best answer.** The author argues that as performers age and extend their networks, those networks produce fewer tangible results and these performers lose favor among directors. Choice A describes a product that tries to adapt to its market in the face of changing preferences, which is similar to the scenario confronting older performers. The politician in choice B, unlike the performers, does not demonstrate adaptability to a changing voter base. Choice B can be eliminated because it does not reflect the labor market described in the passage. Choice C describes a model who is making a change, but the motive behind the change is unclear. Perhaps the model simply wanted to do something else. Choice C is a weaker answer than choice A. Choice D is tempting, but ultimately it is not a strong answer because this individual is less able to compete in his profession due to a loss of function. Older performers likely have not lost their ability to portray roles, but are simply less interesting to the producers and directors who control their labor market. Choice A is the best answer.

21. **D is the best answer.** This question asks the reader to first and foremost consider the strategies themselves. Be sure to answer the question at hand by considering the fundamental qualities of the strategies, rather than the age groups the market may have associated with them. Choice A addresses qualities associated with the age of the actors who use the strategies rather than the strategies themselves. Choice A can be eliminated since it does not directly answer the question. The terms in Choice B describe adaptation as newer and adaptability as dated, but the passage does not describe which of these is more modern. Rather, both strategies are in use at the same time by distinct age groups, so choice B can be eliminated. Choice C reflects the reasons why these strategies are adopted, although it does not speak to the fundamental character of the two strategies. It seems like a possible answer. Choice D is the only answer that provides essential characteristics of these strategies as described in the passage. Actors who use adaptive strategies actively pursue a specific, "telescopic" image of a virtuoso who has performed in the most prestigious venues. Actors who are adaptable, by contrast, accept the more general work that comes to them. When comparing choices C and D, notice that choice C may explain the reasons why one strategy is chosen over the other, but it does not speak to the fundamental character of the strategies as choice D does. Choice D is the best answer since it describes the essential qualities of the two strategies.

22. **C is the best answer.** The author's main point about younger performers is that they can succeed by projecting a very specific professional persona. The author discusses the image that should be cultivated, rather than the quality of the audience that should be sought. For this reason, choice A does not have passage support and can be eliminated. The author says that it is important for musical performers to "stand out from the crowd," but that strategy is not clearly associated with younger actors, so choice B is not well-supported. The author elaborates on the best strategy for younger actors, arguing that they should try to craft an image that associates them with prestigious roles and venues. Choice C summarizes that approach and is the strongest answer thus far. Choice D, in which actors attend opening night galas to expand their networks, may be important for younger actors, but the author recommended that particular strategy for older actors. Choice D is weaker than choice C, which is the best answer.

23. **D is the best answer.** The choices in this question ask test takers to make two assessments: 1) does this information contradict information in the passage, and 2) does it seriously threaten the central thesis (or "main idea")? The author says that networks are less helpful to older actors because, although they result in information about auditions, they do not really provide an advantage in the audition process. The information in the question stem contradicts that claim, so choices A and B can be eliminated. Now consider the central thesis – is it compromised? The main idea of this passage is that networks for older actors are harder to maintain and less helpful for finding roles than are networks for younger performers. If directors were more prone to hiring people they had worked with before, older performers' networks would be very useful for finding work, which contradicts the central thesis. This reasoning eliminates choice C. Choice D is the best answer.

24. **A is the best answer.** It is important to understand the author's argument about younger performers in order to answer this question. The passage states that younger performers should craft a specific public image that is honed like the sights of a telescope. Choice A matches this argument and is a strong answer. While the type of image that should be presented is narrow, the author argues that younger actors must clamor for roles to build out their repertoires, so choice B does not reflect the context of "telescopic" as used in the passage. The author does not provide insight as to younger actors' awareness that the labor market will only toughen as they age, so choice C is not the best answer. While the author may agree that the strategy in choice D would be helpful for a younger actor, that is not the context of the word "telescopic," which refers to a specific public image. Choice D can be eliminated, and choice A is the best answer.

Passage 5 (Questions 25-29)

25. **B is the best answer.** The main idea of the passage is that studies can have non-minimal risks or minimal risks that appear dangerous, and these risks can be justified in environmental studies if the participants are not coerced or wrongly incentivized and if the overall benefits outweigh the harm. The author does not focus on how a specific risk affects distinct individuals, but instead highlights the types of risks, so choice A does not directly relate to the main idea of the passage and can be eliminated. The passage describes a situation in which the researchers and critics of a study have differing opinions of the extent of risk to subjects, making choice B a compelling answer. While the author lists multiple manners of data collection, this data collection is inherent to the study and so does not change the risk of the study. Choice C is not a convincing answer. The risk imposed on third parties is referenced in the passage, but the passage does not discuss minimal risks or how the risk might be dissimilar for the third party. The passage focuses only on the idea that third party risk exists, so choice D is not a strong answer.

26. **C is the best answer.** Part of the main idea of the passage is that non-minimal risks can exist studies, but can be justified in environmental studies if the benefits outweigh the potential for harm. Minimal risk is defined as risk imposed on a subject that is no greater than the risk encountered in daily life. It can be assumed that research conferences are not an everyday occurrence, so choice A can be eliminated. Sleeping on a friend's couch also seems to be a temporary arrangement, so choice B is not the best answer. Stepping in gum on the usual walk to work is a risk of daily life, so choice C is a strong answer. Picking up a friend from jail is hopefully something that is not done every day, so choice D is weaker than choice C.

27. **C is the best answer.** The main idea of the study is that minimal risks can be justified because they are no different than the threats faced in daily life and that non-minimal risks can be justified when they benefit society. In conveying this main idea, the author describes a study that was canceled because critics purported that children were being harmed, when in fact the risks were already part of their daily lives. Combined with the author's description of minimal risk, the tone of this paragraph suggests that the author believes discontinuing this study was unfounded. The author is unlikely to believe this is the typical course of events, meaning choice A is a weak answer. The discussion of minimal risk focuses on how the danger in an observational study is not greater than what the subjects would normally encounter. This does not mean that the researchers believe there is no risk of harm, so choice B is not well-supported. Reviewing the waste water treatment system could lead to it being shut down or replaced, so choice C presents a potential benefit to society and is a strong answer. Choice D describes a potential benefit to the subject, but the benefits described in the passage are primarily medical rather than monetary. Critics in the passage also show concern that monetary compensation could allow researchers to exploit individuals of low socioeconomic status. Since the scenario in the question stem describes a similar situation, the provision of resources could be seen as similarly coercive and may be a reason for opposition to the study. Choice D can be eliminated, and choice C is the best answer.

28. **B is the best answer.** Throughout the passage the author grapples with the idea of minimal risk and suggests that non-minimal risks can be justified if there is a substantial benefit for public health. The passage provides a scenario in which a minimal risk is perceived as more than minimal, but this is not the focus of the passage, so choice A can be eliminated. The author is likely to believe that risks need to be continuously examined, as evidenced by the passage's focus on defining and justifying risk, making choice B a compelling answer. In the passage the author notes that environmental studies are difficult to justify because they do not always have a clear medical benefit like other studies, so choice C seems like a possible answer. Choice B is better than choice C because choice C does not reference risk, which is the overarching theme of the passage. In the conversation about third parties, the author says there are no industry standards to address potential harms or benefits to parties not directly involved in the study. If there are no concrete standards about third parties, then there are no standards to translate to actual studies, and choice C can be eliminated. This makes choice B the best answer.

29. **B is the best answer.** The main idea of the passage is that studies can have non-minimal, but that these risks can be justified in environmental studies if the participants are not coerced or wrongly incentivized and the overall benefits outweigh the harm. The author says that observational studies usually impose only minimal risks, but this is not always true, so choice A can be eliminated. Since the author suggests that observational studies usually have only minimal risks whereas experimental studies typically have greater risks, it could follow that these greater risks require greater justification, making choice B a strong answer. The passage does not imply that observational studies could not lead to new medical treatments, so choice C can be eliminated. Choice D again follows the author's belief that experimental studies usually have more non-minimal risks than observational studies, so it is a well-supported answer. Choice B is better than choice D because it focuses on the process of justifying risk, which is part of the main idea of the passage, and it is not completely clear if the consequences referenced in choice D are risks or potential outcomes of the study.

Passage 6 (Questions 30-35)

30. **B is the best answer.** This passage presents two perspectives on opposite ends of a spectrum. On one end is a critical view on the lavishness of costumes and set design as well as the lack of authentic and substantial 1960s plots. On the other end is the view that the lavish objects have important meanings that bring out complex characters and themes. The author lies closer to the latter side of the spectrum. While the passage spends a significant amount of space being critical of *Mad Men*, it does so almost entirely by quoting critics. The author only seems to share their own ideas in the third and fifth paragraphs where there are original arguments. Thus the author is of the opinion that there is more to *Mad Men* than meets the eye. Choice A sheds a positive light on *Mad Men*, so it could be in line with the author's opinion of the show. Choice B is a better answer than choice A because the passage does not provide much information on the characters in the show, but does attempt to illustrate potential for complexity upon a closer look. Choices C and D assert an opinion opposite to that of the author, and are thus contrary distractors.

31. **D is the best answer.** The author presents a social meme as a cultural phenomenon that extends beyond the confines of its intended medium into many aspects of popular culture. This extension of the phenomenon is due to widespread popularity and desire to emulate the experience. Celebrities are often seen as fashion icons and thus copying their style is not outside the confines of their medium. The author is unlikely to see them as a social meme, so choice A is not a strong answer. In choice B only two people were affected by the movie rather than a larger section of society, so choice B is not a compelling answer. In choice C the picture stays in its original medium, so can be eliminated. Choice D depicts distinct aspects of the book – costuming and lifestyle - extending into multiple facets of many people's lives, and is therefore the best answer choice.

32. **B is the best answer.** In paragraph 2 the author describes consumer nostalgia as a materialistic trade-off for remembering hard-hitting historical themes. It is implied to be a light mask that prevents a viewer from seeing the heavy aspects of the time period, which is one of the main counterarguments that the author presents to their own opinion. The motivations of the show's producers is not the focus of this passage, making choice A a weak answer. Choice B focuses only on the positive aspects of materials from the past and thus fits most closely with the consumer nostalgia counterargument. It is the best answer. Choice C focuses on the producer's perspective instead of the outcomes of materialism, so it is not a well-supported answer. Note that choices A and C are so similar that neither is likely to be the best answer. Choice D centers on personal purchases rather than a greater desire for all things from the past, so this choice can be eliminated.

33. **B is the best answer.** The author uses Greif as an example of a critic who cannot see the greater meaning within *Mad Men*. Greif argues that the intricate costumes and sets distract viewers from the plot of *Mad Men*, and that the plot itself is not substantial. He asserts that the materialistic nature of the show highlights the positive aspects of the 1960s while concealing tough social norms that were rampant at the time. This is one of the major counters to the author's main idea. Choice A speaks to the media's understanding of the plot, not the fans' understanding, and there is not enough information provided to determine how much the show would dive into the issue of gay rights. Choice B illustrates how viewers focus on costumes instead of the underlying controversial theme of war, making it a strong answer. Choice C lacks a material aspect, and thus would not add to the counterargument. Choice C can be eliminated. Discussing the struggle between traditional views of family and modern views of autonomy is a tumultuous topic that Greif would not expect *Mad Men* to tackle, so choice D can be eliminated. Choice B is the best answer.

34. **C is the best answer.** The main idea of the passage is that objects in *Mad Men* possess significance beyond being set pieces. The example provided in the question supports the author's argument that objects can be used as symbols. This means the question is asking the reader to identify a section of the passage that uses an example to support the author's argument. Typewriters are used to support the critic's opinion that the objects in *Mad Men* are alluring and not significant, so choice A is a contrary distractor. The idea that old items carry meaning is the main idea of the passage, so choice B seems to be a strong answer. Choice C is better than choice B, though, because it provides a specific example of the significance of an object from the television show in question, as is the case with the pen in *2001: A Space Odyssey*. Choice D is not as strong as choice C because it again does not point to a specific object in *Mad Men*. It is too vague to be the best answer.

35. **A is the best answer.** The author uses Mendelsohn as an example of a critic who does not see the full potential of *Mad Men*. Mendelsohn believes that the actual climate of the 1960s is diluted by the allure of the sets and costuming, which opposes the author's main idea. The critic asserts that the viewership is too young to remember the turmoil of the time, and so is seduced into pining for the circumstances under false pretenses and pretty colors. In choice A people who are able to remember the 1960s also enjoy the show, so it is a strong answer. Choice B assumes that the older generation has poor memory or was too young to really appreciate the time period as they lived through it. This is not a strong answer. Choice C assumes a stereotype that was not discussed in the passage, and is thus a distractor beyond the scope of the passage. The basis of Mendelsohn's argument is that the age of the viewer affects the viewer's relationship with the content, so choice D can be eliminated. Choice A is the best answer.

36. **C is the best answer.** The author's main idea is that patient malnutrition is a serious clinical issue that goes largely undetected and untreated, and that has consequences not only for patients themselves but also for their hospitals. The author argues that although there are a number of factors that contribute to malnutrition, including staff and patient-related issues, the main route of change must occur through hospital management. Even though patients play a large role in their own lives when it comes to eating, their habits are influenced by hospital policy and protocols. According to the passage, the proportion of the hospital budget devoted to nutrition affects the hospital's ability to meet the diverse needs of patients (paragraph 4), so choice A can be eliminated. The author says that a lack of communication between hospital staff and patients can result in patients receiving food they will not eat (paragraph 3). The passage also states that one of the ways to ensure adequate food intake is to meet patients' cultural and religious needs, implying that patients have dietary restrictions that must be considered. Choice B can be eliminated. Based on the passage, information contained in nutrition-related materials becomes relevant only once a patient is discharged from the hospital. Because the question stem refers to malnutrition in a hospital setting, choice C seems to be a likely answer. The author argues that patients who cannot eat independently and who do not ask for eating assistance from hospital staff are at risk for malnutrition (paragraph 5), so choice D can be eliminated. Choice C is the best answer.

37. **A is the best answer.** The author's main idea is that when it comes to addressing the problem of malnutrition among hospitalized patients, hospital management is most important. Hospital management is responsible for enacting the protocols that protect patients from malnourishment, not only through training and supporting staff around adequate nutrition but also by leveraging patients' own commitment to their health through educating them around food intake. According to the author, hospital staff directly interact with and impact patients, but their actions are largely dictated by hospital policy. The best answer will describe a situation in which a group of people has a similar "middle man" role. In choice A, the sergeants interact with soldiers in a comparable manner, because they cannot address the soldiers' complaints unless there is agreement from management, i.e. their superiors. Choice A is a strong answer. The author does not suggest that hospital staff are part of management or that they own any part of the hospital, so choice B can be eliminated. Based on the passage, the author believes that hospital staff should communicate with patients to determine their food restrictions and requirements. Choice C presents a situation in which the staff make decisions based on their own opinions rather than those of their consumers. Choice C can be eliminated. The author implies that hospital staff do not have a say in budget allocation, but rather that management dictates how much of the hospital's money will be spent on food. Choice D describes a situation in which employees have the same authority as management to dictate how finances are distributed. However, the passage states that staff lack the ability to improve the nutritional culture of the hospital independently. Rather, they need support from management in the form of adequate investment in food. Choice D can be eliminated, and choice A is the best answer.

38. **C is the best answer.** According to the author, tackling malnutrition at the organizational level is the most effective way of decreasing its prevalence. Based on passage information, although patient involvement is a crucial aspect of improved nutrition, patients often must depend on institutional practices to obtain the food they need. The changes needed to lower the rates of malnutrition must occur as an institutional-wide effort involving hospital management. The author believes that a better nutritional culture subsequently impacts patients because of increased funding for food, more complete staff knowledge around nutrition, etc. In this question, a hypothetical study finds that empowering patients with knowledge does not have an effect on nutrition. The best answer will align with the author's main idea that the focus of change in hospitals should be on the organizational level, rather than on patients or individual staff. The author argues that hospital management must be aware of the problem of malnutrition in order to champion improvements in the nutrition culture. Choice A can be eliminated. The author also states that hospitals are crucial for organizing staff trainings and support around techniques to improve eating, such as allowing family members to visit at mealtimes. Choice B can be eliminated. Because the author emphasizes the importance of changes within the hospital rather than changes directed at patients, choice C is a strong answer. According to the passage, hospital budgets greatly affect the ability of a hospital to provide food to a diverse patient population. These budgets are controlled by the institution, which the author stresses is the key focus of change, so choice D can be eliminated. Choice C is the best answer.

39. **D is the best answer.** The author's main idea is that malnutrition has a serious, negative impact on hospitals that affects not only patient well-being but also hospital operations and staff confidence. The author argues that the primary approach to improving malnutrition should take place at an institutional level. Though other factors contribute to malnutrition, including patient and staff actions and priorities, the author believes that the main way to address all of these issues is through revised hospital policies surrounding nutrition. According to the author, malnourished patients have increased costs of care compared to their well-nourished counterparts, but the passage does not indicate that these expenses exceed hospital budgets. Option I is not supported by the passage, and choices B and C can be eliminated. The author states that people who do not receive adequate nutrition are at risk for increased complications related to their preexisting illnesses, so option II is true. Based on passage information, persistent rates of malnutrition and a lack of hospital culture intent on improving nutrition results in low morale for dieticians and diet technicians. Option III is true, and choice A can be eliminated. Choice D is the best answer.

40. **A is the best answer.** Based on the passage, malnutrition is a serious problem with significant clinical and financial implications. The author argues that in order to improve rates of malnutrition, the nutritional culture of hospitals must be altered. The author believes in institutional, rather than staff- or patient-focused change, primarily because of the more sweeping effects that nutrition-focused hospital policy can have on patients and staff at once. Because the ideas presented in this passage concentrate on the ways in which patient nutritional status can be changed at large, they would be most useful to someone working on those broad issues. Compared to individual patients, physicians, or other staff functioning within a single hospital, advocates can have an impact more broadly. The passage does not name just one place that requires policy change, but rather focuses on the improvements needed across institutions. According to the passage, advocates have been pushing for increased awareness of malnutrition, so there exist individuals who are interested in promoting improved nutrition for all patients. Choice A is a strong answer. While there is some passage information relevant to caregivers, the author's main idea about the need for hospital-wide change in nutrition policy does not directly involve caregivers. The author mentions that family members can help patients eat, but is more focused on ways to motivate change within the hospital more broadly. Choice B is not as strong as choice A. Though the author discusses the role of hospital staff in ensuring patient nourishment, they argue that staff cannot effect improvements alone. Staff are responsible for an array of patient-centered responsibilities and for implementing hospital protocols, not necessarily for recommending change. Choice C is weaker than choice A. An underlying theme of the passage is the impact that patient empowerment can have on nutrition, but the author argues that similarly to staff, patients can only be empowered with knowledge if hospital policy dictates that they should get this information. Choice D can be eliminated, and choice A is the best answer.

41. **C is the best answer.** This passage identifies malnutrition as a significant clinical problem with repercussions for both patients and hospitals. The author identifies a couple of approaches that advocates have implemented in the past in an attempt to improve patients' nutritional status. The author states that these efforts have largely failed, however, and that recent studies show that the prevalence of malnutrition remains high. The author then devotes the majority of their discussion to describing strategies they believe could improve the nutritional culture at hospitals. They first and foremost support institutional change at the hospital management level. The best answer will depict a scenario that corresponds to a strategy that has previously been tried. Answer choices can be eliminated if they were not mentioned in the passage or if they were referred to as strategies that should be tried in order to improve rates of patient malnutrition. There is no reference in the passage to community-based social service programs coming into the hospital, so choice A can be eliminated. The author states that a lack of communication between hospital staff and patients is one factor resulting in patient malnutrition. They also argue that hospital policy should include health care providers recognizing the diverse needs of patient diets. However, they focus on deficient communication as an issue they hope will be resolved, not one that has been tackled in the past. Choice B is a possible, but weak, answer. The author explicitly states that advocates have pushed for the inclusion of nutrition curriculum into medical education. Choice C is a strong answer. The passage does not argue that hospitals should change their admissions policies to discriminate against older adults. The author's main argument is that hospitals need to change their structures and protocols to align with patient needs, not that they should selectively treat certain patients depending on their existing capacity. Choice D can be eliminated, and choice C is the best answer.

Passage 8 (Questions 42-46)

42. **D is the best answer.** Although the author discusses various aspects and functions of metaphors throughout the passage, this question is asking for the central thesis specifically. While metaphors are an integral part of university mission statements, that point is not the central thesis of the passage, since the author does not even mention the concept until the fifth paragraph. Choice A is not the best answer. Metaphors might go unnoticed in society, but the author does not suggest that or dwell upon it. The passage demonstrates the societal importance of metaphors, so this answer is contrary to the focus of the passage. Choice B can be eliminated. The author discusses how metaphors can be used as tools of understanding, but he does not mention any other linguistic skills in the passage, so choice C cannot be assumed true. Remember not to consider any previous conceptions about the use of metaphor in writing. The author stresses that metaphors can have different meanings depending on the narrative and how the individual interprets them. A metaphor's social and cognitive influence on individual lives can vary as well. For this reason, choice D is the best answer.

43. **A is the best answer.** The author makes a point of discussing how metaphors can provide a lot of information about the people who create them and the people who interpret them. He thinks they act as a reflection of society in that moment, so choice A is a strong answer. While metaphors may cause individuals to act a certain way, the author does not suggest that the metaphors are explicitly instructive. Individuals can interpret them differently and may react accordingly, because a metaphor is not a specific set of instructions. Choice B is not the best answer. While metaphors may often be intellectual, the author does not suggest that scholarly discussions result from interpreting them, so choice C is not as strong as choice A. Although the author discusses the ideological implications of metaphors, he defines ideological as a set of beliefs that affects social interactions. He does not use the term "ideological" to indicate "spiritual." The author does not suggest the affected societal beliefs must be spiritual, so choice D cannot be assumed true and choice A is the best answer.

44. **B is the best answer.** Although the author focuses on metaphors, which are a literary device, he discusses them in relation to public reactions and their place in society. He does not mention how writers use metaphors in a piece of writing. Remember not to bring in preconceptions of metaphors as a tool for writing. Choice A is not the best answer. The passage mentions how companies create metaphors to appeal to the public, so an advertiser would benefit from learning how to positively appeal to the most individuals. For this reason, choice B is a strong answer. An editor's job is to revise a piece of writing, which is not mentioned in the passage. Choice C is also so similar to choice A that neither is likely to be the best answer, and it can be eliminated. While a dean of a university might benefit from reading this passage, that job entails many responsibilities that may not include creating a mission statement. This argument would not apply to a dean as much as an advertiser, who could apply these teachings to multiple projects. This answer choice might be selected if the discussion of university mission statements is misinterpreted as the main point of the passage rather than an example of the main point. Choice D is not as strong as choice B.

45. **C is the best answer.** The author explains ideology as a shared set of beliefs that can govern society. He mentions this concept to point out how metaphors can cause social change or elicit reactions from individuals. Choice A could be a strong answer choice if it indicated that metaphors were used more often by struggling businesses than by successful businesses, and that the reliance on metaphor was responsible for their inability to attract business. As it stands, the answer choice does not provide enough information to conclude that metaphors do not influence ideology. Choice A can be eliminated. Americans might not explicitly notice metaphors, but they can still subconsciously influence their decisions, so choice B is not the strongest answer. If businesses report that they do not use metaphors to influence the actions of others, then the influential nature of metaphors is called into question. Metaphors would lose their ideological quality, since they could not control social interactions, as suggested in the third paragraph. Choice C is directly contrary to the examples given in the passage to support the author's argument, so it is a strong answer. Businesses from different fields trying to influence individuals in distinct ways are all still utilizing metaphors to generate a reaction. Choice D strengthens the author's explanation of ideology in relation to metaphors, so it can be eliminated, and choice C is the best answer.

46. **B is the best answer.** The author emphasizes how influential metaphors can be, specifically referencing one of the most popular metaphors: "importance is size." He lists many examples to reinforce this metaphor's prevalence and acceptance in society, even if individuals may not explicitly think about it every time they look at a tall building. Although a sports car may be expensive and a CEO may purchase it to show off his salary, the passage does not mention metaphors that relate to money. Do not bring in outside information or stereotypes when answering MCAT® questions. Choice A also lacks a size indicator, so it is not the best answer. Because the author argues that bigger or taller objects display great importance, the CEO would be most likely to purchase a domineering SUV. Choice B is describes a large vehicle, so it is likely the best answer. A compact convertible is much smaller, so choice C can be eliminated. A motorcycle that only holds one individual is not a big enough vehicle to assert one's importance. Choice D is not the best answer and choice B is the strongest answer.

Passage 9 (Questions 47-53)

47. **D is the best answer.** The author argues that the nineteenth century was historically the period in which the British completed their colonization of India, and socially a time for change in India's views towards its female citizens. This change was reflected to an extent in the content of Bengali literature, to which Sharatchandra was a contributor. The author's main idea is that although Sharat was on occasion an advocate for Indian (and especially Bengali) women, perhaps reflecting the dominating sentiment of the times, the majority of his writing reveals his adherence to patriarchal views. The author describes the British domination of India as accompanied by Western efforts to educate the "natives," whom they believed could be transformed into loyal subjects. The use of quotation marks around "natives" indicates that the author may not share the British viewpoint on the original inhabitants of India. Although the author does not portray British domination positively, they do indicate possible gratitude at some points, as in the case of colonization's impact on the education of Indian women. Choice A is a weak but possible answer. While the author disagrees with British colonization, they describe the situation calmly, if sarcastically. Choice B does not match the tone of the passage and can be eliminated. Choice C could be a strong answer, as it matches the author's cynical tone. However, the author presents a more nuanced view: they state that colonization caused Indian society to begin to promote educational efforts for women, in stark contrast to its belief in the past that empowering women would cause them to become either widows or whores. The author supports this societal shift even as they rebuke British colonization. Choice D reflects the complexity of the author's opinion and is the best answer.

48. **D is the best answer.** The author's main idea is that although Sharatchandra raised concerns about women's rights, he did not believe that the patriarchy as it stood needed to be overturned. While Sharat appeared as an advocate for women in at least one venue, his true views—illustrated in his fictional representations of women—were more ambiguous. According to the author, not only do Sharat's female characters represent an adherence to established societal views, but Sharat himself was quoted as saying that it is not cowardly to give up one's rights in order to serve society. Sharat lived and wrote in a time when gender inequities were beginning to be upheaved, and he recognized the injustice of treating women as subservient. However, he did not intend his fiction to upend the status quo or "propose a new utopia." Because the passage does not speak to relationships specifically, choice A does not relate closely to the passage argument about Sharat's views of his writing. Choice A can be eliminated. The author writes that Sharat's literary heroines abided by traditional values, so it is likely that he would have written novels where women remained housewives. Choice B can be eliminated. The author's argument that Sharat did not believe his fiction should cause social change would be unchanged by the assumption that Sharat was praised for raising concerns about women's rights. This argument and the question stem address Sharat's motivations, while choice C speaks instead to the reactions of others. Choice C does not directly relate to the main idea or to the question stem and can be eliminated. Based on passage information, although Sharatchandra at times advocated for increasing women's rights, he never envisioned his books as "propos[ing] a new utopia," or depicting a truly liberal and egalitarian society. The author's main idea would be weakened if Sharat in fact believed that writing female characters who were confined to tradition would create real change in response. Choice D is the best answer.

49. **B is the best answer.** According to the passage, although Sharatchandra at times presented a liberal front, advocating for women's rights and criticizing the misogynistic patriarchy (one end of the passage spectrum), his novels belied this façade. The author argues that Sharat was not as wholly progressive as some of his articles about Indian womanhood seemed to indicate. In fact Sharat believed strongly in the status quo, and his fictional female characters demonstrate that he did not think it necessary to afford Indian women equal rights (the other end of the passage spectrum). The passage states that Sharat's female characters were usually young widows or unloved, married women with high social standing who display filial piety and may have erotic tendencies, but are never overtly sexual. Even the most progressive of his characters abide by tradition, in contrast to his scholarly views on women's rights. A young widow who actively courted men would not be behaving in line with this traditional ethos, so choice A can be eliminated. A married woman who represses her sexuality because she feels a commitment to her husband's parents would be a typical Sharat heroine, so choice B is a strong answer. The passage does not comment on Sharatchandra's beliefs about whether women should obtain an education—and in fact, if he believes in maintaining the current status of women, he would oppose this move. Choice C mistakenly conflates emerging views on women and education in 19th century India with Sharat's own opinions. Choice C can be eliminated. Similarly, because Sharatchandra depicted women as abiding by traditional values associated with love and marriage, his characters would not be expected to seek divorce. Choice D can be eliminated, and choice B is the best answer.

50. **C is the best answer.** The author argues that in India during the nineteenth century, gender inequities arising from a historical patriarchy were coming to light, and women were finally being given more rights, such as the opportunity to obtain an education. Sharatchandra, a contemporaneous writer, was known for his sympathetic views, and at times he demonstrated compassion towards women's societal status. However, the author argues that Sharat's fictional female characters are largely products of a patriarchy, and that he fails to assign them truly progressive identities. The passage spectrum shows that Sharat's views on women are nuanced: his scholarly denouncement of the patriarchy contrasts with his fictional representations of women. The author says that "colonial enlightenment" affected women of the middle and upper classes in India and that these individuals were given the opportunity to receive an education. However, the passage does not comment on women of lower classes and whether they were offered the same opportunities. Choice A is a weak answer. Although the passage implies that women in nineteenth century India were expected to get married, it does not state that there was the same expectation that they would become prostitutes. According to the passage, education was considered a negative influence that would cause women to become either widows or whores, a belief that the author strongly rejects. This choice is attempting to trick the test-taker by mimicking a phrase in the passage. Choice B does not align with the main idea and can be eliminated. The author says that the prevailing belief of the nineteenth century was that women were "nitwits," so choice C is a strong answer. The idea that women were not encouraged to express their sexuality derives from an interpretation of Sharatchandra's work, referred to as his "personal predilection," so it is not necessarily a reflection of real women in India at the time. Choice D can be eliminated, and choice C is the best answer.

51. **C is the best answer.** The main idea of the passage is that Sharatchandra, as a writer in nineteenth century India, was witnessing the beginnings of a social upheaval, including the fight to educate women. However, the prevailing belief of the time—one reflected in Sharat's novels—was still of the historical patriarchy. The author argues that Sharat's fictional female characters were socially conservative and representative of traditional values, an illustration of femininity that gratified the majority of readers. Sharat was popular because he did not challenge the existing state of social affairs. The author does not imply that an author must write female characters in a certain way in order to be a popular writer. Choice A describes only the specific example of how Sharat appealed to readers' traditional sensibilities. Choice A is a weak answer. The author states in paragraph 6 that Sharat gained popularity due to his transparent and simple prose, so choice B can be eliminated. According to the passage, Sharatchandra ensured his popularity by accommodating the inherent biases many of his readers held about women and their role in society, so choice C is a strong answer. Choice D describes the opposite of choice C—Sharat was a well-liked writer because he did not directly challenge the injustices of his time. Choice D can be eliminated, and choice C is the best answer.

52. **B is the best answer.** The author describes Sharatchandra's ideal woman as a maternal figure—someone who obeys the social customs of the time in remaining committed to her husband and their marriage. According to the author, although Sharat is known for vocally advocating for women's rights, his depictions of women in his novels reveal that he did not wholly believe in upending society in order to achieve gender equality. The author implies that Sharatchandra's ideal woman is both a natural mother and wife, though he does not explicitly mention her children. Choice A is a possible but weak answer. Based on the passage, Sharat did not comment on the merits of female education. The desire to educate women is discussed instead in the context of a change in mentality amongst progressive Indians at the time of Sharat's writing. Choice B conflates Sharat's own ideals about femininity with those of a changing Indian society in the 19th century. Choice B is a stronger answer than choice A. The author says that this ideal woman is long-suffering and completely loyal to her husband, so choice C can be eliminated. The passage states that Sharat's beloved female characters actively contained their sexuality, a reflection of Sharat's puritanical beliefs. Choice D can be eliminated, and choice B is the best answer.

53. **A is the best answer.** The main idea of this passage is that although Sharatchandra raised concerns about women's rights in nineteenth century India, based on the characteristics of the heroines in his novels, he actually was more concerned with maintaining societal conventions, even at the price of denying women their due rights. Sharat held complex views about a woman's place in society, represented both in his scholarly work and his literature. Sharat vocalizes one view on gender equality even as he implies an opposing view in another forum. Choice A describes a scenario in which an individual presents contradictory opinions on a gender issue, namely the right to equal wages, in different settings. Choice A is a strong answer. Although this passage comments extensively on Sharatchandra's views on the societal role of women, it is not biographical. Choice B is a weak answer. Although the passage includes information about the time in which Indian women began to gain access to education, there is no reference to the women's suffrage movement. Choice C can be eliminated. The author does not discuss specifics about women's rights outside of increased education, and makes no comment about other countries or the topic of birth control access. Choice D can be eliminated and choice A is the best answer.

TEST ②

ANSWERS & EXPLANATIONS
Questions 1–53

ANSWER KEY				
1. B	12. C	23. D	34. C	45. A
2. D	13. A	24. B	35. B	46. D
3. B	14. C	25. D	36. C	47. C
4. A	15. D	26. C	37. D	48. B
5. C	16. A	27. D	38. B	49. C
6. B	17. C	28. A	39. D	50. B
7. D	18. A	29. B	40. A	51. B
8. D	19. D	30. C	41. D	52. D
9. B	20. B	31. C	42. A	53. B
10. C	21. C	32. C	43. D	
11. A	22. A	33. D	44. D	

EXPLANATIONS FOR TEST 2

Passage 1 (Questions 1-7)

T2 A&E

1. **B is the best answer.** The author make a statement similar to choice A in the first paragraph. In the same paragraph, the author notes that this statement is not supported by robust research. Eliminate choice A. Next eliminate choice C because, although the author makes this statement, they do not provide any further evidence that it is true. Choice D seems appealing at first, but the author describes ethnography as an anthropological approach to learning about other cultures. Choice D is not entirely accurate because ethnography is a part of anthropology as a whole. Eliminate choice D. Choice B is the best answer because the information in the passage about anthropology directly states that cultural beliefs vary among individuals in an ethnic group.

2. **D is the best answer.** The passage describes ethnography as a method of understanding other cultures that emphasizes the importance of the native's point of view and "engagement with the local world." Look for an answer choice where an outsider purposefully attempts to understand the viewpoints of another group. Choice A is appealing because it appears that the police officer wants to understand the "natives," but according to the author an ethnographer is usually an outsider attempting to understand the native population. This choice is not an example of ethnography. Choice B can be eliminated because in this situation, the professor makes no effort to understand the student's opinions. Choice C is appealing because the author mentions learning a local language as a component of ethnography. Using the local language is not enough to constitute learning the viewpoints of the natives, though, so choice C is not the best answer. Choice D is the best choice because it exemplifies the core principle of ethnography: attempting to understand the perspectives of natives to a culture.

3. **B is the best answer.** The author notes that the assumption that an ethnicity can be distilled to a few select traits is a major issue with cultural competency. Choice A can be eliminated. Then eliminate choice C because the author prefers cultural competency to ethnography, and choice C inaccurately characterizes cultural competency as the system that accounts for variations in cultural beliefs. Choice D is appealing because the answer choice uses terms that are mentioned in the passage, but the author does not directly apply these terms to cultural competency. By process of elimination, choice B is the best answer.

4. **A is the best answer.** From the structure of the question, note that the best answer will be one that identifies why anthropologists in particular were employed to educate physicians. The author identifies the problem with the current practice of "cultural competency" as incorrectly equating a culture with a fixed set of beliefs. First eliminate choice B. This statement immediately seems questionable due to its strong language. The MCAT® often provides tempting answer choices that use words such as "never" and "always," but these answers can usually be eliminated because they make statements that are too absolute. In this case, if the author believed that physicians were incapable of learning about cultural variability, it is unlikely that they would have argued for teaching ethnography to physicians. Choice D can also be eliminated because the author does not assert that cultural competency fails to account for the multiple variables that comprise culture. Choices A and C are similar and both are appealing. Choice A better summarizes how anthropologists are trained in a way that eliminates the main weakness of the cultural competency approach. When choosing between two tempting answers, the stronger one usually aligns more closely with the main idea of the passage, which is true of choice A in this instance. Choice A is the best answer.

5. **C is the best answer.** The author does not mention medical issues specific to a particular ethnic group, so choice A can be eliminated. Then, eliminate choice B because the wording suggests that cultural barriers would be uniform among a group of patients. Choices C and D are both appealing, but choice C is the stronger answer because it directly states a way for the physicians to alter their behavior to help their patients. This answer is further supported by the last paragraph in which the author notes that ethnography will help physicians to empathize with their patients.

6. **B is the best answer.** First eliminate choices A and C because the passage attributes this definition of culture to anthropology rather than to ethnography or cultural competency. Next, recall that the author believes ethnography is preferable to cultural competency because patients of a certain ethnicity should not be assumed to have a core set of beliefs about illness. Choice D can be eliminated and choice B is the best answer.

7. **D is the best answer.** Recall that the author advocated for ethnography over cultural competency. The author does not believe patients of a certain ethnicity should be assumed to have a core set of beliefs about illness owing to fixed ethnic traits. Look for an answer choice that allows for variation in beliefs among people of the same ethnic group. Choices A and B can be eliminated because the words "strongly" and "always" do not allow for Chinese people to have beliefs that disagree with the ones presented in these answer choices. Choices C and D both allow for Chinese people to have variation in their beliefs, but choice D is a better answer. The word "most" in choice C is more restrictive than the word "some" in choice D.

Passage 2 (Questions 8-13)

8. **D is the best answer.** The author of this passage agrees with the Supreme Court Justices and their decision to require a warrant to search cell phone, since they reveal a large quantity of personal information. The author lists the various functions of a cell phone in the last paragraph and expresses approval that the law finally discusses cell phone searches explicitly. The author argues that laws are often outdated when it comes to technological crimes, so they are not likely to depict legislators as the heroes of the film. Choice A can be eliminated. Although the author believes Riley was unfairly searched during his arrest, they do not seem to believe that he performed heroic acts. The author's attitude toward Riley appears to be neutral. Choice B can also be eliminated. While the passage recognizes the difficulty placed on police officers by the outcome of *Riley v. California*, the author does not depict them as heroes, since multiple officers looked through Riley's phone without a warrant. Choice C is not a strong answer. Throughout the passage, the author writes with admiration regarding the Supreme Court Justices, specifically Chief Justice Roberts. The author quotes the Chief Justice about the personal nature of cell phones because they agree so strongly with his beliefs. No one else is quoted in the passage, and the author's opinion is particularly apparent in the writing surrounding these quotes. The author is likely to depict Chief Justice Roberts as a hero in a movie adaptation because he makes an argument for privacy, though it may not be a popular opinion with all Americans. Choice D is the strongest answer.

9. **B is the best answer.** The author of this passage emphasizes the multitude of personal information stored on cell phones and argues that a warrant should be obtained before law enforcement can investigate them. The passage does not discuss interrogation, but only searching of property. Choice A does not relate to the main idea of the passage, so it can be eliminated. The author wants law enforcement agencies to arrest and prosecute criminals, but by using the methods permitted by law. They are likely to advise searching any possessions that the law permits, so choice B is a strong answer. The author's argument does not relate to trusting suspects' testimonies, but rather to respecting private property and personal rights under the law. It is impossible to determine how the author would feel about trusting a suspect until proven guilty, so choice C is not a strong answer. The passages stresses the importance of following the law and not infringing upon privacy unless legally allowed, so the author would be unlikely to advise officers to gain information by any means necessary. Choice D can be eliminated and choice B is the best answer.

10. **C is the best answer.** This passage describes the recently imposed requirement of a warrant to search an individual's cell phone. For this reason, option I is true and choice B can be eliminated. The author points out in the fourth paragraph that searching a cell phone without a warrant is a much greater violation than searching an individual's wallet, which is "standard." This suggests that it is standard protocol to look through a wallet without a warrant, so option II can be eliminated. Choice D can be ruled out. In the last sentence, the author compares searching a cell phone to searching an entire house due to the amount of information stored on a cell phone. Since the need for a warrant to search a cell phone was supported by comparing it to a house, a warrant must also be required to search a house. Option III is true. Choice A can be eliminated, and choice C is the best answer.

11. **A is the best answer.** The author argues that the law is constantly falling behind technology and that when one situation is resolved, further technological advancements have already created another gap. For this reason, choice A is a strong answer. The author does not argue that the founding fathers failed to prepare the country for the future, but that the technology of the present day is far beyond what they could have imagined. Choice B is not the strongest answer. The author does not suggest that courts cannot reach an agreement about cybercrimes, but rather that they cannot keep up with the pace of technological development. Choice C is not the strongest answer. In the context of discussing *Riley v. California*, the author points out that cell phones were created 41 years ago, so it reasonable to assume that cybercrimes presented problems earlier than the past five years. Also remember that the best answer on the MCAT® usually does not use extreme language such as "only." Choice D can be eliminated and choice A is the best answer.

12. **C is the best answer.** The author argues that a warrant should be required to search a cell phone because it contains an abundance of personal information. The author does not argue that it contains more personal information than other electronic devices. The scenario in choice A is not directly relevant to the author's argument about cell phones, so choice A is not a strong answer. Needing to obtain a warrant might make law enforcement more difficult, but the author argues that it is necessary to protect suspects' rights regardless of the challenges created for law enforcement. Choice B would not weaken the author's argument and can be eliminated. If cell phones reveal only information that is posted on social media, then a search of a cell phone would not be considered as personal or intimate. Choice C would weaken the author's argument and is a likely answer. The author's argument does not relate to the prevalence of cell phones, but rather the nature of the content on them. Choice D does not weaken the author's main argument about the limits of searches and can be eliminated. Choice C is the best answer.

13. **A is the best answer.** The author argues that police officers need a warrant to search a cell phone because it holds an abundance of personal information. The context indicates that an iPad or tablet is an analogous type of technology. It is reasonable to assume the author would support the necessity of a warrant to investigate an iPad or other tablet. Choice A is a strong answer. While the author admits that law enforcement may become more difficult after the *Riley v. California* outcome, they do not suggest that more money or officers are required. Choice B does not relate to the main idea of the passage and can be eliminated. The author does not suggest that the public need to be educated on what can be searched with or without a warrant. Choice C is not as strong as choice A. Choice D is tempting because the passage opens with an observation about the lag between technological evolution and the fight against cybercrime. The author does not seem to advocate for a drastic rethinking of the legal system to address this discrepancy. Choice A is stronger than choice D because it aligns more closely with the passage's main idea. Choice A is the best answer.

Passage 3 (Questions 14-19)

14. **C is the best answer.** The author covers a spectrum of perspectives from the benefits of perspectival drawing to the benefits of processional drawing. The author appreciates both forms of representation but favors processional drawing because it connects the viewer to the experience of the scene. The author's main argument is that perspectival drawing creates a universal conception of space, but lacks processional drawing's connection to the ways humans utilize space by focusing on the exact geometry of space. Perspectival drawing already exists, so using it more widely would not create a new understanding of space. Choice A can be eliminated. The author acknowledges that perspectival drawing inherently creates a more universally applicable understanding of space, but feels as though the emphasis on exact geometry weakens the connection that humans have to the physical space. The author would not advocate for increased realism, as choice B suggests. Choice B contradicts the author's argument and can be eliminated. The author acknowledges the value of having a human connection to architecture, so choice C is an appealing choice. Choice D neither answers the question nor relates to the additional information. The author would be addressing perspectival drawing, not the tools used for drawing. Choice D can be eliminated. Choice C is the best answer.

15. **D is the best answer.** The author addresses the benefits of digital drawing and paper drawing but favors paper drawing because the materiality of paper allows for greater spontaneity in design and a more tangible connection to the architecture being drawn. The author's main point is that although digital architectural drawing may be faster and more technically accurate, it does not have the tangibility that connects it to the real world. Look for an answer choice that opposes this argument. Choice A aligns with the author's concession that digital drawing allows for complexity of design. Choice A can be eliminated. Choice B illustrates the author's point that digital design is in "simulated space." Choice B can be eliminated. Choice C is appealing because both hand drawing and digital drawing have spatiality, but the author argues that the tactile quality of paper makes its spatiality superior. Choice C is not a strong answer. Choice D directly opposes the author's argument that digital design remains a "simulated space" in spite of its technical superiority. Choice D is the best answer.

16. **A is the best answer.** To find a statement that is not supported by evidence in the passage, look for an answer choice that states an assumption the author uses to further another argument rather than a concluding statement that the author expands upon. Choice A appears to be a strong answer because it is used as an assumption to further the author's argument, but the statement itself is not expanded upon in the passage. The author explains that our current understanding of space assumes that space exists independently of its context. Choice B also seems appealing because it is an assumption described by the author. However, it is later supported by the author's description of the evolution of primordial architecture. Choice A is strong than choice B, so choice B can be eliminated. Choice C is expanded upon as the author explains perspective, a dominant mode of representation for space. Choice C can be eliminated. Choice D is appealing because it is presented in an independent paragraph that does not contain much context, and so appears to be an assumption. However, this statement builds on ideas previously expressed about perspectival representation, namely that it is built on facts abstracted from the human situation. Choice D can be eliminated. Choice A is the best answer.

17. **C is the best answer.** Prior to the Renaissance, images were "processional" rather than "perspectival." The author's main point about space is that the new form of drawing also shifts our conception of space from being temporally ordered to being spatially ordered. Choice A opposes the author's argument and can be eliminated. It is primordial architecture, not modern architecture, that is characterized by temporally structured spatiality. Choice B contradicts the passage. Choice C illustrates the shift in the conception of space that occurred during the Renaissance, and is a strong answer. Choice D contradicts the author's statement that space was understood geometrically following the Renaissance. Choice D can be eliminated. Choice C is the best answer.

18. **A is the best answer.** The author argues that although digital drawings allow for greater complexity of design, they are not connected to the human experience of architecture. Although digital designs are perfect in technique, they are not authentic. Look for an example in which something artificially created is perfect but lacks humanity. Choice A is a strong candidate because the phrase "auto-tuned vocal music" suggests that technology was used to modify music. The word "tuning" suggests that the music was adjusted to be perfectly in tune. This means auto-tuned music may be tonally perfect but loses the human inconsistencies that characterize other music. Choice B is appealing because a facsimile does not carry the value of the original, but the description of the brass miniature as "cheap" suggests that it is not a perfect replica. Choice B can be eliminated. Choice C is another example of an imperfect replica and can be eliminated. The traditional printing press is intimately connected with the human experience of a newspaper, so choice D does not fit the author's argument and can be eliminated. Choice A is the best answer.

19. **D is the best answer.** The author argues that tactile feel of paper allows for a spontaneity of design that cannot be matched by digital design. Choice A is beyond the scope of the passage because the author does not discuss the portability of paper. Choice A can be eliminated. Choice B is similarly out of the scope of the passage because the author does not discuss the availability of paper. Choice B can be eliminated. Choice C is appealing because it mentions physical qualities of paper that are not present in digital design, but it does not directly answer the question. Although various types of paper may be ideal for certain techniques, this does not explain why paper is more appealing than digital design. Choice C can be eliminated. Choice D accurately illustrates the author's argument that paper allows for more spontaneous design than does digital design. Choice D is the best answer.

Passage 4 (Questions 20-24)

20. **B is the best answer.** Based on the passage, the author would likely argue that the reporter needs to be close enough to witness the events but not so personally invested that they cannot analyze the situation. Local Peruvians could provide a close perspective, but would lack the necessary distance from the events to provide a balanced or comparative report. Choice A can be eliminated. Similarly, a native Peruvian in his hometown might not be able to detach himself from the situation to make an analytical report, so choice C is not the best answer. If the studio does not send a reporter to the scene, they must rely on secondhand sources, which the author argues are unreliable. Choice D can be eliminated and choice B is the best answer.

21. **C is the best answer.** The Nativist tradition argues that foreigners are incapable of understanding Latin American culture due a cultural gap. Latin Americans would be the best reporters for Latin American events because they understand the history and way of life in Latin American cultures. Both choices A and D represent people reporting on cultures other than their own native cultures, so they can be eliminated. Choice B presents the issue of Anglo Saxons reporting on issues without traveling to see them up close. This contradicts both the Nativist argument and the main argument of the passage, so choice B can be eliminated. Choice C rewards Latin American reporters who report on Latin American politics with publication in the most prestigious journals, which supports the Nativist argument. Choice C is the best answer.

22. **A is the best answer.** According to the author's argument, secondhand sources are biased by their own political opinions, which are sharply polarized, or one-sided. A liberal Democrat has political opinions on one polarized end of the spectrum, so choice A is a strong answer. A moderate Republican would fall closer to the middle of the political spectrum than a conservative Republican, so choice A is a stronger answer than choice B. A foreign correspondent is reporting for another country and is supposed to remain unbiased in their reporting. Debate moderators are likewise not supposed to express their own political opinions. Choices C and D are not the best answers and can be eliminated.

23. **D is the best answer.** In the second paragraph, the author states that "revolutions tend to question long-standing assumptions, reveal powerful but neglected undercurrents which need to be interpreted in new ways, and can be better understood with the benefit of a comparative perspective." Choices A, B, and C are all benefits of distance from the situation. The author does not discuss the effects that local reporting might have on the reporter, so while choice D may be true, it is not supported by the passage, which makes it the best answer to this question.

24. **B is the best answer.** The author agrees with Bolivar's argument and uses it to add credibility to their own argument, since Bolivar is a well-known Venezuelan and the passage discusses his participation in the War of Independence. The author even relates the concluding paragraph back to Bolivar's initial claim to strengthen the argument. While choices A and D may be true, they do not address the complementarity of the author's argument with Bolivar's. Choices A and D can be eliminated. Because the author supports the claim established by Bolivar, choice C is unlikely to be true. This leaves choice B as the best answer.

Passage 5 (Questions 25-29)

25. **D is the best answer.** The author argues for the necessity of extending healthcare coverage to all Americans because many citizens are uninsured or underinsured for a variety of reasons. The author does not provide supporting evidence for the claim that unemployed Americans make up a large proportion of uninsured citizens. Instead, they list many other factors that can affect health status, such as race or education. Choice A may be true, but it is not supported by evidence from the passage, so it can be eliminated. Although the author realizes that healthcare access is a controversial and complicated topic, they do not suggest it has only recently become controversial, so choice B cannot be assumed true. The author does not give evidence for the assertion in choice C. Instead, evidence is provided for the opposite viewpoint that all Americans should have access to healthcare. Choice C is contradictory to the main idea of the passage and can be eliminated. In the fourth paragraph, the author states that morality will always play a part in the question of healthcare access. He also presents his argument drawing upon human compassion to help one another, because he thinks stressing the moral aspects of this controversy will change readers' minds. For these reason, choice D is the best answer.

26. **C is the best answer.** Throughout the passage, the author argues that healthcare should be a right for all Americans. They describe many reasons why an American may suffer from a poor health status and argue that each human life has worth and should be nourished by others. Though the author acknowledges that new questions would arise from universal healthcare, they still believe it is a right for all Americans. This attitude would not be described as cautious. Choice A is possible, but not particularly strong. The author agrees with the beliefs of Aristotle and Kant about the value of life and their views would likely not be classified as "unsure." Choice B can be eliminated. Because the author so strongly agrees with the concept of healthcare access as a human right, their attitude towards universal healthcare is best described as supportive. Choice C is stronger than choice A. The author's tone suggests anger at the number of uninsured or underinsured Americans, and the questions posed at the end of the second paragraph convey the author's thoughts about the necessity for care for others by any means necessary. Analytical is a neutral word, but the author conveys emotion and passion about this issue. Choice C is a stronger answer than choice D.

27. **D is the best answer.** Throughout the passage, the author argues that universal healthcare access is a right for all Americans, because each soul can and should be nourished by others. The passage does not suggest that healthcare nourishes the soul specifically, but rather the vehicle, or body, that carries the soul. Distractors often use specific phrases from the passage to trap the test-taker, so remember to consider the context. Choice A can be eliminated. The passage does not expand upon the details of universal healthcare access. The author suggests that healthcare coverage would be available to every individual, but not necessarily each incidence of disease. Choice B cannot be assumed true. While universal healthcare access may cost a significant amount of money, the author does not discuss money or expenses. Remember to rely solely on the passage text rather than outside knowledge or opinions when answering questions in the CARS section. Choice C is not the strongest answer. The author suggests that universal healthcare access would complicate healthcare settings, because it would bring up more ethical questions that need to be addressed. Choice D is the best answer.

28. **A is the best answer.** The author argues that universal healthcare should be considered a right for all American citizens because each life has value. They also argue that universal healthcare could address the poor health status of many Americans. If a country with universal healthcare experiences fewer deaths from preventable diseases, the system is working properly by saving lives that may have been lost due to circumstances such as lack of health insurance. Choice A is a strong answer. While the author's argument touches upon human compassion, it is not based upon the idea that all humans want to help one another. The passage focuses on establishing that healthcare access is a right, not considering whether Americans want to help the uninsured. Choice B does not relate to the main idea of the passage and is not the strongest answer. The author does not focus on whether Americans support or oppose universal healthcare. Choice C is not as strong as choice A. Choice D also does not relate to the main idea of the passage: a hospital's ability to treat more patients does not directly support the idea that all individuals have a right to healthcare. Choice D can be eliminated, and choice A is the best answer.

29. **B is the best answer.** The author believes that healthcare access is a human right. There is no reason to assume they would oppose legislation requiring citizens to sign up for health insurance, because health insurance coverage is a step toward the goal of accessing healthcare. Choice A is unlikely. The author reports that many Americans are uninsured or underinsured due to unemployment, so they would not receive insurance through an employer. The author would likely oppose a system in which health insurance is provided to citizens only through their employers, as this would exclude individuals who are unemployed, retired, or unable to work. Choice B is a promising answer. The author would likely support research investigating universal healthcare in other countries, as this could strengthen their argument for universal healthcare in America. Choice C can be eliminated. The passage does not discuss the cost of providing healthcare to all Americans, so there is not enough evidence to determine whether the author would support or oppose the measure described in choice D. The passage provides specific evidence that the author would oppose choice B, so it is a stronger answer than choice D.

Passage 6 (Questions 30-35)

30. **C is the best answer.** In explaining the media attention garnered by gangsta rap, the author points out the association between gangsta rap and the action movie industry. This was not the primary factor contributing to the popularity of rap music in general, though, as it involved only one subgenre. Choice A is too narrow to be the best answer. The author lists popular rappers who emerged from the Golden Era, so choice B describes a result of the mainstream popularity of rap music rather than a primary contributing factor. The author states that the Golden Era of rap involved diversification of the genre into subgenres, such that it reached more audiences. The creation of different rapping styles, then, describes a diversification of rap music. Choice C is a strong answer. While the author mentions that gangsta rap originated from the West Coast, they do not suggest that it was a primary factor contributing to the mainstream popularity of rap music in general. Choice D contributes to the popularity of gangsta rap only, and does not explain the spread of rap music as a whole in the 1980s. Choice C is the best answer.

31. **C is the best answer.** The passage presents a spectrum of characteristics of gangsta rap music, with the author commending Tyler, the Creator for his individuality and well-thought lyrics compared to the gangsta rap music that is less meaningful. The author emphasizes that rappers often use violent themes for no greater purpose than to show power, while Tyler, the Creator utilizes them as a compensatory mechanism for his lack of power. In distinguishing Tyler, the Creator from the rest of the gangsta rap genre, the author argues that audiences might be less offended by his music if they understand its individuality. Option I is true and choices B and D can be eliminated. Although the passage mentions that Tyler, the Creator views his lyrics as fictional, the author does not suggest that the lyrics need to be ignored in order to appreciate his music. Rather, he values the messages presented in the lyrics, so option II is too extreme. Near the end of the passage, the author points out Tyler, the Creator's frustration with stereotypes of Black masculinity. When his lyrics are regarded as compensation for the artist's lack of expected masculinity, audiences would be less likely to be offended. Option III is also true. Choice C is the best answer.

32. **C is the best answer.** The passage argues that Tyler, the Creator's music differs from that of other gangsta rappers, which is why he has experienced such success. The author points out that many rappers discuss acquiring money in their lyrics, but that Tyler, the Creator does not follow that pattern. Though the author mentions that Tyler, the Creator is venturing into the film industry, the passage does not suggest that this is a topic of his lyrics. Choice A can be eliminated. While Tyler, the Creator did become famous from internet exposure, the author points out that he does not rap about his fame like other gangsta rappers do. Choice B can also be eliminated. The author emphasizes that while Tyler, the Creator does use violence in his music, he does so for a different purpose than most rappers. Choice C is a promising answer. The passage does not mention alcohol or partying in relation to rap lyrics. Remember not to bring in outside information or bias when answering questions in the CARS section. Choice D cannot be assumed true and choice C is the strongest answer.

33. **D is the best answer.** Throughout the passage, the author discusses how Tyler, the Creator is unique in his genre of gangsta rap. While the author mentions the influence of Tyler, the Creator's fatherless childhood on his music, the passage does not discuss whether Tyler, the Creator regrets his past. It is impossible to determine how Tyler, the Creator feels about his childhood, so choice A cannot be assumed true. The author emphasizes the success of Tyler, the Creator as a gangsta rapper, but does not discuss other subgenres of rap in detail. A comparison cannot be made regarding the success of rappers from different subgenres. Choice B can be eliminated. While the author commends Tyler, the Creator for his honesty regarding his music and life experiences, those feelings do not necessarily apply to other members of the music industry. Choice C attributes the author's opinion to the other individuals and is too general to be a strong answer. The author opens their argument by discussing the diversification of rap music in the Golden Era, and then details the rise of Tyler, the Creator. It is reasonable to assume that rap music is constantly evolving since Tyler, the Creator only became popular in the last five years. While choice D may not initially seem like an appealing answer, the other choices can be ruled out and choice D can be selected as the best answer.

34. **C is the best answer.** The author discusses the success of Tyler, the Creator in gangsta rap to argue about his individuality in the genre and his value as an artist. The author does not discuss either the censorship of rap music or its appropriateness for children. Since the censorship of rap music is beyond the scope of the passage, choice A can be eliminated. The author points out the association of gangsta rap and the movie industry, but does not express strong positive or negative feelings about this association. Choice B is a weak answer. The passage notes that rap music became popular and entered the mainstream when it diversified into subgenres. The author also values Tyler, the Creator's uniqueness within the subgenre of gangsta rap, so they would likely oppose grouping all rap music together. Choice C is a strong answer because it is directly in line with the main argument of the passage. The entire passage discusses rap music and the unique value of Tyler, the Creator within gangsta rap. The author would be unlikely to oppose listening to rap music, so choice D can be eliminated.

35. **B is the best answer.** At the end of the passage, the author values Tyler, the Creator's lyrics for their inherent opposition to how the artist really feels, which exposes his vulnerability. The best answer will likely involve a person acting one way when they actually feel differently. A boy training hard for a race and winning first place may be compared to Tyler, the Creator's path to success, but not necessarily to how he expresses emotions. Choice A can be eliminated. If a girl brags about her grades but performs poorly, then she is hiding her vulnerability by masking it with confidence. This situation is similar to how the author describes Tyler, the Creator's lyrics, so choice B is a likely answer. A student faking knowledge about a political election does not necessarily harbor opposite feelings, so choice C is not a strong answer. A journalist dreading writing for a new section of the newspaper does not resemble Tyler, the Creator's situation, since the journalist is not hiding true feelings about a topic, but rather is nervous about starting a new project. Choice B is the best answer.

Passage 7 (Questions 36-40)

36. **C is the best answer.** Near the end of the passage, the author makes it clear that religious support and positive familial relationships are the most influential factors on adult substance abuse. The author discusses the influence peers can have on adolescents but implies that the power wanes into adulthood and becomes a less significant factor in social control. Choice A can be eliminated. A strong relationship with his mother or father would be valuable only if it was already developed. If the man must start developing that relationship now, it is less likely that it would provide support in altering drinking behaviors. Choice B is not the best answer. According to the passage, individuals who attend religious services may be more sensitized to moral values and may analyze consequences from a higher being, which can keep them from abusing substances. Choice C is a likely answer. While women tend to consume alcohol in smaller amounts and less frequently than do men, there is not evidence from the passage that female friends and relatives would necessarily be supportive and able to help the man prevent relapse. Choice D can be eliminated, and choice C is the best answer.

37. **D is the best answer.** While the benefits of religion for individuals at high risk for substance use were mentioned in the passage, the passage does not elaborate on how that benefit is affected by age. The contextual factors of life that affect delinquency are discussed in the first paragraph, including the effect of the presence of parents in youth. Choice A can be eliminated. The second paragraph delves into gender patterns with alcohol consumption. Choice B has supporting evidence in the passage. The third paragraph discusses the various factors of religions that influence substance use, such as internalizing social control and accepting consequences from a deity. Choice C can be eliminated. The passage does not offer explanation for why older individuals may be more open to spirituality than younger individuals, so choice D is the strongest answer.

38. **B is the best answer.** In the fifth paragraph, the author stresses that peer influences are the primary factor affecting substance use in adolescents. While the protagonist may be more likely to engage in delinquent behavior if raised by a single parent, that delinquent behavior would not necessarily be drug-related. Choice A can be eliminated. Teens who engage in substance abuse are likely to have friends who also engage in substance abuse. It is likely that the teen in the movie would first try drugs with his friends, since they may already be using and pressure him into it. Choice B is a likely answer supported by the passage. Because social influence plays such a role in adolescent substance use, it is unlikely that the protagonist would start using drugs on his own, so choice C is not the best answer. While religion may help the teen reduce his substance use, there is no reason to assume the film ends with a religious awakening. Choice D can be eliminated.

39. **D is the best answer.** The third and fourth paragraphs discuss the various ways in which a religious institution can benefit its members. Religious institutions especially help older individuals maximize social interactions. They do not help only with stressful life events, so choice A can be eliminated. Religious institutions can inspire individuals through fear by holding them accountable to a higher being, but they can also help with coping or by providing social networks. Choice B is not the strongest answer. While older individuals may value religious institutions more than adolescents, it is not true that only older people participate in religious services. Choice C is not supported by the passage. The author mentions that individuals become attached to religious institutions as organizations and that they can provide social support, so choice D is the best answer.

40. **A is the best answer.** Though the author mentions parenting in the first paragraph, they do not discuss it specifically with regard to substance use. The author does not expand upon supportive parenting or stress that both parents must act a team. Choice A is not a likely reason, and is therefore a strong answer. The author mentions this finding at the end of the passage with the hope that further research will expand upon it, so choice B is not the best answer. The author points out that substance abuse tends to affect families in patterns, which suggest a hereditary component. Choice C is a reasonable assumption. The author concludes by discussing the factors that can affect substance use, of which this finding is one of them. Choice D can be eliminated and choice A is the best answer.

41. **D is the best answer.** The question stem is asking about the author's main idea, which is that the widespread use of models of risk only make the trading environment less certain. This should be kept in mind when evaluating the answer choices since the question is asking for the author's viewpoint. Choice A is tempting because this, ideally, is the role of models of risk as described in the passage, but that is not the reality. The author never discusses how narrow the range of probability is, but based on the information in the passage, it can be inferred that the range is really quite broad since the use of these models makes the system "less predictable." Choice A can be eliminated. Choice B is accurate in arguing that these models destabilize the market, but there is no information given in the passage to suggest that the predictions these models make about traders are necessarily unfounded. Because it is only partially true, choice B can be eliminated. While the widespread use of models indeed impairs their ability to predict the future, as in choice C, there is no discussion of an intent to foil rivals' models in the passage. Choice C is a weak option since it is not supported in the passage. Choice D essentially summarizes the main idea of the passage, so it is the best answer.

42. **A is the best answer.** The second paragraph presents a brief history of the evolution of today's models of risk. Choice A highlights the reason statistical methods started changing, namely that analysts were trying to prepare for the outcomes of a nuclear war. It seems like a potentially strong answer. Choice B suggests that models were created to better understand the national economy, but that ability came from the more sophisticated models developed to study consequences of a nuclear war. Choice B can be eliminated since that was not the original purpose of risk models as presented in the passage. Choice C states that these models were developed to stabilize prices. That is the opposite of the author's central argument that widespread use of these models creates a more volatile market. Choice C can be eliminated . Choice D argues that models of risk are meant to cloud the predictions of other trading models. Notice that the passage neither discusses what other trading models exist nor suggests any attempt to sabotage other models. Choice D can be eliminated, leaving choice A as the strongest choice.

43. **D is the best answer.** First, examine the question stem – what was the intended purpose of models of risk? They are meant to provide information about the future, enabling the institution using them to act on the basis of that information. What is keeping the models from doing that? Choice A suggests that inaccurate government forecasts about the aggregate economy prevent the models' proper functioning. Remember that aggregate data is limited by its inability to predict future conditions according to the passage, so that choice is unlikely. Choice B suggests that obscuring the details of rival models would fix the problem, but no information is given in the passage to suggest that traders know anything about their rivals' models besides that they exist. This option would be no different than what is currently taking place, so it can be eliminated. Choice C presents an option that would be a regression to past methods. Although that could be plausible, the reader is given no details about the difference between present and past models besides that probabilistic models are more complex and ultimately more predictive. This does not seem like the strongest choice because older models were less predictive, so this choice can be eliminated. Consider choice D. The problem with using models, ultimately, is that their widespread use makes the trading environment less predictive. The author implies that if their use were not so prevalent, the models would have much stronger predictive power. If the scenario in choice D were true, it is likely that the models would function better, so that is the strongest answer choice.

44. **D is the best answer.** While reading a passage, it is important to critically evaluate the author's arguments. This passage argues that the overwhelming use of predictive risk models in the financial industry makes all models less predictive. The cause of the problem is the widespread use of models, and the best answer will likely address this root cause. Choice A identifies a solution the author may support, but it is not an appealing choice because it does not propose what the alternative might be. Abandoning models altogether also seems a bit too extreme a remedy. Choice A is a weak answer. Choice B is tempting because eliminating all models would definitely get rid of the problem, but that solution leaves unclear how actors in the financial sector will make predictions. Like choice A, prohibiting models entirely seems more extreme than the tone of the passage. Choice B can be eliminated. Choice C, that financial institutions cooperate to produce less risky models, may also be an appropriate remedy, but how the models will be less risky is left open to interpretation. This proposal also would not solve the problematically widespread use of models among rival traders that is responsible for the difficulties the passage describes. Choice C can be eliminated . Choice D describes another promising solution: prohibiting models from making predictions about rivals' models. This solution, like the others, is not comprehensive, but compared to choices A and C, this choice most directly addresses the root cause of the problem the author describes in the passage. For that reason, choice D is the best answer.

45. **A is the best answer.** The "critical networks" in the passage appears in the context of the shift from models focused on aggregate data to more sophisticated predictive models based on the supply chain. Although the meaning of these networks is not fleshed out in the passage, it appears in a sentence about the supply chain and the institutions that would be affected by a nuclear strike. Choice A alludes to the supply chain and its vulnerability to an attack. This seems like a promising answer choice. Choice B refers to the main idea of the passage, but this idea has not yet been examined in the second paragraph when the author addresses the critical networks. Choice B is not a strong choice . Choice C conflates Americans' development of models in the face of nuclear war with another strategic consideration, the classification of allies and enemies. While determining who is friend and who is foe may have been important, it is a distractor beyond the information presented in the passage. Choice C is a weak answer for that reason. Choice D is not an idea discussed in the passage – that models build upon one another through the use of the information they generate – so it can be eliminated. Choice A is the best choice among those presented.

46. **D is the best answer.** Choice A presents a problem where a leak of information has adverse effects that are isolated to one party rather than an entire system. In the passage, no information is being leaked from institutions using models of risk, and the effects of the widespread use of models reverberate throughout the financial system. Choice A is a weak answer because it describes a problem that impacts only a small subgroup of individuals. Choice B describes a problem of making decisions with incorrect information. In the passage, the information in the models is not incorrect; the problem is that the widespread use of models changes the environment that is being observed on the basis of otherwise correct information. Choice B is not quite similar to the problem described in the passage and can be eliminated. Choice C describes a problem of failing to disclose necessary information. The problems described in the passage do not stem from a failure to share critical information but rather the fact that everyone possesses information from models, so that choice is not sufficiently similar to the problems described in the passage and can be eliminated. Choice D describes a scenario in which collective overuse of a critical, unregulated resource leads to its depletion. That does not fit the problem described in the passage *perfectly*, but it is close – all financial institutions simultaneously dip into a pool of information, which makes the value of that information plummet. Choice D is the best choice among the four answers.

47. **C is the best answer.** The Yogi Berra quote is a paradox because it suggests the future that once was is no longer – but can a future have a present form if it has not yet occurred? Models of risk attempt to paint a picture of the future now, but the argument of the article is that the very existence and collective use of these models changes the future they are meant to predict. Choice A describes the relationship of the past to the present. Notice that choice A does not allude to the future, so it is unlikely to function like the Yogi Berra quote. Choice A can be eliminated. Choice B is tempting because it proposes a malleable future, but the author used the Yogi Berra quote to suggest that events in the present affect the future. Choice B is not a strong answer. Choice C is more like the Yogi Berra quote because, since the present and future are one, and we can influence the events of the present, it follows that the *present* can influence the future. This is very close to the meaning of the passage quote and may be the best answer. Again, the Yogi Berra quote connects the *present* to the future rather than the past, so choice D would be a better summary of the *theoretical* purpose of models. The author makes an argument about how the real effect of their widespread use fails to live up to the theoretical effect, so choice D is contrary to the main idea. Choice C is the strongest answer.

Passage 9 (Questions 48-53)

48. **B is the best answer.** By asking for a summary of a claim the author makes in the passage, the question requires a thorough understanding of the author's position on inviolable rights relative to a more generally held belief. The passage sets up a spectrum of opinions on the topic of inviolable rights, with those who believe such rights ought to derive from sentience on one extreme and those who think markers of higher cognition ought to guarantee inviolable rights on the other. According to the passage, most people are closer to the latter extreme. The author is much closer to the former extreme, which corresponds with the animal rights theorists' approach. Choice A can be eliminated as it aligns with the animal rights position, which, according to the author, is not the opinion most people hold. Choice B suggests most people think that inviolable rights derive from rationality, a marker of higher cognition, so choice B is a strong answer. Choice C, like choice A, better supports the author's side of the spectrum of opinions, not what the author says most people think, so it too can be eliminated. Choice D can be eliminated as it goes beyond the scope of the question, suggesting that inviolable rights are derived arbitrarily, which is not an opinion discussed in the passage. Thus, the best answer is choice B.

49. **C is the best answer.** The question asks about an opinion implied in the passage that is not the author's. The author disagrees with Carl Cohen, the philosopher discussed in paragraph five, who thinks humans and animals belong to different moral categories. The best answer to this question is the one that most accurately summarizes Carl Cohen's opinion. Choice A distracts attention away from the best answer by suggesting that human sentience is the basis for humans' inviolable rights, which resembles information in the passage but does not summarize Carl Cohen's opinion. Choice B can be eliminated as it aligns neither with Cohen's opinion nor with the author's, suggesting that inviolable rights derive from an ability to feel sensations. The author states that Cohen's opinion on the moral difference between humans and animals is that humans and animals are of different "kinds," so choice C, which emphasizes humans as distinctive, is a strong answer. Like choice A, choice D distracts from the best answer by referring to high cognition, a key term from the passage, but in way that does not support Cohen's position as well as choice C. Choice C is thus the best answer.

50. **B is the best answer.** By asking about the author's use of the telepaths as a hypothetical situation, the question requires a solid understanding of the author's main point about inconsistency in the granting of inviolable rights. According to the passage, the author thinks that using higher cognition as the qualifier for inviolable rights immorally privileges some species over others. The author uses the telepaths as emphasis for this argument. Choice A, while true according to the passage, does not answer the question of why the author brings up telepaths, which is to demonstrate the moral inconsistency of awarding inviolable rights based on cognitive ability. Choice B is a strong answer as it supports the author's main idea that granting inviolable rights to beings with higher cognitive capacities is arbitrary and therefore morally inconsistent. Though choice C resembles information in the passage which states that telepaths have higher cognitive abilities than humans, it, like choice A, does not answer the question about why the author brings up telepaths. Similarly, choice D can be eliminated as it does not pertain to the question, even though it seems to align with what the passage says about human rights. On the MCAT®, the best answer choice will always both be true according to the passage and answer the question. Choice B is the best answer because it corresponds to the passage and satisfies the question.

51. **B is the best answer.** A solid understanding of the animal rights opinion discussed in the passage is required to answer this question. The passage states that animal rights theorists argue inviolable rights ought to derive from a being's sentience. According to these theorists, sentience is the ability to experience the world subjectively, regardless of higher cognitive capacities such as reason and language. Option I is correct as it concerns high cognitive capacity in a general sense, which animal rights theorists would not accept as the basis for inviolable rights, so choice C can be eliminated. According to the passage, animal rights theorists would likely consider vulnerability to death as a marker of subjectivity and thus sentience; as such, option II aligns with their approach, so choice D can be eliminated. Option III, like option I, refers to a marker of higher cognition, so the animal rights theorists would not include it in their approach to inviolable rights. Choice A corresponds only to option I, so it can be eliminated. Choice B is the best answer as it corresponds to both options I and III.

52. **D is the best answer.** In order to determine the best answer to this question, it is necessary to understand the author's position that inviolable rights ought to be applied consistently to all sentient beings. The passage states that performing tests on a human against their will violates their inviolable rights. The author believes that, for the sake of moral consistency, all sentient animals deserve similar rights in relation to testing. Because choice A suggests the legislation would limit protection only to animals that can reason, it is too specific to fit the author's opinion, so it can be eliminated. Choice B aligns more closely with Carl Cohen's beliefs than it does with the author's, so it too can be eliminated. Choice C, though it seems to align with the author's opinion that all sentient beings deserve inviolable rights, goes beyond the information in the passage as the author does not discuss the possibility of humane animal testing. Choice D is a stronger answer than choice C as it comes closer to the author's position that all sentient beings ought to have inviolable rights, similar to the rights humans have preventing testing against their wills. Thus, choice D is the best answer.

53. **B is the best answer.** The author describes sentience as the ability to experience the world subjectively. By subjectively the author means with emotions and susceptibility to death. The reason the author brings up sentience is to argue that it is a more comprehensive premise on which to grant inviolable rights than cognitive capacity. Choice A contradicts the author's position, suggesting that sentience is an exclusive condition on which to base inviolable rights when the author means it to be all inclusive. In contrast, choice B concisely supports the author's point that sentience is a more universally inclusive condition than higher cognition on which to grant inviolable rights, so it is a strong answer. Like choice A, choice C contradicts the author's definition of sentience, suggesting that a being must have higher cognition in order to be sentient, so it can be eliminated. The author thinks basic emotions are one marker of sentience, but not that sentience necessarily means a being will feel only basic emotions. By the author's definition, beings that feel more complex emotions, such as humans, are still sentient. Choice D distracts attention away from the best answer by referring to emotion, but in a way that suggests sentient beings necessarily feel only basic emotions. As such, choice B is the best answer.

ANSWERS & EXPLANATIONS
Questions 1–53

ANSWER KEY					
1. B	10. B	19. C	28. B	37. A	46. A
2. C	11. D	20. D	29. D	38. B	47. C
3. C	12. D	21. A	30. C	39. C	48. C
4. D	13. A	22. D	31. D	40. A	49. B
5. C	14. C	23. C	32. B	41. B	50. B
6. B	15. D	24. C	33. B	42. D	51. D
7. D	16. D	25. A	34. D	43. A	52. A
8. C	17. B	26. A	35. C	44. C	53. C
9. A	18. C	27. C	36. B	45. D	

EXPLANATIONS FOR TEST 3

Passage 1 (Questions 1-6)

1. **B is the best answer.** Throughout the passage, the author presents a spectrum of the costs and benefits of mobile technology use by professionals. They argue that mobile technology is often beneficial to companies because employees work longer hours, throughout all times of the day. This benefit often comes at the cost of the employee's personal life, which can lead to stress and confusion. Although the passage spends more time discussing the personal downsides of technology use, it is still fairly balanced in its approach and indicates that mobile technology can be beneficial for the personal lives of some professionals. Remember that answer choices including strong words like "always" are usually not the best answer. Choice A is too far toward one end of the passage spectrum and can be eliminated. Because some individuals can balance their personal lives with mobile technology use while others cannot, it is reasonable to assume that the efficacy of mobile technology use depends on the individual. Choice B is a strong answer. Choice C is the opposite extreme from choice A and also contains the word "always." It is too general of a statement to be true all of the time. If an employee experiences burnout and turns in assignments late or even resigns, the company would not benefit from the mobile technology use. Choice C can be eliminated. The author does not suggest that mobile technology use is only beneficial to the company if the individual possesses work/life boundaries, because individuals who do not possess those boundaries might work the most and benefit the company as well. Choice D can be eliminated, and choice B is the best answer.

2. **C is the best answer.** The author's main argument stresses the importance of maintaining work-life balance, but they do not suggest that mobile technology should not be used in the workplace. Such a belief falls on one end of the spectrum that does not consider the possible benefits of using mobile technology for work purposes. The author is not likely to refuse to use mobile technology, since it can still help them perform some tasks more efficiently. Choice A can be eliminated. The passage does not mention specific technological devices and the author does not suggest that the number of devices used makes work-life balance more challenging. Choice B is not a strong answer. The author is likely to establish certain hours in which others can expect them to work and other hours when they will not use their technology for professional purposes. In the second paragraph, the author suggests that mobile technology can help set up a strong work-life division by maximizing the quality of time spent on each task. Choice C is a possible answer. There is no reason to assume that coworkers have found work-life balance, since the author cites a study in the fourth paragraph that describes how the majority of workers at one company struggle to find work-life balance. Advice from coworkers would not be helpful if they have not found ways to establish work-life balance for themselves, so choice D can be eliminated. Choice C is the best answer.

3. **C is the best answer.** This question is asking for a negative result of increased technology use that specifically decreases personal time. If individuals are exchanging personal communications at work, they are increasing their amount of personal time. Choice A can be eliminated. Choice B could either support or weaken the argument. With more information digitalized, employees do not need to spend as much time physically at work, which means they could save that time and increase personal time. This interpretation would weaken the claim. Choice B could support the claim in question if individuals were using that free time to complete more work while at home. Choice B is a weak answer. Because the work-life imbalance created by mobile technology favors more time spent on work, choice C supports the claim that technology eats away at personal time. The increased workload would decrease the amount of personal time, and choice C points directly to mobile technology as the cause. Choice C is a strong answer. While a time famine results in less personal time, this time famine is not necessarily caused by technology, since it is described as inherent. Additionally, mobile technology is not explicitly referenced in the question stem. Choice C is stronger than choices B and D because it directly links mobile technology to decreased personal time.

4. **D is the best answer.** Do not bring in outside information to answer this question but look for support in the passage only. While many Americans do own cell phones now, as shown by the statistics in the first paragraph, this information cannot be generalized to "most" Americans without information about the American population size. The passage mentions that the majority of South Koreans own a smart phone, but does not make a similar generalization for Americans. Choice A cannot be assumed true. The author does not discuss the imbalance in America specifically. They begin their argument by stating this is a global issue due to the prevalence of technology in many countries. There is no reason to assume the imbalance occurs only in America, so choice B can be eliminated. When the author mentions the time famine, they include the word "inherent," which suggest this feeling is innate and has always existed. While the feeling may be intensified by technology, there is no evidence from the passage that it is a recent development. Choice C is not a strong answer. Throughout the passage, the author suggests that many employees continue work after hours because they carry their work home with them. In the first paragraph, they mention that employees often work beyond the period of paid employment due to the accessibility of mobile technology. Choice D is the best answer.

5. **C is the best answer.** The author suggests that work-life balance is harder to maintain now because technology is so portable and accessible from home. They specifically discuss mobile technology because it is transportable. Because an employee can carry a cell phone to and from work, and is likely to use it for personal reasons in addition to professional reasons, the author would be unlikely to advocate use of a cell phone for the purpose of improving work-life balance. Choice A can be eliminated. Laptops are also portable and are likely to be used for professional purposes that can encroach on personal time, so choice B is not the best answer. If an employee only uses a desktop computer for work tasks, then that object cannot follow them home and they will not be tempted to work during personal time. Choice C is a possible answer. If a company utilizes an online server, it could be accessed from many devices, so employees might devote more personal time to work while at home. Choice C is a stronger answer than choice D.

6. **B is the best answer.** The author would be likely to support the scenario described in the question stem according to the passage argument and the possible benefits of mobile technology use that are described. While employees might still be tempted to work from home using a different device, the temptation will not be as strong if their cell phones are used only for personal reasons. The author is likely to support the proposal because it could help establish work boundaries. Choices C and D can be eliminated. The author mentions the pressure that employees feel to increase productivity and complete tasks after hours if they can access their work. Even if employees are supposed to turn off their work phones at home, they could still be tempted to turn them on to complete more tasks. The passage does not support the idea of turning off personal phones at work, since the author does not suggest they are a distraction. Choice A is not as strong as choice B. If employees have to leave their work phones at the office, they will not be tempted to work as much during personal hours. Choice B is the best answer.

Passage 2 (Questions 7-11)

7. **D is the best answer.** The author argues that the Bhutanese approach to happiness is grounded in an understanding that different fields are interconnected. Look for an answer choice that identifies this emphasis on interdependence. The passage does not indicate what proportion of Bhutanese people believe in Mahayana Buddhism. The passage only notes that Bhutanese policies appear to be derived from this belief. Choice A is out of the scope of the passage and can be eliminated. The passage makes no claim that happiness is a requirement for economic success, but rather notes how economic success can develop even when happiness is made a priority. Choice B is a simpleton distractor and can be eliminated. It is true that Bhutan is influenced by Mahayana Buddhism. The claim that Mahayana Buddhism focuses on individual desires confuses Buddhist principles with those followed by Westerners, though. Loy attributes the reified individual to Western culture. Choice C can be eliminated. Choice D identifies the fact that Bhutanese beliefs are influenced by Mahayana Buddhism and aligns with the author's argument that Buddhist principles contribute to Bhutan's understanding of interdependence. This understanding of interdependence would imply that success in one realm is influenced by success in another. Happiness is interconnected with the policy of the Bhutanese government. Choice D is the best answer.

8. **C is the best answer.** The author argues that it is difficult for Westerners to understand interdependence because their entrenched beliefs emphasize relationships rather than process. In making this argument, the author presents a spectrum of opinions. On one side is Bhutanese process-oriented interdependence, and on the other is Western noun-oriented interdependence. The author favors the Bhutanese conception of interdependence, so the best answer will probably reflect the author's negative view of Western ideas of interdependence. First identify where the answer choices fall on the spectrum. Choice A is strongly negative and appears to be a possible answer because it reflects the author's negative viewpoint on western ideas about interdependence. "Traits" appears to be an example of "nouns" that the author refers to. The author argues that Westerners assign fixed traits to an identity and do not focus on the evolution of that identity. Choice B is slightly positive and contradicts the author's argument, and can therefore be eliminated. Choice C is less negative than choice A. Choice C accurately conveys the author's point that Westerners focus on characteristics rather than on process. Choice C appears to be a strong answer. Upon comparing choice C to choice A, note that choice C makes specific references to the passage. Choice C is a stronger answer, so choice A can be eliminated. The author does not claim that Western ideas of independence assume that a noun's traits do not change. Choice D leans towards the negative side of the spectrum and makes an assumption that goes beyond the scope of the passage. Choice D can be eliminated, and choice C is the best answer.

9. **A is the best answer.** The author argues that a focus on individual pleasure creates a dichotomy between humans and nature that prevents a government from aspiring to the stable, holistic approach to success that is derived from Mahayana Buddhism's belief in interdependence. If GNH focused on individual happiness, it would lose the Mahayana Buddhism conception of interdependence and be subject to the same problems as the Western conception of interdependence, weakening the author's argument. Choice A notes that this statement would weaken the author's argument and shift the Bhutanese emphasis from interdependence to individualism. Choice A appears to be a strong answer. Choice B is appealing at first because it also notes that the author's argument would be weakened, but the author is not arguing that GNH is currently incomprehensible to Westerners. Eliminate choice B. The explanation in choice C contradicts the author's argument. It is *"sukha,"* not individual pleasure, that is characterized by mental stability. Eliminate choice C. The author does not comment on the values held by individual Bhutanese people. Eliminate choice D. Choice A is the best answer.

10. **B is the best answer.** The author argues that Western culture focuses on relationships between nouns rather than on process. This is in contrast to the Bhutanese understanding of interdependence which understands identity as a trajectory and promotes government policy that pursues both economic success and happiness. On the spectrum, the author is more favorable towards the Bhutanese understanding of interdependence. Choice A is appealing because it is plausible that the dichotomy between humans and nature could reflect an inability to understand interdependence. Although choice A supports the claim that Westerners may not understand interrelations, it does not address Westerners' inability to understand evolution. Choice A can be eliminated. Choice B appears to be a strong answer because it notes the fluid nature of identity. Choice C does not answer the question because the statement refers to a result of Western values, not a cause. Choice C can be eliminated. Choice D provides an example that illustrates Bhutan's ability to understand interrelation and evolution. This does not answer the question because Bhutan's understanding is irrelevant to whether Westerners understand interrelation and evolution. Eliminate choice D. Choice B is the best answer.

11. **D is the best answer.** Loy argues that the Western worldview produces a distinction between humans and nature that encourages Westerners to view the environment as a resource. Choice A is appealing, but the word "incapable" is too strong for this situation and does not allow for the possibility that people understand the environment is not solely a resource. Choice A can be eliminated. Loy discussed both individualism and humans' relationship with the environment, but he does not make assumptions about how individual self-preoccupation leads to a cultural disregard for the environment. Choice B extends Loy's argument beyond Westerners' relationship to the environment by generalizing it to their ability to empathize in general. Choice B takes Loy's argument too far and can be eliminated. Choice C covers ideas about how individualism leads to a disregard for the environment. Choice C can be eliminated. Choice D appropriately reflects Loy's point that Westerner's Greek heritage limits Westerner's connection to nature and subsequently influenced their view of the environment as a resource. Choice D is the best answer.

Passage 3 (Questions 12-15)

12. **D is the best answer.** The passage presents a spectrum of influences philosophy has had on neuroscience, ranging from clarifying abstract concepts to questioning scientific laws and hypotheses. Near the beginning of the passage, the author describes aspects of neuroscience that humans now understand more deeply due to the grasp of philosophical concepts. They begin by stating that vision has been clarified due to the philosophical study of perception, so choice A can be eliminated. The author points out that the structure of language, or syntax, is now better understood by examining language from a philosophical point of view. Choice B can also be eliminated. The passage also states that the study of short-term and long-term memory has been strengthened by a philosophical approach. Choice C is not a strong answer since recall describes an aspect of memory. The author points out that the philosophical approach to consciousness, or reflection while thinking, has only led to more questions surrounding the topic. Because this question is asking for the answer choice with the LEAST clarification, choice D is the best answer.

13. **A is the best answer.** This passage discusses how philosophy has influenced humans' understanding of the brain. The author points out that even with these advances, the brain is so complex that it is difficult to find commonalities possessed by all human brains. Forests can be large, complex, and have lots of variability. Because forests possess variable types of trees, it may be difficult to find a single tree that all forests have in common. Choice A is a strong answer. Vast deserts can be grouped together based on their lack of water, so choice B can be eliminated. While swimming pools may differ in size or shape, they are not particularly complex structures. Choice C is not as strong as choice A, because swimming pools are usually not as complicated or vast as forests. Dams may be complex and intricate structures, but the adjective "standard" implies that many dams are built in a common way. The wording of this answer choice suggest that dams do not possess as much variability as forests, which can contain all different types of trees or stages of life. Choice D is not as strong as choice A.

14. **C is the best answer.** Throughout the passage, the author applies philosophical reasoning to understanding scientific concepts. While they discuss the philosophy of neuroscience in detail, there is no reason to assume that they have devoted their studies to only this concept. Be careful not to jump to conclusions or make assumptions about the author. Choice A can be eliminated. In the beginning of the passage, the author proposes that classic neuroscience questions will be answered only with a grasp on philosophical concepts. They do not say the same for all scientific concepts. Choice B can be eliminated. The author draws attention to the flaws of the nomological view of science, because they do not think it necessarily applies to every kind of science, nor does it describe the processes involved in the scientific concept. The author also makes a point of mentioning that the nomological view of science is rooted in early philosophy, so it is reasonable to assume that the author differs from earlier philosophers in this instance. Choice C is a strong answer. At the end of the passage, the author suggests that scientific theories may need to be remodeled to include space models of neural representation, but does not suggest that earlier philosophers believe differently. It is impossible to determine how early philosophers would react to this proposal. Choice C is stronger than choice D since it is directly discussed in relation to early philosophy.

15. **D is the best answer.** The author values studying neuroscience with a philosophical grasp of the concepts. The author primarily discusses neuroscience in the context of philosophy and would not be likely to support a college course studying only the intricacies of neurological processes, because it would not encompass other approaches. Choice A can be eliminated. While the author values the combination of philosophy and neuroscience, they do not mention ethics throughout the passage. There is no way to determine the author's views towards ethical approaches to neuroscience studies, so choice B is not a strong answer. Although the author argues that a philosophical approach to neuroscience often raises questions about the scientific concepts, they do not necessarily promote skepticism. They describe the process as a fluid approach that may raise questions, but raising questions is not the primary goal. Choice C is not a strong answer. The author argues that laws of nature may benefit from expanded definitions, and that accepted hypotheses may need to be rephrased with a philosophical approach. It is reasonable to assume the author would encourage reevaluating basic questions of science, since they suggest these topics need to be revisited. Choice D is the best answer.

Passage 4 (Questions 16-20)

16. **D is the best answer.** The passage presents a spectrum of opinions regarding the efficacy of prostate cancer screening. Some individuals believe that it primarily detects dormant cancer and does not actually improve the survival rate of the diagnosis. The passage does not suggest that neurotic patients' actions have affected the incidence of prostate cancer, since the author does not discuss the causes or predisposing factors of PCa. Choice A can be eliminated. The author does not directly suggest that men are visiting the doctors more often, but it could be that increasing screening causes men to visit doctors more frequently. Choice B is a possible answer. The author argues that the increase in incidence of PCa is caused by more frequent diagnosis, but they do not imply that the criteria for diagnosis has expanded. Choice C is a possible answer, but is not particularly strong. The passage implies that the adoption of screening recommendations has increased diagnoses of PCa, since PSA was adopted roughly 20 years ago, when the incidence started rapidly increasing. The author also mentions that only recently was PSA ruled more harmful than beneficial. Since choice D explicitly describes an increase in screening, it is a stronger answer than choice B.

17. **B is the best answer.** The spectrum throughout the passage relates to the effectiveness of PCa screening when the benefits are weighed against the costs. The author believes that PCa screening can be beneficial for individuals with the personality type to follow through with treatment and maintain a positive attitude. The author does not agree with the U.S. Preventive Services Task Force, which recommends against screening for all men. They do not believe the conclusion in the question stem is necessary since it should not apply to all individuals. Choice A can be eliminated. The author believes that PSA screening can be beneficial to educated, conscientious, and extraverted men who will try to take care of their health. They point out that the screening would not be helpful to neurotic men, who would be too negative and stressed to react appropriately to a diagnosis. Choice B is a promising answer. The author does not suggest that this claim lacks evidence, but simply does not list evidence in the passage. Choice C demonstrates a more extreme view toward PSA screening than is displayed by the author, so it is not the best answer. The author does not discuss cancer treatment in the passage, so it is not possible to determine how the screening technique affects treatment directly. Choice D is not as related to the author's primary argument as choice C, so choice C is the strongest answer.

18. **C is the best answer.** The passage presents the USPSTF on one end of the spectrum, because they recommend no PSA screening for prostate cancer. The author, on the other hand, thinks PSA screening can be beneficial for some men who have the right personality traits. The author suggests that certain characteristics may indicate patient compliance, which could possibly lead to a better outcome if that individual was diagnosed with PCa. The author argues that an individual's disposition affects the benefit/harm ratio for PSA screening, so option I is true and choice D can be eliminated. While the author mentions that a lack of screening can lead to more expenses later if an individual is diagnosed with more advanced prostate cancer, their argument is not based upon this belief. The author does not primarily criticize the USPSTF's recommendation for the possible increase in costs, but rather briefly mentions that possibility to support their primary argument. The passage does not reference the cost to patients, just cost in general. Option II is not necessarily true according to the passage. Choices B and D can be eliminated. The author points out that the USPSTF's recommendation treats men as one homogenous group, when in reality they make up a heterogeneous group with individuals who may react very differently to the same diagnosis. The author primarily criticizes the no screening policy as an over-generalization. Option III is true, so choice A can be eliminated and choice C is the best answer.

19. **C is the best answer.** The passage presents a spectrum of beliefs regarding the benefits of PSA screening. The author believes that it can be helpful to individuals with particular personality traits, but does not suggest that screening should be recommended for every individual. The author argues that patients should be considered on a case-by-case basis, so their argument is not necessarily supported by the results of implementing screening directed toward all females. Choice A can be eliminated. The author's argument relates to government and healthcare recommendations of screening, in addition to patient disposition affecting the benefits of PSA screening. This answer choice supports part of the author's argument, but not necessarily the overarching argument about tailoring screening recommendations according to personality. Choice B is a possible answer but not particularly strong. If physicians can observe patients for five minutes and notice distinct personality traits, it is reasonable to assume that physicians can assess which individuals may benefit from cancer screening. This finding would support the author's belief that PSA screening should be recommended for certain types of people instead of treating all men as a homogeneous group. Choice C relates more directly to the author's view of where screening recommendations should come from and who should implement them, so it is stronger than choice B. While cancer research devoted to screening may possibly support the author's argument, it could also support the argument of the USPSTF. Choice D can be eliminated and choice C is the best answer.

20. **D is the best answer.** The author believes that PSA screening can be beneficial for men with particular personality traits, and thus screening recommendations should be considered on an individual basis. Based on the passage argument about viewing an at-risk group as heterogeneous, the author would likely oppose the scenario in choice A. The author does not address cancer treatment, only screening. If a treatment proves successful for almost all patients, there is no reason to assume that the author would oppose it. Choice B is not a strong answer. The author discusses the USPSTF's recommendation in a calm tone of disagreement, so they might support funding to research the validity their claim. Choice C can be eliminated. The author specifically discusses PSA screening and argues that the recommendations should not be applied to all men without considering other factors. Even though the author believes that PSA screening can be beneficial, they do not necessarily believe that it is beneficial for all men and would be unlikely to recommend screening every man. Choice D is more directly related to the author's argument than choice A and is the strongest answer.

Passage 5 (Questions 21-27)

21. **A is the best answer.** The author of this passage appears intent on setting the historical record straight on the involvement of black churches in the Civil Rights Movement. From her perspective, the body of literature has unfairly treated them as either accommodating or resistant while failing to recognize that many churches used both strategies in their struggle for equality. Because she argues against simplistic labels, choice A is a compelling answer. Choice B, ascribing to white values, falls prey to the "either/or" oversimplification the author argues against, so it is not a strong answer. The author describes the Civil Rights Era as a time whereby black people were oppressed by whites. A negation of this social order would entail a society in which white people are subordinate to blacks, which does not seem to be the intention of black churches at the time. Choice C is a weak answer because its argument is too extreme. The author cites Myrdal's argument that leaders of black churches were not prepared to provide direct resistance to oppression, but she does not appear to share that sentiment. The conclusion of the passage, after all, argues that even accommodating churches could be seen as resistant to the status quo. Eliminate choice D. Choice A is the strongest answer.

22. **D is the best answer.** This question stem asks about the main argument in the passage. Most of the text in the passage is devoted to criticizing scholars who have described the tactics of the black church during the Civil Rights Era as either accommodating or resistant. The final paragraph argues that, while some churches were openly resistant, others offered at least some resistance through challenging notions of black people in American society. The passage says that some scholars assumed black churches completely yielded to Victorian standards of morality, but it never says those scholars assumed that moral system was superior to black values. Choice A can be eliminated. While the author implies that some scholars may treat black values and middle-class values as mutually exclusive concepts, she criticizes scholars for oversimplifying the tactics of black churches rather than for their evaluation of value systems. Choice B is a conflation of two separate ideas in the passage and can be eliminated. The passage presents two black church conventions that did not share a singular vision. That these conventions were at odds is not an assumption of scholars but rather a fact. Choice C does not answer the question stem, so it can be eliminated. Choice D is compatible with a major theme of the passage – namely, that strategies of accommodation and resistance can co-exist. Choice D restates the passage's major argument, so it is the best answer choice.

23. **C is the best answer.** The thrust of the passage argument is that scholars have oversimplified the functions of the black church during the Civil Rights Era. The third paragraph momentarily diverges from this reasoning to discuss specific scholars' observations about the black church. Whereas the first two paragraphs describe two conventions with either accommodating or resistant strategies, the third paragraph presents strengths of these churches alongside their weaknesses. Some of these weaknesses provide clues as to why some churches were accommodating of the oppressive status quo. The author herself does not make a judgment about internal problems in the black church, so there is little basis for concluding that these scholars shared similar viewpoints to her own. Choice A can be eliminated. This paragraph describes challenges within the black church, not outward expressions of resistance. Choice B can be eliminated. The information in the third paragraph gives background about the conflicts facing black churches and insight as to why they may have been accommodating. It paints a fuller picture of these churches, so choice C is a strong answer. The extent to which the author agrees with Du Bois' and Myrdal's views is not clear. She would not be likely to describe the black churches as "unfit" to press for equal rights because she later argues that these churches' strategies were responsive to the plight of the congregation. She also does not contest the scholars' claims about the lack of education and the oppressive tendencies within the black church itself. Choice D is weaker than choice C because the author did not directly assail the claims of these scholars. This makes choice C the best answer.

24. **C is the best answer.** The author has a conflicted relationship with the expectation that blacks should conform to white values. On the one hand, she sees it as falling short of the equal treatment black citizens deserved. The fourth paragraph argues, on the other hand, that this conformity had the potential to validate black people as worthy of civic participation and equality. It is unlikely that she would endorse this approach as the "best" way to win rights, so choice A can be eliminated. The failure of the temperance movement, in addition to alluding to a minor point in the passage, incorporates information from beyond the passage. The passage does not present information about the success or failure of the temperance movement, so choice B can be eliminated as a beyond distractor. Choice C, which states that this expectation was unjust but also provided an opportunity, summarizes the author's complex feelings toward Victorian values, so it is a strong answer. Although the passage addresses gender oppression and classism within the black church, it does not address how significant this issue was in comparison to other challenges the church faced. Choice D can be eliminated in favor of choice C.

25. **A is the best answer.** The argument from the question stem is presented in the fourth paragraph. Envision how the argument would proceed were the passage to continue. What questions linger, and how could points from that paragraph be reinforced? The passage argues that accommodative behavior not only offered protection to members of black churches but also a means of controverting the expectations of the oppressive status quo. Examples that show how protection made the Civil Rights Movement more durable would reinforce that point, so choice A is a strong answer. Churches who believed that Victorian values were the key to liberation were often accommodative churches. The author uses this passage to try to validate the accommodative churches, so her argument would not be served by rebutting them. Choice B can be eliminated. While the author implies that the call for "racial uplift" has an underlying pejorative, possibly racist tone, she believes that this approach had some value. Condemning these undertones would only undermine the reasoning in the fourth paragraph. Choice C can be eliminated. The passage already states that accommodation offered a centralized black community and a compelling narrative that black individuals were worthy of equal treatment, so the strategy in choice D appears to be redundant. It would be a less helpful strategy for developing the argument about accommodative behavior than choice A. Choice D can be eliminated.

26. **A is the best answer.** Consider the methods used by the National Baptist Convention in trying to win equal treatment. Unlike Dr. Martin Luther King Jr.'s rival organization, they advocated assimilation of their parishioners to white norms. Choice A similarly demands that same-sex individuals fashion their marriages around traditional marriages, so it appears to be a strong answer. The passage states that the Progressive National Baptist Convention, not the National Baptist Convention, aligned itself with other organizations and causes. Choice B can be eliminated. Asserting that same-sex marriages are identical to those of heterosexual couples sounds similar to the approach of the National Baptist Convention. There is a subtle difference between choices A and C. The strategy in choice A makes a demand of the minority group seeking equal treatment. The strategy in choice C is to advocate a similarity between the majority and minority groups. The National Baptist Convention made moves to change the behaviors of its member – that is, it looked internally to solve external problems. Choice A is a stronger answer than choice C. Notice that choice D, uniting under an established church, is a method used by both the National Baptist Convention and the Progressive National Baptist Convention. Choice D is less specific to the National Baptist Convention than is choice A, so it is not the strongest answer.

27. **C is the best answer.** If the author were asked what future historians of social movements should keep in mind, what would she likely say? This passage criticized the notion that black churches were either accommodating or resistant – nothing in between. The author demands a complex reading of social phenomena. A call to validate rival movements with differing means to a shared end may refer to the conflict between Progressive National Baptist Convention and the National Baptist Convention, but the author never evaluates one of the conventions over the other. She does not imply that either is worth more or less attention than the other. Choice A is a weak answer. A call to give equal weight to dissenting viewpoints is not a theme addressed in the passage. The author rails against simplistic, binary classification, not that one viewpoint has been privileged over another. Choice B is unsupported by the passage and can be eliminated. The author concludes the passage arguing that accommodation – a strategy that many have seen as counterproductive to winning civil liberties – has been oversimplified in scholarly literature. She calls for a fuller context to accompany descriptions of accommodating black churches. Choice C appears to be a strong answer because it is compatible with the passage's main idea. Choice D argues for an evaluation of scholarship from the perspective of those in the past. Notice that the passage author evaluates scholarship from the Civil Rights Era from the perspective of the present. Although she empathizes with the plight facing accommodating black churches, she retrospectively condemns the scholarship from this era. Choice D is a weaker answer than choice C because the author herself judges previous scholarship from the vantage point of the present.

Passage 6 (Questions 28-33)

28. **B is the best answer.** The main idea of the passage is that stateless people do not receive their right to health because there is no accountability for enforcing equal care for all, and governments do not spend time addressing the healthcare needs of undocumented citizens. While the passage claims that possessing documentation is a requirement for obtaining the right to health, the passage does not offer any information about the ease with which those documents can be acquired, so choice A can be eliminated. The passage mentions that stateless people often have short lives and that these stateless people do not usually have adequate access to healthcare services, so it can be concluded that these people have worse health outcomes and choice B is a strong answer. The author states that politicians believe that their actions are adequate, but then describes the healthcare systems as imperfect and only providing "some" access to legal immigrants, so choice C is not well-supported by the passage. Choice D makes the assumption that being able to access healthcare implies a higher economic status, which on average might be true. However, the passage focuses on the lack of documentation, not money, as a cause of lower healthcare access. Remember not to bring any outside information or assumptions into the exam. Choice D can be eliminated, and choice B is the best answer.

29. **D is the best answer.** The main idea of the passage is that stateless people do not receive the right to health because they do not have rights in the countries in which they reside, and global public health initiatives and legal obligations to provide this right are not being enforced. There is a political aspect to this problem, but the passage suggests it is a structural issue rather than intentional neglect. The passage does not discuss the voting process or suggest that politicians are motivated by winning over votes, making option I a weak answer. Choice C can be eliminated. Part of the main idea is that no one is able to secure implementation of global health policies, so option II is true and choice B can be ruled out. The passage mentions a potential lack of mobility for stateless people, implying that these people are physically stuck in a certain place and cannot move to regions with better healthcare access. This passage implication makes option III true. Since options II and III are both strong answers, choice A can be eliminated, and choice D is the best answer.

30. **C is the best answer.** The main idea of the passage is that stateless people are often denied their right to help for a number of reasons including the absence of rights provided by the country in which they reside and the inability to enforce global healthcare access laws. While universal healthcare would definitely benefit stateless people, they may still have barriers to accessing care such as mobility, as described in the passage. As such, stateless people in countries with universal health coverage may still not receive care and choice A is incorrect. While money is a clear undertone of the passage, it is not specifically expressed as a barrier to care, so choice B is not the best answer. The main idea of the passage includes the concept that there are many barriers to care for stateless people, so choice C is a compelling answer even if it is unclear what is meant by "social barriers." Choice D again neglects to account for possible obstacles to receiving care other than cost, so it can be eliminated, and choice C is the best answer.

31. **D is the best answer.** The passage presents a spectrum of ideas regarding the accessibility of healthcare. The government believes it is doing a good job at keeping its citizens covered, while health advocates believe even the undocumented populations should have access to better care. The author lies somewhere in the middle of this spectrum but leans towards the side of the public health advocates, a tendency revealed in the author's emphasis on the stateless citizen and choice to call current healthcare availability "imperfect." This question thus asks for an argument the author might use to prove her point – something that is not too extreme but emphasizes the need for better healthcare overall. The article does not focus on any particular country and, in fact, tries to talk about healthcare more universally. Further, there is no information in the answer choice to indicate whether the immigrants are documented. For both reasons, choice A can be eliminated. Choice B describes a situation in which the structural healthcare system within a country is failing from overload and not intent, and again it is unclear if the immigrants are documented, so it is not a strong answer. The question asks about the support provided to documented citizens, not illegal immigrants. Choice C does not answer the question. Some of the homeless population in a country are likely to be documented, and dying from preventable diseases suggests they are not obtaining adequate care. This would undermine the argument of adequate access to care, making choice D the best answer choice.

32. **B is the best answer.** Part of the main idea of the passage is that legal obligations guaranteeing the right to health are not always met, and these obligations apply to prisoners. The obligations include preventative, curative, and palliative care for all. The passage states that advocates believe it is the government's responsibility to provide the country's highest level of care to prisoners of war, and by extension this belief is likely to apply to all prisoners. While a case could be made that hormone therapy is not curative, preventative, or palliative, it may be the highest standard of care and thus a right to health violation, making choice A incorrect. Remember not to bring any outside biases about potentially controversial topics into the exam. Choice B matches well with the main idea that the legal obligations are not met, so it is well-supported. There is not enough information in the question stem to know if the prisoner is stateless, so choice C can be eliminated. Not being able to enforce the legal obligations is a point that the author brings up in the passage, so choice D seems like a compelling answer. Choice B is better than choice D because choice D is too extreme, as conclusions about the overall enforceability of the right to health cannot be made based solely on this scenario.

33. **B is the best answer.** Near the end of the passage the author presents guidelines and initiatives that different organizations are laying out to try to improve healthcare access for undocumented citizens. The passage states that the WHO provides guidelines and advises moving towards universal health coverage while the Physicians for Human Rights advocates for the highest standard of care and points out potential barriers to well-being. These organizations provide advice and suggestions, but make no actual structural changes. The organizations are working at the international level, so choice A seems compelling. Pointing out health barriers and healthcare system needs is a way of raising awareness about healthcare, so choice B is convincing as well. Choice B is better than choice A because it is more specific to healthcare and is in line with the implication that the public health organizations speak more than act. Choice C talks about rights, which is the main theme of the passage, but the passage does not specifically mention that the public health organizations protect those rights, so choice C is out of the scope of the passage. Choice D implies that the organizations make actual changes at the country level, which is opposite from the way the passage portrays these organizations, so this choice is a contrary distractor and choice B is the best answer.

Passage 7 (Questions 34-40)

34. **D is the best answer.** The Sungir site comprises three graves, in which were found more than 13,000 ivory beads and over 250 beads made from polar fox teeth. The author says that this find represents more Pleistocene Era beads than has been found in all other contemporary sites combined. Choice A suggests that the three graves are those of ancient kings, which seems possible given that the author remarks on the number of beads (and hours of work) lavished on the burials—but there is no other evidence provided to suggest that the remains were those of kings. Choice A is therefore a weak answer. Choice B says that the graves contained eggshell beads, but in fact they contained ivory and fox tooth beads, so choice B can be eliminated. Choice C suggests that the polar fox teeth were part of polar fox remains, buried with the dead. But the author notes that the teeth were perforated for use as beads, and does not mention any other fox remains. Choice C can be eliminated. Choice D says that the cache of Pleistocene beads at the Sungir site is the largest in the world; since the author says that it is larger than all others *combined*, then it is certainly the largest. Choice D is a strong answer, and it is the best answer.

35. **C is the best answer.** The main idea of this passage is that even though bead remains from the Lower Paleolithic Period are scarce, taphonomic logic suggests that Lower Paleolithic peoples probably did in fact engage in prolific bead-making, and therefore possessed complex cultures and advanced cognitive abilities. The passage does not explicitly define *taphonomic logic*, so its meaning must be inferred. The author says that since ostrich eggshell is fragile, it is likely that only a tiny fraction of the beads made from this material have survived to the present day. This, he says, is what taphonomic logic tells us. Taphonomic logic, then, must be a way of reasoning about how a type of material is likely to hold up in the ground over time, and how we can use that reasoning to derive new information about discovered objects made of that material. The author reports that the society responsible for the El Greifa beads must have been a complex society with accomplished artisans capable of making highly uniform, tiny beads out of fragile material. They would have worn the beads in large numbers for decorative effect, though few beads survive because eggshell is a fragile material and most of them would have been pulverized over the course of tens of thousands of years in the ground. Choice A says that the society probably did not bury their dead with bead adornments. The author says that the Sungir beads were found in graves, but he does not say where the beads at the El Greifa site were found. The passage is unclear on the question of whether the El Greifa society buried their dead with bead adornments. So, choice A is a weak answer. Choice B suggests that the bead-makers had no way of assuring uniformity among the beads they produced, but the author says explicitly that the beads are highly uniform. Choice B can be eliminated. Choice C says that the society probably did not carve beads from stone. The author notes that stone tools were found at the site, and it is reasonable to assume that stone beads, like the tools, would survive in the ground at least as long as the eggshell beads. If no stone beads were found at the site, it is likely that the society did not make stone beads. Choice C is a strong answer. Choice D suggests that the members of the El Greifa society did not wear beads in large numbers, but the author argues that the number of beads found probably does not accurately reflect the number of beads made, since most of the beads would have disintegrated between the time they were made and the time the El Greifa site was found, 200,000 years later. Choice D can be eliminated. Choice C is the best answer.

36. **B is the best answer.** The passage does not explicitly define the term *taphonomy*, so its meaning must be deduced from two related phrases used (but also not defined) in the passage: *taphonomic logic* and *taphonomic threshold*. The author says that since ostrich eggshell is fragile, it is likely that only a tiny fraction of the beads made from this material have survived to the present day: this, he says, is what taphonomic logic tells us. Taphonomic logic, then, must be a way of reasoning about how a type of material is likely to hold up in the ground over time, and how we can use that reasoning to derive new information about discovered objects made of that material. He then says that few ostrich eggshell beads would have survived beyond the taphonomic threshold for ostrich eggshell: this must mean that there is a time span within which a material can be expected to survive more or less intact, and beyond that, we cannot expect to find many artifacts made from that material. Two hundred thousand years, he implies, is beyond the taphonomic threshold for ostrich eggshell: that explains why so few beads were found at El Greifa. It must be that taphonomy is the study of how artifacts change (and how well they hold up) between the time they enter the ground and the time they are excavated. Choice A says that taphonomy is the study of ancient burial sites. This might seem attractive, but it is too specific. Graves are not the only places where artifacts are found, and we do not know whether the El Greifa site contained any graves. Choice A is a weak answer. Choice B says that taphonomy must be the study of how artifacts change over time. This is a vague formulation, but it is accurate, so choice B is a strong answer. Choice C says that taphonomy is the study of how artifacts were actually used by their prehistoric makers. The author talks about how beads must have been used by the El Greifa society, but the author's uses of *taphonomic logic* and *taphonomic threshold* suggest that taphonomy studies what happens after an artifact is interred, not what happens to it while it is in use. Choice C can be eliminated. Choice D suggests that taphonomy is the study of ancient production techniques. There is no basis in the passage for this interpretation of the term, so choice D can be eliminated. Choice B is the strongest answer.

37. **A is the best answer.** The author claims that while it is *possible* that the makers of the El Greifa beads made only around 43 beads (the number recovered from the site), this is highly unlikely. As option I suggests, he argues that eggshell beads would not have been worn in small numbers, as they are very tiny. He points out that intact bead jewelry from the region consists of many tiny beads. Option I is true, so choice D can be eliminated. As option II suggests, the author points out that the beads are highly uniform, suggesting a high level of skill on the part of the artisans—but the author does not present this as evidence that many beads were made. He presents the uniformity of the beads only as evidence that the bead-makers and their society were capable of appreciating an abstract concept. Option II can be eliminated and so can choice B. The author also argues that the meager find at El Greifa should not be taken as evidence that only a few beads were produced there, as ostrich eggshell is not likely to have survived 200,000 years in the ground. But he makes no comparison with ivory beads of the same period, as option III suggests. The only mention of ivory beads is in the discussion of the much later Sungir site. Option III can be eliminated, which means choice C can also be eliminated. Choice A is the only one remaining and it is the best choice.

38. **B is the best answer.** The main idea of this passage is that even though bead remains from the Lower Paleolithic Period are scarce, taphonomic logic suggests that Lower Paleolithic peoples probably did in fact engage in prolific bead-making, and therefore possessed complex cultures and advanced cognitive abilities. A large cache of 250,000-year-old ostrich eggshell beads would be very surprising if the author is right that ostrich eggshell typically does not survive even as long as 200,000 years (the age of the El Greifa site), but it would show that there were prolific bead-making societies even earlier in the Lower Paleolithic Period. Choice A suggests that the new find would refute the author's conclusion about the likelihood of finding large caches of ostrich eggshell beads. This might be tempting, but the word *refute* is too strong. One such discovery would not be enough to completely refute the claim that Lower Paleolithic ostrich eggshell beads are unlikely to be found in large numbers. It is only one site, after all, and there might be explanations for the large find that are compatible with the author's claim. Perhaps there were so many beads there originally that 700 is actually only a tiny fraction of them, or perhaps the soil at the new site is more conducive to the survival of ostrich eggshell. Choice A is a possible answer, but a weak one. Choice B suggests that the new discovery would strengthen the author's claim that Lower Paleolithic peoples possessed complex cultures. Since it shows evidence of bead-making even earlier than the El Greifa site, it does seem to strengthen this claim. Choice B is a strong answer. Choice C suggests that the new site weakens the author's claim about the likelihood of finding large caches of Lower Paleolithic eggshell beads. It could be argued that it does *weaken* it, even if *refute* was too strong a word. However, choice C also suggests that the new discovery weakens the author's claim about Lower Paleolithic peoples' culture and cognitive ability. In fact, it strengthens that claim, so choice C can be eliminated. Choice D says that the new find would strengthen the author's claim that bead production is evidence of a complex culture and cognitive sophistication. But to strengthen that claim, the author would have to say more about what bead-making and bead-wearing imply about a society's technology and culture. Simply finding more beads would neither strengthen nor weaken that claim. Choice D can be eliminated. Choice B is the strongest answer.

39. **C is the best answer.** A discovery of goose eggshell beads at the Upper Paleolithic Sungir site would seem to suggest that the society responsible for the site had made beads from goose eggshell. Choice A compares the soil at the Sungir site to that of the El Greifa site, but this comparison is misleading because the El Greifa site is much older (200,000 years old, compared to the 28,000-year-old Sungir site). Choice A can be eliminated. Choice B implies that the eggshell beads were already ancient artifacts when they were placed in the graves at the Sungir site. This is possible, but seems a bit far-fetched. It not only requires us to believe that a Pleistocene society had the capacity to do archaeology, but also that the goose eggshell beads survived intact in large numbers from some much earlier time period—not just to the time of the burials, but to the time of the discovery of the graves in the present day. Given that ostrich eggshell does not survive that long and goose eggshell is probably not stronger than ostrich eggshell, choice B is a weak answer. Choice C suggests that eggshell was a popular medium in the Upper Paleolithic Period as well as the Lower Paleolithic (the time of the El Greifa site), implying that the bead-makers of Sungir made the goose eggshell beads found in the graves. This seems very plausible, so choice C is a strong answer. Choice D, which suggests that ivory and goose eggshell can survive in the ground for about the same amount of time, might look tempting in the scenario where both are found in the same grave. But it is quite possible that one material would have outlasted the other if the graves had remained undisturbed for a further 5,000, or 20,000, years. Neither the passage nor the question stem provides any basis on which to compare the taphonomic longevity of eggshell and ivory. So choice D can be eliminated. Choice C is the strongest answer.

40. **A is the best answer.** Taphonomic logic suggests that the archaeological record is flawed because not all materials survive intact for the same length of time: just because we have found a large number of one type of artifact and a small number of another does not mean that there were always more of the first type. Fragile objects and objects made from organic materials will not last as long, and so will be underrepresented in the archaeological record compared to objects made of more durable materials. Choice A suggests that archaeologists might never know what the earliest beads were made from. This would seem to be true. Possibly, they were made from leaves, tree bark, or some other substance that has left no trace hundreds of thousands of years later. Choice A is a strong answer. Choice B suggests that Pleistocene peoples were unlikely to use fragile materials like eggshell, implying that this is why those materials are underrepresented in archaeological contexts. But this is precisely what taphonomic logic denies. We cannot assume that fragile materials were used infrequently merely because they have survived in very small numbers. Choice B can be eliminated. Choice C says that once we pinpoint the taphonomic threshold for ostrich eggshell beads, we will be able to determine when bead-making began. This answer choice exploits the difficulty of the term *taphonomic threshold*, which sounds as if it might refer to the time when something (like ostrich eggshell bead-making) began. But the taphonomic threshold of an object type is the time beyond which it cannot be expected to survive intact. Determining the taphonomic threshold of ostrich eggshell beads would only tell us how far back in history (or pre-history) we could expect to find ostrich eggshell beads in significant numbers. It would not tell us when bead-making began. Choice C can be eliminated. Choice D suggests that Upper Paleolithic peoples favored ivory because eggshell was too fragile. In fact, we do not know that Upper Paleolithic peoples in general used ivory. We know that only about the Sungir bead-makers. It is likely that different peoples used different materials, depending on what was locally available. Choice D can be eliminated. Choice A is the strongest answer.

Passage 8 (Questions 41-47)

41. **B is the best answer.** The author argues that newly dead cadaver simulation provides opportunities for medical learners to gain crucial skills without causing harm to living patients. The main idea of the passage is that although newly dead cadaver simulation should be allowed for these educational purposes, the author only condones the practice if the patient gave consent that his body could be used this way or if the family grants consent in the event a patient did not expressly forbid it. The author states that although cadavers do not technically have autonomy, patients have autonomy to decide what happens to their bodies. Based on passage information, consent should be sought when a patient is alive and conscious; the author implies that an unconscious patient cannot ethically give any form of consent. Choice A can be eliminated. The author states that consent should be initiated upon a patient's admission to a care setting, so she would be unlikely to agree with the statement that consent can be sought at any time. She would argue that a patient should be asked about procedures, including newly dead cadaver simulation, as soon as the patient is admitted. Choice B is a strong answer. According to the passage, family members can be consulted about the permissibility of using a patient's body for cadaver simulation as long as the patient never expressly forbade this use. The author asks the question of whether a patient's wishes about his body should be respected post-mortem—and states later that they should. In the event a patient did not provide his opinion on how his body should be treated, his family must grant permission for its use in simulation. Choice C can be eliminated. The author writes that consent for both newly dead cadaver use and medical procedures for living patients should explicitly be described and sought for each simulation/intervention, so choice D can be eliminated. Choice B is the best answer.

42. **D is the best answer.** The author's main idea is that newly dead cadaver simulation offers a chance for medical learners to become competent at a variety of techniques and better familiarize themselves with human anatomy and physiology. Although the passage presents arguments representing both ends of a spectrum (newly dead cadaver simulation should not be allowed because skills can be taught in other ways, i.e. computer simulation, versus cadaver simulations are necessary for medical education), the author has a more nuanced view. She argues that cadaver simulation is necessary but that consent must have been granted by the patient before death. If consent was not sought, the patient's family may also serve as a substitute. The author believes, though, that consent should be obtained if at all possible. The best answer will refute the main idea that newly dead cadaver simulation is appropriate as long as consent has been obtained. Even if cadaver simulation is ineffective at teaching students invasive medical skills, the author states that the practice has also been used for non-invasive techniques and for educating learners about anatomy and physiology. In choice A, only one purpose of cadaver simulation has been demonstrated to be ineffective, but the answer does not state that these simulations are completely useless in medical education. Additionally, choice A does not align with the main idea that a patient must grant permission for her body to be used in order for cadaver simulations to be considered ethical. Choice A is a weak but possible answer. The author in fact agrees with choice B, as she writes that an individual's physical remains do not possess autonomy, implying that they lack the ability to take responsibility in decision-making. Choice B does not weaken the author's conclusions; it fails to refute the passage argument that even though a cadaver does not have autonomy, the patient's wishes must be met after death. Choice B is a weak answer. Although this passage addresses the ethical nature of newly dead cadaver simulation, the author does not reference whether religion must consider the practice ethical for it to indeed be so. Choice C can be eliminated. The author's main idea is that a patient ultimately has control over what happens to her body after she dies, and this dictates whether her body can participate in simulations. If, as in choice D, no one has control over a body after death, the author's major argument would not hold. Choice D is a stronger answer than choice A because it directly addresses the main idea and weakens it by stating that patient autonomy does not extend to physical remains. Choice D is a strong answer, and it is the best answer.

43. **A is the best answer.** The main idea of this passage is that newly dead cadaver simulation provides opportunities for learners to develop a number of skills and gain familiarity with human anatomy without causing harm to real patients. The author argues that while alive, patients have the autonomy to make decisions about how their bodies will be treated, and similarly, after death, their wishes must be honored. Although there are legitimate concerns associated with newly dead cadaver simulation, the author believes that this practice is ultimately beneficial to learners, as well as to society and the people who will receive care from those learners—so long as patients had not explicitly stated their bodies couldn't be used in this way. The author says that newly dead cadaver simulation is often justified as a way to develop health care professionals' ability to perform lifesaving skills and that that practice cannot safely be conducted with living patients, so option I is true. Choice B can be eliminated. The passage does not reference newly dead cadaver simulation as a way to inure students to death. In fact the author writes that critics of this practice believe that cadaver simulation may be counterproductive and lead learners to view patients as "objects," rather than as humans. This statement suggests that desensitizing learners would not be considered a productive advantage of newly dead cadaver simulation . Option II is false, and choice C can be eliminated. Although the author believes that newly dead cadavers provide students with the opportunity to learn accurate anatomical and physiological responses, she does not compare this kind of simulation with dissection of long-preserved cadavers. Option III is not addressed by the passage, so choice D can be eliminated. Choice A is the best answer.

44. **C is the best answer.** The author's main idea is that cadaver simulation can improve the health of living patients because medical learners use simulations to become more familiar with human anatomy and practice life-saving skills without putting patients at risk . However, she argues, patients or their families (in the event a patient did not explicitly forbid newly dead cadaver simulation) must grant permission that their bodies can be used in this way. Physicians, or any other group, cannot dictate what happens to a cadaver because patients have the freedom to decide how their bodies should be treated after death ("autonomy"). This view that no one other than the patient has that right defines antipaternalism. According to the passage, paternalism is the view that a person's stated preferences or choices can be made a lower priority in favor of other standards that person is said to value. For instance, a person may prefer a certain treatment but this preference can be ignored if it upholds another value, like one's own safety or the safety of other living patients. As such, the best answer will describe a situation where an entity takes away someone's autonomy so that she or others may benefit (or be perceived to benefit in the eyes of the entity). Choice A depicts a scenario where individuals lose the ability to decide whether they want to purchase health insurance because the government has dictated that they must. However, in the passage the author emphasizes safety as the value that usurps a person's own choices, while choice A presents financial solvency as that standard. Choice A is a possible but weak answer. Choice B does not reflect the concept of paternalism as presented in the passage; it attempts to trick the test-taker by misinterpreting the word paternalism to mean something to do with an actual father. Choice B can be eliminated. In choice C, a law-making entity has decided that individuals must wear seatbelts while they are driving, regardless of whether people want to or not. As described in the passage, this decision intends to improve the general public's safety. Choice C is a stronger answer than choice A because of its emphasis on safety. Choice D describes a situation that better reflects antipaternalism, because the patient and her physicians are working together to come to a decision about her medical care. Choice D is a weak answer, and choice C is the best answer.

45. **D is the best answer.** Based on the passage spectrum, newly dead cadaver simulation can either be considered an opportunity for medical learners to gain proficiency in difficult medical techniques and thereby become better, safer providers of care or a potentially unethical practice for which there are equally educational alternatives, such as computer simulations. While the author leans more towards the former end of the spectrum, she believes that cadaver simulation is only ethical if patients or their families granted permission for the body to be used in this way. The author acknowledges critics of simulation but implies that the practice is in fact beneficial, as long as it is never concealed and patients' autonomy over how their bodies will be treated after death is maintained. Based on passage information, critics of newly dead cadaver simulation believe that the practice is unnecessary because of a number of reasons, including that computer-based simulations achieve the same educational purposes, especially as the body loses its capacity to realistically teach anatomy and physiology as it ages, and that using cadavers may cause learners to dehumanize bodies and view patients more as objects of analysis than as people. The critics do not comment on cadavers' or patients' autonomy. Additionally, the author believes that cadavers inherently lack autonomy because they cannot make decisions, and she does not state that simulations violate the autonomy of living patients. Choice A is a weak answer. Critics believe that newly dead cadaver simulations may desensitize medical learners and present computer-based simulations as another, better option; they do not think that computer-based simulations have this same negative effect. Choice B can be eliminated. While critics reference the aging of the cadavers as one reason newly dead cadaver simulations are not as effective as they may seem in educating students, they do not comment on how students aging affect their conceptions of the simulations. Choice C can be eliminated. As presented in the passage, critics argue that there is no difference in knowledge gained from computer-based and cadaver-based simulations. Similarly then, critics of a military training program could argue that soldiers can rely on war video games to acquire the same familiarity with fighting strategies as they would from boot camp, the equivalent to a cadaver-based simulation. Choice D is a strong answer, and it is the best answer.

46. **A is the best answer.** According to the passage, one of the major questions involving the ethics of newly dead cadaver simulation is whether cadavers have autonomy. The author presents two views—that because cadavers are incapable of making decisions they cannot be autonomous and that because cadavers are the physical remains of a person that patient's autonomy must be extended to his body even after death. She argues later in the passage that her belief combines these two views: while a cadaver may not be autonomous (in the sense of being able to make decisions), a patient's wishes about how his body should be treated after death must still hold. Because the author states that cadavers lack autonomy as defined in the passage, choice A is a strong answer. The author believes that all patients have autonomy; this is not a right to which patients must consent. Her main idea around consent is that newly dead cadaver simulation serves an important purpose in health care, despite some criticisms of the practice, but that consent from the patient or surviving family must be obtained for the simulation to be ethical. Choice B is a weak answer. Choice C describes paternalism as the author presents the concept. According to the passage, paternalism is the view that an individual's stated preferences or choices can be usurped in favor of promoting other standards that person is said to value. Consequently, an entity other than the individual, such as a group of physicians, can make decisions on behalf of the person that he would not have. The author does not agree with a paternalistic view of cadaver simulation, and choice C does not align with passage information about cadavers' right to autonomy, so it can be eliminated. She also writes that while all living patients have autonomy, cadavers are inherently unable to because they cannot make decisions. Choice D can be eliminated, and choice A is the best answer.

47. **C is the best answer.** The main idea of this passage is that in order for any procedure to be ethical, patient consent must be obtained for it, whether it is newly dead cadaver simulation or medical care. The passage is directed towards individuals who are making decisions about what to do with cadavers; the author writes directives to providers to seek consent from patients. According to the author, a patient or his surviving family must have granted permission for any action. The author does not focus on antipaternalism other than to reinforce her idea that patients' decisions while they were alive should be fulfilled after they have died. She does not reference medical educational outcomes, so choice A can be eliminated. While choice B mentions a provider, this answer has more to do with an individual's decisions about what to do with the body after death. Although the passage centers on newly dead cadaver simulation as the major issue inciting the question of patient and cadaver autonomy, its ideas are more applicable to providers deciding what to do with patients' bodies, rather than their own. The passage does not discuss arguments around whether one should consent to newly dead cadaver simulation, for example, so choice B is a weak answer. Choice C describes a situation where a provider of care (the mortician) must determine how a cadaver should be treated. Based on passage information, consent must have been granted for any decision the patient can no longer make about his body, which the mortician must have previously sought from the patient or must now seek from the family. Choice C aligns with the main idea and is a strong answer. Although the passage references consent for all procedures, including medical interventions, the main idea is not whether or how a patient should consent but rather that for providers, acquiring this consent is crucial. Choice D is a weak answer, and choice C is the best answer.

Passage 9 (Questions 48-53)

48. **C is the best answer.** The author's main idea in this section of the article is that during the early 20th century, African American dancers were forced to confront stereotypes about African Americans during their dance careers. This adds to the author's overall main point that perceptions of dance are shaped by cultural factors. When the African American dancers were encouraged to dance, they were encouraged to do so within narrow culturally accepted dance genres. Choice A refers to one group of people who supported African American dance for the specific purpose of supporting 'leftist culture" through a "cross-class and cross-racial alliance". However, the author does not assert that they solely relied on support from liberals so this choice is an extrapolation that cannot be assumed to be true. Choice A can be eliminated. Choice B summarizes one example of a limitation or prejudiced type of encouragement African American dancers faced. However, the author asserts that these dancers faced challenges so it should not be assumed that these dancers were welcomed. Choice B is not a strong answer. Choice C is appealing because this answer choice characterizes the author's assertion that African American dancers were expected to practice "folk dances," limiting the dance genres they were encouraged to pursue. Choice C is a strong answer. Choice D is very strongly worded and uses absolute language like "inescapable." This automatically makes the choice less appealing. In addition, the author does not mention the effect that prejudices have on the likelihood that an African American pursues dance as a career so this choice goes beyond the scope of the passage. Choice D can be eliminated.

49. **B is the best answer.** The author asserts that the categories human beings use are informative about how they engage with the world and for instance, the classification of dance into art, social, folk, and so on says more about some Western views on class and race than about human movement. Look for an answer choice in which a discipline is divided into sub-disciplines. Choice A is more similar to the author's distinction between dance and sport. Instead of dividing a discipline into multiple categories, this answer choice identifies a difference between two categories. Choice A is not a strong answer. Choice B is an appealing answer because like the author it divides dance into different genres within dance, the field of medicine is divided into different specialties that are each still considered to be medicine. The author does not rank dance disciplines so choice C does not match the author's distinction between different types of dance. Choice C is not a strong answer. Rather than splitting one field into multiple divisions, choice D identifies the factor that unifies different specialties. Choice D makes the opposite point to that made by the author. Choice D can be eliminated.

50. **B is the best answer.** The author asserts that ballet has widespread influence and is now considered to be "universal" even though it was derived from multicultural interactions. The author identifies the standardized teaching of ballet as one reason for its success since it remains consistent as a field even as it spreads. Choice A references ballet's influence on theatrical dance performances around the world but the author cites this as evidence for ballet's influence, not as a reason ballet achieved its influence. Choice A is not a strong answer. Choice B aligns with the author's assertion that its standardized structure facilitated ballet's commoditization. The author writes that ballet is currently universal, not that it was universal from its conception. Ballet was borne of cultural interactions but since it is global now, appears to be neutral. Choice C misinterprets this point to assert that ballet's multicultural origin made it appear universal. Choice C can be eliminated. The author mentions that forbidden folk dances within France may have contributed to ballet's popularity, however, the author does not assert whether this was because ballet could not be affected by folk dances or because there was a greater national focus on ballet or another reason. Choice D is not a point made by the author and so, this choice goes beyond the scope of the passage. Choice D can be eliminated.

51. **D is the best answer.** The author's main idea is that the term dance is problematic because it carries a connotation of what western culture understands to be dance. So by introducing this new term, Kaeppler and William aimed to eliminate that connotation. Look for an answer choice that acknowledges that dance is not solely a western construct and is not necessarily used for the express purpose of entertainment or ritual. Choice A associates dance with Western culture, which is precisely the association that Kaeppler and William tried to eliminate with this term. Choice A can be eliminated. Choice B classifies "body actions" as entertainment but dance can be utilized for purposes outside of entertainment. For instance, ritual or self-expression. Choice B can be eliminated. Choice C inaccurately assumes dances are ritualized and are necessarily multicultural. In addition, it uses the word "dance," which is precisely the term anthropologists were trying to avoid. Choice C is not a strong answer choice. Choice D evades the assumption that dance is a Western construction and keeps the term open to other cultures, making choice D the strongest answer choice.

52. **A is the best answer.** With this question, the goal is to look for an answer choice that describes a categorization that people make and hint at what meaning that categorization reveals. Choice A is an appealing answer since it categorizes dance as a type of physical education but within this category, it is associated with femininity. Choice B is a weaker answer because it characterizes a belief, that ballet is not culturally rooted, but does not associate this with a particular categorization. Choice C similarly illustrates the belief that black dancers are a part of a leftist "cross-racial alliance" but does not clearly categorize black dancers. Choice C can be eliminated. Choice D characterizes ballet training in terms of its standardized nature but does not give any indication as to what this categorization means to the people who created it. Choice D is not a strong answer.

53. **C is the best answer.** David Best distinguished between "purposive" and "aesthetic" sports by focusing on the scoring system. In purposive sports, aesthetics are a by-product of good sports performance whereas in aesthetic sports, artistry contributes to scoring. Look for an answer choice in which this main point, the scoring of sports, is altered so that aesthetics contributes to purposive sport scoring or no longer contributes to aesthetic sport scoring. Choice A is appealing because it references the author's point that purposive sports have an aesthetic quality to them. However, this misses the main point that aesthetic sports are scored on artistry. Choice A can be eliminated. Choice B is appealing because it emphasizes the arbitrariness of the distinction between aesthetic and purposive sports but, the author doesn't mention the connection between aesthetics and performance in purposive sports so this goes beyond the scope of the passage. Choice B is not a strong answer. Choice C is an appealing answer because it addresses the main point of the author's distinction, the scoring system. Choice D, like choice B, addresses how style or artistry affects athleticism but the distinction between aesthetic and purposive sports is based on scoring, not on athleticism. Choice D can be eliminated.

TEST ④

ANSWERS & EXPLANATIONS
Questions 1–53

ANSWER KEY					
1. C	10. D	19. A	28. D	37. B	46. C
2. B	11. D	20. B	29. D	38. D	47. C
3. C	12. B	21. B	30. A	39. C	48. A
4. C	13. A	22. A	31. A	40. A	49. C
5. D	14. B	23. C	32. C	41. B	50. D
6. A	15. C	24. B	33. A	42. A	51. B
7. D	16. D	25. A	34. A	43. D	52. A
8. D	17. A	26. B	35. C	44. C	53. B
9. C	18. C	27. A	36. C	45. D	

EXPLANATIONS FOR TEST 4

Passage 1 (Questions 1-7)

1. **C is the best answer.** The passage assails scholars' characterization of Native reservation schools in the fourth paragraph. The author argues that scholars have been somewhat too eager to call Natives victims, and that tendency has deprived the Native community the credit it is owed for its political maneuvering. While the author certainly believes that scholars have evaluated these photographs with an ideological bent, the primary focus of the scholars is not the memories that these photographs evoke. They appear to study the Native peoples' clash against a dominant culture. Choice A mischaracterizes the academic literature and is a weak answer. While the author suggests that some memories that Native students took from boarding schools were probably positive, she still recognizes that these schools were fundamentally oppressive. She does not appear to advocate that any more deference be given the federal government for that reason. Choice B can be eliminated. The criticism the author levels in the fourth paragraph is that the scholarly literature has told the Native reservation school experience from a singular, oversimplified viewpoint. Because she advocates for a closer examination of the Native students' struggles against the prevailing culture, choice C appears to be a strong answer. Although scholars have characterized students who supported reservation school activities as victims of brainwash, they do not appear to criticize those Native Americans who retain photographs from their days at reservation schools. Choice D misconstrues the scholars' argument, so that is not as strong an answer as choice C.

2. **B is the best answer.** In relating the anecdote of Parker McKenzie and The Pie Club, the author notes that his sister Nellie was one of many Native students that died of tuberculosis at reservation schools and that the disease was dangerously common. The author also argues that the purpose of these schools was to extinguish Native culture, and this idea is reinforced through descriptions of colonial imagery and the gendered nature of the schools' domestic science curriculum. Choice A can be eliminated since it is supported by substantial evidence within the passage. The author makes the claim in choice B in the third paragraph of the passage, but no elaboration on this claim is provided. Choice B appears to be a strong answer. Choice C summarizes a central idea of the passage. All of the anecdotes and evidence are marshalled in support of this overarching point, so this claim is supported by much of the text of the passage. Choice C can be eliminated. The first paragraph argues that the subjects of these pictures wore clothing mandated by non-Native administrators who intended to oppress Native culture. The passage later describes the structure of the domestic science curriculum as further evidence of the schools' suppression of Native culture. The Pie Club photograph contains imagery evincing both forms of oppression, so the claim in choice D is amply supported by text in the passage. Choice D is a weaker answer than choice B.

3. **C is the best answer.** This hypothetical differs from the anecdote about Parker McKenzie in that the doctor is both part of the community that harmed these sharecroppers and not a member of the oppressed group. Analyzing McKenzie's decision to retain photographs through the lens of visual sovereignty, the author argues that this is a strategy oppressed people can employ to reclaim stereotyped images of members of their community. The doctor presumably does not share the heritage of the sharecroppers, so the author's definition of visual sovereignty from the passage does not extend to the doctor. Choices A and B can be eliminated. Because the doctor does not come from the demographic of the sharecroppers, choice C appears to be a strong answer. Although the medical profession is responsible for conducting the syphilis experiments, the author's argument about visual sovereignty does not emphasize the profession of the oppressors and oppressed so much as the family history. Choice C is a stronger answer than choice D.

4. **C is the best answer.** Although the passage suggests several reasons why an individual may keep photographs from schools the author believes to be oppressive – these photographs are sentimental keepsakes, the students have been brainwashed to look on those memories fondly, etc. – the author argues that the exercise of visual sovereignty allows people from oppressed communities to combat oppression. The passage defines visual sovereignty as an act of recontextualizing images that have been used to stereotype communities. Choice A is a tempting answer because the passage argues that ascribing identities to people in the photographs humanizes individuals who have been stereotyped, allowing for the exercise of visual sovereignty. Hold that answer choice for now. It may be the case that these photographs have little personal value for non-Native people, but the passage argues that visual sovereignty is exercised by oppressed people. In other words, Parker McKenzie can give these images a meaning separate from the meaning ascribed by other people. Choice B is a weak answer. If Native parents freely chose to send their children to these schools, this information would undermine the passage question stem's premise that these schools were oppressive. Choice C is a stronger answer than choice A because it more directly contradicts the passage's central argument. Even if the identities of the photographed subjects are forgotten, the author still argues that keeping the photographs in a personal collection is an act of visual sovereignty. By contrast, if the boarding schools were not oppressive, there would be no associated oppression to combat. Eliminate choice A. If graduates of these schools enjoyed a better quality of life than those who did not attend, it may be that this standard of living came at the expense of repressing their personal culture. It is possible that these schools were oppressive but somehow raised graduates' quality of life, so choice D does not weaken the argument as forcefully as the finding in choice C.

5. **D is the best answer.** This phrase could have several different meanings. Use other textual clues to narrow down the answer choices. The author says that "colonial imagery" has dominated historical archives. In the first paragraph, these images are called "propagandistic." This language calls to mind a larger power subverting a smaller group for political ends. Keep that thought in mind while evaluating the answer choices. The author states that some scholars have portrayed some Natives as victims of brainwash. The "non-Native representations" alluded to in the question stem were not carried out by these scholars, so it is unlikely that the author would attach this meaning to the quoted phrase. Choice A can be eliminated. Because these representations aimed to promote a political agenda on the part of the dominant culture, it is unlikely that this dominant group made any attempt to convey the nuances of Native culture. If anything, the goal of this group was to exhibit the subordination of Natives. Choice B is a weak answer. The author suspects that some Natives like Parker McKenzie retained these photographs for partially sentimental reasons, so choice C is tempting. Recognize, however, that prompting feelings of nostalgia was not an intention of the "non-Natives." Choice C can be eliminated. Because the author uses the language of "colonial imagery" to signal the subordination of the Native people to Anglo culture, choice D seems a fitting interpretation of the quoted phrase in the question stem. Choice D is the best answer.

6. **A is the best answer.** In introducing the topic of gender roles, the author acknowledges that this gendered elements of the curriculum were a mechanism of subordinating Native peoples to Anglo culture. The passage suddenly does an about-face and states that, even if this component of the curriculum was oppressive, some students appear to have enjoyed activities that conform to gender roles. The paragraph concludes by criticizing scholars for labeling these students as one-dimensional victims. It appears that the discussion of gender roles serves as a transition to this conclusion, so choice A is a strong answer. While the author recognizes that these gender roles varied between white people and Natives, this observation does not advance the primary argument that Native peoples were more resourceful than scholars have previously described. Choice B is a weak answer. While the author believes that reservation schools were oppressive, there is no discussion of psychological abuse. In fact, the passage provides examples of women in a baking club they appeared to have joined voluntarily and for the purpose of leisure, so it is unlikely that whatever psychological abuse these students faced was unceasing. Choice C can be eliminated. The author acknowledges that enforcing Anglo gender roles at the reservation schools was a mechanism of oppression, so choice D is contrary to the author's argument. Choice D is a weaker than choice A.

7. **D is the best answer.** To answer this question, which asks about an opinion likely held by the author, consider who the author is and her perspective on the Native community. The author argues that, on the one hand, the Natives have been depicted in a highly stereotyped manner by mainstream culture, but, on the other, fellow scholars have been too hasty in classifying Natives as victims. Keep the author's perspective in mind while evaluating the choices. While the author argues in the fourth paragraph that scholars have cried brainwash too frequently, she does not go so far as to argue that students were never brainwashed. The word "never" in choice A hints that this answer is somewhat extreme, and because the choice extends beyond the scope of the passage's reasoning, it is a weak answer. While the author may think that not every aspect of every student's experience at these schools was bad, her description of these schools and their purpose in the first paragraph suggests she thinks they were fundamentally oppressive. It seems unlikely that the author would think that oppressive schools bettered the lives of some students, and if she did, no evidence in the passage suggested otherwise. Choice B is a weak answer. The author certainly characterizes typical historical accounts of the reservation boarding schools as unfairly one-dimensional and perhaps patronizing, but she does not go so far as to say that oversimplifying the Native experience is oppressive. Choice C reflects a harsher stance than the author assumes, so it can be eliminated. The author appears to have written this passage to provide depth to a story she feels has been oversimplified. The third paragraph concludes that simplifying the Native experience threatens to limit discussion about political strategies they employed to survive. This claim implies that Native Americans were more resourceful than previous accounts have described, so choice D is a strong answer.

Passage 2 (Questions 8-14)

8. **D is the best answer.** The author's main idea is that while historically, first in human trials have not been conducted in low and middle income countries for various reasons, including a lack of scientific and clinical rigor and appropriate safety standards, this tradition should be reconsidered as long as certain requirements are met. The author emphasizes the importance of participant safety when conducting trials, so option I is true. Choice B can be eliminated. She states that multinational pharmaceutical companies have in the past attempted to conduct trials in LMICs but that they have failed to ensure the safety of trial participants. The author does not believe that such companies should be responsible for trial development in lower income countries. Option II is false, so choice C can be eliminated. The author stresses that trials require clinical and scientific rigor, or research that is meticulously and accurately carried out. Option III is true, so choice A can be eliminated, and choice D is the best answer .

9. **C is the best answer.** The author's main idea is that FIH trials should be conducted in LMICs as long as certain conditions are met, including the safety of trial participants and more rigorous clinical and scientific research. She argues that the way to achieve these conditions is to establish or improve local regulatory agencies who have oversight of trial activities. If a trial is causing more deaths than expected, as this question states, the author would assume that not all of the necessary conditions are being fulfilled. She believes that ensuring trial safety leads to reduced risk for participants, so choice A is a weak answer. The author implies that increased health literacy in any population will improve trial safety, so she would recommend that trial participants be better educated about the drug they are taking. Choice B can be eliminated. Throughout the passage, the author states strongly that one of the goals of developing FIH trials in LMICs is to reduce the "culture of dependency" that lower income nations have on more developed countries. Rather than suggest that the LMIC in this case seek help from other countries, she would instead recommend that the country bolster its own regulatory agencies. The author states that LMICs have in the past depended on other nations for assistance, for example to ensure that safety standards are met, but she does not believe this is a viable strategy. Choice C is a strong answer. The author believes that clinical and scientific rigor are needed to appropriately carry out trials, so choice D can be eliminated, and choice C is the best answer.

10. **D is the best answer.** According to passage information, the author believes that different population characteristics impact the response to an intervention (i.e. that epidemiology, health services, comorbities, and other factors impact the response to a drug or vaccine). This idea underlies the author's main argument that clinical trials should be conducted in LMICs, especially for drugs that target diseases most prevalent in these lower income countries. The author emphasizes the effect that different population traits can have on a health outcome. Choice A implies that regardless of distinctions between populations of people with diabetes and hypertension (who may differ significantly based on, for example, their socioeconomic status or other concurrent illnesses), lifestyle discussions are beneficial. While this answer choice supports the passage argument about health literacy, it does not specifically address the author's discussion of population-based characteristics, so it fails to answer the question directly. Choice A can be eliminated. Choice B somewhat supports the main idea; however, this answer choice does not explicitly describe what differs between the two groups that may have contributed to one population (the men who lost weight) having a different outcome than the other (the men who did not lose weight) from the same intervention (yoga class). Choice B is a weak answer. Because the author says that genetic makeup can impact the response to a drug or vaccine, choice C does not reflect the main idea. According to passage information, people with a genetic mutation would likely respond differently to the vaccine than people with the wild type gene. Choice C can be eliminated. Choice D reflects the idea that the benefit of an intervention like a job search program depends on the characteristics of the group to which it is applied, in this case college graduates versus high school dropouts. Choice D is stronger than choice B and is the best answer.

11. **D is the best answer.** The author argues that FIH trials should be conducted in LMICs (as long as regulatory standards are met) because they present an opportunity to appropriately test drugs and vaccines for diseases that primarily affect individuals living in these countries. She also believes that encouraging FIH trials in LMICs will drive improvements in all nations conducting trials but especially allow LMICs to become more self-sufficient in running their own trials. The author does not state that trials in LMICs will increase regulatory agencies' knowledge about conditions more prevalent in LMICs; in fact, she believes one benefit of these trials is that LMICs will become less dependent on assistance from regulatory authorities from developed nations. Choice A implies that more intervention from developed nations is a benefit, which counters the main idea. Choice A can be eliminated. While the author argues that FIH trials in LMICs would establish the conditions needed for these countries to become more self-sufficient, she does not, based on passage information, believe that LMICs would be entirely independent. In general, avoid extreme answer choices that imply that something is "always" or "never" the case; these are usually *simpleton* distractors. While choice B is possible, it is a weak answer. The author does not mention whether FIH trials in LMICs would help speed up the clinical trial process for certain products, so choice C can be eliminated. In the last paragraph of the passage, the author emphasizes that benefits of conducting FIH trials in LMICs include more attention to problems in these countries' health systems and ability to regulate trials, which could lead to improved standards for future clinical trials. Choice D is stronger than choice B and is the best answer.

12. **B is the best answer.** One of the underlying themes of the passage is that clinical trials should be conducted in areas that are most affected by the targeted disease because of different factors that can influence how a drug is accessed, administered, metabolized, etc. The author argues that testing a drug only in an area where the disease is not as prevalent (e.g. a developed country) could lead to the production of a drug that may not help most of the individuals who will receive the medication (e.g. those who live in a LMIC). The passage implies that investigational drugs are meant for diseases that are somewhat common in high income countries and even more so in LMICs. Medications that treat rare orphan diseases would not fall into this category, so although choice A somewhat weakens the author's argument, it is a weak answer. Choice B states that regardless of where a drug is tested (in this case, the United States, a developed country), its therapeutic impact on individuals is the same. The author's main argument is that testing a product in a region like the US would potentially ignore factors that could decrease the drug's efficacy once it is used in an LMIC, like India. If there is no difference in health outcome among different populations for a drug tested in only one of those populations, then the author does not need to be concerned about where a trial is conducted. Choice B is a stronger answer than choice A. The author believes that trials are most appropriate when they are conducted in the country where the tested medication will be used, so choice C supports, rather than weakens, her argument. Choice C can be eliminated. The author agrees that FIH trials in LMICs lack regulatory standards that match international requirements, and this is one downfall that must be corrected for trials to be developed in lower income countries. Choice D provides support for the author's argument that these limitations of LMICs must be addressed, and it also does not answer the question stem as directly as choice B does. Choice B is the best answer.

13. **A is the best answer.** Based on the passage, FIH trials have historically been avoided in LMICs because of perceived and actual risks. In addition to concerns over participant safety and the lack of regulatory infrastructure to appropriately monitor trials, the author argues that a major risk that Western companies confront is accurately distinguishing between adverse events caused by the trial drug and by individuals' prior, potentially undiagnosed and untreated, conditions. According to the author, these companies have a hard time isolating risk associated specifically with the trial product; there are other variables that cannot consistently be accounted for. Choice A is a strong answer. The author mentions cultural differences with respect to autopsies but does not address language barriers, so choice B can be eliminated. She states that Western companies often fear they will be perceived as exploiting individuals in LMICs, but she does not say that the companies themselves worry about being exploitative. Choice C can be eliminated. The author is not concerned with the financial risks of conducting a trial and in fact later in the passage argues that more FIH trials in LMICs could stimulate economic activity. Choice D is a beyond distractor and can be eliminated. Choice A is the best answer.

14. **B is the best answer.** The main idea of this passage is that FIH trials should be conducted in lower and middle income countries as long as safety and scientific and clinical rigor can be guaranteed. One reason for this proposed change in tradition, the author argues, is that if LMICs begin developing trials, they will shed light on deficiencies in health systems in other countries, as well as their own, and potentially help improve safety standards everywhere. The author focuses on the role that LMICs can serve as an impetus for change for developed countries. Choice A is a weak answer because it describes a situation where the higher income nation has independently decided to enact improved trial regulations. If the neighboring LMICs serve as an example of safe clinical research, the author argues that other nations will follow suit and similarly reexamine their trial standards to better ensure participant equity and address health system deficiencies. Choice B is a strong answer. The author does not address whether developed nations interact with each other when it comes to evaluating clinical trials, so choice C can be eliminated. Similarly, the author makes no mention of competition between LMICs that are newly establishing clinical trials and other countries. She also makes clear throughout the passage that trial participants are residents of the country where the trial takes place. Indeed, if competition were to exist, it would be anticipated that nations would relax their standards to ensure sufficient participant enrollment. Choice D can be eliminated. Choice B is the best answer.

Passage 3 (Questions 15-21)

15. **C is the best answer.** This question stem proposes an analogous controversy to the one described in the passage. The author expresses suspicion about Eliadian viewpoints on why Ground Zero is a sacred space and prefers to view the issue through an instrumental lens. This perspective argues that people create sacred spaces with social or political motives beyond the spiritual. For that reason, the author would not see the legislature's decision as an attempt to win favors of a deity. Choice A can be eliminated. The author's instrumentalist perspective is skeptical that religious invocation in spaces is meant to make it sacred, so choice B is a weak choice. In the passage, the author implies that invoking a Christian god in this controversy was a move to exclude others, so choice C seems like a strong answer. Choice D proposes that the legislature's motive to suppress dialogue about the validity of other religions. This choice seems a bit extreme. The opponents of the Islamic center in the passage were not explicitly making claims about the validity of Islam, nor does the author see suppression of dialogue their foremost intention. Choice D may sound compelling but is not the strongest analogy to the reasoning presented in the passage. Choice C is the best answer.

16. **D is the best answer.** This question stem presents a situation in which a divine force is invoked in a previously secular space. The passage uses the instrumental viewpoint to interpret the motives of such initiatives as inherently social or political. Choice A is tempting because if all students and teachers were invited, there would be no overt exclusion taking place. In its description of the instrumental perspective, though, the passage argues that individuals designate sacred spaces to separate them from profane spaces. Choice A seems like a weak answer, but keep it while the others are considered. Even if speakers from all religions were brought to school, the question asks about how the prayer circle should be viewed, so choice B does not fully answer the question and can be eliminated. Just because the group does not invoke a divine force by name does not mean that the ritual does not pertain to one particular religion, so the instrumentalist would still view the prayer circle as a move to claim the space and exclude others. Choice C can be eliminated. Compare choice D, which argues that the group is exclusionary regardless of the principal's stated intentions, to choice A. The passage does not give much weight to the viewpoints of those opposing construction of the community center. Certainly no reason to doubt the exclusionary goals of the opponents is presented, so choice D is a stronger answer than choice A because its reasoning most closely parallels the author's.

17. **A is the best answer.** The question stem highlights two arguments from the passage: first, the I-beam was seen as a Christian symbol and, second, this discovery helped Christians lay claim to Ground Zero. Because the assignment of sacred value to this space by Christians helped them lay claim to it, these arguments strongly support the conclusion in choice A. Choice B, that the dominant group will succeed in laying claim to a space valued by many groups, is certainly a conclusion that could be reached on the basis of the passage. However, it is not as strongly supported by the arguments in the question stem as those in choice A because those arguments do not directly address power dynamics between rival groups. Choice B can be eliminated. Choice C also advances a conclusion that could be reached on the basis of the passage, but the arguments in the question stem support that conclusion more weakly than choice A. They do not address the effect of mass tragedy on the nature of a space . Choice C can be eliminated. Choice D addresses the influence a politician can have in making a space sacred and winning favor for his or her views. This answer choice is unrelated to the information in the question stem and is not a conclusion that can be reached on the basis of the passage. Choice A is the best answer.

18. **C is the best answer.** To get the full context of the quoted phrase, refer to the fifth paragraph. The paragraph spends several sentences detailing the death and suffering that occurred at Ground Zero, which makes it different from other burial grounds. While it is true that Ground Zero was the center of a political controversy, that is not the aspect of Ground Zero that the quoted phrase is trying to underscore. Choice A can be eliminated. It is also true that an object interpreted as a divine symbol was found at Ground Zero, but the phrase is not meant emphasize that. In fact, the I-beam cross does not enter the passage narrative until the next paragraph. Choice B can be eliminated. The fifth paragraph describes the aura of awe surrounding Ground Zero because of the incredible suffering that occurred there and the fact that so many people's loved ones lost their lives there. Choice C is consistent with that description, so it is a strong answer. Although the passage does allude to the fact that the media did elevate this controversy to the national stage, that is neither a major point of the passage nor a point that the quote phrase seeks to highlight. Choice D can be eliminated. Choice C is the best answer.

19. **A is the best answer.** The argument of the passage does not present the Eliadian viewpoint as applied to the controversy surrounding the Islamic community center favorably. That being said, the author does recognize the perspective's namesake as a pioneer in her field of Religious Studies. His theories are described as groundbreaking. For that reason, it can be inferred that the author's opinion of the Eliadian perspective is not wholly negative, though it has exacerbated public opinion in a way that the author does not like. Given the mixed feelings that the author appears to have, choice A seems to fit her evaluation of Eliadian viewpoints. Choice A is a strong choice. While the author certainly sees the Eliadian perspective as exclusionary of Islamic groups in the case of the community center, choice B goes farther in arguing that it is responsible for depriving minority groups of civil liberties. The author may well believe that the community center's supporters have been denied civil liberties, but the passage does not go that far. Choice B is a beyond distractor and can be eliminated. Philosophies can be misinterpreted by the masses, and that may have happened in the case of the Eliadian viewpoint. The passage does not address that possibility, so choice C can be eliminated. While the author does not think the Eliadian viewpoint is as helpful a perspective for evaluating a sacred space as the instrumental view in this case, the passage neither calls it naïve nor defines political realities that it overlooks. Choice D is also a beyond distractor and can be eliminated. Choice A is the best answer.

20. **B is the best answer.** It would be helpful to go back to the passage, identify the main idea of each paragraph, and evaluate its relationship with the answer choices provided. Choice A summarizes one of the principal themes of the passage, which is an idea underlying each paragraph. Because the transformation of this site from a secular to a sacred site is the premise of this passage, choice A is supported with ample elaboration and can be eliminated. The passage argues that the I-beam cross helped affiliate Ground Zero with Christian mores, but while it may have exacerbated an anti-Islamic sentiment, that connection is not explicitly drawn in the passage. Choice B seems like a strong choice. Because choice C borrows language from the instrumental viewpoint and the author describes the national discourse around the center as Eliadian, it may seem like choice C's claim is not supported. Remember that the *author* interprets the controversy through the *instrumental* perspective and builds her argument as such. The main idea of the passage is that Ground Zero became a sacred space and that the Islamic center was seen as tainting it. Because that is the central argument of the passage, it is accorded ample support. Choice C can be eliminated. While many people of different faiths lost their lives at Ground Zero, the passage makes it clear that the Islamic organization was unwelcome there, so choice D can be eliminated.

21. **B is the best answer.** The instrumentalist perspective argues that individuals designate sacred spaces for social or political ends rather than for spiritual reasons. The author builds her argument from this perspective in what appears to be a dissent from the Islamic center's opponents. The best answer to this question will likely point to a weakness in the argument that the passage sidestepped or overlooked. Choice A borrows a lot of themes from the passage – taboos, morals, respect – but is ultimately a nonsense distractor. The instrumental view discusses taboos but does not address the moral prerogatives of one group in relation to another. Choice A can be eliminated. The instrumental viewpoint argues that constructing sacred spaces has social or political motives. If the author's stance is that the Islamic organization has a right to exercise their religion in the Ground Zero space, she must address the instrumentalist argument that they must also have non-spiritual reasons for wanting to access that space. Choice B highlights a serious weakness in the author's reasoning, so it is a strong choice. Choice C, viewed in isolation, reasserts the instrumental belief that opponents` of the Islamic center have political motives. Choice C would not weaken the argument but strengthen it, so it is a contrary distractor. Choice C can be eliminated. The passage does call Christianity a historically dominant force, but the instrumental viewpoint does not weigh the influence of groups in resolving conflicts. It rather provides insight into the motives of groups in establishing sacred spaces. Choice D does not have a strong basis in the passage so it does not weaken the author's argument. It can be eliminated. Choice B is the best answer.

Passage 4 (Questions 22-27)

22. **A is the best answer.** The hawkish realists ideologically fall between cautious realists and neoconservatives, so first consider the viewpoints of these two philosophies. Cautious realists want a restrained military, but they recognize that foreign powers will strike if they stand to benefit from an attack (i.e., they are "realists" who recognize that a cost-benefit analysis occurs). Neoconservatives want a dominant global American militia to secure world peace and assert democratic ideals. The inherent tension of this stance is that they are unconcerned with expanding the scope of government, the issue at the heart of conservativism. Hawkish realists, then, fall between these two, so it seems like they want an assertive military in recognition of the strategic calculations of rival states. Choices A and B both advocate for a stronger military, which is a good start. Choice A recognizes that states might attack without provocation, and that argument accords with realist thought. It seems like a strong choice. Choice B presents a position that is identical to the neoconservative stance. It can be eliminated for not falling between the neoconservatives and the cautious realists. Choice C is a position of the non-interventionists , who believe that foreign states only attack in retaliation. This position falls outside the spectrum described in the question stem. Choice C is not a strong choice. Choice D argues that the government should avoid an aggressive military out of respect for other states' autonomy. This may be a position on the spectrum described in the question, but notice that hawkish realists share the "realist" perspective – that is, that states will perform a cost-benefit analysis when deciding whether or not to attack. States will attack even if they are not directly provoked. The "hawkish" ideals likely involve an aggressive military, which is not presented in this answer choice. Choice D can be eliminated in favor of choice A.

23. **C is the best answer.** In the context of the passage, an "offense" refers to the armed forces. The question stem asks which of these three groups would likely agree that military might should be the U.S.'s primary deterrent against foreign attacks. Non-interventionists in option I differ from cautious realists in that they believe that foreign strikes only occur in retaliation, so they believe that declining to attack foreign powers is an adequate deterrent. Option I can be ruled out, so choices A and D can be eliminated. Notice that choices B and C both contain option III, which is true because neoconservatives argue for a very aggressive military stance in order to smother threats before they arise. Now decide whether option II is true. Cautious realists are far more restrained in their use of the military than are neoconservatives, but they also believe that foreign states will attack if it benefits them on balance. A strong American military will likely reduce the benefits a foreign state reaps from an attack, so cautious realists are also likely to see this as a major deterrent to foreign threats. Option II is true, so choice C is a better answer than choice B.

24. **B is the best answer.** The passage implies that neoconservatives object to the ideals of Wilson but share common ground in their desire to use the military to "make the world safe for democracy." This goal has two parts: first, it envisions an active military ensuring global peace, and second, it desires the spread of democracy as seen in the American model. Choice A recognizes the shared desire for an aggressive military, but it does not recognize the second part of the goal. Choice A is a possible answer. Choice B also recognizes the call for military action, but it goes further than choice A and acknowledges the desire to reproduce America's brand of democracy. Choice B is more complete than choice A, so choice A can be eliminated. Choice C acknowledges (what might be) a shared desire to bring about world peace, but allowing foreign leaders to freely govern seems like a mischaracterization. Neoconservatives and Woodrow Wilson would not allow leaders who do not prefer democracy to govern according to their ideals, for example. Choice C can be eliminated. In the author's view, neoconservatives threaten to inflate the size of government, so the passage would not argue that choice D accurately represents their ideals. Choice D is a weak choice, and choice B is the best answer.

25.   **A is the best answer.** The passage's main idea concerning neoconservatives is that their policy preferences violate ideals of limited government and restrained spending at the core of conservative philosophy. The best answer choice will be least similar to this argument. In choice A, a judge relies on core principles of the law to hand down an unpopular opinion. This choice is dissimilar from neoconservatives, who have deviated from fundamental principles in establishing their policy preferences. It seems like a strong answer choice. In choice B, religious dissidents break from a parent organization and form a sect that shares many of the national church's traditions. While the neoconservatives may not be as brazen as the dissidents described, they are similar in that they borrow heavily from the ideology of their progenitors. The passage does not go as far as making the case that neoconservatives are not conservatives; it does, however, sharply criticize their foreign policy. It is implied that neoconservatives still belong in the conservative "big tent" but that they have diverged on this major policy issue. Choice B is analogous to the neoconservative situation and can be eliminated. In choice C, a workers' union diverges from the principles in their charter through a democratic process. Like the neoconservatives, the steelworkers assumed a position that some see as breaking from core principles, so choice C can be eliminated. Choice D describes a head of state who declares a state of emergency in order to circumvent the constitution. This choice may be tempting because this bold move may itself be constitutionally-sanctioned. Because this move may comply with foundational ideals, it could be seen as dissimilar to the neoconservatives. However, the language of the answer choice implies that the head of state's intention is to evade constitutional processes. While neoconservatives may or may not have the intent to flout traditional conservative ideals, the author believes their foreign policy violates those core beliefs in application. Like the head of state described, their actions and beliefs are contrary to foundational principles. Choice D is a weaker choice than choice A because of this similarity. Choice A is the best answer.

26.   **B is the best answer.** The author's main idea concerning neoconservatives is that their foreign policy violates the conservative commitment to small government and fiscal restraint. Neoconservatives want to pursue aggressive military action to establish American primacy and democracy across the globe, according to the passage. While this perspective may arise from their skepticism of foreign powers, as in choice A, the author does not use that as a criticism of the neoconservatives. Choice A can be eliminated. The passage states that conservatives are united in the belief that government should be as small as possible, and the neoconservatives' desire to expand the strength and reach of the military flouts that philosophy . Choice B recognizes that tension and is a good choice. Choice C suggests that their beliefs are out of touch with those of conservative intellectuals, which is true, but that is not the heart of the author's criticism. Ultimately, the author believes that neoconservatives are out of step with conservative philosophy, so their policies might not even be called "conservative." Consider, though, that disagreement with conservative intellectuals is not the strongest argument for rejecting neoconservative policies. It could be the case that these individuals are out of touch with what is needed to promote the common welfare. In that case, the neoconservatives may offer a welcome alternative to the intellectuals' policy preferences. Choice C is not a strong answer because it does not present the best criticism of the neoconservative cause. Choice D could be true, but nowhere in the passage does the author suggest that an oligarchy of major powers would improve the credibility of any of the three types of conservatives. This means that Choice D is an unintelligible distractor and can be eliminated. Choice B gets at the author's primary criticism most directly and is the strongest answer.

27.   **A is the best answer.** In choosing a best answer, look for the choice that would most seriously compromise the author's argument about neoconservatives. He argues that their push to have an aggressive military and therefore broaden the scope of government is misaligned with the conservative commitment to small government. If that conservative ideal only applied to government at home rather than government abroad the expansive neoconservative foreign policy would no longer be incompatible with fundamental conservatism. For that reason, choice A seems like a strong answer. In choice B, if foreign powers only attacked in retaliation to strikes, this would strengthen the non-interventionist position. Neoconservatives pursue an aggressive foreign policy to preempt potential attacks, whatever the reasons for attacking may be. Choice B is unlikely to resolve the tension between conservative beliefs and those of neoconservatives, so it can be eliminated. If a larger domestic government were needed to secure peace for the United States, this would jeopardize the entire conservative establishment – but the disagreement between neoconservatives and their forebears concerns the scope of government abroad. Choice C does not address this tension directly and can be eliminated. If choice D were true and democracy could not thrive in all countries, the neoconservative foreign policy stance would be severely weakened. That would not, however, relieve the tension of those ideals with overarching conservative philosophy, so choice D can be eliminated. Choice A most directly resolves the tension between these two philosophies and is the best answer.

Passage 5 (Questions 28-32)

28. **D is the best answer.** Part of the author's main idea is that the qualities and styles of Hollywood films have come to dominate worldwide. As such, the author believes that audiences outside the United States will think poorly of movies that do not meet Hollywood standards, even if they are produced locally. Choice A can be eliminated because it does not match with the author's point that audiences evaluate domestic movies based on Hollywood, instead suggesting that they judge them based on local criteria. Similarly, choice B contradicts the author's point about how foreign audiences relate to their locally produced films, suggesting that they prefer them over Hollywood movies. Choice C, though it is more in line with the passage than choices A and B, does not provide an accurate reason for why audiences might ignore domestically produced movies; this type of distractor choice—in which the choice resembles the passage but misrepresents the author's reasoning—is common on the MCAT®. Choice D aligns with the author's claim that foreign audiences' negative attitudes toward domestic movies result from those audiences holding domestic movies to Hollywood standards. For this reason, choice D is the best answer.

29. **D is the best answer.** The passage reflects the author's attitude that for movie industries other than Hollywood to project "American values" and "Western ideologies" due to the influence of Hollywood movies constitutes cultural imperialism. Because choice A describes the exportation of an American-style business abroad, the author would likely consider it cultural imperialism, and so the choice does not answer the question well. Similarly, choice B can be eliminated because it deals with the exportation of a product in a way that would likely align with the author's definition of cultural imperialism. Seeing as choice C refers to the popularity of American sport teams abroad, it too likely fits with the author's approach to cultural imperialism, so it can be eliminated. Choice D describes an American individual participating in a Nigerian film, not the exportation of an American or otherwise Western product or business abroad. For this reason, choice D is the best answer.

30. **A is the best answer.** Though the author never states it explicitly, the passage suggests that foreign audiences do not see completely accurate representations of American society in Hollywood movies. Choice A matches with the implication that Hollywood represents America abroad in a way that projects ideals, not realities, so it is a strong answer. Choice B goes beyond the scope of the passage, suggesting that the government controls the production of movies in the United States when the passage does not mention the U.S. government, so it can be eliminated. Choice C seems to get at the author's main idea, but a closer reading reveals that the passage only states that Hollywood has "beguiled" other movie industries into projecting American values, not that it spreads a particular way of life. Choice D is similarly confusing as it seems probable, but, like choice B, it is out of the scope of the passage.

31. **A is the best answer .** The author uses the word "horizontal" to describe a global film industry in which there is a balanced representation of various styles and qualities of movies worldwide. This question asks which of a number of hypothetical trends would indicate an increasingly horizontal global film industry. Even without prior knowledge of the topic, the meaning of an "independently produced" film as one not made in Hollywood can be inferred from the context of the passage and question stem. Choice A suggests that films not from Hollywood are contributing more to the global industry, which most closely matches the author's idea of a horizontal film industry. Choice A is a strong answer Because it only implies that Hollywood is weakening, not that other industries are growing, choice B does not indicate an increasingly horizontal industry as well as choice A, so it can be eliminated. Likewise, choice C provides only a single instance of a non-Hollywood movie being more popular than Hollywood movies, so it does not support the idea of an increasingly horizontal global film industry. Choice D suggests neither that Hollywood's influence is shrinking nor that other film industries are growing, only that individual actors are moving between industries, and so it does not support the idea of a more horizontal industry. Choice D can be eliminated, and choice A is the best answer.

32. **C is the best answer.** Because each option listed bears resemblance to information given in the passage, the question depends on a close reading of the text. Though the author's attitude may appear disdainful, option I is an overly specific characterization; there is no clear evidence that the author strongly dislikes individual Hollywood movies. Choices A and D can be eliminated as they both correspond to option I. Option II does not hold up under close scrutiny as the author never expresses explicit support of non-Western ideologies, only a tacit criticism of the dominance of Western ideologies. Choice B, which corresponds to options II and III, can be eliminated. Choice C is best because it limits the response to option III, which directly correlates to the author's concern about Hollywood's influence expressed in the passage.

Passage 6 (Questions 33-36)

33. **A is the best answer.** The author argues that medicine as a profession must deliver health care that embodies a certain set of values, including altruism, humanism, competency, and trustworthiness (which together constitute medical professionalism). Her main idea is that among the existing methods for teaching professionalism, interactive strategies are most effective for encouraging students to conduct themselves in a medically professional manner and thereby learn those skills. While she implies that strong medical professionalism promotes the health and well-being of individuals and society as a whole, she does not claim that these skills produce improved clinical outcomes. Choice A goes beyond the scope of the passage and is a strong answer. She writes that training around professionalism should begin in medical school but also extend throughout practice, so she would likely agree that even practicing physicians should receive education in these skills. Choice B can be eliminated. According to the author, medical professionalism involves concrete traits of competency and skillfulness as well as abstract principles of humanism, ethics, and altruism. Choice C can be eliminated. The author states that trustworthiness is one of the tenets of medical professionalism, but more importantly, that this professionalism underlies the "social contract" between medicine and society, in which the public trusts medical providers to maintain its overall health. Choice D is a weak answer, and choice A is the best answer.

34. **A is the best answer.** The author's main idea is that teaching professionalism is best accomplished with educational methods that are active, rather than passive. The passage's spectrum spans the two extremes of solely content-based or participatory-based strategies. The author leans more towards the participatory end, as she argues that role modeling is a valuable way for students to view strong medical professional behavior and then, more importantly, mimic it. She also notes that role models have the ability to impart necessary knowledge, whether in a lecture- or discussion-based format. The best answer will refute the conclusion that interactive education allows students to best master professionalism. Choice A describes a finding where students are made more aware of how they can behave professionally after they passively absorb lectures than after actively simulating those behaviors. Choice A aligns with the main idea and is a strong answer. Although the author states that self-assessment questions are an interactive tool that can enhance didactic lectures and web-based modules, she does not believe that these questions are the cornerstone of active learning. Even if self-assessment questions were ineffective at teaching professionalism, there exist other strategies, including discussion forums, role modeling/simulations, and self-reflective writing whose efficacy the answer does not address. Choice B is a weak answer. Because the main idea of the passage emphasizes the way in which medical professionalism should be taught, choice C, which addresses the difference between individuals who have not received professionalism training and those who have, does not directly address the author's major conclusions. Even if patients were to perceive the two groups as equally skillful, they could differ in other, more abstract professional qualities, like trustworthiness. Additionally, choice C does not refute the idea that interactive study is more productive than passive study. Choice C is a weak answer. In choice D, even if role modeling itself were found to be ineffective at teaching professionalism, there exist other interactive educational methods that could still be better than passive methods. Choice D is a weak answer. Choice A is a stronger answer than choices B and D because it addresses the whole of active versus passive learning, rather than specific examples. Choice A is the best answer.

35. **C is the best answer.** The author's main idea is that professionalism should be taught to medical learners in an interactive way. On the passage spectrum of passive and active learning, her argument is that participatory education is more effective at teaching students professional skills, because they actually simulate these behaviors after they have seen the traits modeled by mentors. However, the author also stands by the belief that passive learning plays an important role, for example when students listen to lecture material. If a new project intended to improve professionalism among students, the author would argue that this endeavor include interactive components in order to be most productive. While choice A describes a situation that is similar to role modeling as depicted in the passage, the key difference is that students here would be expected to remain silent during patient interactions. The author would be unlikely to support a project that asked its learners to simply observe care and refrain from participating or practicing professional behaviors. Choice A is a possible answer because it mentions shadowing role models, but it is not a strong answer. Similarly, although the author references discussions as an active educational strategy to enhance passive learning, she implies that professionalism is best taught through role modeling and simulation, which are inherently participatory. These techniques contain some passive components, for example watching mentors and soliciting feedback, but they are more focused on encouraging students to practice professional skills. The author would be unlikely to agree with a project that only involved discussions. Choice B is a weak answer. On the other hand, choice C depicts a scenario where students engage directly with professional behaviors and additionally, actively observe each other's performance and provide feedback. Choice C is a strong answer. Choice D describes a situation that is akin to the didactic lectures mentioned in the passage, which the author believes can transmit large amounts of information about professionalism but are ultimately less effective at actually teaching these skills. Choice D is a weak answer, and choice C is the best answer.

36. **C is the best answer.** The author's main idea is that while there are a number of educational methods available to teach professionalism, the best focus is on actively involving students in observing and modeling professional skills, such that they have the opportunity to refine their behaviors to meet medical professionalism standards. She believes that all of the various strategies she mentions, whether more passive or active, have advantages in teaching learners. While she most strongly supports techniques such as role modeling and self-reflective writing for their ability to engage students in patient care and professionalism experiences, she also lauds educational methods such as didactic lectures and web-based modules for different reasons. In paragraph three, the author describes one of the advantages of lectures as emphasizing the "cognitive base" of professionalism—teaching about the history and framework, for example, of professional behaviors—in order to confer onto them the knowledge necessary to change their actions. While the author does not believe that didactic lectures alone are sufficient to teach professional behaviors, choice A is too extreme; the author believes didactic lectures have merit in being able to teach students factual content. Choice A can be eliminated. The author believes in the importance of educating learners around professionalism, but she does not mention the "cognitive base" of professionalism in relation to this idea. Rather, given that the author already agrees with the information in choice B, she uses the information in paragraph three to describe one method for teaching professionalism that has both advantages and disadvantages. Choice B is a weak answer. The author states that didactic lectures create a "cognitive base" for students learning professionalism. Despite the fact that lectures alone do not teach professional behaviors as effectively as interactive techniques, they are at least able to build a knowledge foundation for students about why professional behaviors are important. Choice C is a strong answer. Choice D is a distractor that interprets "cognitive base" literally; the author does not comment on the intellectual rigor of medical school curricula. Choice D does not align with passage information and can be eliminated. Choice C is the best answer.

Passage 7 (Questions 37-41)

37. **B is the best answer.** Throughout the passage, the author emphasizes the value of research when examining repetition in film. Although he believes it has been unsatisfactory until this point, he remains hopeful about future research. The author does not feel indifferent to film scripts, since he describes them in detail to show their potential use in research. Choice A is not the strongest answer. The author recognizes that transcribed film scripts can greatly help the study of repetition, whether in dialogue or location or props. Even though he thinks Andrew's study did not provided strong results, he views film scripts as useful tools in future research. The author describes film scripts as "compelling" in the third paragraph. Words such as this one that have strong positive or negative connotations are valuable clues to the author's opinion. Choice B is a promising answer. The author does not feel ambivalent about film scripts, since he does not blame their use in Andrew's lack of success. His criticism is directed towards Andrew's method in examining the film scripts, not the film scripts themselves. Choice C can be eliminated. Similarly, he does not resent the use of film scripts—he just thinks they were not used well in that particular study. For these reasons, choice D can be eliminated and choice B is the best answer.

38. **D is the best answer.** The author believes that repetition is a key component of film studies, even if current research does not definitively show that. The author is not likely to recommend avoiding the topic, since he argues about its importance and devotes so much of the passage to the concept. Choice A can be eliminated. The author does not think that recent studies have provided strong evidence. He is not likely to advise a professor to teach based only on anecdotal evidence, but it may be acceptable in order to convey the general concept of repetition. Choice B is a possible answer. While choice C is a tempting answer, the author does not discuss research about repetition in other forms of written text. Even though the author mentions the prevalence of repetition within various forms of narrative, there is no reason to assume that recent studies of those fields have provided stronger results than research of the cinematic arts. Choice C is a possible answer but not particularly strong. Throughout the passage, the author stresses that more research needs to be performed about repetition in film. He lists potential approaches in the third and fourth paragraphs, and hopes that the approaches can be better performed in the future. For this reason, the author would be likely to support students conducting even more research about this important topic with new techniques to avoid the flaws described in the passage. Choice D relates to the main idea of the passage and would provide stronger evidence for the concept of repetition, so it is stronger than both choices B and C.

39. **C is the best answer.** The author believes that repetition in dialogue, music, behavior, objects, or location is an integral part of understanding a film. The best answer choice will probably involve one of these repetitions then. Even if repetitive dialogue might not make sense translated into another language, there could be other types of repetition in a foreign film. It should not necessarily be the hardest genre to understand for this reason, so choice A can be eliminated. Similarly, action films without much dialogue could also show repetitive behaviors or objects, so it should not necessarily be difficult to comprehend. Choice B is not the best answer. Musical films have a musical component that repeats itself throughout the film. The songs themselves might also be repetitive, further enhancing an individual's understanding of the film. This finding strengthens the author's hypothesis so choice C is a strong answer. Although romantic comedies might be repetitive as a genre, the author's hypothesis relates to films individually, not as a whole. Choice D is not as strong as choice C.

40. **A is the best answer.** The passage is based on the assumption that repetition is an integral part of all narratives, which is why the quality of research on the topic needs to improve. The author opens his argument discussing all the different types of work that include repetition—various genres, cultures, and mediums of writing. For this reason, choice A is a strong answer. The author discusses the prevalence of repetition in films, but does not suggest that it is too prevalent. Because he believes that repetition increases understanding of films, there is no reason to assume that there is too much repetition in films. Throughout the passage, the author's criticism is directed toward how repetition is studied, not how it is actually used in film. For these reasons, choice B can be eliminated. While filmmakers might not even realize how much repetition is in their films, this is not suggested by the passage. The author does not suggest that repetition occurs in films without a purpose, so choice C is not the best answer. Although the author criticizes how motifs have been studied in the last paragraph, he indicates that it has been possible for researchers to follow them throughout films. Not enough information is given to support choice D. Choice A is the answer best supported by the passage.

41. **B is the best answer.** The author argues about the importance of repetition in film and the various forms it can take. Even if experienced researchers start a new study, they will not necessarily provide strong evidence of this belief, since past research has fallen short. Choice A is not the best answer. The author argues that research could be improved by comparing repetition in multiple texts rather than focusing on one or two classic works. Because the author thinks repetition is valuable in all films, the study should include multiple films to support this belief. Choice B is a strong answer. While film scripts might be a helpful tool in a study, they might not necessarily provide the strongest results, since the study cited in the passage used film scripts unsuccessfully. Choice C is not as strong as choice B. The author does not believe that repetition in film is limited to language, so linguistic experts are not necessary for a film study. For these reasons, choice D is a weak answer, and Choice B is the best answer.

Passage 8 (Questions 42-46)

42. **A is the best answer.** The author's main argument throughout the passage emphasizes how important and necessary religion is to functioning societies. If a society has been around for hundreds of years and did not fall apart even though they did not have religious beliefs to connect and support each other, then the author's argument would be weakened. Choice A is a strong answer. The author does not make any claims comparing poly-religious and mono-religious cultures. His argument focuses on religion in general rather than specific types of religions, so this finding would not affect the author's argument. Choice B can be eliminated. Even if an atheistic family experiences less conflict than a deeply religious one, that finding does not directly weaken the author's argument because he focuses on society rather than smaller groups like families. Choice C is not as strong as choice A. The author does not differentiate between religions or suggest that only certain religions experience the benefits discussed in the passage, so choice D is not the best answer. Choice A is stronger than the other answer choices.

43. **D is the best answer.** The author believes that having religion in one's life is extremely beneficial. Because the author is such an advocate of the benefits of religion, it is unlikely that he would advise following the same unsatisfying religious path, because the individual would not experience all the benefits discussed in the passage. Choice A is a possible answer but not particularly strong. The author believes that religion provides security, an understanding of human nature, and connections with other beings that are lost if a person is atheist. For this reason, the author is not likely to recommend giving up religion altogether, and choice B can be eliminated. He also points out that religion explains concepts that science cannot, so choice C is not the best answer. In the fourth paragraph, the author states that no one religion is better than another, so it is reasonable to conclude that he would recommend adopting new religious customs to see if they fit the individual's life better. For this reason, choice D is stronger than choice A.

44. **C is the best answer.** According to the passage, Marx does not necessarily suggest that the world would be in chaos without religion, just that it provides some sort of social order. Choice A takes Marx's statement too far and cannot be assumed true. Similarly, Marx believes that man created religion, so there was probably one point when man existed and religion did not. For this reason, choice B is not the strongest answer. One of the greatest benefits of believing in a religion is that it provides an explanation for social inequalities that would otherwise seem unfair. If there is no distinct cause of an inequality, then it can be reasoned that a higher being chose that for a reason in the long-run, which can put an individual at ease. For this reason, choice C is a strong answer. While religious leaders may have a powerful role in society, this is not discussed or suggested in the passage. This answer choice might be selected if the phrase "social control" is assumed to mean control over other individuals in society, rather than related back to the argument in the passage. Choice D can be eliminated and choice C is the best answer.

45. **D is the best answer.** Throughout the passage, the author argues for the social and personal value of religion, which explains why it is human nature to believe in something. The author probably does not mention early societies only to prove that archeological reports can support his claim, because he goes on to discuss human history in general and does not focus on particular archeological findings. Choice A is a possible answer but is not particularly strong. There is no reason to assume that the author is trying to relate his argument to historians or scholars because he does not appeal to those readers anywhere else in the passage. Choice B can be eliminated. While the discussion of early societies might suggest that language is not needed to practice religion, the author does not mention the role of language in religion in the rest of the passage. Choice C does not relate to the main idea of the passage, so it is not the best answer. The main idea of the passage emphasizes the universality of religion, whether geographically or throughout time. Choice D supports the author's main argument, so it is stronger than choice A.

46. **C is the best answer.** In the first paragraph, the author points out that some people still argue that religion is not an innate belief nor necessary to life. Although the author emphasizes the value of religion throughout the passage, this answer choice relates to the beliefs of "most individuals," not the author. For this reason, choice A is not the strongest answer. The author also mentions the differing beliefs of religion, and that some view humans as ambiguous beings that cannot necessarily be characterized in reference to higher beings, so choice B can be eliminated. When discussing the benefits of religion, the author stresses that it provides support and security to those in distress or those asking questions that science cannot answer. Because religion attempts to explain circumstances that cannot be explained otherwise, it is valuable to questioning individuals. Choice C is a strong answer. Lastly, the passage does not suggest that every religion has a god necessarily, just that it provides support and understanding. Choice D cannot be assumed to be true, and can be eliminated in favor of choice C.

Passage 9 (Questions 47-53)

47. **C is the best answer.** The author entertains the argument that weak ties are more important than strong ties before mulling a counterargument with a bit more force behind it. The author, while drawing no firm conclusions about their relative value, appears skeptical of social science research that treats weak ties as intrinsically more useful. Weak ties do tend to connect previously non-overlapping social networks, but that is not the author's primary argument. That point was made to describe a characteristic of these ties and was not treated as a matter of debate. Choice A is a weak choice because it does not strike at the heart of the argument. Choice B also presents a statement that is true but, again, does not address the primary argument. By definition, weak ties exert broader reach within social networks but do not run as deep as strong ties. Because choice B presents a definitional statement about weak ties and does not address a point in contest, it can be eliminated. The passage does not go so far as to call weak ties less valuable than strong ties, but its central argument does call the relative value of these ties into question. Choice C seems like a strong choice. Choice D contradicts definitional information in the passage, which states that both strong and weak ties confer social capital. The argument in the passage concerns the ability of online social networks to augment that social capital. Choice D presents information contrary to what is presented in the passage, so it can be eliminated in favor of choice C.

48. **A is the best answer.** The second paragraph expands on the characteristics of strong and weak ties. Weak ties expose people to new people and ideas whereas strong ties provide emotional support from very familiar relationships. Because strong ties are comprised of familiar, like-minded people, it follows that these ties homogenize the social experience and worldviews to which someone is exposed. Choice A is a strong answer. The passage never reaches a conclusion about which type of social capital is responsible for social adjustment – the author only explores how social media sites can amplify the benefits of social capital. Choice B is a beyond distractor and can be eliminated. It may seem that choice C is supported by the study on college students, but remember that it is social media sites, not strong ties, that reinforce offline networks. Choice C can be eliminated. The passage never discusses which kind of tie is more prone to disappearing from social spheres. The final paragraph argues that all online ties, strong or weak, that cannot be expected to furnish favors are on the chopping block. Because the durability of these ties is not compared in the passage, choice D can be eliminated.

49. **C is the best answer.** The passage discusses the composition of individuals' social media contacts, suggesting that it can be composed of a mix of strong and weak ties. It gives no indication that users with few contacts maintain mostly contacts who are strong ties. The final paragraph opens the possibility that the contacts could all be weak ties who are willing to provide favors. Choice A can be eliminated. The passage also provides evidence that those with many contacts are more willing to delete some, but it does not discuss the behavior of those with few contacts. Choice B can be eliminated. The passage states that social media sites reinforce weak ties. A social media user with few contacts, for that reason, would be expected to derive less benefit from his or her existing weak ties. Choice C is a strong answer. Choice D's reasoning that an individual with few contacts has little need for social support in the form of favors may be borne out by the final paragraph of the passage. It is possible, though, that this person's small ring of social media contacts provides copious social support in the form that the passage references. Choice D cannot be concluded without assuming that each contact provides very little social support. For that reason, choice D can be eliminated in favor of choice C.

50. **D is the best answer.** In light of the question stem, three of the answers will be compatible with the passage's views on how to improve social adjustment. One will not be compatible – or, at least, it will be weaker than the others. In the findings about university students cited in the passage, it was suggested that online social networking sites only improve adjustment for those with more developed offline networks on campus. Living on campus during undergraduate studies might offer students more opportunities to form interpersonal connections. The author would view this policy as helpful for improving social adjustment, so choice A can be eliminated. If online classes had discussion-based meetings, this would add a social element to an otherwise online presence. Choice B does not seem quite as helpful a policy as choice A, so put it on hold for now. The reader might be tempted to recognize choice C as a round-about distractor since it emphasizes broadening students' worldviews, but this proposal increases opportunities for offline socialization by requiring a course based on discussion. The author of the passage may also see this as a somewhat effective strategy based on the passage, so choice C can be eliminated. Choice D may appear tempting since it restricts access to the internet, but that is not the problem underlying students' lack of social adaptation. The problem is that students do not develop sufficiently strong offline interpersonal networks. The study hall in choice D is the policy that goes farthest in restricting those networks. Choice B, at least, leaves some room for social exchange, so that choice can be eliminated. Choice D is the best answer.

51. **B is the best answer.** The social networking skeptics described in the passage believe that online contacts cannot provide emotional support or improve social adjustment. The best answer will present a finding that weakens this belief. Choice A suggests that online gamers meet their closest friends online. This answer choice does not provide information about the gamers' friends offline and support they provide. It might be the case that these gamers have few close friends that provide emotional support, so the friends described in choice A may not be much of an improvement. Choice A is a possibility but seems like a weak answer. Choice B describes a kind of website in which users provide emotional support to cope with loss, and that support is significant in some way. This finding contradicts the social networking skeptics who dismiss the possibility that online networks offer emotional support. Choice B is a strong answer. Choice C describes an online network whereby people support one another in losing weight, and this support helps users achieve that goal. This scenario does not provide an example of *emotional support*, so choice C can be eliminated. Social media sites enable users to stay in touch with relatives and friends, and it might be inferred that this resource then strengthens users' feelings of emotional support. Notice how that conclusion follows from an inference not explicitly stated by the answer choice. Choice D is a possibility, so it should be compared alongside choice B. Choice B offers an instance in which a social networking site provides direct emotional support. Choice D, by contrast, requires a small jump in reasoning to reach the same conclusion. Choice B more directly weakens the skeptics' argument, so it is a stronger answer than choice D.

52. **A is the best answer.** Examining the answer choices in this question, select the choice whose claim is buttressed by the most compelling evidence in the passage. All of the answer choices make strong claims, especially with the words "cannot" and "only," so that may make it easier to determine which have a basis in the passage. The passage describes a study in which university students with more developed offline social networks tend to experience better social adjustment when they have more contacts online. They differ from more junior students whose less established networks are compromised by their intense social media site usage. It follows that these sites may only enhance the social lives of those with more developed offline social networks, so choice A is a strong choice. The final paragraph describes a finding in which contacts are deleted regardless of their status as strong or weak ties. The passage classified these contacts as strong and weak ties, so choice B is a weak choice. Social networks can enhance a user's social capital. The study on college students demonstrated that possibility, so choice C can be eliminated. Choice D is a tempting choice because it almost restates the conclusion of the final paragraph, which argues that online contacts may provide support beyond emotional or informational support. Notice that the last paragraph does not argue that these contacts do not provide these kinds of social capital but rather something in addition to them. A user, for instance, may retain a contact who is a strong tie and provides emotional support. The user might also expect that contact to provide a tangible favor in addition to emotional support. Choice D is a misstatement of the final paragraph of the passage and can be eliminated. Choice A is the strongest choice.

53. **B is the best answer.** This passage explores the nature of social support offered by social networks and what, if any, social capital they confer. The author makes two main points on this question. First, use of online social networks can impede social adjustment and, second, that they offer support beyond the informational or emotional. That social media sites may improve social standing is not without its critics. The author also never speaks to the merit of these sites' reputation or functions, so choice A can be eliminated. The passage does speculate that online networks offer a yet undefined kind of support beyond what strong or weak ties might provide. This support is not given much form but it is implied to be somewhat superficial since it is thought to supply favors. Choice B seems like a possibly strong choice. While social media sites may expand a user's weak ties, that possibility is a beyond distractor because it is never addressed in the passage. Choice C can be eliminated. The article tries to pin down just what kind of social capital these sites supply. It also asserts that weak ties tend to broaden people's perspectives. The passage does not connect those two ideas, though. It does not entertain the idea that users gain social capital by broadening their perspective on these sites, so choice D can be eliminated. Choice B is the strongest choice among those presented.

TEST 5

ANSWERS & EXPLANATIONS
Questions 1–53

ANSWER KEY					
1. A	10. A	19. D	28. B	37. D	46. B
2. B	11. D	20. D	29. B	38. A	47. A
3. B	12. B	21. C	30. C	39. C	48. C
4. A	13. A	22. A	31. B	40. D	49. B
5. D	14. A	23. C	32. C	41. D	50. D
6. C	15. A	24. C	33. A	42. A	51. A
7. A	16. B	25. D	34. C	43. B	52. C
8. D	17. A	26. A	35. A	44. D	53. C
9. A	18. C	27. A	36. B	45. A	

EXPLANATIONS FOR TEST 5

Passage 1 (Questions 1-7)

1. **A is the best answer.** When a CARS passage asks about a quotation from the passage, the context is rarely clear from the question stem alone. This quotation appears in the final paragraph, whose main purpose appears to be rebutting the paragraph preceding it. The third paragraph qualifies the author's main idea that digitization is revolutionizing humanities research, warning that forces outside academia could influence what sources make it into the digital record. The fourth paragraph answers this criticism of digitization, arguing that some amount of chance has always influenced that which makes it into the scholarly record. Choice A restates this function of the final paragraph and the quote drawn from it, so it is a strong answer. The third paragraph, not the fourth paragraph, presents the most "alternative" viewpoint to that of the author, so choice B is not likely to be a strong answer. The author does claim that, like an eagle diving toward prey on the ground, close inspection of the humanities yields new topics for research. That claim is not consistent with the main idea of the fourth paragraph, which responds to what the author apparently believes is the most potent criticism of the main idea. This argument appears earlier in the passage, so choice C is a weak answer. While the fourth paragraph certainly hints that the academic climate is "flippant" because it is at the whim of trends, the passage itself does not address the reasons a scholar may try to publish. Choice D is a weak answer. Choice A is the best assessment of the quote from the fourth paragraph .

2. **B is the best answer.** The passage narrative bobs in and out of the extended analogy of the humanities scholar and the eagle. The author seems to construct this analogy as a vehicle for communicating the main idea. The main idea of the passage is that, like an eagle flying high and low in search of prey, a scholar needs to examine both narrow ideas of interests and broader trends within the discipline to produce the most fruitful research, and digitization allows scholars to more readily understand those trends. Examine the answer choices to see which answer choice is most compatible with the main idea. While the author believes that scholars need to both maintain high-level viewpoints and conduct detailed analyses, the interplay of these two activities does not constitute "interdisciplinary thought." The author argues that both of these activities constitute the work of the humanities. He does not address the question of how cooperation between disciplines may enhance those fields. Eliminate choice A. The author argues that the humanities scholar has a dual role: to both survey the field for research topics that merit consideration and to flesh them out in great detail. This, in his view, is analogous to an eagle that soars in the sky and dives to the ground for prey. Choice B is aligned with the main idea and is a strong answer. The main idea argues that scholars should operate from both "lofty" and "narrow" vantage points; that is, the author does not relegate scholars to just the latter. Choice C is inconsistent with the main idea of the passage and can be eliminated. Choice D is tempting because the author draws a contrast between high-level viewpoints and narrower perspectives, but the second paragraph suggests that the author does not see those activities as dichotomous. In other words, approaching the humanities from two perspectives is not "contradictory" – it is instead a careful balance the humanities scholars must strike. Choice D is weaker than choice B.

3. **B is the best answer.** Refer to the passage to get a handle on the context of the quote in the question stem. The third paragraph poses a potentially serious criticism of the move to digitize humanities sources. While the passage initially appears glowing in its assessment of digitization, this author advances a fear that political circumstances could dictate which sources make it into the digital record, hence the "uneven accessibility" of some texts. The quote acknowledges that this practice has always happened because scholars have had to omit some sources from the record. Find the answer that most closely corresponds with that meaning. While choice A seems to refer to the author's argument about the responsibility of humanities scholars to approach their work from both high and low levels, it does not address the meaning of the quote. Choice A can be eliminated. The third paragraph raises a criticism that the shift to digitized sources could omit important voices from the record, and this quotation acknowledges that this practice has been longstanding. Choice B is a strong answer. Choice C is tempting because it is very similar in meaning to choice B. The shift to digital sources has indeed "filtered" some viewpoints, but the quote refers to events that happened before digitization. Choice C does not account for the pre-digitization era and can be eliminated. While choice D captures the author's cautiously optimistic viewpoint about technological innovations, the quote cited in the question stem is not drawn from a paragraph that projects that optimism. Choice D can be eliminated .

4. **A is the best answer.** When confronting a problem about assumptions in an argument, determine which choice, were it not true, would cause the argument to crumble. The author argues that a humanities scholar needs to both maintain a high-level outlook on broad trends in the discipline and also select specific topics from that overview. He thinks digitization will provide scholars greater clarity about trends in their field. Look for which answer choice, if invalidated, would seriously compromise this argument. If research topics could be generated without a broad overview of the discipline, then the author's analogy of the humanities eagle would be toppled. No longer would the scholar need to have eyes in the sky and on the ground; instead, it would be sufficient for scholars to keep their heads buried in their areas of sub-specialization. Choice A is required by the argument, so it is a strong answer. In the final paragraph, the author explicitly refutes the claim in choice B by stating that humanities scholarship has always been under the influence of these forces. Choice B is a weak answer because the author refutes this claim rather than using it as support for his argument. If the costs of digitization were similar to the cost of archiving paper documents, the barriers to preserving sources in the political record would be similar. The passage concludes with an acknowledgement that, indeed, digitizing and archiving have been subject to the same forces. Invalidating choice C in no way compromises the author's argument, so it is a weak answer. The author certainly encourages scholars in the humanities to maintain a broad perspective on their discipline, but the use of this broad perspective is for finding salient research topics. The author never addresses that which constitutes an "honest assessment" of the humanities. Choice D is a beyond distractor outside the scope of the passage, so it is a weak answer.

5. **D is the best answer.** Although this passage limits its scope to the humanities, it is possible that digitization has influenced scholars in other disciplines. The question requires extrapolation of the professor's deeply ironic situation to the humanities, the field described in the passage. This professor of physics probably has very detailed knowledge of quantum mechanics and is making waves in the physics world, but his or her inability to tutor high school physics suggests a detachment from broader ideas in the discipline. While this scholar's exposure to physics may be limited to quantum mechanics, it is unclear from the information in the question stem that this is a result of digitization. Choice A can be eliminated. The passage indicates that individuals beyond the scholars conducting research have a stake in it, but it never addresses "the drive to publish" or any such incentive facing scholars as they conduct research. Choice B can be eliminated. While the physics professor appears to have a very specialized focus within his or her field, it is unclear that digitization has been responsible for these narrow interests. Choice C is a weak answer. The author argues that humanities scholars need broad understanding in their field to find specific, specialized research questions. That does not appear to be the case for this physics scholar, who enjoys acclaim for his or her research despite an apparent lack of command of general physics. The information in the question stem, for that reason, most challenges the argument in choice D. Choice D is the best answer.

6. **C is the best answer.** To evaluate the humanities teacher's policy from the perspective of the author, consider the author's attitude toward the digital revolution. While the author harbors reservations that political considerations could bar some sources from the digital record, he is optimistic that digitization enables scholars to quickly retrieve large-scale trends happening in the field. These trends will allow scholars to formulate specific research interests. Before the tech revolution, scholars could gain such broad insights, but only with an investment of considerable time and effort. While the author is indeed optimistic about the capabilities, it is a bit too extreme to say that his support is "unequivocal," as in choice A. The author presents a potentially serious caveat in paragraph 3. Choice A is too extreme and can be eliminated. Choice B is tempting because the passage argues that technology quickly enables access to a broad spectrum of ideas. Notice that, although the author argues a broad perspective is necessary to conduct research, he does not go so far as to claim that digitization is necessary to gain this high-level perspective. Choice B is a weak answer and can be eliminated. Choice C recognizes the main idea's nuance that, with time and effort, broad ideas can be gained without the use of technology. It is difficult to say how enthusiastic the author would be about this policy, but choice C reflects a nuance of the main idea more clearly than does choice B. The passage argues that technology allows scholars to acquire a high-level viewpoint of the humanities. The author argues that this broad perspective, not digitization, allows for a more detailed understanding of the field. Choice D is a weaker answer than choice C.

7. **A is the best answer.** When a CARS question presents a new context in which to test the passage's main idea, usually some aspect of the main idea is undermined. Notice that the platform imagined in the question stem differs somewhat from the advantages of digitization enumerated in the passage. Digitization, the author argues, allows for a more readily accessible high-level understanding of the humanities. This social media platform allows scholars to more quickly ascertain research ideas, which, from the author's perspective, comes from high-level knowledge of the discipline. The network effectively short-circuits the pipeline of ideas the author proposes, which is problematic because the author seems to insist scholars have high-level understandings of their discipline. This potential conflict is suggested in choice A, so it is a strong answer. The author does not argue that libraries and archivists have any role in formulating research questions; rather, they build collections that allow researchers to gain broad understandings and then formulate their own research questions. Choice B is not a strong answer. The author acknowledges in the passage that digitization makes research far less "painstaking" and does not appear to take issue with that. It is unlikely the author would raise the objection in choice C, so that answer choice can be eliminated. This social media platform sidesteps the need for a broad understanding of the humanities, so it is plausible to assume that it would allow users to remain more focused on their areas of specialization. This is the opposite of choice D, which can be eliminated.

Passage 2 (Questions 8-14)

8. **D is the best answer.** The last paragraph explains that stories with moral teachings that feature characters humanize lessons in a way that rules cannot give. The author describes moral truths as sometimes paradoxical – like human nature, they sometimes elude understanding. The final paragraph is devoted to the assertion in choice A, so that is a weak answer. The second paragraph addresses the claim in choice B, arguing that literary works allow for a broader range of fictional scenarios to be presented to a reader. Although the justification is present for the claim in choice B, much less text is devoted to that point than there was for choice A. Hold onto it for now. The third paragraph explains that sinners were sometimes described as dogs in ancient times, so Judas' association with the dog may give insight into his wickedness. Historical and literary evidence underpin the argument in choice C, so that answer can be eliminated. The first paragraph examines the argument in choice D that the dog was meant to show that Judas was not one-dimensional. When comparing this choice to choice B, ask "why" – why does the author think this? For choice B, why does the author think that literature is more helpful than other art forms in achieving moral clarity? She feels that way because it more easily allows readers to put themselves in fictional situations. Now, why does the author think that the dog in the Judas painting may underscore the dimensions of his character, as in choice D? The first paragraph does not describe how exactly the dog highlights Judas' redeeming qualities, so that is a tough question to answer. It simply makes the claim without justification. Although choice B lacks much elaboration, the passage provides a little more reasoning for it. Choice D lacks elaboration, so it is a stronger answer than choice B.

9. **A is the best answer.** The main idea of this passage is that art can convey moral teachings and that thematic ambiguity can make art more relevant to a larger audience. That this ambiguity has intrinsic value is the thrust of choice A, so that seems like a strong answer at first glance. While the Rubens painting may not take a clear stance on the nature of Judas, the author encourages viewers to take lessons drawn from their own interpretation of art. The fact that the viewer may reach a different conclusion than would the artist does not lessen the credibility of either person's conclusion, in the author's eyes. Choice B can be eliminated. While the author states that some have interpreted the dog to indicate the many dimensions of Judas' character, that is not necessarily the conclusion *she* reached. She simply argues that multiple interpretations exist and the piece is all the better for its ambiguity. Because the author did not take a stance on the meaning of the Rubens painting, choice C can be eliminated. Choice D similarly makes an argument that the author does not directly address. In the fourth paragraph, the author vindicates works with ambiguous themes, but she does not go so far as to compare the value of ambiguity against overtness. Choice D can be eliminated since it is just beyond the scope of the passage's argument. Notice that choices A and D are similar, but the word "might" in choice A softens the language of that answer. Qualified language like this is often, but not always, a part of strong answers.

10. **A is the best answer.** In the passage, the author does not really evaluate the qualities of parables so much as their potential teaching value. It seems likely that the strongest answer choice will not so much reflect an opinion of the story of the prodigal son so much as a belief about the potential uses of the story. The main idea of the passage is that ambiguous moral overtones in art allow a broad range of people to access moral teachings. The author devotes the final paragraph to defending art that has no obvious moral imperative. Choice A restates this opinion, so it is a strong answer. The passage argues that art allows moral teachings to be transmitted, but it does not argue that one need be a virtuous person to access art. Choice B can be eliminated. The passage defends art that lacks clear moral overtones, but it does not go so far as to argue that this art is more valuable than thematically straightforward works. Choice C can be eliminated. Because it references a very specific hypothetical about whether a dog appears in the parable, choice D seems farfetched enough to be a nonsense distractor. This answer can be further ruled out because the author never takes a stance on what symbolic message the dog is meant to send. Eliminate choice D .

11. **D is the best answer.** Before considering the answer choices, first determine how the author believes art accomplishes its moral objectives. Art allows viewers to ponder nature and new realities, strengthening their grasp on both reality and morality. The passage offers at least two guidelines for works of art that most effectively teach morals: they expose viewers to scenarios beyond their usual experience, and they use characters in place of strict sets of rules. One form of art from the answer choices will stand out as particularly ineffective in light of these guidelines. The author does not necessarily believe that ambiguous moral themes are more valuable than concrete themes. She argues that art is *not less valuable* for thematic ambiguity. Choice A describes an art piece that would not necessarily fail her guidelines, so it can be eliminated. If a song recounted the actions of a knight as a teaching tool about valor, it would anthropomorphize this desirable trait. It is likely the author would think this approach a strong strategy for teaching morals, so choice B can be eliminated. A painting displaying cruelty may be disturbing or in some way objectionable, but this brief description does not necessarily fall short of the guidelines the author established in the passage. Keep it for now but consider it for elimination. Choice D describes a book that expands upon the core beliefs of a religion. The author would likely see this book as an examination of tenets and rules, and she explicitly objects to the use of rules as a moral teaching tool in the fourth paragraph. Choice D more directly violates the author's description of art that transmits morals than does choice C, so choice D is a stronger answer.

12. **B is the best answer.** Although no knowledge of biblical stories was required to answer questions accompanying the passage, familiarity with the topic could ease comprehension. The downside is that readers who are familiar with these stories may be inclined to bring prejudices and outside information to the passages. This question preys on that tendency since those acquainted with the Christian faith likely have strong opinions concerning Judas. In reading the answer choices, contain opinions to those expressed in the passage. While the first paragraph argues that Judas was more complex a character than his brazen treachery would suggest, that was not the connection the author established with the Book of Matthew. The third paragraph raises the possibility that Judas can be interpreted as more one-dimensional. Choice A can be eliminated. The author uses this parable to liken Judas to a rebellious child who throws his food – the teachings of Jesus – to the dogs. That the child would discard his nourishment shows the foolishness of that action. Comparison to this child makes Judas seem similarly ignorant and disobedient, so choice B is a strong answer. The third paragraph explicitly states that the dogs represent the nonbelievers and Judas is the child. Choice C does not seem apt because the dogs, not the child, are the infidels in the parable. Choice C can be eliminated. The wording in choice D suggests that the comparison of Judas to a child is an affront to his mental capacities, which were not assessed in the passage. The author also does not hint at a belief that children are intellectually incapable. Eliminate choice D.

13. **A is the best answer.** The second paragraph argues the point referenced by this question stem. Before reading the answer choices, first evaluate the author's reasoning behind this claim. She argues that art, and literature in particular, allow people to gain exposure to fictional experiences that they could not acquire first—or secondhand. If all artistic themes drew life experiences of the artists, it would be impossible for art to teach lessons that life experiences could not. Choice A seriously weakens the author's argument and is a strong answer. That art is more ambiguous than everyday experience is likely compatible with the author's argument. She claims that ambiguity serves a purpose in conveying moral teachings. Choice B can be eliminated because ambiguity would not negate her claim about the potential of art to teach morality. The author all but acknowledges that other art forms can dabble in fiction but that literature uses fiction more fluidly. Whether literature is a more effective teaching tool than other art is not pertinent to the argument about life experience versus art. Eliminate choice C. It may be that people can recount life lessons better than they can lessons gleaned from art, but it is not clear from the passage that the ability to recite lessons is demonstrative of having taken a lesson to heart. In fact, the passage argues that some art is notoriously ambiguous, which could make describing themes quite difficult. The author appears to think that even obscure themes are solid tools for transmitting moral lessons, so choice D can be eliminated.

14. **A is the best answer.** The third paragraph addresses what some might see as a weakness of the author's argument about art as a teaching tool—namely, that art's themes defy a unified interpretation. The fourth paragraph takes aim at that notion, arguing that art's ambiguity can assist in the learning process. Because that paragraph acts as a rebuttal to an objection, choice A seems like a strong answer. The fourth paragraph is related to the author's argument about the teaching potential of art. It is not a new topic as presented in choice B. Eliminate choice B. The argument in the fourth paragraph is an extension, not a contradiction, of the author's original argument that art imparts clarity. Choice C is misstated and can be eliminated. Although the fourth paragraph focuses on the power of stories as teaching instruments, it seems unlikely that the author's reasoning is confined to parables. Earlier in the passage, the author speculated that stories may be better at transmitting values than other art, but that is not the function of the fourth paragraph. Choice D is a weaker answer than choice A.

Passage 3 (Questions 15-19)

15. **A is the best answer.** Throughout the passage, the author emphasizes how influential skipping through commercials can be. This feature worries advertisement companies because it plays such a role in the use of a DVR. In the second paragraph, the author points out that more than 50% of users appreciate skipping through commercials the most. For this reason, choice A is most likely to be true. The author does not explicitly discuss rewinding live television, so choice B is not the best answer. Similarly, the passage never addresses the free time created by pausing a television program, so choice C can be eliminated. While recording shows for each member of the family may be a benefit of purchasing a DVR, the author does not discuss the DVR's function as it relates to different family members, but rather the family unit as a whole. For this reason, choice D can be eliminated, and choice A is the best answer.

16. **B is the best answer.** The author discusses the drop in viewership of commercials as DVR becomes more popular. He also suggests that commercials can still influence viewers even if they are skipped. While every advertising company would probably also experience a drop in viewership, the author is not likely to suggest inaction, since he mentions the potential influence that advertisements can still have. Choice A is not the best answer. If companies create advertisements with attention grabbing images, then viewers are more likely to pause and actually watch the commercials, or remember the vivid images later. Choice B is a strong answer. The author does mention other devices as another challenge to TV advertising, but the passage does not discuss the effectiveness of advertising on these mediums. It cannot be assumed that advertisements on other devices would increase viewership, making choice C a weak answer. Because the author thinks television advertisements can still have an effect on viewers, choice D can be eliminated in favor of choice B.

17. **A is the best answer.** Although DVR and VCR are common devices outside this MCAT® passage, do no bring in any personal knowledge that is not presented in the passage. The author compares the features of the DVR and the VCR, but discusses the VCR in past tense. He devotes the rest of the passage to recent issues surrounding the popularity of the DVR, so it reasonable to assume that the DVR has essentially replaced the VCR. Choice A is a strong answer. Because the DVR and VCR have similar functions, they are not likely to work together because only one device is necessary. Choice B can be eliminated. There is no mention of how the devices were developed or by whom, so choice C cannot be assumed true. While the DVR may be more expensive than the VCR, that is not suggested in the passage as monetary value is never discussed. Choice D is not as strong as choice A.

18. **C is the best answer.** This question is testing the spectrum of opinions in the passage and where the author lies on it. While some individuals worry that DVRs destroy all advertising efforts, the author leans more towards the other end of spectrum. His main argument throughout the passage involves the influence that television commercials can still have, even if they are often watched on fast forward by viewers these days. Keep this in mind when reading through the answer choices. If companies have devoted more money to advertising, they might be trying to overcompensate for a drop in sales, or they may be trying to take advantage of an effective technique. Similarly, positive ratings by focus groups could have a variety of causes. Choices A and B could each be attributed to decreasing or increasing effectiveness of advertisements. If Americans do not remember the commercials they watched on fast forward, the advertisements do not have an effect on viewers and do not keep them engaged. The author's argument that commercials can still influence viewers would be weakened. Compared to choices A and B, which do not directly weaken the author's argument, choice C is a stronger answer. If children are more likely to purchase toys they have seen on television, then the advertisements do have an effect on viewers and the author's argument would be strengthened. Choice D can be eliminated.

19. **D is the best answer.** Throughout the passage, the author argues that television advertising needs to be adjusted to still be influential to viewers with the increase in prevalence of the DVR. If the sale of DVRs had dropped in the last year, it does not mean that DVRs are not prevalent anymore. Many households may have already purchased one DVR per home and the issues brought forth by the DVR still remain. For this reason, choices A and B can eliminated. While other devices may affect advertising as well, the author's central argument is about the impact of DVRs on the effectiveness of television advertising. For this reason, choice C is a weak answer. The author's concern regarding television advertising in accord with DVR use still applies even if their sales might have dropped slightly in one year. Choice D is the strongest answer.

Passage 4 (Questions 20-26)

20. **D is the best answer.** The author's main argument regarding colonialism is that although there were individual acts of injustice, there were also persistent injustices built into the cultural structures established by colonialism. Choice A is suggested by the author's citation of Edward Said's quote but the first sentence in paragraph 3 indicates that author was more concerned with structural injustice than by cultural homogenization. The author explicitly notes that "colonialism should be mainly understood as a structural injustice." Choice A is not the best answer. Choice B contradicts the passage since the author notes that oppression was more commonly day to day and persistent. Choice B can be eliminated. The author notes that the effects of colonialism are lasting but does not make any arguments about how the effects extend beyond the actual duration of colonial rule. Choice C goes beyond the scope of the passage. Choice D is appealing because this characterizes how the author summarized the different factors contributing to oppression under colonialism. Choice D is the best answer.

21. **C is the best answer.** Miller claims that people within a nation have a common identity and identify with actions on the part of their predecessors. Therefore, national identity allows nations to be held responsible for actions in the past. Choice A refers to Miller's distinction between nations and states but the definition of a state is not crucial to Miller's argument regarding why nations can be responsible for past injustices. Choice A is not the best answer. Choice B is appealing because it summarizes one of Miller's ideas but it leads to some circular logic. If the author were to assume choice B, their argument would be that nations can be held responsible because they are a collective identity that can be held responsible for their past actions. Choice B can be eliminated. The author notes in paragraph 1 that it is because a nation's members act in a way that is connected to their national identity that nations can be conceived of as collective agents who are responsible for their actions. Choice C better characterizes why a nation can be conceived of as a collective identity. If members of a nation did not identify strongly with their common identity, a nation could not be conceived of as a collective agent. Choice C is a strong answer. Choice D is a misinterpretation of the passage. The author notes that according to Miller, nations exist as ethical communities actively created by a body of persons who continuously reshape their common identity. This does not mean that nations must act in an ethical manner, but rather means that nations can determine their own ethical beliefs. Choice D goes beyond the scope of the passage and can be eliminated.

22. **A is the best answer.** The author notes that colonialism led to complex structures of oppression but was characterized by using the resources and labor of the colonized, changing the culture of a place, and establishing new hierarchies where the colonizers are superior. Look for an answer choice that describes a situation in which the culture, practices, and leadership structure would be changed in such a way that the original organization would have effectively been taken over. Choice A is an appealing answer because a company merger would put the smaller company under the larger one's control. In this situation, the smaller company's practices and leadership would change to become that of the larger one. Choice B is appealing because it is an example of a leadership change but the change of one person in one position does not bring about the complete overhaul of established practices. Choice B can be eliminated. Choice C is appealing because it indicates a change in practices but does not necessitate a change in leadership or hierarchy within the company. Choice C is not a strong answer. Choice D is appealing because it involves establishing new hierarchies. However, in this analogy, the new superiors would not be "colonizers" since they earned their positions from within the company. This does not serve as an example of the complete change of culture and leadership that happens during colonialism. Choice D can be eliminated.

23. **C is the best answer.** The author based his or her paper on analyzing Miller's opinions and thus, the author's views are revealed in the way he or she engages with Miller's ideas. The author approved of Miller's correspondence model for redress but questioned Miller's silence on the issue of colonial reparations. Look for an answer choice that respects Miller's work but seeks to improve upon it. Choice A is a potential reason the author cited for why Miller did not discuss colonialism but this does not engage with the author's own perspective on colonial redress. Choice A is not the best answer. Similarly, choice B offers a reason why Miller did not discuss colonialism but does not offer an opinion on why Miller made this choice. Choice B can be eliminated. Choice C offers a judgement on Miller's correspondence model and also notes why colonial injustice does not fit into this model. Choice C is a strong answer. Choice D is a clarification of Miller's liberal nationalistic beliefs but does not offer insight into the author's beliefs. Choice D can be eliminated.

24. **C is the best answer.** The situation in the question stem is an example of a nation offering reparations. This would primarily offer support to passage assertions regarding a nation's responsibility for past injustices. Choice A is appealing because the question stem is an example of reparations but this situation does not provide any information on how the type of injustice corresponded to the reparation. Choice A is not the best answer. Choice B is supported by other information within the passage since the author asserts that colonial injustice was not just composed of individual acts of injustice. However, the question stem does not specify what types of injustices the Apartheid leaders apologized for. So, it cannot be inferred that the Apartheid leaders apologized for structural injustices. Choice B is not supported by the example in the question stem. Choice C is appealing because it appropriately characterizes the question stem as a situation in which a nation is taking responsibility for past injustice. Choice C is a strong answer. Choice D, like choice B, is supported by other information within the passage but again, the question stem did not specifically address structural injustice.

25. **D is the best answer.** The author's main idea with redress for colonial redress is that the complexity of both structural injustice and individual acts of injustice mean that colonialism cannot be clearly classified into Miller's correspondence model. A model for colonial redress must account for reparations for both of these types of injustices. Look for an answer choice that acknowledges this. Choice A relies upon one form of reparation for all the types of injustice so it is not the best answer. Choice B is appealing because it emphasizes the idea of national identity supported by Miller. However, like choice A, choice B relies on one form of reparation for all the types of injustice so it is not the best answer. Choice C is appealing because it refers to Miller's ideas regarding the nature of nationhood and how a nation's citizens' collective identification with the past allows reparations to be made. However, the author does not suggest that individual citizens must organize to establish reparations. Although conscientious citizens are what a nation is comprised of, citizens are not held responsible for acting as individuals to carry out reparations. Choice C can be eliminated. Choice D is the strongest answer because it addresses the author's understanding of the complexity of injustices under colonial rule.

26. **A is the best answer.** As reported by the author, Miller's main point in establishing the correspondence model is that not enough nations take responsibility for the injustices they committed over their history. Those nations must resolve their inherited responsibility by offering the type of redress that corresponds to the magnitude of the injustice. So the author's statement doesn't refer to literal tracking or monitoring of progress, but rather ensuring that the redress is appropriate for the injustice. Choice A is a strong answer because it summarizes this main point. Choice B misinterprets the use of the word "track" and goes beyond the scope of the passage to specifically address the people affected by an injustice. Choice B can be eliminated. Choice C, like choice B, misinterprets the word "track" and assumes that redress will have a positive effect on people previously subjected to injustice. Choice C is not a strong answer. Choice D is appealing because it broaches the idea that the form of redress may differ depending on the form of injustice but choice A more directly summarizes the idea that redress should match the magnitude of injustice. Choice D can be eliminated.

Passage 5 (Questions 27-33)

27. **A is the best answer.** The author implies that advocates of the Fair Innings theory suggest policies that amount to geronticide, but that characterization is a bit extreme. They are actually in favor of rationing expensive medical interventions for the elderly and allocating those funds to somehow improving the quality of life of younger generations. Because the Fair Innings theorists support emphasizing palliative end-of-life treatment over expensive, life-sustaining procedures, option I is a strong choice. Choice B can be eliminated. Option II is tempting because the Fair Innings theorists object to "taxpayer-subsidized" interventions, but it is unclear if they support shifting funding toward younger populations through reallocating taxpayer dollars to other programs or by lowering taxes. Option II is not a fair conclusion on the basis of the passage, so options B, C, and D can be eliminated. Notice that option III is an extreme misrepresentation of the Fair Innings theorists' beliefs. The author introduces their beliefs by likening it to geronticide. Nowhere do they propose mandatory termination of the elderly, though the author appears to equate healthcare rationing as such. Choice A is the best answer.

28. **B is the best answer.** A helpful strategy with CARS questions testing comprehension of the passage is to read the question stem and answer the question before reading the answer choices. The last sentence of the third paragraph suggests that, in the opinion of the Fair Innings theorists, almost nobody would agree that unlimited healthcare resources should be devoted to the care of the elderly. A consequence of that argument is that virtually everybody would limit care provided to the elderly to some degree – that is, the question is not "should we ration healthcare?" but rather "to what degree should we ration healthcare?" This argument treats healthcare rationing as a forgone conclusion, so choice B is a strong answer. That the benefits of expensive medical interventions are too small to justify their cost is indeed a concern of the Fair Innings theorists. The reference to the marginal benefits of healthcare in the sentence was made to set the stage for the broader argument about how acceptable rationing really is. Choice A can be eliminated. While the Fair Innings theory certainly carries undertones about taxation, in the final sentence of the paragraph that point is secondary to the theorists' point about the universality of healthcare rationing. Choice C can be eliminated. While the final sentence alludes to the marginal benefits of some expensive medical interventions, neither it nor the passage compares the cost effectiveness of these interventions to palliative care. What is more, choice D misstates the main idea of the third paragraph. Fair Innings theorists are proponents of palliation, so they would not argue that it should not be pursued. Eliminate choice D in favor of choice A.

29. **B is the best answer.** When an MCAT® question asks about the meaning of a phrase, be sure to refer to it in the passage to put it in context. Several of these choices reflect ideas the author expressed, and to distill the correct answer from among those ideas, context is key. The fourth paragraph stresses the interconnectedness of human beings, and it says that the "social covenant" binds society together. It criticizes the Fair Innings theory for perpetuating the notion that the elderly are a drain on productivity. The paragraph goes on to say that humans support the frail among them. This seems an interesting concession on the part of the author: she appears to agree that the elderly are too frail to be productive, but she argues that they should be provided for anyways. Besides perhaps their past contributions, the elderly do not appear to be productive members of society from the author's perspective. Choice A can be eliminated. The author argues that despite their lack of present contributions, the elderly should be supported just as they supported younger generations in their adolescence. Choice B is a strong answer. While the author agrees that standards of medical care should not be adjusted with respect to age, she uses the fourth paragraph to stress human interconnections on a broader level than healthcare. Choice C is too specific a reading in the context of the paragraph, so it can be eliminated. In suggesting the author calls for economic restraint over familial ties, choice D misrepresents the author's main argument. Choice D can be eliminated.

30. **C is the best answer.** The author believes that cost should not figure into health policy decisions. She makes this stance known in the transition from the third to the fourth paragraph, where she objects to any talk of rationing healthcare on the basis that younger generations owe a debt to the elderly. The Fair Innings theorists, her opponents, argue for limiting the debt burden imposed on society by the elderly's healthcare costs. The best answer will either reinforce her reasoning or weaken the argument of her opponents. That fewer retirees receive support from their families than in generations past may seem like government assistance may be required to fill a financial gap, but choice A seems incomplete. Maybe healthcare has grown cheaper, so the elderly require less financial assistance. Perhaps the elderly have more savings, requiring less monetary support from their families and the government. Choice A leaves open many possibilities about why the elderly receive less support, so it is too vague to be a strong answer. It may seem that more preventative care ultimately results in healthcare savings, but that information was not addressed in the passage. Choice B is a beyond distractor and can be eliminated. For those unaware of the term, the passage implies that palliation is a medical strategy emphasizing comfortable end-of-life care without curative intent. The Fair Innings theorists appear to prefer that route to more expensive curative interventions because of cost considerations, but if palliative care were more expensive than curative interventions, it is reasonable to believe that they would support the cheaper option. Because the finding in choice C would persuade the Fair Innings theorists to support the author's policy positions, it is a strong answer. The author makes an argument about the dependence of the humans on one another at different stages in life to reinforce her main argument. The Fair Innings theorists appear to care more about financial realities than appeals to moral obligations, so the finding in choice D is less likely to persuade them than that in choice C. Choice D can be eliminated.

31. **B is the best answer.** This passage addresses the question of the extent of healthcare to which the elderly are entitled. Although the author does not address physician-assisted suicide directly, her views on end-of-life care may inform that topic. The author appears concerned that the discussion on healthcare rationing overlooks a right of the elderly to maximize their lifespan. She begins the passage with a discussion of the dystopian play *The Old Law* to illustrate how a world without this right would look. From her perspective, rationing care for the elderly is the same as execution against their wills. The author does not appear to support one end-of-life treatment over the other – she is more concerned about the right of the elderly to opt for the care they think best. Choice A is not a strong answer. Coercion is a mechanism to force people into making certain choices. If elderly people felt coerced to undergo physician-assisted suicides, it is reasonable to believe that the author would see that quandary as a forced execution. Because she wants to protect the right of the elderly to receive the care that is best for them, it seems likely that she would campaign for protections against coercion. Choice B is a strong answer. The author does care about individual choice, but because she does not appear to favor one treatment over the other, it is not clear that she would oppose legalization of physician-assisted suicides. Choice C is a weak answer. While the author takes a stance about what she considers "humane," choice D borrows language from the description of the Fair Innings theorists. This choice cannot be eliminated on that basis because the author and the Fair Innings theorists may have some overlapping viewpoints. It is unclear whether the author would support or oppose this measure in the first place, and her chief concern is not the availability of tolerable deaths but rather the ability of the elderly to choose their care. For those reasons, choice D is weaker than choice C.

32. **C is the best answer.** There are two strategies for tacking this problem. It is possible to reread the passage, looking for explicit answers to three of the four questions in the answer choices. That would take far too much time. Instead, use the main ideas of the passage to determine which questions the author answered explicitly. The passage concludes by arguing that total independence is a fiction since human beings go through periods of frailty. The author does not believe any human is totally independent, or autonomous, so choice A can be eliminated. The author never states outright that the elderly are entitled to unlimited healthcare expenditures, so choice B could be very tempting. Consider her viewpoints on the Fair Innings theorists, though. They argue for rationing healthcare. The author thinks that any talk of rationing healthcare overlooks the obligation of the young to care for the old. Because the author does not believe that rationing healthcare should even be entertained, it can be established that she believes the elderly should be able to access unlimited healthcare. Choice B is not a strong answer. Those who support healthcare rationing describe the elderly as a drain on society. Rather than combat this sort of thinking, the author argues that, regardless of their ability to produce or any other qualification, the elderly should be cared for. Because she does not describe whether or not the elderly are productive, the author does not answer the question in choice C. Choice C is a strong answer. In considering the main themes of the passage, why has the discussion about healthcare rationing even gained momentum? The passage argues that the United States is confronting a debt problem and scarce natural resources. The question in choice D is answered, so choice D can be eliminated.

33. **A is the best answer.** Another way of asking this question is, "If the author were in charge of the country, what could be expected to happen?" Of the various viewpoints represented in the passage, none appear to disagree that costly medical interventions extend life by at least a little. The disagreement arises over whether the benefits of those interventions justify their costs. Because it appears that the author would support universal provision of costly medical interventions that prolong life, her policies would likely increase the life expectancy of the country. Choice A is a strong answer. The author's argument does not address how her policy positions would be funded – perhaps she would increase revenues, or perhaps she would allocate resources from other programs. What would happen to the national debt with expansive access to healthcare is uncertain. The national debt is not the author's first concern by any measure, but it cannot be concluded from the limited information in the passage that the national debt would go out of control because of her policies. Choice B is not a strong answer. The author limits her argument to care for the elderly. While it seems likely that she would support universal access to unlimited healthcare, she establishes her argument on the premise that younger generations owe older generations healthcare to reciprocate the care they received when they were little. The passage ideas are restricted to care for the elderly and weak. Choice C is not as strong as choice A because it strays beyond the main ideas of the passage. The author does not explicitly oppose palliative treatments. She is concerned that older people can be coerced into receiving palliative care rather than costly life-prolonging interventions. It may be that some patients desire palliative care, and it appears that the author would support their choice. For that reason, it cannot be concluded that funding for palliation would be reduced. Choice D is a weak answer.

Passage 6 (Questions 34-37)

34. C is the best answer. The main idea of the passage is that high-level literacy is required for full participation in a democracy but poverty prevents many people from achieving high-level literacy. This, in turn, hurts democracy. Or, in short: poverty threatens democracy because it sabotages literacy attainment. According to the author, Hoggart suggests that there are three types of literacy: basic, critical, and cultivated. Someone with basic literacy skills can read signs, forms, instructions, simple news articles, etc. Cultivated literacy is the most advanced. It means being able to understand and intelligently respond to complex written language (as in a novel, or a nuanced work of investigative journalism). This is what is required, Hoggart thinks, for a robust democracy. In the middle is critical literacy, which "allows one to identify and dismiss propaganda, immunize oneself against the hard sell, and recognize the verbal cloaks that liars wear." The best answer is the best paraphrase of this description. Choice A suggests that critical literacy is the ability to read for information. This is a better description of basic literacy, so choice A can be eliminated. Choice B says that critical literacy is responsiveness to complexity. This is a better description of cultivated literacy, so choice B can be eliminated. Choice C suggests that critical literacy is sensitivity to the ways persuasive rhetoric operates. This is a good paraphrase of the sentence used to describe critical literacy, so choice C is a strong answer. Choice D might be tempting because the word "critique" sounds like "critical," and the author is clearly concerned about the effect of literacy on democratic society, so the reference to "those in power" might seem attractive. Choice D is a possible answer. However, choice C better matches the description of critical literacy given in the passage. The author specifically names three kinds of persuasive rhetoric: propaganda, the "hard sell," and outright lying. Further, it is not clear whether the author would say that the ability to intelligently critique those in power is a skill enabled by critical literacy, or whether cultivated literacy would be required. For those reasons, choice C is the best answer.

35. A is the best answer. The Matthew Effect, the author says, is a "downward spiral of poor performance and disaffection" that traps children who are not exposed to language as very young children. The author quotes from the Book of Matthew to explain the effect: "For whomsoever hath, to him shall be given, and he shall have abundance, but whomsoever hath not, from him shall be taken, even that which he hath" (Matthew 13:12). The idea seems to be that adult literacy achievement depends greatly on early childhood language acquisition because children who are lacking in language skills when very young do not ever catch up, but instead fall farther and farther behind. The best answer will explain this phenomenon. Choice A says that children who lack language exposure when young will read less later, compounding their weak language skills. This would seem to be an accurate description of the Matthew Effect, so choice A is a strong answer. Choice B suggests that the Matthew Effect is the claim that poor children are locked into a downward spiral of poor performance. This might seem tempting, but it is not quite right. The Matthew Effect has to do with literacy, not poverty, per se. It is true, according to the author, that low-income children are most likely to experience the Matthew Effect, but it is an effect of not being exposed to enough words as a young child, not an effect of poverty itself. Choice B can be eliminated. Choice C says that it concerns the effect of poverty on children's or families' ability to buy books. This would seem to be a related issue, since having money to buy books probably impacts language development, but it is not an accurate description of the Matthew Effect. Choice C can be eliminated. Choice D says that it is the claim that children who hear fewer words when young are more likely to be illiterate as adults. This is a good answer, but it is not as specific as choice A. The Matthew Effect, according to the author, is not merely a correlation between lack of early childhood language acquisition and later illiteracy. It is a process of increasing failure and disaffection, as early gaps in knowledge and ability lead to broader and broader gaps as time goes on. Choice A is the strongest answer.

36. B is the best answer. The author seems to agree with Hoggart's idea that a high level of literacy is required for advanced participation in a democracy. However, the author also faults Hoggart for failing to ask why different people attain different levels of literacy. The author's attitude toward Hoggart is mixed. Choice A describes the author as uncertain about Hoggart. The author's views on Hoggart are mixed, but this does not mean he is uncertain. The author seems certain that Hoggart is right to say that cultivated literacy is important for a mature democracy, and he seems equally certain that Hoggart should have asked why not everyone is able to attain cultivated literacy. Choice A can be eliminated. Choice B describes the author as ambivalent. Since the author approves of some things Hoggart says and faults him for some things he fails to say, it is accurate to say that he is ambivalent about Hoggart. Choice B is a strong answer. Choice C suggests that the author is approving. The author is somewhat approving, but also somewhat critical, so choice C is a possible answer, but a weak one. Choice D suggests that the author is neutral about Hoggart. The author is not neutral. He thinks Hoggart is right about the need for high-level literacy, but that he failed to ask an important question about how different people achieve high-level literacy or fail to achieve it. Choice D can be eliminated. The strongest answer is choice B.

37. **D is the best answer.** The claim that cultivated literacy is required for mature democracy rests on the assumption that mature democracy cannot be achieved without all or most citizens achieving a very high degree of literacy. The author also appears to be assuming that universal cultivated literacy is very likely to yield a mature democracy, since it would raise the level of political conversation. The best answer will challenge one or the other of these assumptions. Choice A suggests that most people vote for candidates in their own political party. The author would likely say that this is because most people are not sufficiently literate to make political decisions based on more complex factors. This does not appear to undermine the author's claim. Choice A can be eliminated. Choice B says that most political speeches are delivered using vocabulary a 12-year-old can understand. This implies that high-level literacy is not required to understand most political speeches. Perhaps they are delivered using simple vocabulary because most citizens lack the literacy skills to adequately comprehend more complex speeches suited for a mature democracy. This does not undermine the author's claim. Choice B can be eliminated. Choice C says that some of the most highly literate societies are not democracies, but instead are monarchies. This challenges the author's assumption that cultivated literacy is likely to yield a mature democracy. However, the author does not specifically address the question of whether a highly literate society is more likely to be a democracy in the first place. Possibly, the author means just that a universally highly-literate populace is likely to yield a high-functioning, "mature" democracy only if the society is already a democracy to begin with. Choice C is a possible answer. Choice D says that people tend to make political decisions based on emotion, regardless of their level of education. If this were true, then near-universal cultivated literacy might not yield a mature democracy in the way Hoggart and the author believe. If even very literate people still made political judgments based on emotion, then literacy would make little difference to political decision-making or to the quality of the society's democracy. Choice D is the strongest answer.

Passage 7 (Questions 38-41)

38. **A is the best answer.** The author states that dual income families are becoming the norm, but he does not mention whether these households are deciding to have children. Be careful not to reference knowledge not included in the passage when answering CARS questions. Choice A is a strong answer. The author states that school completion rates have increased because of cultural shifts, including the women's rights movement, so choice B can be eliminated. He also writes that inflation has had a strong impact on the need for employment, which has led to more complete schooling for the guarantee of steady wages. Choice C can be eliminated. Educational movements have also promoted school completion; the passage references increased standards and the inclusion of standardized tests to assess student achievement. Choice D can be eliminated. Choice A is the best answer.

39. **C is the best answer.** The main idea of the passage is that while there are a number of factors that contribute to students dropping out of primary and secondary school, pull factors—for example financial concerns, the need to find and keep a job, family changes, and health problems—are the main culprit. The author addresses push and falling out factors as well as part of the passage's spectrum, but his major conclusion is that both male and female students primarily leave school because of reasons intrinsic to themselves, rather than to the school environment, per se. One of the issues the author raises is the difference in perception of school dropout between administrators and students themselves. He states that administrators attribute lack of school completion to both pull and falling out factors, depending on how far a student has progressed in his or her education; however, according to the author, administrators are not correct in their assessment of this trend, as the reasons they identify for dropout are not actually those that students report. Based on passage information, administrators do not want to admit that certain factors cause dropout because they may reflect poorly on administrators. The author does not argue that administrators do not realize what students are coping with when they decide to drop out; rather, he implies that administrators are aware of the real issues leading to dropout but that they do not want to vocalize those problems. Choice A can be eliminated. Choice B aligns with passage information in part; administrators indeed state that students' reasons for dropping out change over time. However, the passage does not mention whether or not students themselves identify a consistent cause for dropping out. Choice B is a weak answer. According to the passage, administrators do not wish to admit that problems such as students' financial and familial concerns lead to school dropout, as it could then appear that schools are not offering these students sufficient academic support. Choice C is a strong answer. The author implies that administrators can determine the factors most causal for student drop-out but that they simply do not wish to acknowledge those issues; they may articulate that it is difficult to pinpoint a reason, but in fact, they know. Choice D can be eliminated, and choice C is the best answer.

40. **D is the best answer.** The main idea of the passage is that although there are three major categories of causes that lead to school dropout, i.e. push, pull, and falling out factors, students, both male and female, are primarily affected by pull factors . The author's argument ranges across the spectrum that push (i.e. elements of the school environment), pull (i.e. events in the student's life), and falling out (i.e. the student does not feel committed to completing school) factors cause students to leave school. His argument is nuanced; he believes that while push factors impact young men more than young women comparatively, overall , pull factors are most significant in causing all students to drop out of school, either directly or indirectly. Because the passage emphasizes that push factors impact young men more than women, this question asks the test-taker to consider this one statement alongside the passage's conclusion that pull factors are most significant in leading students to drop out. The study's findings would not cause the author to change his opinion about what causes students to leave school. Choice A can be eliminated. According to the passage, administrators, not students, report that the reason students drop out changes over the course of their schooling, from pull to falling out factors. However, administrators seem to identify causes that differ from what actually causes students to leave school. Choice B is a weak answer because the study described in the question stem would not cause the author to change his opinion that pull factors are mostly to blame for school dropout and because the reasoning in the answer does not align with passage information. Based on passage information, the author clearly identifies pull factors as the major cause for dropout, although he identifies all three categories as potential contributors (thus creating the passage spectrum). Choice C is a weak answer. The described study would not cause the author to change his opinion about what causes students to drop out because he already argues that they are chiefly impacted by issues such as personal and familial health concerns, marriage and childbirth, and a need to be employed. Choice D is a strong answer, and it is the best answer.

41. **D is the best answer.** Although the passage states that familial obligations are a common pull factor, it does not suggest that most students are affected by this one reason. In addition, the tone of choice A does not match the author's, as he presents the issue of school completion with a more objective, neutral quality. Choice A is a weak answer. The passage does not state that language barriers or immigration policies contribute to school dropout, although dropout rates are high among immigrant students. Choice B can be eliminated. While the author writes that graduating from secondary school guarantees higher wages and access to more education, he does not state that students who drop out fail to realize this association. Choice C can be eliminated. In contrast, the passage describes dropping out as a major issue prevalent amongst certain culturally and linguistically diverse groups, so choice D is a strong answer. Choice D is the best answer.

Passage 8 (Questions 42-48)

42. **A is the best answer.** The passage argues that artists imbue their work with intentions to influence the thoughts and actions of their audience. The author's argument is that the artist's power is quite limited. The artist can make suggestions to the audience, putting the audience in a trance-like state, but the artist cannot predict the audience members' responses. In other words, the artist has the power to make the audience consider his or her suggestions, but that power does not extend to total control of viewers' reactions. The claims do not appear to be at odds, so choices A and B are stronger than choices C and D. Choice A resolves the apparent discrepancy between these claims on the basis of passage information, so it is a strong answer. The passage concludes by arguing that art obscures perception, but that observation does not resolve the apparent discrepancy between the artist's ability to manipulate and the varied reactions of audiences. Choice C's reasoning actually provides the justification that resolves the discrepancy, but it mistakenly concludes that the claims are at odds on the basis of this reasoning. Choice C is a weak answer. Choice D reiterates the supposed discrepancy from the question stem. It does not use any more information from the passage, and it reaches a conclusion the author would not agree with . Choice D is a similarly weak answer. Choice A is the best answer.

43. **B is the best answer.** When reading questions about the assumptions required by an argument, read the answer choices and consider which one, were it not true, would make the argument crumble. When the argument is toppled by an assumption, that is a signal that the assumption is required for the argument to be valid. As stated in the question stem, the author argues that all art –despite the many differences between artists, their artwork, and their techniques – can be recognized as art. If an artist were not equally skilled as another at giving his or her work meaning, that would not necessarily prevent it from being recognized as art. The passage does not define the qualities that make art recognized as such. Choice A is a weak answer. If some viewers did not know how to recognize art, then they would not know how to distinguish "art" from "not art." It would no longer be true that all pieces of art would be recognized as art by all of humanity. Choice B is a strong answer. "Value" is a separate notion from "meaning." An object without value to most people, like a photograph from one's childhood, could hold plenty of meaning. The author does not address the comparative *value of art*. If some art were not intrinsically valuable, there is no basis in the passage to conclude that these pieces would be less likely to be seen as art. Choice C is a beyond distractor and a weak answer. That all artwork would provoke the same reaction in all viewers would certainly contradict a passage claim – namely, that the same artwork may prompt dissimilar responses in viewers. The author argues that, regardless of their responses, all people recognize art as art. Even if the responses to art were the same, this would not contradict the argument in the question stem. Choice D is a weaker answer than choice B.

44. **D is the best answer.** The quality to which the question's quote refers is some unspoken quality that allows art to be recognized as art. The best answer will likely demonstrate some scenario in which some art is not recognized as art. That modern readers are uninterested in Poe's work and find his characters boring speaks to their reactions to the poetry, but it does not speak to their assessment of the poetry as "not art." The passage author even argues that a viewer may find a work revolting and still consider it art. Choice A does not weaken the author's argument, so it can be eliminated. Choice B speaks to viewers' responses to art and not to their understanding of what is or is not art, so it can be eliminated. An "unremarkable" painting in choice C brings to mind a painting that is either uninteresting to viewers or potentially not considered to be a work of art. The latter meaning could be a strong answer, but the meaning is ambiguous. Hold it for now. In choice D, scholarly critics refuse to publish articles that examine pop artists' music through a critical lens, presumably because they do not think they belong in an art journal. The answer choice itself acknowledges that this music was produced by artists, but the critics refuse to accept it as such. Choice D more directly refutes the quoted argument than does choice C, so it is a stronger answer.

45. **A is the best answer.** The universal quality of art to which the question stem refers is the ability of all art to be recognized as art by everybody, regardless of their reaction to the art. If viewers can distinguish modern art from imitations, that would suggest that there is something fundamentally different about the artists' work that the imitations do not have – perhaps that the imitations do not possess the essence of art. The question then arises: are the imitations not themselves art? If the imitations are not art, then that is very likely the difference the viewers are perceiving. That would lend credence to the argument that people can discern art from that which is not art. If, on the other hand, the imitations are art, then the finding would not give evidence that the ability to recognize art is universal. Choice A is a strong answer because the finding requires this assumption. It is probably true that amateur artists are less skilled than professionals, but in the author's eyes, art is art. It does not matter whether some art demonstrates more skill than another. It is still art. Because the author's argument does not rely on the quality of artwork, choice B is not a detail that needs to be true for this finding to contribute to his point. Eliminate choice B. If amateur artwork, like the passage argues about artwork in general, could also disrupt perception, this reasoning would lend credence to the notion that amateur art is itself art. That conclusion would make the finding in the question stem less pertinent to the author's argument because it would not demonstrate viewers' ability to recognize art. Choice C can be eliminated. If imitation artwork conveyed the meaning of the original artist, that would similarly lend credence to the notion that the imitations are indeed art. The finding in the question stem would not demonstrate the viewers' ability to distinguish that which is art, so choice D is not a strong answer. Choice A is the best answer.

46. **B is the best answer.** To paraphrase Picasso, art has qualities that can be seen as misleading but lead to a further understanding of the truth. The question stem asks how this perspective differs from that of the passage author, who believes that artists can manipulate their audiences, affecting their emotional or psychological states. That artists express their true convictions in their work is not necessarily a claim that either Picasso or the passage author refutes. The passage author argues that artists make their pieces with some intention. He neither argues that the intention is to tell the truth or mislead viewers, so whether artists' convictions are true is not an argument in the passage. Choice A can be eliminated. Picasso finds that art reveals some absolute notion of truth to viewers, whereas the passage author believes that art merely stimulates the mindset of viewers. Picasso's argument contradicts that of the author – viewers reach some conclusion independent of the artist. While the author does not argue that artists control viewers' responses, he does argue that viewers' responses are fundamentally conditioned by the artist. Choice B is a strong answer. The author argues that art blurs perception. Choice C is a slight mischaracterization of the author's argument, but more importantly the Picasso quote does not refute that argument. Choice C can be eliminated. That art facilitates the discovery of deeper truths is certainly consistent with the Picasso quote, but the author never claims that artists' audiences learn more about truth. Choice D does not contradict a passage argument so it is a weaker answer than choice B.

47. **A is the best answer.** This question stem presents a situation that challenges an assumption of the passage – namely, that every work of art is created with the intention to impose a viewpoint or suggestion on viewers. To determine how the author might react to a statue without subjective underpinning, look to the author's justification of this assumption. In the fourth paragraph, the author argues that a work of art devoid of an artist's subjective intent is "pointless." The author does not rule out the possibility that art can be created without an underlying message, but he suggests that doing so is without creative merit. Choice A appears to be a strong answer. Because, from the author's perspective, it is possible to create art without subjective elements, the author would be unlikely to disqualify the sculpture as art on that basis alone. The passage also suggests that viewers have responses to art that often differ from the response the artist intended. Viewers would react to this sculpture even if it lacked an artist's message. Choice B is a weak answer. Like any work of art, the sculpture would receive varied reactions from viewers, so choice C can be eliminated. Because the author leaves open the possibility that artwork can be created without a message from artists, it is unlikely that the author would suggest that all art must somehow embody a message from its creators. Choice D is a weaker answer than choice A.

48. **C is the best answer.** Although "liminal" is not a common term, it appears beside "subliminal" in a sentence, which suggests a contrast between the terms. "Subliminal" refers to stimuli that affect behavior below the level of consciousness. If "liminal" is an opposite term, and the question stem asks for the least liminal element, the strongest answer will be the most subliminal element of a painting. Although the symbolism of the general and suitors are not clear from choices A and B, respectively, these are images in a painting that would draw a viewer's attention. They do not appear to be subliminal, so these answers can be eliminated. Choices C and D both describe inanimate objects. If clouds drift in the background, they are not featured prominently. The use of the word "ominous" in choice C, moreover, suggests that these clouds carry a strong suggestive meaning. These are both features of subliminal elements, so choice C appears to be a strong answer. While a bowl of fruit may or may not draw a viewer's attention in a painting, its symbolic meaning is unclear. Subliminal messages make suggestions to viewers without being overt. The meaning of the fruit is less clear than the ominous clouds, so choice D is weaker than choice C.

Passage 9 (Questions 49-53)

49. **B is the best answer.** The main idea of the passage is that the commercialization and marketing of HPV vaccines has misconstrued and undermined the importance of the vaccine as a public health intervention, especially as the marketing campaigns fail to address population health concerns such as accessibility and equity. The author believes that public health education is necessary for the well-being of the population and could rectify some of the problems caused by HPV marketing campaigns. Choice A opposes the author's argument, which makes this answer a contrary distractor. Choice B puts public health education in a positive light. Since the author speaks to the value of parental education in relation to the HPV vaccine, this is a promising answer. Choice C favors public education, so it seems to be a strong answer. Choice B is better than choice C, though, because the passage does not indicate that the author thinks stakeholders are intentionally seeking to undermine campaigns, just that they are manipulating the information provided. Public health education is a tool to aid the decision-making process, but more education and scientific information does not guarantee that the population will make certain decisions. Further, the author focuses on the messages being provided rather than the ultimate effect on the health literacy of the population. For these reasons, choice D can be eliminated.

50. **D is the best answer.** The parental dilemma illustrated in the passage is the struggle of parents to make decisions for their children that will ultimately benefit their health, without sending an inappropriate message of acceptance of sexual behavior at a young age. The author believes that current ad campaigns are causing parents to avoid the vaccine because they fear it will result in promiscuous behavior in their children. In choice A the teen has a history of the potentially detrimental behavior, so the risk assessment is not the same as with vaccinating pre-teens not yet exposed to sexual behavior. Choice A can be eliminated. In choice B is there is no promised benefit to the child, and the potential benefit is social rather than medical. This does not closely fit the parental dilemma from the passage, so it is not a strong answer. In choice C the action could lead to risky health behaviors, but not ambiguously moral behaviors. Choice C can be eliminated. In choice D the marijuana provides health benefits but could possibly lead to taboo behavior such as other drug use, making choice D the best answer.

51. **A is the best answer.** Part of the main idea of the passage is that commercial marketing campaigns undermine the work of population health, which includes aspects such as accessibility and equity. The public health advocates want to raise awareness about HPV and the vaccine so the population can make informed decisions about their health, in the hopes of affecting the greatest amount of people for the greatest amount of good. Vaccination is a simple and time-limited way to stop the spread of disease, so choice A is a compelling answer. Advocates would still be worried about the spread HPV of and accessibility to treatment, so choice B can be eliminated. A cheaper health measure is easier to sell to the public, so choice C appears to be viable. However, HPV could re-occur, requiring a second round of treatment, whereas the vaccine is only required once, so choice A is a better answer than choice C. The vaccines are a more easily distributed health measure. The non-sexually active population would not immediately be affected, since they will not have been exposed to HPV, so choice D can be eliminated.

52. **C is the best answer.** This question can be answered by placing the author on the spectrum from profit-motivated companies to selfless public health workers. The passage provides a range of opinions, but the rhetoric used, such as placing "profit motives" in opposition to "public health value," places the author on the side of the public health workers. The question can be restated as, "With which of the following statements is the author likely to disagree?" The author would probably agree with choice A, making it a contrary distractor. Choice B does not follow the definition of "social marketing" as presented in the passage and has no bearing on the main idea, so it can be eliminated. The author is likely to disagree with choice C because the author argues that the commercialization of the vaccine is detrimental to public health, and by extension to population health ethics, so choice C is a strong answer. The author does not give an obvious opinion on mandatory vaccines and they are a very extreme course of action for both parties, so choice D is not well-supported.

53. **C is the best answer.** The author's main argument is that public health education and advocacy for HPV vaccines is overshadowed by commercial rhetoric. The tobacco public education campaign in choice A is not directly overshadowed by the commercial, and the author is unlikely to go so far as to say that commercial enterprises directly encourage the adoption of a negative health behavior, so this choice can be eliminated. The racist organization in choice B may not be related to population health in the traditional sense, so this is not a strong answer. In choice C a private good replaces a public good. This is in line with the author's argument, so choice C is a strong answer. In choice D there is not an aspect of education or lack of awareness, so it is not a compelling answer.

TEST ⑥

ANSWERS & EXPLANATIONS
Questions 1–53

ANSWER KEY					
1. A	10. B	19. C	28. A	37. C	46. C
2. A	11. C	20. A	29. D	38. C	47. D
3. D	12. B	21. C	30. C	39. A	48. A
4. D	13. C	22. B	31. C	40. B	49. D
5. B	14. C	23. A	32. D	41. D	50. B
6. C	15. C	24. D	33. A	42. C	51. B
7. C	16. B	25. A	34. B	43. C	52. A
8. D	17. C	26. B	35. A	44. B	53. C
9. A	18. B	27. C	36. D	45. A	

EXPLANATIONS FOR TEST 6

Passage 1 (Questions 1-7)

1. **A is the best answer.** While the author ultimately believes that modernist ideals can be useful in building a sustainable future, critics' viewpoints are also acknowledged. The passage sets up a spectrum where modernism's critics describe it as a veil for harmful power structures, while others characterize it as a movement to build a more just society. The author concludes that modernism can adapt by focusing on resource preservation, falling more toward the side of the spectrum that believes modernism can be beneficial. In the second paragraph, in an effort to address the viewpoint of modernism's critics, the passage presents numerous examples of the deleterious effects modernism has had on human society, especially under authoritarian regimes, so choice A is likely. Although the author implies the statement in choice B, this idea is never really fleshed out by examples, so that answer is less supported. Choice C is not necessarily supported by the author – while the success of the Welfare State is "overshadowed in media representations" by its less successful effects, it is unclear how widely this opinion is held. It is a weaker answer and can be eliminated. Choice D can also be inferred, but no example or explanation of modernization's environmental impacts is provided . Choice D can be eliminated, and choice A is the best answer.

2. **A is the best answer.** The author is arguing that, rather than rejecting modernism on the basis of its sometimes oppressive legacy in some parts of the world, we should instead strive to translate its emphasis on improving human wellbeing to the movement to sustain natural resources that improve quality of life. Choice A weakens that claim because it undermines the author's assumption that the use of natural resources necessarily improves the standard of living, so it is a strong answer. Choice B, if true, actually weakens the argument of modernism's critics and strengthens the author's position, so it does the opposite of what the question requires and can be eliminated. Choice C is an argument presented by critics of modernism, as seen in the second paragraph. This choice is less compelling than choice A because the passage already acknowledges this side effect of modernizing. Also note the fact that "some blame" this movement for harmful effects would be unlikely to derail the author's argument; after all, the passage already presents an argument in spite of its dissenters. It can be eliminated. Choice D is tempting because it weakens an argument advanced in the passage – that modernism has worsened human society under authoritarian regimes – but the author, rather than taking that position, merely acknowledges that perspective. Choice D does not weaken the author's main argument , so it is not the best answer. Choice A is the strongest choice among those given.

3. **D is the best answer.** The quotation from the question stem appears in the first paragraph, and although the passage does not really define these power structures, they are nevertheless characterized by hiding behind the veil of something innovative and healthy to mask more insidious motives. Choice A may come close to that idea, but the creation of dangerous neighborhoods was presented as an unintentional side-effect of the social movement that produced the welfare state. The reference to old power structures alluded to ulterior motives, while the negative result of the Welfare State in choice A was not intentional. That choice can be eliminated. Choice B presents a corporation that apparently makes no effort to conceal its desire to implement harmful business practices. The lack of "hiding" makes this scenario different from the power structures in the question stem, so this choice can be eliminated. Choice C alludes to power structures whose harmful effects the passage addresses, but again, the advocacy group does not mask its intention. It can also be eliminated for that reason. Choice D presents a business that purports pro-social goals but has other ends in mind. This choice is most similar to the character of the power structures alluded to in the passage, so it is the best answer.

4. **D is the best answer.** Most CARS passages require readers to consider main ideas, and this passage is no different . The author argues that modernism can be repurposed to enrich the sustainability movement despite the challenges that modernization has presented. Choice A reflects the position of critics of modernism and is not the viewpoint presented in the passage. This choice is a contrary distractor to the question stem and can be eliminated . Choice B alludes to the sustainability movement, but it does not answer the question, which asks about the *modernist* movement in today's context. It is not the strongest answer because it sidesteps the question. Choice C is a position expressed in the passage, but it really addresses the views of modernists rather than the "legacy" of those views. It is a possible answer, but examine the final choice before selecting it. Choice D summarizes the article's main idea, namely, that modernist ideas are still relevant today (its legacy) when applied to the sustainability movement. Because choice D more directly addresses the legacy of the modernist movement itself, it is a stronger answer than choice C.

5. **B is the best answer.** The author argues that the modernist legacy, which some scholars have lambasted, should be reconsidered as human society confronts new challenges of natural resource scarcity. The best answer will likely repurpose something of questionable value to serve new ends. Choice A certainly involves a reconsideration of a prior perception, but it lacks the resolve to use that new perspective in new contexts. It is not the strongest choice for that reason. Choice B involves something outdated but useful and devotes it to a renewed purpose to meet the demands of present society. It seems like a good possibility. Choice C reflects a changed perspective on pre-existing notions, but the change suggested only mitigates the symbol's further harm rather than using it proactively to improve society. Furthermore, the author argues for modernism to play an important role, not to be hidden away. Because this choice is only partially correct, it is not the strongest answer. Choice D also reflects a new perspective on something "longstanding," but the advisor is not recycled for a new purpose; rather, the advisor is replaced. It is a weak choice because it is only partially analogous to the question stem. Choice B presents the best analogy to the argument in the passage, so it is the best answer.

6. **C is the best answer.** Although the idea of the social contract is frequently invoked in public dialogue, it is important to constrain pre-existing notions surrounding this idea to the information presented in the passage. The passage describes a re-envisioning of the social contract that included measures to ramp up various social services, so think about the connection between the social contract and social programs to mitigate hardship as each answer choice is considered. Choice A preys on knowledge readers may have about World War II, but the passage implies that the social contract is related to social programs rather than international accords. Choice B also alludes to wartime, and it can be eliminated by recognizing that the social contract was invoked in the passage in reference to a time *after* the war. Choices A and B are incorrect because they are not related to major ideas discussed in the passage in reference to the social contract. Choice C may not appear to suit the passage at first glance because the passage only discusses what society gives its citizens under the new social contract, but the word "contract" alludes to a two-way agreement. Contracts contain obligations on the part of multiple parties. Choice D is tempting, but again, it does not speak to a truly contractual relationship. The passage, moreover, does not invoke a government's "obligation" to provide these services on any moral grounds. For those reasons, choice D can be eliminated, and choice C is the best answer.

7. **C is the best answer.** When considering an author's tone, take into account the choice of words in the passage. This author argues that the legacy of modernism should not be tarnished by its failures, but he lends critics a fair, thorough (if brief) representation of their views. Choice A would not work because this approach to critics' viewpoints is in no way vitriolic. Choice B is tempting, but ultimately the passage disagrees with the degree to which critics take modernism to task . The author's viewpoint on the legacy of modernism is unambiguous at the end of the passage; the argument does not suggest a "tentative" stance but rather a firm (if respectful) disagreement with the critics. Choice B is not the best answer because it mischaracterizes the author's argument as less resolute than it is laid out in the passage. Choice C is a good choice because the passage lightly disagrees with the critics while still giving them the respect of a kind portrayal. Choice D is unlikely because the author never employs language that indicates hurt. Choice C most accurately characterizes the language of the author and is the strongest answer.

Passage 2 (Questions 9-13)

8. **D is the best answer.** The author strongly believes that a human organ market would have major benefits. They mention the opposition to the proposal so that readers know the potential risks of a human organ market. The author does not suggest these opposing beliefs are unjustified, since the passage does not specifically address and disprove the concerns. The author would not call the concerns unjustified, since they later discuss the lack of adequate information and negative outcomes from organ donations in India and Iran. Choice A is not a strong answer. Although potential arguments for unethical aspects of a human organ market are listed in the first paragraph, the author does not suggest agreement with those judgments. They believe that the market could save lives and as long as it is regulated, it should maintain quality of care. Because the author argues for the creation of a human organ market, they do not view this practice as unethical. Choice B can be eliminated. The author does not suggest that those beliefs are old, because the passage presents the concerns as current opposition and does not try to argue that they are out-of-date. Choice C is not a strong answer. The author presents the opposing beliefs to show that there could be negative outcomes of establishing this market, but they can be avoided if they are considered throughout the process. The author thinks the concerns are represent unwarranted assumptions to make since there is no reason to assume that they will all come to fruition. For these reasons, choice D is the strongest answer.

9. **A is the best answer.** Remember that this question is asking about the author's opinion specifically. The author's main concern relates to regulation, because if there is not a competitive market, then the cost of buying a human organ will be too expensive and the demand will not meet the supply. If the market is going to help both patients and donors, then there must be regulations on costs and quality of services. The author also believes that regulation can eliminate some of the concerns raised by people who oppose an organ market. Option I is a strong option and choice B can be eliminated. The author presents other individuals' concerns about the inequality that might be created by a human organ market if only some humans can afford to purchase the organs or if poor individuals donate organs for money without realizing the negative side effects. However, the tone of the passage does not suggest that the author agrees with this concern. The author also proposes that regulation would make this risk acceptable. Option II is untrue and choice C can be eliminated. The author believes that an individual can decide for themselves if the payment is sufficient for the risks of donating an organ in less developed countries, as discussed in the fourth paragraph. The passage does not suggest that individuals will be forced to donate organs there or in more developed countries. Because the author is not primarily concerned that coercion may result from a human organ market, option III lacks support. Choice D can be eliminated and choice A is the best answer.

10. **B is the best answer.** The author argues that although creating a human organ market could be dangerous and presents some ethical concerns, the number of lives saved would outweigh the risks. The best answer choice should relate to this argument specifically. While an increasing death rate from lack of organ availability does suggest that an organ market could be beneficial, it does not provide evidence that the benefits would outweigh the costs. Choice A can be eliminated. If countries with black markets for human organs experience lower death rates from organ unavailability, then the sale of organs is associated with more lives saved. This supports the author's argument because it relates directly to a benefit of a human organ market, so choice B is a strong answer. The statement in choice C does not directly support the idea that healthy individuals would be more likely to provide their organs if they were compensated. An organ donation involves a major surgery and lifestyle changes, which are likely more intense risks than participating in a research study. For this reason, choice C is a not strong answer. Even if hospitals have the resources to perform more organ transplants, that statement does not suggest that the overall benefits of a human organ market outweigh the costs. Choice D does not directly support the author's argument. Choice B is the best answer.

11. **C is the best answer.** The author criticizes the current practice of donating organs after death because the organs are often not healthy, and more importantly, family members usually object or cannot agree, delaying the process until the organ is no longer viable. The author does not suggest that more family members should be involved in the process or that some family members feel left out of the decision. Choice A is not supported by the passage. The author proposes that the family should actually make money if an individual is paid to donate an organ after death, which does not correspond to the process being too expensive. Choice B can be eliminated. The author stresses that when the family disagrees or objects to the donation, it can lessen the success of the donation. If a family cannot agree where to vacation, they may never actually go on the vacation. Choice C presents a reasonable analogy, and is a strong answer. If a family does not plan well and is rushed at the airport, their blunder is not caused by indecision or disagreement, which are often the causes of problems in organ donation after death. This answer choice might be selected based on the fact that organ donations have to occur quickly, but the author's criticism is most directly related to indecision rather than speed. Because choice C describes an indecision that jeopardizes the outcome, it is more relevant to the author's criticism than choice D. Choice C is the best answer.

12. **B is the best answer.** The author stresses that a human organ market cannot be limited to one organization or there will not be regulations to ensure quality of service and proper payment. However, the passage does not focus on the actual regulations that can ensure quality. It is unknown whether the author would support or oppose this specific legislation. Choice A is not a strong answer. If the government controlled the price of organs, they would be the only agency in the market. Because the author believes a competitive market would result in the best outcome, they would likely oppose this situation. Choice B is a strong answer. Health insurance is not mentioned in the passage. Since there is no way to determine how a human organ market would affect health insurance, choice C is not the best answer. Remember that questions in the CARS section are limited to the information provided in the passage. While the author might oppose less government spending on health care, this is not suggested by the passage since it does not discuss government spending. According to the passage, the money for organs would come from competitive agencies, not the government. Choice D does not relate to the author's argument, so it can be eliminated. Choice B is the best answer.

13. **C is the best answer.** Throughout the passage, the author argues that a human organ market would benefit donors with monetary support and patients with healthier organs that are delivered to them more quickly. They believe that the medical benefits outweigh the risks or ethical concerns. Even if donors do not feel as fulfilled as they expected, they still successfully donated organs that helped another individual, so the author's argument would not be affected. Choice A can be eliminated. Even if most individuals report they do not support the idea of a human organ market, there are still some individuals who would support it and donate, and those donations could positively impact the lives of many individuals. Additionally, it is not possible to predict how individuals would actually react if the market were established and normalized, because their opinions might change. Choice B is not a strong answer. If the death or complication rate increases when a hospital performs more organ donations, then establishing a market could do more harm than good. The higher rate of organ donations would not yield greater medical benefit, so choice C is a strong answer. Even if scientists are close to creating artificial organs with new technology, they likely could not be sold to the public for years and would likely be too expensive for most individuals. A human organ market could still be beneficial to the public in this case, so choice D is not as strong as choice C.

Passage 3 (Questions 14-17)

14. **C is the best answer.** The passage presents a spectrum of the benefits of female principals versus male principals. The author does not suggest that one gender is better than the other at this career, because they present the varying strengths of each. The author would not likely suggest that a woman should not pursue a career in this field, since the passage shows that female principals can succeed. Choice A can be eliminated. While choice B is a tempting answer, the passage actually suggests that female teachers, like male teachers, prefer working for male principals. There is no reason to assume that a female principal is more likely to succeed if she works with female teachers instead of male teachers, so choice B can be eliminated. The author argues that women can be effective as principals when they are working with certain populations, such as younger children, students of lower socioeconomic status, or involved and enthusiastic parents. If a woman applies to jobs serving these populations, then she is more likely to succeed as a principal. Choice C is a promising answer. While the author describes male principals as more assertive and aggressive, they do not suggest that women should try to adopt these characteristics, since their own strengths come from different traits like compassion and sensitivity. Choice D is not suggested by the passage, and choice C is the best answer.

15. **C is the best answer.** The passage discusses the different strengths of male and female principals that were studied because of the No Child Left Behind Act. The author introduces the National Defense Education Act to compare its scope as an education reform bill to that of No Child Left Behind. The passage not suggest that NCLB was inspired by NDEA, and the acts were established almost 50 years apart. Choice A is not a strong answer. The passage mentions the belief that Black students, particularly male ones, were struggling due to the "feminization" of public schools with female principals. The passage does not suggest this belief is necessarily true, since the author later lists the strengths of female principals and does not explicitly state that male principals interact with Black students better. Choice B can be eliminated. The author points out that the No Child Left Behind Act intended to improve school performance by focusing on school principals and the effects they have on an entire school. Choice C is a possible answer, even if it seems counterintuitive. The author describes the goal of NCLB as increasing school performance, but the passage does not evaluate how successful the act has been in this regard. There is insufficient support for choice D, leaving choice C as the strongest answer.

16. **B is the best answer.** The author believes in the influence of principals on student and teacher performance. Given the discussion of negative beliefs about feminization of schools, choice A is a possible answer. The author believes that the gender of a principal is an influential characteristic, but the passage also discusses the influence of every principal, regardless of gender. The author opens their argument by describing principals as the thrusters steering a spaceship, and concludes their argument by stressing that principals affect both teachers and students in a school. Choice B is a stronger answer than choice A because it is more related to the main idea. The author does not describe the background needed to become a principal, nor do they suggest that teachers often become principals. Choice C can be eliminated. While the author suggests that the No Child Left Behind Act was created in response to the failure of Black male students, they only suggest that this failure could be caused by the feminization of schools. They do not imply that education reform aims to change the feminization trend specifically. Choice D is not supported by passage information. Choice B is the best answer.

17. **C is the best answer.** Throughout the passage, the author stresses the value and influence of principals on student and teacher performance. They describe the No Child Left Behind Act because it focused on improving school performance by targeting school principals. The author compares the legislation to a spaceship and describes the principals as the thrusters guiding the ship in the right direction. Although it is tempting to equate a principal to a captain, the author suggests that the principals lead a school in the right direction—they are not necessarily in the highest position or most influential role in a school network, as there could be a superintendent with more power. Choice A is not the best answer. The author does not explicitly discuss the hierarchy of power in a school network, so there is no reason to assume that a principal is second-in-charge after the captain. Choice B can be eliminated. The author stresses that principals direct schools towards goals, so it is reasonable to compare their role to that of a navigator . Choice C is a strong answer. A principal is probably not similar to a crewman, because there are generally multiple crewmen on a ship but only one principal in a school. Choice D can be eliminated and choice C is the best answer.

Passage 4 (Questions 18-22)

18. B is the best answer. This passage discusses the reasons why decreasing numbers of Canadians attend services at Evangelical churches in the present day. Some scholars believe that Canadians do not feel a sense of belonging to a church, as defined by a need to physically attend services. They do mention the social interactions that can affect a sense of belonging. Option I is outside the scope of the passage, so choices A and C can be eliminated. Other researchers propose that Canadians feel more independent and do not need to consult a higher being as often as in the past. This independence could be described as a change in lifestyle that has affected Evangelical church attendance. Additionally, integration with new cultures by forming friendships with immigrants could contribute to a change in lifestyle. Option II is supported by the passage. While the author states that there are more Canadians who claim they have no religion, that finding does not necessarily mean that fewer Canadians are attending any religious service. Those individuals might not have been attending a religious service even when they claimed to believe in a religion. Additionally, there has been an increase in Eastern non-Christian religions in Canada, so option III does not have strong support from the passage. Choice B is the best answer because it only includes option II.

19. C is the best answer. The passage presents a spectrum of the reasons why Evangelical church attendance has declined in the last sixty years. Some scholars believe that Canadians are more independent and decisive, while others think that Canadians can express their faith from locations other than church. The author ultimately concludes that the feelings of inclusivity and tolerance in Canada have contributed the most to this decrease in church attendance. While some Canadians may view attending church as an unnecessary act, the author does not express similar feelings to that sentiment. The author's assessment of the decline in attendance does not pass judgement on the worth of attendance, so choice A is not supported by the information presented in the passage. The author only discusses friendship and pleasant exchanges with regard to the impact of immigration to Canada and the appreciation of different cultures. The author does not discuss the interactions that occur at church specifically, so choice B is not a strong answer. Some individuals train months for a marathon, while others recognize that dedication but do not feel the same need. Choice C is a strong answer. Nowhere in the passage is being religious equated with growing or becoming one's best self, so choice D brings in assumed knowledge of religion. Since choice D is not supported by the passage, choice C is the best answer.

20. A is the best answer. The author of this passage argues that Evangelical church attendance in Canada has decreased because the citizens are more tolerant of others' beliefs, rather than whole-heartedly supporting every aspect of Christianity. Canadians also feel that they can practice their faith in settings other than religious services. Based on these changes, it is reasonable to describe religion as more individualized now than in the past. Choice A is a promising answer. Even though Evangelical church attendance has dropped, the value of that religion has not necessarily also dropped. Individuals may still value their religion, but for different reasons or in different settings. Choice B is not a strong answer. The author points out that 84% of Canadians still believe in God, and that Eastern non-Christian religions have increased in popularity. Though the final paragraph describes an "emerging secular society," the passage overall does not support the idea that religion does not fit into a secular world. Choice C can be eliminated. The author does not suggest that the religions are constantly expanding, but rather that Christians' views of their own religion and others is changing. Choice D can be eliminated and choice A is the best answer.

21. C is the best answer. The main idea of the passage is that Evangelical church attendance has dropped due to Canadians' enhanced tolerance and acceptance of other beliefs as they have forged friendships with immigrants of diverse backgrounds. The author does not explicitly discuss the Eastern non-Christian religions that have gained popularity in Canada nor does the passage discuss any religious services or practices. While choice A may be a true statement, it is not supported by the passage. Remember not to bring in outside information to CARS passages. The author discusses how Christians' tolerance of other beliefs has increased, but does not discuss that same trend for believers of other religions. It is impossible to compare the religions in this regard, so choice B can be eliminated. The author stresses that immigrants have brought other religions with them, and Evangelical church attendance has declined because native Canadians recognize the importance of immigrants' religious beliefs as well. The author discusses Christianity with regard to native Canadians and Eastern non-Christian religions while referencing immigrants, so choice C is a strong answer. The passage describes how Eastern non-Christian religions are accepted by Canadians who recognize there are many possible paths to God. It is reasonable to assume that Christianity is accepted well in Canada, since the passage states that it is still popular, so the religions do not differ in this regard. Choice D is not the best answer and choice C is the strongest answer.

22. B is the best answer. The passage presents a spectrum of opinions regarding the reasons why fewer Canadians attend Evangelical churches in present day. Some scholars believe that Canadians do not need a physical location to practice faith anymore, or that they are more independent and do not need guidance from higher beings as much. The author believes that the primary factor behind this trend lies in the inclusivity of Canadians resulting from positive interactions with immigrants. While the author discusses this increased tolerance, he does not suggest that Christians are more likely to convert to the other religions, but simply recognize their value for other individuals. Choice A takes the author's opinions too far and can be eliminated. The author points out that this recognition of multiple paths to God has led to more personalized beliefs, so it is reasonable to assume that members of the same religion might have religious practices that are dissimilar. Choice B is a promising answer. The author does not focus on the publicity or religious discussions of Canadian Christians, only on their church-going tendencies. It is impossible to determine how their religious discussions in public compare to those of other Canadians. Choice C is not a strong answer. Even though Canadian Christians are less likely to attend religious services, they do not necessarily believe in their religion any less. Choice D is not supported by the passage, and choice B is the best answer.

Passage 5 (Questions 23-28)

23. **A is the best answer.** Throughout the passage, there is a spectrum of beliefs presented regarding the cause of NCDs. Some individuals attribute the diseases simply to personal failures, while others propose that multiple factors could play a role. The author falls on the latter end of the spectrum. They stress that in order to prevent NCDs, humans must adopt a new perspective about their origin. In the second paragraph, the author points out that NCDs were previously thought of as resulting from gluttony and sloth, which implies that these diseases were the individual's own fault. Choice A is a strong answer. The passage suggests that NCDs were previously viewed as avoidable by altering gluttonous lifestyles, so choice B can be eliminated. While NCDs might be influenced by genes and location, the passage does not imply that those were the main considerations in previous attitudes. In addition, the influence of genetics is more consistent with the author's viewpoint than the "recent" views referenced in the question stem. Choices C and D are not supported by the passage. Choice A is best answer.

24. **D is the best answer.** This question can best be approached by process of elimination. Remember that the author introduces the passage by discussing diabetes as an increasing problem for developed and developing countries. Choice A can be eliminated. The author then suggests that calorie-dense foods and low physical activity, both characteristics of developed countries, can increase an individual's likelihood of developing diabetes. Choice B is not the best answer, since the lifestyle of a developed country can contribute to NCDs. The author does not agree with the individuals who believe personal failure leads to diabetes, but rather falls on the other end of the spectrum. Since the author does not identify a single common cause for the development of diabetes, choice C is not the strongest answer. Throughout the article, the author stresses how many factors can influence the development of diabetes, such as maternal and paternal health in addition to childhood lifestyle. For this reason, choice D is a stronger answer than choice C.

25. **A is the best answer.** The author proposes the idea that childhood habits strongly affect adulthood likelihood of developing diabetes because children maintain more plasticity than adults who are set in their habits. The evidence shows that adults who were obese at one point but lost the extra weight have a lower risk of developing diabetes than adults who are still obese. This shows how environment, or personal choices, can affect the occurrence of NCDs. Choice A is a strong answer. The research shows that adult body weight can be vastly different from childhood body weight, since it considers both non-obese adults who were obese children and obese adults who were non-obese children. Choice B can be eliminated. While bodyweight may be a primary risk factor for diabetes, the author does not cite this study to prove that point, but rather to stress that childhood habits must be addressed for the best prevention of NCDs. Choice C is not a strong answer. The author similarly does not reference developed or developing countries in this context, so choice D can be eliminated. Choice A is the best answer.

26. **B is the best answer.** Throughout the passage, the author stresses the importance of breaking bad habits while children are still young before they reach the constancy of adulthood. While educational brochures might reach a lot of pregnant women, the author argues that the lifestyle changes are more effective when they are taught before pregnancy. Choice A is not the best answer. If educated parents can teach their children to use sunscreen, then it is reasonable that they could teach them how to eat a healthy diet and incorporate physical activity into everyday life. Since the author believes that establishing healthy habits early on would most effectively prevent diabetes in adulthood, choice B is the best answer. Medical trips to developing countries may decrease their rates of diabetes, but they would not decrease rates of diabetes worldwide. Choice C can be eliminated because it does not fully answer the question. The author's tone in the last paragraph suggests that they do not endorse making pregnant women feel self-conscious. The author is also opposed to the view that individuals are personally responsible for their obesity, so it unlikely that their argument would be supported by acts of shame. Choice D can be eliminated.

27. **C is the best answer.** Criticizing the driver for not cleaning his car is similar to the biblical view of NCDs, by emphasizing the importance of the owner's habits. The author does not believe personal failure is the cause of NCDs so they would not agree with a statement that solely faults the car owner. Choice A can be eliminated. The author does not criticize the biblical view for its emphasis on the future, so choice B is not the best answer. The author argues that it is unfair for biblical believers to blame the NCDs entirely on the individual's bad habits, since genetic predisposition greatly affects these diseases. They point out the significance of early life influences, which is similar to the importance of the history of the car and its parts. Choice C is a strong answer. If fault is placed on a driver who has not spent enough money on his car, then the criticism mirrors the biblical view of NCDs that solely blames the individual's choices. Choice C is a better answer than choice D.

28. **A is the best answer.** Throughout the passage, the author stresses that early intervention is the best strategy to implement healthy life choices. If schools can sell cheap junk food to children, then it is likely to influence children's taste preferences and neuroendocrine pathways. The author would be likely to oppose this practice, so choice A is a strong answer. Limiting the amount of food one family can buy in a week could affect many aspects of family life, including social interactions. This proposal does not relate as closely to the author's argument as choice A, so choice B is not the best answer. While the author would be unlikely to support buffet halls at colleges, they may argue that the students are adults and have established habits already. The author would probably not oppose that practice as strongly as choice A. Choice C can be eliminated. The author would likely support choice D, since it could influence the way parents raise their children and would establish an early intervention program. The program would not start until children are about five years old, so the major pitfall of the 1000 Days Campaign would be avoided. Since the author would support choice D, it can be eliminated. Choice A is the best answer.

Passage 6 (Questions 29-35)

29. **D is the best answer.** This question depends on a solid understanding of the author's main idea. Against the claims of several other literary critics, the author sees distinctly Irish qualities in Beckett's body of work from the years following the Second World War. On one side of the spectrum of opinions in this passage are the critics who see Beckett's work as wholly universal. The other extreme would be those who think Beckett is an entirely Irish writer; the author's opinion sits closer to this side of the spectrum than to the other. Since choice A contradicts the author's characterization of Beckett's writing as abstract and intellectual, it can be eliminated. Likewise, choice B has no firm basis in the passage, as the author never discusses acclaim or adoration for Beckett's work, only its critical merit. Neither choice A nor choice B is related to the author's main point that Beckett's Irish nationality influenced his work throughout his career. Choice C reduces the author's main idea to one side of the spectrum of positions in the passage. In most cases, such extreme answer choices are distractors. In contrast to choice C, choice D matches the author's position on the spectrum: on neither extreme, but closer to the side that acknowledges the Irish qualities in Beckett's work. Choice D is the best answer because it comes closest to the author's position along the spectrum.

30. **C is the best answer.** The author discusses previous scholarship of Beckett's work as lacking in its consideration of the Irish qualities of his writings. The author cites attitudes of *ressentiment* as evidence that Beckett's work contains Irish elements. Though the author states that *ressentiment* imparts a certain Irish quality to Beckett's work, he does not claim that this quality was either historically more common in Ireland or unique to the Irish. Because choice A suggests that there is a historical preponderance of *ressentiment* in Ireland, it can be eliminated. Similarly, choice B makes the claim that *ressentiment* is uniquely Irish—a more extreme version of choice A—so it too can be eliminated. Choice C matches well with the author's belief that the Irish qualities of Beckett's work have not been adequately addressed, so it is a strong answer choice. Choice D suggests that *ressentiment* is the main characteristic of Beckett's work when the author only argues that *ressentiment* is one Irish facet of Beckett's style. Answer choices like choice D distract attention away from the best answer by going beyond the scope of the passage or otherwise exaggerating the author's position. Choice C is the best answer because it accurately summarizes the author's point that attitudes of *ressentiment*, which the author identifies as an Irish trait in Beckett's work, have been overlooked in previous scholarship.

31. **C is the best answer.** The author introduces a discussion of begrudgery to previous scholarship of Beckett's work, and uses it as evidence of the Irish quality of that work. The author is arguing, in a sense, with earlier scholars about whether Beckett should be considered an Irish writer. The discussion of begrudgery serves only as evidence within that argument. Option I identifies begrudgery as the main point of contention between the author and the other scholars rather than approaching it as a piece of evidence within that argument. Choice A can be eliminated. Option II accurately characterizes the debate between the author and the "critical orthodoxy" as having to do with the Irish qualities in Beckett's work. Choice D can be eliminated. Option III mistakes evidence within the argument for the argument itself, so choice B can be eliminated. Choice C, which includes only option II, is the best answer.

32. **D is the best answer.** By including information about Nietzsche's "creature of *ressentiment*," the author elaborates on their own concept of begrudgery. The citation from Gilles Deleuze provides explicit information about the "faculty of forgetting nothing" of the "man of *ressentiment*," which provides evidence that holding a grudge is one aspect of *ressentiment*. *Ressentiment*, in turn, is an aspect of begrudgery, the sociological phenomenon that the author identifies as an Irish element in Beckett's writing. Choice A is overly general in its explanation of Moran's statement, suggesting that qualities of *ressentiment* are central to the Irish literary character when the author only states that they are one aspect of that character. Answer choices like choice A that make broad, overarching statements appear frequently on the MCAT®. While they may seem relevant to the passage, they often serve to distract attention away from the best answer. Choice B, on the other hand, is too specific. While it is probably true that Moran is resentful in *Molloy*, that does not explain Moran's underlying character, and so does not answer the question. The best answer for an MCAT® question will both be true according to the passage and answer the question. Choice C provides an extreme characterization for Moran, suggesting that begrudgery is a dominant aspect of his character. In contrast, choice D states only that Moran embodies aspects of *ressentiment*, which is consistent with the quote in the question stem. On the MCAT®, answer choices that use extreme language distract attention away from the best answer by appearing to align with the author's position, but in an exaggerated or otherwise manipulated way. Choice D is the best answer because it is true according to the passage, answers the question, and avoids extreme language.

33. **A is the best answer.** The question asks for the statement that provides the best evidence *against* the author's claims about Ireland's influence on Beckett. The author claims that Ireland remained influential on Beckett's work throughout his career, even in his later works. Contradictory evidence for this claim would demonstrate that the literary qualities associated with Irish influence diminished in Beckett's later works. Choice A states that envious characters were not present in Beckett's later works. This is a strong answer because it suggests a diminished presence of begrudgery which, for the author, would also mean the diminishing influence of Ireland. Choice B can be eliminated as it does not contradict the author's claim: it is possible that Beckett wrote Irish themes in French. The use of Irish names in Beckett's novels points to the influence of Ireland, so choice C can also be eliminated. Since Beckett could have considered himself a universalist and yet still have been influenced by Ireland, choice D does not demonstrate a diminished Irish influence as well as choice A. Choice A is thus the best answer because it provides the clearest evidence to contradict the author's belief that Ireland continued to influence Beckett throughout his career.

34. **B is the best answer.** The question asks for a generalization concerning the author's approach to sociology and literature based on a close reading of the passage. The author's discussion of begrudgery as a sociological phenomenon indicates that they think sociology is an important element of literary scholarship. Choice A contradicts the author's apparent position that sociology is important to literary scholarship, so it can be eliminated. In contrast to choice A, choice B suggests that a "thorough understanding" of a piece of literature can be attained in part from considering the sociology surrounding that literature, aligning with the author's belief that sociology is important to consider when discussing literature. Choice C takes the author's opinion too far, suggesting that sociology is the most important lens through which a piece of literature can be examined, a claim that the author does not make. The author likely agrees that Beckett critics have *some* understanding of his work, even if they are less familiar with the sociology of the Irish. On the MCAT®, the answer choice with less extreme language—in this case "important" as in choice B rather than "central" as in choice C—is more likely to be the best answer. The fact that the author does not discuss other writers does not mean the author would not consider sociology important to understanding their work as well. There is not enough information in the passage to determine how the author would approach the works of other writers. Choice D does not have enough basis in the passage to make it a valid claim, so it can be eliminated. On the MCAT®, the best answer choice will both answer the question and be valid according to the passage. Choice B is the best answer because it most closely aligns with the author's position that sociology is an important aspect of literary scholarship.

35. **A is the best answer.** The question asks for an application of a central concept in the passage—begrudgery—to a context outside of literature. The passage describes a few specific characteristics of begrudgery, one of which is jealousy. Choice A is a strong answer because it applies jealously, an aspect of begrudgery mentioned in the passage, to answer the question. Because the author never explicitly discusses how begrudgery manifests in the dialogue of *Molloy*, choice B does not have a basis in the passage and can be eliminated. Choice C resembles information presented in the first paragraph concerning Beckett's work, but does not relate to what the passage says specifically about begrudgery. Choice C does not satisfy the question. Though the author identifies begrudgery as an Irish aspect of Beckett's work, the author never states that begrudgery is uniquely Irish. Choice D inaccurately suggests that the trait of begrudgery is necessarily linked to Ireland, so choice D can be eliminated. Choice A is the best answer because it most clearly adapts information from the passage to the scenario in the question.

Passage 7 (Questions 36-41)

36. **D is the best answer.** Choices A, B, and C could all contribute to individual happiness, and could be true about Shakespearean actors, but they are never suggested by the passage. In the fourth paragraph, the author discusses how reading Shakespeare's works stimulates the brain by forcing it to quickly understand confusing words in familiar contexts. The author later cites how these positive brain waves can help individuals develop happy dispositions. The Shakespearean actors would have to read his work during rehearsals, and then continue to listen to it for months, frequently stimulating those brain waves. Choice D is the best answer.

37. **C is the best answer.** In the first paragraph, the author discusses how *Romeo and Juliet* remains popular today because it uniquely engages the audience. Later, the author discusses how Shakespearean works force the reader to consistently analyze and pay attention to the text. If a study found that *Romeo and Juliet* was not actually more engaging than a non-Shakespearean play, the author's central argument would be weakened. Choice C is the best answer. While the play is popular in high schools, the author does not mention the relatability of the characters or how frequently it is a part of a school curriculum. These statements do challenge the idea that *Romeo and Juliet* is still popular, but they do not directly challenge the author's central claim and are beyond the scope of the passage. Choices A and B are not as strong as choice C. If readers had difficulty understanding the play at first, the author's argument about how much thinking the text requires would be strengthened rather than weakened. Choice D is not the best answer.

38. **C is the best answer.** Although people live their lives differently depending on their environment, this statement does not explain the lifestyle of most Shakespearean professionals, as they could still reside in completely different cultures. Choice A is not the strongest answer. There is no reason to assume that actors, directors, or designers associated with a Shakespearean performance must be older, so choice B can be eliminated. In the fourth paragraph, the author describes the challenge that Shakespeare poses to the brain by forcing it to consider new possibilities and constantly keeping it "on its toes." It is reasonable to assume that the adventure posed by dramatic works carries over into personal life, as the brain adjusts to adapting to new stimuli. Choice C is the best answer. The author does not state that adventure helps alleviate depression, but rather that drama does, so choice D is also not the best answer.

39. **A is the best answer.** Ackerman stresses that all thoughts, sensations, and desires stem from the brain. Since she uses such exaggerated language in the quotation, Ackerman wants to remind individuals how complex the brain is, presumably because it is often taken for granted. Choice A is supported by the passage. Ackerman does not mention that the body must be functioning for the brain to be important, so choice B can be eliminated. Similarly, she does not stress the differences between bodies, but rather the complexity of the brain. Choice C can be eliminated. It is the passage author, not Ackerman, who states that more research should be done about the brain, so choice D can be eliminated. Choice A is the best answer.

40. **B is the best answer.** This question requires a close reading of the author's word choice and tone when describing the puzzles. The author discusses how keeping the brain "fit" is a cliché, and it seems as though every business is marketing their own model. The passage specifically states how the products are "mass-produced" and seems to list out the possibilities with disdain. The author thinks these puzzles are created simply to be sold, and that they are advertised to help the brain stay "fit" but are not supported by science, like reading Shakespeare. Choice A can be eliminated and choice B is the best answer. The author does not seem to think these puzzles are successful for any individuals, as the passage does not mention any responses to or results from the products. Choice C can be eliminated. Because the author describes the games with a disapproving tone, choice D is not the best answer.

41. **D is the best answer.** Although the passage mentions the brilliant costumes from *Romeo and Juliet*, the author does not stress their importance as much as language in the play's success. Choice A is not the best answer. While choice C is an appealing answer, it would actually allow the audience to forget about the language and just watch the actions. This would not keep them as mentally stimulated, and in the author's opinion, would not result in as successful of a performance. Choice C can be eliminated. The author stresses how stimulating the text from a Shakespearean play can be. By having to figure out what each word means, the play keeps readers engaged. In order to keep audience members engaged, actors need to enunciate their lines well so the audience can follow along and keep stimulating their brains. Choice D is the best answer. Experienced actors may be able to enunciate better than novice actors, but choice B does not relate as directly to the author's arguments about language as choice D. Choice D is a better answer than choice B.

Passage 8 (Questions 42-46)

42. **C is the best answer.** The passage presents a spectrum of characteristics of metafiction, ranging from self-conscious language to challenging the distinction between reality and fiction in characters' own lives. Ian McEwan falls on the latter end of the spectrum, describing the tragedy of one character's blunder. He does not suggest that the character is dishonest or purposefully lying about the incident in *Atonement*, so choice A is not a strong answer. Similarly, he does not suggest that Briony's personal bias influences her interpretations of the events. Choice B is not a particularly strong answer since it is not explicitly discussed in the passage. McEwan attributes the tragedy in the novel to Briony's wild imagination and failure to take the facts into account. Although choice C may not seem like an obvious societal critique, it does encompass McEwan's concerns regarding fact and fiction. Choice C is stronger than choice B since it is more directly in line with the author's point regarding McEwan's metafiction. McEwan does not specifically blame Briony's storytelling for the incident, since storytelling can involve recalling the truth. Choice D does not necessarily involve imagination or fantasy, so it is not as strong an answer as choice C.

43. **C is the best answer.** The author discusses the characteristics of metafiction in the spectrum of the passage because McEwan examines the line between fact and fiction more so than other authors. While the author mentions respected postmodern writers in the British literary pantheon, the passage does not suggest that writers utilize metafiction simply to be compared to those successful authors. Choice A assumes too much from the information presented in the first paragraph. The author mentions how influential postmodern writing can be, but later specifies how it influences readers. Choice B is too general to be a strong MCAT® answer. The passage points out that authors use metafiction to influence readers to inspect both their own perceptions of reality and fiction and the juxtaposition of the two. Choice C is more specific than choice B and directly aligns with a main idea of the passage. While authors often utilize metafiction to question fantasy and reality, they do not go so far as to question man's existence. Choice D is too extreme and takes the argument too far. Choice C is the strongest answer.

44. **B is the best answer.** The author argues that McEwan took metafiction to the extreme by examining the relationship of reality and imagination in the process of writing. They point out that one person's reality may be influenced by external factors, so that people actually "create" their own reality. This is comparable to creating a reality for a fictional character, so the best answer will likely involve an artist constructing an original storyline. Do not get distracted by the works of the art described, as the concept applies to any form of storytelling. A dancer performing a classic piece is not creating a new reality, so choice A can be eliminated. If a director is in charge of a new movie, then it is reasonable to assume that he or she is creating the reality of the original characters. Choice B is a promising answer. If an actor is reprising a role, then he has already created that character's reality years ago and is not currently composing reality. Choice C is not a strong answer. Similarly, a screenwriter adapting an old movie may be altering the reality of the characters, but did not create it. Choice D can be eliminated and choice B is the best answer.

45. **A is the best answer.** The author discusses McEwan's novel *Atonement* to exemplify the metafictional concept of confusing imagination for reality. The situation is described as one that gets out of hand due to a misunderstanding caused by misinterpretation based on Briony's fictional writing. It is reasonable to assume that women may have more active imaginations if they understand Briony's situations because their own imaginations may have gotten them into similar situations. Choice A is a promising answer. Reading more metafiction does not necessarily mean that an individual will have a greater appreciation or understanding of it. It is impossible to determine if reading more metafiction would influence one's feelings towards this situation, so choice B can be eliminated. Fiction writers may have active imaginations and experience sympathy for a character caught up in her own confusion of reality and fiction, but choice C does not specify that women are more likely to become fiction writers, just writers in general. Choice C is too general of an answer. While women may be more sympathetic than men in general, that is not discussed nor suggested by passage discussion, and cannot be assumed as true. Remember not to bring in outside information or personal bias to answer the question. Choice D can be eliminated and choice A is the strongest answer.

46. **C is the best answer.** The author discusses the characteristics of metafiction throughout the passage, and focuses on the work of Ian McEwan because he so successfully utilizes the devices of metafiction. In the beginning of the passage, the author mentions McEwan's multiple awards and the respect he has earned in the literary community. Choice A can be eliminated. The passage details the intertwining of imagination and the retelling of events when describing the plot of *Atonement*. Choice B can also be eliminated. While the author discusses the complicated relationship of reality and fiction in storytelling and writing, the passage does not relate that complexity to any other forms of art. Additionally, the author does not expand upon the theory of writing or how it has changed. Choice C is a strong answer as it is not supported by passage discussion. The author devotes an entire paragraph to discussing how creating a reality, like writing metafiction, is similar to a person's own reality, as they are both a combination of truth and fiction. Choice D can be eliminated and choice C is the best answer.

Passage 9 (Questions 47-53)

47. **D is the best answer.** The passage presents a spectrum of theories regarding mate preferences for men and women. While the author believes that men and women may value different traits in long-term partners, they do not think that this theory applies to initial meetings in live settings. The parental investment theory is only discussed with regard to heterosexual couples, so it cannot be determined whether it applies to same-sex couples as well. The passage directly states that parental investment theory applies to heterosexual couples, but this does not necessarily correspond to an assumption that it could not apply to same-sex couples. Choice A is possible, but is not a particularly strong answer. While the author believes that initial feelings of romantic attraction may not follow a pattern and therefore may be difficult to predict, they think that explicit preferences can predict the outcome of long-term relationships or marriages. Choice B may be selected if initial feelings of attraction are confused for long-term romantic attraction. Near the beginning of the passage, the author points out that men value attractiveness in a partner more than women do, but does not say that it is the trait *most* valued by men. Choice C can be eliminated. The main idea of the passage argues that patterns of gender mating preferences are not apparent in live, short-term situations because individuals may not be looking for a long-term partner right away. This argument assumes that individual preferences, rather than overall gendered preferences, are most relevant to live romantic interactions. Choice D is stronger than choice A because it directly relates to the main idea of the passage.

48. **A is the best answer.** The author discusses the concept of parental investment theory because it helps predict the qualities men and women look for in a long-term mate based on the different resources they contribute to ensure the success of their child. According to this theory, women select partners with financial and material resources because these contributions from the father increase the child's likelihood of survival into adulthood. This is the only trait mentioned in regard to women's mating preferences, so it reasonable to assume that the material goods are the father's biggest contribution according to the parental investment theory. Choice A is a strong answer. There is no mention of a father's selflessness in order to ensure childhood survival, so choice B is not supported by the passage. While parental investment theory proposes that men are more likely than women to value attractiveness in a mate, the first paragraph explains that attractiveness conveys information about reproductive health. The passage does not suggest that the attractiveness will be inherited, so choice C is not a strong answer. The first paragraph discusses how men and women face different challenges to reproductive success, but does not expand upon the concept of paternity uncertainty and how it affects a mother's financial support. Choice D may be true, but is not implied by the first paragraph. Choice A is the best answer.

49. **D is the best answer.** The main idea of the passage is that explicit partner preferences only have predictive value for long-term, heterosexual partners. Because the author points out that the theories discussed in the passage apply only to heterosexual couples, it is impossible to determine how the concepts apply to same-sex couples. Choice A and B are not strong answers because the author's argument no longer applies. If a heterosexual couple is being introduced by friends, then they are meeting for the first time. In such a scenario, gut-level preferences would have better predictive value and explicit partner preferences may not be relevant yet. Choice C is not a strong answer. If a heterosexual couple is moving in together, they are likely in a more long-term relationship and explicit partner preferences would have better predictive value. Choice D is stronger than choice C because of the long-term nature of the couple's relationship. Although the complicated wording of this question may make it confusing, the best answer can be determined by eliminating choices that are not addressed in the passage or are not directly in line with the main idea of the passage.

50. **B is the best answer.** The author argues that parental investment theory can predict mating preferences when applied to long-term relationships, but not when applied to short-term situations. Even if a study found that initial feelings of attraction can be predicted by explicit partner preferences, the theory's validity would not be strengthened since the two situations are not related. Choice A can be eliminated. Parental investment theory proposes that women tend to be choosier when looking for a mating partner since raising a child requires a bigger investment from them. If women take longer to decide if an individual can be a potential partner, it would strengthen the claim that women are more selective in mating preferences. Choice B is a promising answer. The parental investment theory would not be strengthened by the finding that men desert their children more often because according to the theory, men contribute material and financial resources to a child. Choice C can be eliminated. In the first paragraph, the author states that women put greater investment into caring for a child. Choice D would not be a new finding, nor would it strengthen the validity of the theory since has already been established. Choice B is stronger than choice D because it would provide *additional* evidence for a concept proposed by the parental investment theory.

51. **B is the best answer.** Because this question is looking for an answer with the LEAST evidence, the best answer will likely be mentioned but not expanded upon in the passage. In the beginning of the passage, the author points out that paternity uncertainty is a challenge to reproductive success that only men face. Choice A is a possible answer since it is an assertion supported only by one example. While the author believes that men choose attractive women to ensure reproductive health, they do not explain exactly how youth and attractiveness convey information about reproductive fitness. This statement is mentioned but not further explained, so choice B is stronger than choice A. Many times throughout the passage the author cites studies showing that women favor partners with social status and resources. Choice C is in line with the main argument of the passage and can be eliminated. Similarly, the author argues that expected mating preferences cannot be seen in short-term, face-to-face encounters, and discusses construal-level theory to explain this divergence. Choice D is also a main argument of the passage and can be eliminated. Choice B is the strongest answer.

52. **A is the best answer.** The author argues that parental investment theory does not predict initial feelings of attraction because people may have different long-term expectations from short-term interactions. Similarly, a woman who valued owning a cat in the abstract may alter her values when she interacts with cats at a pet store. Choice A is a strong answer. A baseball fan who is disappointed may not necessarily alter his values based on that interaction, so choice B is not a strong answer. A coffee drinker changing her order one day may or may not be changing it permanently. Also, this change is unlikely due to abstract expectations or values. Choice C is too general to compare the situation described in the passage. Even if a college student is changing his preferences by switching majors after live interactions, there is no reason to assume that these values differ from abstract or long-term goals. Choice D also does not have enough detail to compare to the situation of changing expectations based on live interactions. Choice A is the best answer.

53. **C is the best answer.** According to parental investment theory, which has been supported by many studies evaluating mate preference in long-term relationships, women value social status and material resources in a partner. While the theory only applies to long-term relationships and the patterns may not be seen in a short marriages, there is no reason to assume that the woman would not expect the marriage to last long. Choice A is a possible answer but is not very relevant to the main idea of the passage. The passage does not suggest that women alter their values in long-term relationships based on their own attractiveness. That trait is only discussed in reference to men's partner preferences, so choice B can be eliminated. If the man was also working for a successful business, then the woman's selection could be explained by the parental investment theory, since she would be more likely to receive financial and material support. Choice C is stronger than choice A because it directly follows the patterns proposed by the parental investment theory. The theory does not discuss love affecting mating preferences, so choice D is not suggested by the passage. Remember not to bring in outside bias or information. Choice C is the strongest answer.

TEST **7**

ANSWERS & EXPLANATIONS
Questions 1–53

ANSWER KEY					
1. D	10. C	19. D	28. C	37. B	46. A
2. B	11. A	20. C	29. C	38. C	47. C
3. A	12. B	21. B	30. B	39. A	48. D
4. A	13. A	22. A	31. D	40. B	49. B
5. D	14. D	23. D	32. A	41. D	50. B
6. D	15. C	24. D	33. D	42. C	51. C
7. B	16. B	25. B	34. A	43. B	52. A
8. C	17. D	26. B	35. C	44. C	53. C
9. C	18. C	27. C	36. D	45. B	

EXPLANATIONS FOR TEST 7

Passage 1 (Questions 1-5)

1. **D is the best answer.** This passage presents a spectrum of various musical activities that can help cement abstract concepts in the minds of children. The author focuses on the benefits of music education in children, but does not suggest that there is a time frame in which the exposure must occur. The passage does not mention any other age groups in the discussion of music education, so choice A cannot be assumed true. While the author emphasizes music creation, they also mention the sociocultural implications of listening to music near the end of the passage. Choice B is too extreme in its wording and can be eliminated. Throughout the passage, the author discusses the various concepts that children can learn by participating in music, but does not discuss intelligence or academic performance in relation to it. Choice C takes the author's argument too far and lacks direct support from the passage. When listing the benefits of music education, the author points out that children learn to balance the various aspects of music, which teaches them about turn-taking. They specifically mention that this can improve classroom interactions because the children have already begun to understand the need for taking turns. Choice D is a reasonable assertion and is the best answer.

2. **B is the best answer.** The author presents a spectrum of activities that can positively contribute to the cognitive development of children, but ultimately focuses on the range of benefits of music education. While the author stresses the importance of these potential benefits, they do not suggest that these benefits are undervalued or unrecognized by the community. The author makes no mention of individuals disputing the claims. Choice A is not supported by the passage. The passage does argue that there is a need for music education to be established within early childhood learning programs, so it is reasonable to conclude that the author believes music education is necessary. Choice B is a strong answer. The author only presents the positive aspects of music education and writes with a supportive tone throughout the passage. Choice C is directly in opposition to the main idea of the passage. While the author compares music-making to artistic endeavors in the beginning of the passage, they do not discuss the specific benefits of art education. They compare the two activities, but not necessarily their formal education processes in learning environments. Choice D is not as strong as choice B because choice B has stronger support throughout the entire passage.

3. **A is the best answer.** Throughout the passage, the author discusses the many benefits of music education for children, ranging from increasing literacy to cementing confidence. While all of the answer choices are positive effects of music education, the question stem asks specifically about benefits that can be experienced by children of all ages. The author opens their argument by stating that music is a resource through which meaning is made, but they discuss this concept in relation to young children. It is reasonable to assume that older children have already established understanding of concrete and abstract concepts. Choice A is too narrow to explain why they focus on gathering musical instruments for all ages. Remember that this question is asking for the answer that LEAST explains the situation in the question stem, so choice A is a strong answer choice. It is reasonable to assume that children of all ages could improve communicational skills through music education, as the passage does not suggest this is age-specific. Choice B can be eliminated. Similarly, the end of the passage points out that music creation fosters creativity in children, and does not discuss this concept with regard to a specific age. Choice C can also be eliminated. The author mentions that music education can help children develop the concept of turn-taking, which can improve classroom interactions. They also stress the sociocultural development that can stem from music engagement, so this benefit could spread to children of all ages. Choice D can be eliminated. Choice A is the best answer, as it is the only positive influence that is specific to young children.

4. **A is the best answer.** The author's primary argument centers around the skills children can develop from actively engaging in music. Children can improve social skills by understanding the concept of turn taking when playing different notes and rhythms. The author also points out that active music engagement is learning through play, so it is reasonable to assume that the preschools in choice A would experience less conflict due to the improved social skills. The author never mentions intelligence or academic achievement in relation to music engagement, so choice B can be eliminated. Middle school students who play an instrument did not necessarily actively engage in music during younger childhood, so their maturity would not necessarily be linked with the author's discussion of music education for children. Choice C is not a strong answer. While the author suggests that music education can increase confidence in children, they do not discuss this finding in relation to teenagers or young adults. Additionally, high school students may not have engaged in music during their formative years, so choice D can also be eliminated. Choice A is the best answer.

5. **D is the best answer.** The main idea of the passage is that music education should be established for children due to its countless developmental benefits. Teachers in charge of the music curriculum can only alter an already-established program; they do not decide whether a school will have a music education program or not. Choice A can be eliminated. Principals who run the daily activities at a school may or may not have control over the establishment of a music education program. Choice B is a possible answer, but is not particularly strong. The administrators who make schedules for students can assign children to music education programs, but cannot necessarily create those programs if they are not already in place. Choice C can be eliminated. The information presented in the passage would be extremely helpful to parents deciding where to send their child to school, because they can learn about the importance of music education and look for schools with strong music education programs. Choice D is stronger than choice B because the parents have the power to decide whether their children receive music education, while a principal may not have that power.

Passage 2 (Questions 6-12)

6. **D is the best answer.** The passage presents a spectrum of opinions regarding the skills that can be developed by playing chess and the relationship between chess ability and general intelligence. The author presents evidence showing that skills gained from chess often do not transfer into other domains. The fourth paragraph discusses how chess players often do not have exceptional skills at recall of digits or visual memory of shapes. There is no reason to assume that chess players are, as a group, talented at memorizing patterns in general. Choice A can be eliminated. Chess players also did not score especially well on the Tower of London test, which examines executive functioning and planning skills. While the author concedes that playing chess requires planning, they do not believe that this skill translates to other types of planning, so choice B is not a strong answer. The author concludes their argument by stating that chess players can probably still learn new skills from the game, but only if they have not fully developed those skills yet. According to the passage, only children learn from each game of chess, so choice C can be eliminated. The author believes that chess does not directly increase general intelligence, but recognizes that there is a strong correlation between the two variables. Note that the question stem does not specify a causal relationship. By this reasoning, choice D is the best answer.

7. **B is the best answer.** The main idea of the passage relates to the investigation of the positive correlation between chess ability and general intelligence. The author suggests three theories to explain the finding. They think there is a possibility that playing chess could increase people's IQs, so if they have been playing for years, then it is reasonable to assume their IQ scores may have improved. Choice A can be eliminated. Throughout the passage, the author only discusses playing chess and never mentions the learning process or who teaches an individual how to play. There is no reason to assume that individuals with low IQ scores are not taught how to play chess. This answer choice preys upon a misunderstanding of what it means for smart players to be "selected" for chess. Smart chess players are selected by their talent at the game, not by the people teaching them the game. Choice B is a strong answer. The author also suggests that chess could "select" players with high IQ scores because they feel encouraged to keep playing when they perform well. Choice C is not the best answer. The author also believes that chess players may generally have higher IQs because playing the game of chess requires a high degree of intelligence, so smart individuals are more likely to play. Choice D can be eliminated, and choice B is the best answer.

8. **C is the best answer.** The passage presents the cognitive skills that could possibly be learned by playing chess. The author believes that valuable skills can be gained only if the chess player is still young and not fully developed. Even if high school students are quick learners, they are not "at the beginning of their development," as the author emphasizes at the end of the passage. Choice A can be eliminated. Students who already know how to play chess are unlikely to benefit because they are probably not at the beginning of their development. Choice B can also be eliminated. Elementary school-aged students are still developing and are likely to gain cognitive skills from chess that can be transferred to other aspects of life. Choice C is a promising answer. Even if a child's parents have high IQs, there is no information in the passage to suggest that the child will also have a high IQ. Remember not to bring in outside information or assumptions. Choice D also does not specify the age of the children, so it is not as strong of an answer as choice C.

9. **C is the best answer.** The author's argues that chess skills are only likely to be transferred to other skill sets by children who are not fully developed. The best answer will likely provide evidence of this inability to transfer skills for the rest of the population of chess players. The correlation between chess ability and general intelligence does not relate to the transfer of chess skills, so choice A can be eliminated. If the transfer of skills is limited to the extent of overlap between two domains, then it would likely limit the ability of chess to be transferred, but not if the two activities are related. Choice B is a possible answer, but is not particularly strong. If studies have conclusively found that chess players' planning and memory skills do not transfer to other tasks, then the statement in the question stem is directly supported. This evidence directly relates to chess skills, so choice C is stronger than choice B. Even if a specific skill is less likely to be transferred to another domain, there is no reason to assume that the skills gained from playing chess are very specific. Choice D does not relate to chess as much as choice C, so choice C is the best answer.

10. **C is the best answer.** The author argues that while chess players may typically have high IQs, the skills they develop from playing chess may not always transfer to other tasks. The author does not discuss the amount of time a chess player usually spends playing the game, so choice A can be eliminated. While the student in question may not have as high of an IQ score as the average chess player, that fact does not necessarily relate to the result of one specific test in school. Choice B is unlikely. If the subject of the test required different skills from those required by chess, it would offer explanation for why the student performed poorly, as the author points out that chess skills often do not transfer to other domains. Choice C supports the main idea of the passage, so it is a stronger answer than choice B. The author's argument is not based upon the relationship between the subject matter and chess, but rather their use of similar skill sets. The same skills could be required even if the subjects are dissimilar. Likewise, tests on the same subject could require distinct skill sets. Choice D can be eliminated, and choice C is the best answer.

11. **A is the best answer.** The author argues that chess skills can only be transferred to other domains when the chess player is not fully developed. If children cannot proficiently develop skills from playing chess, then there would be no skills to transfer to other domains and no obvious benefits of teaching chess to young students. Choice A is a promising answer. Even if there is not a correlation between chess ability and IQ, the author's argument about skill transfer would not be weakened since chess players do not need to have a high IQ to be able to transfer skills from chess. Choice B can be eliminated. Even if more adults play chess than children, those children could still transfer chess skills to other domains. The author's argument is not weakened since it is not based upon the number of children who play chess. Choice C is not the best answer. The author's argument does not relate to the level of intelligence of the children playing chess, so there is no reason to assume that children lower IQs cannot still develop transferable chess skills. Choice D can be eliminated, and choice A is the best answer.

12. **B is the best answer.** The passage presents evidence claiming that no studies of adults have found direct evidence of memory or planning skills transferring to other tasks. While the author believes that children might be able to transfer skills developed from chess to other domains, they do not present evidence supporting this claim. While choice A is a tempting answer, the author would probably expect other skills to be transferred as well, not just memory skills. The author does not differentiate between chess skills when discussing their potential to be transferred in children. Choice A is possible, but unlikely. The author would likely conclude that the chess player's memory skills were strengthened by another factor that the small sample shared in common, rather than being transferred from chess to another domain. The author presents evidence claiming that skills gained from playing chess often do not transfer to other domains, so the author would not expect the memory skills from chess to affect memory skills in other aspects of life. Choice B is stronger than choice A because it is more in line with the author's belief that skills gained from chess are usually not transferrable. There is no reason to assume the chess players in the study played one another, because the author does not discuss the importance of an opponent in developing chess skills. Choice C can be eliminated. The author is not likely to attribute the finding to luck, since they write in a tone that indicates respect for the findings of research studies. Choice D can also be eliminated, and choice B is the best answer.

Passage 3 (Questions 13-18)

13. **A is the best answer.** In the second paragraph, charisma is described as unstable, as it typically results from leading people in distress, and that distress will not last forever. The author suggests that charismatic leadership will eventually peter out, so choice A is the best answer. Narcissistic leadership, not charismatic leadership, is characterized by exploiting others for personal gain. Choice B can be eliminated. The author discusses ineffective and immoral leadership in the fourth paragraph, but does not mention that they usually involve charisma, so choice C is not the best answer. In the first paragraph, the author discusses the existence of destructive leaders with charisma. Since there is no evidence in the passage indicating they are rare, choice D is not as strong as choice A.

14. **D is the best answer.** The author states that narcissistic individuals often feel inferior and so depend on external admiration and praise. They are likely to surround themselves with people so they can receive the most compliments and encouragement, rather than feeling inadequate on their own. Choice D is the best answer. While choice A is tempting, there is not as much support in the passage for the assertion that narcissistic leaders feel the need to dominate as many subjects as possible. Narcissistic leaders often put their needs above those of a group, so it is unlikely that they want to enact the most change in a society, and choice B can be eliminated. These leaders are probably not popular, since they exploit subjects and are self-centered, so choice C is not the best answer.

15. **C is the best answer.** This question, like many on the MCAT®, can be answered with an understanding of the author's main idea alone. The author argues that regardless of charisma, a leader must establish and maintain trust to lead other individuals in the most beneficial way. If a commander loses trust by lying to her soldiers, then she can no longer be an effective leader, so choice C is the best answer. If a CEO is forgiven for his wrongdoings, then it is implied that a leader can lose trust and recover, which would weaken the author's argument. If an ineffective mayor does that much damage, even though he is not immoral, the author's argument about the harm of unethical leaders would be weakened. Choices A and B can be eliminated. Even if a narcissistic actor learns that the quality is harmful to himself and others, that realization does not necessarily affect his or others' leadership, so choice D is not the strongest answer.

16. **B is the best answer.** In the second paragraph, charismatic leaders are described as "leaders followed by people in distress." The politician has the best chance of being viewed as a charismatic leader when her followers are searching for guidance, so choice B is the best answer. Though the author states that subordinates often view charismatic leaders as uniquely qualified, they do not suggest that the leaders must actually be experts on the subject. Choice A can be eliminated. The author does not suggest that indecision is a detractor from charisma, so choice C is not the best answer. While charismatic leaders are described as enthusiastic, they are not necessarily enthusiastic in a positive way. They could be influenced by injustice and let their followers see how upset they are in order to inspire them. For this reason, choice D is not as strong as choice B. Choice D also uses the word "never," and the best MCAT® answers are rarely so extreme.

17. **D is the best answer.** In the final paragraph, the author suggests that individuals may have to tolerate narcissistic leaders if it is for their job, since that is their source of income. While they may be true statements, the passage does not suggest that politicians or professionals in the entertainment industry are tolerated more even when they are egotistical. Choices A and B can be eliminated. The author specifically compares the workplace to home life, suggesting that in personal settings these selfish qualities are tolerated even less, so choice C can be eliminated. Choice D is the best answer.

18. **C is the best answer.** In the fourth paragraph, the author discusses ineffective and immoral leaders because the two categories are destructive in different ways. Immoral leaders do not put other individuals above themselves, while ineffective leaders can harm an organization's structure or profits. Choice C is the best answer. The author mentions in the first paragraph that destructive leaders can be charismatic or not, and does not suggest that the former is more common. Choice A cannot be assumed to be true. While the author discusses these leaders as a problem in the Western world, the leaders do not necessarily come from the Western world. Choice B is an assumption not supported by the passage. Ineffective leaders could have good intentions, but poor actions and results. Choice D is not the strongest answer.

Passage 4 (Questions 19-22)

19. **D is the best answer.** This question is asking about one of the major deterrents to implementing new teaching strategies for middle school students. The best answer must both be presented in the passage and indicate that educators do not know the most effective teaching practices. The author argues that middle school educators recognize that their students are at a unique stage of development, which should help them teach their students more effectively. Choice A can be eliminated. The passage does not offer support for the idea that educators who have not recently engaged in play cannot implement it in their classrooms. Choice B is not the best answer. While there is pressure to teach professional development during middle school, that fact does not support the claim that educators do not know the most effective teaching methods, but rather they are forced to implement different teaching methods. Choice C is not as strong as choice D. Throughout the passage, the author stresses that the research about engaging teaching methods for middle school students has not been publicized enough because educators are not aware of all of the benefits. Their lack of understanding is due to lack of awareness about the research and various interpretations of the findings. Choice D is the best answer. Note that since the author is biased in favor of the importance of play-based learning, it is not surprising that the best answer to this question points to teachers' lack of knowledge about this educational tool.

20. **C is the best answer.** The main idea of the passage points to the importance of learning through play during development so that students are more prepared for success in the educational and professional environment. The author does not suggest that the educational games must be multiplayer or involve teamwork, so choice A cannot be assumed to be true. The author points out that these games teach cognitive flexibility, but not necessarily flexibility in attitude. Picking an answer based on recognizing a phrase from the passage is a common pitfall on the MCAT®. Make sure to read each question and answer choice carefully. Choice B can be eliminated. The author stresses that playing educational games teaches students focus and determination, since they must plan strategies and adapt throughout the process. They suggest that this perseverance and preparation is applicable to professional situations. Choice C is a strong answer. While engaging in play might teach motivation to students, the author does not suggest that this skill is most helpful for professional careers. Choice D is not as strong as choice C.

21. **B is the best answer.** This question may seem specific but can be answered with information from the main idea of the passage. "Pedagogical" is used to describe a type of expertise, and because the educators do not know how best to support students at unique stages of development, the word probably does not describe developmental psychologists. Choice A is not the best answer. Because teachers are trained in education and learning, in addition to their specific subject matter, it is reasonable to assume that "pedagogical" is analogous to "instructional." A martial arts instructor would be an expert in their specific subject, martial arts, and how to teach that skill to others. For this reason, choice B is the best answer. The passage does not suggest that educators are experts in social interactions, so "pedagogical" probably does not relate to social behaviors or societal changes. Choice C cannot be assumed true. Choice D can be eliminated according to the same reasoning as choice A, since developmental psychologists and school counselors have overlapping roles. Note that choices D and A are so similar that neither is likely to be correct.

22. **A is the best answer.** The author presents engaging learning as a method to improve learning in middle schools in general—they seem to think it can apply to almost every situation. If this method only benefits a certain subset of middle school students, then it is not as helpful as the author believes and they would have to reevaluate their proposal. For this reason, choice A is the best answer. Even though students are graduating high school with higher GPAs, that does not mean they did not struggle in middle school. The author's belief that engaging learning could have helped them could still be valid. For this reason, choice B is not the strongest answer. If high school drop-out rates have increased, then that could mean more students fell behind during middle school, which would strengthen the author's argument. Choice C can be eliminated. Even if more students are attending college than in the past, the increase could be explained by many factors unrelated to the author's argument. Those students also could have benefitted from engaged learning, so choice D is not the best answer.

Passage 5 (Questions 23-29)

23. D is the best answer. The main idea of the passage is that Voltairine de Cleyre is an anarchist whose feminist tendencies arose from her anarchist ideals of equality for all humans, instead of a traditional feminist agenda. The author believes that de Cleyre can be construed as a feminist of sorts, but this feminism is rooted in her anarchism. Choice A agrees with the author's sentiment that she is more an anarchist than a feminist, but uses extreme language. In contrast, the author tone is more balanced and incorporates tentative words like "may" when discussing the interpretation of de Cleyre's feminism as part of her anarchism. Choice A is a weak answer. Choice B describes the opposite opinion of the author and is a contrary distractor. While the author believes that de Cleyre does have some feminist tendencies, the author thinks that de Cleyre's writing was driven by more than feminism, so choice C can be eliminated. Since the author's main argument is that describing de Cleyre as a feminist fails to accurately account for her anarchism, the author would probably agree that concluding that de Cleyre is a feminist neglects a certain ideal – anarchism. This is the sentiment expressed in choice D, making it the best answer.

24. D is the best answer. Remember not to bring in any outside information or opinions about anarchism when considering the answer choices for this question. The main idea of the passage is that de Cleyre's feminism is rooted in her anarchism, and to make this point the author alludes to the definition of anarchism. The author notes that de Cleyre does not think that a true anarchist utopia will necessarily ever be achieved, but this is de Cleyre's utopia, not the author's. Further, de Cleyre did live by anarchist-inspired ideals that she thought could actually be obtained. For these reasons, choice A is an unlikely answer. Choice B mentions violence, which is discussed in the passage in the context of de Cleyre's support of activists and disdain for government, so this is a possible answer. The author describes de Cleyre as an enemy of government, the current economic system, and her Catholic education, so choice C is compelling as well. The author's main argument, though, is that equality of all individuals is the tenet of anarchism that leads to de Cleyre being misconstrued as a feminist. The author mentions that de Cleyre's pursuit for the abolition of marriage was based in her desire to fight for liberty from all forms of sanctioned repression for people of all genders, not just women. Choice D is stronger than choices B and C, and so is the best answer.

25. B is the best answer. The main idea of the passage is that de Cleyre's apparent feminism is actually just a manifestation of her individualistic anarchism. The author argues that this individualism can be traced back to her disdain for authority and the need to blindly follow instructions in her Catholic education. Choice A assumes that her writings mark the beginning of her individualism, and as such, the answer choice could either be interpreted that her Catholic education spurred her individualism or that the absence of earlier writings makes it impossible to determine if the individualism originated earlier. Either way, choice A is not a strong answer. Since the author argues that de Cleyre's dislike of the constraints of Catholicism spurred her individualistic tendencies, continuing with this oppressive culture would oppose her belief system, making choice B a compelling answer. Choice C seems to indicate a possible source of de Cleyre's individualism, but does not preclude the Catholic school as a stronger influence. Choice C is a weaker answer than choice B. Choice D also offers a potential source of de Cleyre's individualism before her Catholic school education. However, the role of her education could still be a more powerful influence, and eccentricity in early childhood does not necessarily mean preclude conformity in adulthood. For both reasons, choice D is not the best answer. Choice B is better than choices C and D because it more closely relates to Catholicism as mentioned in the question stem.

26. B is the best answer. The passage presents a spectrum of ideas about how to characterize de Cleyre. On one end of the spectrum are arguments that she is solely an anarchist, while on the other end of the spectrum are arguments that she is solely a feminist. The author lies somewhere in the middle of this spectrum, leaning towards the anarchist side. This tendency towards anarchism makes option I possible, especially because both de Cleyre and Kropotkin are both anarchists. However, while the passage describes anarchism, it never speaks to the role of the political movement in society as a whole. In particular, Kropotkin's conception of anarchism in society is not fully discussed. Option I is beyond the scope of the passage, and choices A and C can be eliminated. While de Cleyre's idea of the role of women is that of equality with men, Kropotkin's perception is less well defined. The author only alludes that Kropotkin thinks women are being exploited, but offers no other suggestions as to their role in society. Option II is not a strong option. Choice D can be eliminated. Both de Cleyre and Kropotkin believe that women and laborers are forced to work too long in boring jobs, so option III is a good option and choice B is the best answer.

27. C is the best answer. The main idea of the passage is that de Cleyre's feminist tendencies are rooted in her anarchist idealism. The author argues that de Cleyre believes in equality for all humans, and as women are humans, they fit into this belief system. A situation that is similar to de Cleyre's would thus involve a misinterpretation of the motivations of an advocate because of a greater identity or circumstance that was overlooked. In choice A the carnival worker presumably opposes the bureaucracy of the carnival to support their own well-being, not for some greater purpose, so it is not a compelling answer. In choice B there is not enough information to know if the man is a human rights supporter over all, or if he is an advocate for only the LGBTQ population, so it is not a convincing answer. Choice C at first glance appears to be the same as choice B, but the medical student is working under the greater umbrella of patient advocacy for all, making it a stronger answer than choice B. Choice D again does not provide enough information to determine if the writer has greater equality ideals or is just a champion of immigration, making it a weak answer.

28. **C is the best answer.** The main idea of the passage is that de Cleyre's feminist ideals were in fact just individualist anarchist ideals in disguise. De Cleyre supported equality and individuality for all people and disliked all forms of conformity, an ethos that applied to both men and women. As a woman, her distaste for conformity led her to reject traditional female roles. Choice A shows a continued rejection of gender roles by having a child out of wedlock, so it appears to be a possible answer. Choice B assumes that having a child is the role of a women, but it could be just a biological consequence of other "non-feminine" sexual choices. Since the passage does not discuss childbearing as one of the "traditional expectations of females," choice B is not a well-supported answer. Remember to leave behind potential biases and only consider passage information when answering CARS questions. Choice C speaks to de Cleyre's individuality ethos, making it a strong answer. Choice C is better than choice A because it is more in line with the main idea of the passage - it has a more anarchist tone than feminist tone. Choice D is a confusing answer because it implies that a child takes away individuality rather than independence, making it a distractor.

29. **C is the best answer.** The passage presents a spectrum of ideas about the definition de Cleyre, a woman who did not like traditional categories. One end of the spectrum argues that she was completely an anarchist, while the other end argues that she was solely a feminist. The author lies somewhere in the middle of this spectrum, but leans toward the anarchist side. The author describes de Cleyre's feminism as a manifestation of anarchist ideals. However, saying that feminism and anarchism are linked for everyone, not just de Cleyre, is an extreme take on the author's view. Choice A is not well-supported. The author does believe that de Cleyre is a feminist, just within the framework of anarchism, so choice B again supplies too extreme of a viewpoint. Atheism is only explicitly mentioned once in the passage, but the author attributes a distaste for her Catholic education as an instigator for her individuality, making choice C a compelling answer. Choice D uses the term "traditional feminism" which the author specifically argues does NOT apply to de Cleyre, so it is a contrary distractor.

Passage 6 (Questions 30-34)

30. **B is the best answer.** The author describes the relationships involved in symbolic patriarchy, and argues that they involve unequal power relationships between men and women. The author is proposing their own idea throughout the passage—they do not cite any other authors or mention other beliefs. Choice A can be eliminated. The author uses the descriptor "so-called" before the phrase in question, so they are skeptical about the concept of a "gendered world." They do not believe that dichotomized gender roles are accurate representations of the interactions involved in symbolic patriarchy. Choice B is a strong answer. The author draws attention to gender inequality in the beginning of the passage, but not by using quotations in this sentence. They are starting to list examples of symbolic patriarchy instead of describing discrepancies between the genders in the workplace like they did in the first paragraph. Choice C is not the best answer. The author is likely not proposing a new term since they describe the term as "so-called," which implies both that other individuals have used the term before and that the author does not agree with it. Choice D is not as strong as choice B.

31. **D is the best answer.** The author argues that symbolic patriarchy is based upon ideas of dominance and hierarchy, not necessarily limited to familial interactions. They point out the prevalence of symbolic patriarchy in the workplace and society, which indicates that it does not always involve familial relations. Choice A can be eliminated. In the third paragraph, the author argues that symbolic patriarchy can no longer be viewed in terms of dichotomized gender roles, but rather on social interactions. Choice B is not the strongest answer. The author mentions the existence of patriarchal bargaining, or a willingness to submit to power in order to receive protection, but does not suggest that this occurs in every case of symbolic patriarchy. Choice C is not the best answer. Throughout the passage, the author stresses that symbolic patriarchy can take many different forms, but is based upon dominance in relationships. A specific power arrangement, or hierarchy, can lead to oppression and symbolic patriarchy, so choice D is the best answer.

32. **A is the best answer.** Throughout the passage, the author argues that symbolic patriarchy is prevalent in society and explains the various forms it can take. While they begin their argument by stating that many problems for women in the workplace revolve around gender, they do not delve into these problems. They do not list examples of negative outcomes or psychological effects of working in these conditions, so choice A is a promising answer. The author discusses symbolic patriarchy in the context of multiple social systems. Choice B relates to the main idea of the passage and can be eliminated. In the fourth paragraph, the author describes different forms of symbolic patriarchy, such as patriarchal bargaining. Because they stress that symbolic patriarchy can take place in many different situations that may not resemble one another, choice C is not a strong answer. The author concludes their argument by discussing the necessity of further research and advising the direction that research should take. They argue that research must examine symbolic patriarchy in social relations and interactions, so choice D can be eliminated. Note that choice A stands out from the other answer choices because the author uses the example of the workplace as a lead-in to the larger issue of symbolic patriarchy, which is the real focus of the passage. The other answer choices specifically reference symbolic patriarchy and are supported by explanation, so choice A is the best answer.

33. **D is the best answer.** Throughout the passage, the author argues that symbolic patriarchy is not confined to familial relations, and that it establishes a hierarchy favoring those in masculine roles. The author mentions employment experience only in relation to gender roles. Choice A is not related to the main idea of the passage and can be eliminated. Similarly, the author does not discuss personal feeling of like or dislike in the workplace, but rather focuses on feelings of power. Choice B is not a strong answer. Throughout the passage, the author suggests that symbolic patriarchy is a current problem in the workplace, not one that only "outdated" companies would experience. Choice C is a possible answer, but not particularly strong. In the second paragraph, the author discusses the concept of masculinity and states that it unfairly rewards men over women in the workplace. Choice D is also consistent with the main idea of the passage. For these reasons, choice D is the strongest answer.

34. **A is the best answer.** The best answer will both be consistent with passage information and correctly assess the impact on the author's argument. The author believes that symbolic patriarchy is based upon dominating male roles, but that it can occur in situations outside of home life. In the third paragraph, they argue that patriarchal interactions are often caused by fatherly figures or the oldest male in a situation. If a man had younger siblings, then he is more likely to have experienced one of those roles at some point, and the author would expect him to express greater dominance. Choice A is a strong answer. The author does not discuss preferences in the passage, nor do they suggest that men are more likely to be dominating towards other because they like it. Remember not to bring in any outside bias on this topic. Note that the author specifically indicates a focus on large power structures rather than individual dominance. Choice B is not supported by information in the passage. While it is true that symbolic patriarchy is not confined to familial relations, this concept is already discussed by the author and does not weaken their argument. Choice C is not the best answer. The author stresses the role of a fatherly figure and the power hierarchy that usually places men on the top, so this finding does relate to the author's argument and choice D can be eliminated. Choice A is the best answer.

Passage 7 (Questions 35-40)

35. **C is the best answer.** The passage presents a spectrum regarding the influence of Feng Shui in Chinese culture versus other cultures. The author argues that Feng Shui has played an important role in Chinese societies, since it has existed for so long, but that its reach outside China is limited by ignorance regarding Feng Shui. The author mentions that the western world is aware of the original Luo Shu and the concept that the chart adds up to 15 in each column and row. The passage also argues, though, that other cultures do not recognize other variations of the chart that add up to other numbers. For this reason, the western world is not necessarily supportive of variations of the Luo Shu due to lack of understanding on the topic. Choice A can be eliminated. There is no way to determine if the western world opposes the concept, since the author believes the western world is unfamiliar with the variations of the Luo Shu. Choice B can also be eliminated. The author suggests that other countries are mostly unaware of the variations, likely because Feng Shui originated in China and is most studied and understood in its country of origin. Choice C is a strong answer. The passage does not suggest that the western world is uninterested in learning about Feng Shui, because it does not mention any attempts or rebuttals to educate them on the subject. Choice D is not supported by the passage. Choice C is the best answer.

36. **D is the best answer.** This passage discusses the usefulness of Feng Shui in different. The author stresses its importance in Chinese cultures but suggests that it might not carry the same weight in other cultures that have less knowledge of the concept. Near the beginning of the passage, the author suggests that multiple societies discovered magic squares, but only Chinese societies pursued their practical applications. The ancient foreign scholars probably did not think magic squares could be applied to all aspects of life, since they did not pursue the concept of Feng Shui. Choice A can be eliminated. The passage does not suggest that the ancient scholars viewed magic squares as confusing topics or that they did not investigate them further. Even though they did not reach the same applications as Chinese cultures, scholars may have investigated magic squares and there is no reason to assume they viewed them as a confusing topic. Choice B is too extreme in its wording and can be eliminated. The passage also does not imply that ancient scholars believed that magic squares only related to Chinese cultures. This is not suggested by either the passage content or tone, so choice C can be eliminated. The passage states that ancient foreign scholars studied magic squares like Chinese scholars did, but that they did not propose practical applications of the squares as the Chinese scholars did. Choice D is the strongest answer.

37. **B is the best answer.** Throughout the passage, the author considers the influence of Feng Shui in Chinese societies, both past and present. The author concludes their argument by suggesting that this influence is positive in nature and can benefits individuals. For this reason, the author's tone while discussing the two schools of Feng Shui would not be described as detached. Choice A can be eliminated. The author writes with a respectful tone, since they provide such detail and value Feng Shui so strongly. Choice B is a promising answer. The author already seems informed about the two schools of Feng Shui, since they describe them in the passage. Choice C is not as strong as choice B because it does not relate to the author's views towards Feng Shui. While the author does strongly support Feng Shui, their tone would not best be described as enthusiastic, since they do not use passionate wording or punctuation. Choice D is more extreme than choice B, so choice B is the better MCAT® answer.

38. C is the best answer. The author describes the two primary schools of Feng Shui because they believe in their potential to help the residents of a building. It is the Form School that values the energy flow between mountains, rivers, and valleys. Choice A describes a position attributable to the Form School, and can be eliminated. While the Compass School does consider timing, the recommendation from choice B may not necessarily apply to this situation since the construction workers have to erect the building quickly. Choice B is possible, but there may be a stronger answer. The Compass School stresses the orientation of the building and the rooms inside, since each building is divided into "mountains" that can oriented with a compass. Choice C is stronger than choice B because the passage does not discuss how timing affects building development as much as orientation does. While the Compass School heavily utilizes a compass, the passage does not suggest that every building must be in the shape of a compass in order to benefit from this practice of Feng Shui. Choice D can be eliminated and choice C is the best answer.

39. A is the best answer. The author stresses that the Form School determines how best to harness the Qi, or energy, from the surrounding natural environment. Option I is true and choice D can be eliminated. The author states that all energy comes from mountains and ridges in Chinese beliefs, and that water flow can alter that energy as well. If a location is not near mountains, ridges, or water flow, then it is impossible to determine if Form School Feng Shui masters can offer suggestions. Because option II uses extreme wording like "any," it is unlikely to be included in the best answer, and choice B can be eliminated. It is the Compass School that considers timing, as the Form School is not concerned with temporal information. Option III is not true and choice C can be eliminated. Choice A is the best answer.

40. B is the best answer. The passage presents a spectrum regarding the value of Feng Shui in various cultures. Although Feng Shui originated in China, the author believes it can benefit individuals from various countries. The passage suggests that Feng Shui is most often practiced in Chinese cultures, so that finding would not add support to the author's argument. Choice A can be eliminated. If foreigners are as satisfied with Feng Shui as Chinese citizens, then the author's argument about the universal value of the practice would be strengthened. Choice B is a strong answer. The author's argument is not founded upon an individual's feelings toward Feng Shui—even if individuals doubt its efficacy, the author might still view it as a beneficial practice. Choice C is not a strong answer. The finding that ancient cultures also discovered Feng Shui would not necessarily strengthen or weaken the author's argument. More information would be necessary about the popularity and success of Feng Shui in ancient cultures. It is unclear how this finding would affect the author's argument, so choice D can be eliminated. Choice B is the best answer.

Passage 8 (Questions 41-46)

41. D is the best answer. Throughout the passage, the author discusses the multitude of reasons why critics disagree with the mainstream climate change thesis. In the conclusion, they emphasize that having a discussion with the skeptics is the best method to possibly change their minds because they will not feel threatened or insulted. According to the passage, if scientists acknowledge the arguments and address them with evidence and good-will, they can decrease the number of skeptics. Choice D is the best answer. In the first paragraph, the author introduces the concept that climate change is primarily caused by human activities. Choice A can be eliminated. The author also stresses the importance of accepting the standard thesis about climate change so it can be arrested, or slowed down. This does not imply that past destruction can be undone, so choice B can be eliminated. In the fourth paragraph, the author points out the genuine nature of skeptical scientists compared to greedy professional skeptics. There is no reason to assume that scientists' skepticism hurts the cause more, so choice C is not as strong as choice D.

42. C is the best answer. This question is best approached by process of elimination. Some skeptics, like scientists, feel it is their duty to question the thesis to help humankind. They want to completely understand the concept before agreeing, so that if any others are influenced by their decision, they can have confidence in their conclusions. The second paragraph points out that some critiques are raised by concerned and responsible citizens. For these reasons, choices A and D can be eliminated. In the fourth paragraph, Rahmstorf mentions "Don Quixotists," who have committed to one belief and refuse to consider other options. Choice B is not the best answer. Although the passage discusses how some skeptics argue only for personal gain or financial benefits, the author never proposes that they argue out of ill-will or animosity. Choice C is not suggested by the passage and is the best answer.

43. B is the best answer. Although the author suggests that the mainstream thesis is legitimate, they also mention that some critics are merely unconvinced or unsure. They do not necessarily reject the thesis, so option I is not part of the best answer. Choices A and D can be eliminated. In the last paragraph, the author discusses the negative consequences of questioning motivations, as the skeptic will not be engaged and open to a conversation. Option II is true. The author never mentions how many skeptics eventually change their minds, so option III cannot be assumed true. Choice C can be eliminated and choice B is the best answer.

44. **C is the best answer.** The author describes the different kinds of climate change skeptics in detail so mainstream exponents will understand their reasoning and the best way to engage with each skeptic. Choice C is the best answer. While lobbyists probably do have too much control over this scientific issue, the author does not suggest that the government should step in to decrease the skepticism. While the author believes in the mainstream thesis and the importance of convincing critics of its validity, their tone does not suggest frustration over its seriousness. Choices A and D might be true statements, but they do not reflect a theme of the passage, so they can eliminated. The author does not suggest that every single critic can be convinced, because some of them are motivated by money or may have to argue against the mainstream thesis for their jobs. For this reason, choice B is not the best answer.

45. **B is the best answer.** The author stresses that in order to change a skeptic's mind, there must be education and engagement. By bringing her grandfather to a practice, the granddaughter could show all the hard work and physical activity that goes into a cheerleading competition. The granddaughter would not be questioning or attacking the grandfather's reasoning, but rather presenting her information in a respectful way. Choice B is the best answer. If the granddaughter does not try to engage her grandfather in a conversation, then she is making the assumption that he is ill-intentioned rather than ill-informed. Refusing to engage in conversation will not change the grandfather's beliefs, so choice A can be eliminated. While the granddaughter should inform her grandfather of her reasoning, the grandfather would feel attacked and insulted if she does not let him respond. This response would be unlikely to result in a change of opinion, so choice C is not the strongest answer. By questioning her grandfather's favorite sport, the girl is likely to push her grandfather away. This response also changes the topic and fails to address the grandfather's beliefs about cheerleading, so choice D is not the best answer.

46. **A is the best answer.** Although the author supports the mainstream thesis about climate change, their argument pertains to methods of dealing with skeptics. The author believes that recognizing a skeptic's argument is the best approach. In this case, scientists could have learned from those critiquing certain parts of the mainstream thesis, so the author's argument about the importance of a discussion is strengthened and choice A is the best answer. The author believes in the mainstream thesis, because they want to convince skeptics in the last paragraph, so choice B can be eliminated. The author's argument does not hinge on the validity of the mainstream thesis, because they do not discuss evidence supporting or refuting it. Instead, they discuss how to interact with individuals who have different beliefs. Choice C is not as strong as choice A. Though the author's argument does not focus on the certainty of the mainstream thesis, their argument would be affected by this information. Choice D is not the best answer.

Passage 9 (Questions 47-53)

47. **C is the best answer.** The passage presents a spectrum of treatment options for obese children, including parental control, exercise, and psychological intervention. The author argues that children may have an addiction to food, which is why weight loss interventions may not be successful. The author focuses on how food addiction affects eating behaviors, without much discussion of how it affects exercise ability. Choice A is not a strong answer. The author discusses the importance of proper treatment for obese children with a food addiction because they believe that proper intervention can provide health benefits. The author opens their argument with a statistic showing that not every obese child grows into an obese adult. Choice B has a tone of finality about obese children that the author does not employ throughout the passage, so it can be eliminated. Near the end of the passage, the author discusses the promising results of therapy for obese children, and suggests that standard interventions could be strengthened by combination with psychological treatment. Choice C is in line with the author's main argument and is a strong answer. The author primarily discusses the benefits of psychological treatment for obese children with a food addiction. A strict lifestyle change could be necessary to lose weight, but this approach is not specifically argued by the passage. Choice D is goes beyond the central argument of the passage and can be eliminated. Choice C is the best answer.

48. **D is the best answer.** The main idea of the passage is that obese children may have an addiction to food and could benefit from additional interventions beyond standard weight loss techniques. The author points out that parents may not recognize emotional eating until their child has noticeable weight gain. The author would not likely advise waiting to see if this action is a new habit because the child may benefit from treatment as early as possible. Choice A can be eliminated. Parents buying healthier snacks is similar to parental control measures that the author describes as ineffective, so choice B can also be eliminated. There is no reason to assume that the child discussed in the question stem is obese or has progressed to the point of food addiction. There could be many reasons why the child is snacking more, so choice C is drawing a conclusion that is not supported by the passage. The author believes that successful weight loss may be hindered by the parents' inability to understand and recognize emotional eating. If the parents ask their son about his motives for eating, they may learn about stress or discomfort that could be the motivation behind emotional eating. This would be the best start in addressing a possible food addiction. Choice D is the strongest answer.

49. **B is the best answer.** The author argues that obese children may have a food addiction and could benefit from psychological treatment in addition to standard interventions. They do not suggest that every overweight or obese child has a food addiction, because they point out that there are many potential reasons for unsuccessful weight control. Choice A can be eliminated. The author stresses the benefits of emotion-focused family therapy for obese children with food addictions, and believes that parents who recognize emotional eating may be able to intervene more successfully. Healthcare professionals and family members might become more involved if the child undergoes addiction treatment. Choice B may be misinterpreted as the kind of parental intervention that encourages clandestine eating patterns, but the further intervention in the answer choice may refer to professional intervention. Choice B is a possible answer. The author does not believe that every obese child grows into an obese adult, as they point out that only 40-70% actually do. This might be a reasonable answer choice if it had a softener like "may," but as written choice C is not supported by passage information. While the author discusses the likelihood of food addiction with other disordered eating, they do not discuss any relationship to substance addiction. Choice D is beyond the scope of the passage. Choice B is the best answer.

50. **B is the best answer.** In the first paragraph, the author establishes the health complications of obesity for children and adults. They state that childhood obesity is a global priority due to economic burden of medical care for obese children. Although the author discusses the economic implications of childhood obesity, they do so with regard to medical costs rather than the cost of food. They also do not suggest an inconvenience from grocery shopping, so choice A is not a strong answer. Because the author uses this term to describe a global priority, it is likely referring to public health concerns that affect communities rather than individuals. Choice B is a promising answer. While familial relationships may be strained due to childhood obesity, that is not suggested by the first paragraph. Choice C is not as strong as choice B since this concept is suggested later in the passage. Bullying may be considered a burden of childhood obesity, but is not discussed or suggested by the author. Remember not to bring outside information or bias into the CARS section of the MCAT®. Choice D can be eliminated, and choice B is the strongest answer.

51. **C is the best answer.** In the main idea of the passage, the author argues that childhood obesity is often caused by a food addiction that requires psychological treatment in addition to standard methods. While the author draws comparisons between disordered eating and addiction, they do not discuss predisposing factors or conditions that lead to either. Be careful not to bring in outside knowledge about the development of addiction, as the answer to the question can be found in the passage alone. Choice A is beyond the scope of the passage. The author only discusses medical conditions caused by childhood obesity and does not suggest that they are worsened by other medical conditions, so choice can be eliminated. The author discusses food addiction with a tone of seriousness and suggests that a commitment to treatment is necessary to maintain a healthy weight. Near the end of the passage, the author suggests that psychological treatment may help weight maintenance into adolescence, implying that treatment is ongoing and does not necessarily end in childhood. Choice C is a promising answer. While the author mentions that childhood obesity is a global priority, they do not suggest it is increasing in prevalence. Choice D can be eliminated, and choice C is the best answer.

52. **A is the best answer.** The author believes that children with a food addiction could benefit from psychological treatment in addition to standard weight loss measures in order to treat the underlying disease longitudinally. If children are too young to benefit from professional counseling, then there would be no added benefit of psychological treatment for children. Choice A would weaken the author's argument about the value of psychological treatment of childhood obesity, so it is a possible answer choice. If children with food addictions believe their habits are out of their control, they might benefit from psychological treatment to address those feelings of helplessness. Choice B would strengthen the author's argument and can be eliminated. Even if most children do not have a food addiction, they could be screened for disordered eating habits, as the author suggests at the end of the passage. Those children who do have food addictions could still benefit from psychological treatment. Choice C does not weaken the argument as much as choice A and can be eliminated. The finding that adults can also develop food addictions does not affect the value of psychological treatment for children, so choice D is not a strong answer. Choice A is the best answer since it casts doubt on the value of psychological treatment for childhood obesity.

53. **C is the best answer.** The author describes children who crave, desire, and work to get food as displaying characteristics of addiction. Remember to answer this question based on the author's definition and not information from outside of this passage. Someone who drinks coffee every morning is not necessarily craving, desiring, or working to get the drink. Choice A is a possible answer but is faily vague since the individual's motivations for drinking coffee are not specified. If a person eats chocolate after completing a task for work, he or she may be using chocolate as a reward for completing a mandatory assignment. This situation does not closely resemble those described by the author, so choice B is not a strong answer. Someone who thinks about lunch hours in advance is likely craving food, similar to the author's description of individuals with food addictions. Craving food is a specific example of a trait described by the author, so choice C is stronger than choice A. The author points out that there are many reasons why weight loss interventions may not be successful. The individual in choice D may not necessarily have a food addiction, but could have extenuating circumstances explaining the unhealthy behavior. Choice C is the best answer because it describes a scenario directly suggested by the author as characteristic of a food addiction.

TEST 8

ANSWERS & EXPLANATIONS
Questions 1–53

ANSWER KEY					
1. A	10. D	19. B	28. C	37. A	46. B
2. C	11. C	20. B	29. C	38. C	47. B
3. D	12. B	21. C	30. D	39. D	48. D
4. D	13. D	22. A	31. B	40. D	49. C
5. B	14. D	23. A	32. A	41. C	50. B
6. B	15. C	24. C	33. D	42. B	51. D
7. A	16. A	25. C	34. B	43. B	52. C
8. C	17. B	26. D	35. A	44. C	53. A
9. B	18. A	27. A	36. A	45. C	

EXPLANATIONS FOR TEST 8

Passage 1 (Questions 1-6)

1. **A is the best answer.** The author's main idea is that when it comes to defining love, one can use a model to derive a consistent definition, even though people throughout history have primarily used their own experiences as the basis for their definitions, rendering this abstract concept unique to the individual. Although the author states that philosophers of language have long debated the concept of love, they do not mention moral philosophers. The passage's primary focus is on the linguistic definition of 'love,' rather than how concepts of morality have been applied to the study of love, so choice A is a possible answer. Based on passage information, arguments about the definition of love have moved from the field of philosophy to those of biology, sociology, and psychology. Choice B can be eliminated. The passage focuses on the difference between people's conceptions of love based on their own relationships and the author's proposed formula for defining love, so choice C can be eliminated. The author states specifically that philosophers who study language have sought to define love, so choice D can be eliminated. Choice A is the best answer.

2. **C is the best answer.** The author's main idea is that although individuals define love based on their personal experiences ("everyone has a conceptual image of love")—which leads to definitions that are different depending on the person—love can in fact be defined in a more all-inclusive and precise manner. The author puts forth a model in which all forms of love and all features of those forms are identified, and then commonality between the features is found, thereby producing a definition for love. The answer that most weakens the author's conclusions will argue that individual definitions of love are in fact valid and that there does not need to be a theoretical model to define love. Regardless of whether everyone has a conceptual image of love, the author's argument would still stand that a definition for love can be derived from a model. For those individuals who have personal conceptual images, the author would nevertheless state that their definitions are incomplete. Choice A is a weak answer. Choice B describes a situation where the passage's definition of love needs to be altered to incorporate new information. Choice B is a possible answer, though a new form of love would neither weaken the author's claim that love should be defined in an all-inclusive and precise manner, nor affect the proposed model. The passage also states that its given definition is based on current knowledge. On the other hand, if individuals' conceptions of love in fact produced a comprehensive and precise definition for love, then there would be no need for the author's theory. Choice C is a stronger answer than choice B because it directly addresses—and weakens—the main idea. Choice D does not speak to the main idea. Even if philosophers have stopped debating love, the author believes the question of how to define this concept is noteworthy. Choice D can be eliminated, and choice C is the best answer.

3. **D is the best answer.** The author's main idea is that despite how love has largely been defined throughout history (namely, by individuals based on their personal experiences), a more comprehensive and precise way to arrive at a definition is to use a model in which the common features of all forms of love are identified. The author argues for this systematic approach, rather than one that may vary significantly between people. Based on the situation described in the question stem, the author would not agree with the philosopher's approach because the author construct their definition for love from their own experiences. Choice A attempts to trick the test-taker by directly referencing the triangular theory. While the theory is itself described as an accepted form of love, the author would not agree with the decision to define love based on personal experience. Choice A is a weak answer. The author states at the end of the passage that love can be defined as a state of intimacy (or affection) and passion (or attraction). However, they would not agree with the philosopher's finding, so choice B is a weak answer. Choice C attempts to distract the test-taker by capitalizing on the fact that the philosopher's three components of love directly match those of the triangular theory. The author would not find fault with this finding because there are other types of love that the philosopher does not seem to reference. Even if the philosopher were to define love as including the components of, for example, care and sacrifice (central features of altruism) based on his experience, the author would still disagree with him. Choice C is a weak answer. Choice D addresses the author's main idea and specifically reflects their argument that abstract definitions should derive from a formula rather than from personal conceptions. Choice D is the best answer.

4. **D is the best answer.** The author's proposed model for defining abstract concepts essentially seeks to determine all forms of that concept, identify the respective features of those forms, and then find commonalities between the features. Those features then comprise the concept's definition. The author's main idea is that contrary to popular belief, an abstract concept like love can have a single definition, which is not based off of individual experiences and conceptions. Based on passage information, most people believe that love is defined at a personal level. Similarly then, individuals would likely formulate their ideas about the concept of friendship based their reactions to their actual friendships. Choice A is a weak answer. The passage states that philosophers of language believe they must establish the meaning of a word before they discuss it. It is unlikely that such a philosopher would conclude, rather than open, her presentation on loyalty with the definition of the word. Choice B is a weak answer. The passage emphasizes that abstract concepts, in contrast to concrete ones, lack tangibility. Choice C does not align with the passage's ideas on abstraction because it refers to a concrete item, a city mural. Choice C can be eliminated. The author's model for defining concepts supposes that if a definition of a word (i.e. the mind) has certain forms (i.e. sentience and willfulness), the components share features. The author states that because the forms of love include the triangular theory, altruism, and erotic love, and because these forms share the features of affection and attraction, then love can be defined by these features. Choice D is the best answer.

5. **B is the best answer.** The author argues that people define love based on their prior experiences. Consequently, people tend to believe that their definitions of love are unique and variable, and that the concept of love cannot be described by a formula. The author states, on the other hand, that this mode of thinking is both incomplete and imprecise. They believe that love can be defined singularly with a systematic mode of reasoning. The best answer will reflect passage information that people conceive of ideas based on their own experiences rather than on a theory. Choice A describes a situation where a man derives his definition of love from a hypothesized model. It does not align with the passage's ideas that people generally conceive of love from personal encounters and relationships. Choice A can be eliminated. On the other hand, choice B matches the author's description of people changing their opinions depending on the condition of their relationships. Based on the passage, the general public would swing from one extreme to another in defining love if their own experiences mirrored that shift. Choice B is a strong answer. Because the author focuses on how the general public changes its views on love due to the quality of personal relationships, choice C is a weak answer. Choice C describes a scenario in which an individual defines love based on an influence—romance novels— external to her own life. Choice B is a stronger answer than choice C because it references the impact that individual experiences and personal relationships have on people's definitions of love. Remember that the author's main idea is that the general public conceives of love according to the outcomes of current and/or previous relationships. Choice D attempts to trick the test-taker by focusing on "variables," which are only used in the passage to represent different features of the forms of an abstract concept. The author does not suggest that people or things should be assigned such variables. Choice D does not align with passage information and can be eliminated. Choice B is the best answer.

6. **B is the best answer.** Based on passage information, philosophers of language have long debated the concept of love, believing that the meaning of a word should be ascertained definitively before it can be discussed. The author states that over time, this study has shifted from the world of philosophy to also penetrating the empirical fields of biology, sociology, and psychology. They identify certain questions that philosophers of language have addressed, but they do not state how the study of these questions related to the researchers' own interests. Choice A is a weak answer. On the other hand, the author contrasts the study of love within philosophy with that of the evidence-based sciences, which have utilized quantitative and qualitative approaches. Choice B is a strong answer. The author references love as a concept only in the context of being abstract and does not imply that it can be considered concrete as well. Choice C can be eliminated. Although the author mentions the progress that empirical researchers have made in broadening understanding of love, they do not suggest that philosophers of language no longer debate love or that they have been somehow supplanted in this area of study. Choice D is a weak answer, and choice B is the best answer.

Passage 2 (Questions 7-13)

7. **A is the best answer.** Throughout the passage, the author discusses the use of technology in the classroom with excitement and possibility. They treat the topic as inevitable, especially when companies like Apple are working on extending technology's reach in education. For this reason, choice A is the best answer. The author does not go so far to suggest that teachers will be fired for failing to adapt, so choice B is not the best answer. The author also points out that not enough research has been to done to understand the benefits of using this technology, so there is no reason to assume that students cannot learn well without it. Choice C can be eliminated. In the last paragraph, the author does not use the phrase "teach the way they've been taught" to excuse educators who were not taught with technology, but rather to stress that technological advances should be incorporated as soon as possible so educators feel familiar with them. Choice D is not as strong as choice A. Keep in mind that choice D is a distractor answer choice that references a point the author made, but in a misleading way – a common MCAT® device.

8. **C is the best answer.** This question requires a close reading of the third paragraph. The author points out that the students responded positively and acknowledged aspects they liked about the course, so they must have reviewed the course in order to convey this information. Choice C is the best answer. Though the passage mentions that the course was entirely paperless, it is unlikely that achievement was the only criteria for success, so choice B is not the best answer. The passage does not ever mention the grading of the course nor its popularity with the university, so choices A and D can be eliminated. Remember not to make assumptions that go beyond the information provided in the passage.

9. **B is the best answer.** Read the quotation about Apple's plan carefully. The passage states that Apple wants to create interactive digital lessons rather than rely on textbooks. Because Apple mentions textbooks as non-interactive learning materials, option I can be eliminated. Educational games are interactive and digital, so option II is correct. While Apple might create applications for time management, this is not suggested by the passage. For this reason, option III can be eliminated and choice B is the best answer.

10. **D is the best answer.** Throughout the passage, the author discusses many challenges educators will face in implementing mobile technology, including its rapid pace of change. For this reason, choice D is the best answer. The author mentions multiple times that not enough research has been done on the effects of technology and that direct benefits have not yet been determined, so choice A can be eliminated. In the last paragraph, the author questions whether technological innovations are better than the previous model, so choice B is not the best answer. Choice B also uses the word "always," and the best answer on the MCAT® is unlikely to use such extreme wording. Finally, the author mentions that students and universities must work with teachers to adapt to new educational technology, so choice C is not as strong of an answer as choice D.

11. **C is the best answer.** Throughout the passage, the author remains hopeful about the benefits that can come from using technology to facilitate learning. They do not mention how the approach would need to change depending on the age group, so there is no reason to assume that the practice cannot be successful with young children. For this reason, choice C is the best answer. The author might recommend parental locks for younger children as the best way to stick with the program and hopefully see benefits, so choice A is not the best answer. The author stresses that using technology will be a big change for all parties involved, so it make take time for the students to adjust. Choice B can be eliminated. Because the program would be such a change for the students, the author would likely recommend discussing it with the students to hear their feedback and improve the program. For this reason, choice D is not the best answer.

12. **B is the best answer.** The fourth paragraph discusses how universities or school districts must decide the best way to use technology at their institutions. These university and school districts are also responsible for providing technological devices for teachers and students alike, so choice B is the strongest answer. The author does not mention how students' intelligence would affect either the technological programs or the school subject. Choice A and C can be eliminated. While the mobile program might affect the success of educational technology, the author does not discuss this as a major factor, as there is not enough research about these programs yet. Choice D is not as strong as choice B.

13. **D is the best answer.** Throughout the passage, the author stresses that adapting to changes in technology as soon as possible will lead to the greatest success in using technology for education. The author thinks that if a teacher is familiar with using mobile programs themselves, they are more likely to successfully implement them in their own classrooms. For this reason, choice D is the best answer. The author is unlikely to advise a computer coding class because knowledge of coding is not necessary to use technology efficiently. Choice A can be eliminated. If the student only studied books about teaching from the last twenty years, he or she would be unlikely to understand how to use technology effectively while teaching, especially given the rapid pace of change in educational technology. Choice B is not the best answer. Although some older professors may not be experts in using technology, that does not mean that they do not have valuable knowledge about becoming an effective teacher. The author is unlikely to advise a student to completely avoid older professors, so choice C can be eliminated. The use of the word "never" in this answer choice also makes it extreme and unlikely to be the best answer.

Passage 3 (Questions 14-18)

14. **D is the best answer.** The main idea of this passage is that Kierkegaard's idea of solitude, which the author calls "imagined solitude," and *King Lear*'s idea of solitude, which could be called "abandonment solitude," seem different but have a common element: both view spatial solitude, and the social isolation that comes with it, negatively. The main difference between the two views, according to the author, is that Kierkegaard believes solitude can be positive as long as it is imagined solitude, while *King Lear* presents a view of solitude that is entirely negative. Choice A says that *Lear* treats spatial isolation as a kind of punishment. This is true, but it also says that Kierkegaard's vision of solitude requires spatial isolation, and according to the author, Kierkegaard says exactly the opposite. Choice A can be eliminated. Choice B suggests that *Lear*'s vision of solitude does not require spatial isolation but Kierkegaard's does. *Lear*'s conception of solitude does include spatial isolation, but Kierkegaard's does not. Choice B can be eliminated. Choice C says that Kierkegaard and *Lear* both view spatial isolation negatively. This is true, but the question asks for the *difference* between the two, so choice C can be eliminated. Choice D says that *Lear* views solitude as punishment, while Kierkegaard views it positively. This is the main difference between them, so D is the strongest answer.

15. **C is the best answer.** According to the author, Kierkegaard thought that proximity to other people was important to achieving imagined solitude, a state in which a person can contemplate spirituality and the nature of humanity. The question proposes that some other scholar thinks the author is wrong about some essential part of Kierkegaard's view. The best answer, therefore, will be as close to the *opposite* of what the author says as possible. Choice A says that Kierkegaard believed that being alone in a crowded city means still being close to others. This is not the opposite of what the author says. In fact it is almost exactly what the author says. Choice A can be eliminated. Choice B suggests that Kierkegaard was more interested in the contemplation of God than of human affairs, but there is no reason why Kierkegaard's view of solitude would have to change to accommodate this information. While in a crowded city, a person could achieve imagined solitude and contemplate God. Choice B can be eliminated. Choice C suggests that Kierkegaard did not think there was anything special about solitude within a large city. Instead, he just thought it was easier to get his writing done in a place where it is hard to get to know other people and therefore easy to stay anonymous. If that is all that Kierkegaard meant, then the author's interpretation of Kierkegaard is questionable. The author suggests that Kierkegaard places a special value on *imagined* solitude, a state that is only possible in the midst of other people. Imagined solitude gives rise to "creative contemplation" and "compassion," while spatial solitude, a state of physical separateness from other people, is "spiritually arid and necessarily self-involved." According to the author, the creative contemplation Kierkegaard values *requires* closeness to other people. If this is not what Kierkegaard meant to convey in his letter to the Danish king, then the author might be mistaken about Kierkegaard's view. Choice C is therefore a strong choice. Choice D says that Kierkegaard was not as interested in solitude as he was in the nature of God, but this would not mean that the author was wrong about Kierkegaard's views on solitude. Choice D can be eliminated. Choice C is the best answer.

16. **A is the best answer.** The sentence "Solitude is the wage of disloyalty" is the closing line of the paragraph on *King Lear*, in which the author argues that Lear is punished for disinheriting his daughter with increasing isolation and eventually death. Option I says almost exactly that: Lear earns his fate. Answer choices that do not contain option I—namely choice B and D—can be eliminated. Option II mixes up all the ideas. It suggests that people who want to be alone risk alienating others. That might be true in some contexts, but it has nothing to do with *King Lear*. Lear does not betray his daughters by wanting to be alone. He betrays Cordelia by disinheriting her, and is punished with isolation. Answer choices containing option II can be eliminated, though in this case that means choices B and D, which have been eliminated already. Option III says that the quotation is intended to critique Kierkegaard's view of solitude. This might be tempting because the passage is clearly contrasting the visions of solitude offered by Kierkegaard and *King Lear*, but the author seems equally interested in both conceptions of solitude, and the final paragraph proposes an idea that is common to both. While the phrase "solitude is the wage of disloyalty" certainly presents a view of solitude that differs greatly from Kierkegaard's, it is not at all obvious that the author prefers Shakespeare's view. Option III—and choice C—can therefore be eliminated, leaving choice A as the best answer.

17. **B is the best answer.** According to the author, *King Lear* is a play whose moral is that disloyalty leads to isolation and death. Lear betrays his loving daughter, Cordelia, and is then betrayed by his other two daughters, Goneril and Regan, leaving him completely alone. The question asks for the description the author would probably *disagree* with, so the incorrect answer choices will match that description of the play, and the best one will contradict it. Choice A says that *King Lear* is the story of a father betrayed by his children. The author would likely disagree somewhat with this description, because it makes Lear sound innocent and the author thinks he is to blame for his fate. Lear *is* betrayed by two of his children, though, and the author would not disagree with that. Choice A is a possible answer, but a weak one. Choice B suggests that Cordelia, the disinherited daughter, seeks revenge on her father. The author tells us that this is not true. Instead, he reports, Cordelia is consistently loyal to Lear. Choice B is a strong answer. Choice C says that *King Lear* shows why loyalty is important. The author would agree with that, since they think the play is about disloyalty leading to isolation and death. Choice C can be eliminated. Choice D says that *Lear* is about the downfall of a king. This is a vague description, but given what the passage reveals about the play, it is not inaccurate and it is hard to see how the author could disagree with it. Choice D can be eliminated. Choice B is the strongest answer.

18. **A is the best answer.** In this passage, the author compares Kierkegaard's "imagined solitude" to the kind of solitude suffered by Lear in the play *King Lear*, which might be called "abandonment solitude." The best answer will give a reason why this comparison is misleading or poorly done. Choice A says that Kierkegaard and Shakespeare are not addressing the same concept. While the author claims that they are both concerned with the idea of solitude, it is arguable that imagined solitude, which is chosen, and abandonment solitude, which is forced on a person, are too different to call them both "solitude." To put it another way, it seems quite possible that Kierkegaard and Shakespeare could agree with one another about solitude. They might both believe that chosen solitude is good but forced solitude is bad. If it is possible that no disagreement exists between Kierkegaard and *King Lear*, then the author's choice to present them as having differing visions of solitude is questionable. Choice A is a strong answer. Choice B suggests that the author has misunderstood Kierkegaard. If the author's understanding of Kierkegaard is inaccurate, that would certainly affect their comparison of Kierkegaard and *King Lear*. Choice B does not match the question as well as choice A, because it does not specifically concern the comparison of the two views. Choice B is a weak answer. Choice C says that philosophy and drama cannot be compared because they express ideas differently. This is a "beyond" distractor. It requires an opinion about whether philosophy and literature can be compared, and forming such an opinion would require information well beyond what the passage addresses. The phrase "It is not possible" is also far too strong. Perhaps comparing philosophy and literature is *difficult* or *complicated*, but to say that it is not possible goes too far. Choice C can be eliminated. Choice D suggests that the author's presentation of *King Lear* was incomplete, implying that their interpretation of the play is therefore suspect. This has the same fault as choice B. If *King Lear* is inaccurately described, then perhaps the author has misunderstood or misrepresented what Shakespeare meant to convey. This does not directly the address the question, which asks about the author's comparison of Kierkegaard and Shakespeare. Choice D, like choice B, is a weak answer. Choice A is the best answer.

Passage 4 (Questions 19-24)

19. **B is the best answer.** The author argues that Chinese children born throughout the one-child policy era are ungrateful, especially towards their parents. Although the Chinese government has attempted to instill feelings of gratitude in young people through gratitude education campaigns, the author's main idea is that these campaigns are ineffective. The passage states that gratitude campaigns strive to increase awareness of gratitude among children, but that only focusing on awareness is insufficient. For children to be grateful, they must first develop a strong sense of justice, which produces a strong sense of responsibility. Responsibility drives true acts of gratitude. According to the passage, the idea that discipline engenders a sense of justice derives from Kohlberg's theory of moral development. This theory involves three stages, the first of which involves children developing an understanding of justice by being taught to follow strict rules and obey authority. Once children have reached this stage, they have grasped the concept of justice and can move on to a second level of mutual understanding and social conscience. This second level, based on the passage, is crucial for the third level, autonomy, but is not necessary or related to a sense of justice. According to the passage, the first stage is the only stage that is needed to instill in children a sense of justice. Option I is a weak answer. Choices A and C can be eliminated. According to passage information about Kohlberg's theory of moral development, justice is fundamental to the development of morality. The passage does not conversely state that moral values are crucial for justice. As such, the theory does not comment on whether there can be justice without morality. Option II is false, and choice D can be eliminated. Kohlberg's theory involves discussion of the role of discipline in moral development. The passage specifically emphasizes the idea that discipline produces a sense of justice, which promotes the development of moral values, including gratitude. Option III is true, and choice B is the best answer.

20. **B is the best answer.** According to the author, gratitude education campaigns seek to raise awareness of the necessity of gratitude, in part by engaging parents and children in activities. However, these campaigns fail to achieve their purpose because gratitude must be trained through discipline, which establishes in children a sense of justice. Based on passage information, the campaigns rely too much on schools and parents to enact this training, neither of which accomplishes the goal effectively. The author argues that respect for authority engenders a sense of justice, which itself promotes responsibility and provides the foundation for grateful actions. While the passage states that the "little emperors syndrome" is a result of the one-child policy, the author is less interested in this supposition and more focused on why efforts to curb the ingratitude problem are ineffective. Choice A addresses the author's introduction to the passage's central argument but does not align with the passage's main idea about the efficacy of gratitude campaigns. Choice A is a weak answer. Choice B accurately describes the thesis of this passage: that gratitude education campaigns do not achieve their purpose of teaching Chinese children to return kindnesses. According to the passage, the campaigns rely on parents and schools to instill the value of justice, but at least in the case of parental involvement, this aim is thwarted by the fact that many parents do not want to discipline their children or do not know that they need to. Without discipline, the children do not develop a sense of justice, and so they behave ungratefully. Choice B is a strong answer. The author argues that discipline imbeds in individuals a strong sense of justice, and that justice underpins responsibility, which drives gratitude. Based on this sequence of reasoning, disciplinary practices indirectly produce feelings of gratitude. Choice C is a weak answer. Although the author focuses a significant amount of attention on the lack of discipline exercised by Chinese parents, they do not believe that parents are entirely to blame for the ingratitude problem. They imply that a lack of knowledge about how to teach gratitude stems from the campaigns themselves. The passage identifies a lack of justice training in schools as another contributor to the issue of ingratitude. In general, be wary of answer choices that present an extreme opinion, as choice D does. Choice D is a weak answer, and choice B is the best answer.

21. **C is the best answer.** The author's main idea is that gratitude education campaigns do not achieve their intended purpose because they fail to promote a strong sense of justice in Chinese children born throughout the one-child policy era. The passage's spectrum ranges between the argument that gratitude can be taught through government campaigns and the argument that gratitude necessarily arises from a background of discipline, primarily rendered in the home. While the author identifies certain benefits of the campaigns, they believe strongly that they are insufficient for teaching gratitude because they do not promote the necessary precursors to gratitude (including justice). According to the author, parents can be effective at educating children about gratitude within the home if—and only if—they promote justice training. The author states that the campaigns are the product of the Chinese Communist Party, who established this initiative ostensibly to solve the ingratitude problem but also because they hoped to promote a certain ideology. The quotations around the Chinese government's claims about what has caused this social problem, as well as the use of the term "self-interested interpretations" indicate that the author does not agree with those sentiments or the campaigns. Although choice A, like the campaigns, includes parents in an effort to help teach their children, the author does not view the motivation for the campaigns in a wholly positive light. They believe that while the campaigns could promote improved interactions between children and parents if they were implemented differently, they were not created solely for this reason. Choice A is a weak answer. Choice B tries to trick the test-taker by incorporating mention of education reform. However, choice B does not align with passage information about what the campaigns intend to do. The tone of choice B is too positive, and the passage does not state that the campaigns are based off of empirical research. Instead, the author implies, they are inherently biased because they are meant to promote the Chinese government's ideology. Choice B is a weak answer. Like the gratitude campaigns, propaganda endorses an ideal that is perceived to benefit society (e.g. grateful children), even while it more insidiously pushes a different agenda (e.g. the Chinese Communist Party's ideology). Choice C presents an example that is as nuanced as the author's depiction of the function of the gratitude campaigns. Its tone, similarly, matches the author's. Choice C is a strong answer. Like the social media initiatives described in choice D, gratitude campaigns have widely broadcast the existence of a social problem, although the author does not state whether the campaigns first made people aware of children's ingratitude. Unlike choice D, though, the author says that the government has launched efforts at all levels of education and across the country, mandating gratitude-oriented activities, to solve this problem. Choice D does not match passage information, so it can be eliminated. Choice C is the best answer.

22. **A is the best answer.** The author's main idea is that the major reason the Chinese government's gratitude campaigns are ineffective is that they do not promote the values necessary to create grateful children. Based on the passage, gratitude campaigns seek only to increase awareness of gratitude and operate on the mistaken assumption that gratitude can be taught in this manner. According to the author, though, gratitude must be trained. Specifically, when children grasp a strong sense of justice early on, that leads them to develop a strong sense of responsibility. Responsibility is what causes people to act selflessly, rather than selfishly as human nature dictates. The author believes that people only understand justice when they are disciplined and have self-control. Choice A describes a situation in which two individuals set aside their considerations of personal gain in order to repay a kindness. Choice A aligns with passage information that responsibility involves repressing the instinct to indulge oneself and instead serve others. Choice A is a strong answer. In choice B, a woman makes sacrifices on behalf of her grandmother, but the answer choice states that she does so out of personal affection, or love. According to the author, for someone to act out of a strong sense of responsibility, they do so without regard to personal affection. Choice A is stronger than choice B because the former better aligns with passage information. Choice B can be eliminated. Choice C describes a scenario in which a child behaves in a certain way because he knows he will receive praise. The author writes that people with a strong sense of responsibility make sacrifices without regard to personal gain, including in the form of spiritual acclamation, which the child in choice C is seeking. Choice C is a weak answer. Choice D depicts a situation that matches a colloquial definition of "responsibility." Be careful not to incorporate outside knowledge when answering questions. Instead, refer only to passage content. In their description of responsibility, the author does not reference whether people act because they feel they must. Rather, they imply that they repay kindnesses because they want to. Choice A is a better answer than choice D because it more directly matches passage information. Choice A is the best answer.

23. **A is the best answer.** The author argues that Chinese parents are not disciplining their children or instilling in them a respect for authority. According to the author, discipline produces a sense of justice, which underpins the feeling of responsibility, which drives gratitude. The passage's main idea is that gratitude campaigns are unsuccessful because they do not emphasize the justice training needed to engender gratitude. The author argues that kids are unable to conceptualize justice because parents are not exercising authority over their children's actions. The best answer will describe a situation where Chinese parents discipline their children. In choice A, Chinese parents with only one child in fact punish their child when they have committed wrongdoings. If true, choice A would weaken the author's belief that Chinese parents' decision not to discipline their children contributes to these young people's ingratitude. Choice A is a strong answer. Choice B explicitly mentions parents who are born in a specific period, which falls outside the range of years the author identifies in the passage as a time of upheaval. According to the passage, people born in China from the 1950s to the 1970s suffered a great deal growing up, which is the primary reason why they choose not to discipline their own children. Choice B is a weak answer because it assumes that if parents of the 50s to 70s behave a certain way, individuals born after that time will as well. The author says certain parents avoid disciplining their children because they were raised in an authoritarian environment and do not want their children to suffer the way in the same way. However, they do not reference how these parents feel about failures or challenges in life in general. Choice C does not directly address the author's claims about Chinese parents, so it is a weak answer. Choice D presents a statement that reflects what Chinese children feel. The extent to which they feel controlled could vary significantly from the degree to which their parents are actually disciplining them, though. Choice D does not weaken the author's claims as much as does choice A. Choice A more specifically refutes the conclusion that Chinese parents do not exert authority over their only children. Choice D can be eliminated, and choice A is the best answer.

24. **C is the best answer.** The main idea of the passage is that gratitude education campaigns are ineffective because they do not promote the values necessary to engender grateful feelings and actions, specifically, that of justice. According to the author, children develop a strong sense of justice if they are disciplined. The problem in China for children of the one-child policy era is that neither schools nor their parents (the two main actors in the gratitude campaigns) promote justice training. Parents are also loathe to exercise authority over their kids. As a result, children are ungrateful. The author states explicitly that authority imbeds in children a sense of justice. In the first stage of the moral development theory, children come to understand justice by being disciplined when they behave poorly. Based on this framework, commending children when they behave well would not instill a sense of justice, so choice A can be eliminated. Although the author mentions that gratitude campaigns include the activity of parental story-telling, they do not believe that such efforts are productive. Telling morality stories to children does not align with the passage's idea that justice is borne out of discipline, so choice B can be eliminated. Choice C describes a scenario that matches passage information: the author writes that for children to understand justice, they must follow strict rules. When they commit wrongdoings, they receive punishment so that they understand the error of their ways and adjust their behavior in the future. Thus they can understand the meaning of justice. Choice C is a strong answer. Choice D does not directly address the passage argument that justice develops out of being disciplined appropriately. Although involving one's teachers could be viewed as punishment, choice C is a stronger answer because it is more specific.

Passage 5 (Questions 25-30)

25. **C is the best answer.** Throughout the passage, autonomy is discussed as a right of both the patient and the physician. In countries where physician-assisted suicide is legal, physicians are not required to perform the services. The physician is allowed to refer the patient to someone else, so choice A can be eliminated. In the author's opinion, the duties of a physician are unclear, so choice B is not the best answer. Choice C illustrates the autonomy of the physician, making it the best answer. Choice D is a weak answer because the physician is not required to perform services and, instead, can make a referral. Remember that when two answer choices are quite similar to each other, it is often the case that both can be eliminated.

26. **D is the best answer.** The author presents arguments both for and against physician-assisted suicide, but the main idea of the passage is that autonomy is the most important factor to be considered when discussing PAS –autonomy of both the patient and the physician. The passage is inconclusive about the definition of harm and whether physicians may sometimes be involved in processes that are harmful to the patient, such as assisted suicide, so choice A can be eliminated. Choice B is contradictory to the main idea because the author thinks patient autonomy is very important and only speaks of physicians as chaperones that lead patients through the decision-making processes. Choice C supports the autonomy of the patient while denying the autonomy of the physicians, so it can be eliminated. Choice D does not deny either the patient's or the physician's autonomy and alludes to the author's idea that a balance between the two is still being negotiated, making it the best answer.

27. **A is the best answer.** The concern for "vulnerable persons" is listed along with worry about patients' consent and the necessity of PAS in a world with increasingly effective palliative care. These concerns are reported as reasons for healthcare workers to oppose assisted death. Being dependent on others makes the patient vulnerable, and the author appears to be concerned about the well-being of patients, so choice A is a strong answer. The passage describes different factors in decision-making, but never attributes a value such as "rash" to these decisions, so choice B is not well-supported. Choice A is also better than choice B it uses the term "often" rather than more absolute phrasing. The MCAT® usually prefers answer choices that leave room for ambiguity. Choices C and D are not as strong as choice A because the healthcare workers would be unlikely to describe themselves as vulnerable, and would be more likely to focus their concerns on the people in their care. While legality was mentioned in the passage, Choice D is also weak because malpractice is not related to the main idea of the passage.

28. **C is the best answer.** The main idea of the passage is that the autonomies of the patient and physician are important factors to be considered when discussing physician-assisted suicide. The author does not place one autonomy over the other, so choice A can be eliminated. Choice B denies the patient's autonomy in favor of an institution's decision, and is contradictory to the information in the question stem, so it can be eliminated. If the hospital had determined that PAS ultimately harmed patients, there would be a legal policy prohibiting it. Choice C is better than choice A because it values the physicians' autonomy without as forcefully suppressing the patient's autonomy, though this answer may seem to contradict the implication in the question stem that the hospital as a whole refused to assist in the patient's death. Although the sanctity of life is briefly referenced in the passage as an argument against PAS, choice D is not the best answer because it does not allude to the main idea of autonomy. Also, like choice B, choice D is not consistent with the fact that the hospital does not have a policy for or against PAS. By process of elimination, choice C is the best answer.

29. **C is the best answer.** The main idea of the passage is that the autonomies of the patient and physician are paramount to the discussion about the legality and morality of physician-assisted suicide. The "other experts" are included in this passage as a counter to the argument that denying physician-assisted suicide denies autonomy, and thus they pose an opinion opposite to the main idea. The experts, in contrast to the author, focus on physician autonomy rather than patient autonomy, so choice A is not a strong answer. The experts also assert that rights over our own bodies are different than the right to ask others to severely alter those bodies. This assertion brings the discussion away from autonomy and towards a separate moral argument. As the experts are not focused on societal views of autonomy, choice B is not a compelling answer. The experts assume that physicians would have a power over death, instead of highly regulated laws and formalities that are standards for other aspects of care, making choice C the best answer. While the experts use the word "demand," choice D is a distractor using similar verbiage, and can be eliminated because the experts also speak about the power and autonomy of the physician.

30. **D is the best answer.** The argument posed in paragraph 4 is that allowing physician-assisted suicide would change a physician from a healer to a killer, and that morality would be lost. Stated more generally, this means a profession would change from something usually seen as positive to something usually seen as negative because of a change in the profession's duties. In choice A the banker changes professions entirely, so the answer choice can be eliminated. In choices B and C the stimulus for the change was not the duties of the job, but the people involved in the job, so these choices can also be eliminated. In choice D the computer specialist gained skills for a job that can be seen as negatively impacting society and a potential impetus for losing morality, making it the best answer choice.

Passage 6 (Questions 31-35)

31. **B is the best answer.** Throughout the passage, there is a spectrum of opinions regarding the value of reading books that are self-selected, even in the context of the classroom, and reading those that teachers feel pressured to assign. The author's main argument revolves around the importance of an individual choosing what he or she wants to read. The passage mentions many benefits of this self-selection, such as increased reading skills and the development of a love of reading. Since choosing literature can result in a valuable experience, choice A can be eliminated. The author does not argue that reading in the classroom cannot be valuable. An individual may enjoy a book assigned for class or may gain skills by selecting a book to read to complete an assignment. For this reason, choice C is not as strong as choice B. Because self-selected reading can increase literary skills, choice D can also be eliminated. Choice B is the best answer.

32. **A is the best answer.** When discussing the benefits of self-selected reading, the author points out that children with shared literary interests often form friendships because they like to talk about their reading material. These children have developed a love of reading and seek out one another, so choice A is a strong answer. Although the passage suggests that avid readers like to interact with one another, it does not suggest that they are more social in general. Choice B cannot be assumed true. While students with similar reading skills may work together on assignments, that is not supported by the passage since it does not discuss group assignments or overall academic ability. Choice C is not the strongest answer. Students who enjoy reading may share similar values about other aspects of life, but that is not suggested by the author since the passage focuses on reading skills specifically. Choice D is not as strong as choice A.

33. **D is the best answer.** This question relates to the author's main argument about the value of self-selected reading, because Serafini is cited to support the author's argument. Serafini is not suggesting that an individual must actively concentrate on improving reading skills, but instead they must put in the effort to read more. Choice A is not a strong answer. Serafini does not suggest all reading skills are inborn, but rather that they can improved. For this reason, choice B can be eliminated. Serafini does not address the different effects of reading fiction versus non-fiction or magazines versus novels, so choice C cannot be assumed true. Serafini acknowledges that most strong readers pick up a book because they enjoy it, and that their skills are enhanced naturally because they read more often. For this reason, choice D is the strongest answer.

34. **B is the best answer.** Throughout the passage, the author describes the benefits of self-selected reading for children of all different ages and personalities. The author points out that children these days are exploring more genres than in the past, so there is no reason to assume choice A is true. In the first paragraph, the author discusses all the factors that influence self-selection for reading. Although personality can affect reading preferences, it is not the only contributor, as previous experiences and even formatting can have an influence. Choice B is the best answer. The main idea of the passage concerns enjoyment of reading rather than book sales, which could be affected by many factors. For this reason, choice C is not as strong an answer as choice B. Lastly, the author emphasizes that all children can enjoy some form of reading. Choice D is not the best answer.

35. **A is the best answer.** Throughout the passage, the author argues that allowing children to select their own books to read will result in the greatest improvement of literary skills. Allowing a child to share that enjoyment with another individual increases their excitement to read, so their literary ability will continue to grow. If a child gets to select her own book and discuss it with another individual to enhance her understanding, then she will see the greatest increase in her reading skills. Choice A is a strong answer. The author emphasizes that social interactions about novel topics can increase the desire to read. If the father suggests the girl read alone, then the pair will not be able to discuss the girl's book as much and it will not benefit her reading skills the most, so choice B is not as strong as choice A. The author stresses that if a child has the desire to read and can select the book, then it will benefit reading skills the most. If the father suggests a more challenging book, then the child might feel like it is assigned and not enjoy the material as much or read as often. Choice C can be eliminated. If the father suggests that he read his own novel beside the girl, they will not be able to discuss her reading and the lack of social interaction will not increase her desire to read. Choice D is not as strong as choice A.

Passage 7 (Questions 36-41)

36. **A is the best answer.** The main idea of the passage is that something must be done to assure that Mexican nationals detained in the US receive the rights assured to them by the Vienna Convention. The author describes the treaty signed at the convention as proclaiming the rights and responsibilities of consuls, or representatives of one state residing in another. The treaty also includes a provision that accused foreign nationals need to be made aware of their rights to contact the consulate for assistance. Choice A has an element of bringing a person from the researcher's homeland to support the researcher, so it is a possible answer. In choice B the tourist does not have the *right* to use resources from their own country but can *only* use those resources, so it is not similar to the Vienna Convention and can be eliminated. In choice C, the children are provided with their detainment rights but do not have a representative or peer to help them through their detainment process, making it a weak answer. In choice D the student is allowed to bring something from a familiar place to a foreign place, but there is no suggestion of advocacy, so it is not the most convincing answer. Choice A is the best answer because the interpreter could potentially help out with tricky situations.

37. **A is the best answer.** While this question directs the reader back to paragraph 4, it can be answered without referring back to the passage by remembering the stance of the author and the main idea of the passage. The author's main argument is that something must be done to assure that detained Mexican nationals receive their rights as provided by the Vienna convention. Throughout the passage the U.S. is depicted as a stubborn country adverse to change, and the author specifically mentions that additions to the Miranda Rights might be resisted, make choice A a possible answer. As the country is depicted as individualistic and stubborn, police officers may choose what they will do regardless of written or oral materials. While the author insinuates that the Vienna Convention education materials are not used by police officers, the author does not speculate if they just did not reach the officers or if the officers chose not to read them. Further, the author is only concerned with consular rights and not all police procedures, so choice B is an extreme distractor. Throughout the passage, the author places blame on the actions of the U.S. on the state, federal, and individual levels, such as when citing federal unwillingness to control the state's execution of criminal law, making choice C a weak answer. Near the end of the passage, the author suggests that if the nationals had proper attorneys or were not already incriminated by the arresting officers, the nationals may have had a fighting chance, making choice D a possible answer. Choice A is better than choice D because it correlates better with the theme that the U.S. is adverse to change, and the author does not suggest the confessions given to the police officers were false, just that these confessions were just inappropriately obtained before counsel was available to the defendants.

38. **C is the best answer.** Part of the main idea of the passage is that the United States is denying foreign nationals the rights assured to them by the Vienna Convention. The author argues that the U.S. denies Mexicans their rights because the U.S. believes that the states should have power over their own jurisdiction and the federal government does not want to risk their reputation by exerting power over the states. The U.S. agrees to the terms of the treaty, but then does not think these terms apply to the U.S. because they do not fit with current in-country legal procedures. In choice A, the soccer coach had presumably agreed to the terms of the game but decided to lead the team down an illegal path, so it seems like a good answer. In choice B the mother had different standards for her own child than someone else's child, but the passage focuses on the U.S.'s treatment of the treaty in its own country, not the U.S.'s opinions on treaty enforcement in other countries, making this answer not well-supported. In choice C the teacher continued to follow his own ways in spite of new demands on student performance, which is similar to the way the U.S. continued to prosecute in the same manner it did before the Vienna Convention, so it is a compelling answer. Choice D again illustrates a double standard, but it is unclear which underlying doctrine the doctor is failing to uphold, so it is not a compelling answer. Remember not to bring outside opinions into the MCAT®, such as beliefs about the unwritten responsibilities of physicians. Choice C is better than choice A because its defiance illustrates a refusal to change one's ways, whereas it is unclear if the soccer coach championed tripping before she knew the rules of the game.

39. **D is the best answer.** The passage presents a spectrum of ideas about the way Mexican nationals are treated in the U.S. On one side of the spectrum are the Mexico sympathizers who believe the Vienna Convention should always be upheld. On the other side of the spectrum are the U.S. supporters who champion an individualistic government and just application of constitutional law. From the author's tone and provided examples, the author appears to be very much on the side of the Mexican sympathizers, but still closer to the middle of the spectrum because of their recognition of the necessity for justice to be served in the U.S. Since the author has a somewhat moderate view of the U.S., a reader should be wary of choosing an answer that is too extreme. The author does imply that the federal government is wary to step on the state's toes, so choice A is a promising answer. The passage cites the U.S.'s attempt to education law enforcement about the Vienna convention, so the author is unlikely to agree that no intention exists at all, making choice B a weak answer. The passage focuses on foreign detainees, not all foreign visitors, so choice C takes the author's opinion too far. The author does think that the U.S. cares more about its own rules than its promises, which can be seen as "selfish," so choice D is a compelling answer. Choice A is not as strong as choice D because the passage also states that the U.S. defends its actions to the world, so it is difficult to determine which image the country is more worried about.

40. **D is the best answer.** The focus of the passage is on the need to rectify the U.S.'s disregard of detained Mexican national's consular rights, so this question turns the tables and asks the reader to show how much they understand about the disposition of the U.S. and Mexico as presented in the passage. Choice A is tempting because the author portrays the U.S. as a potential perpetrator of a double standard, but the passage never actually reflects on how the U.S. believes the Vienna Convention should be carried out in other countries, so it is not a strong answer. Throughout the passage the author appears to put Mexico in a positive light by emphasizing the injustices the U.S. is placing on Mexican nationals, so choice B is a possibility. Lack of knowledgeable representation is a problem the passage attributes to U.S. law, while Mexican officials are depicted as well-informed in the Vienna Convention and capital law, so choice C can be eliminated. Choice D again puts Mexico in a positive light. Choice D is better than choice B because it is a more moderate positive response.

41. **C is the best answer.** The main idea of the passage is that something needs to be done to stop the U.S. from continuing to violate the Vienna Convention, particularly in the case of foreign nationals. Choice A is almost verbatim part of the main idea of the passage, so it could be argued that the entire passage is evidence to support it, and the answer choice can be eliminated. The U.S. claims to have supplied pamphlets to its law enforcement, but the author argues that there is a disconnect between this claim and Vienna Convention enforcement, so choice B seems to be a possible answer. One of the arguments supporting the U.S.'s actions is that if a defendant was justly tried, then their constitutional rights were preserved. The supporters of this argument believe that breaking the treaty is just a technicality, and not to be worried about since the constitutional rights were upheld, but the author immediately points out that upholding the treaty could have benefited the defendant. This means there was passage support *opposing* the claim presented in choice C rather than supporting it, making it a strong answer. Choice C is better than choice B because the latter provides specific statistical evidence, even though the author does not necessarily agree with the evidence provided. The author explains that information about past experiences, such as childhood trauma, could influence sentencing, so choice D can be eliminated.

Passage 8 (Questions 42-48)

42. **B is the best answer.** The main idea of the passage is that the obesity epidemic is caused by a mixture of intrinsic and extrinsic factors, but much of the blame can be placed on extrinsic entities such as agribusiness and major food companies. The researchers have a similar opinion, citing genetics, metabolism, and the environment as the perpetrators of obesity. The author and researchers are likely to believe the cure to obesity will involve multiple factors, so choice A is not a strong answer. The passage presents a spectrum of etiologies for the obesity epidemic from entirely extrinsic factors to entirely intrinsic factors. The author lies near the middle of this spectrum, leaning towards the extrinsic side. Choice B shows this interplay of intrinsic and extrinsic factors, making it a good answer. As the author believes that extrinsic entities play a role in obesity, the author would agree that obese people are not entirely at fault, but would not go so far as to say that they have no fault at all. Choice C is a conclusion that is too extreme. Choice D is not as strong as choice B because it does not illustrate the roles of both intrinsic and extrinsic components.

43. **B is the best answer.** The main idea of the passage is that a complex interplay of extrinsic and intrinsic factors has led to the current obesity epidemic. The author uses our Paleolithic ancestors as an example to highlight this main idea, as the presence of obese ancestors suggests a genetic or metabolic propensity towards obesity, and the low prevalence of obese ancestors suggests some outside change in diet and lifestyle over the years that lead to today's epidemic. Choice A is irrelevant to the main idea of the passage and is not the best answer. The passage does suggest that the diet of Paleolithic ancestors was more healthy than the current "toxic" diet, so choice B is a suitable answer. The lack of agribusiness should lead to fewer obese people, making choice C a contrary distractor. Choice D uses words similar to the passage but ultimately does not make sense, making it a nonsense distractor.

44. **C is the best answer.** The main idea of the passage is that the current obesity epidemic was caused by a variety of intrinsic and extrinsic factors, with an emphasis on outside players such as agribusiness. In the passage, agribusiness is described as affecting food by genetically modifying it, sending it around the world out-of-season, employing mass marketing, and promoting unhealthy foods as "part of a balanced diet." Option I is supported by the passage because genetically modifying crops changes their biological make-up. Since option I is correct, choice B can be eliminated. Option II is also supported because of corporations' ability to market out-of-season foods. As option II is also correct, choice A can be eliminated. The passage does not provide any information to indicate that corporations influence portion sizes, so option III is not well-supported, and choice D can be eliminated. Choice C is the best answer because it includes options I and II.

45. **C is the best answer.** The passage presents a spectrum of evidence for the cause of the current obesity epidemic, from only intrinsic factors to only extrinsic factors. The author shows that they believe the obesity epidemic arises from both intrinsic and extrinsic factors, but leans towards the extrinsic side. The fact that some Paleolithic ancestors were obese could point to the role of intrinsic factors, so choice A is a possible answer. Because global corporations are an outside entity, and one of the major extrinsic factors discussed by the author, choice B can be eliminated. Mental health is introduced in the passage outside of other extrinsic factors like agribusiness, and seems to be an example of an intrinsic factor. Choice C points to an intrinsic factor that may play an important role in obesity, undermining the passage argument about extrinsic factors playing the greatest role. Choice C is stronger than choice A because Paleolithic ancestors are only mentioned briefly at the beginning of the passage with no reference to intrinsic factors involved. The fact that an undefined number of Paleolithic individuals were obese does not necessarily weaken claims about the extrinsic causes of obesity. Choice C is the best answer. Choice D also seems to be a possibility because the lack of physical activity could be due to intrinsic decision-making. Choice C is better than choice D because choice D is also consistent with the extrinsic theory, as diet and the ability and the exercise have been shaped by societal pressures.

46. **B is the best answer.** The author presents a spectrum of reasons for the current obesity epidemic, from solely intrinsic factors to solely extrinsic factors. From the emphasis and tone in the passage the author shows that they lie somewhere in the middle of this spectrum, leaning toward the extrinsic factor side. Choice A is not a good answer because genetics are intrinsic factors. The author's reaction would more likely focus on the extrinsic factors that have led to the contestants' obesity. Choice B is a strong answer because agribusiness is the focus of the author's argument. Choice C is not compelling because lifestyle choices and eating habits are intrinsic factors. The author is unlikely to place blame entirely on the obese people, making choice D a weak answer.

47. **B is the best answer.** On a spectrum of entirely intrinsic causes to entirely extrinsic causes, the author believes the cause of the obesity epidemic lies somewhere in the middle, but towards the extrinsic side. Throughout the passage the author emphasizes the role of agribusiness as an instigator for the epidemic, but also points to decreased physical activity, epigenetics, metabolism, and mental illness as factors. Choice A seems to be a strong answer because the population could be influenced by outside Western ideals. Choice B also seems to be a strong choice because the growing economy would be receptive to agribusiness. Choice B is stronger than choice A because an expanding economy, and the potential for agribusiness, is more likely to influence the population than is an influx of tourists. Choice C might be tempting based on the inference that computer programmers are sedentary, but they may not be, and their Internet access could lead them to informed food consumption. While the author thinks the obesity outlook is bleak, the author believes the solution will be multifactorial with a focus on agribusiness, not genetics. This reasoning suggests that choice D is not a strong answer.

48. **D is the best answer.** The main idea of the passage is that the current obesity epidemic arose from both intrinsic and extrinsic factors, but especially outside players such as agribusiness. Where mental illness falls on this spectrum is not explicitly stated in the passage. The author argues that extrinsic commercial factors are the main focus for ending the obesity epidemic, not the eradication of mental illness, so Choice A can be eliminated. Though the role of mental illness is unknown, it is still a factor considered by the author, making choice B a weak answer. The author never speaks about treating mental illness and focuses on commercial enterprises as a mediator for change, so choice C can be eliminated. Choice D is the best answer because the role of mental health in the rise of obesity is unknown, but it is still a factor worth mentioning.

Passage 9 (Questions 49-53)

49. **C is the best answer.** The passage presents a spectrum of approaches of how best to interpret past historical events. On one end of the spectrum lies those that think historical writings are completely objective, and on the other end lies those who think historical writings are completely subjective. The author lies somewhere in the middle because she believes the past objectively happened, but there can be more than one interpretation. The author does not believe there is one objective report of the past, and that works of fiction can remind readers of the various interpretations. If the professor only reads history textbooks, then he is likely to learn about one interpretation of history that is common to textbooks. The author would likely not recommend limiting the reading to one genre, since the professor would only be exposed to one report of the past, so choice A can be eliminated. Similarly if a professor only interviews historians, then he will likely hear the scholarly opinion of past events. The historians could present a spectrum of opinions, but it is impossible to be sure. Choice B is a possible answer. The author emphasizes that works of fiction often present a new view of past events, and prevents them from being interpreted only one way. Choice C is stronger than choice B because it is more in line with the main idea of the passage, since it recognizes the value of fiction in interpreting history multiple ways. The author does not propose that fictional accounts should be interpreted literally, but rather be considered to remind the reader of the subjectivity of documenting history. Choice D is not as strong as choice C since it is more extreme than the author's opinion. Choice C is the best answer.

50. **B is the best answer.** Throughout the passage, the author stresses the importance of considering different accounts of history because each is tainted with subjectivity. The author does not mention any other historical theories, nor does she make any comparisons between postmodern theory and any others. Choice A can be eliminated. At the end of the passage, the author emphasizes that postmodern theory prevents history from being conclusive, because new interpretations should be considered. Choice B is a strong answer. The author does not suggest that theorists are more valuable than historians, because historians are needed for some interpretations of history. Choice C is not supported by passage information. Similarly, the author recognizes the value of postmodern theory but does not discount the value of other theories in the process. There is no reason to assume that the author would not encourage the development of new historical theories. Choice D cannot be assumed and choice B is the strongest answer.

51. **D is the best answer.** The main idea of the passage is that fictional works can help readers reach various conclusions about historical events, instead of believing in one objective truth. The author mentions the novel *The Passion* to give an example of fiction questioning past interpretations of history by utilizing subjective narrators. The best answer will likely involve subjectivity—a quality that the author of the passage values, even if some readers do not view the details as important in the scheme of the novel. A description of the setting is not necessarily biased by the narrator, since it could written in the third person. Choice A can be eliminated. Similarly, intricate character networks are dictated by the author, not the narrator, so choice B does not involve narrator subjectivity. Choice B can also be eliminated. The author stresses that the first narrator of *The Passion* does not recount historical events, but rather shares unnecessary details, which can be used by the reader to interpret the historical events. Choice C is not a strong answer. Because the first narrator writes in a diary, it is reasonable to assume that he is sharing persona feelings and thoughts, and that those subjective matters could be deemed unnecessary by some readers. Choice D involves a subjective point of view rather than an objective view of past events, so it is the best answer.

52. **C is the best answer.** The passage presents a spectrum of how best to reach conclusions about the past. Some individuals believe that the past can objectively be reported while others think that documentation of history is subjective in nature. The author proposes that multiple interpretations of historical events should be considered due to their subjective nature. She believes that historical accounts can rarely be considered facts, but she does not suggest that is the case with non-history subjects. Choice A is too general of a statement to be true. The author does not suggest that historical accounts are often inaccurate, only that they are clouded with bias. Choice B is too extreme of an answer choice for the author's tone throughout the passage. Near the end of the passage, the author proposes that skepticism can be helpful when considering historical accounts, so individuals can come to their own conclusions rather than blindly accepting others' views. Choice C is a promising answer. The author does not discuss honesty throughout the passage. She does not suggest that historians are lying or purposefully being untruthful, but rather they may alter accounts based on personal thoughts and beliefs. Choice D is not in line with the main argument of the author, as it does not relate to the concept of subjectivity in reporting historical events, so choice C is the best answer.

53. **A is the best answer.** The author believes that fiction is especially valuable when interpreting historical events because it presents new opinions and ideas. Because she stresses this value, it is reasonable to assume that historical textbooks do not necessarily present new opinions or ideas. If historical textbooks did propose multiple theories regarding the past, then works of fiction would not be as valuable when interpreting the past, because the historical textbooks would provide the distribution of judgments. Choice A is a strong answer. Even if historical textbooks are often reprinted with new information, that information is not necessarily presenting a new view, but rather could be expanding upon an objective point of view. Choice B is not a strong answer. The author believes that fictional works are useful because they emphasize the subjective nature of accounting history, so choice C would not weaken the author's argument since it is discussed in the passage. Even if fiction authors do not purposefully write characters with bias, they are still presenting new opinions and interpretations. The author of the passage would not value fiction any less, so choice D can be eliminated. Choice A is the strongest answer.

TEST **9**

ANSWERS & EXPLANATIONS

Questions 1–53

ANSWER KEY					
1. A	10. B	19. D	28. B	37. D	46. C
2. B	11. D	20. B	29. C	38. C	47. D
3. C	12. D	21. A	30. B	39. A	48. D
4. C	13. B	22. C	31. D	40. B	49. A
5. A	14. D	23. B	32. A	41. A	50. B
6. C	15. A	24. D	33. D	42. B	51. A
7. B	16. B	25. A	34. B	43. D	52. B
8. D	17. B	26. C	35. A	44. A	53. B
9. A	18. C	27. D	36. D	45. C	

EXPLANATIONS FOR TEST 9

Passage 1 (Questions 1-7)

1. **A is the best answer.** The author's main purpose in this passage is to draw attention to Watkins's novel approach to the history of places. His writing is at times overly enthusiastic, so it is important for the reader to keep his main idea in mind. In this question, the test taker is asked to express the author's ideas in different words. Choice A captures the author's key interpretation of Watkins: that history does not need to be imposed on an environment. Instead, it can arise naturally from it. Choice A is closest to this sentiment. Considering choice B, the author does not use the word "biography" in the literal sense (to refer to noteworthy people). He in fact uses "biography" to speak of place as though it was a person. For this reason, Choice B is out of scope. Choice C is tempting because it recognizes the originality of Watkins's outlook, but the author would not agree that Watkins's ley lines are "personalized" to him. Choice C is probably not the best. Choice D implies the existence of other mapping techniques in addition to Watkins's, but no others are mentioned by the passage. Choice D can be eliminated. Choice A is the best answer.

2. **B is the best answer.** It can be helpful to understand the tone of a passage to get a better sense of the author's attitude toward his subject. Imaging how the author would sound if the passage were read aloud. Bored? Factual? In fact, this author seems pretty enthusiastic about Watkins, and hopes to encourage other historians to think carefully about his approach to history. With this reading of tone in mind, it is easier to see that the author's main purpose in writing this passage is to draw attention to Watkins's novel approach to the history of places. While the author presents a variety of refined views about the implications of Watkins's ley lines, it is an overstatement to say his goal is to "critique," when in fact his views are quite positive. Choice A can be eliminated. Choice B better captures the author's chief sentiment about Watkins—that his was of approaching history is interesting and worth considering further. Choice B is promising. While the author does spend some time establishing Watkins's historical credentials, and elaborates a little on Watkins's technique, it would be inaccurate to say the goal of his passage was to introduce the reader generally to cartography—in fact, he is only interested in a very specific kind of English cartography, namely Watkins. Choice C can be eliminated. Choice D is tempting in that it says the author's goal is to "open a debate," a sentiment consistent with the author's desire to draw more attention to Watkins. However, the author never comments on whether not ley lines are historically legitimate, only that they are worth additional study, so choice D can be eliminated. Choice B is the best answer.

3. **C is the best answer.** This question asks the reader to adapt the author's argument to a new situation. A good technique for combined answer choices is to first see if any of the options appear in all of the choices. Cartography (Option II) appears in every choice, so the reader can turn to consider choices I and III. It is also reasonable to think that a cartography, or the study of maps, would be relevant to a history like Watkins's, which relies on a spatial relationship between places. It is unlikely that the author would think Urban Design as a crucial field to the study of ley lines. The author states that ley lines would be "lost in the contemporary urban existence." Option I is unlikely, so choices B and D can be ruled out. Because Watkins's original research dealt with matters of local history, and his ley lines linked various aspects of history, it is reasonable to think that a historian would be in attendance. Option III is likely. For this reason, we can rule in option III, and rule out choice B. Choice C is the best answer.

4. **C is the best answer.** The passage's main idea is to advocate for Watkins's unique way of imagining history through geography. This question asks the reader to imagine how the author would respond to an objection to Watkins's technique. Choice A suggests that the author advocates for Watkins's method because it actually establishes causal links between different eras. The author does not advocate for Watkins for this reason—rather, it is how Watkins thinks about the project of history as a whole that the author finds appealing. Choice A can be eliminated. Choice B suggests that the author thinks Watkins's account is autobiographical, but there is no evidence to support this idea—in fact, Watkins's himself thought that his project was rather objective, a notion that the author does not contest. Choice B is not the best choice. Considering choice C, the author is excited and enthusiastic about drawing attention to Watkins's ideas, and would likely describe them as "alternative" and "enriching," with regard to the general practice of history. Choice C does a good job capturing the main idea of the passage, so it is very promising. Choice D temptingly borrows language from the passage, but the categories of historical evidence proposed toward the beginning of the passage are Watkins's, not the author's. The claim is also in overstated terms. Given the MCAT®'s dislike for oversimplification of views, it is unlikely that "only" one historical approach accounts for "all existing" evidence. Choice D can be eliminated. Choice C is the best answer.

5. **A is the best answer.** The author likely has many goals in quoting Daniels near the end of the passage, and this question asks you to choose the one that fits the main idea the best. The author's goal is to draw critical attention to Watkins's original approach to history by way of geography—allows the best answer choice to become apparent. Of the options given, choice A most directly expresses this sentiment, so it is very promising in this regard. Choice B is very tempting, in that does accurately describe one of the notions proposed by Daniels, but it does not capture the author's main idea. Choice B can be ruled out. Choice C characterizes Daniels's reading of Watkins as more "skeptical," but the language of the quotations do not show any skepticism—in fact, Daniels seems about as enthusiastic as the author. Choice C can be eliminated. The idea expressed in choice D is not unique to Daniels, as similar notions are expressed by the author throughout the piece, and the question stem specifically asks what new idea the author is trying to point out. This option also does not acknowledge the author's primary aim to advocate directly for Watkins's ideas, so choice D is not the best. Choice A remains the best answer.

6. **C is the best answer.** The passage's main idea is to advocate for Watkins's particular way of practicing history through ley lines. The author describes not only Watkins's attitude toward geography and history, but also provides some insight into what Watkins's thoughts about his own idea. Considering choice A, there is no direct reference to Watkins choosing among equivalent ley lines. Choice A can be eliminated. While there is some reference to Watkins's large amounts of recorded material in the passage, there is no indication that any of his writings were personal. Choice B can be eliminated. Choice C does a good job capturing the author's description of Watkins's attitude. The word "objective" reflects the author's characterization that in creating ley lines, Watkins was interested in "a diagnosis of the facts as they presented themselves to him." Choice C is promising. Choice D is tempting because it sounds plausible in the context of a history passage, but there is no comment at all on Watkins's idea about creativity, so this answer choice is out of scope. Choice D can be ruled out. Choice C is the best answer.

7. **B is the best answer.** This question asks the reader to apply Watkins's method of examining history to a different context. The passage's main idea is that more contemporary critical attention should be paid to Watkins's geographic approach to history, so this question asks the reader to consider several options as to how that might be done today. Choice A may be tempting because Watkins's travels took place in England, but the analysis described in this choice has little to do with his idea of geography and ley lines, so it can be eliminated. Choice B is plausible because it seeks to pursue the object of study (in this case, literature) by way of a geographical association (Park Avenue). Choice B is promising. Choice C is out of scope, because there is no indication in the passage that ley lines are related to the loss of draft materials. Choice C is unlikely. Choice D is interesting because the project implies travel with the phrase "varying distances." However, the study does not capture notion of a history organized by linear geography, which is central to Watkins's idea. Choice D can be eliminated. Choice B is the best answer.

Passage 2 (Questions 8-13)

8. **D is the best answer.** The main idea of the passage is that some form of structured standards and education needs to be integrated into the architecture profession to promote horizontal sharing and overall awareness of individual failures so that these failures can be avoided in the future. While the author is likely to agree that building failure happens overly frequently, it is too extreme to say it happens all the time, so choice A can be eliminated. The author states that both small and big problems can lead to large scale failures, but provides an example that suggests that these failures are more due to lack of knowledge than lack of detail, so choice B is not well-supported. While the author says that building failure is recently gaining more attention, there is not information in the passage to suggest that the problem in and of itself is new, so choice C is a poor answer. Part of the main idea is the need for education reform, so choice D is the best answer.

9. **A is the best answer.** The main idea of the passage is that organized and clear guidelines and education changes need to be incorporated into the architecture profession to prevent future building failures. The author mentions an example in which a building failed because the type of failure was unfamiliar to the architect. Choice A also relates to the lack of continuous education that the author cites in the passage. For these reasons, choice A is a strong answer. Choice B seems similar to choice A, but the author never implies that architects need to be trained in all things, just that they should be able to access information and have set standards for possible projects, making choice B a weak answer. The author does emphasize the importance of a mentor, but there is not enough information provided in choice C to assume that a mentor would have provided information about another architect's mistakes. In fact, the passage suggests that current mentors do not provide such information, so choice C can be eliminated. Choice D mentions poor guidelines, so it seems to be in line with the main idea of the article. However, the author says that the current standards are incomplete, whereas the word "flawed" in choice D suggests that they are altogether wrong, so it is a weak answer. Choice A is the strongest answer.

10. **B is the best answer.** Part of the main idea of the passage is that architecture education needs to be adapted so that new and current architects create fewer situations that lead to building failure. The author suggests that if students have a specific mentor who makes a point to teach a student about their own mistakes, the student may not make the same mistakes in the future. Choice A does not mention mentoring in the sense that it used in the passage, so it is not a strong answer. Choice B describes a situation where students perform better in a traditional educational setting instead of a mentorship, so it is a compelling answer. Choice C also details a situation where more learning happens in the classroom than on the wards, but the knowledge being spoken about is not necessarily crucial to functioning well on the wards, whereas avoiding building mistakes is knowledge crucial to building in the real world, so choice C is not the best answer. Choice D again suggests better outcomes in classrooms than in the real world and highlights the main idea of finding out information to avoid mistakes. However, choice B is better than choice D because choice D does not specifically mention the role of a mentor in the inability to troubleshoot.

11. **D is the best answer.** The main idea of the passage is that formal standards and education reform need to be integrated into the architecture profession to promote awareness of building failures by sharing them among architects in a non-generic manner. The author says that architects should have "continuous education" and then suggests that "continuing education" only affects one generation or individual, but knowledge is not shared within or between generations. Choice A suggests a reasonable distinction between continuing and continuous education, but does not reflect the distinction the author describes in the passage, so it is out of the scope of the project. Resources outside of the curriculum could mean gathering information from other architects, so choice B seems to be a possible answer. Choice C is in line with the main idea of the passage but does not obviously answer the question about the difference between continuous and continuing education, so it can be eliminated. Choice D is also in line with the main idea because the author believes that sharing details between architects continuously will lead to fewer building failures. Choice D is better than choice B because it suggests an ongoing sharing instead of a case-by-case sharing, and it answers the question more directly by speaking to the author's core point, rather than focusing specifically on continuing education classes.

12. **D is the best answer.** The author mentions a new Google Feed that lists specific building failures in real time, which suggests that architects can access this feed, see others' failures, and not repeat the same mistakes in the future. The author appears to offer this feed as a possible solution to flaws in the current education and architecture standards that have led to the occurrence of similar building failures among various architects. The security camera in choice A has the continuous monitor or reference, but it does not lead to quality improvement outside of that manager's business, so choice A is not a strong answer. The teleconference in choice B allows for sharing within the field, but it likely will not lead to fewer failures in that field, so choice B is not the best answer. Choice C describes the meeting of several administrators to horizontally share information about avoiding mistakes and creating better outcomes, so it appears to be a good answer. Choice D offers a hotline that can be referenced at any time to help make a good decision, so it is also a possible answer. Choice D is better than choice C because it has the element of continuous updates within a field – other drivers – whereas choice C is only annual. This means in choice D the hotline is "continuous" while in choice C the meeting is "continuing", so choice D most accurately represents the Google Feed and is the best answer.

13. **B is the best answer.** The main idea of the passage is that long-term educational and guideline changes need to be implemented in the current architecture profession to avoid building mistakes. The author contends that one of the main causes of these mistakes is the inability or unwillingness among architects to share their failures with each other, so other architects are doomed to make the same mistake. The author does state that the current teaching of building mistakes is often too general, but the author also mentions building mistakes on structures as small as decks. This means that the author is unlikely to be most supportive of an education that only mentions the biggest building mistakes, making choice A a weak answer. The author believes that the architects need to learn from and share with each other, so the author would probably support starting that sharing at a networking event, making choice B a strong answer. The author provides a possible solution to the lack of sharing among architects by mentioning the new Google Feed of industry mistakes, so accessing information in choice C makes this answer appealing. However, choice B is better than choice C because the answer choice does specifically mention what kind of resources are being obtained and it cannot be assumed that these resources will lead to intra-professional sharing of mistakes. The author does state in the passage that the lack of clarity in standards and protocols may lead to certain building failures, but the author is unlikely to believe a single lecture will cure this long-term problem, so choice D can be eliminated. Choice B is the best answer.

Passage 3 (Questions 14-19)

14. **D is the best answer.** The author's main goal in writing this passage is to draw attention to the fact that while much recent art has failed to be correctly inspired by technology, some new art is (specifically, "Techno Art" and "Sci Art"). The author contrasts these promising modes of expression with older forms of art that have failed to make use of technology properly—namely, post-modernism. While the author expresses himself enthusiastically, with imaginative and flowery language, he is not enthusiastic about post-modern art. Choice A can be eliminated. Considering choice B, "inhibited" suggests that the author's tone is restrained, which is the opposite of the enthusiasm he actually shows, so choice B can be eliminated. The wording of choice C is a little too strong—the author does not dismiss post-modern art: in fact, he spends much of the passage engaging with its problems. Choice C can be ruled out. It is fair to say that the author does not think much of post-modern art, and a good synonym for this is "unimpressed." Choice D is the best answer.

15. **A is the best answer.** This question asks the reader to adapt the information found in the passage to a new and imaginary situation. A clear conception of the author's main idea—that several newer forms of art do a better job at integrating technology than other forms—is crucial to picking the right answer. Considering choice A, it is true that the forms of art that the author admires use technology in new and novel ways. It is possible that a collage of images made from the readouts of a scientific instrument would be inspiring to a practitioner of "Sci Art," so choice A is promising. Considering choice B, the author introduces the passage with a description of how the chariot affected many generations of artists, so it is easy to imagine that the water wheel, as a similar piece of inspiring but rudimentary technology, might do the same. But it is important to keep in mind that the author's primary goal is not to celebrate old art that used ancient technology correctly, but to introduce new art that uses current technology in meaningful ways. Choice B is tempting but probably not the best. Choice C may be appealing because the word "Apollo" is mentioned in relation to an artistic exhibition earlier in the passage, but such recognizable words can often be a trap. The author actually criticizes the Apollo exhibition mentioned, so it is not probable that he would approve of this one. Choice C can be eliminated. While the scarecrow found in choice D might be seen as another piece of primitive agricultural technology, it is important to remember the author is not interested in how art can be adapted to make technology, but how technology contributes to the creation of art. Choice D can be eliminated. Choice A is the best answer.

16. **B is the best answer.** Recall that the author's central claim is that newer forms of art (like "Techno Art" and "Sci Art") do a better job engaging with contemporary technology than other forms of recent art ("Post-modernism" and "Conceptualism"). While several of these answer choices are plausible, only one effectively challenges that main idea. Considering choice A, the author's example of the chariot does not express the main idea of the passage, because the author is interested in the art of the future, not the art of the past. Whether or not chariots were new technology does not affect his main contention, nor does it challenge his more minor point that technology has been inspiring to artists of the past. Choice A is not the best. Choice B argues that recent art like post-modernism—contrary to the author's claim—actually integrates new technology into its mode of expression. This is a key quality that the author reserves for the newer forms of art he wants to endorse, so if this were to be true, his argument would be significantly impaired. Choice B is promising. Choice C is tempting, because it claims to establish a link between a form of art the author admires ("Techno Art") and an aspect of postmodernism the author dislikes ("abstraction"). But the fact that other scholars have argued this point does not necessarily make their claims true, so C is not the best choice. Considering choice D, it might be reasonable to infer that some understanding of technology is important to creating art based on technology, but the author does not claim this to be true. Choice D can be eliminated. Choice B is the best answer.

17. **B is the best answer.** This question asks the reader to understand how the author has made use of an example when building his argument. Even though a specific part of the argument is addressed by the question stem, a clear understanding of the main idea is the most effective way to eliminate weak or unsupported answer choices. Recall that the author thinks that a meaningful engagement with technology is important to good art, and seeks to advance contemporary art forms that he feels does this well. He brings the artists Monet and Rivera into the middle of his discussion to illustrate how technology was properly integrated into art in the past. Choice A attempts to confuse the test taker by moving around in time: Monet and Rivera are not current artists that the author is interested in, so they cannot be a part of new artistic movements. Choice A is not the best. Choice B expresses the author's goal for the main idea, and correctly positions Monet and Rivera as artists who are in line with his ideas. It also correctly identifies them as artists of the past, not the present. Choice B is promising. Choice C temptingly engages some ideas associated with the author's argument, but the author never mentions a pre-technological period of art—in fact, his description of the chariot refers to artistic practices that are quite old. From what can be found in the passage, it is not clear if the author would agree that a pre-technological period of art even exists. Choice C can be eliminated. Choice D is tempting because it uses the word "Renaissance," which appears in the same paragraph as the artists mentioned. But there is no indication that Monet and Rivera are Renaissance artists, so choice D can be eliminated. Choice B is the best answer.

18. **C is the best answer.** It is clear that the author believes art needs to engage technology, but that does not necessarily mean that he is single-minded in a belief that all technology is good. Remember that the author's goal is not to talk about technology, but technology's role in the creation of art. Choice A is tempting because the statement in itself is true—he and the Futurists would agree that the future of art relies on bringing technology into art. But this does not mean he agrees with the Futurist's enthusiasm for technology in general. Choice A is probably not the best. Choice B may tempt those readers who bring in outside knowledge: while Cubism and Futurism are related historical movements, and Cubism is even mentioned in the passage, there is no link in the passage between these two forms of art. It is not safe to infer that the author's approval of Cubism would extend to Futurism, so choice B can be eliminated. Choice C is expressed simply, but it does effectively capture the author's complex feelings toward the role of technology in the world. Notice that the author does not necessarily think that technology is good—he agrees with another writer who characterizes technology as a "whirlpool"—but he does think art that engages with technology is good. Choice C is promising. Choice D may be tempting because the author may seem like the type who may resist nationalistic forms of cultural explanation, beware of extrapolating too much: nationalism is not mentioned at all in the passage. Choice D can be eliminated. Choice C is the best answer.

19. **D is the best answer.** Recall that the author's main purpose in writing the passage is to argue for the meaningful incorporation of technology into contemporary artistic expression. In this question, the reader is asked to imagine a new piece of art, and consider whether or not it would satisfy the author's expectations. Choice A is tempting because it endorses the use of current technology in art. But it is important to notice that the author believes that there are good and bad ways of integrating art, and in fact the "assimilation" or "transubstantiation" of technology into art is crucial. The artwork provided would probably not satisfy the author because the technology is not being significantly altered by the artist. Choice A is unlikely. Considering choice B, while it is true that the artist feels that technology is brought into human life by art, it doesn't necessarily follow that any introduction of technology to a general public with satisfy him. Choice B is not sufficient to satisfy the author. Be careful not to draw upon outside knowledge when considering choice C: while it may seem tempting to conclude that book is not a form of art that would belong in a museum, this may not be the case for the author. There is no discussion of the difference between visual and printed artwork, so it is unlikely that a question would ask you to conclude some difference between the two. Choice C is probably not the best. Choice D contends that the author would not find the artwork meaningful because the artists is not "engaging" with the images. The passage shows that the author thinks there are more and less effective ways to bring technology into art, and that some kind of give-and-take between technology and art—communicated by words like "assimilation" and "transubstation"—is important to meaningful expression. Choice D is the most promising of the options given, and is the best answer.

Passage 4 (Questions 20-24)

20. **B is the best answer.** Throughout the passage, there is a spectrum presented between the concept of identity proposed by the author and the two prior concepts, which had a simplistic individual versus social conception, and did not focus on change over time. The author's main argument revolves around how identities can change when an individual is part of a team. Because the author believes the team members have an influence on one another, he would probably not suggest studying the individuals on their own. Choice A can be eliminated. The author believes that an individual's identity can be altered as a result of participating in team activities, so he would probably suggest studying the team members over a long period of time to establish a baseline identity and note the changes that occur. Choice B speaks to the main contrast between the author's beliefs and previous conceptions, so it is a strong answer. Although studying team members during training sessions might be helpful, it would not provide a full scope of identity change since it would just relate to one aspect of an individual's life. Choice C does not include the sequential analysis that the author values, so it is not as strong as choice B. The author does not suggest that interactions with a coach are most responsible for an identity change, so choice D is not the strongest answer. Additionally, choices C and D are so similar that neither is likely to be the strongest answer, since they would both involve studying team members at group practices. For these reasons, choice B is the best answer.

21. **A is the best answer.** The passage presents a spectrum of approaches to the psychology of sports. Previous researchers focused on only individual or social effects, but the author complicates this approach by proposing a conception of individual identity that is socially negotiated. Throughout the passage, the author argues that individuals must be studied in the context of the team to correctly note identity changes. He proposes this perspective because he believes that past research has not focused on the correct interactions; either they have been too individual or too social. He believes they must be combined to note the effect of team participation on each individual, so choice A is a strong answer choice. The author does not suggest that team members should only be studied as a group, because he wants to track each team member's personal identity change. He suggests studying team members individually and in the team context, so choice B is not the most contrary to the author's opinion. Though choice C seems like an overgeneralization, the author does not address group dynamics from team to team, so it does not directly oppose his opinion. The author believes that individual identities change while on a sports team, he does not believe that a sports team identity has to necessarily change. Choice D is not as strong as choice A.

22. **C is the best answer.** Throughout the passage, the author argues that team interactions can change an individual's identity. The author's main idea relates to identity in team sports, but he does not discuss how identity changes over a lifetime. Choice A is too general of a statement to be true. The author discusses the effects of these social interactions that happen naturally—he does not suggest that the individuals are trying to change one another. This answer choice misinterprets how "negotiation" is used in paragraph three, because the author does not suggest it is an intentional interaction between individuals. Choice B is a possible answer, but not particularly strong. If athletes describe themselves before and after joining the team, then their personal identity changes caused by team interactions will be evident. Choice C relates to the author's main argument, so it is stronger than choice B. The author does not discuss the identity of the team as a whole, but rather those of members of a team. Choice D is not discussed in the author's argument, so it is not as strong as choice C.

23. **B is the best answer.** The author believes that team interactions affect an individual's social identity, so athletes should be studied across time while participating in a team sport. Even if athletes prefer to participate in research studies individually, the author would still believe they should be studied in a team context too, even if the athletes do not prefer it. The author does not discuss athletes' preferences in research, so choice A is unrelated to the author's argument. If individuals experience identity change regardless of participation in team sports, then there is no reason to assume that the team interactions affected social identity. There would be no need to adopt to the author's proposed method of studying team interactions since they are not necessarily influential. Choice B is a possible answer. The author's argument relates to an individual before and after participating in a team sport—it does not relate to the identity of all individuals playing team sports. Even if those athletes have similar identities, those identities are not necessarily developed discursively through the team experience, as the author argues. The argument does not depend on personality differences, so choice C can be eliminated. The author does not address how team dynamics might change as individual identities change, so choice D does not relate to the main idea of the passage. For these reasons, choice B is the best answer.

24. **D is the best answer.** The author's argument revolves around the influence of team sports on self-identity. He does not suggest that the participating in team sports results in a positive change, but rather he argues that it results in some sort of change. The author does not suggest that team sports build character, but rather alter it. Choice A is attempting to appeal to personal opinions or biases, but it is not supported by the passage and can be eliminated. While leadership roles may alter an individual's personality, the author does not propose this idea. He believes that team participation can alter an individual's personality, not necessarily a leadership role. Choice B is not a strong answer. The author's argument relates to social interaction in a team context, not as a whole. Though social interaction might be necessary to self-development, the author does not make suggestions about social interactions in general, so choice C can be eliminated. The author believes that team sports change an individual's identity, and even states that identity is "not a pure and stable unit." Choice D agrees with the passage since the author specifically states that identities are often changing. For these reasons, choice D is the best answer.

Passage 5 (Questions 25-31)

25. **A is the best answer.** The passage sets up a spectrum between Buddhist and Western ways of understanding the world. The author favors the Buddhist understanding, and defends Buddhist ideas against the claims developed by Western science's expectations. The main idea is that a Buddhist attitude establishes no hierarchy between subjective and objective experiences, which in contrast to Western science's acceptance of only physical phenomena as the basis for truth. Given the development of these terms in the passage, neuroscience is best associated with a Western scientific worldview, and the author's purpose is to question the notion that such a worldview ought to be automatically accepted. Answer A is consistent with this main idea, in that it questions whether the physical world can support claims to truth on its own, so is a likely candidate. Considering choice B, it is true according to the passage that a Buddhist does believe that the mind arises from the body, but this answer choice is expressed in extreme language ("entirely"). It is also true that a neuroscientist would agree with this statement, so this answer does not effectively challenge neuroscience's assumptions. Choice B can be eliminated. Choice C is a distractor that attributes a Buddhist belief—that matter is a phenomenological event—incorrectly to neuroscientists. Choice C can be eliminated. Choice D adheres closely to language found near the end of the passage, but misrepresents Buddhism as favoring a monist view of the world, when in fact the author explicitly states that a Buddhist worldview is not monist. Choice A is the best answer.

26. **C is the best answer.** The main idea of the passage is that Buddhism does not prioritize external events over internal events, unlike Western science. The word "phenomenological," appearing as often as it does, is important to the author's expression of this main idea. Choice A is tempting because the root word "phenomenon" puts the test-taker in mind of an extraordinary event, but there is no notion in the passage that external events of any particular magnitude are more important than any other. Choice A can be eliminated. Considering choice B, the test-taker should note that the author's main idea is to downplay the automatic legitimacy that Western thought confers on external events, so it is unlikely that the author would recognize a substantial difference between the physical world of reality and the internal world of imagination. Choice B can be eliminated. Choice C does the best job leveling the difference between internal and external events, which is consistent with the author's point, and is the best choice. Choice D is a weak answer because according to the passage, Buddhism rejects the notion of all essences, including the soul. Though the tone of reverence may sound religious, its claim is opposite the author's intention. Choice D can be eliminated, and choice C is the best answer.

27. **D is the best answer.** This question asks the reader to adapt the passage to an imaginary situation. Answering the question requires extrapolation from several views presented in the text. It is important to distinguish the author's position from the vision of Western science presented in the passage. According to the authors, Buddhist thought does not automatically recognize the legitimacy of physical phenomena without a consideration of internal states. Choice A is tempting, in that a Buddhist would generally approve of the interrelatedness of the internal and external worlds, but the strong language of causality ("bear directly") makes it unlikely that Buddhists would express themselves in this way. Buddhists would be reluctant to prioritize one event (cause) over another (effect), as this an attitude better attributed to Western science. The MCAT® typically favors choice that are less extreme, so choice A can be eliminated. Choice B is out of scope, because there is no discussion in the passage that a Buddhist's idea of truth requires a clearly defined question. Choice B can be eliminated. Given the main idea of the passage, choice C is not the best, because a Buddhist probably would not say that an experience "does not qualify" as legitimate, as this attitude is part of the author's criticism of Western science's view of subjective experience. Choice C can be ruled out. Choice D captures both the ambivalence to individual experience that the author attributes to Western science, and also restates the central Buddhist idea that events in the world always take place within individual experience. The best answer is choice D.

28. **B is the best answer.** The main idea of the passage is that Buddhism does not prioritize external experiences over internal experiences, as does Western science. Psychology is a division of Western science, and so is legitimately subject to the author's criticism. The question asks the test-taker to identify the most problematic aspect of this science. Choice A is not on its face objectionable to the Buddhist ideas presented in the passage, in that it accounts for subjectivity. This aspect of psychology might even be appealing to Buddhists, so choice A can be eliminated. Choice B is worth careful consideration. Psychology is subject to the same demands to prove causal relationships as other divisions of Western science, and from the passage we know that Buddhism is reluctant to automatically accept causal relationships as legitimate ground for claims about truth. Choice B is the best option. Choice C is not the best choice because Buddhists are not concerned with the ability to replicate outcomes—they are more interested in the nature of experience itself. In fact, this choice expresses a Western criticism of psychology, not a Buddhist criticism. Choice C can be eliminated. Choice D is out of scope, as psychoanalysis is not mentioned anywhere in the passage, and the author makes no claims as to whether or not its attitudes and methods are compatible with Buddhism. Choice B is the best answer.

29. **C is the best answer.** Recall that the author's central contention is the Buddhism, unlike Western science, does not prioritize external over internal experiences. The best answer choice will somehow extrapolate from this idea. Choice A is tempting as the author mentions mental representation within the passage, but it is to assert that Buddhism does not reduce outward events to internal mental states. Choice A dramatizes precisely this phenomenon, and so can be eliminated. Choice B draws attention to the establishment of a Western scientific fact, and so would do best to illustrate one of the Western scientific viewpoints that the author disagrees with, rather than the Buddhist point of view the question stem asks for. Choice B can be eliminated. The scenario presented in choice C presents a world in which internal and external experiences influence each other, which is consistent with the author's main idea. Choice D draws the reader's attention to the passage of time and punishment, neither of which is addressed in the passage. Choice D is out of scope, and can be eliminated. Choice C is the best answer.

30. **B is the best answer.** The passage's main idea is that a Buddhist attitude establishes no hierarchy between subjective and objective experiences, which is different from Western science's preference for physical rather than mental phenomena as the basis for truth. While it may be tempting to return to Barash's quotation to approach this question, a solid understanding of the main idea allows the elimination of most answer choices. Choice A is not the best because the author states that Buddhism does not allow for essences, of which the soul is given as an example. Choice A can be eliminated. Choice B is promising because it avoids the hierarchical language that might indicate a preference for external over internal experiences, which the author claims is Western science's mistake. Considering choice C, it would be inaccurate to say that the passage engages religion as a whole, so claims comparing religion and science in general (instead of, specifically, Buddhism and Western science) are likely out of scope. It is also inconsistent with the passage's main idea to say that Buddhism departs from the spirit, when the language of essences is explicitly non-Buddhist. Choice C can be eliminated. Cartesianism is mentioned only once, at the very end of the passage, and elaborates a position that is not central to the main idea. It is never said to bear at all on the differences between physical and mental phenomena, and so choice D is out of scope, and can be eliminated. Beware of answer choices that use complicated vocabulary from the passage. Choice B is the best answer.

31. **D is the best answer.** This question requires reconciliation of the two contrasting views presented in the passage. The passage has set up a spectrum between Buddhist and Western ways of understanding the world, and the author favors the Buddhist understanding. The author's central contention is that Buddhism, unlike Western science, does not emphasize a difference between internal and external experiences. Looking for the best answer, it will be important to acknowledge this central difference. Choice A would not be agreeable to a Buddhist, as challenging the legitimacy of those claims is the central goal of the passage. While choice B offers a balanced view of internal and external states, it recognizes the central role of causality in connecting those states, which would be agreeable to a scientist but not a Buddhist. Choice C is tempting in its appearance of fairness, but it is safe to conclude that neither a scientist nor a Buddhist would agree: the Buddhist would object to the characterization of a purely mentally determined worldview, and the scientist would likely refuse the notion that Western science's claims to truth were in any way provisional. Choice C can be eliminated. Choice D, worded as it is, would in fact be agreeable to both scientists and Buddhists, but for different reasons. Near the beginning of the passage, the author recognizes that Buddhism sees the mind as arising from the body, but suggests that this view is not to be collapsed into the basic mind-brain materialism assumed by Western science. The wording of choice D does not exclude this interpretation, however, so would be acceptable to a scientist. Choice D is the best answer.

Passage 6 (Questions 32-36)

32. **A is the best answer.** The passage presents a spectrum of opinions regarding the value of dance programs as physical activity for female adolescents. While the author argues that dance can positively contribute to both the physical and mental health of women, they do not believe it has accomplished these goals yet. The UK school system has implemented dance programs for six weeks in order to satisfy the physical activity requirements in the national curriculum. Although the author suggests that the programs have not been very successful at inspiring young women, they do not imply that they do not fulfill the physical activity requirement. Option I is true and choices B and D can be eliminated. Near the beginning of the passage, the author discusses the benefits of dance, like creative thinking and teamwork. However, the author does not believe that school dance programs have been successful and rather discusses teamwork as a possible future benefit if different dance programs are implemented. Option II is not a strong answer. The author similarly believes that dance programs have the potential to motivate young women and build confidence, but that current programs have not been successful in this endeavor. The author discusses the need to alter school dance programs so that they can have longer-lasting benefits, like those mentioned in Option III. For this reason, choice C can be eliminated and choice A is the best answer.

33. **D is the best answer.** There is a spectrum of opinions in the passage regarding the value of dance programs in UK schools, with the author ultimately concluding that current programs could greatly be improved to better motivate young women physically and mentally. The author does not suggest that dance programs in the UK are unsuccessful, but that school-based programs are not very successful. Choice A is too broad and can be eliminated. The author believes that the dance programs in schools need to be altered, but does not necessarily suggest that they require more funding. Choice B is not particularly strong. While the author discusses the statistics regarding the lack of dance teachers in physical education roles, they do not elaborate on this shortage. There is no reason to assume that dance teachers do not apply for those jobs, because there could be other factors that determine why they are not hired. Choice C can be eliminated. Throughout the passage, the author suggests that dance teachers have the potential to inspire and motivate young women. The author specifically suggests implementing programs with passionate dance teachers so that adolescents are more likely to have a positive experience and continue to dance as a form of physical activity. Choice D is suggested by the passage and can be selected as the best answer.

34. **B is the best answer.** The author argues for the implementation of more effective dance programs in schools so that more young women can experience the benefits. While the author suggests that dance can improve creativity, it is not necessarily classified as an "outlet" in the passage. The term "outlet" could apply to anger or sadness instead. Choice A is too vague to be the best answer. Throughout the passage, the author mentions that dance can enhance teamwork and interpersonal interactions. On this basis it is reasonable to assume that dance serves as a connection, since it brings women closer together. Choice B is a strong answer. The author only discusses school-based dance programs, so there is no reason to assume that it serves as a lifestyle. Choice C is too broad and cannot be assumed from the passage. The author also does not discuss dance as a form of relaxation for adolescent women. Although choice D may be true, it is not supported by the passage. Remember not to bring in personal opinions or outside information when answering questions in the CARS section. Choice B is the best answer.

35. **A is the best answer.** The author of this passage argues for the implementation of stronger school-based dance programs because they believe these program have the potential to inspire young women and improve both their physical and mental health. The author believes that PA interventions should be targeted at youth to instill healthy habits. Although the author primarily discusses PA in secondary school student, the finding in the question stem still supports the author's argument about the importance of strong school-based dance programs because these programs could be geared towards young children to inspire them to keep dancing throughout secondary school. Choice A is a promising answer. The study finding strengthens the need for successful PA programs in schools for young children, so choice B can be eliminated. The finding is relevant to the author's argument since they discuss the potential of one particular sport in improving childhood/adolescent health. Choice C can also be eliminated. This finding does not repeat earlier points in the passage because the author does not state that the altered dance programs need to be implemented in primary schools to have the greatest effect. Choice D is not supported. Choice A is the strongest answer.

36. **D is the best answer.** The author opens their argument discussing the health benefits of moderate-to-vigorous PA each day, such as an association with lower levels with type 2 diabetes. While adolescent women may experience less PA than adolescent men, they are not necessarily at greater risk for type 2 diabetes because it is influenced by many factors. There is insufficient evidence in the passage to support choice A. Although adolescent women experience a sharper drop in PA than adolescent men, that finding is not necessarily due to a lack of participation in sports. There is not enough information in the passage to conclude that adolescent men participate in sports to a greater extent, so choice B is not a strong answer. The author discusses the current school-based PA programs with disappointment, but does not suggest that adolescent women have expressed the same disappointment. Choice C confuses the author's opinion with that of adolescent women and can be eliminated. The author points out that dance is a popular form of PA for adolescent women, even if it is not implemented well in school-based programs. It is reasonable to assume that adolescent women recognize the value of dance since they favor it as a form of PA. Choice D is the strongest answer.

Passage 7 (Questions 37-41)

37. **D is the best answer.** In the passage the daughter is described as identifying with her adoptive culture. It is coincidental that this culture is Scottish; her adoption of Scottish culture does not have anything to do with any of the qualities specific to that culture. Therefore, choice A has limited relevance to the passage. The passage states that the daughter developed her sense of ethnic identity based on the linguistic identity of her adoptive mother, which would not necessarily have to be specific to a certain country. Keep in mind that the daughter's father is Nigerian, and she specifically seeks information on her *matrilineal* relatives; who are Scottish, like her adoptive parents. Her mixed racial background is not a focus of this passage. Therefore, choice B is not the best answer. Choice C might be tempting because the "fictional nature of our identities" is a phrase directly from the passage, but the argument made by the author is that it is logical to have anxieties and questions about one's identity, regardless of how superficial the concept may be. The passage discusses the conflicting feelings within the daughter regarding whether her identity lies in biological heritage or adoptive family. If she did not culturally and emotionally identify so strongly with her adoptive mother, it is implied that such an internal conflict would not exist. Choice D is the best answer.

38. **C is the best answer.** It is true that the daughter's biological mother is Scottish, but the evidence provided by the passage indicates that the use of Scottish language is an overt adoption by the daughter of the adoptive mother's cultural identity. Therefore, choice A is not the best answer. The content of choice B was never addressed in the passage. Choice C is a strong answer because it is most supported by the text of the passage. Choice D is true according to the passage, but not used as evidence to support Kay's use of Scottish language in the daughter's voice, so this would not be the best answer to this question. Because choice C is better supported by the passage and more directly answers the question than choice D, choice C is the best answer.

39. **A is the best answer.** This question requires you to think about the spectrum of ideas presented in the passage, and figure out where on the spectrum the author lies. At one end of the spectrum is the statement expressed by option I; that the daughter's identity is primarily dictated by her adoptive mother's. At the other end is option II, that the daughter feels such a strong identification with her biological heritage, that she has become one with it. Recall that the main idea of the passage as well as the place on the spectrum occupied by the author is that identity is a fluid concept, and oscillation between identities is common. Options I and II are not sufficiently supported by the passage, as the author never selects a clear preference for one or the other. Option III is correct because it does not compromise the author's position on the spectrum, and cites the sentiment made in the passage that the daughter longs for information about her matrilineal relatives. Choices A and B both contain option III, but choice A is the best answer. Choice B might be tempting since it encompasses three viewpoints that were expressed in the passage to *varying* extents, but it is important to recognize that I and II are not true statements.

40. **B is the best answer.** It is true that this particular passage discusses the case of an adopted child, but the overall conclusion being drawn is not specific to adopted children. This makes choice A a weak answer choice. Choice B is a restatement of the main idea of this passage; that identity is a fluid concept. Choice C is close to the main idea of the passage, but not as fitting of an answer as choice B. While the passage does discuss an individual with a multifactorial concept of identity, the main idea of the passage is that there is a tendency to oscillate between multiple concepts of identity. The passage goes beyond mere acknowledgement of multiple components of identity. Choice C can be ruled out in favor of choice B. Choice D focuses on a detail presented in the passage, rather than the main idea. In addition, it expresses a conclusion that is only tangentially relevant to the passage. Thus, this choice is not the best of the options presented. Choice B may not feel comfortable because of its relatively mild language, but it is most in accordance with the main idea, and is the best answer of all of the options offered.

41. **A is the best answer.** This is a main idea question. Choice A is a succinct summation of the main idea presented in this passage. Choice B is not the best choice because it represents an extreme place on the spectrum, while the author makes a more moderate argument. Choice C is not something that is explicitly refuted by the passage, but it was also never elaborated upon. This answer choice is ill-fitting in comparison to some of the other options offered. Choice D is an overly extreme restatement of the idea presented in the passage that identity is fictional in nature. The author also concedes that the craving for identity is legitimate, making this answer choice too radical. For all of these reasons, choice A is the best answer.

Passage 8 (Questions 42-47)

42. **B is the best answer.** Part of the main idea of the passage is that the debate about teaching evolution vs. creationism in public schools has become so polarizing that each side equally devalues the other. This means that the author believes that evolutionists and creationists treat each other with identical distaste. The author also says that some evolutionists believe in God, so choice A is not a strong answer. Choice B is better than choice A because it talks about the evidence for the arguments instead of fundamental belief system, and the author describes the creationists' evidence to be "scientific blogs" or God, whereas the evolutionists cite Darwin and scientifically proven evidence. Choice C is opposes the author's view that creationists and evolutionists are equally scornful - it is a contrary distractor. The author uses the examples of anti-evolutionist biologists to show that there is an overlap between science and religion, making choice D weaker than choice B.

43. **D is the best answer.** While not directly related to the main idea of the passage, the author's opinion towards the creationist's arguments is condescending and sarcastic, such as when the author snidely refers to blogging as a scientific enterprise. As such, the author believes that the evolutionists are correct. The author only talks specifically about atheists being antagonistic and it is unlikely the author believes *all* evolutionists are inflammatory, so choice A can be eliminated. There is information in the passage about evolutionists who also believe in God, making choice B a weak answer. Choice B is also likely to be a weak answer because it uses strong language like "only." Choice C appears to be well-supported because the author agrees with evolution as a scientific theory. Choice D also supports the author's opinion on evolution. Choice D is better than C because the author says the best solution for deciding on a curriculum is for both sides of the controversy to work together.

44. **A is the best answer.** Choice A is strong because uninformed voters are also relevant to the evolution vs. creation debate today. It is true that the 1925 Scopes trial was a pivotal moment in the early 20th century evolution debate, but this information is not provided in the passage, so choice B is a distractor beyond the scope of the passage. The author does not imply that the public is uneducated, just uninformed about the complexity of the issue, so choice C is a weak answer. Choice D appears good because the debate is largely between scientists and nonscientists. Choice A is better than choice D because the John Dewey example is used as a lead-in to the author's main idea about extremist views running the debate, not that scientists and nonscientists have different points of view.

45. **C is the best answer.** The author describes the creationists' belief in Intelligent Design as the idea that everything was created the way it currently is for a purpose. The passage does not specify that creationists only believe in 7 days of creation, so choice A is not well-supported. While many creationists may indeed want prayer to be included in schools, the focus of the article was on giving children "misleading" information in the current curriculum instead of adding to other parts of the school day, so Choice B can be eliminated. The author also states that creationists misunderstand the use of the term "theory." Choice C is the best answer choice because it implies that a theory is unfounded and that the changing of the landscape over time is unlikely to fit in with God's intelligent decision. The creationists do not believe that we should not change our future; they only believe that our present was not developed by many biological changes in the past. This makes choice D a weak answer.

46. **C is the best answer.** The main idea of the article is that the evolutionists and creationists have too polarized of opinions to listen to each other. The creationists want to blend the possibility of God into the curriculum, while the evolutionists insist that scientific integrity should be maintained in science education. In the author's opinion, creationists do not have valid evidence for their theory. Choice A is true, but it does not answer the question and thus is a weak answer. Choice B uses academic buzzwords and shows both evolutionists and creationists as extremists, but ultimately it does not make sense with the main idea, making it a distractor. Choice C is most in line with this main idea and is strongly supported by the statement at the end of the passage that science and religion are separate and that the focus of the debate should revolve around quality education for the children. Choice C is also better than choice D because choice D refers to all extremists, not just the two types of extremists described in the passage. Choice D also uses the term "always," and strong answer choices on the MCAT® usually do not include an absolute.

47. **D is the best answer.** The author is of the opinion that the debate about the science curriculum in public education is too extreme, and that debaters need to find a middle ground if they are going to put the education of students first. The study about the pledge of allegiance only shows that the creationists are religious traditionalists. The finding thus supports the author's view of creationists as well as the author's argument that the focus in the school curricula debate is misdirected. However, the study does not relate to evolution so is not connected to the author's main idea, making choices A and C weak answers. Similarly, the finding does not negate any inference about the author's opinion of creationists in terms of their opinions about science education, so choice B has no bearing on the author's main argument and can be eliminated. Choice D shows the irrelevance of the study to the main idea of the passage and is the best answer choice.

Passage 9 (Questions 48-53)

48. **D is the best answer.** The passage sets up a spectrum between Positivistic science and indigenous African fortune telling practices. The author's main idea is that while basket divination has some outward aspects in common with secular science, these two approaches to understanding the world should not be likened to one another. Ultimately, the author comes down on the side of indigenous fortune-telling practices, because these practices have the power to console, unlike Positivistic science. In this question, the reader is asked how basket divination is different from typical séances. Choice A is unsupported by the passage, because the verifiability of predictions is not mentioned. Choice A can be eliminated. While it seems that basket diviners are respected, there is no sense given that similar roles are not respected in other traditions, so choice B is not the best option. While a reader may be tempted to bring in a western view of fortune telling, in which mystery would be an expected component, this is not described as a part of basket divination, so choice C can be ruled out. In fact, the opposite is true of basket divination: the author mentions that it is quite dry and secular. This is expressed most clearly by choice D, which is the best possible choice of the options given.

49. **A is the best answer.** The author's main idea is that while basket divination has some aspects in common with science, likening one to the other should not be done. This question asks the reader to understand the dynamic between the basket diviner and his clients, and imagine a similar scenario in the Western world. The author describes the basket diviner's behavior as more of an act of calm interpretation than heightened emotions. Choice A describes a situation in which test results are being interpreted by a figure of authority (a physician), so it is a promising choice. Choice B describes a situation of open emotional expression, which is inconsistent with the description of a basket diviner's interaction with his clients. Although what sets basket divination apart from positivistic social science is its involvement with human suffering, it is the non-emotional aspect of divination that prompts the comparison to social science in the first place. Choice B can be eliminated. Choice C is tempting, in that it is likely that the behavior of the family will be formal and reserved in the manner attributed to a basket diviner's clients. On the other hand, the idea of a business transaction is not well developed by the passage, and unlike a bank lender, the basket diviner plays no active role in the outcome, so C is probably not the best choice. Choice D presents a situation that is openly antagonistic, which does not capture any aspect of the relationship between a basket diviner and his clients. Choice D can be ruled out, and choice A remains the best.

50. **B is the best answer.** The passage sets up a spectrum between indigenous fortune-telling practices and Positivistic science. This question asks the reader to identify the author's central idea about science. It is useful to remember that the author finds a direct comparison between science and basket divination to be unfair to the unique practice of basket divination. Choice A tries to tempt the reader by confusing terms: the author expresses disapproval of Positivistic social science throughout the passage. Choice A can be eliminated. Choice B suggests that basket divination, as a form of fortune telling, can do more to calm emotions than science. This idea is expressed affirmatively toward the end of the passage. Choice B is a good option. Choice C suggests that Positivistic science came out of basket divination, but nowhere in the passage is this notion supported. Choice C can be eliminated. Choice D is tempting because is it expressed in neutral terms, but in fact the author's main idea is that Positivistic science and basket divination are not so easily reconciled. Choice D can be ruled out, and choice B is the best answer.

51. **A is the best answer.** This question asks the reader to imagine a new situation and evaluate whether or not the author's central argument would be strengthened or weakened if it were true. Recall that the passage sets up a spectrum between western science and indigenous fortune telling practices. The author's main idea is that although basket divination has some similarities with western science, it is ultimately unique. Choice A argues that the situation presented would strengthen the author's argument. An important part of her argument is her objection to the notion (advanced by other scholars) that African ways of understanding the world are not open to alternative ways of understanding the world. If basket diviners had training in other forms of knowledge, basket diviners would have chosen their craft with the awareness that other forms of knowledge exist. This situation would weaken her opponent's point that their worldviews are "closed," and so strengthen her own. Choice A is promising. Choice B states that the author's argument would be strengthened by a closer association between science and basket divination, but the author's goal in writing the passage is to distinguish them. Choice B can be eliminated. Choice C claims that basket diviners are scientists—not just similar to scientists—which is a view better attributed to the scholars that the author disagrees with. Choice C can be ruled out. Choice D is tempting because it seems to recognize the distinction that the author is arguing for. But it is inaccurate to say that her argument would be unaffected by this piece of evidence, because if it were true, it would strengthen her argument by directly challenging the views the author positions herself against. Choice D can be eliminated, and choice A remains the best answer.

52. **B is the best answer.** The author's main idea is that although basket divination has some similarities with a western, secular attitude, it has important differences. This question asks the reader to demonstrate an awareness of the ways that basket divination appears outwardly secular, like western science. Choice A is directly supported by the passage, and is consistent with the view of basket divination as a straightforward, unemotional practice. Recall that the question stem asks for the least likely option, so choice A can be eliminated. Choice B depicts a situation opposite what is presented in the passage. The author describes basket divination as an unemotional, restrained social encounter. While it is true that basket divination does address human suffering, which sets it apart from Positivistic science, this does not automatically mean that that suffering is shown outwardly—in fact, the opposite is true. Choice B is promising. Choice C closely matches the language presented in the passage, describing a situation that is quite likely during a basket divination. Given the question stem, which asks for the least likely of the given scenarios, this answer choice is probably not the best, and so choice C should be eliminated. While it is mentioned that basket diviners are men, it is not necessarily true that women cannot be clients of basket diviners. The passage offers no comment on this issue, so D is unlikely to be the best choice. Choice B is the best answer.

53. **B is the best answer.** The passage's main idea is that a direct comparison between western science and basket divination is unfair to basket divination as a practice. This question asks the reader to understand and express the essence of a position that opposes the author's. A spectrum can be a helpful tool in recognizing that the test taker is being asked to characterize an extreme position—that of Positivist social scientists. Choice A is tempting because the author redeems some of her opponents near the end of the passage by providing a refinement of their argument, but this statement cannot be applied to all scholars who have compared Positivist social science and basket divination. Choice A can be eliminated. Choice B captures the author's chief criticism in the passage, which is that a lot of the meaning of basket divination is lost when it is compared to social science. Choice B is promising. Choice C expresses the opposite of the author's main idea—the point of the passage is to argue that basket divination offers more than its similarities so Positivist science. Choice C is probably not the best choice. Choice D is tempting because it borrows language from the final paragraph, and even repeats a criticism of Positivist science mentioned by the author. But this criticism is secondary to the main idea of the passage, so the reader should consider other options carefully before selecting it. Choice D is not the strongest option of the answer choices presented. Choice B is the best answer.

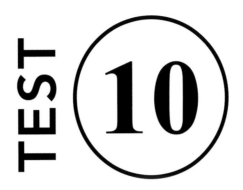

TEST 10

ANSWERS & EXPLANATIONS
Questions 1–53

ANSWER KEY					
1. C	10. C	19. A	28. B	37. D	46. D
2. D	11. C	20. C	29. A	38. C	47. B
3. B	12. A	21. B	30. D	39. D	48. D
4. C	13. C	22. C	31. C	40. A	49. A
5. B	14. D	23. A	32. C	41. C	50. C
6. D	15. B	24. B	33. B	42. D	51. B
7. D	16. C	25. C	34. B	43. D	52. A
8. C	17. D	26. C	35. C	44. C	53. B
9. B	18. D	27. D	36. D	45. C	

EXPLANATIONS FOR TEST 10

Passage 1 (Questions 1-6)

1. **C is the best answer.** The author argues that hard work goes into performing comedy as a profession, and discusses stage personas to demonstrate how much thought goes into an act that may be viewed as inconsequential by the audience. While the author mentions the turnover of material and the necessity to generate unique jokes, they differentiate this from creating a comic persona. Audiences may value uniqueness in comic material, but not necessarily in personas, so choice A is not a strong answer. The author does not discuss audience members identifying with comedians onstage, so there is no evidence to support the claim that audiences value identifiability in comic personas. Remember not to bring in personal bias or experience when answering CARS questions. Choice B can be eliminated. The author points out that comic personas are presented to the audience as truthful representations, so it is reasonable to assume audiences value some degree of authenticity—otherwise, comedians might present more outrageous personas. Choice C is a strong answer. While the author values hard work in comic personas, they do not suggest that the audience necessarily feels the same way. Choice D may be selected if the author's opinion is inaccurately attributed to the audience as a whole. Choice D is not as strong as choice C since it is not directly suggested by the passage.

2. **D is the best answer.** The spectrum in the passage ranges from a view of comedy as a side project that does not involve much time to the author's opinion that comedians devote themselves to their profession more than other people may expect. The author points out that a comedy show may last only a few hours to set up a contrast with the amount of time the comedian spent preparing for the show. The passage does not criticize audience members for the amount of time they devote to a comedy show, so choice A can be eliminated. The author mentions unpaid comedians to concede that not every performer is a professional devoted to comedy writing, so choice B is central to the author's argument and can be eliminated. The author believes that critics and TV commissioners should discuss more than just the content of a comedic performance, but this critique does not necessarily generalize to society. Choice C can be eliminated. The author points out that comedy writers spend a great deal of time and energy on material that may be forgotten or underappreciated by audiences. Choice D is an assertion that criticizes the dismissive attitude of society towards comedians, so it is the best answer.

3. **B is the best answer.** The main idea of the passage is that professional comedy requires hard work, time, and energy, even though audience members may not realize it. While choice A is an assertion made by the passage, it is not necessarily challenged by this example, as the comedian may still work very hard at her career. It is impossible to determine how her work load is affected by improvising a performance, so choice A is not a strong answer. The author points out multiple times that writing jokes takes up a great deal of time, and that many comedians find that their more successful jokes are the ones that require revision. A comedian who is successful by improvising rather than devoting time to pre-writing jokes challenges the passage assertion that professional comedy requires a great deal of preparation time. Choice B is a strong answer. A comedian who improvises may still create a comic persona, so choice C can be eliminated. The author mentions one comedian whose jokes are better received after social media approval, but does not assert that this finding is universal. Choice D does not describe a passage assertion. Choice B is the best answer.

4. **C is the best answer.** Throughout the passage, the author argues that professional comedy requires a great deal of time and energy. Bethany Black's threefold formula exemplifies this requirement, as a comedian needs writing skills, joke turnover, and a comic persona to succeed. She does not specify a particular quality for that comic persona, so there is no reason to assume that a dark personality would not qualify. Choice A can be eliminated. The threefold formula requires fresh material for joke turnover, and this could come from stealing another comedian's jokes. The passage does not address joke theft, so there is insufficient support for choice B. Choice B is also too specific, as it addresses only one component of the threefold formula. If comedians have not practiced their routines, they may make mistakes in their pace, tone, and rhythm, which could throw off their comic persona. They may also resort to reusing old material or borrowing jokes from other comedians. Choice C shows why the three components of the formula are necessary, so it is the best answer to this question. The passage does not discuss the success of comedians who do not write their own material, so choice D cannot be determined from passage information.

5. **B is the best answer.** The passage presents a spectrum of opinions regarding the ease of performing comedy, with the author arguing that more work goes into the act than people might think. While the author mentions the amount of material comedians write that has to be cut from performances, he does not focus on the mindset required to cut jokes . Choice A is therefore a possible answer but not particularly strong. The author stresses the amount of time that goes into creating a single joke or a few minutes worth of material. Choice B strengthens the author's primary argument regarding the validity of the comic profession and the time and effort comedians must devote to their careers. Choice B is stronger than choice A since the author's main purpose does not relate to preparedness to omit material that comedians have worked hard on. While the author focuses on comedians who write their own material for hours at a time, he also mentions that one comic gives his rejected jokes to other comedians—implying that not every comedian writes his/her own material. Choice C can therefore be eliminated. Finally, the author discusses Bethany Black posting jokes online looking for favorable responses in order to emphasize the effort that goes into joke-writing, not to suggest that every comic must do the same. He does not mention comedy on social media again in the passage, so choice D is unsupported and can be eliminated. For all of these reasons, choice B is the best answer.

6. **D is the best answer.** In the main idea of the passage, the author stresses the time and energy that goes into comedy writing for professionals. He notes specifically that comedians who make heavy use of one-liners must generate an enormous amount of them because each joke takes up so little time. He also mentions that many of the jokes are discarded before reaching a performance, making choice A tempting. According to the passage, however, the primary motivation for writing many one-liners is to fill the required time. There is no suggestion that the artist in choice A has had to paint a great many landscapes in order to fill space—only that he or she has chosen to paint more than needed (perhaps to have the option to discard some). Choice A is therefore not a particularly strong answer. Filming one scene multiple times relates to delivery and performance rather than the creation of the material to be performed, so choice B can be eliminated. There are few restrictions on or expectations for the length of pop music albums, so an artist who chooses to write short songs does not necessarily need to write many of them in order to fill the album. Choice C is therefore not a strong choice. If an individual is designing the sets for a play involving many short scenes and multiple storylines, then he or she will have to generate a lot of ideas because the style of the play requires it. Choice D is the best answer because it describes a case in which many ideas are required by the genre in which the artist is working.

Passage 2 (Questions 7-12)

7. **D is the best answer.** While positive psychology can help increase happiness, it is not the only method for becoming happy. The article points out that this is a recent method, and happy individuals have existed for a long time, so choice A can be eliminated. Religious individuals may find happiness through believing in a higher being and the promise of happiness in the afterlife, but that does not necessarily result in the most happiness. This concept is also contrary to the main argument that humans should consider ways to achieve happiness in this lifetime, rather than relying on later judgment. Choice B is not the strongest answer. The authors include longevity as a benefit of living a happy life, but that does not mean that every elderly person is happy. Choice C is not supported by the passage. The authors point out that the U.S. Constitution guarantees only the pursuit of happiness because the founding fathers knew they could not promise happiness to every individual. For this reason, choice D is the best answer.

8. **C is the best answer.** In the fifth paragraph, a positive intervention is defined as an intentional act that specifically tries to increase happiness. Taking medication to prevent another heart attack increases health, but not necessarily happiness. Choice A can be eliminated. Training for a marathon because a doctor recommends it is not an act motivated by achieving happiness. Choice B can be eliminated. If individuals played a sport in high school and decide to play it again of their own accord, it is likely because they enjoy playing that sport and will be happier with it back in their lives. Choice C is the best answer. Although not drinking soft drinks may be healthier, it will not necessarily make an individual happier if that choice is forced on them by another individual. Although the authors point out the positive effects of happiness on health, the positive psychologists' main focus is on happiness, not health. Choice D is not the strongest answer.

9. **B is the best answer.** The author devotes the second paragraph to presenting religious views on happiness, focusing on arguments that it can only be attained after one or many lifetimes. The author then considers whether it can be achieved in this lifetime and presents evidence stating that this is possible. Because the author thinks humans can be happy on Earth, they are skeptical about religious teachings regarding happiness. The author does not support these religious beliefs, so choice A can be eliminated. While the author does not agree with the religious views, they present their beliefs calmly and respectfully, so it is unlikely that they are outraged. Choice C is not the best answer. Because the author supports positive psychology and happiness in one lifetime, they disagree with the religious views and do not express mixed feelings. Choice D can be eliminated and choice B is the best answer.

10. **C is the best answer.** The authors do not suggest that the stories must be happy in order to influence readers, so choice A can be eliminated. Though these individuals do have story-telling in their lives, which may increase their levels of happiness, the story-telling is not necessarily the cause of their increased longevity. The individuals could all have a similar healthy lifestyle or diet. According to this reasoning, choice B can be eliminated and choice C is the best answer. Remember not to make assumptions about causation from correlation. Because the authors emphasize the power of story-telling, whether fictional or narrative, a finding relating to reading is not completely unrelated to the passage. If the study were able to show that there was a causal relationship between reading and lifespan, the authors' argument would be strengthened. Choice D is not the best answer.

11. **C is the best answer.** Physical pleasures, relationships, and achievement of goals can result in varying levels of happiness, as discussed in the first paragraph. Choice A can be eliminated. The authors do not suggest that positive psychology will necessarily be helpful for individuals of all backgrounds, so choice B is not the strongest answer. In the first paragraph, the authors point out that the current methods for achieving happiness are not always reliable or sustainable. Positive psychology is a new approach that is supposed to have long-lasting effects. Choice C is the best answer. The passage does not discuss happiness rates in America over time, so choice D can be eliminated.

12. **A is the best answer.** The author argues throughout the passage that it is natural for humans to desire happiness, and that happiness is possible during this lifetime. They list many benefits of leading a happy life, such as being kinder and establishing better relationships. The author would likely support a method that could instill these values in children and would justify the cost by the number of lives they would be changing. Choice A is a strong answer. The author does not mention the finances of this research throughout the passage, so it is unlikely that they would be discouraged by the cost. Choice B can be eliminated. The author cites other researchers' studies and does not suggest that they have completed their own, so it unlikely that they would assume they are more qualified. Choice C is not as strong as choice A. Note that choices B and C are similar enough that neither is likely to be the best answer. The author supports positive psychology strongly, as conveyed by their enthusiasm and tone throughout the passage. There is no evidence from the passage that the author would hesitate to act. Choice D is not the best answer.

Passage 3 (Questions 13-19)

13. **C is the best answer.** The author discusses the threshold model, a long-standing belief that prolonged moderate daily smoking is required to trigger tobacco addiction, as a way to set up his argument that publications like the DSM should not be relied on as the sole source of knowledge for any mental disorder, including addiction. According to the author, the DSM uses the threshold model's tenets as its basis for describing tobacco addiction because this model is accepted wisdom. However, the model is not supported by research, and there have been studies refuting some of its aspects. As the story of tobacco addiction indicates, the DSM is not entirely an evidence-based document and as such should not be taken to represent the entire human experience, even if the DSM has the merit of allowing researchers to better communicate with one another. The author argues that the articles equating moderate daily smoking with tobacco addiction were notable for their lack of references. He does not say that the findings in the articles were wrong, but rather that they were not supported by data. Choice A is a weak answer. The passage states that the articles forming the foundation for the threshold model were based on the idea that moderate, not light, daily smoking is correlated with tobacco addiction, so choice B can be eliminated. Because the author emphasizes the lack of references in the articles that initially established the threshold model, choice C is a strong answer. The author says the authors of the 1970 articles could not have known how tobacco addiction develops because research into the process did not emerge until the 2000s, so choice D can be eliminated. Choice C is the best answer.

14. **D is the best answer.** In this passage, the author describes an ongoing debate over the threshold model and the question of how much tobacco utilization is addictive. Despite a public belief in the validity of this model, he believes it has significant problems due to the fact that it was established without clinical data. The author later employs this debate in his argument for why the DSM, which describes tobacco addiction as if the threshold model were true, should not be considered an evidence-based document or taken to entirely represent human experiences with mental illness. While the author says that social influences including peer pressure and pleasure-seeking behavior may promote smoking, these influences have an effect before addiction is established. Based on the author's description of recent studies around chippers and their symptoms of addiction, he believes that tobacco itself has the greatest impact on continued addiction. Choice A can be eliminated. The author mentions symptoms of withdrawal as a sign of addiction but does not explicitly describe what those symptoms entail; choice B is a *beyond* distractor because it supplies information beyond what is given in the passage. Choice B is a weak answer. Similarly, the author does not discuss the rate at which individuals become addicted, regardless of how much tobacco they consume. Choice C can be eliminated. The passage says that chippers, individuals who smoke fewer than five cigarettes a day and report no addictive symptoms, initially supported the threshold model. However, recent studies have shown that even chippers indicate that they have difficulty not smoking and experience withdrawal symptoms when they do not consume tobacco. The author does not believe the threshold model is true and uses these recent studies as evidence to support his claim. Choice D is the best answer because while chippers were thought to be atypical individuals, in fact they have a similar experience with tobacco addiction as other smokers.

15. **B is the best answer.** According to the author, the history of research and diagnosis of tobacco addiction shows that the DSM should not be relied on as the sole source of knowledge about any mental disorder, because it is not entirely an evidence-based document and does not always base its descriptions of conditions on clinical studies. The author discusses the threshold model and tobacco addiction as a way of demonstrating how the DSM includes theories that are not necessarily supported by data. The answer choice that most weakens the author's ideas about the DSM should address his concerns that the DSM does not reflect the outcome of scientific studies. Choice A could weaken the author's argument; however, the author uses tobacco addiction as an example of his larger belief that the DSM does not sufficiently incorporate data around all mental disorders. On the other hand, if choice B is assumed to be true, then the DSM does reflect characteristics of mental conditions as revealed by clinical studies. Choice B is a better answer than choice A because it aligns more closely with the author's general argument about the DSM, rather than solely focusing on the absence of data around tobacco addiction. Choice B is a strong answer. Throughout the passage, the author expresses his skepticism for the threshold model (that moderate daily smoking is a prerequisite for tobacco addiction), so choice C can be eliminated because it not only counters the threshold model but also fails to address the author's main idea. The author believes that DSM definitions are designed to foster communication among researchers and do not reflect clinical studies of experiences with mental disorders. Even if choice D were true, the author's arguments about the DSM's lack of research-based legitimacy would still hold. Choice D can be eliminated. Choice B is the best answer.

16. **C is the best answer.** A major theme of this passage is that the DSM's descriptions of mental disorders is not necessarily based on demonstrable data, as shown by its acceptance and promotion of the threshold model (which itself was established by articles lacking references). However, the author states that the DSM represents a common vocabulary and as such was designed to improve communication among researchers and clinicians. Although the definitions in the DSM may not be based on scientific studies, they nevertheless make it easier for scientists to discuss and research mental disorders. While choice A is a possible answer because it at least includes one reference, the author would be unlikely to support a project that did not consider the entire breadth of teenagers' interactions with adults (similarly to how he believes the DSM should not be taken to represent the entire human experience with mental illness). He would find fault with the fact that other research exists but was not considered in the creation of the project. Choice A is a possible answer. The passage mentions organizations because the author does not think that people should blindly accept definitions of mental illness but rather consider whether those definitions are supported by data. He does not relate good communication with the role of such organizations. Choice B can be eliminated. The author says the DSM improves communication by representing a common usage of language. Choice C describes a similar situation where the current vernacular is clarified with standard definitions and can help the social service organizations communicate with one another as well as their clients. Choice C is a stronger answer than choice A because the question stem indicates that the goal of the document is to improve adults' communication with teenagers, rather than to accurately represent a natural phenomenon. The author would be likely to support this project because it establishes a common vocabulary for the document's users. Choice C is a strong answer. Although the author says the DSM contains factual errors, he does not state that these errors impede the document's ability to communicate. Rather, these errors indicate that the DSM should not be considered an entire or true spectrum of human experiences with mental illness. Choice D can be eliminated. Choice C is the best answer.

17. **D is the best answer.** While the passage focuses on tobacco addiction, this question asks how passage information can be applied to addiction in general. According to the passage, smoking researchers have long believed in the threshold model, which states that individuals who become addicted to tobacco necessarily smoked more than five cigarettes each day for a prolonged period of time. The author writes that both the threshold model and new research have demonstrated that withdrawal symptoms occur very quickly after an addicted individual stops smoking, due to the fact that nicotine levels decline rapidly in the blood. This information indicates that nicotine has a short half-life and that withdrawal occurs quickly as a result, so choice A can be eliminated. Despite the existence of some research in support of the threshold model (the original "chipper" study) for tobacco, the author does not advocate for this model. Additionally, there is no evidence in the passage that suggests that the model could be applied to or modified with another drug. Choice B can be eliminated. Choice C is a *simpleton* distractor; people smoking cigarettes with reduced nicotine would certainly not have as much nicotine in their systems (unless they smoked more of those cigarettes), but this is an answer choice that does not require passage information to be true. Choice C can be eliminated. In contrast, the passage explicitly states that before individuals become addicted, certain factors impact the motivation to continue using a drug, including peer pressure and loneliness. Choice D describes a situation that addresses and ameliorates those factors specifically. Choice D is the best answer.

18. **D is the best answer.** The author's main idea is that while the threshold model has dominated the field of tobacco addiction research, even to the extent that it was used as the basis of the definition of tobacco addiction in the DSM, it was not established with much empirical evidence, and there have recently been studies refuting its assertions. As this history of tobacco addiction research shows, there are problems with considering the DSM an evidence-based document. Because of the lack of data supporting claims in the DSM, the author argues that the DSM should not be regarded as a wholly accurate representation of human experiences with mental illness. This question asks how new clinical evidence supporting the threshold model would affect the author's arguments. The author does not believe the threshold model is a legitimate way to study tobacco addiction because he says the original articles describing the model did not have sufficient references. Choice A can be eliminated. Even with this new evidence supporting the threshold model, prior studies refuting it would still hold true, so choice B is a weak answer. Similarly, the author states that the DSM's assertions about the threshold model are not supported by references. Even with the study described in the question stem, the DSM's current definition of tobacco addiction would not change. Choice C can be eliminated. The new study does not change the fact that there are, according to the author, content errors and a lack of clinical evidence in the DSM that render it an incomplete catalog of human experiences with mental conditions. Choice D is the best answer.

19. **A is the best answer.** The main idea of the passage is that based on the history of tobacco addiction research, it is clear that the DSM includes theories like the threshold model that may be widely believed but are not in fact supported by clinical data. According to the author, the threshold model, which states that prolonged moderate daily smoking is required to trigger tobacco addiction, was published without references. Yet it currently forms the basis of the definition of tobacco addiction in the DSM. The author argues that the DSM is not an evidence-based compilation of information about mental disorders but instead serves as a way for scientists and clinicians to communicate with one another. He believes the lack of evidence for theories in the DSM is especially troubling because mankind can hypothetically describe the experience of living with a mental disorder accurately—the DSM just fails to accomplish that goal because it does not derive its definitions from accepted research. Option I is true. Choices B and D can be eliminated. The author does not believe that the DSM should be ignored when researching mental conditions; rather, he believes that the DSM plays a specific role in facilitating conversations between scientists and physicians. Option II is not true. Choice C can be eliminated. Although the DSM takes many tenets of the threshold model to be true, it does not reference the threshold model specifically. The author also makes clear that the threshold model preceded the DSM by roughly a decade; the original articles about the model were published in the 1970s, and the author implies that the DSM takes many of the tenets of the model to be true because it gained so much popularity when it first entered the research consciousness. The DSM did not introduce the threshold model but rather, since the 1970s, has given it more exposure. Option III is not true. Choice A is the best answer.

Passage 4 (Questions 20-25)

20. **C is the best answer.** The passage presents a spectrum of ideas about when and how ART should be initiated in resource limited settings. On one end of the spectrum are those who believe that everyone worldwide should receive the same care of early ART initiation. On the other end of the spectrum are those who believe that ART should be rationed and delayed in resource limited countries. The argument the latter side lays out is that limiting treatment in some areas could lead to better treatment in both rural and urban areas if all patients were held to the same CD4 standard. While early initiation of ART therapy leading to lower viral transmission is a positive consequence, this result is not connected to the rationing of ART, making choice A a weak answer. Increasing resources in rural populations is the goal of ART rationing supporters, so choice B is compelling. Choice C offers a negative consequence of ART overuse, so it too seems like a probable answer. Choice D again references rural areas, but does not specify what resources and cannot be directly linked to ART, making it a poor answer. Choice C is better than choice B because it directly references ART usage and provides a concrete reason to suggest that ART rationing could be positive.

21. **B is the best answer.** The main idea of the passage is that the decision of when to start ART in resource limited areas is complicated by a number of factors, but population health agencies need to come up with an implementable plan so that more patients receive the care they deserve. One of the complicating factors the author mentions is the criteria for initiating ART. While major public health entities have provided the same laboratory guidelines for populations worldwide, resource limited areas may not have access to facilities with those laboratories, and the clinical diagnosis is not enough to start their therapy. This means that patients in these populations are potentially receiving ART later than their developed world counterparts. In choice A, inner talent is not valued as highly as outer beauty, which is opposite to the value of clinical vs. laboratory diagnoses, making it a contrary distractor. In choice B people with an added resource – a good sense of smell – have better odds of knowing what is in the milk carton than those who can only look at it, so it seems like a strong answer. Choice C values what is on the inside but only when there are markers on the outside, which is similar to the situation in resource limited areas, so it could be a good answer. In choice D the outside appearance is again valued over the inside, making it a weak choice. Choice B is better than C because choice B specifically refers to an unfairness based on a difference in resources, which is analogous to the lack of laboratory facilities (good noses) necessitating clinical diagnoses (best-by dates). In contrast, in choice C the cream filling (an analogue of laboratory findings) is only found when the donuts are a different color (an analogue of clinical findings) but there is no inherent inequality of that resource. For this reason, choice B is the best answer.

22. **C is the best answer.** The passage presents a spectrum of ideas about when to start ART. On one end of the spectrum lies those who believe ART should be deferred and rationed in resource limited settings because of complicating factors in those settings. On the other end of the spectrum lie those who believe ART should be initiated early worldwide. The author lies somewhere in the middle of this spectrum but leans towards early initiation for everyone, as suggested by the stipulations and necessity for a specific situation the author refers to when discussing ART rationing. As such, the question could be rephrased to "Which of the following provides the MOST support for the author's argument without being too extreme?" The best answer to this question also has to be an idea presented in the passage – an answer choice that supports the author's argument but was not presented in the passage can be eliminated. Choice A provides a reason to provide ART to everyone, but not a reason to start it early, so it can be eliminated. The author does mention stigma, so choice B is a possible answer. The author argues that early ART therapy can lead to decreased opportunistic infection, so choice C is a well-supported answer. Choice C is better than choice B because the author is unlikely to believe stigma is an issue in all cases and in all developing countries, so choice B is an extreme distractor. Having a global health organization support early initiation is a compelling reason to implement that plan, making choice D a strong answer. Choice C is better than choice D because the author points out that guidelines are not always implemented in certain countries, so the author is unlikely to think the WHO's support is the best evidence for early ART initiation.

23. **A is the best answer.** The passage presents two sides of the human rights perspective. One side argues that, in an environment where full access for all is unachievable, ART rationing should be invoked to assure that both urban and rural populations receive ART. The other side argues that ART for all should always be the goal, which is the focus of this question. Choice A is in line with the idea that everyone deserves a chance to receive ART, so it is a strong answer. The more frequent diagnosis of cancer does not necessarily indicate a more frequent occurrence of cancer, just better ability to recognize it. This means that the ART may still be helping, not harming as insinuated in choice B, so that choice can be eliminated. The study may suggest that people are living long enough to develop cancer, but may also suggest that more patients are being diagnosed because of more contact with healthcare facilities, making choice C an improbable answer. Choice D suggests that there are enough resources available to diagnose cancer, so there may also be enough resources to diagnose ART, but since the answer choice does not specifically spell out this inference and connection to ART, so choice D is a simpleton distractor and choice A is the best answer.

24. **B is the best answer.** The main idea of the passage is that while initiating ART in resource limited countries is a complex problem with many different facets, public health agencies should work towards and implement an achievable plan that benefits the most HIV patients in both developing and developed countries. The author cites longer survival times, decreased susceptibility to opportunistic infections, and decreased stigma as reasons why ART should be initiated early. The passage does not suggest that earlier initiation will lead to earlier or better education, so choice A is beyond the scope of the passage. Choice B assumes that the decreased compliance is caused by decreased access to something, such as education, support services, or healthcare facilities, so it is compelling in its vagueness. If the patients are inconsistent with their use of ART, early initiation may not reduce their symptoms, so choice C seems to be a likely answer. Choice D uses terminology from the passage and is confusing, but ultimately it does not make sense that noncompliance leading to drug resistant strains means that patients do not experience reduced symptoms, so this choice can be eliminated. Choice B is better than choice C because early ART initiation *can* still lead to lower symptom rates if the patient is compliant.

25. **C is the best answer.** The passage presents a spectrum of ideas about when to start ART in developing nations. One side of the spectrum believes that ART initiation should be deferred and rationed. The other side of the spectrum believes that ART initiation should be early and for everyone. The author lies somewhere in the middle of this spectrum but leans toward the early initiation for everyone side, as evidenced by the stipulations mentioned about rationing and the emphasis on the human rights burden of not treating eligible patients. The author would agree that ART for everyone is the ideal, but would probably believe that in the current environment giving ART to every patient in developing countries is too extreme, so choice A can be eliminated. The author specifically points to how the guidelines provided by the AIDS Society and WHO cannot always be implemented in developing countries, making choice B a well-supported answer. Choice C presents a moderate view of how to get ART to the most people, so it is a compelling answer. The author does mention cost as a big factor preventing ART initiation, but placing all the blame on drug companies is a view that is likely too extreme for the author and not the focus of the passage, making choice D a poor answer. Choice C is better than choice B because while part of the main idea is that public health agencies should make achievable plans, the author is more likely to believe they should be implemented at the level of each country, as the author highlights possible differences in access and laboratory facilities from country to country.

Passage 5 (Questions 26-30)

26. **C is the best answer.** The passage presents a spectrum of theories analyzing the value of playing video games, ranging from capitalists pursuits to engaging in a fantasy world. In the third paragraph, the author discusses the theory of Malaby that attempts to connect the value of market and social interactions, which he considers to be cultural capitalism. Although the passage mentions that this theory was recently published, he does not state that it is the most recent theory proposed regarding the value of gaming. Remember to read the passage closely and not jump to conclusions. Choice A can be eliminated. The author believes that the cultural capital theory does not account for individuals' own values—he does not suggest that the theory is too detailed to apply to every individual. He believes that it does not recognize individuality as a whole. Choice B may have been selected if the use of the word "individual" had not been recognized from the passage and not read closely in the answer choice. The author believes that the cultural capital theory does not account for individual values because it focuses on virtual interactions rather than interactions in reality. The individuals' values must be considered outside the virtual world, so choice C is a strong answer. Although the term "cultural capital" does not necessarily include social values, the description in the third paragraph includes the value of social networking in the virtual world, so choice D can be eliminated. For all of these reasons, choice C is the best answer.

27. **D is the best answer.** In the spectrum of the passage, the author presents various theories regarding the value of video-gaming. He opens his discussion presenting the capitalism that the individuals experience playing the game and also producing the game from across the globe. He does not suggest in the first paragraph that there are other values besides capitalist ones, because he does not discuss or suggest other values until later in the passage. Choice A does not describe the author's attitude at this point in the passage. The author does not suggest that only certain individuals playing video games experience the value of capitalism, because he discusses them as one group and does not suggest there is variability. Choice B is not a strong answer. While the author discusses this value with almost a negative tone, as he mentions the individuals who must work in sweatshops for this value to be experienced by people playing video games, he does not go so far as to say that the value should not be encouraged or that game researchers are responsible for promoting certain values. Choice C is too extreme to be the best answer. The author mentions the sweatshop workers in the first paragraph to suggest that the capitalist value of video-gaming is probably only a value to individuals playing the game. They are learning capitalist concepts while playing the game and benefitting from their purchase of the game, while game developers and technicians in another country may earn a very small amount of money for their time-consuming creation of a product. The game developers and technicians may not consider their involvement with capitalism a value. Choice D is the strongest answer.

28. **B is the best answer.** Throughout the passage, the author presents various theories to determine the value of video-gaming. Ultimately, he concludes his argument pointing out that users do not necessarily need to determine why they value video-gaming, because the virtual value will come regardless to fill in what they are missing from reality. This discussion of fantasy compensating for reality is not discussed earlier in the passage, so choice A can be eliminated. The author uses this quotation to propose a new approach to value theory, since it is not suggested earlier in the passage and the author discuss this concept as a final conclusion. Choice B is a promising answer. The theory discussed previously includes the cultural and capital values of playing video games but this quotation does not directly question those values. Additionally, the author quotes the philosopher Zizek to conclude his argument throughout the entire passage, not just from the previous passage. Choice C is not a particularly strong answer. While the author proposes that outwardly determining value may not be necessary, he does not suggest that concept with a defeated tone. He does not suggest that the theories presented were worthless or unhelpful at determining value, so choice D can be eliminated and choice B is the best answer.

29. **A is the best answer.** Throughout the passage, the author presents theories finding different values in playing video games. He concludes his discussion by emphasizing the postmodern capitalism of video games, because individuals can engage in negotiations and interactions they cannot in the real world. Because the author describes the social interactions of individuals playing video games as "transactions," and describes negotiations as "slippery," it is reasonable to assume an aggressive attitude may benefit a player when making deals with other players. Choice A is a possible answer. The author proposes that individuals do not need to be aware of their values of video gaming while playing, so choice B is in direct opposition of the author's argument. While the author mentions the value of interactions in a fantasy world, he does not suggest that individuals should play video games to escape the real world. The last paragraph discusses how video games manufacture value in relation to the real, so the real is still involved in fantasy games. Choice C takes the author's beliefs too far and can be eliminated. A friendly attitude while playing video games may or may not increase the value of video-gaming, as it is not directly discussed in the passage. However, the business-like tone and word choice mentioned before suggests a more competitive attitude is involved in the value of video-gaming, so choice A is stronger than choice D.

30. **D is the best answer.** The author argues that the value of video-gaming comes from postmodern and capitalist beliefs near the end of the passage. The author does not mention the content or plot of the video game throughout the passage, so choice A can be eliminated. Avoid bringing in outside assumptions or personal bias from experience. The author only mentions differences in individuals with the value of video-gaming when discussing the sweatshop workers across the globe, so choice B is a possible answer but not particularly strong. Throughout the passage, the author does not discuss an individual's motivations for playing a game affecting its value, so choice C can be eliminated. The author points out multiple times in the passage the capitalist value of video-gaming. He mentions the sweatshop workers across the globe to suggest that not every location experiences the benefits of capitalism, which then may lessen the value of playing video games. Choice D is stronger than choice B because it accounts for the variability of capitalism depending on location, which is suggested more strongly than the variability depending on the individual.

Passage 6 (Questions 31-36)

31. **C is the best answer.** The author's main idea relates to the question of how political participation takes shape. The discussion in most of the passage is focused on defining CM and explaining how it has been applied. The author's original commentary comes primarily in the last paragraph. The main idea of the passage can be stated as: Cognitive mobilization and political sophistication are both high in the younger generations, resulting in expressions of political opinion and engagement other than voting. Most of the answer choices would support the author's argument. Therefore, the question becomes selecting the one that is the most supportive. Choice A acknowledges the repositioning of political parties to address this younger demographic, who do not turn out to vote unless they see a direct goal being achieved. It also focuses on the political parties which were mentioned earlier in the discussion, which can make it sound like a plausible answer. However, since the author is focusing on the actions of the younger generations themselves, it is a possible answer, rather than a strong one. Choice B focuses on the rate of young people voting. The author specifically mentions that young people can be very interested, but fail to participate in elections, choosing instead to express their opinions more directly through nontraditional channels. This makes it a possible, answer choice, but not a strong one. Choice C accurately reflects the discussion put forth in the final paragraph, and adds that the young who do not vote might do so if they had more appealing candidates, making it a strong choice. Choice D is directly contradicted by the information in the passage, which acknowledges that political participation is high, it just comes in nontraditional forms. This makes it the weakest answer in that it least supports the author's argument. Since choice C closely matches the passage, and adds additional, relevant, information, it best strengthens the author's argument and is the best answer.

32. **C is the best answer.** Choice A may sound attractive because it recalls information that is presented in the final paragraph about emergent trends in participation. However, this is not the tone in which the discussion of political parties is presented, which focuses on explaining their existence. It is also presented by the author, rather than as part of the discussion of Converse's argument. This makes it a weak answer that can be eliminated. Choice B describes the theoretical purpose of organized political parties, and is a common defense put forth by their spokespeople when they receive criticism on the news. However, it is not supported by information from the passage and can be eliminated. Remember not to allow information from outside the passage to influence decision making on the CARS section. Choice C accurately summarizes the information that is presented in the passage, and is specifically attributed to Converse. For the average person, politics are too big to engage with. So, instead, they align themselves with a group that puts forth a set of declared philosophies with which they agree. Cognitive dissonance means when a person holds two or more conflicting ideas, not when they have a hard time engaging with complex ones. This is a good example of a more subtle 'unintelligible' answer. In general, if the precise meaning is not known, do not choose an answer unless all other options have been definitively eliminated, or at the very least discounted. Since choice C accurately reflects Converse's explanation for the development of political parties, it is the best answer.

33. **B is the best answer.** For questions that ask the reader to go beyond the information presented in the passage, asking which answer choice best matches the passage/main idea is the best approach. The main idea of the passage is about the nature of cognitive mobilization, and how its progress has changed the way people that interact with their societies. The author argues that today's citizens have transcended traditional participation models, desire more direct modes of engagement, and tend not to hold strong party loyalties. Choice A suggests that political sophistication is a replacement for CM. In fact, it is a separate but closely related idea that builds upon CM, as summarized in the first sentence of paragraph 5. Choice A is a weak answer. Choice B reflects the discussion of the lesser importance of voting to people in the younger generation, who only go to the polls when they see an issue that they care about at stake. This implies that they often do not cast their votes otherwise, which in turn means the interests and opinions of the whole population are not necessarily represented, making choice B a strong answer. Choice C sounds like it could be a strong answer because of the increasing cynicism present in the population of developed countries, and which is frequently discussed in the media. However, it is not mentioned in the text, allowing for it to be eliminated. Remember not to bring in any outside information when answering CARS questions. Choice D takes the author's point too far. While the youth may certainly prefer being able to cast their votes directly on certain issues, that does not mean that the entire system can be eliminated. The rest of the population is not discussed, and there is no passage support for such sweeping change. This makes choice D weaker than choice B, which proves to be the best answer based on the information presented by the author in the passage.

34. **B is the best answer.** The discussion of political sophistication explains the ability of well educated and informed people to engage with politics at a higher level, and make their own decisions about their affiliations and beliefs. Therefore it makes sense that they could hold a more complicated and subtle set of opinions, making choice A seem like a strong answer. However, while cynicism might be commonly associated with greater understanding of politics, it is not mentioned in the passage, which weakens choice A. Choice B integrates information from much of the paragraph focusing on political sophistication, which made a specific point of the politically sophisticated's ability to transcend party affiliation. This makes it a strong choice as well. Choice C implies that political sophistication is new, when in fact none of the components under discussion are necessarily associated with the modernity. Though sophistication is high amongst the young, it is not a new concept. Choice D speaks more to CM than it does political sophistication. Political sophistication is the next level after CM, and is not required for making a decision. Rather it allows for individuals to make more individual and more complicated decisions. CM is the paradigm needed for understanding the situation overall, which makes choice D a weaker answer. Also, be very careful when choosing any answer that contains extreme phrases like 'the most significant.' If there is a single instance where it may not be true, then the answer choice should be eliminated. This leaves choices A and B as viable options. Due to the lack of passage support for cynicism, and because choice B is more specific, B is the best answer. On the MCAT® always choose the most specific, supportable, answer. When making a decision between two strong possibilities, look for any features that would make one or the other less accurate or true.

35. **C is the best answer.** CM refers to the skills that are needed to engage with the modern political landscape, and is an emergent feature of the complicated modern system. Therefore, this question is asking which of these would add the least to the understanding of this system. Choice A would not necessarily produce major gains in CM, but being active on the internet discussing politics would likely add at least a little to CM. This makes it a possibility. Choice B would add significantly to CM, in the form of an organized and specific education. The widespread literacy and education presented in the first paragraphs align well with this idea. This makes it the weakest. Choice C, the deployment of advertising, does not focus on something that would seek to educate the public and allow them to better understand the political situation. Instead, it refers to an attempt by an individual or group to draw attention to something. This may possibly educate someone, but it is the most likely to be biased or contribute to an asymmetry of public information, making it a very strong answer choice. Choice D sounds like it could be a strong answer because it discusses something that is not specifically in the passage. However, political discussion in any form would increase CM. No matter the location, it would be more likely to result in education than C, making it less strong.

36. **D is the best answer.** CM focuses on the abilities of citizens to engage with and understand the complex political environment they operate in. While most of the discussion focuses on the circumstances that allow for an individual's participation, if they are interested, voting is in fact specifically mentioned to be on the decline with ad-hoc and nontraditional modes of engagement becoming more popular with increased CM. This eliminates choice A. Choice B speaks to interest in politics, which is also not supported. An individual who is well educated about the political system can choose not to care or not find the issues under discussion particularly relevant to their lives. This allows for choice B to be eliminated as well. Choice C accurately describes the results of greater political sophistication as presented in the fourth paragraph. It is more specific to these ideas than cognitive mobilization, the overarching topic of the passage, which is being addressed in this question. While it is likely that a higher level of CM would likely result in an individual being less reliant on parties, this is not specifically addressed, making this a possible answer, but not a strong one. Choice D suggests that citizens who have a high CM would be more efficient in communicating with their government. This may take the form of nontraditional, nonvoting, engagement as with the younger generation. However, they are still able to communicate their ideas. With their greater understanding of the issues and the political system this a logical conclusion, which makes choice D the strongest answer. The other possibility, choice C, is not as specific to CM and would require more assumptions be made beyond the information in the passage.

Passage 7 (Questions 37-43)

37. **D is the best answer.** In the passage the conservationists fight the developers on the basis of incomplete information about a new terminal site and because the proposed site is environmentally sensitive. While the military does want this site, the author implies that the victory belonged to the conservationists, not the MOD, by describing the Gas Council and Total as "refusing to concede victory to the conservationists." Further, choice A has a condescending tone toward the academics that is not found in the passage, making this answer weak. The word "ideology" in choice B is confusing – it is difficult to determine what ideology is being referred to, making it an unintelligible distractor. Choice B can be eliminated. While choice C is true, this victory of the developers does not cancel out the victory of the conservationists, making it a weak answer. Choice D suggests that the developers are trying to save face, protect their egos, and protect their company, which is consistent with their earlier refusal to provide full information that could be used to derail their development plans. These are likely reasons to fail to acknowledge the victory of a grass-roots opposition, making choice D the best answer.

38. **C is the best answer.** The main idea of the passage is that detailed information should be passed from the commercial enterprises to the public so everyone can make an informed decision about the costs and benefits of potential industry. The author shows how the conservation groups require these details so they can determine how the potential terminal will impact local wildlife. This question asks the reader to select the answer choice that the conservationists would emphasize the least. Choice A illuminates the conservationists' desire to maintain a home for the local wildlife, so the conservationists are likely to include it in their argument and it can be eliminated. Choice B is in line with the main idea that details of the operation should be made public, so it is not a strong answer. Choice C focuses on local botany, which is likely a concern of the conservationists, but it does not mention the destruction of plant life nor is botany a focus of the conservationists in the passage. Choice D is very similar to choice C in that it relates to the main idea of the passage – transparency – and can be eliminated. Choice C is the best answer choice because it is not as forceful of an argument as the other answer choices.

39. **D is the best answer.** In the passage the conservationists are worried about a large scale disruption of local wildlife, so their argument would be best supported by economic development harming a large population or habitat. While the conservationists would be worried about the loss of a rare species, it is difficult to pin the lack of bear sightings on the coal plant, so choice A is not a strong answer. In choice B a large area of an ecosystem is destroyed, but the environmental impact of this loss of grass is unclear, so it is not the most convincing answer. Choice C only includes a select number of a non-endangered animal species and the impact of petroleum is not identified, so it is not a compelling answer. In choice D an entire flock of rare birds may not be able to mate because of the wind turbines, and this direct and large scale correlation of development and destruction makes choice D the best answer choice.

40. **A is the best answer.** The passage presents a spectrum of ideas about what should be valued more highly. Conservationists are on one end of the spectrum, arguing that the local environment and especially rare species should be preserved. The commercial company is on the other end of the spectrum and believes that job growth and industrial development are more important that maintaining local habitats. The author lies somewhere in the middle of the spectrum, leaning towards the conservationists' side because of their emphasis on learning all the details. However, the author does note that the environment can thrive with the new industry, and seems to take more issue with the industry's lack of communication than its impact on the environment. Choice A shows this balance between the author's conservation and commercial tendencies, so it is a strong answer choice. Choice B includes a view that is more extreme than that of the author as evidenced by the author's suggestion that animal habitats and industry can coexist, so this answer can be eliminated. Choice C also reflects the fact that the author has some commercialism tendencies. Choice A is better than choice C because the passage does not address globalization. Choice A is also more in line with the main idea of the passage – that obtaining accurate information is essential to informed decision making. Choice A talks about "considering" alterations to the environment, implying that there will be a cost-benefit analysis. While the author does show that some wildlife thrive at the new terminal, the author would be unlikely to believe that this would occur in all cases, making choice D an extreme distractor.

41. **C is the best answer.** The main idea of the passage is that the public should be made aware of the details of large industrial projects so that informed decisions about the fate of those projects can be made with adequate information. In the passage, the conservationists argue that they did not have enough time with the plans, and thus cannot make appropriate decisions. Choice A does not put the short review time in a negative light so it is contrary to the tone expressed in the passage and can be eliminated. The passage explicitly states that the conservationists did not have enough time with the plans so choice B is not an assumption but a directly stated fact, making it a weak answer. Both the author and the conservationists believe that Gas Council and Total was intentionally hiding information, as evidenced by the author's description of the lack of detail provided and avoidance of questions by the Gas Council and Total, making choice C a strong answer. The main idea of the passage was about the level of detail disseminated, not the length of time to interact with that detail, so abolishing short review times was not a focus of the passage. Further, providing an opinion about how to change the protocols for review times is more of an argument than an assumption, making choice D a weak answer. Choice C is the strongest answer.

42. **D is the best answer.** The passage presents a spectrum of ideas about the risks and benefits of building a terminal. On one end of the spectrum are the conservationists who demand detailed plans of the site and protection of local wildlife. On the other end is the commercial company that only worries about making money and creating jobs. The author lies somewhere in the middle of the spectrum, as his main point is that the details of any big industrial plan should be made available to the public—and, if this is done correctly, industry can coexist with the local environment. The author probably would not advise terminating the project entirely because of a new pack of weasels, so choice A is not a compelling answer. Choice B is in line with the passage's main idea that information should be made available to the public, so it is a possible answer. Since the author does not completely agree with the extreme conservationists, and this group would likely suggest the course of action described in choice A, choice C can be eliminated. The author believes that wildlife and industry can coexist, making choice D a well-supported answer. Choice D is stronger than choice B because the author would not likely agree that the developers should act entirely according to public opinion. Since he falls in the middle of the spectrum of opinions between conservationist concerns and commercial concerns, he would not think that a potentially extreme public opinion should govern the decision. Choice D is more in line with the author's moderate views and is thus the best answer.

43. **D is the best answer.** The main idea of the passage is that the details of a large industrial plan should be made public so that an informed decision can be reached. In the passage, the conservationists believe that all industrial enterprises should undergo such scrutiny in their planning phases. Choice A does not focus on the dissemination of detailed information, so it is not a strong answer. Choice B speaks about making the plan public, so it is a compelling answer. Choice C does not relate to the main idea, and knowing that Nature is a legitimate, peer-reviewed journal is beyond the scope of the passage, so choice C can be eliminated. Choice D emphasizes the theme of public awareness, which relates to the main idea of the passage. Choice D is better than choice B because the conservationists are unlikely to have any subtleties to convey to the public: their argument is that the gas company is not providing the public with details of their plans. Choice D also includes both the goal of the conservationists and the main idea of disseminating information, whereas choices A and B do not link these two ideas together. For these reasons, choice D is the best answer.

Passage 8 (Questions 44-48)

44. **C is the best answer.** In the main idea of the passage, the author argues about the uniqueness of steampunk doctors. Though he mentions that steampunk works started appearing in the 1970s, he does not specify when a novel must be published to be considered steampunk. It is impossible to determine if publishing a steampunk novel later would lessen its distinction from popular imagery. Choice A is not a strong answer. The author discusses the cautionary tone of 19th century works and how it differs from the often positive tone of steampunk doctors, but the tone of contemporary works is not discussed. Choice B might have been chosen if the distinction between 19th century characters and steampunk doctors is considered. The author describes contemporary images of doctors as benevolent healers, but then reiterates the mysterious and shadowy nature of steampunk doctors. This distinction is directly discussed in the passage, so specifying the doctor's motivations would take away some of the traditional steampunk mystery. Choice C is a promising answer. The author only discusses a doctor's effect on society, or lack thereof, in relation to 19th century characters. No conclusions can be drawn about a steampunk or contemporary doctor's effect on society, so choice D can be eliminated and choice C is the strongest answer.

45. **C is the best answer.** Throughout the passage, the author discusses the unique characteristics of steampunk literature. He begins by describing it as "transfictional," which suggests that it crosses multiple genres of fiction. The author mentions that historical fiction is often one of those genres, so option I is true and choices B and D can be eliminated. Similarly, the author points out that steampunk literature often reimagines popular fictional characters from the Victorian era, so this connection to previous works of fiction would qualify as transfictional. Option II is true and choice A can be eliminated. While steampunk literature is related to previous works of literature, it is not this quality that would necessarily be described as transfictional. The transfictional aspect involves combining different types of fictional genres, not specifically reimagining old ideas from the past. Option III is not as strong as options I and II since they describe the types of fiction that are combined in steampunk literature. For all of these reasons, choice C is the strongest answer.

46. **D is the best answer.** The author details specific 19th century characters in order to contrast them with steampunk doctors. He discusses their eventual demise and provides some information about each's original experiments in relation to their failures, so choice A can be eliminated. He also emphasizes that the characters' hubris, or arrogance, results in their downfall. It is reasonable to assume that the characters' had overconfident attitudes, so choice B is not a strong answer. The passage lists the moral offenses of the characters, such as inflicting pain on innocent people, so choice C can be eliminated. Although the author describes the cautionary endings of each tale, he does not discuss the ethical dilemmas of the 19th century characters. He describes the characters as almost ignoring ethics until their experiments failed, so choice D is the strongest answer.

47. **B is the best answer.** Throughout the passage, the author describes the unique qualities of steampunk literature. He opens his argument discussing the Victorian influence on steampunk literature, because it often takes place in a setting inspired by the 19th century. It is reasonable to assume that the setting is realistic, so choice A can be eliminated. The author emphasizes that steampunk literature often contained magical events that extended beyond the realm of most science fiction. Choice B is a promising answer. Similar to choice A, choice C can be eliminated due to the Victorian inspired realistic setting. The author does not specifically discuss the believability or absurdity of characters in steampunk literature. Choice D is not as strong as choice B, since choice B is more in line with a point made directly by the author.

48. **D is the best answer.** In the main idea of the passage, the author discusses the particular qualities of steampunk literature, especially in comparison to similar genres. The author is not specifically arguing for the value of steampunk literature, because he does not suggest that belief is in doubt. He does not propose counter arguments or views devaluing steampunk literature, so choice A is not a strong answer. Although the author does seem to prefer steampunk literature's potentially positive consequences to the destruction of 19th century works, he does not make this argument throughout the passage. Choice B is a minor point of the author's and can be eliminated. The author does not mention the role of the reader in relation to steampunk literature, and does not write with an advisory tone. Choice C is not particularly strong. Throughout the passage, the author discusses similarities and differences between steampunk literature and other genres in order to emphasize its unique nature. Choice D is the strongest answer.

49. **A is the best answer.** The passage presents a spectrum of opinions regarding the spirituality of music. One end of the spectrum recognizes the idolization of celebrities and that spirituality can be found in activities that differ from everyday life. The author lies closer to the other end of the spectrum, arguing that singers inspire fans because of their intrinsic charisma, and that the previous definition of spirituality is too broad. The author presents the relationship of a singer and a fan as a pull towards the singer because the interactions can feel personal for the fan. He contrasts this with spirituality, which can push people away from God since the relationship is one-sided with the deification of a higher being that is inherently sacred. Choice A is a strong answer. The author describes how Christopher Partridge believes that the sacred applies to anything set apart from daily life, only to disagree with this definition in the concluding paragraph by stating that everyday events can be divine if they are viewed that way by the individual. Choice B is not a strong answer because the author ultimately argues against this definition. Similarly, the author's argument about Elvis proposes that fans did not actually worship him, but rather became emotionally invested in him. Choice C is in direct opposition of the author's primary argument and can therefore be eliminated. Although the first paragraph states that there is an inherent spirituality in West African music, the author is quoting another individual that he does not particularly agree with, since he does not believe listening to music is a spiritual act. Choice D is not supported by the author's argument, and can be eliminated. Choice A is the strongest answer.

50. **C is the best answer.** The passage discusses the spirituality of listening of to music and becoming a fan of singers, with the author ultimately concluding that those actions are not spiritual since the singer is not viewed as a deity. Music fans who are very religious may not necessarily deify their favorite singers, as their religion does not necessarily affect music fandom. Choice A can be eliminated. Even if music is frequently used in worship settings, that does not mean that the singer or band is being sacralized. While the lyrics or subject matter may worship deities, that does not necessarily mean that the fans of the music are deifying the singer. Choice B does not directly weaken the author's claim since he discusses the singers rather than lyrics of songs. If singers are asked to bless fans at concerts, then those fans are deifying the singers and believe they are inherently sacred. This finding would weaken the author's claim because the musical fandom is a spiritual practice. Choice C is a strong answer. The author states that spirituality does not involve a mist settling over individuals as they experience an event that differs from everyday life. Choice D is mentioned in the passage and does not weaken his claim. Choice C is the best answer.

51. **B is the best answer.** The spectrum in the passage relates to the spirituality of musical fandom. While the author does not believe in this concept, professor Gary Laderman falls on the side of the spectrum that believes fan inherently deify their heroes. Laderman does not compare Presley's fandom to the artist's own expectations, so choice A can be eliminated. Instead, he argues that the spiritual inspiration and deification was not necessarily done on purpose, but just naturally occurs in these situations. Choice B is a promising answer. Presley's lyric content is not discussed or hinted at in the passage. Choice C takes Laderman's quote literally but out of the context of his argument regarding unconscious worshipping by fans, so it is not a strong answer. Laderman discusses the unconsciousness of deifying Presley, so the fans probably did not even notice that their admiration was not secular. Choice D can be eliminated and choice B is the strongest answer.

52. **A is the best answer.** The author argues that musical fandom is not a spiritual practice because fans do not deify singers even when they admire them. Near the end of the passage, the author proposes that famous singers are not even socially sacralized, so society does not view as sacred beings. If celebrities are treated like regular citizens, then they are not being deified. Choice A is a strong answer. If celebrities feel infallible and like they can do no wrong, then they likely are being sacralized because they are not held to the same standards as everyone else. Choice B can be eliminated. While the general public may have different views regarding what is spiritual, that finding does not support the author's conclusion that celebrities are not socially sacralized. Some individuals could view them as sacred, so choice C is not a strong answer. The author argues that Presley was not actually deified and neither are contemporary boy bands. If the general view of spirituality has changed since Presley's time, then One Direction would be deified. Choice D would weaken the author's claim, and Choice A is the best answer.

53. **B is the best answer.** Throughout the passage, the author argues that musical fandom is not a spiritual practice because the act does not involve worshipping a deity, since a singer is not a deity. The author discusses neo-religiosity scholarship because he disagrees with its definition of spiritual being anything that differs from everyday life. This problem does not suggest that religion is too complex to define, since he thinks the definition is too broad. Choice A can be eliminated. The author believes that the neo-religiosity scholarship definition of spiritual allows too many concepts to be spiritual—such as listening to loud music. Choice B is a strong answer. The definition recognizes many events as spiritual, so choice C does not support the central problem of neo-religiosity scholarship. The author does not argue with the definition because he thinks that religion and scholarship do not relate. Choice D is outside the scope of the passage and choice B is the best answer.

TEST **11**

ANSWERS & EXPLANATIONS
Questions 1–53

ANSWER KEY					
1. B	10. A	19. D	28. B	37. C	46. B
2. C	11. D	20. C	29. C	38. B	47. D
3. A	12. C	21. B	30. A	39. C	48. C
4. D	13. A	22. C	31. C	40. D	49. B
5. A	14. D	23. D	32. B	41. B	50. C
6. D	15. C	24. B	33. B	42. D	51. B
7. C	16. B	25. D	34. A	43. D	52. B
8. C	17. B	26. B	35. C	44. A	53. D
9. B	18. D	27. A	36. B	45. D	

EXPLANATIONS FOR TEST 11

Passage 1 (Questions 1-7)

1. **B is the best answer.** The author's main idea is that strong school leadership creates an environment conducive to academic success. They also say that such a climate can overcome other factors influencing student achievement. There is no support in the passage for the impact of parental involvement on students' academic lives. Choice A, which is a beyond distractor, is not the best answer. The author refers to socioeconomic status as one of the factors that can impact achievement—though school climate has a greater effect. Choice B is the best answer. Choice C contradicts the author's main idea, because they argue that student achievement is unrelated to trust in school leaders and is actually more directly related to trust relationships with teachers. The author does not address student motivation in the passage but rather focuses on external variables that affect student achievement, such as school environment and trust relationships between principals and teachers. Choice D can be eliminated.

2. **C is the best answer.** The author mentions a "climate of trust" throughout the passage as part of their main idea that principals can create an environment that promotes student achievement. While schools encourage students to become engaged members of society, the passage does not support the idea that schools urge students to become politically active. Choice A can be eliminated. The author emphasizes the importance of the teacher-principal trust relationship, but also mentions other interactions, such as those between parents and faculty, that impact the climate of trust. Avoid answer choices that represent extreme ends of the spectrum, in this case that only principal-faculty or only teacher-student interactions determine a school's climate and, consequently, the level of student achievement. Based on the passage, the author believes principals are primarily responsible for the nature of a school's environment. They also describe the importance of other trust relationships, though, such as between teachers and students, whose quality is influenced by the actions of the principal. Choice B is not the best answer. The author says that an environment that promotes achievement is open and motivational, characteristics that are established and modeled by school leaders. Choice C is the best answer because it reflects the author's argument that principals are primarily responsible for the nature of their school's environment. Choice D uses a phrase directly from the passage, which makes it seem plausible, but the passage actually says that academic press, rather than school climate, is leveraged by school policies.

3. **A is the best answer.** An underlying theme of the passage is that a trusting environment is one that embraces openness and that such an environment encourages individuals both to acknowledge their weaknesses and to strive to improve them. The author implies that leaders who themselves share information encourage those working under them to be similarly open about the challenges they face. Choice A is the best answer because it describes a situation in which a leader promotes an open climate that is likely to foster success. Choice B can be eliminated because the author supports leaders who are open with those they work with. They believe that information sharing stimulates problem-solving. The author does not believe that cultivating relationships between leaders and members of the community is as significant as the leader-employee interaction, as leader-community relationships are mentioned only once in the passage. Choice C is not the best answer. Choice D can be eliminated for a similar reason: the author does not speak to the importance of school leaders establishing trust with their students directly.

4. **D is the best answer.** Based on the passage, "collective teacher efficacy" occurs when teachers believe their shared efforts will positively impact students. The author says this construct arises when teachers work in a climate of trust. They argue that a trusting environment keeps teachers honest about their weaknesses. When they work to resolve those weaknesses, they are rewarded with greater student achievement, which then creates a stronger sense of collective efficacy. Conversely, if a group of individuals tries to have a positive impact but fails, they may lose their sense of efficacy and behave in accordance with that feeling. Because the concept of collective teacher efficacy speaks to how the shared perceptions of a group impact its behavior, choice A is not the best answer. Based on the concept of collective efficacy, the group of physicians in choice B should feel an increased sense of ability to help patients. Choice B contradicts the idea that a group's prior success creates the perception that they can do more for people. Choice C describes academic press, a concept addressed earlier in the passage. Choice C does not answer the question and can be eliminated. Choice D presents a situation in which a group of individuals is unable to achieve its intended goals and as a result loses its sense of being able to help others. Choice D is the best answer.

5. **A is the best answer.** The author suggests that various interactions—between principals and teachers, between teachers and students, and amongst teachers—contribute to student achievement, but they argue that principals are primarily responsible for creating a climate conducive to academic success. Throughout the passage, the author says that when principals are trustworthy and open, teachers strive to be the same. When teachers model their behavior after these principals, students act according to their teachers' behavior and are more likely to succeed academically. Choice A is the best answer. The author does not mention studies that have demonstrated a correlation between school leadership and teacher achievement. Instead they suggest that a principal's behavior can indirectly influence student achievement. Choice B is not the best answer. Because the author emphasizes relationships within the school community that promote achievement, principals who rely only on themselves would not be expected to lead successful schools. Choice C can be eliminated. The author does not make a judgment about whether principals deserve respect, regardless of how well their schools perform, so choice D is not the best answer.

6. **D is the best answer.** The best answer will both reflect an idea in the passage and weaken the main idea. The author argues that principals create the kind of school environment that promotes high student achievement by establishing strong trust relationships with teachers. Choice A somewhat weakens the author's argument. However, while the author discusses the concept of academic press—the importance of teachers believing their students can succeed—academic press is born out of outstanding school leadership. A teacher who does not help students achieve academic expectations may be functioning in a school where there is a strong climate of trust, and based on the passage, students would then be expected to succeed anyway. Choice A can be eliminated. According to the author, students indirectly benefit from trust relationships between principals and teachers, so choice B supports the passage argument and can be eliminated. The author's main point is that a strong school environment can promote student success, regardless of socioeconomic status. In the right school climate, students of all backgrounds would demonstrate similar academic performance. Choice C can be eliminated. Choice D weakens the author's main idea to a greater extent than choice A. If a strong climate of trust causes students to relax their academic motivations, then principals should not try to achieve such an environment.

7. **C is the best answer.** The main idea of the passage is that principals are primarily responsible for creating a climate of trust in their schools. The author implies that when this climate is established, trust relationships between other members of the school community are strengthened as well. Choice A agrees with the main idea that students achieve academically when they are in schools with a climate of openness and motivation. The author states that teachers' trust in their principal is related to teachers' trust in one another. Choice B is not the best answer because it supports the main idea: when principals create an environment of trust, others within the school are likely to trust one another as well. The author writes that principals have only an indirect impact on student success, primarily through direct interactions with faculty, so choice C is not supported by the passage and is the best answer. The author stresses that in a climate of trust, both teachers and principals are more open about their vulnerabilities. If these two groups did not trust one another, they would, based on passage information, be defensive and closed off. Choice D can be eliminated.

Passage 2 (Questions 8-12)

8. **C is the best answer.** In the third paragraph, the author discusses the challenge that editors face when reviewing articles to be published. They may not be able to recognize that an article has a ghost writer because it is well written and subtle in its pharmaceutical suggestions. This makes choice C the best answer. The passage suggests that editors only ignore ghostwriting if there are not policies in place to emphasize the importance of determining authorship, so choice A is unlikely to be true. The passage does not address the quantity of articles that pharmaceutical companies ghostwrite, or their desire to publish in other outlets, so choices B and D are beyond the scope of the passage and can be eliminated.

9. **B is the best answer.** This question asks about the process of selecting nominal authors and incorporating their contributions. In the fourth paragraph, the passage states that the nominal author can edit an article only after the marketing goals have been met and the legal department transfers ownership to the nominal author. Choice B is the best answer. Choices A and C are too early in the process, since the author is selected after the first draft is complete and the company has already developed and implemented the marketing goals. Because the nominal author does not contribute to that first draft, he is not involved in the entire process, and choice D can be eliminated.

10. **A is the best answer.** Throughout the passage, the author argues that ghostwriting is a corruption of literature because it is sponsored by a company with ulterior motives—those articles are not actually beneficial for the medical community, so knowledge is not gained from them. This makes choice A the best answer. If a pharmaceutical company writes an article marketing their drug, they can become more well-known and sell more of their product, so choices B and D can be assumed to be true. If a scholarly article promoting their drug is published in a respected journal, the company can also gain prestige, so choice C is likely to be true as well.

11. **D is the best answer.** This question asks about the specific legal punishments that Stern and Lemmens have suggested. In the last paragraph, the author states that the journals that publish ghostwriting would have to reduce the cost of subscriptions, so they would make less money from each person who subscribes to the journal. The passage acknowledges that the individual authors involved with ghostwriting would pay a minimal fine, so choice A can be eliminated. The author stresses the importance of legal punishments because government regulation has failed in the past, so choice B is not the best answer. The author does not suggest an extreme punishment like shutting down companies, so choice C is unlikely to be true. Choice D is the best answer.

12. **C is the best answer.** Throughout the passage, the author primarily argues that journal editors should be stricter in regulating ghostwriting because it undermines the integrity of medical literature with dishonesty. The author does not discuss how frequently the journals publish their editions or if pharmaceutical companies are trying to ghostwrite less often. Choices A and B can be eliminated because they are not addressed in the passage and do not directly affect the author's argument.

   If the pharmaceutical companies that are guilty of ghostwriting actually produce effective drugs and help patients, the threat to the medical community is lessened. Choice C is a strong answer. If the journal editors were friends with pharmaceutical representatives, that could lead to them publishing even more dishonest ghostwriting to placate their friends. The author's argument would be strengthened, so choice D can be eliminated. Choice C is the best answer.

Passage 3 (Questions 13-18)

13. **A is the best answer.** In the passage, the author states that the current Dalai Lama encourages the Tibetan Buddhist monastic community to approach scientific ideas openly but with skepticism. The author argues that this critical approach to science comes from the Dalai Lama's sense of morality, which requires him to put concerns of human need before the advancement of knowledge. Choice A contradicts the author's position as it suggests the Dalai Lama wants to see scientific concerns influence Tibetan Buddhist theology rather than the other way around, so it is a strong answer. Choice B aligns with a part of the author's main argument: that the Dalai Lama sees value in science inasmuch as it propounds Buddhist thinking. Since choice B does not contradict the author's position, it can be eliminated. Choice C goes beyond the scope of the passage, exaggerating the author's claims concerning the Dalai Lama's guardedness with respect to scientific thinking. As such, choice C is not as strong as choice A. By aligning with the author's view instead of contradicting it, choice D distracts attention away from the best answer. Close readings of questions are important in order to avoid distractors such as choice D. Choice A best satisfies the question, and so it is the best answer.

14. **D is the best answer.** In order to answer this question, it is necessary to understand the spectrum of ideas the author establishes in the passage, specifically in paragraph two. One extreme of the spectrum values the growth of empirical knowledge over all other considerations, while the other end of the spectrum values the well-being of life over all scientific pursuits. According to the author, the Dalai Lama is closer to the latter extreme as he believes scientific knowledge is only valuable if it benefits the needs of all beings. Choice A does not have a strong basis in the passage, suggesting that the Dalai Lama thinks scientific ideas should be evaluated based on their compatibility with Tibetan Buddhist doctrine. The author does not make this claim, arguing instead that the Dalai Lama evaluates scientific ideas based on how much they benefit life, so choice A can be eliminated. Choice B likewise suggests that the Dalai Lama would accept scientific knowledge that points to the reality of intangible matter, irrespective of whether or not that knowledge benefits living things, so choice B can also be eliminated. Since the passage does not discuss technology in relation to the Dalai Lama's idea that scientific knowledge ought to benefit the needs of all beings, choice C goes beyond the scope of the passage, and so it too can be eliminated. Choice D suggests that the Dalai Lama would be open to a scientific discovery that benefits human beings, aligning with the author's point that the Dalai Lama values science inasmuch as it benefits life and making choice D a strong answer. Thus, choice D is best.

15. **C is the best answer.** The best answer to this question requires an understanding of the author's main point concerning Tibetan Buddhists' approach to science. According to the passage, Tibetan Buddhists, in accordance with the Dalai Lama's thinking, see value in scientific knowledge only so long as that knowledge fulfills moral responsibilities. Choice A suggests acquiring knowledge is more important than anything else, including morality, so it can be eliminated. Choice B can also be eliminated because it implies that Tibetan Buddhists value science only insofar as it spreads Tibetan Buddhists thought, whereas the passage states that the Dalai Lama has called on his monastic community to recognize the value of basic scientific principles both in their capacity to propound Tibetan Buddhist idea and in their own right. Choice C is a strong choice as it concisely aligns with the author's main point that Tibetan Buddhists' value scientific knowledge based on its moral worth. Like choice B, choice D implies that Tibetan Buddhists only value science if it supports their beliefs and principles, which contradicts the author's claim that the Dalai Lama has called on Tibetan Buddhists to value science in its own right as well. As such, choice C is the best answer.

16. **B is the best answer.** The author explains that the Dalai Lama's belief that science is only valuable inasmuch as it benefits life comes from his philosophical and religious obligations as the leader of Tibetan Buddhism. Since the Pope is in a parallel position of religious leadership, it is reasonable to infer, based on the information in the passage, that the author would think that the Pope's obligations as leader of the Catholic Church likewise influence his approach to scientific thinking. Choice A suggests that the Pope would have to concede his theological beliefs in order to endorse a scientific belief, so it can be eliminated as it does not align with the author's view that people can hold both theological and scientific beliefs simultaneously. Choice B is a strong answer as it does align with the author's point that theological thinkers evaluate scientific knowledge based on its ethical implications, as illustrated by the Dalai Lama's relationship to science. Choice C, like choice A, can be eliminated as it implies that religious leaders must make concessions to scientific beliefs in order to endorse particular aspects of scientific knowledge, in this case by feeling compelled to be responsible to scientific conceptions of knowledge. Choice D goes beyond the scope of the passage by explicitly linking the hypothetical of the Pope's endorsement of scientific research into climate change with Tibetan Buddhist thinking about science, a connection which the author does not explicitly make. Choice B, therefore, is best.

17. **B is the best answer.** According to the author, the Dalai Lama values scientific knowledge inasmuch as it makes life better for people. The author does not view scientific and theological beliefs as inherently contradictory. Based on the author's reasoning in the passage, for a scientist to believe in reincarnation suggests that the scientist values unempirical, ethical thinking as well as empirical, scientific thinking. Choice A can be eliminated as it implies that scientific knowledge is limited and that theology fills in what science cannot explain, a claim that the author does not make. Choice B is a strong answer because by suggesting that the scientist would recognize the ethical implications of scientific thinking it aligns with the author's main idea that people who hold both scientific and theological beliefs—such as the Dalai Lama—value science according to its impact on living beings. Choice C claims that scientific knowledge ought to serve as the basis for moral thinking, which, like choice A, is not a claim the author makes. Choice D suggests that scientific and theological beliefs are fully separate from one another, a claim that contradicts the author's argument that science and theology are not mutually exclusive and in fact can inform one another. Choice B is thus the best answer.

18. **D is the best answer.** The author's main idea is that the Dalai Lama values the improvement of human life more than the growth of scientific knowledge. In the Dalai Lama's view, science is valuable when it serves to improve human life. Choice A can be eliminated as it exaggerates the Dalai Lama's approach to science, suggesting that scientific thinking can never be used to improve life. On the MCAT®, choices that overstate the main idea of a passage often distract from a better, more subtle answer. Choice B can also be eliminated as it neither supports nor contradicts the author's main argument, instead claiming that Tibetan Buddhist beliefs are unscientific, a claim that the author does not discuss. Likewise, choice C does not answer the question as it neither opposes nor supports the author's argument, stating that the Dalai Lama's ideas are unusual in Tibetan Buddhism, a statement that is irrelevant to the author's main idea. Choice D, which implies theological thinking cannot lead to ethical conclusions, satisfies the question by contradicting the author's main idea that the Dalai Lama believes ethics based on theological reasoning should guide science. Thus, choice D is best.

Passage 4 (Questions 19-24)

19. **D is the best answer.** The main idea of the passage is that, while psychogeography is an amorphous concept negotiated by each individual practitioner, psychogeography still has some basic components. One of the components that the author emphasizes is a tendency towards radicalism, which some pseudo-psychogeographers fail to uphold. This means that all options can be correct depending on the user and choice D is the best answer choice. Option I is a strong option because the author describes psychogeography as a nuanced literary form, which is a type of art, so the author would probably agree it is a form of art. Throughout the passage, the author describes psychogeographic works as narratives of the practitioners' wanderings, so option II is also a good option. Option III is a good option because the author mentions that Ackryod's writing lacks political subversion when describing the author as a poor example of a psychogeographic writer. All options can be correct, making D the best answer choice.

20. **C is the best answer.** The author is of the opinion that Ackroyd is not a good example of a psychogeographic writer as he lacks and political or radical motivation in his writing. Rephrased, this question asks, "With which of the following statements is the author most likely to disagree?" Choice A is a weak answer because the passage mentions the fragmentation of pscyhogeography several times, and the author would agree that these fragments are not reconcilable. Choice B can be eliminated because the author would agree that London is unpredictable. In the passage, the author describes Ackroyd's inclination to write about fragmented characters and pervasive atmospheres in London, making choice C a strong answer choice. Choice D is a weak answer because the author agrees that psychogeography should be radical, while Ackroyd has a conservative and historical view.

21. **B is the best answer.** This question asks about the author's opinion of Sinclair and why the author tends to favor this writer. The main idea of the passage is that while the definition of psychogeography is ambiguous, there are certain tenets a work must have to be considered psychogeography. The author emphasizes the necessity of radical and politically subversive themes, and in so doing makes it clear that they believe Sinclair is a good example of a psychogeographic writer and Ackroyd is a bad example. Choice A seems to be a strong answer choice because the author believes that Sinclair presents a narrative of his wanderings, as opposed to Ackroyd who adds an idealistic spin. Choice B is also a strong answer choice because the author believes that Sinclair is true to the psychogeographic spirit. Choice B is better than choice A because the author does describe some of Sinclair's writing as subjective, and the idea that Sinclair is a good example of a psychogeographic writer is part of the main idea of the passage. The subjectivity Sinclair includes does not appear to bother the author, so choice C is not a strong answer. Choice D is a weak answer because the author describes all of psychogeography as fragmentary, and the author concedes that Ackroyd provides only fragments as well.

22. **C is the best answer.** Part of the main idea of the passage is that psychogeography is amorphous but has the common themes of urban walking, political subversion, mystery and occult, and rediscovering the past. Choice A is not the best answer choice because it only involves haphazard political protests with no clear connection to the past or the occult, so it is unlikely to fit into the author's idea of what makes a traditional psychogeographic piece. Choice B is weak because the answer choice suggests that fragmented lives become interwoven. The connectivity is in line with Ackroyd's style, not the style of traditional psychogeographers. Traditional psychogeographers would leave the characters separate and fragmented – puzzle pieces that do not fit together. Choice C is likely the best answer choice because it includes elements of wandering, potential occult history, and room for political commentary and reform. Choice D is a less appealing answer choice because, though it is founded in geography, it has no clear subversive political ties nor does it suggest anything mysterious.

23. **D is the best answer.** This question asks about why the author believes Ackroyd is not a good example and how writing about the end of a political riot might change this perspective. Part of the main idea of the passage is that the author believes psychogeographic writings have certain necessary components, especially radicalism. Choice A seems to be a strong choice because the absence of political subversion breaks one of the fundamental components of psychogeography. Choice B is weak because the author believes Ackroyd already employs urban walking; this would not affect the author's opinion. Choice C is not a good answer choice because chaos is not described as one of the fundamental principles of psychogeography. Choice D is better than choice A because there is not enough information in the question stem to know if the writing is politically inflammatory, and the author faults Ackroyd for more than just his lack of political motivations.

24. **B is the best answer.** Part of the main idea of the passage is the psychogeography is difficult to define and writers use the fundamental components differently, though there are some fundamental components that are necessary for true psychogeographic writing. The author believes that Ackroyd is not a good example of a psychogeographer because he is traditional instead of radical, but the author does admit that Ackroyd employs some of the basics of psychogeography. On a spectrum of quintessential psychogeographers to not-at-all psychogeographers, the author would place Ackroyd on the latter side but close to the middle. Choice A is not a strong answer choice because it conveys a more extreme view of Ackroyd than the author actually has. Choice B is the best answer choice because it fits with the main idea of the passage. Choice C is not a strong answer because the author describes Sinclair's writings as fragmentary and inconclusive. Choice D is weak because the author believes only Ackroyd strives to connect all of the stories together, while others in the movement leave their characters unconnected.

Passage 5 (Questions 25-30)

25. **D is the best answer.** The author's main idea is that health care professionals and family members should cooperate to provide the best possible end-of-life care for patients with ID. Despite the challenges that may arise due to this joint effort, both parties must communicate and depend on one another to ensure that the patient's medical and emotional needs are met. According to the author, one of these challenges is that family members may feel that physicians are intruding on them and providing unwanted advice. The best answer will present a similar objection to the guidance counselor's attempt to suggest an educational strategy for the student. Based on passage information, family members do not perceive that physicians spend inadequate amounts of time with patients; on the contrary, the author implies that one of the reasons joint collaboration is difficult is that relatives would prefer that physicians spend less time with the family and reserve their opinions about patient care. Choice A is a weak answer. Similarly, although the author identifies patient stress as one negative consequence that can result when care staff and relatives do not work well together, she does not write that family members are concerned about this issue. Choice B can be eliminated. The author also does not mention lack of expertise as a reason why relatives do not want physicians to be involved in patient care. In fact, the main idea of the passage is that physicians have more medical experience than family members and can contribute this knowledge to improve end-of-life care for people with ID. Choice C can be eliminated. The passage states that relatives often feel health professionals' presence and advice infringe on their rights as representatives. Choice D describes a situation where similarly, parents are irritated because they perceive school staff as interjecting unwanted opinions about a sensitive topic. Choice D is a strong answer, and it is the best answer.

26. **B is the best answer.** According to the passage, the main reason family members and ID care professionals should collaborate in providing end-of-life care for people with ID is that they can combine their strengths: relatives with a life-long relationship with the patient are likely more attuned to symptoms of pain and distress, while even ID physicians without extensive experience in end-of-life care can help family members make difficult medical decisions. The author says that patients with ID may not demonstrate very visible signs of distress, not that they are completely unable to communicate that they are experiencing pain. It is precisely because family members can pick up on patients' subtle cues that they are valuable to the care team. Choice A is a possible but weak answer; it would be stronger if it said that people with ID are unable to *verbally* communicate that they are experiencing pain. The author states that end-of-life care for people with ID is especially challenging because they may not understand the implications of their care, in other words, that they are dying. Choice B is a strong answer. While the majority of this passage focuses on the conflicts that can arise between ID care staff and relatives when they try to provide end-of-life care together, the author says these problems are not unique to patients with ID. Note that the question asks why end-of-life care provision is challenging specifically for people with ID. Choice C is a weak answer. The author explicitly states, rather than implies, that people with ID are a uniquely vulnerable patient group, especially when they age. Choice D is a weak answer. Choice B is stronger than choice D because it more specifically identifies the reason why providing end-of-life care to people with ID is challenging. Choice B is the best answer.

27. **A is the best answer.** The author describes the concept of 'two families' as the joint effort of the groups who know the patient the best—the ID care staff and relatives. This passage focuses on the advantages and disagreements these groups may face when working together to provide end-of-life care for people with ID. Ultimately the author argues that in terms of true patient-centered care, the benefits of collaboration outweigh the problems. Choice A describes a scenario where an individual (the student) confronts an issue that the author would argue both his family and the professionals who work with him should address jointly. According to the concept of 'two families,' these groups, who know the student best, can communicate openly about the approach that is best suited to meet his needs. Choice A is a strong answer. The author focuses on the role that family members, rather than friends, play. In addition, the passage describes the emotionally charged and difficult decisions involved in end-of-life care, which harbor a different tone from the scenario described in choice B. Choice B is a weak answer. Although the author mentions cooperation among professionals, she is much more interested in the relationship between professionals and family members. Choice C is a possible answer, but it is weaker than choice A, which emphasizes specifically an interaction between a professional and a relative that is intended to improve an individual's health. Similarly, the author describes the personal relationship that the ID care professionals have with the patient, which is not mimicked by the interaction between the homeowner and the makers of the online videos. Choice D is a weak answer, and choice A is the best answer.

28. **B is the best answer.** According to the passage, health professionals and family members may confront certain tensions when they seek to jointly provide end-of-life care for patients with ID. These problems range from a feeling that health care providers are intruding on a family during an extremely difficult time to doctors viewing the inclusion of families as a waste of time. However, the author argues that these problems must be overcome or overlooked; the two groups must combine their knowledge to provide quality care to the patient. The author says that the different parties may not use the same language to talk about the patient's condition, so choice A can be eliminated. Based on passage information, family members are often more attuned to how patients' symptoms present. The author believes this difference is a reason why professionals and relatives should work together, not a conflict that emerges from their interaction. Choice B is a strong answer. The author states that both parties may not proactively seek contact with one another; relatives may be unwilling to communicate because they want time alone with the patient, while care staff may remain reticent because they feel they can provide medical care more efficiently when they work independently. Choice C can be eliminated. Similarly, the author references the feeling relatives may have that providers are infringing on a family's privacy. Choice D can be eliminated, and choice B is the best answer.

29. **C is the best answer.** The author's main idea is that health care professionals and family members should cooperate to provide the best end-of-life care possible to patients with ID. She argues that although this relationship can be emotionally taxing for relatives and time-consuming for physicians, a joint effort is necessary to ensure that the patient's needs are met. The author says upfront that end-of-life care is not a field that naturally aligns with ID care and that studies have shown that ID providers lack experience in symptom and pain management. However, the passage focuses on what ID care professionals can do in spite of that lack of expertise (e.g. work with family members to identify symptoms of distress). The author does not oppose ID physicians working with their dying patients, so choice A can be eliminated. The author admits that physicians may need to spend more time working with family members than they would if they were to provide care without consulting relatives. However, she believes this extra effort is necessary and would support, rather than oppose, family members utilizing physician knowledge to appropriately administer oxygen, regardless of the time "burden." Choice B can be eliminated. The author says that doctors may feel they can provide the best care to their patients without input from family members, but she implies that this is not how they should behave. The passage's main idea is that a patient will receive the best care when her 'two families' (ID care staff and relatives) come together. Regardless of the time burden placed on the patient's physician, he must cooperate with family members to provide pain medication. Choice C is a strong answer. The author does not make a judgment about whether patients should seek palliative or treatment-oriented care or how physicians should react to their patients' wishes around this matter. She bases her argument off of the fact that as more ID patients have lived longer, they have simply required more health services associated with end-of-life care. Choice D does not align with the main idea, so it can be eliminated. Choice C is the best answer.

30. **A is the best answer.** One of the underlying themes of the passage is that family members constitute an important part of the end-of-life care team because they, having had a life-long relationship with the patient, are most aware of the patient's needs and how those needs are expressed. The author argues that despite the problems that can emerge when ID professionals and relatives jointly provide end-of-life care, this collaboration is necessary. If the family members who spend the most time with dying patients have been estranged for decades—in other words if they lack the crucial life-long relationship—it is likely these relatives will not be as attuned to a patient's subtle signs of pain and distress as the author believes. Choice A is a strong answer. The author's main idea is that regardless of conflicts that arise between physicians and relatives, this joint effort is necessary to ensure that patients receive the best possible care. Even if the collaboration is fraught, the author would argue that this antagonism on the part of the relatives can, at best, be resolved, and at worst, overlooked, for the sake of the patient. Choice B can be eliminated. If family members cannot explain why they are attentive to a patient's small changes in mood and behavior, but they are still able to realize when these changes occur and notify the patient's physicians, they remain a necessary part of that patient's care. Choice C can be eliminated. Regardless of how many relatives a patient has, or what proportion of patients with ID at the end of their lives have family member visitors, the author still believes that when these family members are present, they should be included in care provision and discussion around medical decisions. Choice D is a weak answer, and choice A is the best answer.

Passage 6 (Questions 31-35)

31. **C is the best answer.** Throughout the passage, the author argues that it is difficult to determine the effects a coach can have on a Master athlete, especially compared to younger athletes. She does mention self-reported data from the Master athletes in the second and third paragraphs. The passage states that coaches can makes sports more enjoyable, but it does not suggest that Master athletes utilize them for that reason—it might just be an added benefit. For this reason, option I is not true and choices A and B can be eliminated. The third paragraph specifies that Master athletes strategically use coaches to motivate themselves. Option II is true, and choice D can be eliminated. The author points out that Master athletes with coaches report higher levels of self-determination, and that they specifically utilize their coaches to improve internal determination. Although this finding might seem counter-intuitive, since athletes are using other individuals to increase their own self-determination, it is clearly stated in the passage. For these reasons, option III is true and choice A can be eliminated. Choice C is the best answer.

32. **B is the best answer.** Throughout the passage, the spectrum of differences, or lack thereof, between coaching Master athletes versus younger athletes is discussed. The author believes that Master athletes have different needs and experiences, so that the coaching style needs to be altered. The best answer has to satisfy both criteria of being a point made in the passage and also supporting the author's argument. The author does not suggest that master athletes do not benefit from coaching, as she lists possible benefits in the third paragraph and states that coaches can be an instrumental resource for Master athletes. Choice A is not in agreement with the author's views, so it can be eliminated. The author opens her argument stating that the Master athlete cohort is growing, which is why she believes more research should be done about how best to coach them. Choice B is a strong answer as it is a point made in the passage and in agreement with the author's argument. The author believes that coaches are a valuable resource, but does not distinguish their value from age group to age group. Choice C is not a point made in the passage, so it can be eliminated. While the author suggests that coaches might need special training to work with Master athletes, she does not state they should focus on coaching only one age group. A coach may be able to alter his/her coaching style depending on the athlete cohort, so choice D is also not suggested by the passage. For these reasons, choice B is the strongest answer.

33. **B is the best answer.** The author argues for the need of research examining the needs of Master athletes and how best to coach them, because they represent a very different population than younger athletes. Although Master athletes are often older than 35, the author does not suggest that the physicality of a sport must be altered to accommodate their age. Remember not to bring in outside assumptions. Choice A is not suggested by the passage and can be eliminated. The author believes the psychology of coaching Master athletes is unique, because this group probably has special needs and preferences that should be addressed. Choice B is a promising answer. While the author suggests that Master athletes might also have different social needs, as suggested in the second paragraph, she mentions this concept in reference to coaching, not team interactions. Teamwork is not discussed in the passage and choice C can be eliminated. While coaches may need to motivate Master athletes differently than younger athletes, this concept does not encompass all the points made by the author. It is not simply the motivation that differs between the cohorts, so choice B is stronger than choice D because it is a more inclusive answer choice.

34. **A is the best answer.** The author argues that Master athletes have different coaching needs than younger athletes due to their psycho-social state. Lifelong athletes and new athletes probably also have different psychological needs since their experience in that particular field can vary immensely. The author might agree with this advice since it recognizes the importance of coaching to fit accommodations. Choice A is a possible answer. The author does not discuss the distinct needs of Master athletes in regards to their experience in the sport, but rather their psychological state, so choice B is not as strong as choice A. This advice is not likely to worsen coaching for Master athletes, since this distinction could apply to athletes over age 35, so more Master athletes may receive more tailored coaching. Choice C can be eliminated. Even though this advice does not necessarily take age into account, the author would not disagree with it on that reason alone, since it could still improve coaching for specific populations by considering psychological needs. Choice D is not a strong answer. Although it may not be obvious whether or not the author would agree with this advice, choice A is similar to a point made in the passage so it is the best answer.

35. **C is the best answer.** Throughout the passage, the author argues that Master athletes have different psycho-social needs than younger athletes, and that coaching should be adjusted for this cohort. The author points out that there is a lack of research discussing the effects of having a coach for Master athletes, so the benefits are not completely obvious at this time. Even if athletes' performance declines as they get older, this finding could be caused by many different reasons. It could be due to worsening health, or inexperience in the field, or difficulty learning new techniques as an individual is more set in his/her ways with increased age. The performance decline is not necessarily due to inadequate coaching, since the passage also mentions that some Master athletes do not have coaches. This finding is not likely to support the author's claim, so choice A can be eliminated. Similarly, the finding does not specify whether or not these athletes have coaches, so it does not question the importance of coaches for Master athletes. Choice B can also be eliminated. The finding does not strongly affect the author's argument, since the performance decline could be caused by a variety of factors and the author would likely still argue for coaching adjustments. Choice C is a promising answer. The author does not suggest that athlete performance necessarily declines with age, as she describes Master athletes as competitive and dedicated, as seen in the first paragraph. For these reasons, choice D can be eliminated and choice C is the strongest answer.

Passage 7 (Questions 36-40)

36. **B is the best answer.** The author emphasizes the cultural significance of the Ojude Oba festival because it brings the community together for a day, to celebrate their society and also their differences. Regberegbes, or age groups, especially bond with one another throughout the day. While the author suggests that many of the groups dance for the king, he points out that they simply must perform for the king and they often rely on dance. Not every age group necessarily dances then. Remember to read the passage carefully and not jump to conclusions when reading the question stems. Choice A can be eliminated. The author stresses the unifying nature of the festival, as each regbergbe renews their allegiance to the king every year, often with a meaningful dance. Choice B is a promising answer as it emphasized in the passage. Even though the regberegbes are age-specific groups, the passage does not discuss what they talk about amongst each other, so choice C cannot be assumed true. The author mentions that the king opens the festival with a prayer, but he also points out that members of different faiths are welcomed at the celebration. It is reasonable to assume that not every single member of the community is Muslim, so they may not all pray for the king. There is not enough information to support choice D, so choice B is the strongest answer.

37. **C is the best answer.** Throughout the passage, the author argues for the cultural significance of a festival that was once only an extension of religion. Currently, the festival welcomes members of all faith and encourages cultural contact. The author does not highly value the festival's religious significant in today's society, so choice A is not a strong answer since it is in direct opposition of the author's argument. The passage does not discuss the positive implications of recognizing Ijebu history, so choice B cannot be assumed from the passage. The author believes that the cultural aspects of the festival are the most significant for the community, like how it brings people together of all faiths and backgrounds. Choice C is supported by the main idea of the passage. The author mentions that the festival has economic significance, but does not stress this point throughout the passage. The economic implications of the festival are only mentioned near the end of the passage, so choice D is not as strong as choice C.

38. **B is the best answer.** In the spectrum of the passage, the author discusses the religious foundation of the Ojude Oba festival and how it has become a tolerant and unifying celebration. It is impossible to determine which aspects of the festival were created by the settlers of the Ijebu community or have been adopted over the years, besides Islamic aspects that have always been a part of the celebration. The newly discovered festival may or may not involve singing of the national anthem, so choice A is not particularly strong. The author points out that the festival always start with a prayer from the Imam, or Islamic leader, so it is reasonable to assume that the Muslim settlers of the Ijebu community brought this aspect of the celebration to another land. Choice B is a strong answer. Performing for the king is an act to renew allegiance, not necessarily to express faith or Islamic beliefs. Choice C may or may not be influenced by the religious roots of the festival, so it is also not a particularly strong answer. The author points out that the festival today is a welcoming experience for believers of all faiths, so it is reasonable to assume that that was not necessarily the case when it was created. Choice D is not a strong answer and choice B is the best answer since it acknowledges the religious creation of the festival.

39. **C is the best answer.** In the main idea of the passage, the author argues that while the Ojude Oba festival started as a religious event, it has grown into a cultural celebration. If a festival in the Ijebu community does not include a prayer, then it probably does not have its roots in a religious origin. The Ijebu community could have a celebration that is old and not based on religion. Choice can be eliminated. The passage does not discuss the religions or festivals of nearby regions so no assumptions can be made about their customs. Choice B is not a strong answer. The Ojude Oba festival celebrates a Muslim holiday and does include a prayer, so it is reasonable to assume that a festival without a prayer is rooted in a cultural original rather than religious one. Choice C is a strong answer. Only the Ojude Oba festival and its ability to unite the Ijebu community are discussed in the passage, so it is impossible to determine how unifying other festivals are for the Ijebu community. Choice C is the best answer then.

40. **D is the best answer.** In the main idea of the passage, the author argues that the Ojude Oba festival celebrates the uniqueness of the community and acts as an all-inclusive event. Even if Ijebus report this festival as their favorite of the year, that does not support the proposal that OJude Oba has cultural and spiritual significance. It only tells of enjoyment of the festival compared to other festivals, so choice A is not a strong answer. If Ijebus feel unified during the festival, then that would support the proposal that it is a cultural event but does not provide information regarding its religious significance. Choice B can be eliminated. Similarly, if Ijebus feel close to Allah during the festival, then that finding would cement the festival's religious significance, but not necessarily its cultural impact. Choice C can also be eliminated. If Ijebus bond with one another during the festival, then it would have cultural significance, and if they bond with visitors during the event, then it would have religious significance since the visitors often bring other religious ideas and values with them. Choice D is the best answer because it strengthens both aspects of the proposal.

Passage 8 (Questions 41-46)

41. **B is the best answer.** This question asks about information implied in the passage. A close reading of the third paragraph is required to answer this question. The first sentence of the third paragraph refers to the 1950s and 1960s as a time of "pioneering" research. The author goes on to discuss the shortcomings of the research, but qualifies that statement by pointing out that the records collected during that time constituted the "official" body of research until the present day. Choice A does not match the passage because it ignores the author's point about the research being flawed, so this answer choice can be eliminated. Choice B best fits with the author's implied meaning and tone, attributing both a positive and negative quality to the research. Choice C, on the other hand, attributes only negative qualities to the research, contradicting the author's point. In general, avoid answer choices that sit at either extreme of the spectrum of opinions of a passage. Choice D both ignores the negative aspects of the research that the author discusses and does not match factually with the information in the passage.

42. **D is the best answer.** The question asks for the author's perspective on newly proposed research. Given the author's support for the application of advanced methodologies to existing data, they would likely support new research that incorporates improved techniques. Choice A does not relate to the author's main point in this respect, though it does deceivingly resemble information in paragraph three. Similarly, choice B relates to information in the passage but does not satisfy the question; distractor answer choices such as choices A and B are common on the MCAT®. Choice C goes beyond the scope of the passage by suggesting that the author would support a specific component of the proposed research. Choice D is best for the reason that it accurately applies the author's main idea - that advanced methodologies should be applied to existing data - to the question.

43. **D is the best answer.** The "long chronology" discussed in the fourth paragraph is an opinion on the origins of Saharan rock art that holds that hunter-gatherer societies began creating the rock art before and during the early Holocene. Though it mentions hunter-gatherer societies, choice A does not provide evidence that weakens this position, so it can be eliminated as it does not satisfy the question. Because they reference neither hunter-gatherer societies nor time before the Holocene, choices B and C do not weaken the "long chronology," and so they can be eliminated. Choice D is best because, of all the choices, it is most contradictory to the position referenced in the question. Questions such as this one, in which the prompt asks for the most *contradictory* choice, are common on the MCAT® and require especially close readings of both the question and the answer choices to avoid confusion.

44. **A is the best answer.** Because the question asks about implied information, it depends on a close reading of the passage as well as a solid understanding of the author's main idea. Choice A is best because it relates most closely to the author's focus on improvement in analysis and methodology since the 1960s. Choice B can be eliminated because it contradicts the author's point that the research was influential at first and only later contested for its methodological and analytical flaws. Choice C is not as good an answer because the author suggests that the early research was important and influential, but also that the methods used in the first decades of study have been heavily criticized. The description of this research as "authoritative" ignores the author's main point about improving methodologies. Choice D goes beyond the scope of the passage as the author states that the early research marked the beginning of rock art research in the area, not that it was foundational to the field rock art studies as a whole. Choice A is a better answer. Many MCAT® questions have distractor answer choices such as choices C and D that come close to the author's position but are either too strongly worded or overly general to be the best answer.

45. **D is the best answer.** The passage implies the author's position in the last paragraph: the author thinks the "huge amount" of archaeological data should be "re-analyzed" in order to secure "sounder conclusions" on the rock art chronology. Based on this information, the author's main argument in relation to rock art chronology is in favor of advanced methodologies and analysis of available data. Because option I contradicts the author's statement that available data is sufficient for the application of advanced methodologies, answer choice A can be eliminated. Option II does not align well with the statement in paragraph five about research on the timing of the Wild Fauna style being highly contested, so choices B and C can also be eliminated. Option III aligns with the author's point that stronger conclusions can be drawn through the application of advanced methodologies and analysis to existing data. Choice D is best because it limits the answer only to option III, the most clearly supported of the three options.

46. **B is the best answer.** This question asks for evidence from one part of the passage to support a statement made in a different part. The claim referenced in the question is made in the first sentence of the second paragraph, and the best support for this comes later in the passage. The author argues for the importance of Tadrart Acacus in ongoing research based on the diversity of rock art it contains. Choice A, though factually supported in the passage, does not relate to the author's argument in this case. On the MCAT®, keep in mind that the best answer choice has to be true according to the passage and also answer the question. Choice B is best because of all the answer choices it most clearly matches the author's point that the diversity of artworks at the massif makes it a good case-study for further research. Neither choice C nor D is supported by information in the passage, so they can both be eliminated.

Passage 9 (Questions 47-53)

47. **D is the best answer.** This question asks the reader to consider how this new piece of information would affect the arguments that were presented by the anti-Tocquevillians. The group described in the fourth paragraph argues that there are many additional modes of participation that a strict Tocquevillian interpretation ignores. For the Tocquevillians only public discussion of politics counts as engagement. This means people talking about politics in a place where they could be seen and heard to do so like a café, church, or village meeting. However, according to their opponents, many additional types of participation also count. If most modern discussion takes place in digital media, it would indicate that the observed crisis of public involvement may be, at least in part, due to a failure to analyze the change in communication mediums. Choice A sounds familiar because it uses specific terms from the end of paragraph 4, but does not make sense in the context of the argument being made there. Choice B makes a true statement about the Tocquevillians, and therefore seems like it might be a strong answer. It does not, however, directly answer the question about the opposition. Choice C offers an explanation of the phenomena involved, but it mistakenly identifies it as damaging the opposition perspective. It may seem reasonable because it is a common argument heard against the public outcry against the lack of social involvement amongst the millennial population. Especially in CARS, always be careful not to allow outside information or background knowledge to bias your decision making.

48. **C is the best answer.** This question asks the reader to interpret how the author would respond to a new piece of information. The main idea of this passage is about participation, what it means, and how it should be evaluated. Having a well informed electorate/population is not the same as having an actively engaged one. Therefore the trend toward a more informed public would only tangentially affect the arguments presented in the passage. This makes choice C the strongest answer. Choice A recalls the claims of the Tocquevillian opposition in the passage due to its similar content, however it misses the thrust of the passage by focusing on the information in a debate, rather than the importance of that debate itself. Choice B sounds like it may be a strong answer because it is mentioned that the Tocquevillians have ignored studies in the past. However, this is less likely to receive the support of the author as it is focused on only one party, and misses the main idea of the article. Choice D sounds like it could be a plausible answer because the debate described would be logically tied to the information presented, and would likely resonate within academic circles of discussion. However, insofar as it is less closely related to the passage, and relies upon additional assumptions, it is less correct. Many times the MCAT® will ask for a choice between two or more compelling options or several poor choices. In these cases, evaluating which is less wrong and which has the most support in the passage is the best approach.

49. **B is the best answer.** This is asking for what the definition of an 'affirmative state' is in this context. With a close reading of the sentence in the passage and the answer choices, the answer becomes apparent. 'Efforts to shrink the affirmative state' implies that there is at least some entity that believes it is a not a positive institution. Choices A and B both describe situations which have parties advocating scaling back. Choice A would be in the context of encouraging intellectual criticism, which runs contrary to the idea of decreased participation opportunities. The actor in Choice B would be a party advocating for a smaller less involved government. This also fits with the fewer participation opportunities, making Choice B the most accurate Additionally, efforts to shrink it result in less interaction between the public and the state, as described by the fewer egalitarian participation opportunities. There would not seem to be an incentive to shrink the state described in Choice C. There is no support for Choice D as shrinking participation in a participatory state does not make sense.

50. **C is the best answer.** Like an assumption, an inference is not stated in the passage. Instead it is an extension of the logic and arguments presented in one. Choice C is not specifically stated however it does stem from the passage arguments found in the third paragraph. Choices A and B are both specifically mentioned in the passage, found in paragraph 2 and 5 respectively. Choice D is more difficult to eliminate however. It summarizes points that are made in the passage about losing the original venues of discussion and debate as presented in paragraphs 3 and 4. An inference will provide additional analysis on what was presented in the passage. Rephrasing information is not the same as drawing an inference from it. When answering questions on inferences, assumptions, implications and similar language, the key is often close attention to what information relates closely to the passage without being stated in it.

51. **B is the best answer.** This option succinctly and accurately summarizes the concerns of the author in the final paragraph, making it the strongest answer. The passage presents two different models of how to think about participation. This establishes a spectrum from de Tocqueville's very restricted definition, which only included political discussion in a public community venue, to the more inclusive version including 'thinking and talking' and other 'citizenship activities' advocated by the opposing side. The author only makes his own perspective clear in the last paragraph. Here, he discusses modern participation, and expresses a concern about the unintended consequences that may come from actively trying to stimulate participation. Choice A ignores the author's concerns in the final paragraph, and is not specifically advocated by either party. Choice C contains judgments that are not reflected in the passage, making it less unique to the author's main idea. Choice D summarizes only the non-Tocquevillian argument, but then claims that it supports neither. This makes it both a weak answer and not consistent with to the author's arguments.

52. **B is the best answer.** An assumption has two key features: it is left unstated, and it is a prerequisite to the argument. Choice A fails the first of these tests as it is de Tocqueville's thesis. Choice B relates to the reasons people avoid politics and choose not to engage in political discussion. It also informs the argument about civic organizations. Choice B is thus a strong answer. Choice C fails for the same reason as Choice A: it is directly stated in the passage. Choice D is unstated, but it is an inference rather than an assumption. This means that it is a conclusion that can be logically reached from the passage, not a prerequisite to the passage argument. Choice D could be inferred from the arguments of the anti-Tocquevillian advocates, but it is not an assumption made by the author. Choice B is the best answer.

53. **D is the best answer.** After presenting both sides of the debate, the author reveals his perspective in the last paragraph. Up until this point, the passage is largely concerned with the opinions of the Tocquevillian and anti-Tocquevillian factions of the intellectual debate. The author argues that attempts to resolve the participation deficit in the modern context will create more opportunities for those with vested interests in the system to manipulate outcomes. This is best addressed, and countered, by choice D. The two camps agreeing on many or even most issues would not change the fact that they have a fundamental disagreement on the subject of the article: participation. Choice A can therefore be eliminated. Choice B recalls a commentary about hard-to-define subjects, such as beauty, art, and pornography. It does not, however, address the author's claim—only that of the anti-Tocquevillians. Choice C is likely true, but it is also not relevant to the author's main idea. Choice D is the strongest answer.